The History of
Folklore in Europe

Translations in Folklore Studies

DAN BEN-AMOS, *General Editor*

ADVISORY BOARD

The History of Folklore in Europe

Giuseppe Cocchiara

Translated from the Italian by

John N. McDaniel

A Publication of the
Institute for the Study of Human Issues
Philadelphia

Copyright © 1952, 1971 by Editore Boringhieri
English translation and new material copyright © 1981
by ISHI, Institute for the Study of Human Issues, Inc.
All Rights Reserved
No part of this book may be reproduced in any form or by any
electronic or mechanical means including information
storage and retrieval systems without permission in writing
from the publisher, except by a reviewer who may quote brief
passages in a review.

Manufactured in the United States of America

Originally published in Italian as *Storia del folklore
in Europa* by Editore Boringhieri, S.p.A., Turin, Italy

Library of Congress Cataloging in Publication Data

Cocchiara, Giuseppe, 1904–1965.
    The history of folklore in Europe.

    (Translations in folklore studies)
    Translation of Storia del folklore in Europa.
    Bibliography: p.
    Includes index.
    1. Folklore—Europe.   I. Title.   II. Series.
GR135.C613   1980   398'.094   80-17823
ISBN 0-915980-99-1

Publication of this book has been assisted by a grant from the
Publications Program of the National Endowment for the Humanities.

For information, write:

Director of Publications
ISHI
3401 Science Center
Philadelphia, Pennsylvania 19104
U.S.A.

For my parents

(

CONTENTS

vii

III / Europe Between Religion and Superstition   44

IV / Error in the Light of Reason   61

V / Encounters Between Nations and Civilization   77

PART TWO / THE SEARCH FOR ORIGINS BETWEEN THE
ENLIGHTENMENT AND PRE-ROMANTICISM

VI / Man and History   95

PART SIX / ASPECTS OF FOLKLORE IN THE LAST FIFTY YEARS

FOREWORD

by Dan Ben-Amos

This volume marks the first publication in English of Giuseppe Cocchiara's seminal work *Storia del folklore in Europa*. In a bold fashion Cocchiara describes the emergence of "folklore" as an intellectual force throughout European society. The wide scope of his book, spanning many historical periods, scholarly traditions, and divergent philosophies, is unmatched in any language.

Since the work's first publication in Italian in 1952, interest in the history of folklore studies has increased, and a number of fine books devoted to the subject have appeared. Most of them, however, concentrate on the history of folklore in a particular country or area. For example, Inger M. Boberg, *Folkeminde-forskningens historie* (Copenhagen: Einar Munksgaards Forlag, 1953), focuses on folklore studies in Nordic countries. A later book edited by Dag Strömbäck, *Leading Folklorists of the North* (Oslo: Universitets-forlaget, 1971), complements Boberg's volume by discussing more recent folklore scholars, yet has a similar geographical limitation. Other volumes include Paulo de Carvalho-Neto, *History of Iberoamerican Folklore: Mestizo Cultures* (Oosterhout, Netherlands: Anthropological Publications, 1969); Jouko Hautala, *Finnish Folklore Research 1828-1918* (Helsinki: Societas Scientiarum Fennica, 1968); and Richard M. Dorson, *The British Folklorists: A History* (Chicago: University of Chicago Press, 1968). All of these works, excellent as they are, lack the breadth and diversity that characterize Cocchiara's volume.

Cocchiara does not start his history of folklore
with the coinage of the term by William Thoms in 1846.
By that time, he assumes, the main paradigms of the
discipline had been formulated. The scientific research and theoretical debates that occupied folklorists and anthropologists at the end of the nineteenth
century appear only in the fifth part of the book,
almost as a postscript to the history of European
folklore. Cocchiara reaches as far back as the
Renaissance to find folklore's real intellectual roots.
Among the forefathers of the discipline he counts such
major thinkers as Montaigne and Montesquieu, Voltaire,
Rousseau, Vico, and Herder. In other words, Cocchiara
finds a common source that folklore shares with other
European trends of thought. Unlike many American
universities, which regard folklore as an academically
deviant discipline, he treats its concepts and concerns as an integral part of European intellectual
history.

In Cocchiara's view, the geographical finds of the
Age of Discovery--the revelations of unknown human
societies with strange languages, religions, and cus-
toms--spurred a new interest in "the folk." Paradoxi-
cally the contact with the New Man from the New World
brought about a concern for European indigenous cultures and languages; the Noble Savage molded by
Renaissance humanism would become the Noble Peasant of
Romantic humanism. A parallel trend was the preoccu-
pation with ancient Greece and Rome--cultures exotic
on the surface, yet clearly related to modern Europe.
In the same era, Europeans began to make "discoveries"
in their own backyards: ancient runes, popular proverbs, peasant songs, all of which focused attention
on vernacular cultures and languages. For thinkers
and artists searching for their national heritages,
folklore became an important resource. All of these
concerns--the ancient and exotic, the local and the
popular--merged in the growing fascination with the
folk.

By the late eighteenth and nineteenth centuries,
as Cocchiara demonstrates, folklore was strongly
linked with emergent nationalism, offering people a

new pride in their own traditions. Under the impetus
of nationalism in northern Europe, folklore research
shifted its focus from the classic shores of the
Mediterranean to the forests and fjords of the Nordic
countries. At the same time, however, the new concept
of an "Indo-European" language and culture--a common
ancestor for both classical and Nordic societies--
reunited nationalism with exotic fascination. These
twin strands of interest, like the rose and the briar
in folk motifs, have twisted round each other to form
the modern discipline of folklore, in which historical
studies of specific national traditions have been
complemented by comparative and cross-cultural researches.

Cocchiara's broad theoretical and historical perspective thus enables him to bridge the humanistic
ideas of the Renaissance, the European Romantic notions
of man and nation, and the social scientific theories
of the late nineteenth century. Yet he concludes his
study with a discussion of his own countryman, Benedetto Croce, who is known more as a philosopher than
as a folklorist. Fortuitous as this may be, Croce's
aesthetic ideas pertaining to folklore make Cocchiara's
history even more relevant to current research, which
centers on such issues as the poetics of culture and
folk aesthetics.

In this way, *The History of Folklore in Europe*
itself represents the course that folklore studies
have followed: from a concern with religious ideas
and mythic beliefs to an interest in the symbolic
significance, the aesthetic aspects, and the artistic
performance of folklore; from involvement with national
origins and comparative histories to an analysis of
folklore as art in culture. Cocchiara's *History* places
folklore, once again, at the center of the discussion
about man and his world.

TRANSLATOR'S INTRODUCTION

Giuseppe Cocchiara, author of *Storia del folklore in Europa*, dedicated his life to the study of folklore. Born in Mistretta (Messina) in 1904, he developed an early interest in Italian and, more particularly, Sicilian folklore, as is evidenced by his first book, *Popolo e canti nella Sicilia d'oggi*, published when he was only nineteen years of age. After receiving a degree in jurisprudence, he went to Oxford in 1929 at the urging of Raffaele Pettazzoni, where he studied under R. R. Marett and Bronislaw Malinowski. During his three-year apprenticeship in London he concentrated on legends, folksongs, and *chansons de geste*, producing works clearly influenced by the evolutionistic and comparative principles so central to the English anthropological school. In 1933, Cocchiara returned to Sicily to become director of the Pitrè Ethnographic Museum. In addition, he served as Professor of History of Popular Traditions at the University of Palermo from 1946 to 1965, the year of his death.

During the course of his career, which developed under the influence of Giuseppe Pitrè's cultural historicism and Benedetto Croce's ideal historicism, Cocchiara produced a number of important volumes, including *Genesi di leggende* (1940), *Storia delle tradizioni popolari in Italia* (1947), *Il mito del buon selvaggio* (1948), *Pitrè, la Sicilia e il folklore* (1951), *Il paese di Cuccagna* (1956), *Popolo e letteratura in Italia* (1959), *L'eterno selvaggio* (1961), *Il mondo alla rovescia* (1963), and the posthumously published *Le origini della poesia popolare* (1966). The most significant of his works, however, is his history of European folklore, *Storia del folk-lore in Europa*, first published in 1952 by Paolo Boringhieri (Turin) in its Biblioteca de cultura scientifica series. Since the initial publication, Cocchiara's compendious study has been translated into Russian (*Istoriǐa fol'kloristiki v Europe*, trans. A. Benediktov and M. Kirillova, Moscow: Izdat'elstvo inostrannoy literatury, 1960), Hungarian (*Az európai folklór története*, trans. János Balázs and László Lontay, Budapest: Gondolat, 1962), and Polish *Dzieje folklorystyki w Europie*, trans. Wojciech Jekiel, War-saw: Pánstwowy Instytut Wydawniczy, 1971). In 1971 the text was reissued in a second Italian edition, with an extensive introduction by Giuseppe Bonomo, Cocchiara's colleague, collaborator, and friend.

The extraordinary interest generated by Cocchiara's *History of Folklore in Europe* can be explained in part by the uniqueness of his effort to describe the origin and development of folklore as a scholarly discipline in Europe. Foregoing the more usual arguments that folklore is a recent and subsidiary science or merely a casual conglomeration of genre studies (the ballad, the folksong, the folktale, the myth, and so on), Cocchiara places the birth of folklore at the moment of Europe's awareness of itself as a historical and cultural entity. He begins his study, then, by taking us back in time--not to the Age of Romanticism or the rise of nationalism or the beginning of myth and bal-lad study, where other folklorists have taken us, but back to the sixteenth century and Montaigne's essays on the noble savage of the New World. Cocchiara thus provides a study that is large in dimension, grand in design, and rich in its promise to place folklore against the expansive background and foreground of philosophy, literature, ethnology, cultural anthro-pology, and above all, history itself. Perhaps Cocchiara had his own text and his own discipline in mind when he said, near the end of his life, "History is the story of all--of rulers *and* the ruled, of scholars *and* peasants. In this story, the history of man, the need to discover the primitive and the popular is not some superficial whim; indeed, the

desire to gain new and original experiences is deeply
imbedded within the consciousness of us all."

The reader of *The History of Folklore in Europe*
will find himself confronted with something more than
the dry bones of abstract theory and minute historical
fact. What one encounters is the history of an *idea*,
the idea of "the folk" as an increasingly influential
force in European life and thought. The "folk" that
emerges from Cocchiara's pages is a living embodiment
of a collective ideal. Those who sing, tell tales,
and teach simple but essential truths do so, Cocchiara
believes, with a spirit unique to the oppressed, the
impoverished, the alien, the ignored. The genuine
interest with which European poets, patriots, and
scholars viewed the folk and its lore--an interest
compounded of appreciation, nostalgia, and at times
a touch of envy--is captured and thoroughly explored
in Cocchiara's text. From his initial discussion of
travelers and missionaries, through his assessment
of various romantic and nationalistic movements, to
his analysis of systematic twentieth-century folklore
studies, Cocchiara insistently reminds us of the fascination with which the "civilized" European has witnessed the often mysterious works and workings of the
folk. To miss that fascination is to miss the attitude that invigorates Cocchiara's *History* and the
discipline of folklore itself.

Despite its obvious merits, *Storia del folklore
in Europa* poses some difficulties for the translator.
Cocchiara's style, for example, is occasionally dense,
often elliptical, always complex--and a characteristic
sentence might well run upwards of a hundred words,
with numerous embedded clauses, parenthetical observations, and elusive allusions. In conveying his erudition and his obvious enthusiasm for his subject,
Cocchiara resorts to the stratagems and devices of the
lecturer: rhetorical questions, repetition, and
poetic, impassioned prose serve to enliven his presentation with a personal charm that is at once con-
versational, dramatic, and provocative, while his
argument develops in labyrinthian twists and turns
that can both confuse and delight. Although I readily

confess to taking liberties in sentence and paragraph
structure, I have attempted to retain those stylistic
qualities that give *Storia del folklore in Europa* its
particular vigor and warmth.

Another difficulty results from Cocchiara's casual
handling of titles, names, and citations of source
materials. To provide consistency and to facilitate
further research by English and American readers of
Cocchiara's text, I have inserted the first names of
those to whom Cocchiara refers only by surname, and
I have brought names and works in line with the Library
of Congress system of capitalization and spelling. A
related problem is that although Cocchiara occasionally
cites the source of quotations either parenthetically
within the text or in appropriate sections of his
bibliographical notes, at other times he does not do
so--especially for quotations taken from non-Italian
sources. To assist English and American readers, I
have located all passages originally written in English, and I have supplied bibliographic information
for such passages in footnotes at the bottom of appropriate pages. Too, I have "silently" corrected small
errors of fact here and there, in an attempt to offer
the reader a translation that is accurate yet unencum-
bered by brackets, explanatory footnotes, asterisks,
and other devices often used to indicate correction
and modification. When such editorial devices as
brackets and emphatic italics do appear within quotations, the reader may correctly assume that they have
been supplied by Cocchiara.

In addition to Cocchiara's bibliographic notes,
the reader will find an "Annotated List of Names"
appended to the text. The first version of these notes
was prepared by L. B. Rosenberg for the Russian translation of *Storia del folklore in Europa*. The notes
appeared in modified form in the Hungarian translation,
and they were subsequently translated into English by
Andrea Nemeth-Newhauser. Using the English translation as a starting point, I have introduced additional
bibliographic material and deleted unessential or
inaccurate information, and in many cases I have re-
written the entries entirely. For the convenience of

English and American readers, I have modified titles
and names in conformity with the Library of Congress
system.

In completing this translation, I have incurred
many debts of gratitude. Douglas Gordon, in his role
as managing editor at the Institute for the Study of
Human Issues, has provided helpful guidelines for
preparing the manuscript. The typing of the manuscript was carried out, more cheerfully than I had
any right to expect, by Brenda Bimson, Jane Davis,
Bernice Burns, and Jean McDaniel. The preparation
of the manuscript was supported by grants from the
National Endowment for the Humanities and the Middle
Tennessee State University Faculty Research Fund.
Linda Dégh, Ralph Hyde, Larry Burk, Mimi Hunter,
Vilmos Voigt, and Roy Shelton have given their time
and expertise generously, and Cindy Hall has assisted me in matters of indexing and bibliographic
verification. I am particularly grateful for the
encouragement offered by Richard M. Dorson, whose
enthusiasm for the project provided impetus and
inspiration, and for the guidance given by Dan
Ben-Amos, who, as general editor of the Translations
in Folklore Studies, helped me turn inspiration into
execution. I also appreciate the close reading of
the text and the helpful comments provided by William
E. Simeone and Wayland D. Hand.

Two chapters of my translation that have appeared
elsewhere have been reprinted with permission. Chapter Eight, "The Poetic Revolt," appeared in *Tennessee
Folklore Society Bulletin*, 39, No. 4 (1973), 119-128,
and Chapter Twenty, "The Teachings of Pitrè," appeared
in a special issued on Italian folklore studies in
Journal of the Folklore Institute, 11, Nos. 1 and 2
(1974), 123-139.

John N. McDaniel
Middle Tennessee State University
Murfreesboro, Tennessee

PREFACE

*The science of folklore and its subject. What
the "folk" of the folklorists is. The history
of folklore, the history of the dominated.
Folklore as an ineliminable aspect of the
history of culture and of civilization. The
historiography of folklore as an integral part
of the history of historiography. Europe in
search of itself.*

In his *Vorlesungen über die Geschichte der Philosophie*,
Hegel observed that it is impossible to write an introduction to the history of philosophy without first considering the concept of philosophy itself, particularly
because philosophy "has the characteristic and, if you
will, the drawback of lending itself, from the very
beginning, to the most varied opinions about its essential nature, what it can and should do." Similarly,
it is impossible to establish the history of folklore
without first identifying the concept underlying this
discipline, whose definitions are often so much at var-
iance.

Originated for the purpose of collecting and studying various manifestations of folklife found in various
historical civilizations, folklore is seen by many of
its adherents as an autonomous science with its own
methods and laws. Others, however, see folklore as a
subsidiary science that takes its laws and methods
from ethnography, ethnology, psychology, or sociology.
There is often a certain natural interplay between
folklore and these disciplines because they have many
common concerns. Consequently, many scholars believe
that folklore is resolved in philology when it collects

and interprets folksongs, fairy tales, short stories,
and legends; in the history of art when it studies
rustic architecture, folk pottery, and handmade products; in the history of religion when it studies
spectacles and festivals; in the history of ethnography when it studies habits and customs--and so on.
In a word, folklore should be the whole of various
elements, whose study one would undertake in the
various disciplines mentioned. Ultimately, however,
the limits of a discipline are established by the subject itself. If we regarded folklore only in terms of
philosophy, ethnography, sociology, or psychology, we
could only explain its philological, psychological or
ethnographical history--not the history of folklore.
For the history of folklore to be studied as such, it
must offer its own particular problem. But, we have
to ask, what *is* this problem?

Before answering this question, we should observe
that the history of folklore has often been presented
as a veritable monster that lives in and for itself,
like certain protagonists in Norse legends. But this
is not the way to understand folklore, much less the
science of folklore. At other times, facile theories
of folklore are offered, against which it is then easy
to argue, perhaps because in doing so one believes
himself capable of destroying the very subject of
folklore: the folk. This, a worse method than the
first, not only disorients scholars but also dis-
credits a discipline on whose systemization generations of scientists have worked.

We can also say that the discipline of folklore
has evolved, in the midst of doubts and uncertainties,
along two parallel lines, each often ignoring the
other: on one side is the oral tradition, explored
with philological or aesthetic aims, and on the other
side are the objective traditions, whose research is
associated with historical or historical-ethnographical
interests. Of course, folk literature does give us
many individual texts, some of which are artistic in
nature. So considered, those texts are merely selec-
tions of literature; but for the folk from which they
derive they are an inseparable part of a heritage in

which, instinctively but unitedly, the manifold values of the human spirit are reflected. Hence, a unity between folk literature and ethnic tradition exists, as is evidenced by the fact that popular oral productions (songs, legends, and proverbs) often appear as lifeless organisms when they are not illuminated by the custom, usage, or belief that harmonizes them, enlivens them, and often explains them.

Thus (to return again to Hegel) just as it is impossible to write the history of philosophy if diverse concepts exist within it (because given concepts, in themselves diverse, produce more philosophy, which would result in obscuring each concept), so is it impossible to establish a history of the study of folk traditions if there are diverse concepts within it (because it would then be necessary to explain the philological or ethnographical or sociological history of the study of folk traditions). To be written effectively, the history of the study of folk traditions must be guided by a problem that unites and combines the others and whose resolution depends on its own subject, folk traditions--which presupposes not only a tradition but a tradition that is "popular," or "of the folk."

I am saying, of course, that one has to look for the unity of folklore in the unity of its subject, in the heritage, that is, of the so-called common folk of civilized nations (generally recognized as the working class). But it is an error, in my opinion, to enclose folklore (that is, the material of folklore) within the circle of those common people to whom, rightly or wrongly, the folklorists give the name of folk. This is so because the concept of folk, even though it is reflected principally in the *vulgus*, is not exclusively sociological. The term *folk* can, in fact, assume quite different meanings: the sociologist, the historian, and the political scientist speak of a folk that always corresponds, in their views, to something in particular, to certain ethical or spiritual interests related to the aim of their work or their thought. The scholar of popular traditions does indeed address himself to specific classes, but for him the folk is not merely the

whole of these classes. The folk is the expression
of a certain vision of life, certain attitudes of the
spirit, of thought, of culture, of custom, of civilization, which appear with their own clearly delineated
characteristics. Here is the very nature of folklore,
which, as Antonio Gramsci warned (and a similar warning
still has validity, especially in Italy), "should not
be thought of as an oddity or an eccentricity or as a
picturesque element, but as something that is to be
taken seriously and earnestly," especially since it
points to a "conception of the world and life."

A folk, after all, is what its history has made
it, not only political history but historical life in
all its manifestations, from language to economics,
from law to customs. It is true that the history of
folklore is occasionally vitiated by premises that are
the very negation of history and aesthetics, with the
result that many persist in the absurd idea of a minor
history in contrast to a major history, of a minor art
or literature in contrast to a major one. But it is
also true that folk traditions, whatever they may be,
are always historical formations, as are language,
economics, and law. Nor is it possible for these
"spiritual" facts—documents of life, thought, or
art—to live outside (or above) history, which is not
only made by rulers but also and above all by the
ruled. History provides their life and their spirit.

If folk traditions must be considered as historical
formations, the fundamental problem that they present,
given their nature, is a historical one. Hence, the
task of the scholar of folk traditions is to see how
they are formed, why they are conserved, and what
necessities contribute not only to their conservation
but also to the continual and, I would say, *natural*
re-elaboration containing the very secret of their
existence: a continuous dying for an eternal rebirth.

Indeed, it is this continual re-elaboration that
sets folklore apart, providing it with a specific
quality that renders it unmistakable. While folklore
scholars have often been anxious to give mysterious
origins to folk literature (for example), the origin
cannot be separated from the essence and nature of the

historical "fact" of that particular literary phenomenon. Although folk literature arises spontaneously
through the originality and freedom of the creative
act and cannot repeat its causes outside of itself,
its roots nevertheless are sunk in the tradition of a
specific cultural environment.

In this sense the problem of folklore is to define
these characteristics, to define what can be called
folk and what cannot. Certainly it is necessary to
consider as *folk* everything that, from a creative
standpoint, is presented as elemental and artless,
directly adhering to the real, to the sensible, to
what concretely and immediately solicits our feelings
and emotions. It is impossible, however, to define
the folk without considering values inherent in the
tradition--in, that is, the continuous vitality and
presence of the past. It is necessary, then, to see
in the concept of *folk* the disposition, need, and
demand of the individual who lives with others, of
one who contemplates, with a spirit that is his spirit
and that of others, the vast little world that sur-
rounds him, "the world in which his reality and his
history exist.

When the *popular* and *folk* are understood in this
way, we derive a clearer concept of folklore, along
with a more precise understanding of the relationships
between folklore and philosophy (broadly speaking),
between folklore and the history of religions and
therefore of mythology, and so on. The same is true
for the term *primitive*, into which the term *folklore*
is often converted. Primitivism has been understood
at times as a "first age" and, as such, is recognized
in "savage" nations--nations different from those of
Western Civilization. Additionally, the concept of
the primitive has been very prolific in the history of
folklore. But isn't there something more than that
involved here, as eighteenth-century historians,
particularly Giambattista Vico, understood quite well
--if not an ideal "fact" of our conscience and our
being, then a specific stage through which we have
been or are now passing, one that lives and relives
in us?

Unlike folklore, ethnology, the study of primitive
nations, cannot have empirical confines in which relative comparisons are legitimate. It is a fact, however, that both ethnology and folklore are specific
fields of possible historical investigations with the
purpose of explaining and illuminating civilization
itself. It has been said, and rightly, that if this
were not the case ethnology would be an idle field
of study indeed. But is the position of folklore any
different? And isn't it therefore impossible to trace
the history of folklore without coupling it to the
history of ethnology, even though folklore studies do
not always require its help?

This being the case, it seems to me that the problem that confronts folklore is not a philological,
sociological, psychological, or ethnographical problem; rather, it is essentially a historical problem,
one that combines and transfigures all the others.
In making this claim, I do not wish to deny the validity that various philological or naturalistic disciplines assume in the field of folklore; of these, when
and where appropriate, the folklorist should avail
himself, but without mistaking the instruments of his
work for the work itself. It is the duty of the folklorist, in fact, *not* to isolate those inquiries but to
integrate them, particularly because in the field of
folklore the intrinsic interplay of the various disciplines is forever dominated by the very nature of folklore, by the concept of the "popular."

The task of the folklorist is and must be, in my
opinion, the task of the historian of folklore, who
naturally must refer to specific chronological limits
in his narration, inasmuch as these, finally, are
simply reference points for our understanding. In
light of our desire to understand the character of a
discipline, the historical method is especially appropriate, for it is necessary to see the particular
moment in which the discipline becomes an autonomous
field of research.

In searching for the roots from which folklore
grew into an autonomous discipline, scholars have
almost always professed agreement in believing that

the ethnic tradition (usages, customs, beliefs) goes
back to the philosophical movements of the seventeenth
and eighteenth centuries, while popular literature
(songs, legends, proverbs) is related to Romanticism.
Thomas Mann recently asserted that Romanticism extracted "the treasures of fairy tales and songs from
the depths of the past" and "was a great patron of the
science of folklore, which in its own variegated lumi-
nosity appears to us as derivation of the exotic."
But the moment at which the science of folklore began
to acquire critical and historical awareness of itself
cannot be traced back, in my opinion, to the philosophical movements of the seventeenth and eighteenth
centuries and much less to Romanticism, since from this
movement it drew the nourishment that in part fed it.
The person who realized this was a perceptive French
folklorist, Pierre Saintyves, who believed that geographical discoveries of the sixteenth century, particularly the discovery of the New World, obliged
scholars of the time to reconsider many issues related
to the history of institutions, and they developed a
means of investigation, that of comparison; from this,
modern ethnography and folklore were born.

　　After the discovery of America, the struggle
against the bonds and the inheritances of a culture
that seemed, politically and socially, to deny the
human spirit and all original freedom became increasingly alive in the European conscience. It was then
too that ethnographical literature took shape and
developed, entering into European culture as a stimulus to research even though it ranged within the confines of the exotic. The Enlightenment, Preromanti-
cism, Positivism, and Evolutionism were merely stages
of this research, which underwent the various modifications of historiography and entered into a general
evolution that reached fulfillment in the European
spirit. In such research, the study of folklore gradually assumed its own particular characteristics,
enmeshed as it was in an intricate network of "myths
and messages" in which politico-social, philosophical,
and artistic experiences were confirmed. These myths
and messages managed to end up uniting Europe, however,

binding it in an ideal unity while they assumed their
own validity in their very errors--in the sense that
these errors were a necessary and constant stimulus
for the progress of our discipline. In these myths
and messages each nation gave or believed it gave the
best of itself, and they coincided with the advent of
the Age of Reason, the theory of the social contract,
idol worship, the mission of peoples and nations, and
the formation of the working class. Furthermore, new
impulses were derived from the traditions of the folk,
which resulted in the renewal of poetry, literature,
and music.

It would be naive to isolate folklore studies from
all these experiences that give them their life; such
studies must not be considered as so many distinct
fabrics but as a unified fabric. The various threads
intertwine, of course--not giving us different threads,
however, but rather the fabric itself. The historian
who wishes to investigate the origin and development
of European folklore studies must turn to the methods
that have gradually characterized these studies, considering them not as a series of magical recipes ("do
this and you will get that") but as a sum of experiences and personal interpretations. It is obvious
that the history of folklore can be considered only as
an intellectual history concretized in the personality
or the cultural world of individual scholars, whose
work should be judged not only for what it *was* worth
but especially for what it is *now* worth.

It is in the light of these criteria that I set
about to study how an awareness of folklore first
developed in Europe and how as a result the science
of folklore began. Furthermore, my investigation is
by design an internal history, or perhaps I should
call it (in Vico's phrase) an "ideal history" of a
whole movement of studies that brought Europe to the
discovery of itself, of what it has in its innermost
soul. As such it has its unity and vital center in
European culture; additionally, it necessarily must
concern only those scholars who lived and thought in
the historical climate of that culture in whose service

they put to themselves the problems with which they were occupied.

Finally, I ought to say, as the end *ad quem* of my narration, that although I have considered it appropriate to examine recent phases of folkloristic studies, I have limited my examination to those figures whose work is or can be considered to be concluded. This is not because the immediate past cannot become history (a commonplace denied by all the history of historiography, old and new); rather, this is so because often we are dealing with inevitably controversial theories and doctrines, with hypotheses that, although containing sharp and brilliant conjectures, need a scientifically grounded confirmation. At other times, we are dealing with interpretative beginnings that could lead to further development or with polemics or polemical suggestions that might well offer individual scholars the possibility of clarifying their thinking to themselves and to their readers. In this respect, the work of each of us is like a book that has not come to its last, concluding chapter. Because of the regard that we owe to the intense, impassioned work of those who today represent the science of folklore, I have preferred not to write the final chapter of this book.

PART ONE

SOURCES OF A NEW HUMANISM:
  THE STUDY OF PEOPLES

CHAPTER I

THE "DISCOVERY OF THE SAVAGE"

1. *A New Province of Knowledge*

In Europe the discovery of America nourished a new
humanism, one that added the study of the folk and of
more remote civilizations to the study of the classical world. It was, above all else, the period of
primitive man, who was not sought, as in the medieval
age and in the Renaissance itself, in the tradition
of Adam and the concept of original sin; rather, he
was sought among the remote forests of America where
harsh European domination had not extinguished the
fundamental character of those who came to be considered the representatives of nature: the primitive,
the barbarian, the savage.

In the preface to the second edition of *The Golden
Bough*, Frazer says that to humanists "the rediscovery
of ancient literature came like a revelation, disclos-
ing to their wondering eyes a splendid vision of the
antique world, such as the cloistered student of the
Middle Ages never dreamed of under the gloomy shadow of
the minster and within the sound of its solemn bells."
In speaking of primitive peoples, he adds: "A greater
panorama is unrolled by the study which aims at bringing home to us the faith and the practice, the hopes
and the ideals, not of two highly gifted races only,
but of all mankind, and thus at enabling us to follow
the long march, the slow and toilsome ascent, of humanity from savagery to civilisation. And as the scholar
of the Renaissance found not merely fresh food for

thought but a new field of labour in the dusty and
faded manuscripts of Greece and Rome, so in the mass
of materials that is steadily pouring in from many
sides--from buried cities of remotest antiquity as
well as from the rudest savages of the desert and the
jungle--we of to-day must recognise a new province of
knowledge which will task the energies of generations
of students to master."[1]

In the competition between ancient and modern
historians--to which Frazer alludes--the discovery of
America placed its chroniclers and its historians in
an unusual position, inasmuch as the ancients obviously made no comments about the American Indians; nevertheless, the discovery of America created and
strengthened a myth that was to become very prolific
in the history of European culture: the myth of the
noble savage. The most perceptive interpreters of the
Indian life of America (for example, Pietro Martire,
Jean de Léry, and Bartolomé de las Casas) not only
defended the primitive Americans, excusing them from
charges that generally degraded them, but they also
exalted these primitives for their own particular virtues, making--note well--their primitiveness coincide
with their nobility. This is the dominant note in
innumerable travelogues and diaries published in different languages and containing the most piquant
details of the beliefs, myths, and customs of the
American population; this is also the dominant note
in the "Accounts of New France" and in "Edifying
Letters" written by missionaries and dedicated, for
the most part, to the study of primitive peoples.
Thus, primitive man, the very ideal of humanity but
of a humanity better than the one in the midst of
which he lived, was born--and with him came a new
province of knowledge in which the study of the folk
was no longer merely an idle pastime.

[1]*The Magic Art*, Vol. I of *The Golden Bough* (1900;
rpt. New York: The Macmillan Company, 1935), p. xxv.

2. The Savage as Historical Document

The primitive thus became a document, we might even say
a historical document. But as such, he was also to
become an instigator of controversy. Travelers, missionaries, and historians of the American Indian, furnished as they almost always were with a classical
culture, one of the links unifying Western Civilization,
idealized the distant people that they described or
studied (following the tendency, so prevalent in Greco-
Roman times, of citing distant people not remembered by
civilization). They perceived their hero, the savage,
as a noble creature, and they compared him to the
Greeks and Romans. They remind us, as someone has said,
of "those poets of the Augustan Age who sang the praises
of the rustic life and dreamed that the Golden Age was
near." But there is a difference: for them the Golden
Age was not a dream but a reality. Understand that I am
not saying that the concept of the Golden Age formulated
by the Classical Age coincides (as Gonnard believes)
with the concept of the noble savage. I wish only to
set up a basis of comparison. The concept of the noble
savage, whatever its direct or indirect antecedents may
be, originated with the discovery of America, originated
with ethnography, or, to be more precise, with
geographico-political tendencies that were emerging in
the history of modern ethnography.

On this subject, we should not forget the work of
Montaigne that contributed to these tendencies. Montaigne, one of the most perceptive late Renaissance
scholars, was extremely interested in the folklife of
Europeans and savages. For example, he was very interested in folk poetry, which he felt comparable to
artistic poetry: "Folk poetry has such grace and
ingenuousness, for which it may be compared with the
principal beauty possessed by the poetry of art; as is
seen in the villanelles of Gascony and in the songs imported from the nations that do not have knowledge of
any science or even of writing" (*Essais*, Book I, Chapter LIV). Above all, however, he was aware of the *human*
values in nations that, as he says, do not have either
knowledge or writing. "I have had," he asserts, "beside

me a man who had been ten or twelve years in that other
world that has been discovered in our century in the
place where Villegagnon landed, which he called Antar-
tic France." After noting that each writer ought "to
write what he knows and as much as he knows about it,"
he takes aim at the "haughtiness of civilized nations":

> Now I find that there is nothing barbarous and
> savage in this nation [Brazil], going on what was
> reported to me about it, except that each man calls
> barbarous whatever is not his own custom. Indeed,
> it seems we do not have any other test of truth and
> reason than the example and pattern of the opinions
> or customs of the country where we live--because
> here for us is the perfect religion, the perfect
> politics, the perfect manners in all things. They
> [the Brazilians] are wild, just as we call wild the
> fruits that nature has spontaneously produced;
> actually, however, those that we have altered by
> our artifice and led away from the common order are
> the ones we should call wild. The former retain,
> alive and vigorous, the truths and the most useful
> natural virtues and proprieties which we in our
> society have adulterated and modified to please our
> corrupted taste. (*Essais*, Book I, Chapter XXXI)

Montaigne's portrait of these savages is suggestive and
poetical. For example, he observes, "Some one of the old
men, in the morning before they begin to eat, preaches
to everyone in the hut, walking from one end to the
other and repeating one single sentence several times,
until he has finished the circuit. . . . He recommends
only two things: valor against the enemy and love for
their wives." It almost seems to be a picture from the
Bible. Commenting on their songs, he compares them to
an Anacreontic image, noting in them "a soft language,
with an agreeable sound, somewhat like Greek in its
endings." This is the spirit with which Montaigne
approached the world of the primitives; and, as if to
tie together the threads of his discourse, he adds:

> Epicurus said that while things here are as we

see them, at the same time they are all exactly
alike and of the same fashion in many other worlds.
And in so many instances do we not see today similarities and resemblances between this new world of
the West Indies and our own?

In truth, considering what has come to our
awareness about the course of this civilization,
I am often astonished to see, at a great distance
in time, the coincidences between a great number
of fabulous popular opinions and savage beliefs.
The human spirit is a great worker of miracles.
(*Essais*, Book II, Chapter XII)

Thus, Montaigne not only gave vigor and emphasis
to the comparative method, but he also brought within
the confines of European culture a document that at
that time was validated only by travel books and stories of distant peoples. It is said that basically
Montaigne viewed the world of the primitives with a
certain tinge of humor. But wasn't his humor aimed
as much at his contemporaries as at the savages? And
didn't this "other world," as he called it, reflect
what he felt to be a new and refined emotion?

3. Savages in the "Essais" of Montaigne

In approaching the primitives, these *homines Dei
recentes*, Montaigne was especially fascinated by a
work that marked a decisive advance in the field of
ethnography, the *Histoire d'un voyage fait en la
terre du Brésil, autrement dite Amérique*, narrated
in 1578 by Jean de Léry. Unlike Martire (who wrote
Decados de orbe novo, published between 1511 and
1530, a work that assumed a preëminent place among
contemporary explanations of the discovery of America), Léry did not limit himself to the observation
that American Indians lived contentedly with the gifts
of nature. Indeed, he went beyond that; he excused
them of all the charges that had begun to weigh heavy
on them. Although his investigations were restricted
to Brazil, he recognized that his savages were no less

barbarian than we ourselves often are; nor did he hesitate to address uncivilized Europeans with the impreca-
tion of a savage: "You are great fools. Are so many
riches needed by you or by your sons or by those who
will come after you? Will not the land that has nourished you be equally sufficient for nourishing them?"

In Léry one finds the impetuous, heroic attitude
that we also find in Bartolomé de las Casas--not the
attitude of a fighter who justified his hatred of his
neighbors (the Spaniards) with his love of the foreigners (the American Indians), but of a fighter who
was quick to put his contemporaries in confusion so
that they would know what kind of civilization they
had taken to a nation that did not really need it at
all. Casas's *Historia de las Indias*, published between
1552 and 1561, is the work of an anticonquistador who
did not miss any occasion for praising the life of the
American savages, who seemed to him, as to Léry, to be
patient, shrewd, obedient, industrious, fair, and so
on. The Spanish conquistadores, intent on making slaves
of the American Indians, did not, needless to say, support the work of the missionaries. Casas said in his
famous letter of 1555 that "the *encomenderos* justified
their tyranny with the excuse of teaching the Ave Maria
to the Indian *encomendados*." He adds: "Imagine that
doctrine for people who did not know if the Ave Maria
was wood or stone or something to eat or drink."

Although using the work of Léry, Montaigne was closer
to Martire, who did defend the savages, but only for what
they could teach us. But in Montaigne's work the controversy over the conquest and exploitation of American
savages was toned down to a serene contemplation, which
was simultaneously an evasion and a solution; both the
evasion and solution were placed, however, on politico-
social ground relating to the Western World:

> The laws of nature, less corrupted than ours, rule
> the savages. And they are in such a state of purity
> that I am sometimes vexed that knowledge of them did
> not come earlier, in the days when there were men
> able to judge them better than we. I am sorry that
> Lycurgus and Plato did not know of them because it

seems to me that what we actually see in these
nations [those of the American savages] surpasses
not only all the pictures with which poets have
idealized the Golden Age and all their inventions
for representing a happy state of man, *but also the
conceptions and the very desire of philosophy.*
They could not imagine a naturalness so pure and
simple as we see by experience; nor could they believe that our society could be maintained with so
little artifice and human welding. There is a
nation, I would say to Plato, where there is no
sort of traffic, no knowledge of letters, no science of numbers, no name for a magistrate or for
political authority, no custom of servitude, no
riches or poverty, no contracts, no successions,
no divisions, no occupations but leisure ones, no
regard for any but common kinship, no clothes, no
agriculture, no metal, no use of wine or malt.
They have not even heard the words that signify
lying, treachery, dissimulation, avarice, envy,
calumny, pardon. (*Essais*, Book I, Chapter XXXI)

For Montaigne the world of the primitives was still
that of the travelers and missionaries who journeyed
among the American Indians. We must observe, however,
that nature as he conceived it was no longer that, for
example, of Marsilio Ficino. Charron, a friend and disciple of Montaigne, realized this when, in his *De la
sagesse* (which came out in 1601, and which not insig-
nificantly opened the seventeenth century), he decisive-
ly asserted that man is naturally good.

4. An Ethnographo-Folklorist: Lescarbot

Montaigne, whose voice and spirit echoed the classical
idea--but a classical idea already decanted in the
"other world"--closed the sixteenth century. But his
argument, or rather, his message (in which, whatever
his sources were, the experience lived by the missionaries and travelers who thrust themselves among the
Indians of America was summarized), was accepted

completely by the next century; however, in that next
century the comparisons between us (civilized men) and
the savages (a new acquisition of European culture)
increasingly assumed the character of a political and
cultural revolt. In 1609, for example, *Histoire de la
Nouvelle France* was published in Paris, narrated by
Marc Lescarbot, an imaginative Parisian lawyer as well
as a good poet. He was concerned, of course, with giving a report of "customs of New France compared with
those of ancient peoples," but was this comparison an
end in itself? In describing the attitudes of American
savages, as articulated in all their living, manner of
dress, family life, established institutions, and rites
and ceremonies, Lescarbot continually turned to Herodotus, Pliny, and Tertullian. His explanations, however,
were often quite odd: a tribe has the custom of burning
the furniture and possessions of those who die--clearly
a lesson for European misers! Additionally, Lescarbot
was not content to compare primitive customs with those
of the Greeks or Romans. He also focused on the popular
traditions of Gascony. Here, too, his comparisons are
rather mnemonic and vague. What is important, however,
is that his was one of the first works in which the
study of primitive peoples coincided, although somewhat
timidly, with the study of commoners among civilized
peoples.

In his comparisons Lescarbot was following in the
footsteps of the Jesuits. He compared primitives to
the Greeks and Romans in order to exalt them. And although he did not have theological concerns to sustain,
he too insisted on a common origin for the primitives
and the Greeks, one of the theses that Jesuits themselves had proposed. But just when it seems to us that
Lescarbot, with his idealization of the savage, is going
to take us back to a kind of Arcadia, we suddenly discover that his comparison touches two worlds, ours and
that of the savages--to the detriment of the first,
naturally. Do you wish to know, he wonders, why savages
are happy and live in a Golden Age? The reason is that
they have no sense of "mine and thine." We Europeans
are always in discord about everything. For the savages
however, concord is the predominant factor of life. All

Europeans are tormented by vanity and ambition, but
savages are not familiar with this torment and are
happy.

In Lescarbot's work, comparison between primitive
customs and those of our own takes place on a social
level. Baron Lahontan placed himself on precisely this
same level, as if to conclude another century of experience concerning travels among American Indians. He
was a violent type, like Casas, but he was also eccen-
tric, like Lescarbot.

5. *Dialogue Between a Huron and a European: The*
   Political-Social Controversy of Baron Lahontan

Having lived for a long time among American Indians--
an adventurous soul, he even fought against the good
Iroquois--Baron Lahontan, after returning to Paris,
became fascinated with those distant countries where
he had gained a new cultural awareness. His *Voyages*
and his *Mémoires*, published in 1703, reflect this
state of mind. His savages are the very same as those
of the missionaries, Léry, and especially Lescarbot.
Open, for example, *Nouveaux voyages de M. le baron de
Lahontan, dans l'Amérique Septentrionale, qui contien-
nent une relation des différens peuples qui y habitent,*
where we are introduced to his savages: "they live
happily"; "they are an example for us"; "they have no
sense of 'mine and thine'"; "they live in a kind of
equality consonant with natural sentiments." His books,
which so excited his contemporaries, are, however,
labored inquiries, rich in detail, massive. But what
is their gist? Gueudeville will tell us in *Dialogues
de Monsieur le baron de Lahontan et d'un sauvage, dans
l'Amérique*, published in Amsterdam in 1704. The savage
that Gueudeville placed on stage is a Huron who has
visited Europe, and he therefore can relive his experience in the talks that he has with the Baron. This
Huron is an imaginary character, of course; but doesn't
he emerge as a living presence from the *Voyages* and
Mémoires of his interlocuter, from whom he receives
imagination, reasoning, impulses, and energy?

The dialogue between the savage and the Baron is
alive, dynamic, dramatic. It confronts the most lively
problems of the time, even though solutions certainly
are not given; what we *do* find here, however, is a
beginning, the message of new hope--and you can feel
it: Europe prides itself in owning a wonderful page
of humanity in the Bible; the savage answers with his
natural religions, in which there are no impostures,
in which all is clear, luminous. The European prides
himself in possessing the best laws in the world, and
all that need be said is that it is an inheritance from
Rome. Well and good, but Europeans do not apply the
laws that they have. The savages do not have laws, but
they *do* have a natural morality, which has the weight
of a law--a law that *is* observed. The European has a
civilization? Which one? "Look at the European," the
savage will say to you; "he is a carnival clown with a
blue suit, black cap, white feathers, and green ribbons."
On the other hand, the savage is an ephebus in the sun.
True enough, the savage does not know how to read; but
as a result he avoids a sea of trouble. The moral:
only savages can help us discover liberty, justice, and
equality.

A natural man with his natural religion and natural
laws, the savage who converses with Baron Lahontan seems
to have come from the Sorbonne where he had read Montaigne. This savage actually is not a savage at all.
He is a fine philosopher who has summarized and developed ideas that increasingly came to be affirmed in the
awareness of the age, which desperately invoked a better
world--what had essentially been imagined in the utopias,
from Plato's *Republic* (which Montaigne had considered
earlier) to Thomas More's *Utopia* (the basis for Gueudeville's *Dialogues*). Much later, in 1714, Gueudeville
translated More's book, which is not only an imaginative undertaking but also a text of religious literature emphasizing the strength and nobility of natural
religion (even though it remains subordinated to the
Revelation). Plato's *Republic*, observed Gaetano Salvemini, inspired "Thomas More's *Utopia*, Campanella's *La
città del sole*, and Bacon's *New Atlantis*, and it has
continued to serve as a model for similar writing.

Additionally, the second half of the seventeenth
century possessed, in Vairasse d'Alais' *Histoire des
Sevarambes* (1677), some parts of Fénelon's *Les
aventures de Télémaque* and other such romances, its
apologetic descriptions of countries that owed their
happiness to economic equality and lack of individual
property." And now Gueudeville, with the help of Baron
Lahontan, violently grafted the concept of the noble
savage in America on this trunk.

6. The "Lesson" of the Savage

The discovery of America, then, gave a new vision of
the world in which we live. The comparison between
us civilized men and American Indians raised some
problems in culture and politics never raised by other
primitive peoples. Missionaries--shown especially in
the case of Father Le Jeune, author of the notable
Relations de ses voyages de 1632 à 1661--were so increasingly concerned with loving the savages, regarding
them as the sons of God and our brothers, that they
endeavored to "tolerate their imperfections without
saying a word," thus giving a humane character to
colonization. And as Antonello Gerbi well knew, they
were also preoccupied with praising the evangelical
mildness of savages in order to save them from the
avidity of merchants and the tyranny of rulers. But
did they ever think that their idealizations would
become extremely valid arguments against contemporary
institutions and their own beloved religion, for the
diffusion of which they had traveled into distant
lands, facing sacrifice and suffering?

Missionaries had not always been cautious in considering the religion of primitive peoples. Some,
armed with holy fervor, saw it as a mass of pagan
superstitions. But didn't the more intelligent ones
attempt to transfer the characteristics of primitive
Christians to American Indians? For example, consider what Charles Lallemant, in his *Relation des
Jésuites* (1648), said about the savages of that Canada
so beloved by Baron Lahontan:

> To tell the truth, no knowledge of a God had been
> handed down to these people from their fathers;
> before we set foot in their country, they knew
> nothing but vain fables about the origin of the
> world. Nevertheless, savages as they were, lodged
> in their hearts was the secret feeling of a divin-
> ity, a first principle, an author of all things,
> whom they unconsciously invoked. In the forest,
> on the hunt, on the water, in dangerous storms,
> they called to it to help them.

This was the taking of a clear, distinct, categorical
stand. But despite the cautious observations of Martire and the more decisive ones of Lallemant, the
theory that primitive people were atheistic got a
footing and was asserted. This theory had been broad-
cast about the American Indians by Antonio Pigafetta,
who said of the inhabitants of the Marianna Islands,
"They worship nothing." But how did Pigafetta presume
to know this, if, as he admitted, he had been on these
islands for only a few hours? And later Léry, refuting
Cicero, asserted that in recent times (we are in 1609)
nations in which no religious sentiment exists had been
discovered. He referred especially to Brazil--where,
he immediately added, the hereafter is believed in (as
if this did not constitute a religious sentiment!).
     No matter what the truth was, no matter whether or
not there was a religion among the American Indians,
it is a fact that with the appearance of travel books
about primitive peoples the idea of nature as an antidote to evil crept into the conscience of the time,
even though a growing skepticism crept in as well.
In one of his fables La Fontaine tells us of the man
who runs after fortune, and he says of him:

> . . . Les mers étaient lasses
> de le porter: et tout le fruit
> qu'il tira de ses longues voyages
> ce fut cette leçon que donnent les sauvages;
> "Demeure en ton pays par la nature instruit."

Thus, doubt and nature were intertwined. But the lesson

that savages gave to Europeans was now clear, and even
poets like La Fontaine and Montaigne had accepted it.

7. From "Oroonoko" to "Robinson Crusoe"

The concept of the noble savage, meanwhile, passed
from France (which had imported it from Spain, especially from Casas) into England. In England, however,
this concept took on what I would call a romantic
aspect. The denunciations of Casas, Léry, and Lescarbot were softened in England into a pathetic story that
came out as early as 1688: Aphra Behn's *Oroonoko*, the
story of an English merchant youth who embarks from
London for trading in the West Indies. His companions
are massacred on an island, but he is saved by a savage
girl, Yoriko, for love. When finally the young merchant is able to board a vessel, he takes along Yoriko,
who follows him humbly and submissively. But once back
on his ship, "home territory," the youth--with the
river now passed and God forgotten--reflects on his
lost time and on his affairs ended in smoke; subsequently, he sells his loved one as a slave. Thus we
see the European, vile and infamous, and the savage--
a noble and generous soul.

The story of the love of a European and a savage is
one England knew as early as 1624 when in his *General
History of Virginia* Captain John Smith, the author,
related his famous adventure with an Indian girl, Pocahontas. But in Behn's narrative this story was not
only of literary interest but also a spur to politico-
social controversy. Behn's story contributed the firm,
strong framework to another work from the same country
that soon appeared on the literary scene: *Robinson
Crusoe*. Its author, Daniel Defoe, had lived in an environment from which he had gleaned only despair. He
had gone ahead despite political libels. But at the
age of sixty he felt a nostalgia that was very much in
the spirit of utopians and travelers. Having seen the
liability of his actions, he, as a good Englishman,
counted on new experience as a probable asset.

At that time in England people were talking a great

deal about the adventures that befell a Scottish sailor,
Alexander Selkirk, who had been abandoned on a deserted
island by the captain of a ship--an island on which he
remained alone for four years. This story was narrated
in the second edition of a book by Woodes Rogers entitled *A Cruising Voyage Round the World*. From this
book Defoe drew the inspiration for writing, in 1719,
the volume entitled *The Life and Strange Surprising
Adventures of Robinson Crusoe, of York, Mariner*. But
wasn't this volume--which inspired a whole series of
Robinsons, even though none of them approached the color
and warmth of the first--still, in its way, on the same
road already traveled by a whole literature that had
delighted in describing happy countries distant in time
and in space and not yet corrupted by civilization?
Consider, as far as France is concerned, the already
cited *Histoire des Sevarambes* of Vairasse d'Alais,
which was published in 1677, and Fénelon's *Télémaque*,
published in 1698. For an even better example, consider
Voyages et aventures de Jaques Massé, published in 1710
by Tyssot de Patot. But what was the essential spirit
behind these writings, and what was the dominant force
in the writings of Defoe? The French obviously felt
compelled to stake a new claim, to escape to a new
world, however imaginary, from which they could see
their own world. The spirit of Baron Lahonton, whether
as forerunner or follower, was in them, and, like him,
they entertained a desperate desire to live according
to and in the midst of nature. We might say that
Robinson Crusoe captures the same desire--but it follows another course. In describing the adventurous
life of their hero, French utopian writers dogmatized
against all dogmas; additionally, they made of his ship-
wreck--generally the dominant note in their works--the
shipwreck of Western Civilization. Robinson's shipwreck, on the other hand, is indeed a liberation from
society, but it is simultaneously an approach to God.
Robinson is not alone on the island on which he is
shipwrecked, for he is with nature, which nourishes,
saves, redeems him. For him, however, nature is God.
     It will be suggested, perhaps, that one apply the
Calvinistic interpretation of the Adam and Eve story to

Defoe's tale. Robinson is an Adam without Eve. He too undertakes the conquest--the practical conquest-- of a world that is to be built from nothing. But whatever echoes we today might recognize in *Robinson Crusoe*, the crux of the novel is in Robinson's meeting with Friday, whom he saves from cannibals. Friday, a savage with the features of an ephebus, generous and loyal as Europeans rarely are, is himself a representation of a return to civilization, when the latter has been conquered not outwardly but from within.

This is the message of Robinson. On the island on which he lands, he encounters neither king nor shepherds as happens in the widespread myth, extending from Italy to Greece, of the boy abandoned on the riverbank; he does not encounter magicians as does the protagonist of *The Tempest*; nor, finally, does he encounter those sages who preach morality to remote Westerners, who are dissatisfied with their governments and monarchies. What he encounters is man's conscience, the conscience that he had vainly sought in the bosom of his civilization and his world. After twenty-eight years, Robinson returns to his country. But when Defoe returned to his civilization, he could see only criminals and prostitutes.

8. The Impact of the "Noble Savage" on the European Conscience

Civilization and the world of Defoe were not, in fact, Eden--by now left in the past--but rather Europe. As Christopher Dawson observes, after the rapid advance of evangelism in lands on the other side of the Atlantic, Europe stopped being a Christian continent and lost one of its exclusive and typical characteristics, even though it still kept its loyalty to the classic tradition and to humanism. It is true, Dawson adds, that society generally continued to be dominated by religious ideas just as it had been in the medieval age and that "indeed it may be doubted whether religion has ever excited a more passionate interest in men's minds than during the century that lies between the years

1560-1660, the age of the Puritans and the Jansenists,
. . . of St. Teresa and St. Vincent de Paul."[2] But in
the midst of this society wasn't there already a seeth-
ing of ideas, anticipations, and intuitions destined
to shape a new society in which the notion of the noble
savage certainly would not be foreign? Of course this
concept brought into the European conscience problematical issues that changed with the historical phases in
which it was articulated. One certainly can say, however, that from its inception this concept identified
the savage as the authentic "natural" man (with his
laws and with his natural religions); moreover, it
emphasized an interest in everything relating to man,
everything *human*.

By this point the savage was a touchstone with
which the classical and modern worlds could be measured.
This constitutes the beginning of the history of folklore, especially when coupled with ethnology. The concept of the noble savage contained the affirmation of a
new set of values from which the history of folklore
was to gain a vigorous impulse: the affirmation of all
that is simple and elemental, as opposed to all that is
artificial and farfetched.

[2]*Progress and Religion* (1929; rpt. Westport, Conn.:
Greenwood Press, 1970), p. 187.

CHAPTER II

THE MESSAGE OF THE ORIENT

1. *The "Symbolic Foreigners"*

After the discovery of America, anyone living in Europe
must have felt that he was living in a dissatisfied,
turbulent new world. The concept of the noble savage
served, among other things, to contrast Europeans to
American Indians (exactly as Casas, Léry, Montaigne,
and Baron Lahontan have documented for us). However,
we must ask a question about this contrast in which
the comparative method has its first unsophisticated
but rich application: how many other concepts are
related to the concept of the noble savage--accompany-
ing it, complementing it, perhaps even perfecting it?
Such concepts are not only the result of an elementary
civilization like that of the American Indians but also
of refined civilizations like those of the Orientals,
civilizations whose historical development took place
well before Europe had its own cultural unity.

A perceptive and sensitive French thinker, Paul
Hazard, observed that, along with the concept of the
noble savage, "Symbolic Foreigners" arrived at that
time in Europe. He adds: "They arrived with their customs, laws, and original values, and they brought themselves to the attention of a Europe eager to question
them about their history and origin. They gave the
requested answers, each his own." This interest was
not, however, merely an erudite interest in the usages,
laws, and spiritual values in which the life of "Symbolic Foreigners" was realized; more importantly,
such interest pointed to a deepening of the European
conscience. It is an error, then, to think that

sixteenth- and seventeenth-century Europe considered
"Symbolic Foreigners" as an expression of inferior
peoples, whoever they were; in fact, the contrary is
true. On the one hand, such comparisons emphasized
Europe's interest in primitive *and* in Oriental peoples
(that is, nations in varying degrees remote from the
West); on the other hand, these comparisons generated
a new ethical awareness in Europeans themselves.

We know that even back in the medieval ages Europe
had possessed a literature that made the Orient its
object, a flowering tradition that continued into the
Renaissance; hence, ancient Oriental civilizations,
particularly Arabia and India, had long been generally
present in the European mind. After the discovery of
America, however, the Orient became accessible not
only to those who maintained trading and dwelled on
the various interests of the visited countries when
they returned home but also to the missionaries whose
attention again turned to the Orient, spurred by the
hope of spreading Christianity there. The commentaries
of the former and the latter did not remain as dead
letters or idle curiosities; rather, as had previously
occurred in commentaries on primitive nations, they
penetrated the culture of the time, of which they
represented one of the most disquieting aspects. As
the Arabian expert Francesco Gabrieli observes, this
renewed discovery of the Orient was not "a direct and
unreflective contact as in the medieval ages but
rather an aware expansion of the Western spirit
towards worlds distant in time and place; knowledge
and scientific exploration corresponded to the intellectual and moral needs of a society and an era that
cannot be adequately studied without investigating
the whole phenomenon of the *filorientalismo*." Gabrieli goes on to comment on an entire world that,
while full of exotic reality, constitutes, like the
world of the primitives, another acquisition of the
reawakening European culture.

2. The Orient as a Cradle of Forces, Ideals, and Religions

The Orient viewed by travelers after the discovery of America was no longer, then, merely a comparative point signifying, as happened in the medieval ages, something radically different from the customs and beliefs of the West; rather, the Orient now came to be viewed as a cradle of forces, experiences, ideals, and religions. The attitude of those who went to the Orient was generally that of cautious observers who tried to become aware of those forces, to make those experiences their own, and to outline those ideals. Let us open, for example, the reports entitled *Delle navigationi et viaggi* (1556-1606), a work that a geographer, Giovanni Ramusio, assembled, or Richard Hakluyt's account entitled *The Principal Navigations, Voyages and Discoveries of the English Nation*, published in 1589. Here the Orient is no longer the dimly outlined country of Utopia; rather, it is clearly separated into various nations. Each nation has its own distinct features--not self-contained, distant, impenetrable features but something close to the spirit of whoever observes the people in order to analyze and understand them.

In the travel accounts collected by Ramusio and Hakluyt, an indomitable spirit of adventure is undeniably present. In addition, these writers often demonstrated a great desire to understand. The Orient was most available to those who visited it with numerous interests in mind, especially ethnographical interests, and perhaps no other traveler was as analytical in this regard as Pietro della Valle. *Viaggi di Pietro della Valle il Pellegrino . . . descritti da lui medesimo in 54. lettere familiari*, first published in Rome between 1650 and 1658, was translated into French, German, English, and Dutch, and it attained an uncommon popularity.

Valle had no commercial interests to satisfy, except that of acquiring a series of Oriental manuscripts, still conserved today in the Vatican. He was a pilgrim of love who viewed the Orient "as a fabulous

world, in many respects still primitive and savage," a
world that nevertheless preserved "vestiges and echoes
of the oldest and most glorious European civilization."
This belief led to his comparisons between holidays in
Persia, Turkey, and India, on the one hand, and those
in Europe, on the other; however, along with holidays,
he compared the totality of Oriental life with the
life of the West in perceptive critical observations
expressed in a style in which one senses both the
learned humanist and a modern mind imbued in the scientific interests of ethnography.

3. *"The East Is God's, the West Is God's"*

An ethnographical interest in the Orient was expressed
by another Italian, Daniello Bartoli, who, unlike
Valle, was never in the Orient, although he provided
a lively picture of it through the accounts and
letters of his Jesuit brothers. Having the task of
writing a *Dell'historia della Compagnia di Giesù*, he
planned to organize the work in sections corresponding
to the branches of the institutions whose events he
narrated. Although he spoke of his brothers' "intent
to convert idolaters" or people who were "still barbarians"(as he considered the Indians), he focused
sharply on the usages and customs of the people that
he described. It is true that Bartoli had his prejudices, but these he transformed into edifying literature. As a result of these prejudices the apostleship
of his brothers took on the epic tones heard in so many
accounts of this period--and his missionaries sometimes
asked only that they be allowed to shed their own blood
for the good of souls. For the most part, however,
they were pioneers who again, although perhaps for
religious reasons, joined the East with the West.

In drawing up the works entitled *La Cina* and *Il
Giappone* (which followed his *L'Asia* and which were published between 1653 and 1661), Bartoli made great use
of Matteo Ricci's letters and accounts (only recently
made known to the public, along with many other travel
documents). But did he ever come to understand the

apostleship of this learned missionary? Along with
his companions of the faith, Ricci had tolerated the
national practices of his neophytes even though he
himself considered them examples of superstition and
idolatry. In this respect he was followed, as far as
India is concerned, by Father Roberto de Nobili, who
was willing to make certain concessions to customs
and local ideas. This was the basis of the sharpest
criticism directed at the two missionaries, who were
accused of actually practicing paganism, and it was
the basis of the controversy raised by the so-called
Chinese and Malabar rites, which raged as much in the
Orient as in the West. But if such controversy resulted in establishing the superstitious character of
these rites (in respect to Christianity), it also
revealed the spirit of the civilization coursing
through them. Additionally--and a distant echo of
this is heard in some of Bartoli's own writings--from
such controversy came an understanding that missionaries, particularly the Jesuits, responded sensitively
to the moral depth of some religions (especially
Asiatic ones), even if of natural rather than supernatural character; the missionaries were sensitive,
then, to the problem of natural religion, which indeed
is always worthy of respect even if incomplete in
respect to the Revelation. Thus, the Oriental may
have been idolatrous and superstitious, as the missionaries believed, but he was a soul of God. Goethe
would say later, "The East is God's, the West is
God's." The Oriental, in essence, is as noble as the
savage!

4. The Turk and the Persian Give Lessons to Europe

The Oriental was not merely noble. He was wise and
vigorous, despite the millennia that he carried on his
shoulders, and he was capable of teaching Europeans a
thing or two. Travelers and missionaries had tried to
see how much of the West was in the East and how much
of the East was in the West. Now, however, we are at
the point where an Oriental enters the European scene

in order to criticize the oddities and prejudices of
Europe. The Oriental now wants the upper hand--and
he will have it.

In 1684, for example, a Genoese, Giovanni Paolo
Marana, published an interesting book, *L'espion du
grand-seigneur*, a work in which something is said
about Turkey, of course, but even more is said about
Europe. The Turk here is not the one that Jean
Rotrou jestingly portrayed in *La sœur* (1645). It
seems that he has emerged, rather, from certain pages
of Paul Rycaut, whose *l'Histoire de l'état présent de
l'Empire Ottoman* (first published in English in 1666)
had been published by Briot in 1671, or from the
atmosphere which Jean Baptiste Tavernier had created
for him; in 1676, Tavernier had published a book that
is surely one of the most intriguing works of the
French, *Les six voyages de Jean Baptiste Tavernier,
ecuyer baron d'Aubonne, en Turquie, en Perse, et aux
Indes*.

Marana's intentions were not those that Rycaut
and Tavernier had set their minds on. Indeed, his
Turk is not in Turkey at all but rather in France,
in Paris, from where he sends secret accounts to the
Council of Constantinople. Nor is it without significance that one of the numerous editions of *L'espion*,
the edition of 1710, carried the addition *dans les
cours des princes chrétiens*. The courts, especially
those in Paris, are his observatory. His letters are
brief, stringent, and full of facts. He is a liberal
thinker who judges Christians without animosity, but
he is more concerned with morality than with dogma.
He would like to reconcile all religions, since there
is always something good in them. The customs of
Europe interest him. But, after all, isn't Turkey
with its simpler traditions preferable to this very
complicated Europe?

Two years after the publication of *L'espion*, in
1686, *Voyages du chevalier Chardin en Perse, et
autres lieux de l'Orient* appeared in France. Sir
John Chardin, a man motivated by his interest in gem
commerce (as was Tavernier), was rather unusual in
that he wasn't Catholic. A fervent Protestant, he

was fascinated by distant countries, as many before
him had been. The country of his heart, however, was
Persia, whose inhabitants, he felt, had no reason to
envy Europeans, however different their customs were.
In his accounts (occasionally long-winded but often
delightfully refreshing and light), he attempted to
instruct himself in order to instruct his readers
"about everything that might deserve the interest of
all of Europe concerning a country that we could call
'another world' because of its remoteness and its
unusual customs and laws." He adds that "the climate,
the climate of each people, is always, it seems to me,
the chief cause for the tendencies of the people's
customs." Although he explained the difference
between European and Persian customs, he concluded
that Persia was a country that had no reason to envy
Europe.

5. Egypt: Fountain of Youth

In addition to the Chinese, the Japanese, the Indians
(of historical India), the Turks, and the Persians,
we must also consider other heroes: the Egyptian, the
Siamese, and the Mohammedan Arab. Marana himself, the
inventor of the Turk, published a romance in 1696,
*Entretiens d'un philosophe avec un solitaire sur
plusieurs matières de moral et d'érudition*, whose hero,
a nonagenarian, is "fresher and rosier than a little
girl"; this is so because he has lived in Egypt, a
country where one learns "true philosophy, which has
nothing in it of Christianity." But was Egypt merely
a fountain of physical youth? Or was it not also a
fountain of intellectual youth? In an old work published in 1551 and dedicated to the *Mythologiae, sive
Explicationum fabularum*, an Italian humanist, Natale
Conti, had proposed the idea that ancient fables were
artificial productions intended to transmit the teachings of philosophy. He was convinced, however, that the
knowledge of the Jewish patriarchs had passed into Egypt
and then on into Greece. It is true that many scholars,
such as the famous Jesuit Anthanasius Kircher (whose

Oedipus aegyptiacus was published in Rome in 1652),
believed that idolatry, under the influence of the
devil, came from Egypt (a thesis renewed in 1711 by
Antoine Banier, who, in his *Explication historique
des fables*, identified this idolatry with sun worship).
But in 1670 another gem merchant, François Bernier, in
his *Histoire de la dernière révolution des états du
Grand Mogol*, picked up on an idea that was common to
other travelers: specifically that one must search in
Egypt for the origin of music and geometry. In 1681,
Jacques-Bénigne Bossuet's *Discours sur l'histoire
universelle* was published. In the tradition of St.
Augustine, Bossuet followed the road of humanity, imagining himself to be under the powerful and triumphant
guidance of God. Of all the nations that he described,
the one in which he was most interested was the Egyptian. Naturally Bossuet knew Herodotus and Strabo, but
he also had other texts, including the accounts of the
Capuchin missionaries, at his disposal. Relying on the
evidence that these sources offered him, he refused to
believe that Egypt had a philosophy, old or new; however, he did believe that it had an architecture that
could be a source of inspiration. He hoped, therefore,
that Thebes would rise again:

> If our travelers had pushed as far as the place
> where this city rose, they would certainly have
> discovered something incomparable in its ruins,
> because the works of the Egyptians were made for
> resisting the changing times. . . . Today, now
> that the name of the king has spread even into
> the most obscure parts of the world, and now that
> the sovereign pushes just as far for an investi-
> gation of the most beautiful works of nature and
> art, shouldn't a worthy aim of this noble curios-
> ity be the uncovering of the beauties that Thebes
> contains in its deserts and the enriching of our
> architecture with the inventions of Egypt?

To all of this we must add the fact that in 1685 an
Anglican theologian, John Spencer, published his vast
De legibus Hebræorum ritualibus et earum rationibus.

In this work Spencer asserted, contrary to Bossuet,
that the Mosaic religion was not wholly founded on the
Revelation; furthermore, he emphasized the important
influence that the Egyptians have had in the realms of
law, precepts, and rites. In looking at all of these
facts, we surely begin to have an idea of what Egypt
represented.

Because Marana was neither a scholar nor a philosopher, he most probably did not know all the books
previously written about Egypt. It is a fact, however,
that he gave us an Egyptian who, while judging Europe
in much the same way as the Turk had judged it, could
do so "thanks to God" with a "noble title"--he, the
son of a pagan yet blessed land.

What is said of the Egyptian can also be said of
the Siamese, who descended into the field accompanied
by a clever French writer, Charles Dufresny. In 1699,
in his *Amusements sérieux et comiques* (a novelette that
often reminds us of Marana's *Entretiens*), Dufresny
resolved to join forces with a vigorous, wise Siamese
in order to criticize contemporary customs, somewhat
in the manner of Jean de La Bruyère (to whom we owe
some of the most beautiful passages ever written about
French peasants). Siam was held in high esteem at
that time. Just think of it! In 1684 Parisians saw
the first mandarins arrive, and in 1685, 1686, and
1687 French missionaries had gone to Siam. From Siam,
then, came accounts written primarily by the ecclesiastical scholars of the day. At the heart of these
accounts one is able to ascertain that the Siamese,
despite their ridiculous religion, had pure, austere
customs, and they were both tolerant and wise.
Dufresny grasped and skillfully disseminated these
ideas, at the same time (aware as he was of the inner
workings of the French court) rebelling against the
"softened" customs of his time.

In the midst of this flowing of interests that
multiplied daily, the presence of the Arab also had
a place. At first he did not make his presence known,
but soon he clearly emerged in the awareness of the
European world, particularly because Corano was to
stand as godfather to a work destined to make an

enormous impression: *Contes Arabes*, translated by
Antoine Galland. Galland was a disciple and successor
of Barthélemy d'Herbelot de Molainville at the Collegio
Reale in Paris, who already had contributed so much to
a greater awareness of Oriental civilization with his
Bibliothèque orientale in 1697.

6. Fairy Tales and the Orient

Contes was published in Paris between 1704 and 1717,
a period in which admiration and excitement had continued in France for a *genre* whose characters were
accustomed to living in hovels among the poor folk,
for the pleasure of children who had no other dreams.
Madame d'Aulnoy had begun this mode, which was further developed by Mademoiselle Le Force, Comtesse de
Murat, Chevalier de Mailly, and especially Charles
Perrault, who published *Histoires ou contes du temps
passé* in 1697 under the name of his son, P. D'Arman-
cour (who was then only ten years old). For these
people the past appeared in an atmosphere of dream
and poetry.

In the introduction, in which the son, or rather
Perrault, dedicates his *Histoires* (subtitled *Contes
de ma Merè l'Oye*) "to the Grand Madamoiselle," he
says: "On ne trouvera pas étrange qu'un enfant ait
pris plaisir à composer les contes de ce Recueil."
It is like reading La Fontaine:

>   . . . et moi-même
>   si Peau d'ane m'était conté
>   j'y prendrais un plaisir extrême.

Perrault, however, recognized this publication as
useful because his fairy tales "renferment toute une
morale très sensée." He creates these prose and verse
stories with elegance and grace, setting them in a
misty morning atmosphere. The heroes of his fairy
tales belong to all social classes. At times they
live in "reality," but they invest this reality with
a marvelous supernatural significance; and the moral

of the tales is realized in virtue, in the struggle
against vice and evil.

Like other storytellers of the period, Perrault
drew his material from the folk. In fact, in this
respect his *Histoires* continued a tradition that had
previously reached its height in Italy in the sixteenth century with Straparola and a century after
with Giambattista Basile, from whose *Lo cunto de li
cunti* Madame d'Aulnoy herself had taken a good part
of her *Contes de fées*, which came out between 1682
and 1690. I have hinted at relationships and deriva-
tions among French and Italian fabulists, which is
incontestable. However, both generally drew from
one common source, and these fabulists were certainly
not folklorists; rather, they were writers or poets
whose work nevertheless interests folklorists because
it documents, in a definite period and specific
environment, the diffusion of prolific and vigorous
narrative motifs existing among the folk.

It is true, of course, that French fabulists
sometimes dressed their fairies in French fashion,
making them speak as if they had been actually ladies
of Versailles. But what were these fables, and where
did they come from? In 1688 La Fontaine, who had
been fascinated by such fables as "Peau d'âne," published the first edition of his *Fables choisies, mises
en vers* (which later became the famous *Contes et
nouvelles*). Two years later--nor is it without significance that we point out this date--a learned Frenchman, Bishop Huet, appeared on the scene. Throughout
his life, Huet tried to demonstrate that the gods of
the Phoenicians, Egyptians, and Persians descended
from Moses, since he was convinced that beneath even
the most diverse inventions one could find the unique
figure of God. In his curious *Lettre sur l'origine
des Romans*, first published in 1670, he expressed the
opinion that fairy tales are the inventive products
of the human spirit but that the spirit of imitation
is common to all peoples and all times. Nor is it to
be doubted, he adds, that, this being the case, many
fairy tales originated in the Orient. "And when I say
the Orient," he concludes, "I mean the Egyptians,

Persians, Indians, Syriacs, and Arabians." It is true
that the time was not ripe for raising a question of
this kind. But Huet had already perceived the problem,
and La Fontaine himself, a few years later, would also
perceive it. In the preface of 1678, which preceded a
new edition of his *Fables*, La Fontaine asserted: "I
owe a large part of my fables to Bidpai, the Indian
sage."

7. The *"Thousand and One Nights"*

Given the atmosphere created by travel books about the
Orient and by the interest in fables that these books
aroused, one can understand and explain the success of
Galland's *Contes*. But what are the *Contes*? They are
Les mille et un nuits, the stories of the *Thousand and
One Nights*. In this book we hear the civilizations of
India, Persia, Iraq, and Egypt speaking--the result of
a slow, laborious process of formulation realized "in
an area of diffusion and transmigration that transcends
to a large extent, the sphere of one human life and one
specific country."
     Galland, as Gabrieli has noted, "was neither a sci-
entific translator with scruples of literalness and
completeness nor, on the other hand, a manufacturer and
falsifier of his manuscripts; rather, he was a literate
educated man of the great century who, in his travels
in the Orient, had observed that world with the objec-
tivity and interest of a Valle. He disclosed the
exotic narrative treasure that he came across without
giving in to romantic abandon and with a vigilant
awareness of historical and moral requirements that had
to be safeguarded to make the work acceptable to his
contemporaries." Those contemporaries, we should add,
were immediately interested in the *Contes*, in which the
folklife of Oriental metropolises is animated by the
most extraordinary and incalculable things. We are
meant to be entertained by the book, but we are also
meant to learn. The *Thousand and One Nights* opens like
a poem, with an invocation to Mohammed; but after this
invocation there immediately follows the foreword:

Praise to God, Lord of all worlds, benediction
and health to the Prince of Prophets, to our Lord
and Patron Mohammed, to whom God grant continuing
and incessant benediction and well-being until
the day of judgment. May the deeds of the
ancients serve as examples to the following generations so that man may see the warning events
that have happened to others and take warning
from them and, reading the history of past peoples, receive healthy restraint from them. Praise
be to those who from the histories of the ancients
have made an example to the future. Of such exemplary narrations are the accounts of the *Thousand
and One Nights* with the marvelous adventures and
fables contained in them.

No other word found in the *Thousand and One Nights*
is used so much as the word "marvelous." The stories
are all "marvelous." Every listener "marvels at the
tales." The *Thousand and One Nights* is the temple of
the "marvelous," a temple through which all classes
parade: kings, queens, princes, ministers, courtiers,
viziers, fakirs, tailors, merchants. All, to use a
phrase from the book, love "poetry and sententious and
admonishing talk." Occasionally the events have nothing of the extraordinary: they are events of all days
and times. But they are then invested with the supernatural, with the "marvelous," so that along with kings
we find birds who read, along with slaves demons who
change into lions, and so on. Genies and goblins fly.
Along with religion, white or black magic presides over
human events in a combination of evocative power. The
popular style in which past events are expressed nevertheless maintains a certain reality: kings, for example, always have a kingdom. This reality is charming
in a hallucinating atmosphere of wonders and genies,
and the background against which the events are set is
an Orient that also contains a bit of the West. All
this makes the *Thousand and One Nights* a prodigious
work indeed.

On the one hand, the *filorientalismo* with its travels
put forth non-Christian values, nourishing, through a
love for the exotic, an idea that the concept of the
noble savage had previously sustained--the idea of a
natural religion; on the other hand, the *filorien-*
talismo undoubtedly aided growth of a new philological awareness through its emphasis on language study.
All of this, moreover, also gave the beginning to a
history of religions, which is precisely what the
works of Kircher and Spencer demonstrate. Consider
the fact that the former, in accomplishing his encyclopedic work, related the beliefs of China and Japan
to those of the American Indians, while the latter
tried to establish systematic relationships between
the customs of the Hebrews and those of other Semitic
peoples.

It is generally argued that theoretical ethnography and consequently the comparative method have
not been influenced by Orientalism. But can this
thesis be accepted? Orientalism has, in my opinion,
a significant relationship to theoretical ethnography
and to the comparative method that accompanies and
guides it, inasmuch as it presents the same instances
inspired by the concept of the noble savage. If we
take a retrospective look at all the travel books
about the Orient, we realize that many travelers
stopped to look at only what was strange and new, in
the manner of Marco Polo; but we also perceive that
others (for example, Valle and Chardin) went well
beyond that, clearly demonstrating their intent to
appraise the institutions of Oriental countries.
This approach inevitably promoted the investigation
not only of the differences among these institutions
and ours but of the similarities as well. The similarities, in turn, clearly gave rise to the principles
of humanity and brotherhood that the concept of the
noble savage had previously proposed. The differences,
on the other hand, help us understand why beliefs and
practices must be placed in their historical context,
in order that their nature, which is never despicable

or ridiculous, may be revealed. In both cases, how-
ever--in the feeling that the voices of others were no
longer curiosities but contingent and actual voices--
was the powerful presence of the *filorientalismo*. The
filorientalismo reconciled, in the conscience of the
time, those motivating forces that later gave a new
organization to the study of peoples, in the sense that
at last this study would come to include usages,
beliefs, superstitions--everything that is, if not the
whole tradition of the people, certainly an indelible
part of it.

Oriental peoples, like the primitives, would become
a touchstone with which popular European life could be
tested. Meanwhile, however, what difficulties would
accompany the development of such a life?

CHAPTER III

EUROPE BETWEEN RELIGION AND SUPERSTITION

1. *The Struggle Against Error*

As the love for travel books, distant countries, and
the most dissimilar civilizations and cultures grew
stronger and stronger in Europe, we are presented
with a most interesting phenomenon: the examination
that Europe makes of itself and its tradition, which
was partially recognized in the survival of ingenuous
residue from medieval life. The American Indians and
Oriental peoples (the "Symbolic Foreigners") had
already pointed out certain evils *via* travelers, missionaries, observers-philosophers, and romancers. But
theirs had essentially been a retrospective examination. It was necessary to put the examination on other
bases. This, strange to say, would be accomplished not
only by a number of rebels who saw the Catholic Church
and its dogmas as an end to all civilization but also
by religious thinkers who wanted to free the Church
from prejudices that hindered or compromised its authority. Both of these movements initiated a struggle
against certain traditional beliefs, a struggle founded
on principles and purposes that were opposite yet converging. But what, we first must ask ourselves, was
the origin of such a struggle, and what were the spiritual movements behind it?

The discovery of America, scientific advances, and
the Reformation were the fundamental stages giving impetus to the battle against traditional beliefs, in the
midst of which European awareness grew. But, if we wish
to clarify the origin and development of this struggle,
we also have to consider the Counter Reformation and

movements associated with the advent of modern thought
--those that emphasized observation or experimentation
(Bacon), those that expounded on the autonomy of science in regard to faith (Galileo), those that were
inspired by methodical doubt (Descartes), those that
attempted to reconcile faith with science by identifying God with nature (Spinoza), and those that pointed
toward a new conception of religion (Locke).

2. *The Reformation and the Comparison between the*
   "Marvelous" Christian and the "Marvelous" Pagan

The Reformation had been inspired by a critical spirit
that, paralleling the humanistic movement, attempted
to return to sources and origins, to the documents and
authentic testaments of faith. Humanists and humanistic historiographers--and it would be sufficient here
to cite Valla and his *De falso credita Constantini
donatione*--were trying to open the eyes of all who had
inherited the old legends and ancient traditions,
blindly and passively accepted for generations and
generations. Sixteenth-century reformers--Luther,
Calvin, Zwingli, and others--approached the texts in
much the same way, accepting only what, in matters of
faith, were explicitly contained in them. Everything
else was emphatically rejected. It clearly was not a
question of analytically examining religion, which
was to be the work of the following centuries. Indeed,
the Reformation critically analyzed only a very few of
the dogmas it accepted. What we must see, however, is
the fecundity of such a movement in respect to the
subsequent course of European culture. But one must
also note yet another aspect of the Reformation, for
which we must refer not to Lutheranism but to Calvinism: individualism--the fact that man comes to find
himself alone in the presence of God. Luther considered religion to be the concern of the State, nor would
he allow that the subject of a reformed prince should
profess a different religion; for Calvin, on the other
hand, political communities (like the religious) were
a free expression of the individual. It is precisely

here that we should see the origins of what would
become, in doctrine and political procedure, European
liberalism.

Although humanism appears to us, at least in certain respects, as the exaltation of human nature under
the inspiration of a classical paganism, we know that
the Reformation regarded paganism as the basic corruption of man. This was the basis of the struggle that
the Reformation undertook against Roman idolatry, an
idolatry imbued with paganism and characterized by a
mass of rites and foreign cults to which folklife
especially adhered. Accepted by the people (at least
at first) because it signified a rebellion against the
clergy and the authority of Rome (we know, however,
that Luther would throw himself against the *ladresco
ed assassino tumultuare del contadinume*), the Reformation resumed an attack previously initiated against
idols by Byzantine Christianity as far back as the
sixth century--an opposition to images with bobbing
heads, miraculous cures, and so forth, of which monks
had been the most zealous advocates. To this was
added the veneration of saints and of the Virgin Mary.
But in resuming this controversy, which merged with
the controversy over pagan papism and the attendant
criticism of papal theology, didn't the Reformation
provide us with an inventory of such beliefs?

The most significant movement deriving from this
critical attitude was the proceedings of the famous
Centuriatores Magdeburgi, which examined a tremendous
amount of material relating to Christian martyrdom,
miracles, legends, and so on. Nor should one forget,
in this regard, the close ties between the theories
of Erasmus and the Reformation, since Erasmus's broad-
minded humanism (which is not to be confused with
Luther's rigid theology) clearly led to the new tendencies of the century.

This inventory, and with it a study of traditional
beliefs, was not, however, an end in itself; one must
remember that the "protesting" writers had the well-
resolved goal of recognizing in ancient philosophies
and religions those superstitions found in the Roman
liturgy, which the people naturally enough accepted

and adopted. On the one hand, the arguments raised
against Roman idolatry encouraged the study of Biblical
texts and Semitic languages; on the other hand, such
arguments initiated comparisons of cults and the study
of their antiquity, an investigation already undertaken
with amateur curiosity by humanists (for example,
Boccaccio, Pictorius, Sardi, and Conti) who had been
interested in classical legends, beliefs, and rites.
From the comparison between the "marvelous" Christian
and the "marvelous" pagan a whole series of tracts on
comparative religions, mythologies, and rites came into
being, although it was frequently a matter, as Eduard
Fueter defines it, of a partisan historiography.

From this point of view the Catholic Counter Reformation is not of minor importance. We know, for example, that the Council of Trent aggressively opposed the
consuetudines non laudabiles, especially devil worship
and witchcraft. But in point of fact this opposition
was sustained as much by the Reformation as by the
Counter Reformation, which continued to see in witchcraft something that approached heresy.

3. The "Malleus maleficarum" and Demonological Literature

The fight against witchcraft found one of its principal
sources in the *Malleus maleficarum* of Jakob Sprenger and
Henricus Institoris, first published in 1480, which was
a virtual gospel for the tribunals of the Inquisition.
The mentality of Sprenger (under whose name the *Malleus*
generally goes) was essentially the same as Luther's.
Sprenger was a Dominican scholar who comfortably moved
between the Bible and the works of St. Thomas Aquinas.
He simultaneously represented, as Jules Michelet says,
"good sense and the negation of good sense." But leaving aside these qualities, there is a very good reason
for our remembering his *Malleus*: it is the richest
encyclopedia that we have about the prejudices not just
of Germany but of the entire fifteenth century. It
seems that Sprenger, who sent so many sick paupers to
the stake with heroic fervor, possessed an overwhelming

concern, the concern of the folklorist who collects
contemporary superstitions, compares them to each
other, places them in the past from which they derive,
and finally (canonists and glossarists by his side)
considers them as heretical phenomena against which he
hurls his inexorable condemnation. In this respect
the *Malleus* is a work of considerable interest to the
scholar of popular traditions. But we must also note
that this work contains elements that were later picked
up not only by the so-called *Fontes, Marteaux, Fourmu-
liers, Fustigationes,* and *Lanternae,* but also by different *Disquisitiones* (the most famous being the one
by Martin Del Rio)--demonological literature in which
prejudices about the devil, witches, and witches'
sabbaths are exposed to a disconcerting examination,
via an impassioned dialogue with the devil.

The inquisitors were not the only protagonists in
this dialogue: the devil affects everybody a little
bit! Very instructive in this regard is *Demonomanie
des sorciers,* a work that Jean Bodin published in 1580.
Bodin was an advocate of natural religion, which he
considered innate in humans and therefore anterior to
all historical forms of religion; furthermore, he was
an admirer of the Judaic religion because it contains
the simplicity of primitive religion. This was in
antithesis of the utopianism of the time (in which,
as Roger Chauviré correctly noted, all one's ideas
supposedly begin with the family and with respect for
natural law). When the struggle in France between
Catholics and Huguenots began, Bodin joined the political group that hoped to reconcile the demands of the
two groups, proposing religious tolerance as an instrument of pacification. He had, then, an open mind. But
when it came to witches and the prejudices surrounding
them (which he approached with the same earnestness
that he had for politico-doctrinal subjects), he did
not have the least tolerance.

In his *Demonomanie*--an earlier work than *Heptaplomeres,* in which he was concerned with religion and
natural law--Bodin asserted, like Luther, that the persecution of witches is sacred and indispensable (didn't
Bacon, after all, say the same thing?); moreover, he

immediately became incensed with those who did not
believe in witchcraft, or who only believed "up to a
certain point." Believing that to make France peaceful one must rid the country of all witches, Bodin did
not want to hear reasons. Even Aristotle wearied him,
as did all those who appealed to the laws of nature and
reason: "Now it is almost no less impious to doubt
that it is possible that there are some witches than to
ask skeptically if there is a God. But the accumulation of these errors has come because those who have
denied the existence of evil spirits and witchcraft
have attempted to contend physically with supernatural
and metaphysical things, which is a notable indecency."

4. Bodin and the Witches

But there are more matters to consider. All of Europe
was then at the mercy of "sorcerers," and all of Europe
was full of witches and stakes. In Bodin's view, these
witches came from Italy, a country that actually had
been, in comparison with other nations, the most skeptical about witchcraft, which is, as we know, the decadent part of magic. The Renaissance, as its greatest
representatives have demonstrated, was actually not
much concerned with witchcraft, while it always sought
to give a scientific character to magic. Of course
this did not stop many from believing in omens and in
auguries--a result of the classical tradition (the
Greco-Roman), strengthened by the diffusion that humanism itself had given to Chaldean, Hebraic, and Neo-
Platonic systems of knowledge. But it is also true
(as evidenced by Galileo's strong opposition to the
decadent tradition of magic) that the Renaissance threw
many ashes on the red hot flames of the devil.
   But what did all this matter to Bodin? He had a
sure target to aim for in Andrea Alciati, who, although
believing in witches, begged a little common sense for
them, as opposed to the blind fury of those who would
attack them with flames. Since Alciati was Italian,
Italy, argued Bodin, was also responsible for the crime
of exculpating witches. Some years later witches did

in fact find an able defender in a learned German
Jesuit, Friedrich von Spee, whose *Cautio criminalis*,
published in 1631 and written in a deft, smooth Latin,
is an answer as much to the *Malleus* as to *Demonomanie*,
an answer that one could place beside Beccaria's *Dei
delitti e delle pene* in the history of legal procedure.
(It is a fact, however, that in Italy Galateo, also
known as Antonio de Ferrari, had relegated belief in
witches to the field of hallucinations in his *De situ
Iapygiae*, published in 1511.)

Spee, who was also a skilled poet, had observed
many trials, and he could not tolerate the spectacular
quality that executions for witchcraft had assumed in
Germany as well as in Spain; consequently, he had
fairly well made up his mind about the beliefs and
prejudices involved in such trials. It should be added
that he had the scholarly temperament of a folklorist,
one who did not mind interrupting his prose to introduce some anecdotes like the one about the monk and the
prince, which is the best remark in his *Cautio*. A
German prince, Spee reports in his work, asked a monk
if a person who has been denounced by twelve witches
and who has participated in a witches' sabbath could
be arrested. The monk answers, "Certainly." The
prince then replies, "Very well, reverend, you should
be arrested because you have been denounced not by
twelve but by fifteen witches."

5. *Anticipators of the Enlightenment: Browne and
   Sprat*

The times, however, were not completely ready for
Cautio criminalis to sweep away the unfortunate persecution of witches. We should not be surprised, then,
that a cultured, refined scholar like Thomas Browne,
one of England's greatest essayists, believed in
witches. In England too, after all, witchcraft was
not just a literary expedient in the hands of Shakespeare; indeed, it came under the rule of common law.
Elizabeth had virtually memorized the articles from
the statutes of Henry VII about the condemnation of

whoever practices witchcraft. Later, James I in his
Daemonologie directly cited the devil as having the
greatest responsibility for witchcraft, with the result
that he did not hesitate to legislate:

> Whoever shall use, practice, or exercise any Invo-
> cations or Conjuration of any evill and wicked
> Spirit, or shall consult, covenant with, intertaine,
> employe, feed, or reward any evill and wicked Sprit
> to or for any intent or purpose; or takes up any
> dead man, woman or child, from his sepulcher or
> other place in which a cadaver reposes, or the skin,
> the bones, or other parts of the corpse where it
> might to be employed or used in any manner of Witch-
> crafte, sorcery, enchantment, or spell--such trans-
> gressors duly or legally convicted and sentenced
> through trial by jury shall suffer death.[1]

Browne, a member of the Reformed Church, had very
fertile ground under his feet, for in England the worst
period of that horrible mania was during the rule of
James I (1603-25). But Browne was no less credulous
than James I; let the proof of this be that in his
Religio Medici he did not hesitate to assert:

> For my [owne] part, I have ever beleeved, and doe
> now know, that there are Witches; they that doubt
> of these, doe not onely deny them, but Spirits;
> and are obliquely and upon consequence a sort, not
> of Infidels, but Atheists. Those that to confute
> their incredulity desire to see apparitions, shall
> questionlesse never behold any, nor have the power
> to be so much as Witches; the Devill hath them
> already in a heresie as capitall as Witchcraft,
> and to appeare to them, were but to convert them.[2]

In 1646 Browne, in a volume entitled *Pseudodoxia
Epidemica*, was quick to expose what he calls "common

---

[1] I Jas. I, C. 12.

[2] *The Works of Sir Thomas Browne,* ed. Geoffrey Keynes
(Chicago: Univ. of Chicago Press, 1964), I, 40.

and vulgar errors" to the light of experimentation.
He used the word "reason" many times; but unfortunately
he observed that, although the "multitude" is "flattered with that aphorism" that the voice of the people is
the voice of God, the multitude cannot give us truth.
Browne was convinced that books could not amend the
multitude. In fact, he wrote only for those who constituted "the knowing and leading part of learning."[3]
His works are whimsical, interesting, clever, and
tastefully written. But although he gives us a certain
inventory of the errors and commonplaces that the folk
believes in--and educated people, as well--Browne did
not really involve himself in either their origin or
their character, which he considered from an outsider's
point of view. He was more of a moralist than a historian, and he felt compelled to address his morality to
a cultured public, a specific class--the one to which
he belonged. This does not alter the fact, however,
that in matters of witchcraft he was like the folk.

Equally vigorous was the battle against errors that
an English theologian initiated some years later, in
regard to the High Church. This theologian was Thomas
Sprat, who later became the Lord Bishop of Rochester.
He was closer to Spee than to Browne, but from Browne
he inherited a love for experiment and science. His
History of the Royal Society, published in 1667, is an
energetic, courageous attempt to reconcile religion
with science. George M. Trevelyan notes, "Like Locke
and Newton a few years later, the Bishop concedes to
'the ancient miracles' of Bible times a passport as
privileged phenomena, unusual interferences of God with
His creation"; but it is a fact, he quickly adds, that
"modern miracles were no longer to be expected in the
Protestant, Anglican climate."[4] Sprat said that "the
course of things goes quietly along, in its own time
channel of natural causes and effects."[5] The world of
Shakespeare, he added with saintly naiveté, the world

[3]*The Works of Sir Thomas Browne,* II, 5.
[4]*English Social History* (London: Longmans, Green
and Co., 1943), p. 288.
[5]Quoted by Trevelyan, *English Social History,* p. 258.

of fairies, witches, love potions, and charms, is gone.
In Sprat's view, fairies and witches were only illusory
daydreams. Of him, certainly, Lord Shaftesbury could
not write what in 1707 he wrote to Lord Summers: "I
could put your lordship in mind of an eminent, learned,
and truly Christian prelate you once knew, who could
have given you a full account of his belief in fairies."[6]   But in regard to the matter of witches, it
wasn't until 1736 that the English Parliament abolished
the law punishing witches, even though it had been a
dead issue for quite a while.

6. Bekker and Thomasius

Following a somewhat different course from that of the
two Thomases, Browne and Sprat, were two rebellious
intellectuals, Balthasar Bekker, a Dutchman, and Christian Thomasius, a German. They too were opposed to and
fought against error. Neither, however, had theological concerns to serve. Bekker, disavowed by his church,
did indeed repudiate Spinoza, who had put traditional
beliefs on trial in his *Tractatus theologico-politicus*;
but he was a dyed-in-the-wool Cartesian, as is evidenced
by the fact that in 1668 he published his *Admonitio
sincera et candida de philosophia cartesiana*. Thomasius, although educated in the rigid canons of Lutheran
Protestantism, neither had nor desired bonds that might
restrict him.
     Bekker had an adversary to shoot at, the devil--an
adversary at whom he took deadly and open aim in *De
betoverde Weereld*, a bulky text published in 1691 and
translated in all European languages. This work was,
we could say, the first scientific attempt in which the
story of the devil was drawn not from books of the Bible
but rather from traditions and beliefs that various
countries held about the devil. As for the first part,
Bekker was convinced that the Holy Scripture, which

[6]*Characteristics of Men, Manners, Opinions, Times,
etc.*, ed. John M. Robertson (Gloucester, Mass.:   Peter
Smith, 1963), p. 7.

always makes an appeal to a belief in the devil, "considered in its substance and without prejudice, does
not attribute to the devil that power and those works
that the prejudices of commentators and translators
have attributed to him." As for the second point, he
maintained that belief in the devil, which he traced
to some degree in all European countries, was of pagan
origin and therefore had polluted Christianity. His
was a continual colloquy with the devil, but this colloquy was an attentive, scrupulous investigation into
all prejudices in which one could recognize the humbugs
of ignorant people who had no relationship with the
devil and whom it was inhuman, therefore, to condemn
for this alleged relationship.

A few years later, Thomasius expressed the same
opinion. Going back to Spee, he aggressively fought
against witch trials and the use of disgraceful punishments and torture. One of Thomasius's greatest works,
in which we hear echoes of Bekker, is his *Dissertatio
de crimine magiae*. But the work that gives a legacy
to his name is undoubtedly his *Fundamenta juris naturae
et gentium*, published in 1705. In this work he considered law as a social phenomenon; further, as has been
observed, he clearly distinguished morality from law,
in contrast to Italian political thinkers (from the
beginnings to St. Thomas Aquinas) who had distinguished law from morality. He thus became an advocate of
natural law, with which he had already struggled in
his *Institutionum jurisprudentiae* and which had previously found its most illustrative exponents (after
Bodin) in Johann Altusio, Alberico Genitili, and Hugo
Grotius.

Going back to these predecessors, Samuel Pufendorf,
who held the first professorship of natural law, published *De jure naturae et gentium* in 1672. The ideas
in this work were certainly not limited to the ruling
monarchy (Bodin) or to the intransigent confessional
(Altusio) and even less to the conviction that "natural
law is imposed and willed by God, the author of nature,"
and that "the Bible is the one and only source of law."
Pufendorf, Hazard observes, "does not deny divine power;
rather, he puts it on another level: there is the level
of pure reason and that of Revelation, the level of

natural law and that of moral theology, the level of
obligations placed on us because terms of natural law
make us consider them essential for the conservation
of human society in general, and the level of obligations placed on us because God prescribes them for us
in Holy Scripture." Here, then, was a clear distinction between natural and divine law. Now, Thomasius
had read Pufendorf, and the secularization of studies
attracted him and won him over. Thus, his investigations took a new direction:

> Never again will any belief be received dogmati-
> cally. When I examine a doctrine, no longer will
> I ask about the reputation that it enjoys or the
> authority that supports it; rather, I will ask
> what degree of evidence is presented. I will
> study the various arguments, pro and con, and I
> will decide myself, in accordance with my own
> understanding. Instead of remaining the obedient
> subject of the dictators of thought, I will be
> like those ancient heroes who took up arms against
> the tyrant and contributed to the triumph of
> liberty.

Like an ancient hero, then, he donned armor and
helmet, ready to descend into battle. His enemies
were prejudices, the source of all evils, and reason
was the faith for which he fought. It was this faith
that led to his insatiable love for society and humanity.

7. Deism and Natural Religion

Of equal interest for contemporary scholars, meanwhile,
was the desire to systematize natural religion. In
this regard, we should not forget the work of Herbert
of Cherbury entitled *De Veritate*, published in 1624,
which has been regarded as the manifesto of the intellectual current called deism, predominant in the seventeenth and eighteenth centuries. Cherbury emphatically
rejected the concept of the Revelation. He said that
the Revelation was nonexistent in natural religion,

which has no need of superstitious practices. Cherbury
denied the existence of a God, the God of Abraham,
Isaac, and Jacob--but he did believe in God. It is
absurd, he said, to think that man must have the Revelation in order to follow a morality: man can govern
himself quite well with only his reason. What truly
interests God is that we follow the sentiments of
religion and morality that he has impressed in our
souls. What good is it to believe in the Revelation
and then not follow such sentiments?

John Toland was apparently more cautious about
the Revelation. In 1696, he published *Christianity
not Mysterious*, in which he asserted that the mystery
does not exist and that the Revelation, while "undoubtedly a source of information," is not a "foundation," which only reason is competent to give us. He
added that reason is always superior to Revelation
"just as a *Greek Grammar* is superior to the *New
Testament*; for we make use of *Grammar* to understand
the language and of *Reason* to comprehend the sense of
that Book."[7]

Leaving aside these essentially theological discussions, it is a fact that Cherbury and especially
Toland have left to us, submerged in their dissertations, the description of usages, customs, and practices that illuminate the popular life of the time.
In *Letters to Serena* (1704), addressed to Queen Sophia
of Prussia, Toland concerns himself with the power
that prejudices have. He observes:

> The very midwife hands us into the world with
> superstitious ceremonies, and the good women
> assisting at the labor have a thousand spells to
> avert the misfortune, or to procure the happiness
> of the infant; making several ridiculous observa-
> tions, to discover the omen of his future state
> of life. Nor is the priest in some places behind-
> hand with these gossips, to initiate him betimes
> into his service, by pronouncing certain forms of
> words or so many powerful charms, and using the

[7]*Christianity not Mysterious* (London, 1696), p. 141.

gentle symbols of salt or oil, or the severer
applications of iron or fire, or by marking him
after some other manner, as his own right and
property for the future.[8]

But Toland did not merely compile an inventory of prejudices and general beliefs in the midst of which he
lived, disgusted as he was by the fact that responsible
poets and professors were forever speaking of genies,
nymphs, and metamorphosis; he also tried to see what
the origins of those beliefs were--and here his examination was perceptive even though his conclusions
offered too-open criticism. This deserves an example.
In *Letters to Serena* Toland proposes to explain the
origin of the idea of a disembodied soul. This belief
itself was already incorporated in the heritage of the
rough, uncultured folk. According to Toland, however,
it derives from the Orient and more specifically from
Egypt, from which it was taken, along with funeral
cults.

Although such research is often very ingenuous, we
must always be aware of the importance of deism in that
research. In one way or the other, deists were especially interested in liberating religion from all the
dogmatic overlay and superstitions that accompanied it.
In the last analysis, Cherbury and Toland believed in
miracles, but didn't they still look at them with a
critical eye? They were convinced that cults and rites
were the impostures of priests.

Deism was criticized not only in the satires of
Swift but also in the commentaries of numerous scholars
(although some considered deism to be only a deviation).
Too, there is much available research aimed at establishing the historical precedents of deism, which are
often recognized in specific intellectual currents (the
religious philosophy of the Italian Renaissance) or in
the works of specific authors (for example, More's
Utopia, Bodin's *Heptaplomeres*, and Locke's *Reasonableness of Christianity*). But isn't it more accurate, as
we have already seen in our investigations of Orientals

[8] *Letters to Serena* (London, 1704), p. 3.

and American Indians, to think that the beginning of
deistic solutions had been raised by investigations
that travelers (directly) and missionaries (indirectly)
had conducted into primitive and Oriental religions,
which have their own morality, even though of "natural"
composition?

8. *Folkloristic Theology*

We should not forget, however, that the superstition
against which battles were fought was nestled in
country houses, in villages where parishes agreed with
those Jesuits who "welcomed as good external practices
even the superstitions of a pagan flavor" because
"they considered them a useful basis for religious
life." This was the origin of the persistent substitu-
tion of pagan rites for Christian ones, although in
such substitutions the spirit that had animated preceding protagonists was changed; additionally, this
attitude generated the rising reaction at the heart
of the Jansenist movement and the harsh criticism of
the morality of the Jesuits, which has its most
famous expression in Pascal's *Lettres écrites à un
provincial.*
      In France, however, there were two theologians,
Jean Baptiste Thiers and Pierre Le Brun, who did not
agree with these opinions. In contrast to Browne, they
wished to educate the folk, liberating it from all
prejudices that fetter spiritual life. Like Sprenger,
Bodin, and Browne, moreover, they believed in witches.
Thiers, who published his copious *Traité des superstitions* in 1697, believed: (1) that a thing is superstitious and illicit when it is accompanied by certain
circumstances that have no natural virtues for producing desired results; (2) that superstition ruins faith
in the Church and worship of God; and (3) that superstition is the result of a pact between man and the
devil. No less important is Le Brun, to whom we are
indebted for *Histoire critique des pratiques superstitieuses qui ont séduit les peuples et embarassé les
savans*, first published in 1701-02.

Thiers and Le Brun did not fail to point to the
work carried out against superstitions by the members
of councils, especially the Council of Trent. They
(especially Thiers) emphasized the ideas of the Holy
Fathers and ecclesiastical writers, in respect to
superstition. But their work was not exhausted here.
They attempted to discover practices and beliefs, the
remains of paganism, heresies, deviations, and degenerations introduced by the folk ("par les rustres,"
says Thiers) into the bosom of religion (it would be
better to say the detritus of dead religions). Thus,
they relegated superstitions and beliefs to the kingdom of error, and, as Bodin and Browne had also asked,
isn't error perhaps the son of the devil?

Arnold van Gennep has recently observed that the
works of Thiers and Le Brun go back to demonological
literature for their subject matter. But here it is
best to be very precise. However we may regard the
subject matter, there is no doubt that the works of
Thiers and Le Brun basically follow the same tradition
as the works of Sprenger and Bodin, although the former two paid more particular attention to the problem
of popular errors. But doesn't their methodology, the
systematic gathering of traditions, conclude and perfect the work of Browne, Spee, Bekker, and Toland,
those who, while they must be included among the
anticipators and initiators of the Enlightenment, are
clearly the true precursors of European folklore?
Browne, Bekker, and Toland did not content themselves
with inventorying or collecting materials related to
cults, rites, and so on; rather, like Thiers and Le
Brun much later, they attempted to produce an answer.
It is precisely because of this that we can say that
the works of these two French theologians smoothed the
way for works such as Henry Bourne's *Antiquitates
vulgares, or The Antiquities of the Common People*,
published in 1725 (and reprinted later in many editions by John Brand, beginning in 1776). In Bourne's
text we see the concept of antiquity clearly formulated for everything that is popular (although, as we
know, Bacon already had discussed many of the popular
traditions and etymologies found in the *Antiquitates*);

moreover, we here see commemorated, with poetic accents, the holidays and beliefs of the English people,
which still today provide a sure reference point for
scholars of folklore.

CHAPTER IV

ERROR IN THE LIGHT OF REASON

1. Bayle: Precursor of European Folklore

The ongoing battle that Europe waged against traditional beliefs after the discovery of America took a
distinctive turn in eighteenth-century Catholic France,
the France of Thiers and Le Brun. This distinctive
turn was shaped by the work of the Enlightenment, whose
spiritual leader was Pierre Bayle. Even though Bayle
was most attracted to the works of Spinoza and Descartes, he was extremely interested in travelers, missionaries, American Indians, Oriental peoples, and the
naturalistic theology of deists.

The period in which Bayle lived nourished many
deists and liberal thinkers--a fact, he quickly adds
in his work against the revocation of the Edict of
Nantes, which has caused "many to be astonished. But
I am even more astonished that there are not more
deists and liberal thinkers, considering the devastation that religion accomplishes throughout the world
and the kind of morality that seems to be the inevi-
table consequence. To secure its own temporal well-
being, religion encourages every offense imaginable
--assassination, robbery, exile, and other violent
acts--producing an infinite number of other errors
such as hypocrisy, heretical practices, and so forth."

There was an episode, a neglected episode if you
will, that compelled Bayle to descend into battle
against this "devastation." In the *Journal des Savantes*
of January 1, 1681, one can read this announcement:
"Everyone is talking about the comet, the most important news at the start of this year. Astronomers are

observing its course, and the people are predicting a
thousand calamities." After that announcement a full
year passed before Bayle wrote a *Lettre à M.L.A.D.C.
docteur de Sorbonne. Où il est prouvé par plusieurs
raisons tirées de la philosophie et de la theologie
que les comètes ne sont point le présage d'aucun
malheur*. But this was not enough for him; in 1683 he
followed closely with *Pensées diverses, écrites à un
docteur de Sorbonne*; in 1694 with an *Addition aux
Pensées diverses*; and finally in 1705 with a *Continuation* to *Pensées diverses*. The comet, however, is not
the only concern in his discourses; his topic is much
broader than that. On the one hand, his argument
involves the larger question of belief, while on the
other hand (and this is what particularly interests
us), it attacks this concept at its core because the
superstition associated with the comet, attached as
it was to pagan beliefs, afforded a fortunate occasion for undertaking a study of prejudices and tradition itself.

Bayle asks himself what tradition *is*, in the first
place, and he concludes that it is "the assertion of
two or three persons repeated by a numberless throng
of credulous people." He adds: "Do you wish to
relate tradition to astrology? What is astrology
itself, this cause and source of so many prejudices,
if not something truly laughable?" You want to go
back to other sources, to accounts of poets and historians? If you do so, you will quickly discover,
Bayle asserts, that many poets and historians are
professional liars. Bayle laughed at everything, but
his machinery was now in motion. The interest (I
would call it a scientific interest) in the name of
which he entered the debate was transformed in his
hands. It was not enough for him to conclude that
attitudes toward comets belonged to the vast estate
of superstitions that has become an integral part of
Christianity (the object of study by Thiers and Le
Brun); he went on to address a question to himself:
"Do we wish to suppose that the comet is truly an omen
of misfortune?" The answer was precise, unequivocal,
and dogmatic: "In this case God would be performing

miracles in order to confirm idolatry in the world."
Here he was operating on an anatomical table; his investigation was made quite incisively, for he attempted
to dissect piece by piece an idolatry that was even
worse than the atheism of which he was accused. With
contemporary travel books in hand, he placed this atheism on the throne--if not the throne of glorification,
at least the throne of consideration.

2. Superstition as an Element of Power

Bayle's *Pensées* is an extensive and useful accumulation of popular beliefs of the time. Stripped of controversy, the *Pensées* offers us sharp investigations
aimed at penetrating the secret of prejudice. But it
is in the entries of the *Dictionnaire historique et
critique*, perhaps a form more suitable to his mentality,
that we must search for the folkloristic Bayle, who
even here did not hesitate to combat error with the
critical knowledge that by now his awareness of prejudice afforded him. Bayle felt that falsehood always
renders bad service to the truth. But read, for example, the "Takiddin" entry:

> The lot of mankind is unfortunate since the knowl-
> edge that frees it from one evil drops it into
> another. *Destroy ignorance and barbarities and
> you thus destroy the superstition and the foolish
> credulity of the people so useful to their minds*,
> whose power they share by sinking into laziness
> and dissolution. In revealing such confusions to
> men, you inspire in them the desire to examine
> everything; they then investigate and subtilize so
> much that they do not find anything to satisfy
> their miserable reason.

Previously, even Plutarch had granted to superstition only one extenuation: in the hands of a statesman, it can be an instrument of domination. Bayle did
not have the gods of Plutarch in front of him. His was
a God who could not possibly be credited with beginning

those religions that contain the seeds of war or witchcraft. But did that God live in the Catholic religion
of his time, in the France of Louis the Great? Or was
the Catholic religion itself the source of errors? In
his *Commentaire philosophique sur ces paroles de Jesus-
Christ, Contrain-les d'entrer*, which attacks the dogmas
of the Church (although he recognized the validity of
some of these dogmas), he asserts: "One of necessity
must admit that any particular dogma, whether or not
presented as being contained in the Scripture, is false
when it is confuted by the clear, distinct knowledge of
'natural' understanding, principally that of morality."

Notice the key word: morality. But was he perhaps
unaware that Spinoza, going back to Plutarch, had
asserted that religious superstitions are especially
useful to kings for stifling the people? Superstitions,
nevertheless, have always had undeniable fascination.
And, Bayle asks, isn't man himself, this "most difficult mouthful to digest, with which all systems must
contend" (as he says in his "Réponse aux questions
d'un provincial"), perhaps a pillar composed of truth
and falsehood?

3. *Fontenelle and "Histoire des oracles"*

Bayle's argument was taken up and skillfully continued
by one of the most perceptive scholars that the Enlightenment has given to us, Bernard de Fontenelle, who,
unlike Bayle, grew up in a Catholic environment and was
educated by Jesuits.

In the "Discours préliminaire" at the beginning of
the *Encyclopédie*, it is asserted that "without having
the dangerous ambition of tearing bandages from the
eyes of his contemporaries, Fontenelle prepared from
afar, in shadow and in silence, the light with which
the world was to be gradually illuminated." This is
true up to a certain point, inasmuch as he was much
more cautious in accounting for dogmas and revealed
religion than Bayle had been, and he knew how to mask
his destructive criticism with a worldly smile that
straightway served his purpose. One cannot say, however, that his *Histoire des oracles*, published in 1686,

was presented "in shadow or in silence," when it is
remembered that he was violently attacked by Catholics,
especially the Jesuits. On the contrary, I suggest
that as a consequence of the publishing of *Histoire
des oracles* he came to be incarcerated in the Bastille.
In 1707 (however much Fontenelle might have remained
secluded, perhaps to make people forget what he had
written), Father Jean-François Baltus published a
Réponse a l'histoire des oracles de Fontenelle, in
which he accused Fontenelle's *Histoire* of being a
detestable, impious work that, in his view, was one
of the most important sources of anticlericalism in
the eighteenth century. This judgment was later
adopted by an outspoken critic of Fontenelle, Louis
Maigron.

   In the preface to *Histoire des oracles*, Fontenelle expressly tells us what compelled him to write
this work:

> Some time ago there fell into my hands a Latin
> book on the oracles of pagans recently written by
> Dale, a doctor of medicine, and printed in Holland.
> It seemed to me that the author vigorously demol-
> ished everything commonly believed about demonic
> oracles and their total disappearance with the
> coming of Jesus Christ; the entire work seemed to
> me enriched by a great knowledge of antiquity and
> by much erudition. I thought about translating
> it, so that women as well as those men who could
> not easily read Latin would not be deprived of
> such pleasing, useful literature. But then I
> reflected that a translation of the book would not
> have had the effect that I wanted. Because Dale
> had written only for the literate, he rightly
> omitted embellishments and decorations that could
> not have had great importance for them. He refers
> to a great number of passages and cites them very
> accurately in excellent translations when they are
> translated from the Greek; in many passages he
> debates on critical and exegetic topics, sometimes
> unnecessarily but always inquisitively. This is
> what scholars need. . . . Moreover, Dale never

hesitates to interrupt the thread of his discourse
to introduce some other subject, and within this
parenthetical insertion he will insert another
parenthesis, which is not always the last one.
. . . I therefore have put away the thought of
translating it; I have decided that it would be
better to give it another form, while conserving
the content and the principal material of the
work. I confess that one could not have taken
greater freedom than I have done. I have changed
the order of the book entirely; I have removed
everything that seemed to me inherently of little
use or too unstylish to compensate for its slight
usefulness; and I have added not only all the
extras that seemed to me most suitable but also a
good many things that strengthen or emphasize the
argument. . . .

Antonius van Dale's work, to which Fontenelle
alludes, had been published in Amsterdam in 1683 under
the title *De oraculis ethnicorum dissertationes duae:
quarum prior de ipsorum duratione ac defectu, posterior
de eorundem auctoribus.* It was translated into English
by Aphra Behn in 1688 as *History of Oracles.* Fontenelle did not much differ from Dale in the latter's
fundamental treatment of the subject. Both, in fact,
attempted to demonstrate that pagan oracles were not
demonic in origin but rather were effected by the will
of the mighty and the imposture of priests. Thus, the
arguments of reformers and deists continued. But,
while Dale was stopped by the controversy, it is clear
that Fontenelle critically attacked the entire problem
of error and superstition.

4. The Character of Oracles

In *Histoire des oracles*, which combines the best qualities of the litterateur and the scientific popularizer,
Fontenelle, like Dale before him, did not hesitate to
transfer his judgment from paganism to Christianity.
However, he took a more categorical position: "In

essence the question of oracles, of religious character
for pagans, has become unnecessarily of a religious
nature for Christians, and in all respects prejudice
has obscured clear truth." And he immediately added:
"Still, these prejudices that impugn true religion
manage to get confused with it, gaining the devotion
that religion itself should have. One does not dare
refute them for fear of offending something sacred.
I do not exactly blame this excess of religiosity;
indeed, it is commendable. But as commendable as it
may be, one must agree that it is better to distinguish
error from truth than to respect the error confused
with the truth."

Fontenelle was concerned, he said, "with defending
the authentic interests of Christianity." But did he
really defend these interests? Like Bayle, Fontenelle
well knew what power custom has. He observed that it
"has an impact on humans without requiring the support
of reason." However, he emphatically said, "If man
will consult his reason, he will not need demons either
for understanding God's actions toward man or for putting between God and us something that approximates
him more than we can."

Histoire des oracles is related to Bayle's *Pensées*,
then, in that it not only attempts to eliminate the
miracle from history but also renders suspect any
religion whatever that believes in miracles. "The
deceptively profound thought of Fontenelle," Hazard
observes, "merges with Bayle's views on comets. It is
easy to see the relationship. Both appeal to a broader
audience than just philosophers and theologians, and
both are united in the desire to denounce the weakness
of human nature, the first cause of error, and the
blindness of tradition, which collects the error,
strengthens it, and makes it almost invincible." The
comets of Bayle are, in essence, the oracles of Fontenelle. Both men believed in "miracles," but only, to
use Leibniz's expression, in miracles of reason.

5. *"De l'origine des fables"*: A Contribution to the
    History of the Ancients

Fontenelle did not concern himself only with oracles.
Indeed, one of his greatest essays is *De l'origine des
fables*, which he wrote for the purpose of demonstrating
that fables, too, should be considered as a page from
the history of the errors of the ancients. Fontenelle
had a markedly negative attitude toward fables, even
though these fascinating works invested classical peoples with poetry, theater, and the plastic arts. The
fables of which Fontenelle speaks are not the same as
myths (studied widely by the Jesuits, as is especially
evidenced by Natale Conti's famous *Mythologiae*). There
are, however, some passages in his essay suggesting
that his eye was clearly fixed on fables that were then
circulating in France. For example, he asserts that
"even today the Arabs fill their stories with wonders
and miracles, most often ridiculous and grotesque."
Additionally, he wasn't ignorant of the religious
fables of his own country, like the story of the tree
on which Judas was hanged (recounted by François Luzel).
    Fontenelle was certainly fascinated by these tales,
but what particularly fascinated him? Generally speaking, he was most interested in the ways in which error
is sustained by fables. In Fontenelle's *Dialogues des
morts anciens avec des modernes*, Homer says to Aesop:

> Don't think that man just looks for the truth. Man
> and error are great friends. If you wish to tell
> the truth, it would be best to plant that truth
> within fables to make it more pleasing. But if you
> wish to relate these fables, they will please even
> if they do not contain any truth. Indeed, truth
> must be transformed into error in order to be well
> received by men; error, on the contrary, comes to
> man quite naturally, because that is the place of
> its birth and its habitual abode, while truth is a
> stranger.

In *De l'origine des fables* he again resumed and developed this idea, concluding that the motive that furthers

error, and therefore fables, is owed to the respect
that we have for the ancient past. Have our fathers
believed it? Do we dare pretend to be wiser than
they? Fontenelle was convinced that if a people were
placed on the earth today, its first stories would be
fables, regardless of the environment. But he was
also convinced that in the development of the human
race--and we know that he was more concerned with the
concept of progress than was Bayle--true stories were
blended with ancient ones, and the "marvelous" over-
powered the truth; this is demonstrated to us, he
adds, not only by the myths of the Egyptians, Phoenicians, and Greeks, but also by the facts that historians have told us about the Augustan Age.

In this opinion Fontenelle was evidently in agreement with Bayle, who in his *Dictionnaire* (the "Pheron"
entry) was skeptical about the heroic legends of the
Greeks and those of the first kings of Rome, and with
Charles Saint-Évremond, the most typical representative
of free-thinking Frenchmen, who said in his *Réflexions
sur les divers génies du peuple romain, dans les dif-
férents temps de la République*, "I detest the admiration lavished on fables and the chance for error in
false judgments. There are so many true things to
admire in the Romans that to favor them with fables is
a great wrong." On the other hand, this was not the
opinion of Fontenelle's companion in battle, Charles
Perrault. Both of them opposed everything that was
ancient. In 1688 Fontenelle had published his *Digression sur les anciens et les modernes*, as if to
strengthen the idea that Alessandro Tassoni had proposed on the subject in Italy in 1620. And in 1690
Perrault published *Parallèle des anciens et des
modernes*, in which he maintained that the best way to
compete with the ancients was to draw inspiration from
customs and usages of one's own age. Perrault well
knew, however, that the ancient could also be made
modern and current. In his blind refutation of the
ancient world, in which he saw falsehood everywhere,
Fontenelle made a serious mistake: he came to see
ignorance where there was actually a refreshing
ingenuousness, and he confused modern superstitions

with things that were not originally superstitions.
It goes without saying, then, that to see only error
where there is life, whatever it is and however it
develops, is to negate that life; moreover, he ignored
the ethical importance of fables, which have their
own truth even in their errors; but most of all he
failed to perceive the aesthetic importance that fables
increasingly assumed not only in scholarly literature
but in popular literature as well.

6. *"De l'origine des fables"*: *Primarily
   Ethnographical Incunabulum*

The importance of *De l'origine des fables* is not to be
found, however, in Fontenelle's negative attitude
toward fables. For him, as well as for Bayle, error
contributed to the discovery of truth, even if in
another sense. In this respect, *De l'origine des
fables* can be considered as the first attempt in which
the study of fables was undertaken as an ethnographical
problem.

Fontenelle was convinced that fables are not merely
fantasy. In his view--and here certainly is the
essence of the ethnographical aspect of fables--they
were the result of everything that fathers tell sons.
And what is it that fathers tell sons, if not what they
themselves have done and seen? We must establish, then,
a starting point in this investigation; that is, we
must return to our earliest ancestors, the first people
who populated the earth. But here, Fontenelle immediately adds, we must be specific. The first humans to
whom he turns are not the Kafirs, Laplanders, or Iroquois. Of course these are ancient peoples, but,
precisely because they are, they have necessarily
arrived at a degree of civilization that the first
humans did not have. This is yet another proof of his
idea on progress.

When Fontenelle's essay came out, two works had
already been published in which, for the first time,
theories on the subject of the savage were supported,
although these theories had passed almost unnoticed.

In 1702 Father René Joseph Tournemine, Fontenelle's good friend, asserted in his copious and courageous "Projet d'un ouvrage sur l'Origine des Fables" (published in *Mémoires de Trévoux*) that if we wish to initiate a genuine comparative study of fables, we must return to the customs of American savages and to the *Avventure* of merchants who had discovered the new people. Two years later, there appeared, anonymously, a work by Father La Créquinière, *Conformité des coutumes des Indiens orientaux, avec celles des Juifs et des autres peuples de l'antiquité*; in this work the author, while professing (rather strangely) that he had given up studying the Indian religion because it was absurd, says that if we want to find some vestige of antiquity, we must go back to uncivilized peoples.

Now we know, of course, that *De l'origine des fables* first appeared in 1724, but it is difficult to ascertain whether it was actually composed in 1680, as J. R. Carré thought (his supporting evidence, however, has not persuaded many), or between 1691 and 1699, as the Abbé Trublet thought. In any event, it is a fact that, whether or not he had known the sources, Fontenelle went beyond those simple pronouncements, which, however, he stated with critical acumen.

7. *Fables Are Only Fantasies?*

The innovation on which Fontenelle insisted--an extremely significant one in the fields of ethnography and folklore--is that we can determine the level of civilization of our earliest ancestors, the true creators of fables, by going backward, imagining ourselves in an "état d'esprit" through which all peoples have passed and which even today is not completely extinguished in our midst. On the one hand, then, he gave scientific weight to the relationship between us and savages; on the other hand, he gave no weight whatever to the concept of the noble savage. On the contrary, Fontenelle placed at our origin a crude man who, in comparison to the American Indian, did not even have words for justice and liberty in his vocabulary. This,

evidently, was altogether an invention. But to this
man Fontenelle attributed his own philosophy and even,
as he says, some "systems" of philosophy, which were
combined with facts related by fables. Fontenelle did
not deny that even in the distant past there were men
who had a touch of genius, who looked for the cause of
everything that they saw (and that they narrated). But
it is clear enough to everyone, he asserts, that our
research must not be conducted with our heads filled
with the vagaries of the Phoenicians or the Greeks;
rather, it is best to proceed by seeing what has led
the Greeks or Phoenicians to these vagaries.

Fontenelle observes that, as far as the first
hypothesis is concerned, there is no doubt that the
savages who first inhabited the world were fascinated
by actions that they did not have the power to perform:
the hurling of lightning bolts, the unleashing of
winds, the stirring of ocean waves. Because all this
was beyond their power, they imagined some beings more
powerful than they who were capable of performing such
acts. It was necessary that these beings should behave
as if they were themselves human--for what other shape
could they possibly have? From the moment that they
took on human shape, the imagination attributed to them
everything that is human. Along with divinities, then,
prodigies were born; but aren't prodigies the leaven
of fables, and don't they bring out the fact that from
the beginning fables were permeated with errors or
erroneous beliefs, which are the foundation of fables?

Thus, what we call the philosophy of the prehistoric age is discovered to be related to stories about
how the world works. For example, a youth has fallen
into a river and no one can fish out his body. What
has happened? The philosophy of the time (but read,
"the belief of the time") teaches that there are divinities (actually, Fontenelle says "des jeunes filles")
governing the river. They have taken the youth, which
is natural enough, but to where is he taken? Why, to
an inaccessible palace under the river.

It happens, then (and we are at the second hypothesis), that man's imagination, which never proceeds
in accord with reason, gets heated up with its subject,

magnifying that subject and adding whatever is needed
to make it still more marvelous, since we are ever
flattered by the admiration that we can inspire in our
listeners. The fable thus renews itself but conserves
its secrets, which succeeding ages adopt and pass
along. In this treatment we find a truly striking
resemblance among the fables of different countries;
however, they also can be the result of that one "état
d'esprit," as Fontenelle calls it:

> The Americans send the souls of sinners to certain
> lakes, just as the Greeks sent them to the rivers
> Styx and Acheron. The Americans believe that
> rain is produced by a little girl who, while play-
> ing among the clouds with her little brother,
> breaks her jug of water. And does that not
> strongly resemble those fountain nymphs who pour
> water from their amphorae? According to the tra-
> ditions of Peru, the eloquent Inca Manco Guyna
> Capac, son of the Sun, convinced the primitive
> inhabitants of the country to live under reason-
> able laws. Orpheus, also the son of the Sun, did
> as much for the Greeks. This demonstrates, then,
> that the Greeks were savages at one time, just as
> much as were the Americans, that they left the
> state of barbarianism by the same means, and that
> the imaginations of these two so distant peoples
> shared in believing the son of the Sun to be one
> who had an extraordinary talent. Since the Greeks
> with all their *esprit* did not think more reason-
> ably when they were still a young people than did
> the barbarians of America (who were, to all appear-
> ances, quite a young people when they were discov-
> ered by the Spaniards), there is reason to believe
> that the Americans would have eventually come to
> think as reasonably as the Greeks, if they had had
> the time.

Fontenelle thus gave a universal, eternal value to
the primitive world, even though he considered this
world as being a chronological "first age." In doing
so, he brought this age into the realm of folklore--

inasmuch as one must remember, he adds, that old ideas
are always latent in present life, and a return to
superstition is always possible. This concept is the
most important contribution of his work. Moreover, it
was the first time, in a period in which all mythology
was subject to allegorical interpretations, that an
interpretation *began* with primitive peoples and was
related to their own beliefs. Although he recognized
this merit in Fontenelle, Lang suggested that Fontenelle's investigations should also have approached
zoomorphic beliefs and magical works in addition to
anthropomorphic beliefs. True enough, but isn't this
just too much to ask?

*8. The Historicism and Anti-historicism of Bayle
     and Fontenelle*

The search for truth, which at that time was the search
for history, became an all-consuming project for Bayle
and Fontenelle, because the search for error was transformed, in their view, into the history of errors.
Both of them had a sacred concept of truth, but they
also had a sacred concept of history.
     In his *Dictionnaire* ("Husson" entry) Bayle asserted
emphatically:

> Whoever knows the laws of history will agree with
> me that a historiographer faithful to his mission
> must rid himself of an interest in flattery and
> gossip. As far as possible, he must put himself
> in the condition of one who is never overly emo-
> tional. Putting aside everything else, he must
> pursue only the interests of truth, for the love
> of which he must sacrifice his sensitivity to the
> wrongs that he may have suffered, the memory of
> good received, and even love of country. He must
> forget that he belongs to a certain nation and that
> he was educated in a certain faith, since both the
> former and the latter are composed of his parents
> and friends. A historian, then, is like a Mel-
> chizedek--without father, without mother, without

child. If he is asked his origin, he should reply:
I am neither French nor German nor English nor
Spanish; I am cosmopolitan. I am in the service
of neither the emperor nor the king of France;
rather, I am exclusively in the service of truth.
Truth is my only queen, to whom I have pledged my
oath of obedience.

In this way Bayle, as Ernst Cassirer observes, not only
anticipated the idea of a (hypothetical) universal history from a cosmopolitan perspective, but in a rigidly
rationalistic century he became the first convincing
logical positivist, one who "did not turn doubt against
historical fact, but one who himself served as an
instrument for discovering truth." Here was a new his-
toriographical concept, even though history then broke
down, in his view, into a heap of ruins, impostures,
and falsehoods; additionally, however, a new position
was taken, that of considering the ruins, impostures,
and falsehoods in which beliefs and prejudices are
articulated as pages alive and pulsating with the history of the human spirit--a history that includes both
truth *and* error.

No less significant on this subject was the lesson
of Fontenelle. He too was convinced that it is impossible to investigate truth without being aware of error.
He too had a cosmopolitan concept of history, with the
result that he began with a past that was generally
neglected and ignored, the past of the primitives. But
was he perhaps attempting to resolve his own personal
doubts and fears by formulating a problem like that of
the origin of religion and myths?

We must recognize that for Bayle and Fontenelle the
quest for truth was not merely a scientific project; it
was above all else a political and social project,
because both of them intended, fundamentally, to renovate society so that a new will and a new faith might
develop within it. It is precisely this intention that
led them, on the one hand, to attack the spirit of error
in the name of liberty and, on the other hand, to
broaden their examination to all peoples of the earth,
each of which, positively or negatively, has something

instructive to say to social reformers. There is
surely a false premise in such an attitude, an indis-
criminate identification of superstition with tradi-
tion--as if it were possible to consider the past
only as a past and then afterwards identify that past
with Catholicism, which the Enlightenment attacked
while disregarding the influence that it has exercised
in various historical periods. But in spite of this
premise, can we deny to Bayle and to Fontenelle their
desire to renovate society, their desire to call attention to national usages and customs?

CHAPTER V

ENCOUNTERS BETWEEN NATIONS
AND CIVILIZATION

1. *A New World Is Born: Montesquieu and Voltaire,
    Historians of Man*

The concept of a universal history from a cosmopolitan
perspective, hinted at in the works of Bayle and Fontenelle, was expressed by two liberal thinkers, Montesquieu and Voltaire. These latter two clearly had an
elevated concept of history; but, like Bayle and Fontenelle, they (especially Voltaire) did not know how to
account for traditional values or beliefs, which they
generally recognized in Catholicism. Both of them,
like Bayle, loved minute facts, curiosities, and unpublished documents, but both saw such facts as coinciding
with laws or customs.
     In the preface to *De l'esprit des lois* Montesquieu
seems to provide the very basis of his work when he
says, "I have begun with a consideration of mankind,
and the result of my thoughts has been that, in the
midst of such an infinite variety of laws and manners,
man was not solely conducted by the caprice of fancy.
I have laid down the first principles, and I have discovered that the particular cases follow naturally
from them, that the histories of all nations are only
consequences of them, and that every particular law is
connected to another law or depends on some other of a
more general extent." In his *Essai sur les mœurs*,
Voltaire protests against the once-held view of history
as an alternating pattern of political events, kings,
battles, and destruction. The words *homo sum*, he adds,
should be the teaching of every historiographer worthy

of the name; he continues, now descending into the
heat of battle: "Instead of amassing a pile of facts,
some of which are always destroyed and negated by
others, one must choose the most important and the
most certain in order to offer the reader a controlling thread, enabling him to form an opinion of the
extension, revival, and advances of the human spirit,
and in order to make him see the characteristics of
nations and their customs."

Like Bayle and Fontenelle, then, Montesquieu and
Voltaire were convinced that reason, which presides
over the study of nature, must also preside over the
study of history. Both of these men had the greatest
faith in the rational validity of "universal laws,"
which accounts for their optimism. This optimism is
displayed in rationalism's faith in the unlimited
progress of man--not the dialectic process of history
but the quasi-mechanical result of knowledge acquired
down through the ages.

On this subject Cassirer observes that for
Montesquieu political events were the center of the
historical world, the State was the one true object
of universal history, and thus the spirit of history
coincided with the spirit of laws; for Voltaire, on
the other hand, the concept of the spirit of history
was more extensive, since it included all the changes
through which mankind had to pass before it could
reach a true awareness of itself. This awareness
arises not from political events but from an understanding of religion, art, science, and philosophy,
from which one can derive a full picture of all the
individual phases that the human spirit has had to go
through and overcome before arriving at its present
state. But could we argue with Cassirer's contention
that in turning to the political realm Montesquieu
ignored religion, art, and science? And even if Montesquieu and Voltaire had a preference for the specific forms of the State, didn't both of them see
history as a function of civilization, and civilization as the harmonious meeting of progress and man?

2. *"Lettres Persanes" and Their Argument*

In the name of this civilization, Montesquieu, like
Bayle and Fontenelle, dismissed all theological considerations from history; but he also focused on those
peoples who had previously been brought to Europe's
attention for the purpose of attacking absolutism and
dogmas--peoples in whom nature and reason or at least
a life lived according to natural laws had occasionally
been recognized. Consider his *Lettres Persanes*, published in 1721. Here it first seems that his intent
is to rebuke Marana, Baron Lahontan, and Dufresny himself. He has too much pride in his country, too much
pride in being French, not to acknowledge that he lives
in a great century in which art, philosophy, and science have attained a preëminent position. But then,
like Marana, Baron Lahontan, and Dufresny, he, as
Albert Sorel has observed, "feels the old social
institutions of most centuries dissolving around him,
those beliefs, habits, and customs that have supported
the French monarchy." His argument is inexorable,
resolute, stinging.

In *Lettres Persanes* Montesquieu imagines that two
Persians, Rica and Usbek, have stopped in Paris while on
their trip through Europe, and from here they send their
impressions to their friends. Thus, after the savage
of missionaries, of travelers, and of Baron Lahontan,
after Marana's Egyptian and Dufresny's Siamese, it was
now the turn of the Persian, who had already been idol-
ized by Bernier, Chardin, and Tavernier. And the Persian is the equal of his colleagues in that he is
outspoken and goes directly to the bottom of things,
once and for all. Listen to this: the king in Paris
is a man who "makes his subjects think what he wants
them to." Similarly, the Pope in Rome is capable of
"making people believe that three and three add up to
no more than one" and that "the bread that is eaten is
not bread." Priests hardly deserve mention, for they
are a "pack of misers who forever take and never give."
And what could be said of the ladies? Their manner is
so capricious that if a lady returns to Paris after
spending some time in the country, she will discover

that her manner of dress will make her look like she
has come from another world. Now, the lifestyle of
the French is like their fashions. They change customs according to the dictates of their sovereign,
who could make his people more serious if he wanted.
But what do you expect from a nation?

In a series of pictures and images reminiscent of
the art of La Bruyère, the life of a society and a
people parades by us. And while the voices of the
sitting rooms and of the courtiers are united with
shouts of the Rue Quincapoix, Montesquieu shows us,
in contrast, the idealized life of the Persians, their
principles of government and politics, along with
copious disquisitions on various peoples, the origin
of republics, and the government of the Goths. Too,
Lettres Persanes provides some lively, vivid comments
on the three forms of government (despotism, monarchy,
and democracy), the main topic of the *Esprit des lois*.

Lettres Persanes attempted to strike the spirit of
the French at its core and to destroy a specific
society. The *Esprit des lois*, on the other hand, took
up the issue of the recreating of society. Like the
historian cherished by Bayle, however, Montesquieu did
not write this work merely for the French, no matter
how much the Enlightenment thinkers believed that
France was Europe and that everything French was European. (Here there was a certain tinge of malice mixed
with truth, inasmuch as France succeeded in influencing
all European classes with its fashions, art, *causeries*,
and so on.) His work was by design a universal
entreaty directed at men of good will.

3. *The Comparative Method in Montesquieu*

In the *Esprit des lois* there are, of course, many comparisons between and discussions of distant peoples,
including primitives. Georges Hervé, a French sociologist who investigated Montesquieu's ethnographical
sources, observed that long before the *Esprit* Montesquieu was delighted by actual travel accounts as well
as imaginary journeys. It would be better to say,

however, that he enthusiastically *continued* such literature, since the ethnographical documentation of
Lettres Persanes is travel literature, as Gennep and
Hervé suggest. It should be added that between 1728
and 1731 Montesquieu visited Austria, Hungary, Italy,
Switzerland, Holland, and England, countries that he
discovered from personal observation to be very useful
for his ethnographical documentation.

Such literature and travel gave Montesquieu the
bases of comparison suggested to him by different
societies and provided him with the notion that different civilized societies could find a reference
point in primitive societies. It is true that Montesquieu usually applied the comparative method to the
accomplishments of great civilizations like those of
Persia (already dear to his heart), China (about whose
history he wrote some still current pages), Mexico,
and the Mongolians. But it is also true, as Hervé
says, that although he rarely cited the accomplishments of the savages, when he *did* do so he presented
the primitive world as a paradigm of wisdom and virtue. His primitives, then, were essentially those of
the missionaries and travelers. After asserting that
all nations have a "national law," for example, he
went on to say that this was true even for the Iroquois, who ate their prisoners. Nor did he hide his
admiration for the colony of Paraguay, instituted by
the Jesuits, which suggested to him the following
maxim: "It is always good to govern humans by making
them happy."

This was precisely the task that he assigned to
laws. Of course one can assert and demonstrate that
his sources were not always exact and that he regarded
all travel descriptions in the same way. The more
important fact, however, is that Montesquieu's comparisons were only a pretext and a stimulus for investigating the juridical institutions of various nations.
He considered these institutions as social forms
directed and guided by a norm even though that norm
might be in contrast to specific cases in which the
empirical existence of laws is realized.

4. The *"Esprit des lois"*

Believing that laws were essential statements deduced
from the nature of things, Montesquieu thought laws
were in harmony with the very nature of men, influenced by the nature of the soil and the climate.
For example, in speaking of the Oriental peoples, he
observes, "If to that delicacy of organs which renders
the Oriental people so susceptible to every impression,
you add a certain indolence of the mind, naturally
connected to that of the body, by means of which they
grow incapable of any exertion or effort, you will
understand how the person who has received impressions
is then unable to change them. For this reason, laws,
customs, and maxims, even apparently unimportant ones
such as their mode of dress, are the same today in the
Orient as they were a thousand years ago." His admiration, however, went out to the Chinese legislators,
those who "acted most reasonably by considering men
not as being in the peaceful state in which they will
be one day or the other but as needing direction in
fulfilling the duties of life; thus, these legislators
made their religion, philosophy, and laws wholly practical."
   Although his investigation was primarily aimed
at discovering the spirit of laws, many of his references are more specifically related to folk beliefs,
those related to metempsychosis, for example, which
he considered to be suited to the climate of the
Indians:

> Excessive heat burns the entire country; the
> livestock provides little nourishment, and there
> is always the danger that it will fail because
> of the cultivation of the land. The oxen are
> not plentiful, and they are subject to many
> diseases; therefore, a religious law that pre-
> serves them is more suitable for the policy of
> the country. While the meadows are scorched,
> the rice and vegetables grow in abundance with
> the help of water that has been conserved; a

religious law that permits only this kind of
nourishment is useful to the men who live in this
climate.

It is clear that Montesquieu did not make the climate
an exclusive, absolute, static factor; rather, he
related it to spiritual causes underlying both laws
and customs. He asserted, however, that not all soils
or climates are suited to a given governing regulation
or a specific constitution. He admired the English
constitution, for example, but he certainly did not
advocate that it be applied to the entire world. It
is the duty of the legislator, however, not to become
entangled in these causes since, he emphatically says,
"if it is true that the character of the spirit and
the passions of the heart are different under different skies, the laws must take account of these differences in character and passions and be adapted to
them." Furthermore, we should add, Montesquieu
believed that laws were related to customs but were
not themselves customs. Although he wished to reform
certain contemporary customs, he was quick to offer
the categorical warning: "When a people is conquered,
it is not necessary to leave them their laws. It is
necessary, however, to leave them customs because a
nation knows, loves, and defends its customs much more
than its laws."

Montesquieu believed, then, that laws, like customs, were not the result of license or whim; rather,
they were vital, prolific forces. They are subject,
of course, to some external conditions, but it is not
only those external conditions that have formed laws
(as some hasty readers of Montesquieu think). He
appeals *to* the reason to make the law a product *of* the
reason. But hadn't experience--a fundamental "fact"
of laws--already come to the reason? Naturally, he
was led to generalize and to create a sociological
typology; the great virtue of this typology, however,
is that it advanced those investigations of his that
he considered secondary: specific investigations of
laws and customs.

5. *Voltaire and Fanaticism*

Montesquieu's interest in laws and customs was fully
shared by Voltaire. In his *Lettres sur les Anglais*,
published in 1734, Voltaire idealized contemporary
England just as Montesquieu had idealized Persia, and
he graphically depicted its industrial activities,
institutions, and customs. It is in the *Lettres* that
one still finds the assertion that liberty coincides
with the rights of man. But this work is now admired
not merely for maxims of this sort, but also because,
as in *Lettres Persanes*, each chapter offers criticism
of the lifestyles and customs of France.

Such criticism continues in *Le siècle de Louis XIV*,
published in 1751; here the history of commerce,
finance, and ecclesiastical matters is integrated with
the history of the arts, dress, and customs—although,
in the last analysis of this work (which certainly is
not one of the usual compilations of the time), we see
that Voltaire allowed himself to be seduced by the same
sociological typology that Montesquieu loved so much.

Leaving aside the many allusions in his *Dictionnaire philosophique*, dialogues, tragedies, and minor
works, which are his most vivid, the major work in
which Voltaire particularly gives attention to customs,
laws, and constitutions is his *Essai sur les mœurs*.
Some of the essays were published between 1745 and
1748, and the entire work appeared in 1758, with the
significant title of *Essai sur les mœurs et l'esprit
des nations et sur les principaux faits de l'histoire
depuis Charlemagne jusqu'à Louis XIII*. In Voltaire's
view, not all usages and customs are explained by what
their actual tradition is; so much did he believe this
to be the case that, to advance his argument, he
broadened his historical vision to all peoples, whose
religious and moral opinions he attempted to describe.
He did so, however, with the specific purpose (as a
fine critic of Voltaire, Raimondo Craveri, has noted)
of illuminating the history of religion and natural
morality, as opposed to the corruptions of fanaticism.

Believing that men shape society and perceiving
men within the context of human history, Voltaire

concentrated as much on morality as on religion. But
what are these two entities? Voltaire thought that
just as the foundation of morality is the same for all
people, so are civilized usages common to the entire
world. This idea is predicated on the assumption of
human equality, a theory offered by Claude Adrien
Helvétius. He adds, however, that even though all
things that depend on nature resemble each other, the
same cannot be said for all things that depend on custom; rather, resemblances between customs, he says,
are due to chance. In the summary concluding his
Essai, he clarifies some of the resemblances that we
share with savages, the Japanese, and others in regard
to New Year's Day omens, the judgments of God, art,
and so on. Nevertheless, he says in this summary:

> The conclusions of this work are that all things
> that are intimately related to human nature resem-
> ble each other throughout the universe, while
> those things that depend on custom are different;
> if customs resemble each other, the resemblance is
> merely a matter of chance. The empire of custom
> is a good deal broader than that of nature. It
> extends to all beliefs and usages, and it spreads
> variety over the face of the earth; nature, which
> spreads unity, establishes a small number of
> invariable principles everywhere. Thus, the
> foundation is the same everywhere while culture
> produces variations.

Just as Montesquieu distinguished customs from
laws, then, Voltaire distinguished customs from nature,
crediting the resemblance to chance while forgetting
that the result is that no one can be held responsible
for his own customs. It is also to custom that Voltaire attributed the evil found throughout the world.
Although he believed that nature is always the same,
he also believed (here we return to Montesquieu) that
it is perfectible and that one should hold morality to
this perfection. He observes, we should add, that
religion should teach the same morality to all peoples:
"I only say that there is no religious society or rite

in the world instituted for the purpose of encouraging
humans to vice. Religion serves us throughout the
world to produce evil, but it was wholly instituted to
produce good. And while dogma and fanaticism lead to
war, morality inspires harmony everywhere."

The conclusion: reduce natural law to positive
principles, and you will have the religion and morality
suited to a civilized people, who thus will not believe
in such crafty devices of priests as oracles, human
sacrifices, and miracles, nor in the tricks of the
kings of France, who attempted to cure the sick
(beliefs and tricks to which Voltaire gave particular
attention in chapters XVII, XXXII, and XXXVI). Voltaire knew, then, how to fight against all errors--
especially, as he promised his readers in the preliminary discourse in his *Essai*, against a "host of absurd
fables that continue to infect the youth." However,
this scorn for fables, a term obviously used here in
the generic sense, did not prevent him elsewhere from
expressing a nostalgic hope for the happy time of
fables:

> *O l'heureux temps que celui de ces fables*
> *Des bons démons, des esprits familiers*
> *Des farfadets aux mortels secourables!*
> *On écoutait tous ces faits admirables,*
> *Dans un château, près d'un large foyer:*
> *Le père et l'oncle, et la mère et la fille,*
> *Et les voisins et toute la famille,*
> *Ouvrait l'oreille à monsieur l'aumônier,*
> *Qui leur faisait des contes de sorcier.*
> *On a banni les démons et les fées;*
> *Sous la raison les grâces étouffées*
> *Livrent nos cœurs à l'insipidité;*
> *Le raisonneur tristement s'accrédite.*
> *On court, hélas! après la vérité*
> *Ah! croyez-moi, l'erreur a son mérite!*

Although these seem to be Perrault's verses, they are
in fact Voltaire's, reminding us of a beautiful passage by Alessandro Verri; commenting on "Saggio sugli
errori popolari degli antichi," which Giacomo Leopardi

had written under the direct influence of the Enlightenment, Verri stated: "We boast of reason so much,
yet we owe our greatest achievements to error. Enthusiasm and sublime passions are usually the daughters
of error, with whose aid the greatest enterprises are
accomplished."

6. *Voltaire and the Savages*

The "daughters of error" (or of the history of errors)
are precisely what Voltaire collected in his investigation of the usages and customs of all peoples, thus
broadening the province of historiography. He said in
Essai sur les mœurs that so far (that is, up to his
own time) historians had neglected three-fourths of
the world. Therefore, in his narrations he contrasted
American Indians and Oriental peoples to such countries
as France, England, Spain, and Sweden (rendered in
short, lively sketches), and he took advantage of the
researches of missionaries and travelers. For example,
in his *Essai* the American Indians are presented as
people devoid of the concept of one God—but aren't
these the ones about whom he had sung in *Alzire*?

> *L'Américain farouche en sa simplicité*
> *Nous égale en courage et nous passe en bonté.*

In the sketches preceding his *Essai* (which were first
published in Kiel's edition under the heading of
"Advis des éditeurs"), he drew an amusing picture of
primitive peoples in general, especially those of
Africa and Asia. He concludes:

> The populations of America and Africa are free,
> yet we ourselves have no idea of liberty. They
> are aware of honor, a word that European savages
> seem not to have understood. They have a coun-
> try which they love and defend; they make treaties,
> fight courageously, and often speak out boldly.
> Is there an answer more attractive than the one
> that a Canadian ruler gave to the representative

of a European nation who had suggested that the
Canadian give up his patrimony to him? "We are
born on this land and our fathers are uncivilized.
We will give ourselves to the bones of our fathers.
Will you rise and come with us to a strange land?"

These delightful episodes pleased Voltaire--and in
this respect he was similar to Montaigne and Baron
Lahontan. But although he resorted to savages to ridicule Europeans (those uncircumcised Jews, as he often
called them), he believed, like a good bourgeois, that
a sense of "mine and thine" existed in the heritage of
the primitives. Too, he believed that ownership is a
natural right, a point that had also been made by
Locke, who, like Voltaire, thought that only action
conforming to law can express human freedom. Relat-
edly, we should not forget what Voltaire wrote in his
dialogue "Un sauvage et un bachelier":

> If, after a war has ended, someone should ask
> about his part of the fifty units of the 50,000
> millions to be distributed between a billion men,
> he will be answered that the divisions have already
> been made among us and that he can go to get his
> among the Hottentots. But even among these peo-
> ples, there are some who have and some who do not.
> A bachelor asks the savage, "Who has made the laws
> in your land?" The savage replies, "Public inter-
> est. Everything that I have seen in my country
> teaches me that there is no other motive behind
> laws."

7. *Voltaire and the Oriental World*

Voltaire assumed this same attitude toward the Oriental
peoples, each of which is invoked for their religious
tolerance, customs, and natural laws. Consider, for
example, his comment on Asiatic ceremonies: "Asiatic
ceremonies are bizarre, the beliefs absurd, but the
principles just. Some travelers and missionaries have
foolishly represented Oriental priests as preachers of

iniquity. It is impossible, however, that any religious society could be constituted for the creation of sin." When he turned to the Orient for inspiration prior to writing his *Essai*, it was said that he dressed his Oriental characters according to French fashion (the same accusation leveled at Galland after he translated the *Thousand and One Nights*). Whether or not this was so, what most interested Voltaire about the Orient was that it strengthened his argument against religious fanaticism.

For Voltaire, the Orient continued to be a Utopia, as did the world of the savages. Too, he thought of the Orient as a complex of nations that could be compared, in a given epoch, to our own historical vicissitudes. He argued, for example, that in the medieval age we Europeans resembled the Chinese and that India of the eighteenth century was governed like Europe in the age of feudalism. But he also noted that the Orient was a complex of civilizations in which feudal privileges did not exist; rather, it was characterized by benevolence and liberty. The most important point, however, was what was at its base or, rather, what was *not* at its base: it was not Christian. He even regarded Mohammed as an enlightened despot, since it was convenient to his political viewpoint. These distortions, as Gerbi has observed, "were not errors but longings; the 'reality' and efficiency [of the Orient] were being given a retrospective examination, after the passage of many years. Each improvement in the 'reality' of China expressed the desire for a similar improvement in the 'reality' of Europe." To say that "in the Orient there are no Bastilles" was actually Voltaire's desire to say "let us destroy the Bastille."

8. *From the Inquiry into the Spirit of Nations to the Distinction Between the Bourgeoisie and the Folk*

Voltaire continued the politico-social controversy that had existed in the sixteenth and seventeenth centuries. Beyond the controversy and the longings that he set forth, however, it is a fact that the encounter

between peoples and civilization, when viewed historically, demonstrated that one cannot hazard a theory,
whatever it may be, that is limited by a narrow local
perspective. This was the essential point of Voltaire's inquiry into the spirit of nations. This
"spirit" remains (as the spirit of laws did for Montesquieu) an empirical concept if one looks only at
the external, naturalistic factors; but it is so much
more profitable to consider the concept, from time to
time, in connection with the concrete expressions of
history. Voltaire, however, did not always capture
the spirit shaping the civilization of the individual
nations that he considered.

It has been observed that in 1665 Charles Saint-
Évremond (who gave evidence of having read Paolo Sarpi
in his *Discours sur les historiens français*), remembering that Caesar had not lost the occasion in his
Commentaries of speaking of the usages, customs, and
religion of the Gauls, praised Hugo Grotius "for penetrating the most hidden causes of war, the ruling
spirit in Spain, and the character of the Flemish
people"; he also praised Grotius for "penetrating the
true genius of nations," for "capturing the correct
character of society and principal persons," and for
"explaining different states of religion." Because
of their merits and faults, we could say the same of
Montesquieu and Voltaire. But for them did the nation,
which they defined as a collection of people characterized by specific spiritual or moral features, include
the folk, the "small" people?

Bayle and Fontenelle were convinced that the folk--
and their allusion referred to the "little" people--is
everyone's victim. Montesquieu firmly asserted that
"it is not unimportant that the folk be enlightened."
Voltaire, however, was not entirely of this opinion,
as is evidenced by his warning in *Le siècle de Louis
XIV* that "within the nation there is a group of people
with no access to reason." Despite proposing the
universality of reason, Voltaire was not, in the last
analysis, asking for equality for all citizens. Browne
had asserted that enlightening the people was not worth
the pain--but Voltaire went further, suggesting that if

you enlighten the people, you will have revolution.
Voltaire was too peacefully middle class to want revolution. His Enlightenment was embodied in the *honnête
homme*, the middle-class man, whose ideal image was
contained in Voltaire himself:

> *Jaime le luxe, et même la mollesse,*
> *Tous les plaisirs, les arts de toute espèce,*
> *La propreté, le goût, les ornaments.*
> *Tout honnête homme a de tels sentiments.*

This was a period during which the middle class
secured a sharp self-awareness. The middle class
wanted to distinguish itself clearly from classes that
were or that they believed were inferior; that is, the
middle class wanted to distinguish itself from the
people who (as Voltaire said) steadfastly believed in
everything that Enlightenment thinkers wished to abol-
ish. A perceptive historian, Bernhard Groethuysen, has
recently brought this conflict to light, a conflict
which underscores precisely this distinction between
these two classes. In his examination Groethuysen
makes use of the sermons of country curates, material
that is seldom brought into historical investigations.
Through these sermons we are able to follow the folk,
those living in the hamlets and the country, the humble
people who had their pilgrimages and their holidays,
rooted as they were in traditional beliefs. To assert
his distinctiveness, then, the middle-class man felt he
had to become a religious skeptic. As Groethuysen
observes, "If religion is good for the folk, and even
necessary, the middle-class man must be able to dis-
pense with it, while remaining what he is: a perfect
honnête homme. The distinction between the two classes,
the bourgeoisie and the folk, is an acquired accomplishment, and it is the attitude of these two classes toward
religion that permits us to distinguish them. He adds:
"This does not mean that all members of the middle class
are necessarily skeptics. It means that if a member of
the middle class has conserved something from the old
faith, he has done so as an individual rather than as a
middle-class man."

The Enlightenment certainly had not failed to
bring usages and customs into the study of history,
even if it did so only for the purpose of criticizing
them. These usages and customs belonged, in part, to
a class of people that now, through political and
social misunderstanding, was addressed with scorn
because only error was to be found there. But for
the time being, in this distinction between the middle
class and the folk, the Enlightenment placed its attention directly on the folk, now no longer *the* nation
but a *part* of the nation. This attention was focused
on the humble ones, members of the lower class who had
their own moral and intellectual heritage--a heritage
that the humanists did not understand but for which,
in their heart of hearts, they felt a secret fascination.

PART TWO

THE SEARCH FOR ORIGINS BETWEEN THE
ENLIGHTENMENT AND PRE-ROMANTICISM

CHAPTER VI

MAN AND HISTORY

1. Toward a New "Science of Customs"

During the period in which the Enlightenment formulated
and exalted its dogmas, some intellectual tendencies,
characterized by irrationalities that Enlightenment
thinkers rejected, or at least believed to be harmful,
were emerging in European intellectual history. The
study of primitive and Oriental nations, the comparison
of their usages and customs with those of Westerners,
and the battle against error that led to a critical
investigation of errors (or of spiritual manifestations
considered to be such) point to the clear beginning of
the science of customs. Whatever its contingent concerns might have been, the Enlightenment must be credited with bringing into the field of history those
problems related to the origin of social, religious,
and political ideas, quite often stretching all the way
back to the life of primitive peoples. From Bayle to
Fontenelle, from Montesquieu to Voltaire, French Enlightenment thinkers attempted to give an essentially
rational interpretation to the life of those peoples--
peoples who, considered as a whole, are like a crucible
in which everything could be melted down.
    Not everyone, however, shared this rational inter-
pretation, as is shown, for example, in a work by a
learned Jesuit, Joseph François Lafitau, entitled the
*Mœurs des sauvages amériquains, comparées aux mœurs
des premiers temps*, perhaps the first document in
modern ethnology. Understandably, Fontenelle never
cited this work, nor was it cited by Montesquieu, who
loved to look in current ethnographical literature for

inspiration for his politico-social concepts. In the
"Avant-Propos" that was added to his *Essai*, however,
Voltaire demonstrated that he was familiar with
Lafitau, even drawing a whimsical profile of him:
"Lafitau saw the Americans as coming from the ancient
Greeks, for the following reasons: just as the Greeks
had their own fables, so do the Americans; the earliest Greeks went hunting, and the Americans do the same;
the earliest Greeks had oracles, and the Americans have
magicians; dancing took place during the Greek festivals, and dancing takes place in America. Surely we
must agree that these are convincing reasons indeed!"

But was Lafitau really like Voltaire's portrait
of him? There is no doubt, let us hasten to add, that
in reading the *Mœurs* one discovers an attentive,
scrupulous ethnographer who displays the world of
primitives in all its variety. Lafitau responded to
the human side of this world, examining it with the
knowledge of the scholar--one who balanced his particular preparation in Christian theology with frank
statements of his personal opinions.

Lafitau had been in Canada for a long time as a
missionary, where he had had the fortune of being
guided in the study of savages by an old *confrère*,
Father Julien Garnier, who, after sixty years of
living in those places, knew the languages of the
Algonquins, the Hurons, and five Iroquois dialects.
Although somewhat removed from the savages, Lafitau
was not content to describe them in the way that the
usual traveler had. His ambition, as he declared,
was to give a sketch of the "science of usages and
customs of different peoples," which had "something
of such usefulness and interest that even Homer made
it the object of an entire poem," the *Odyssey*; this
work, he said, should be considered as the first
ethnographical work. We see, then, that he was keenly
aware of how much had been written about primitive
peoples, and he willingly turned to the works of
Martire, Casas, Gómara, Léry, and Vega. But it would
be erroneous to think that he only concerned himself
with writers who had a recognized scientific importance; he also occasionally turned to the works of

Lescarbot, and he did not neglect the amiable (though)
polemical) disquisitions of Baron Lahontan.

Lafitau certainly knew how much had been written
about the life of savages in the field of ethnography;
moreover, he could call upon his direct experience.
His savages seem to have come from a fresco whose background is animated by but not submerged in nature. He
follows them leisurely from birth to death, in their
occupations and entertainments, in all the particulars
of their lives. He was spurred by an anxious, persistent desire to penetrate into a world that is not ours
but that reminds us of our own. The world of the
savages, *his* savages, was not, for Lafitau, a bizarre
fact. Like ours, it is a world containing spirits
rather than things, humans rather than objects of curiosity. The primitive, the noble savage, had not merely
been studied prior to Lafitau: he had also been
invented. Yet when we study the savage (and to study
him one must know the language in which his thought is
articulated), shouldn't we perhaps realize, Lafitau
asks, that the savage's most essential customs, like
ours, are rooted in religion, in the worship of spirits
and the dead, and in social organizations?

2. Lafitau and his "Mœurs des sauvages amériquains"

The *Mœurs* was the most perceptive, attentive investigation of primitive religions at the beginning of the
Enlightenment. This was a period in which deists and
atheists saw primitives in general and the American
Indians in particular as deists or atheists. Lafitau
was convinced that those who saw the primitive as an
atheist basically had good supporting evidence, inasmuch as some ethnographical literature suggested the
existence of people who had no religion, and he concluded that religion is a creation of legislators who
"have invented it to lead people by fear, the mother
of superstition." But, he asks himself, where is the
truth to be found?

The truth is to be found precisely in the midst of
his savages, his Americans, whom he had studied for
years and whom, in fact, both deists and atheists had

often known only on the basis of cursory information.
Lafitau tells us at the very beginning of the *Mœurs*,
"I have become painfully aware that those who concern
themselves with savages in their accounts paint them
as people who have no religious sentiment, no knowledge
of the divine, no object to whom they render any worship; they paint them as people with no laws, no civil
order, no form of government--in a word, as men who
have almost nothing of man except the form. This is
an error for which many people are responsible. . ."
(I, 5). Shortly thereafter, as if to draw an ideal
picture, he says that the savages "have a good disposition, a lively imagination, facile thought, and
admirable memory. All have some traces of an ancient
hereditary religion and a form of government. . . .
They have brave and proud hearts that have been tested
by everything, an intrepid valor, a strength in difficulty that is heroic, . . . a respect for their elders,
a deference for their equals--all of which is truly
astonishing" (I, 97).

Lafitau came to consider religion as both a spiritual and a social phenomenon binding the life of his
savages together, accompanying them from birth to
death, and consecrating all the solemn moments of life.
In some of them one can even find the idea of a Great
Spirit, a Supreme Being (I, 111-17). Numerous, however, are the olympuses of their gods, for their
mythology is fused with religion in an intricate network of cults and rites, all based on a certain conception of the world and life. Spirits dominate
nature--and it is primarily here, in this domination,
that Lafitau brings in the belief of a soul separable
from the body:

> The soul for the Americans is a good deal more
> independent from the body than is the case for
> us, and it enjoys greater freedom. It leaves the
> body to make excursions where it wishes. Great
> travels do not affect it; it moves in the air,
> crosses the seas, and enters into the most incred-
> ible places. They [the savages] are convinced
> that the soul, seeing the body immersed in sleep,

benefits by taking a trip, after which it returns
to its abode. At their awakening they believe
that the soul has really seen everything that has
passed in their sleep, and they behave accordingly.
(I, 132)

We clearly see that, although Lafitau did not draw
clear theoretical conclusions from his observations,
his thought contains the seeds of modern ethnology.
In his view, the American primitive was neither a
monotheist nor an animist; if anything, the American
primitive was both a monotheist and an animist who
also believed in the worship of the dead (one could
observe this, for example, in the Iroquois, who, in
honor of the dead, threw a certain quantity of wheat
in front of the door of the hut). Lafitau also noted
that there was a rigid social organization existing
among American primitives, one in which (in general)
the most absolute chiefs were regarded as fathers of
their people and therefore had the right to apply the
most rigorous justice. Nor were other organizations
merely religious in nature, as is especially demonstrated by the family structure. "It must be remembered," Bertrand de Jouvenel has recently noted, "that
as early as 1724 Father Lafitau had observed in the
Iroquois the phenomenon of uterine filiation and
revealed that, in consequence of this, the woman was
the center of the family of the people. He concluded
the comparison with what Herodotus reported about the
Lyceum." But even here Lafitau was far from theorizing
or at least from generalizing (as Johann Bachofen and
Lewis Morgan did later). Indeed, let us open his
Mœurs :

In the customs of the Iroquois there are some
degrees of kinship that are actually a bit different from those of the Hebrews and the Chaldeans,
but to which they are comparable in that they produce misunderstanding because of their terms.
. . . It is necessary to know that for the Iroquois and Hurons all the children of a tribe
consider as their mothers all the sisters of their

mothers and as their uncles all the brothers of
their mothers; for the same reason they give the
name of father to all the brothers of their
fathers. . . . All the children who descend from
the mother and from her sisters and from the
father and from his brothers are considered to be
brothers and sisters. But they consider as cousins
the children of their uncles and of their aunts,
which is to say the children of the brothers of
their mothers and of the sisters of their fathers,
although the level of their relationship be identical. At the third generation all this changes,
with the uncles and aunts of the parents becoming
grandmothers and grandfathers. (II, 243)

Lafitau thus excludes the possibility that matrimony can be considered only as a natural phenomenon.
In fact, he relates matrimony to religion. In his
view, this religion is not a meaningless issue, however it may be articulated in the life of savages;
rather, it is a woof in which threads thin as air but
hard as steel end by entwining all social institutions.
Lafitau did not ignore the fact that there are also
some "lower" forms of thought among the savages, such
as those involving magic (or so he erroneously judged
it), and he thought that the savages, like the ancients,
had occasionally erred in the kind of faith and worship
that they rendered to God. This opinion, however, did
not prevent him from justifying, explaining, and understanding that religion. This was to be, in fact, precisely one of the results of his comparative approach.

3. Ethnography and History

In reading the *Mœurs*, we immediately recognize that we
are in front of a pleasing, robust narrative. Because
of this quality, the *Mœurs* reminds us of Martire, the
author of *Decados de orbe novo*. Additionally, Lafitau,
like Martire, was a humanist who was well aware of the
classical world, its institutions, practices, and
beliefs. Homer, Herodotus, Varro, Diodorus Siculus,

Strabo, Plutarch, Pliny the Elder, Tacitus, and Caesar
are the sources from which he drew his information;
these sources carried him confidently into the classical world, the knowledge of which was always indispensable to the preparation and spiritual training of
Jesuits. Living in the midst of savages while fully
admiring classical antiquity, the Jesuits, as we have
already seen, went into raptures over the potential
analogies between savages and the peoples of Greece
or Rome. These comparisons and references are significant because they were used to demonstrate two theses,
one about the classical world itself and the other
about the primitive world. On the one hand, references
to the classical world constituted a title of nobility
for the savages; on the other hand, they established a
presupposed community of origins for the savages and
the ancient Greeks and Romans, one that demolished, to
use a phrase from Gerardus van der Leeuw, the wall that
had separated them.

Like his predecessors, however, Lafitau provided
only superficial accounts, for which he was criticized
by Voltaire. But did Lafitau perhaps have other purposes in mind? We should note that the learned Jesuit
did not hesitate to declare at the beginning of his
work:

> I am not satisfied merely with knowing the charac-
> ter of the savages and accounting for their customs
> and practices. I have looked for vestiges of the
> most backward antiquity in these practices and cus-
> toms. I have read with particular attention those
> ancient authors who have dealt with the customs,
> laws, and usages of peoples of whom we have some
> knowledge. I have made comparisons between these
> customs and confess that while ancient authors have
> given me some explanations for supporting some
> likely conjectures about savages, the customs of
> the savages have also given me some explanations
> for more easily understanding and explaining much
> of what ancient authors talk about. (I, 3)

In other words, the savage represented not only the

present, with which he was interested, but also, in
certain respects, the past. Thus, one could find
explanations for many rites, usages, and institutions
not only in the world of the savages but also in the
world of classical civilization and, therefore, in our
own. Lafitau was not satisfied, however, with merely
investigating the Greeks and Romans; he also investigated such ancient European peoples as the Gauls, the
Tracians, and the Sciti. He asked for an understanding
of all these peoples, even occasionally referring, like
Lescarbot, to the commoners among civilized peoples,
especially the French peasants (whom he cited for their
funeral laments). These peoples seemed to him to be
fundamentally united under a common denominator.
Hence, he did not hesitate to assert:

> . . . Not only do the people we call barbarians
> have a religion, but this religion shares some
> striking similarities with primitive religions,
> with those that in ancient times were called the
> revels of Bacchus and of the Mother of the Gods,
> the mysteries of Isis and Osiris. . . . In
> matters of religion we do not have anything older
> in profane antiquity than the mysteries and revels
> comprising the religion of the Phrygians, the
> Egyptians, and the first Cretans, who regarded
> themselves as the first peoples of the world and
> the first authors of the worship of the gods;
> these mysteries and this worship passed from them
> to all nations and were spread throughout the
> world. (I, 7)

It follows, then, that the religions of barbarians and
pagans have the same base and the same principles. We
know that Fontenelle--and we must allow for the fact
that his *De l'origine des fables* preceded Lafitau's
Mœurs--observed that even the Greeks went through a
savage stage, and we know that he searched for this
base and these principles in human nature, more specifically in man's reason. This search would later be
repeated by Enlightenment thinkers, often using materials provided by missionaries, with the result that

they could compare the facts of natural religions with those of revealed religion. But even here, argued Lafitau, there was some error. This base and these principles, he asserted, are in fact related specifically to Catholicism, and Catholicism should therefore be called to explain them.

4. The "Scienza Nuova"

The perceptive, conscientious study given to the world of the primitives and the world of ancient European civilization was thus transferred by Lafitau to a strictly theological level. Even on such a level he did not forget that he was an ethnographer, one who well knew that "the subject of customs is a very broad subject" joining "the most disparate things." His work was essentially a series of investigations and comparisons demonstrating that there is not a single example of savage customs that does not have its parallel among ancient peoples. But even here he did not generalize, because his studies led him to the conclusion that within the broad category of usages one must distinguish between characteristics deriving from human nature (which sends us back to the Revelation) and characteristics deriving from contacts or migrations among peoples.

Lafitau's mission was to explain classical civilization by drawing parallels with savages, but he also attempted to explain savages in terms of the Bible, the Revelation, and the will of God. Bosseut's argument was thus transferred to the field of ethnography. Lafitau, a good theologian, began the history of mankind with the Revelation, to which he traced not only the most general customs and beliefs (for example, sacrifices, initiations, and belief in a Supreme Being) but also the communal elements that we find as much in Christianity as in pagan religions. This suggests that mankind began not with error (as Enlightenment philosophers would have it) but with truth--which from the very beginning is articulated in religion and mythology. But there is an additional factor that must be remembered:

in Lafitau's view, God's "revelation" was made not to
Moses but to the first man. "The study that I have
made of pagan mythology," he asserts, "has given me
an avenue to another system, and it has led back beyond the times of Moses, back to our first parents,
Adam and Eve, in order to reach God." In saying this
he did not exclude the conjecture that lawmakers after
Moses had taken advantage of man's ignorance in order
to create new usages. But when we go back to Adam and
Eve, he adds, we will see "a religion pure and holy in
itself and in its principles, a religion willed by God
and transmitted to our first parents. In fact, there
can be only one religion; this religion, being *for* men,
must have started *with* men, and it will survive as long
as they. This is what faith teaches and reason tells
us" (I, 13).

The changing of religion with time and with men is
the transformation that has brought about many usages;
and if these usages are errors, they are so as much
among savages as among Greeks and Romans. He acknowledged, for example, that crude and criminal superstitions are occasionally to be found among savages.
However, he afterwards immediately observes: "Are they
any cruder or more criminal than those of the Greeks
and Romans, who, after carrying the sciences and the
arts to the highest perfection, failed to draw any
result from all their enlightenment and philosophy
except the tainting of their religion with a multitude
of extremely ridiculous, insipid fairy tales?" (II,
157). As ridiculous and insipid as such fairy tales
may be, they have served a historical function, and
they have their own nature and office. The task of
the historian is to see precisely what this nature and
office have been throughout history. In its course of
development, the human race has certainly had some
moments identified with error; but these deviations
must be studied without rationalistic recriminations
because even when such deviations involve corrupt and
monstrous forms of religion, what counts is always the
search for truth, although such deviations may strike
us as being ridiculous and disgusting. Indeed, it is
the search for truth that actually binds these

"deviations" to revealed religion.

Religious faith thus gave impulse in Lafitau's work to a theory that could be called historico-ethnographical. What is important, as Arnold van Gennep has observed, is not the fact that Lafitau related his parallels (although cautiously and prudently) to a traditional orthodox theory opposed by Enlightenment philosophers; rather, the important point is that he had clearly perceived much that his predecessors had missed. Further, he had a unique method of investigation, one that employed comparison to illuminate relationships and processes that otherwise would have remained hidden, even though such comparison does not clearly establish when some sketchy idea found among savages became a conscious development in the classical world. In any event, Lafitau must be credited with studying pagan religions as the vestiges of revealed religion, with the result that, for him (as previously for Fontenelle, in another sense), the significance of the surviving elements became clear. It is also to his credit that he perceived the relationship between ethnology and folklore. Most of all, he must be given credit for clearly bringing ethnology into the realm of history. This is the most significant aspect of his method, which later influenced ethnological and folkloristic studies. Indeed, Lafitau had viewed ethnology not only as a tool but also as a criterion for a new interpretation of history. This interpretation became the central concern of an Italian thinker, G. B. Vico, who, a year after the *Mœurs* came out, published a work in Naples under the following title: *Principi di una scienza nuova.*

5. Vico and the Primitive World

The *Scienza Nuova*, in this regard, is a veritable war machine, which, although not perfect in all its contrivances, was a powerful instrument of assault. Vico represented a new voice in the history of European thought, as new as he wished his science to be. For

him there were no limits to investigation. He had the
spirit, the fervor, I would even say the voice of those
Enlightenment philosophers who synthesized innumerable
interests. But unlike Enlightenment philosophers, he
perceived the importance of tradition, which he regarded as an alive, fertile element in history. Like
Enlightenment thinkers, he abhorred the idea of a
"miraculous" history. But unlike Enlightenment thinkers (or at least many of them), he claimed that fables,
proverbs, and anecdotes were a part of history, and he
did not consider them, in the manner of Fontenelle, as
errors of the human spirit. Nor did he believe that
religions based on the impostures of other religions
could exist. If they do exist, they come only from
the credulity of men. Man, in his view, is the measure
of history, and history should therefore be the "science" of man; this "science" should study the products
of the human spirit, only those things made by man.

The "new science," the "knowledge" that would serve
to pose the question of man's origins in an altogether
new way, imposed a specific task on Vico, the convert-
ing of the certain (a philological proof) to the true
(a philosophical proof). In the *Scienza Nuova* Vico
notes:

> The unhappy cause of this is that there has not
> been until now a science that is both a history
> and a philosophy of man. Thus, philosophers have
> meditated on a human nature already civilized by
> the same religions and laws that have permitted
> the philosophers themselves to become such, and
> they have not meditated on the human nature that
> created those religions and laws that now surround
> these philosophers. Philologists (because of the
> common fate of everything ancient, which, as it
> gets further away from us, becomes lost from sight)
> have handed down ancient popular traditions that
> are so inexact, torn, and split that, if their
> proper aspect is not restored, the shreds cannot
> be reassembled and put in place. Whoever considers
> this with some seriousness will conclude that it is
> altogether impossible that popular traditions were

originally thus, not only in the allegories that
have been attributed to them but also in the common sentiment of many ages. This can be explained
by the fact that they have been passed down to us
by uncultured people. (The first *Scienza Nuova,*
ed. Nicolini, § 23)

From this new horizon, which became broader yet
more precise in later editions of the *Scienza Nuova*
(re-edited first in 1730 and then in 1744), Vico viewed
the history of humanity, the history of nations and
men, the history of the past that forever becomes the
present. He was not concerned with either the problem
of ethnology or the problem of folklore. He sensed,
however, the presence and the incidences of both. But
what was the world of the primitives for Vico, the
world that Lafitau emphatically placed in the field of
history? Vico's historicism certainly remains incom-
prehensible, or at least unclear, if it is not seen in
the light of a "document" that helped Vico to animate
it: the brute, primitive man with his obtuse imagination. This brute, this primitive, is not, however,
merely a chronological determination for Vico; it is
an ideal determination, in that the primitive world
not only can be *in* us but also continually *returns* in
us. This is his discovery (previously suggested by
Lafitau, but carried out by Vico on a higher level).
Vico often speaks in his work of the constant
effort that he had to make to penetrate this world,
granted that to us "the capability is naturally now
denied to enter into the vast imagination of primitive
men, the minds of whom had nothing of the spiritual,
because everything was in the senses, everything was
contained in the body," so that "one can hardly understand how the earth's first humans thought." But the
world of which he speaks, the world in which he is
interested, the world that he tries to understand and
therefore to comprehend, can and does have its own
voice; it is a primitive world that became civilized,
thus entering into history as an aspect of the development of the universal spirit, which embraces in its
humanity both the civilized man *and* the savage.

Comparisons between us and the primitives, which gradually became immersed in social controversies after
the formulation of the concept of the noble savage,
were exalted by a historical vision. It is our mind
that goes out to search for this world, penetrates it,
and makes it our own. Vico, like Lafitau, perceived
the importance of the study of religion in understanding the primitive world. And, like Lafitau, he did
not believe that there could be people without religion. His argument against Bayle and the libertines
in this regard was as strong as the argument made by
Lafitau:

> Let not our first principle be accused of false-
> hood by modern travelers who report that the
> peoples of Brazil, Kafiristan, and other nations
> of the new world (and Antoine Arnauld believes
> the same thing about the dwellers of the islands
> called the Antilles) live in society without any
> knowledge of God; perhaps persuaded by these,
> Bayle asserts in the *Treatise on Comets* that peo-
> ple can live with justice without the light of
> God; not so much did Polybius venture to assert,
> whose dictum, acclaimed by some, is that if there
> were philosophers in the world who lived with
> justice by force of reason and not of laws, reli-
> gions would not be necessary in the world. These
> are the fictions of travelers who fill their books
> with ridiculous information. (The second *Scienza
> Nuova*, ed. Nicolini, § 334)

With these words, as we see, Vico demonstrates that
he was well informed about some of the ethnographical
tendencies of his time. But what was primitive religion for him if not one form of the human spirit, an
aspect of the imagination? It is the imagination that
creates myths and religions. And doesn't the brute,
the primitive, perhaps become immediately human when,
with fear and wonder, he raises his eyes and notices
the sky, taking the world around him into himself and
making it a part of his mental life? Thus, religions
are always present, in a positive fashion, in the

history of the human race and therefore in its institutions (for example, matrimony). But what are languages--whose etymology helped him to discover the meanings of myths, those uneliminable "moments" of each religion--if not part of the documents, part of the fragments that, in giving the origins of the names of things, reveal all that has struck the imagination of man?

The very nature of religions is reported by Vico as that of poetic language. This point of view, Fausto Nicolini observes, serves "to demonstrate that in Vico's system religions cannot have anything but a human (rather than divine) character in that they have languages." But for Vico isn't the divine, in all its forms, contained in mankind or, we should perhaps say, in the man who historicizes the divine?

6. At the Origins: Poetry

In reporting the world of "beasts," primitives who live in a world that is itself the work of the imagination (that is, of poetic wisdom), Vico considered poetic language, specifically the metaphors for emotions and feelings, as the natural language of primitives, the one and only expression of a disturbed and moved spirit that, in its own way, interprets the darker aspects of the world. The world of man, which is as much as saying history, was not at first familiar with reason (an idea to which Vico often appealed) but rather with imagination. This is true in the sense that even in the light of reason the imagination eternally renews itself. When poetizing, when singing, doesn't the rational man turn young and therefore irrational?

In these premises--although erroneous because there is no man who is not a combination of reason and imagination--was the clear formulation of a theory about primitive and barbaric poetry, undoubtedly one of the most ingenious insights of the *Scienza Nuova*. There was in such a formulation, Mario Fubini correctly observes, the recognition of poetry as a primitive form, anterior to reflection; poetry that is close to the

origins is less threatened by reflection, and therefore is the most poetic and pre-eminent poetry. But
there is an arguable point here, given the fact that
Vico not only subverted the very concept of classical
poetry but also regarded a poet such as Homer as a
barbaric bard who sang of crude, fierce customs,
transfiguring the most elementary instincts of life.

In Vico's view, poetry, the most valid work of the
imagination, is not merely in contrast to reason; true,
it thrives and develops primarily in essentially barbaric ages, but it also explains the beginning of history itself, a history that from the start was exactly
reported by poets whose allegories contained significant accounts of the first ages. Like Lafitau,
Vico was opposed to allegorical exegesis. Unlike
Lafitau, however, he saw a precise relation between
reality and myth, with myth serving as a mirror that
reflects the entire history of man. One could indeed
say that no one had perceived the vast scope of myth
as Vico had. In his view, myth, like language and
poetry, was a mirror reflecting primitive peoples--
their religions, customs, and traditions. Myth thus
becomes an element of history that the historian must
interpret.

It was Vico's opinion that the historian neither
can nor should neglect the popular traditions that
Enlightenment thinkers had rejected, or at least were
in the process of rejecting. In fact, Vico took pleasure in turning to such traditions as a "common ground
of truth": he took pleasure in the balladeers of his
city, who reminded him of the rhapsodies of the Homeric
poets; he was delighted when confronted with the stories that his fellow citizen, Giambattista Basile, had
reworked into literature; and the mythology of the
fireside reminded him of log customs in the age of
Boccaccio. It is true that Vico saw the folk, the
commoners among civilized people, as astonished (like
his "brutes") in the presence of an eclipse or a
calamity; but for him impostures or allegories did not
exist; or, to put this another way, impostures or
allegories are not what have made languages, religions,
customs, and traditions, which derive, rather, from

the imagination. This was to pose man's creativity as
the very foundation of history, a part of the humanity
of every man.

It has been said that in relating the imagination
to an everlasting moment of human activity, Vico not
only confused poetry (which has an imaginative value)
with myth (which, on the contrary, has a practical
value), but he also confused the autonomy of poetry
with what we could call its mythologizing activity.
We do know that he called poetry to an educative function for the common people (how different is this from
what Enlightenment thinkers said?), since it invents
"sublime fables proper to the folk understanding; it
agitates in order to attain the goal that it has set
for itself, of teaching the common people to act
virtuously" (the second *Scienza Nuova*, ed. Nicolini,
§ 376). But did Vico really confuse myth with poetry?
Or did poetry help him to understand myth, which (like
religion) in its primitive stage is absorbed by poetry;
and didn't the subsequent formulation of his myth-
poetry theory help him to explain the very origin of
spiritual life?

Leaving aside these distinctions, it is a fact that
Vico focused on the primitive world and popular traditions in his work. The pariahs of society (the primitives, on the one hand, and the commoners among civilized peoples, on the other) break into the *Scienza
Nuova* not as things but as people--as historical people.
History, in his view, was not a proceeding *ad infinitum*
but an alternating of historical eras in which we occasionally become barbarians again--not because of reason
but rather because barbarity is the moment in which the
spirit flows into the world and the mind with an indomitable power.

7. *Vico: Civilized and Barbarous Nations*

It was in the light of these concepts that Vico viewed
human institutions, which, precisely because they *are*
human institutions, he considered objectively in both
civilized and barbarous nations. Too, it was in the

light of these concepts that he contributed ideas,
principles, and corollaries to the facts that previously had been predominant in descriptive ethnography. Thus animated, the world of history itself,
the history of barbarous and civilized nations, springs
forth:

> We observe that all nations, barbarous as well as
> civilized, although separately founded because
> remote from each other in the immensities of space
> and time, preserve three human customs: they all
> have some religion, they all contract formal mar-
> riages, and they all bury their dead; nor are
> human actions celebrated with more elaborate cere-
> monies and more consecreated solemnity among
> nations, however savage and crude, than the rites
> of religion, marriage, and burial. The axiom that
> "uniform ideas born among peoples unknown to each
> other must have a common ground of truth" should
> suggest to everyone that from these three institu-
> tions all humanity began, and therefore they must
> be jealously guarded by everyone so that the world
> does not revert to the jungles again. Thus, we
> have taken these three eternal and universal cus-
> toms for the three first principles of this sci-
> ence. (The second *Scienza Nuova*, ed. Nicolini,
> § 333)

Vico acknowledges, then, that the uniformity of
customs must be related to the universal tendencies
of man. But accustomed as he is to seeing both sides
of the coin, he goes on to say the following about the
origins of language, which he traces back, as he does
with poetry and myth, to the heroic period, specifically man's primitive period:

> The greatest difficulty still remains: how is it
> that there are as many different common languages
> as there are peoples? To solve the problem, we
> must establish this great truth: just as peoples
> because of the diversity of climates have acquired
> different natures, from which have sprung as many

different customs, so from their different natures
and customs as many different languages have
arisen. Because of this diversity of their nature,
they have seen the same utilities or necessities of
human life from different viewpoints, and there
have thus arisen so many national customs, usually
different from and occasionally contrary to one
another. Only in this way have there arisen as
many different languages as there are nations.
This is found in the proverbs, which are the maxims
of human life, the same in substance but explained
from as many viewpoints as there have been and are
different nations, as is seen in the Bible. (The
second *Scienza Nuova*, ed. Nicolini, § 445)

Thus, the problem of human origins becomes the problem
of its historicism. Vico, like Lafitau, had a vivid,
profound perception of everything human. He perceived
the fascination that the most remote periods exercise
on our imagination. But do facts like those glimpsed
by ethnographers exist? Or do processes exist, historical processes that are to be evaluated in terms of
their genesis and development? The *Scienza Nuova* is
an admirable temple that could carry this most solemn
and austere inscription: "The nature of institutions
is to be found in their birth at certain times and
under certain guises; whenever the time and guise are
thus and so, such and not otherwise are the institutions that come into being" (the second *Scienza Nuova*,
ed. Nicolini, § 147).

The thinker who had always been surrounded by a
"sea of doubts" here had no doubts. In this his
"Bible" he singled out the very essence of history:
to know the nature of institutions means to perceive
them in their birth and therefore to historicize them.
This, indeed, is the most significant contribution of
the *Scienza Nuova*, a work in which human institutions
find a comprehension and justification of their own.

8. Muratori's "Antiquitates"

It is significant that almost contemporaraneously Lodovico Muratori set out to complement his *Annali d'Italia*,
which is concerned only with political history, with
his historico-cultural *Antiquitates Italicae Medii
Aevi*. Published between 1738 and 1742, the *Antiquitates* is a perceptive, scholarly investigation that has
particular interest for folklore. Availing himself of
parchments, chronicles, and ancient laws, Muratori
took delight in reconstructing the fashions of dress,
wedding customs, spectacles, games--in other words, the
common traditions of the Italian people. But what
value do his reconstructions have?
     In Italy Vico had previously asserted that to study
languages and institutions one must know the institutions themselves; therefore, one must consider not only
wars and trades but also customs, whether barbarous or
civilized. To a degree Pietro Giannone and Carlo Troya
had given support to Vico's idea--but even before Voltaire had rendered the concept popular (although it had
been a concern of ancient historians, from Herodotus to
Caesar to Tacitus), Muratori was at work reconstructing
the customs of the Italian Middle Ages. In the
Antiquitates, however, he was not only an extremely
learned, eminent philologist but also a historian pon-
dering the past, a past consisting of more than superstitions (which he sometimes regarded only in terms of
external characteristics, inasmuch as he, like the
Enlightenment thinkers, considered them a product of
ignorance). The past, as he says in Dissertation LIX,
has not developed merely from ancient customs "whose
names endure without the facts" (which demonstrates how
he viewed the concept of survivals); rather, the past
is the result of a collective heritage and human mentality that, while reconstructed in certain documents,
we should be able to assess exclusively with our own
minds. In short, the *Antiquitates*, however much the
result of erudition, was meant to be an amplification
of the confines of history, the complement of *Annali
d'Italia*, in which he had previously pictured the

Middle Ages as a not entirely barbaric period. On the
subject of Odoacer, for example, he observed that "the
Latins and Greeks called whoever was not of their nation barbaric," whereas in fact one must recognize that
"there have been barbarians wiser and more sophisti-
cated than the Latins and Greeks themselves." In
Antiquitates (Dissertation XXIX) he concluded, finally,
by identifying barbarity with simplicity, an identification that joins him with Vico. And, like Vico, he
understood the importance of folk poetry, inasmuch as
he considered both mimes and *histriones* to be poets of
the folk.

CHAPTER VII

NATURE, CIVILIZATION, AND PROGRESS

1. *Rousseau and the Apologia of the Savage*

In the eighteenth century, the impact of Lafitau's
Mœurs and Vico's *Scienza Nuova* did not damage the
theoretical constructions of the Enlightenment.
Rather, the schism in this century was represented
primarily by J. J. Rousseau, who perceived the noble
savage--the barbarian, the native--in the manner of
Lafitau and Vico, whose works synthesized the ethnographical efforts of the preceding centuries, although
in different ways; furthermore, he contributed perhaps
more than anyone else to spreading the concept of the
noble savage, popularizing it and making it familiar
throughout Europe.

The *Journal Encyclopédique* of January 1, 1768
(which a year before had carried Voltaire's judgment
on Lafitau), emphatically stated that G. B. Vico was
the first thinker who had dared to pretend that
"originally men lived exactly like beasts." And
immediately after: "A man most prolific in paradoxes,
the eloquent Rousseau of Geneva has spread this idea
in his *Discours sur l'origine et les fondements de
l'inégalité parmi les hommes.*" As we have seen, however, this was not the case. Vico compared the world
of nature to the world of history, which is concerned
not with beasts but with humans, their institutions
and their customs. But did Rousseau--who had as much
in common with Lafitau as with Vico--actually envision
original man as a beast? Wouldn't it be better to say
that all of his work was a program attempting to give
dignity to man, liberating him from the superstructure

of society in order to give him back to society pure
and uncontaminated? In his program the primitive (the
barbarian, the ingenuous man) was clearly fashioned on
a paradigm of science and human knowledge. Rousseau
transported reason, to which Enlightenment philosophers
had given their own particular "rational" interpretation, to a distant world of primitive peoples, where he
found a state of charm that made man human long before
he had been corrupted by society and by the progress of
the arts and sciences.

Rousseau's savage is brought to our attention within a frame that seems made for containing an idyl by
Gessner or a painting by Greuze. This savage is the
very perfection of humanity, stripped of all supernatural gifts and artificial powers acquired only by means
of long progress. In short, this is man, as Rousseau
often asserts, as he came (theoretically, at least)
from the hands of nature. He sees him "as resting
under an oak, quenching his thirst at the first brook,
finding his bed at the foot of the same tree that has
furnished him his meal." He follows the savage's life,
which, exposed to the intemperances of climate and the
vigors of the seasons, has given the savage a robust,
virtually indestructible constitution. In this apolo-
gia of the savage, which Rousseau always made aggressively and insistently, there are specific reference
points; for example, he cites the Caribs of Venezuela
who live in absolute tranquility, the Hottentots of
Good Hope who can see ships on the high seas with the
naked eye--ships so far away that the Dutch succeed
in sighting them only with a spy glass--and the American savages, so dear to all the literature of the age,
who could detect the Spanish by smell, like blood-
hounds.

Rousseau loved to go from particular facts to
general ones. His savage, who has whatever the best
in all savages might be, is always pictured as man
abandoned by nature to his instinct and feelings. In
contrast to those Enlightenment writers who had made
the savage into a thoughtful philosopher, Rousseau
wished to see him as he is, "wandering in the forest
without work, without language, without domicile,

without war, and without friendship, without need for
his own fellow men and without any desire to harm them,
perhaps even incapable of recognizing any one of them,
individually; subject to few passions and sufficient
unto himself, he does not have anything but the feelings and understanding proper to this state." Reflecting further, he goes on to observe:

> One finds that this state was the least subjected
> to revolutions, the best for man, and that he must
> have left it only by some tragic accident, which
> for the common good should never have happened.
> The example of savages, who have almost all been
> found at this point, seems to confirm the fact
> that mankind was made to remain in it always, that
> this state is the true childhood of the world, and
> that all subsequent progress has been, in appear-
> ance, moving toward the perfection of the individ-
> ual, but in reality the progress has been toward
> the decrepitude of the species.

He adds, pleased and disturbed at the same time (hence
his anguish), that as long as men were content with
their rustic huts and lived without arts requiring many
workmen, they were free, good, healthy, happy. But
alas: "From the moment that a man had need of help
from someone else, from the moment that it was profitable for a single person to have provisions for two,
equality disappeared, property was introduced, work
became necessary, and vast forests were changed into
smiling fields that had to be watered with sweat of men
and that soon were seen to germinate and grow with
bondage and misery."

The world of primitives or savages was not a world
where there was, as Voltaire had thought, a sense of
"mine and thine"; rather, it was the primitive world
depicted by Casas, Léry, and Baron Lahontan. But what
was this primitive world for Rousseau--this world that
he conjured up with such excited accents in his *Discours sur l'origine et les fondements de l'inégalité
parmi les hommes*, which was published in 1755 and which
included and documented the conclusions he had reached

four years before in the first *Discours sur les sciences et les arts*?

2. The Primitives and Us

In the preface to the second *Discours* Rousseau notes
that the state of nature, in which he had placed his
primitive, "no longer exists" and "perhaps never existed." He adds, however, that "it is necessary to have
specific concepts in order to judge our state correctly." Thus, it was the present, the civilization in
which he lived and with which he struggled in the name
of another civilization, that drove Rousseau to his
investigation. But is it possible to have a specific
concept of a state of nature that never existed and
perhaps never will? Rousseau himself apparently gives
us the answer when he says in *Discours sur l'inégalité:*

> O man, whatever country you may come from, whatever
> your beliefs may be, listen: here is your history
> as I believe it to be read, not in the books of
> your fellow men, which lie, but in nature, which
> never lies. . . . The times of which I speak are
> extremely distant: how much you are altered from
> what you were! It is, so to speak, the life of
> your species that I am about to describe according
> to the qualities you received, which your education
> and your habits have corrupted but not destroyed.
> There is, I feel, a period in which the individual
> would wish to remain. You will look for the period
> in which you would desire that your species had
> remained.

After drawing some pictures of primitive life, he seems
to resume the same discourse: "I have taken considerable time to present the supposition of this primitive
state because I have felt obliged to destroy some old
errors and some ancient, inveterate prejudices, and I
thought I should dig to the roots to demonstrate, in a
panorama of the true state of nature, how far even
natural inequality is from having as much reality

and influence in such a state as our writers claim."

Clearly, the world of primitives, at least as he
represented it, was not a historical fact as it had
been for Lafitau, even though Rousseau blended ethnographical accounts (for example, the *Histoire générale
des voyages*) with imaginary travels of utopian literature; rather, this world is the rational reconstruction
of the condition in which men would have found themselves if their pure human nature had not been altered.
As such, the primitive world was for him, as it had
been for Vico, an ideal state, a touchstone with which
mankind itself could be measured.

Vico's beast, the primitive man who is totally
"sense and imagination," was not, in Rousseau's work,
simply a combination of the irrational elements that
Vico had proposed as fundamental to poetry, myth, and
religion: he was also a *free* individual, which is the
very basis of the state of nature. This freedom of the
individual consequently became the basic assumption
underlying the social contract, with one qualification:
while the state of nature was for Rousseau a quest for
what Kant called the philosophical basis of human freedom, the social contract was a quest for the philosophical basis of public rights--for in his view natural
law itself, whose purity and shape he found in the concept of the divine, was no longer the gift that God
makes to man as soon as he is born; rather, it was in
"the individual himself, potentially." This struck at
the heart of old ideas about natural law, ideas that
had been exceedingly suggestive even for Vico.

The search for human liberty, the search for our
moral life, is the *deus ex machina* of all Rousseau's
work, which was presented in a number of paradoxes
that he clarified and resolved. Rousseau saw nature
as the antidote for all evils. There he also found
the ideal of liberty, which was, in his eyes, the very
mark of the life of the savage. We should note that
the savage was contrasted to civilized man not because
he was dominated by a natural life but because he
dominated nature through his own genuine impulse to
work and live freely.

In regard to his predecessors, this was Rousseau's

great innovation. On the experiences of the two *Discours* he planned to complete a work of restoration in
respect to society, re-establishing relationships between the state and the individual (*Le contrat social*);
in respect to family, encouraging the love and fidelity
of husband and wife (*La Nouvelle Héloïse*); in respect
to the individual, educating him so that he might develop freely, according to nature (*Émile*). But in such
innovations we find the old idea that the primitive
world always lives in us or at least can return in us.
To Vico, certainly, this world and its relationship
with man were strictly of historical interest. Rousseau was following another line of thought, for he was
not particularly interested in history. But didn't
this "uninteresting" history provide him with a way of
approaching old ideas? And didn't Rousseau choose the
primitive world and "natural man" (as he called him,
using a somewhat equivocal expression) to be our guide?
It was not a matter of waiting for that world to return
to us; rather, it was a matter of *making* it return in
us, rediscovering and promoting it so that men might
again find their own way--in the manner of Robinson
Crusoe, whom Rousseau dearly loved. And when Rousseau
spoke of man, he did not exclude the plebeians, the
humble ones, the pariahs of society. In contrast to
the Enlightenment, which certainly did not acknowledge
that all men were equal, he proposed human equality as
the very basis of the moral and social life of the
people. So much, then, for the *honnête homme*!

3. *Popular Tradition as a Human and National Factor*

Rousseau much preferred the plebeians to other classes.
The citizen of Geneva hated Paris and its weak, corrupt
society with the instinctive vehemence that the savage
had expressed in his long colloquies with the European.
Rousseau, however, did not have to take recourse to the
pretense of a savage who could see what Paris and the
old European world did not see, for he made *himself* a
savage. Rousseau believed that the savage, who helped
him to know man and who served as a spur to his

political and pedagogical theories, was vibrantly alive
in the middle of the countryside among the humble folk,
in whom neither sentiment nor poetry is dead.

Rousseau has left us inspired descriptions of the
landscapes that he liked best: hills mirrored in the
lakes among the rays of the dying sun, fields shadowed
by trees and knolls, forests that invite us to a dream
--to a dream, one should note, that is both an evasion
and a rediscovery of the self. The "nature-civiliza-
tion" antithesis, the dominant intellectual concern of
his time, became a central theme in his work. This
theme, however, was often transformed into poetry, not
an unseemly lyricism nor an Arcadian pastoral but an
affirmation and celebration of a profoundly human
sentiment.

In some of Rousseau's descriptions nature seems to
unfold just as he saw it, as if he were enjoying it in
a distant past: "In the earliest times . . . the
stars, the winds, the mountains, the rivers, the trees,
the villages, the dwellings themselves each had its
soul, its god, its life. The teraphim of Laban, the
manitos of savages, the fetishes of Negroes--all the
works of nature and man were the first gods of mortals,
and polytheism was their first religion" (*Émile*, Book
IV). Viewed as an element of religion, nature is the
measure of human simplicity, the source of man's moral
energy, the faith that drives man to work well. The
savage thus lives again in the rustic or the pastoral,
and Rousseau occasionally united the two: "Émile, who
has been brought up in full freedom like young peasants
and savages, should behave like them and change as he
grows into manhood. The difference is that instead of
being active merely in playing sports or searching for
nourishment, he has learned to think in his work and
his play" (*Émile,* Book IV).

But in this "learning to think," what was the importance, in Rousseau's view, of what Vico called
"popular traditions"? In Geneva, in his little country where the corruptions of Paris did not exist and
life still had its own unspoiled taste, Rousseau, as
Karl Vossler observes, seems to admonish his fellow
citizens: "Remain faithful to your national usages,

to your national customs, to the spirit of your country. Think of your Genevan character and do not ape
the French. Be proud of being Genevans. However much
the French exalt their own admired culture, they are
not free; they are slaves of their lords, while we
Genevans in our modest little State, in our own State,
are free men and citizens." Geneva was intended to be
a reference point, as the primitive world previously
was, even though it may appear to us (as, for example,
in his *Lettres sur les spectacles*) to be a veritable
Cockaigne, a Bengodi. To Rousseau Geneva was indeed
interesting, but national usages, national customs,
and devotion to one's own country are always interesting, wherever they be. In his work, moreover, these
forces were introduced by being made a part of the
political heritage of a nation, and thus they were
given the historical dignity that Vico had previously
given them and that Rousseau emphasized as national
will and thought.

   As is seen in the first *Discours*, Rousseau was
convinced that old customs, those customs reflecting
our deepest feelings, are a genuine treasure, which,
once lost, can never be recovered. He was convinced
also--and this is the warning that he issued to the
Polish in his *Considérations sur le gouvernement de
Pologne et sur sa réformation projetée*, published
posthumously--that a nation, in order to be such,
absolutely must have an education that permits the
people to appreciate the power that traditions have
in national life. Indeed, traditions concretize life
and make it worth living. Rousseau therefore reminded
the Polish how much the Homeric poems and the tragedies
of Aeschylus and Sophocles (but when we read those
pages, our thoughts especially go back to Plato's *Republic*) influenced the education of the Greeks, who
rediscovered themselves in these works--their own
beliefs and their fathers' beliefs, which were rooted
in them like a tree in the earth. Rousseau was pleased
with the Polish because they conserved national customs,
the very symbols of their country.

   Now, it has of course been said that for Rousseau
popular traditions (or national traditions, as he called

them) have significance only when they are deeply felt;
if they die, however, it is necessary to allow them to
do so, since they no longer answer to the needs that
first made them both social and historical forms of
thought. It is a fact, though, that Rousseau relied
on these social forces, a lesson given by the Enlightenment. Moreover, as Vossler says, one sees "from
these surprisingly modern proposals that Rousseau was
not imprisoned by his own abstractions, but possessed
a fine sense of style with which to awaken and strength-
en the ideal of the community, the national will, the
general will; that is, he was well aware of the bonds
that link the moral will of personal autonomy with the
cultural or popular traditions of a nation."

Just as Émile had to find the strength of his education in himself, so a people, the folk, can and must
find in itself what is reflected in its usages and customs. Vico had previously stated that poetry instructed
the common people to work virtuously. Rousseau went
further: he transformed the poetry that he perceived
in all nature--in the forests and hills, in a tree or
a lake--into the traditional treasures of the folk.
And the folk, unlike the middle-class people who reside
in great cities, live in the country and in small towns
where man is still a part of nature, the nature of God.

4. Goguet and the Origin of Humanity

In studying the future of man, Rousseau came to regard
the past and its tradition as a human element. It has
been said that Rousseau denied progress. But didn't
he support the idea of progress through his faith in
human nature and its perfectibility? The concept of
progress held by Bayle, Fontenelle, and Voltaire obviously does not coincide with Rousseau's concept,
even though he shared these men's optimistic view of
life; but he believed that progress is to be sought
within us, while for the Enlightenment progress was
generally believed to result from a superimposition
of acquisitions successively accumulated and conserved
for the future. Had such an idea been shared by those

contemporaries of his who undertook the study of past and present usages and customs? Or did they evade it?

A good indication of what initially seems to be Rousseau's idea is provided by a work published in 1758, some years after Rousseau's *Discours* were published. It is credited to Antoine Yves Goguet and is entitled *De l'origine des lois, des arts et des sciences, et de leurs progrès chez les anciens peuples.* This work conveys the experiences of an *Encyclopédie*, of one who attempted to understand the quality of these manifestations in the manner of Bayle, Fontenelle, Montesquieu, or Voltaire. But in the midst of those experiences, which conclude in a reliance on the unlimited progress of the human race (the very aim of civilization), a refreshing note was sounded in Goguet's work: he did not ridicule the past; rather he approached it timorously, with the same sense of *pietas* that had compelled Lafitau, Vico, and Rousseau to look there for the "life" of our institutions. Nor is it without significance that he often cited the work of Lafitau, although he did not remember the name of the author. In inquiring into the origin of laws, arts, and sciences, Goguet focused his attention on the primitive world, which he thought of as a fundamental "fact"--a world to which we must return if we wish to take our own civilization into account. About this point he is quite explicit: "As soon as I found myself almost completely without sources, especially for the earliest times, I consulted everything that ancient and modern writers have told us about savage peoples. *I believe that the conduct of these nations enables us to put some sure and correct lights on the state in which primitive peoples were found immediately after the confusion of languages and the dispersion of families.* Accounts of America have been particularly useful to me" (I, xxx-xxxi).

Goguet here seems to be echoing Lafitau, but actually he was far from considering the first moment of mankind in the way that Lafitau, Vico, and Rousseau had considered it. True enough, that world is a simple state, but in his opinion such simplicity, as he himself said, is merely a synonym for crudeness and

ignorance. We could say that in his view Lafitau was
right about an idea that Enlightenment thinkers from
Bayle to Montesquieu had previously brought into intellectual history, the idea of progress from "low" to
"high"; thus, everything "original" is "inferior,"
even though it provides a concept of life that needs
to be looked at without Enlightenment bias. He goes
on to say that even classical peoples passed through
a savage period during the times of their first existence. At this point, however, we hear the echoes of
Fontenelle and Lafitau.

Because of these often provocative comparisons,
Goguet's work can be considered as one of the first
treatises of general ethnology--an amplification,
Arnold van Gennep rightly calls it, of Lafitau's
Mœurs, but the *Mœurs* of a Europe seen through the
lens of the Enlightenment. Additionally, we can here
find some sharp, penetrating investigations into customs, beliefs, and ceremonies of different historical
periods, investigations which actually constitute the
real value of the work (several editions were made in
France, and it was also translated into English and
Italian). But his weakness was that he insisted on
relating customs, beliefs, and ceremonies to the idea
of ascendant progress. He glides right over Rousseau,
and Vico is of no importance at all. Progress--a
specific idea that he has about progress--is all that
matters.

We must observe that Goguet did share with Lafitau
(and in part with Vico) the belief that the Deluge
might have been a historical reality, a belief unifying his investigations. But the advancement of laws,
arts, and sciences, which he could observe in his own
enlightened century, required a thoughtful pause: as
one who moved between the Bible and Voltaire, between
Lafitau and Montesquieu, he did not want to compromise
in religious matters. This is one explanation for his
rather superficial examination of the origin of arts,
customs, and beliefs.

5. A New Religious Phenomenology: Fetishism

The study of religious beliefs initiated by Lafitau,
Vico, and Rousseau, which demonstrated that religion
is an essential moment in the life of man, was boldly
continued by Charles de Brosses in his treatise *Du
culte des dieux fétiches, ou Parallèle de l'ancienne
religion de l'Egypte avec la religion actuelle de
Nigritie*, first published in 1760 (it had been presented to and rejected by the Académie des Inscriptions in 1758). Naturally, Brosses believed in
progress, like a good Enlightenment thinker, but, unlike Goguet, he did not believe in an absolutely uniform progress. Goguet had asserted that the customs
of a nation are not corrupted (as Rousseau believed)
but rather perfected by the progress of the sciences
and arts. Brosses, on the other hand, denied this
connection, in any form. With Goguet, and therefore
with Lafitau, he shared a belief in the Deluge. After
the Deluge, he asserts, peoples began on a journey that
led them from barbarity to civilization. He goes on
to say, however, that this does not obviate the fact
that in the midst of the so-called "nations" there remained a uniform state that may be called "barbarity."
It was not necessary, then, for Brosses to go among
barbarians (or among those whom we call barbarians)
to find what is primitive: the primitive can be seen
in some individuals who have lived or who continue to
live in the most illustrious of centuries among the
most civilized of nations. This interesting notion
derived from the concept of "survivals" previously
suggested by Fontenelle. Furthermore, Brosses compared such barbarity to the state of infancy. This
was a speculative theory already hinted at by Locke
(along with Vico and Rousseau, whose concept of barbarians was, however, quite different from Fontenelle's) when he compared savages to babies in his
Essay Concerning Human Understanding.
     Proceeding in his investigation, Brosses himself
remembers that "a foreign writer" from whom he took
"some assertions" had observed that man does indeed
progress from low to high, from inferior to superior,

but that man nevertheless can express perfect ideas
by proceeding from what is not perfect. Such a writer
is David Hume, the most vigorous supporter of natural
religion, who had also given attention to folk customs
and superstitions in such works as *The Natural History
of Religion*.

Brosses was a spirited free thinker, and his essay
has the vitality of *Lettres d'Italie* and *Correspondance*,
in which one recognizes a wealth of knowledge about
usages and customs of Italy, France, and so on. Because
of his method of investigation, Brosses was quite similar to Lafitau, whom he often cited and discussed. We
must observe, however, that he rigorously applied this
method only to specific religious phenomena. From
Lafitau Brosses took the maxim that "ways of behaving
correspond to ways of thinking," and from Lafitau he
took the idea that is at the center of his own book:
"An opinion found diffused in all barbarian climes is
also found in all ages of barbarity." But while Lafitau
was always cautious in illustrating this idea, Brosses
followed through, taking it to its extreme consequences.

Brosses acknowledged the Revelation, to which he
traced many contemporary absurdities; but, unlike
Lafitau, he acknowledged it only for the Hebrew people,
since he was convinced that human civilization must
date from a post-Deluvian barbarity that had not yet
received the Revelation. He associated this civilization with Egypt, a country whose animal cults caught
his attention; these he regarded as a species of
fetishism, a phenomenon that he believed to be of a
religious character and that in his own age he found
to be alive and present among the inhabitants of the
Portuguese colonies of Africa.

In any event, Brosses' major concern was to search
for the origin of religion, which he traced back to his
phenomenological supposition, not an organized system
of cults and beliefs but a particular mental attitude
revealed in particular acts and gestures that are the
same for everyone. In his opinion, all nations have
passed through the same "mental state" (to use Fontenelle's expression), recognized in the unchanging uniformity of the savage and demonstrated when, through

fear, the savage peoples nature with genies and
spirits. This thesis was renewed some years later
by Nicolas Bergier in *L'origine des dieux du paganisme*. In Brosses' opinion, fetishism was the first
form of idolatry and therefore the first form of
religion, which is not recognized in the doctrines of
revealed faith but rather in those "lower" religious
elements constituting the common basis of all religions. This is an altogether arbitrary theory, however, because fetishism, which Brosses (who compared
Egyptian gods with African fetishes) extended "to all
the uncouth peoples of the universe in all times and
places" to make his hypothesis valid, is not even
recognized in all primitive peoples.

Despite the negative comments that may be made
about Brosses' phenomenology, one must observe that
his parallelism, although a deviation from Lafitau's
method, is also a perfection of this method in some
respects, inasmuch as it is based on a more systematic procedure. This method of his, this fetishism
of his, was a flag under which ethnology and folklore
began their march in the investigation of origins and
future developments.

6. *Boulanger and Antiquity Unveiled*

Fetishism did not merely help Brosses to inquire into
the first form of human thought; it also helped him
to analyze the origin of arts, sciences, and institutions. These were later related to the Deluge (which
is to say, to a collective emotion of mankind) by one
of France's greatest geniuses, N. A. Boulanger, whose
principal work, *L'antiquité dévoilée pas ses usages*,
was published posthumously in three volumes in 1766.
An Enlightenment thinker (about whom Diderot wrote a
delightful biography), Boulanger traced the course of
the Enlightenment in this work, giving new consideration to the origins of religion. As has been noted
by Franco Venturi, his most perceptive biographer, in
Boulanger's work "superstition, which formerly appeared to many of his generation as an obstacle that could

only impede the growth of knowledge, took on a new and
central importance." In contrast to Goguet (and like
Lafitau, Vico, and Brosses), he believed that religion
has shaped all human institutions throughout the ages.
This explains the importance that he assigned not only
to cults and rites but also to myths and fables. In
one of his earlier works, *Recherches sur l'origine du
despotisme oriental*, Boulanger underscored the absurdity of regarding ancient fables as ridiculous, since
they were originally based on some principles that do
credit to mankind. And now in *L'antiquité*, which can
be considered, as he says, as a general mythology of
mankind, he becomes specific:

> The most useful part of history is not a dry
> knowledge of customs and facts. The most useful
> part is the identification of the spirit that has
> given rise to these customs, along with the causes
> that have led to certain events. All customs have
> motives, which are more important than simple
> opinions or facts; these opinions, on the other
> hand, have been initiated or raised by certain
> facts. If it sometimes seems that there are cus-
> toms without motives, it is because the motives
> have been forgotten, and the customs are so
> disfigured that nothing of the motives has been
> conserved. . . . Each custom, then, has its
> particular history or at least its own fable;
> each custom goes back to a particular fact. Per-
> haps there is a secret and common connection that
> joins the general mass of all customs with that
> of all facts. The history of customs and of
> their spirit is a new principle for constructing
> the history of man.

It was precisely this idea that initiated the work
some years later, in 1776, of an inquiring youth, Jean
Nicolas Demeunier; in his book entitled *L'esprit des
usages et des coutumes des differéns peuples*, he extended his investigation to many manifestations of
contemporary folklife, and he insisted that customs
are to be judged not only for what they represent

today but also (even more importantly) for what they
represented in the past.

7. The Form and Essence of Festivals

Boulanger's works, especially *L'antiquité dévoilée pas
ses usages*, suggested to some of his contemporaries
that he was familiar with Vico's *Scienza Nuova*. "The
Frenchman," wrote Ferdinando Galiani, the Abbot of
Tanucci, "has stolen from G. B. Vico, and he has not
cited him." Moreover, as Finetti correctly stated,
both began with the feral state, and for both the
Deluge deserved serious consideration. We should add
that (as Venturi has observed) Boulanger's investigations into the primitive mind, the logic of myths, and
the religious origin of man's political institutions
were much in line with Vico's investigations. It is
a fact, however, that Boulanger had nothing in common
with Vico in the formulation of such issues.
    Although Boulanger's studies cannot be compared to
those of Vico and Rousseau, they nevertheless indicate
an advance in respect to Goguet's efforts, and in their
ethnographical importance they are as significant as
those of Brosses. Furthermore, Boulanger, like his
immediate predecessors, was convinced that only savage
customs could "explain the uniformity that we see in
the customs of the ancients." This idea underlies his
comparisons between Mexicans and Greeks, for example,
and between Peruvians and Christians. But who *were* the
primitives, in his view? They were "descendants of
those hordes of men who escaped from the Deluge but who
could not form nations and bring about civilization."
This, however, does not obviate the fact that those
hordes, as a result of their original purity, believed
in an omnipotent God (a belief which is at the center of
all religions). In Boulanger's opinion, then, primitive
societies, even if overcome by the Deluge, lived with
their eyes turned to the heavens. Nor is it without
significance, he adds, that such a lifestyle can also
be discovered among contemporary American savages--
which is not to deny them an idea of progress. When

the faith of the savages began to weaken, they conserved customs from their primitive society but not
the spirit of those customs. It is precisely then
that the savage state was born, which one can investigate as much among us civilized people as among
savages.

Related to this idea is Boulanger's classification
of festivals and myths, which, on the basis of the
memory inspired by the Deluge, are pervaded with a
certain *esprit:*

> In the first book I examine institutions created
> by different peoples of the earth, in order to
> retrace the memory of the Deluge; this constitutes
> everything that can be called a society's "com-
> memorative spirit." In the second book it will
> be shown that all ancient institutions and feasts
> have a somber quality of sadness, which penetrates
> into even the gayest and most dissolute ceremonies;
> this I call the "funereal spirit." In the third
> book I will proceed by examining the oldest cri-
> teria and by exploring the true motives of enigmas
> arising among peoples; this I call the "mysterious
> spirit," and I believe that these "mysteries" have
> had no other purpose than concealing those dogmas
> that would threaten the people's tranquility. In
> the fourth book I consider the motives that have
> caused peoples to hold certain specific ideas
> about changes of ages and periods; this I call the
> "cyclical spirit." In the fifth book I examine
> the nature of festivals and ceremonies instituted
> for special yearly, monthly, and daily events; and
> this I call the "liturgical spirit." (I, 39-40)

In a note explaining the precise nature of these
cyclical festivals, he adds:

> In this work I call "cyclical festivals" all those
> festivals associated with the conclusion or re-
> newal of months, years, centuries, or other peri-
> ods. The word "cyclical" is a general term that
> will be used to indicate all periodical festivals,

especially those associated with the conclusion or
beginning of a period. If the ancients had not
brought so much confusion into their festivals,
which obscured the spirit and motives, it would be
easy to make this distinction. A festival celebrating the end of a period is sad and funereal;
one celebrating a beginning is devoted to joy and
happiness. But because the conclusion and the
beginning of a cycle are joined and because the
festivals celebrating the two extremes of a period
are related to and follow one another, each has
caused this confusion, of which we have a thousand
examples. Conversely, once we are familiar with
the nature of customs and understand the true
spirit of these festivals, then we can call those
that have been associated with the concluding
periods "oeno-cyclical" and those that have been
associated with beginning periods "neo-cyclical."

In these classifications Boulanger, whose treatment of basic religious and mythological issues was
clearly influenced by Lafitau, came quite close to
Montesquieu, who had placed *la vertu, l'honneur et la
crainte* at the base of various political structures.
But, Venturi observes, "as previously in the works of
Montesquieu (whom Boulanger had always respected and
admired), such a sociological position is transformed
by a lively interest in described phenomena and by a
sympathetic concern that modifies these initial schematic classifications." All of these classifications
concluded, then, in a broad perspective, with the
result (and here the influence of Rousseau is evident)
that true progress was seen to begin not when man
credited the power of action to the heavens--but
rather to himself.

8. *The Idea of Progress as a Philosophical Element*

Like Goguet and Brosses, Boulanger saw the idea of
progress as essentially a philosophical issue. This
placed him in contrast to Vico (who recognized the

principle of progress in the human mind) and Rousseau
(who recognized it in the sentiments of the natural
self); nevertheless, Boulanger's studies illuminated
usages and customs of different nations, especially
their survival, although his evidence was not always
exact because taken out of general context. This is
the case, for example, when he asserted in *L'antiquité*
that even a defamed astrology put man in touch with
the cosmos (although in a way that we consider superstitious); he added, however, that he was interested
in tracing the origins of beliefs to a reasonable
beginning rather than to the folly or stupidity of
men. Boulanger adopted an approach that previously
had been in opposition to the Enlightenment and that
at the height of the Enlightenment was dictated, as
in Goguet and Brosses, by a new need, an ethnographical need, one perceived not as an exclusive function
of reason but rather as an emancipation *from* reason.
By this time ethnology had begun to give importance
to reason *and* imagination, for now imagination was no
longer regarded as a regression in respect to progress.
Rather, it was now regarded as an eternal fact of the
spirit--precisely the message of Lafitau, Vico, and
Rousseau.

CHAPTER VIII

THE POETIC "REVOLT"

1. A Taste for the Popular and the Mediation of Ossian

In 1760, the same year that Rousseau's *La Nouvelle Héloïse* and Brosses's *Dieux fétiches* were published in Paris, *Fragments of Ancient Poetry Collected in the Highlands of Scotland, and Translated from the Galic or Erse Language* appeared in England. These fragments were examples of lyrico-epic poetry attributed to an ancient bard, translated by an anonymous person, and derived from a group of manuscripts dating between the twelfth and sixteenth centuries. Their success, however, drove the "anonymous" translator, James Macpherson, to publish in 1762--this time with his name--an ancient poem in six books, *Fingal*, along with the beginning of another poem entitled *Temora* (published completely with the name of the translator a year later). Finally, in 1765, *Fragments*, *Fingal*, and *Temora* appeared together in a volume, preceded by some introductory essays by Macpherson himself (who had published them previously in *Fingal* to establish the authenticity of the songs that he presented) and by Doctor Hugh Blair, who had improved their quality.

Thus, a new poet, Ossian, was born. It was a period during which Europe was shaken by a continual, incessant effort to clarify issues related to the origin of ideas, poetry, society, religions, and customs. The Enlightenment was a force that spurred, directed, and shaped initial approaches to these issues. The concept of the noble savage was by now

linked to the history of mankind, and man was the very
center of an investigation that both reflected and
placated the unrest of the age. It was on this foundation, within this broad European picture that had
its lights and shadows, in an England where the middle
class had become rich through trade and commerce--
joined, indeed, to the classical world but also concerned about the new world (which was at the same time
old)--that the songs of Ossian, a disguised bard,
resounded like a voice that rises in the chorus, exalting the primitive. But in the very moment that *Ossian*
proposed a return to the primitive, it invoked still
another return: a return to a national heritage.

2. The Significance and Value of a "Joke"

In his foreword to the 1765 edition of *Ossian*, Blair
compared this new bard, who looked on the scene from
his vantage point in Scotland, with Homer--a comparison
that was in itself significant. We must remember that
with his collection Macpherson did not merely propose
to offer his fellow countrymen an ancient poetry that
would place Scotland among those nations that had their
own poetry in ancient times; he also wanted to put them
in contact with a fresh, free poetry, which was made,
as Vico would have said, by the demands of nature, with
nature itself assuming the function of a poetic character.
     Macpherson well knew that his contemporaries were
not predisposed to recognize in a new poet anyone who
could be compared with Homer. He therefore had to
invent this new Homer, clearly contrasting him to Pope.
Pope's poetry, a mirror of the prevailing classes, is
perfect, precise, well-molded, which is appropriate for
classical poetry inspired by specific models; Pope's
poetry, however, was tightly restricted by these models
It is true that, as if in contrast to the strict domin-
ion of Pope, a voice had been raised that seemed genuinely new--the voice of James Thomson, who spoke in moving accents of the grand and humble life of Scottish an
English peasants in his *Seasons*. He obviously wanted t

free himself from the usual reinvocation of a world
by now exhausted in the work of Pope and his followers.
But wasn't Thomson--who perceived the importance of
nature in its various aspects before Rousseau did--
bound by poetic diction in his expression?

Contemporaneously another poet, Thomas Gray,
rebelling against poetry permeated with classicism,
brought to English poetry the motifs of a Celtic world
that, in his eyes, was a barbaric realm untouched by
artificiality and conventionality. This was the
message in his translation of ancient Norse poetry
(also much beloved by William Temple), and this was
the message of his ode entitled "The Bard," which came
out in 1755. Observe: it is the return of the bard,
the ancient poet, the old rhapsodic singer of the folk.
And he returns when Edward Young takes refuge in the
kingdom of nocturnal melancholy, wearing an expression
of deep sadness. But the bard now has his own name,
clear and ringing. He is called Ossian, and he was
born from the confluence of these yearnings. Ossian
was the product of a joke, as it has been called, but
a noble joke through which Macpherson called the attention of England and Europe to the Gaelic poems that
inspired him to create *Ossian*. In light of his poem,
it seemed as if the Norse peoples had their own personality and original civilization. It was, in short,
the utilization of one's own national epopee. The long
arguments made for and against the good intentions of
the translator, Macpherson, neglected the fundamental
fact that *Ossian* could be judged as a good or bad work
whether created by Macpherson or by an ancient Gaelic
bard. Another fundamental fact, however, was also
neglected: this work was intended to be a national
Iliad near at hand, an *Iliad* that needed only to be
discovered, not created. Ossian, in fact, was meant
to be the folk-singer of a heritage that had a poetic
and a *national* value, inasmuch as he wished to use his
songs to take Scotland and England back to the sources
of their own history and tradition. The medieval age,
considered by the Enlightenment as a period of darkness,
came to life again through *Ossian* (at the very moment
in which an admiration for Gothic cathedrals arose).

The medieval age, which Vico had earlier viewed as a
heroic age, thus became the heroic age of the English.

Let us welcome Homer back then--a primitive and
barbarous Homer as Vico had imagined him, a Homer
whose heroes are fresh and elemental, precisely as
Thomas Blackwell had seen them in his *An Enquiry into
the Life and Writings of Homer* (1735), which Johann
Winckelmann later called "one of the most beautiful
books in the world." Thus, one may go back, to use
the apt expression of Madame de Staël, to a Homer of
the North, and through him, most significantly, we
return to poetry reconstructed from Gaelic songs and
festivals. In other words, it is a poetry that goes
back to national sources, back to the origins.

3. *"Ossian" and the Discovery of a New "Poetic" World*

Ossian clearly reveals a refined sensibility that,
through the primitive and the barbarous, attempted to
appeal to the instinctive values of the human spirit.
Its poems seem to plunge us immediately into those irrational springs of life where Vico placed the beginnings of poetry. And as the argument for the state of
nature became more vocal, we find that *Ossian* (let us
not forget that England was the country of deism) takes
us back to the primitive feelings of man, making us
perceive the grandness of natural phenomena and a vital, deeply felt religious sentiment. One of the most
cultured men of Europe, Melchiorre Cesarotti, who was
fascinated by *Ossian* and translated its poems into Italian, said, "Ossian is the genius of savage nature. His
poems are like the sacred woods of the ancient Celts;
they inspire horror, but one feels a divinity living
there in each step" (*Poesie di Ossian*, I, Pisa, 1801,
p. 107). It is nature as envisioned by Rousseau and
Brosses. But in the poems of *Ossian* we seem to have
Rousseau and Brosses as influenced by the brilliant
pages of Edmund Burke, who published his short tract
entitled *Philosophical Enquiry into the Origin of Our
Ideas of the Sublime and Beautiful* in 1757.

The sublime dominates the poems of *Ossian* much the
way that the marvelous dominates the *Thousand and One
Nights*. It is a spellbound realm, as if the poetic
world of Thomson were enlivened by a great creative
capacity. In this world the dreams of warriors, their
hopes and loves, are presented with pure melancholy.
Cesarotti, whose commentaries on the poems of *Ossian*
always refer to Homer, rightly or wrongly (but more
wrongly than rightly), was certainly correct when, in
a letter that he sent to Macpherson in 1763, he identified the characteristics of the sublime in *Ossian*
and gave some indication of its underlying flavor and
sensibility:

> Permit me in the name of Italy to say that I am
> happy about the fortunate discovery that you have
> made of a new poetic world and about the precious
> treasures with which you have enriched literature.
> Morven has become my Parnassus and Lora my Hippo-
> crene. . . . All this grand, dark spectacle is,
> to me, more fascinating than the island of Calypso
> and the garden of Alcinous. Granting preference
> to ancient or modern poetry has been disputed for
> a long time, perhaps with more harshness than good
> intent. Ossian, I believe, will help the cause of
> ancient poetry, without the supporters of the
> ancients gaining much. It is necessary to see,
> beyond his example, how the poetry of nature and
> sentiment is above the poetry of reflection and
> *esprit*, which seems to be the heritage of the
> moderns. But if the superiority of ancient poetry
> is to be demonstrated, it will be necessary to
> understand the shortcomings of ancient poets even
> better than criticism has so far understood them.
> Scotland has shown us a Homer who neither naps nor
> stammers, who is never vulgar or languid, but
> always grand, simple, quick, precise, varied and
> yet the same (trans. from the French, *Epistle*, I,
> 7-8, Firenze, 1811).

Walter Binni, who carefully studied the impact of
Ossian, *via* Cesarotti, on Italian poetry, commented:

"Cesarotti was on the right track when he asserted that
although *Ossian* happened to agree with the partisans
of the ancients, it also brought out the defects of the
ancients; namely, that if it made those qualities of
the sublime discovered in the ancients acceptable (and
actually it is born from the labor of a common dispute
more than from one of the two theses), it also demonstrated that such sublimity was quite different from
the sublimity that one could actually identify in the
classics." *Ossian*, then, conveyed the desires of a new
age, and those desires were articulated in the language
of a "new" Homer who had rubbed elbows with the Celts.
One could find a similar language in the Bible. In
fact, in 1753 a learned professor from Oxford, Robert
Lowth, had demonstrated in *De sacra poesi Hebræorum*
that the poetry of the Hebrews had flourished among
specific individuals in a "nation of husbandmen and
shepherds"[1]--which was to historicize the Bible itself.
And now from a people of warriors, peasants, and shepherds comes Ossian, whose solemn language echoes the
language of Homer and the Bible.

It cannot be denied that Macpherson has given us
some lively, pleasing prose in *Ossian*. But the turgidity of certain passages clashes in our ears, even
though some contemporary critics mistook this turgidity
for genuine creative impulse. *Ossian*, nevertheless, is
not to be judged only for its poetic worth (whatever it
may be) but also for what it introduced into the poetry
of the age, for we must remember that it encouraged an
interest in new poetry *and* folk poetry.

4. The Investigation of Popular Poetry

Actually, many people had praised such poetry long be-
fore *Ossian* had been published, particularly in Spain.
As early as 1511, Hernando del Castillo had published
Cancionero general, a collection of some old romances

[1] *Lectures on the Sacred Poetry of the Hebrews*,
trans. G. Gregory (New York: Garland Publishing, Inc.,
1971), p. 146.

handed down from the oral tradition. The collecting
of these romances was continued, in 1550, by Estéban
de Nájera in *Silva de varios romances*, a year later by
Lorenzo Sepúlveda in *Romances nueuamente sacados de
historias antiguas de la crónica de España*, and by the
anonymous collector of *Cancionero de romances* in 1655.
Such collecting was continued gradually but increasingly
until, in 1700, the first *Romancero general*, edited by
Pedro Flores, was published. It was a question, Cesare
de Lollis has observed, of "a poetry of the people, a
grave and serious people who for seven centuries never
put down shield and armor." He adds, "Those who reno-
vated the *genre* were learned poets; however, everyone
forgot that these were cultured poets, as was even
Góngora, the author of *Soledades*, a work that no one
would understand without the help of commentary."
But wasn't the epic poem echoing within the walls of
ancient Spain simply, in the view of the collector,
an epic poem without its Homer? Nevertheless, this
epic poem was inherently linked to its own country as
the inheritance of a people who saw it as a reflection
of their own moral and spiritual past.

The same thing happened in Great Britain, where the
vitality of popular poetry was especially reflected in
a series of poems composed on very different themes,
some of which could be traced all the way back to the
eleventh century. Although cultured poetry pleased the
upper class, the lower and middle classes were always
delighted by

> The ballads, posted on the wall,
> Of *Joan of France*, and *English Moll*,
> Fair *Rosamond*, and *Robin Hood*,
> The Little Children in the Wood. . . .[2]

Some of these ballads, from the beginning to the seventeenth century, had been collected by Selden, Roxburghe,
and Wood, but the first who paid critical attention to

[2]Jonathan Swift, from "Baucis and Philemon," in
Swift: Poetical Works, ed. Herbert Davis (London:
Oxford Univ. Press, 1967), p. 80.

them was Addison.   In 1711, in two numbers of his *Spectator* (numbers 70 and 74, which correspond to the 21st and 25th of May), Addison pointed out two of these ballads to his readers, "Chevy Chase" and "Two Children in the Wood," which, he said, are among those "most in vogue among the common people. . . ."[3] He also compared some passages from these ballads with others by Homer and Virgil.   It has been argued that he made the comparison to justify his appreciation of these ballads, but the real reason was to introduce citizens to such poetry, to the *genre* of old ballads.   His contemporaries did not think that this was the reason; indeed, his comparisons were parodied in a very popular work, *A Comment upon the History of Tom Thumb*, which appeared anonymously in 1711.   This parody caused Addison to reconsider his opinions, with the result that when he published the *Spectator* in volume form, he toned down and qualified his praise; but he still remained firm in his high regard for the profound, intense poetry of his fellow citizen who turns from work and modulates his song naturally, simply, and effectively.

The same considerations had been made in the preface to *A Collection of Old Ballads*, published in three volumes between 1723 and 1725.   The anonymous collector did not hesitate to compare his unknown singers to Homer: "The very Prince of Poets, old *Homer*, if we may trust his ancient records, was nothing more than a blind *Ballad-singer* who writ songs of the siege of *Troy*, and the adventures of Ulysses. . . .   At his Death somebody thought fit to collect all his Ballads, and by a little connecting 'em, gave us the *Iliad* and *Odyssey*."[4]   The anonymous collector viewed the oral tradition as being more significant than the written tradition, an opinion that was fully shared by Macpherson.   In addition, this anonymous collector thought the importance of these ballads was to be found in their antiquity and their naturalness.   A dedicated Scottish poet, Allan Ramsay,

[3]*The Spectator*, ed. Donald F. Bond (Oxford: Clarendon Press, 1965), I, 297.

[4]*A Collection of Old Ballads*, I (London, 1723), iii-iv.

followed him in this opinion. Ramsay collected the old
popular English and Scottish songs, along with his own
and those of his contemporaries, in an anthology entitled *The Ever Green* (2 vols., Edinburgh, 1724)--the
first example of an anthology in which popular poetry
did not cut the figure of a poor relative. Ramsay also
referred to the subject of Homer. In treating these
ballads, however, he deleted and added verses with the
patience of a goldsmith who had been transformed into
a poet, when in fact he should have remained only a
collector.

The significance of these early collections, nevertheless, is that they provided the perspective of a
native medievalist, a perspective revealed in an effective and highly imaginative poetic representation. Nor
can we forget that the end toward which the collectors
aimed was to put the ingenuous freshness of this popular poetry in contrast to classical poetry. Addison,
for example, observed that classical poetry is indeed
a copy of nature, but one "destitute of all the Helps
and Ornaments of Art"[5]--which suggests how these early
collectors viewed the study of folk poetry. They were
the true precursors of Macpherson, in whose *Ossian* the
myths and ballads loved by Addison were revived. The
rough, archaic tone in these ballads was pleasing, and
if their authors had no name, as Ossian had, they too
were the product of the minstrels who had cooperated
in creating *Ossian*. Ossian now returned the favor,
for it was because of him that folk poetry in Addison's
Spectator began to have a new, genuine appeal in England. Folk poetry was no longer a curiosity, although
it was still capable of arousing curiosity; rather,
folk poetry began to be a poetic and cultural concern.

5. Percy's "Reliques"

Given this atmosphere, one can understand the inevi-
table success of Thomas Percy's *Reliques of Ancient
English Poetry*, a three-volume work (each volume

[5]*The Spectator*, I, 362.

divided into three parts) in which English and Scottish
ballads were collected. The *Reliques* was first published in 1765 (the same year that the complete edition
of *Ossian* was published), with a preface in which the
collector insisted on the originality of this popular
poetry. He considered such poetry to be the detritus of
the forgotten art of ancient scalds (hence the importance given to the oral tradition). In the introduction
to the first volume, in which he discusses the ancient
English minstrels (with Ossian looking over his shoul-
der), Percy observes, "The old minstrel ballads are in
the northern dialect, abound with antique words and
phrases, are extremely incorrect, and run into the
utmost licence of metre; they have also a romantic
wildness, and are in the true spirit of chivalry."[6]

Percy was quick to comment on the national character
that these ballads conserve. "Chevy Chase" and "Robin
Hood" were at this time preferred to the magniloquent
heroes of *Ossian*. But who was Robin Hood, as the anonymous collector of *A Collection of Old Ballads* had previously asked, if not a typical national hero to whom the
folk imagination, out of love for the folk, had given
an ideal, legendary character? In the preface to his
ballads, Percy naturally did not hesitate to recognize
the importance of poetry that is both old and new: "In
a polished age, like the present, I am sensible that
many of these reliques of antiquity will require great
allowances to be made for them. Yet have they, for the
most part, a pleasing simplicity, and many artless
graces, which in the opinion of no mean critics have
been thought to compensate for the want of higher beauties, and, if they do not dazzle the imagination, are
frequently found to interest the heart."[7] Percy was
convinced, then, that these ballads, although extremely
"incorrect," were also extremely charming. What method
did he adopt to emphasize their artistic value?

[6]"An Essay on the Ancient Minstrels," in *Reliques
of Ancient English Poetry* (New York: Dover Publications, 1966), I, 380.
    [7]Ibid., I, 8.

6. *The Popularity of Ballads Is Born*

Percy collected the *Reliques* primarily to demonstrate
the genuine voice of the English people of earlier
centuries, which explains the title of his collection.
He was well aware of the argument about the origins of
chivalric romance, which was then in vogue. Indeed,
the *Reliques* constituted *his* argument. He had also begun to collect old broadsides, which ultimately came
to integrate the oral tradition. As has been correctly
said, the first popular printings in the last years of
the fifteenth century and the first years of the sixteenth century transcribed scarcely readapted popular
ballads (for example, the "Gest of Robin Hood"); but
re-elaboration was becoming increasingly important.
The ballad writer, an Elizabethan, was influenced by
two streams of thought, that of the fifteenth-century
folk and that contemporary with the new culture, and he
directed these two streams into the broadside ballads.
Broadside ballads are somewhat similar to those popular
printings and folio sheets of ours--where, however, the
light of true poetry seldom shines. It was logical,
then, that Percy planned to go back to the sources, to
manuscripts that conserved these ballads or to the oral
tradition, where the material of the broadsides was
reshaped and transformed into something truly popular.
Aided in this research by David Dalrymple and Thomas
Warton, he took great care and effort to review old
collections of existing manuscripts in the libraries
of his country. But one day while in the house of a
friend, Humphrey Pitt, he noticed that the housemaid
appointed to light the fire in the fireplace snatched
some leaves of an old manuscript from the flames.
Percy wanted to see what she had found. It was a manuscript containing almost two hundred English and Scottish ballads by a folksinger of Lancashire in the middle
of the seventeenth century. Not only were there ballads
of the pure fifteenth-century tradition, however; there
were also ballads antedating the broadsides of the time,
along with other non-popular compositions that nonetheless were related to the oral tradition.
   The *Reliques* is merely a selection of these various

materials, many of which were damaged with the passing
of time. At this point came the intervention of Percy.
In the preface to the first volume of his anthology
(where there are occasional allusions to the folk
poetry of other people), Percy said that he considered
his obligation as editor to be the correcting of those
texts that, in his opinion, were marred. In his collection there are many texts preceded by the notation
"given some correction." In this respect he was following Ramsay. But to what extend did he have this
right?

A perceptive philologist, Joseph Ritson, violently
attacked Percy, disputing even the existence of the
famous manuscript (it was later published by Child,
however) and denouncing the imprudence of the forger.
Introducing and identifying the philological requirements of popular poetry, Ritson emphasized the necessity of being absolutely faithful to the text. But
Percy held to his previous statements. In the adver-
tisement to the fourth edition of the *Reliques*, he
observed with conviction:

> These volumes are now restored to the public with
> such corrections and improvements as have occurred
> since the former impression; and the text in par-
> ticular hath been emended in many passages by
> recurring to the old copies. The instances, being
> frequently trivial, are not always noted in the
> margin; but the alteration hath never been made
> without good reason; and especially in such pieces
> as were extracted from the folio manuscript so
> often mentioned in the following pages. . . . The
> MS. is a long narrow folio volume, containing 195
> Sonnets, Ballads, Historical Songs, and Metrical
> Romances, either in the whole or in part, for many
> of them are extremely mutilated and imperfect. The
> first and last leaves are wanting; and of fifty-four
> pages near the beginning half of every leaf hath
> been torn away, and several others are injured
> towards the end. . . . Even where the leaves have
> suffered no injury, the transcripts . . . are some-
> times extremely incorrect and faulty, being in such

instances probably made from defective copies, or
the imperfect recitation of illiterate fingers.[8]

Thus presented, Percy's innovations are no longer
such. Wherever possible, however, Percy should have
restricted himself to reconstruction (even though this
is debatable in the field of popular poetry, where each
text is always a restored creation). But when he said
in the first edition of the *Reliques* that the poetry
of the ballads is like a young girl who comes from the
fields with wind-blown hair, didn't he believe he had
discovered something that was, in his view, "suited"
to English society? Even though there are some ballads
subjected to his "refinement," there are undoubtedly
other accurate ones in the *Reliques*.

7. The Importance of the "Reliques" in the History of Poetic Taste

Despite its defects, the *Reliques* had the great merit
of emphatically calling scholars' attention to popular
poetry, the poetry that flowed in the midst of the
people and that was rightly considered the people's
sacred heritage. Percy's work was not a philological
one; but didn't he inspire in England the kind of research to which David Herd first contributed with his
Ancient and Modern Scottish Songs, published in 1766,
and to which Ritson himself contributed numerous collections between 1783 and 1795? Nor was the *Reliques*
of interest only to scholars; it also made a great impression on the poets of the time. Edmund Gosse has
said, quite rightly, that it immediately opened a new
era for European as well as English literature.
Precisely for this reason, the *Reliques* must be
considered as the expression of a sensibility that
viewed popular poetry as true poetry and that tended
to emphasize all that was thought to be old and popular; thus, popular poetry became a source to which
legitimate poets could turn. This lesson, before

[8]*Ibid.*, I, 4-6.

Romanticism confirmed it as canon, also came from the
great Scottish poet Robert Burns, whose poetry had
been, we could say, watered by that spring. Johann
Peter Eckermann, in one of his colloquies with Goethe,
made a very fine comment on the subject:

> Now take Burns. Wasn't he a great success because
> the songs of his predecessors lived on the lips of
> the folk and were sung next to his cradle and be-
> cause from youth he grew up among those songs, with
> those excellent models living in him and giving him
> a foundation with which he could begin? And wasn't
> he a great success because his own songs found
> similarly receptive ears among his people, and the
> mowers and reapers re-echoed them to him through
> the fields, and he was greeted in the taverns by
> cheerful companions? All this must indeed be sig-
> nificant. . . . (*Colloqui col Goethe*, trans. T.
> Gnoli, Firenze, 1947, p. 562)

There was something new, then, that came to be felt
at this time by the more sensitive men in England; and
in this "something" was hidden, in its primitive form,
what later became the concept of popular poetry. Consequently, popular poetry would be called to invigorate
and refreshen poetry that was not popular. This new
sensibility was revealed even in the changing connota-
tion of the word *Gothic*: throughout the first half of
the century it had been understood as a synonym for
barbarian (in the pejorative sense), but now it came to
represent the age in which these ballads were conceived
and produced, as if to signify a specific direction of
art.

8. *England's Place in the History of Pre-Romanticism*

In my opinion, it is an error to argue that the exaltation of the primitive created a dilettantish mode in
England. Nor is it exact to argue that *Ossian* and
the *Reliques* sustained an exclusively aesthetic interest in popular poetry. In those works arising from an

interest in primitivism there was a national and social
argument that must not be forgotten. This argument
certainly was not circumscribed within one "mode," if
to this word we give a restricted meaning in time, one
that changed with the changing of sensibilities.

The Enlightenment, with its iron-clad laws about
reason, did not seem to participate in this lively,
influential movement that broke from the past. David
Hume, for example, one of the Enlightenment's greatest
exponents, declared that England's *Ossian* gave Europe
a good laugh; nevertheless, one sees that Europe recognized all this enthusiasm for the past, accepted it,
and drew new energy from it. Enlightenment writers
themselves had been much influenced by their love for
distant things, but things geographically distant; in
England, however, this love became a love for things
distant in time, especially certain Norse legends that
contributed a new aura to poetry. A deep feeling for
tradition was thus contrasted to the concept of reason.

"The rightness," observes Friedrich Meinecke, "of
our speaking not only of an English but of a European
pre-romantic movement in the eighteenth century strongly suggests that behind the play and the amusement
occasionally moved something that actually could be
considered to be the prelude to authentic Romanticism:
the reaction of the irrational against the cold rationalism and the refined, purified civility of the age."
He adds, "In France this pre-romantic impulse led a
secondary existence at the side of the reigning Enlightenment. In England it acquired an almost equal
existence with the Enlightenment from the middle of the
century on. Of course it did not produce figures of
the stature of Hume and Gibbon (as the Enlightenment
had), but it did produce some fine talents who, with
imagination, sensitivity, pleasure, and love, contributed to the already evident cherishing of the value of
the past." He concludes, "England was, at least up to
1765, the guide and pioneer of the European pre-
romantic movement."

The most energetic representatives of this movement
were Vico and Rousseau (besides a host of scholars, from

Lafitau to Goguet, from Brosses to Boulanger). But
while the above-mentioned had undertaken speculative
investigations, the English must be credited with providing the documents to which those speculative investigations directly or indirectly appealed. Their
battle was not conducted in the name of ethnography or
philosophy. It was conducted in the name of poetry--
popular poetry.

When England gave new importance to the simplicity
and sentiment emphasized by Macpherson in *Ossian* and
by Percy in the *Reliques*, it made itself the crier of
a new credo, one that provided a thought-provoking
look at tradition and an admonishment to Enlightenment
philosophers, teaching them that the "beautiful" is
not a matter of progress but rather a fact of the
spirit. In the apparent atmosphere of the idyl, in
the apparent "joke" of research about its own past,
we do indeed find a prelude to the *Sturm und Drang*.

CHAPTER IX

POETRY AND TRADITION

1. *The Primitive in His Proper Home*

The explosion of the *Sturm und Drang* moved from the
tranquil shores of England to the skies of Germany.
Switzerland, a small nation surrounded by diverse
cultures that threatened its survival, especially contributed to this explosion. Béat Louis de Muralt, a
strict, austere citizen of Berne and a disciple of
Saint-Evremond, announced the great birth of England
in his famous *Lettres sur les Anglois et les François*
(which influenced Voltaire in his *Lettres* addressed
to the English), and he contrasted England to the
growing decadence of France. More importantly, however, he investigated the character and individuality
of his own country, whose origins he praised.

On the one hand, Muralt is associated with approaches that often, particularly during the Renaissance, had led philosophers and historians to study
national characteristics (which is the significance
of the assertion that his *Lettres* should be considered
the first and most famous example of research into the
characteristics of various nations); on the other hand,
he is associated with authors who, in attempting to
identify such characteristics, compared Europe with
the savage and the French with the Egyptian or the
Persian, as Baron Lahontan, Marana, and Montesquieu
had done previously. But there is a difference: for
Muralt the study of national characteristics evolved
into an awareness of the unity of nations, while the
concept of the noble savage helped him shape the myth
of his own country's origins. Thus, those who previ-

ously had been called "the savage and the European" or
"the Egyptian and the Frenchman" now, although still
in contrast to France, came to be called "the English
and the Swiss." It was no longer necessary to voyage
over the seas, delving into American Indians or savages
in general or rediscovering Egypt or Persia, in order
to instruct France about her most fundamental beliefs.
All one had to do was to look in his own backyard.

2. Muralt and Haller

To his *Lettres*, which first appeared in 1727, Muralt
added a "Lettre sur les voyages," which apparently was
written some years before. In this "Lettre" (which is
the key to his *Lettres*), he deplored the influence that
the French style had begun to exercise on Swiss minds,
and he subordinated the refined French civilization to
the peasant civilization of his own country, a civilization dominated by an unswerving faith in its mountains and traditions. Switzerland, his Switzerland,
was not afflicted with the "diseases" of France: "It
seems that the Providence governing the world has hoped
that nations might produce directness and simplicity.
He has provided us with a remnant of order for all the
world to see, a characteristic lost among rich and
extravagant nations. . . . A happy obscurity, a life
removed from all ostentation and weakness, must join
us to our mountains." Muralt did not merely confront
the emerging Enlightenment with his notion of a "happy
obscurity" of ancestral traditions and old liberties;
he went further:

> When man lost his own employment and dignity, he
> also lost sight of his principal concerns; in the
> disorder in which we now find ourselves, we have
> all lost sight of our purpose and worth. Since
> only order can procure such awareness for us, I
> think that there is only one means for retaining
> order: we must follow our own instinct, a divine
> instinct that is perhaps the only legacy from the
> original state of man left to us in order to bring

us back to this state. All known living creatures
have instincts that do not mislead them. Could it
be that man, the most elevated of all creatures,
does not have his own instinct, one that is clear,
certain, and pervasive?

It would be impossible, Hazard observes, to make
the call for a "return to the primitive" heard more
clearly than this, a call that resounded even before
Rousseau raised his voice. But what was the irrational
primitive for Muralt, if not a yearning to perceive his
own nation and everything that contributed to its original character? This desire explains the connection he
made between ancient traditions and his mountains and
his linking of the concept of "tradition" to the concept of "nation." Nor is it without significance that
three years after the publication of his *Lettres* the
poem *Die Alpen*, by another patrician of Berne, Albrecht
von Haller, came out. Carlo Antoni comments:

It is clear that Haller was influenced by Muralt.
He had read the *Lettres* shortly before. . . . However, unlike his teacher, he wrote in German, a
language that another Muralt, Johannes, had used
for modest literary and social purposes just a few
years before. To the idea of national "character"
he added an integral element, language. . . . The
moralist's call for a return to the old virtues,
to the sober, happy life of the old nation, is
broadened in *Die Alpen* to a universal principle:
civilization corrupted man, and the innocent life
of the state of nature is true happiness. This
idyllic motif echoed throughout the philosophical
climate of the age. The idea of a happy state of
nature, of virtue impressed in the hearts of wise
and beneficent legislators, is best revealed in
the pure nostalgia of Arcadia. It is the denial
of the old Christian dogmas of the Fall and Grace;
it is the new ethic of an earthly happiness and
virtue arising from human nature itself.

It was the triumph once more of the concept of the noble

savage, which had now become a poetic inspiration for
Haller, just as later it would become a philosophical-
political inspiration for Rousseau, another Swiss who
was, as we have seen, much attracted to Switzerland's
mountains and traditions.

Like Muralt, Haller investigated the primitive in
his own backyard, among peasants and shepherds who
reflected the very spirit of nature, its dawns and
sunsets. Traveling among mountaineers, he had often
exclaimed: "Oh happy people that ignorance preserves
from evil. . . ." With the simple spirit of a peasant,
he was fascinated by the peasant world. His mythology
was rooted in those homey mountains, the very pillars
of nature, liberty, and happiness:

> Oh blind mortals, whom avarice, honor, and extrava-
> gance have brought to the grave with vain delusions,
> who poison the gift of brief and exactly numbered
> days with new cares and empty efforts, who scorn
> the quiet happiness of a modest fortune, who demand
> more destiny than nature demands from you and who
> make yourselves subject to foolish desires. Oh
> believe it, no ribbon of an order makes for happi-
> ness, nor do ornamental pearls make for riches!
> Look at a scorned people, happy in work and in
> poverty. Only natural reason can make you happy.

This is the essence of Haller's mythology. It seems
as if he were interpreting the thought of Muralt, who appealed in his "Lettre sur les voyages" to "a kind of life
removed from all weakness" that "would join us to our
mountains." Haller's *Die Alpen*, however, is not merely
a poem about the ideal happy state of nature. It is the
glorification of a people whose nature is partially a
reflection of its character, and, as such, it was the
beginning of a new poetry. The Swiss, however, also
sought for their poetry elsewhere--and they found it.

3. *Bodmer and the Folklore of Switzerland*

In focusing on the old "local" freedoms, Muralt again

found himself sharing with the English in the desire
to reassess the medieval age, which for the Swiss was
the heroic age as well. Basically, this called for a
revival that would provide them with a historiographi-
cal ideal. And wasn't this the central interest of
another great Swiss, Jakob Bodmer?

Even before Muralt's *Lettres* were published,
Bodmer, in collaboration with Johann Jakob Breitinger,
had founded the *Discourse der Mahlern*, a journal based
on the example of Addison's *Spectator*. In the *Discourse* (which, like the *Spectator*, was published in
volume form), the compilers indicated that they planned
to dwell especially on "different styles of speech and
dress, the diversions of lords, the middle class, citizens and women, engagement and wedding ceremonies, and
funeral rites. . . ." Increasingly they illustrated
such matters with a taste for the particular and the
unpublished, which reminds us of Bayle and Fontenelle,
despite differences in their intentions.

The *Discourse* was published between 1721 and 1723.
Later, however, Bodmer's activity took on a greater
scope. In 1727, two years after the publication of
Muralt's *Lettres*, Bodmer established a society of
national history in Zurich called the Helvetische
Gesellschaft, one of the first if not the first of its
kind, which published a series of works that included
the *Thesaurus Historiae Helvetiae*. Subsequently, with
the help of the trustworthy Breitinger, he promoted the
Helvetische Bibliothek. In 1739 his four volumes of
*Historische und kritische Beiträge zur der Historie der
Eidgenossen* were published. But what was the purpose
of these studies, which provided vignettes of the
peasant civilization idealized by Muralt and praised
by Haller?

Believing that a history should also consider the
life and history of peasants "because they are the only
ones to whom nature imparts its language," Bodmer, in
speaking of the Swiss in his *Discourse*, exclaims with
the same enthusiasm found in Muralt and Haller: "What
savage but natural manners! What peasants, but so
magnanimous! What glory, what magnificence!" Bodmer
discovered this glory and magnificence in what then

were called local *Antiquitates*, which had been studied
just about everywhere.

In England, as we have seen, such studies were
exemplified in the work of Browne and Brand. Before
Bodmer's *Beiträge* was published, Thiers and Le Brun
had studied *Antiquitates* in France, and Muratori had
done the same for years in Italy. But what was Bodmer's attitude toward his *Antiquitates?* What *pietas*
did he show in evaluating and making them an element
and monument of national history? And to what extent
do his researches have a genuine importance in the
historiography of folklore? The studies of Browne,
Thiers, and Le Brun were not actually scholarly, although some, like those of Le Brun and Thiers, were
motivated by a religious (Catholic) interest. Brand
was more objective, for in dealing with his people's
traditions he assumed what I would call a "contempla-
tive" attitude. Muratori's studies, however, were
quite different; although his studies of *Antiquitates*
were scholarly, he enlivened them with his good taste,
a taste that most often was philological and historical. And it is to Muratori that Bodmer is most closely
related. In his studies, Bodmer, like Muratori, attempted to illuminate his country's folklore by using
archivistic documents, and he also made use of old
chronicles and parchments. But in regard to *Antiquitates*, he had an attitude that was neither the contem-
plative one of Brand nor the scholarly, historical one
of Muratori. The contemplation of the ancient customs,
usages, and freedoms of his country was for him primarily a political activity. *Antiquitates*, particularly
customs, are the very pillars on which his country's
past is supported, the columns on which its future must
stand. His work, then, anticipated Rousseau's *Considérations sur le gouvernement de Pologne*. But especially following him were Muralt and Haller.

4. Poetry and National Sentiment

Equally exciting was Bodmer's study of poetry, his
most important and best known activity. We know, for

example, that his *Von dem Einfluss und Gebrauche der Einbildungs Krafft*, written in 1727 in collaboration with Breitinger, shows the influence of Addison's *Spectator* essays about the pleasures of the imagination, in which he argued for a return to nature that was, in his view, a return to poetic sincerity; on the other hand, this work goes back to the discourses of Muratori, Gian Vincenzo Gravina, and Pietro Calepio on the rights of the imagination, which Enlightenment thinkers wanted regulated by reason. But this work, which also conveyed a strong attack against Gottsched's steadfast appeal to Aristotelian rules and French models, primarily signified Bodmer's entrance into the field of aesthetics (a word that would be used later by Breitinger) in order to establish laws for everything that is "original" and "characteristic"--those original and characteristic elements that he had found in rustic usages, the very models of simplicity and "naturalness."

This obviously accounts for Bodmer's idealization of poets like Homer and Dante, in whom one can indeed recognize a simplicity and a naturalness of inspiration. Bodmer, however, perceived these poets as representatives of a heroic age, placed them within their historical context, and considered them as powerful forces in the life of their nations. Like Vico, he also returned to the age of the fierce and virtuous barbarian, and it was precisely on this ground that his angle of approach (fully treated by Blackwell) led him to react against Enlightenment pride. Just as he had related rustic usages to a nation's history, he now extended this concept to poetry: poetry too is an integral part of a nation's history, and each nation must recognize itself in its poets. But in this respect Dante and Homer pointed him toward further work. In 1732 he translated Milton, of whom he said later in his *Kritische Geschichte des Verlorenen Paradieses*, published in 1754, "In the rebellions that the English nation provoked against Charles I, Milton demonstrated that he was an advocate of all kinds of liberty--religious, domestic, and civil--through the many writings that he produced in their defense. . . . He was in all

things a republican, and he thought of a public matter
like a Greek or a Roman, of whom he was perfectly
aware."

5. *Bodmer's Discoveries*

Bodmer's greatest discoveries, however, lie elsewhere,
in *Parsifal*, *Minnesang*, and the *Nibelungenlied*. True
enough, he was also much interested in Percy's *Reliques*, which he translated (although without specify-
ing its particular characteristics) and in which he
saw a reflection of the "fabulous" element that served
as the basis of his aesthetics. But he was especially
taken by the epic. In that same Switzerland where a
Genevan, Paul Henry Mallet, praised the Norse world of
the *Edda* and Scandinavian mythology, brilliantly reinvoking it in *Introduction à l'histoire de Dannemarc*
(published in 1755) and *Monumens de la mythologie et
de la poesie des Celtes* (published in 1756 and then
translated in England in 1770 by Percy himself with
the title *Northern Antiquities*), Bodmer turned to
Parsifal, *Minnesang*, and the *Nibelungenlied* as texts
of true poetry. Here he found not only an escape from
the rules dictated by Gottsched but also an austere,
solemn sense of life that imbued everything with the
simplicity and sincerity of proverbs. Moreover, Bodmer
was convinced that these texts contained the documents
of an ancient poetry mirroring the German revolts. He
believed that such poetry "surely must have voiced the
fearless, powerful sentiments and the violent, warlike
spirit of those autonomous little states that wished
to shake the yoke of Rome and fulfill their strong
desire for liberty."
    Bodmer smelled something fishy about *Ossian*; but
when he concluded his argument on the relationships
between poetry and nations by asserting that the
Nibelungenlied is the German *Iliad*, didn't he antici-
pate Macpherson by some years in thinking of his own
country's ancient poetry as "national" poetry? In
Bodmer's view, poetry was a virtual mirror of customs,
which explains its historical importance, but it was

also the sacred heritage of a nation. This idea is
similar to the one offered by Justus Möser, who, while
praising *Minnesang* poetry, lamented the fact that Germany unfortunately was imitating foreign poets and forgetting its own sources. Möser was quite interested in
folk traditions, although he never attempted to escape
through poetry in particular or through folk literature
in general. He made the argument of the Swiss his own.
His Switzerland, however, was Westphalia.

6. The Historiographical Work of Möser

The work most often associated with the name of Justus
Möser is undoubtedly his *Osnabrückische Geschichte*,
published in 1768. Instead of exalting the chivalric
medieval age, Möser praised local self-governments in
rural communities, where custom carried the weight of
law. As Antoni says, Möser, like his Swiss predecessors, was a "patriot"; he too defended the uniqueness
of Switzerland's national character against the influences of the French style, and he too championed ancient liberties against all despotism. This *advocatus
patriae* had his eye cocked at the citizens of his Westphalia, whose conditions "were different from those of
the serfs of large estates in Eastern regions" because
they "were proprietors, semi-proprietors, and tenants."
In these citizens he saw the key to German history,
which he recognized in the fundamental institution of
landed property, *mansus*--a key revealed by the participation of the *homo œconomicus* in the "glory of the
nation"; furthermore, here he became sensitive to mankind itself, which had to be saved from the invading
rationalism of the day. This "mankind" was at the
center of his studies. He attempted to so illuminate
"German antiquity" that its original purity would
emerge, even though such constructions often caused
history to look like a continual decline.
    All of this explains Möser's persistent, impas-
sioned defense of traditions, in which he recognized
the purity of history. Nor was this defense, like
Bodmer's, concentrated only on the discovery of the

original spirit of his people. It was also a defense
of German art. In essays published in the *Hannöver-
isches Wochenblatt* and then collected in 1747 under
the title *Versuch einiger Gemälde der Sitten unserer
Zeit*, these convictions of his were already in hand,
partially supplemented by the discourses of Bodmer
and Breitinger. Two years later, in the introduction
to *Arminius*, he presented a vivid, lively *excursus* on
the Germany of Tacitus, deploring the fact that the
highest Germanic classes acceded to the Roman style
but asserting that the rude protagonists of this book
were not dead; indeed, they lived again in the low-
Saxon citizens, those citizens whom his predecessors
had idealized and whom he had learned to know and to
appreciate daily in the city of his birth, Osnabrück,
where he was a lawyer.

Like the Swiss, Möser had some strong aesthetic
interests. In *Gemälde* he confessed to favoring Haller's poems and praised the noble simplicity of true
poetry, and in *Harlekin*, published in 1761, he rejected the aesthetic simplicity of *imitatio naturae*.
In *Gemälde* he first took a position against the rules
of French poetics, and *Harlekin* was intended as an
answer not only to Gottsched but to Voltaire, to whom,
years before, he had addressed a "Lettre sur le car-
actère du Dr. Luther et sa réformation." We know that
Gottsched wanted mask-characters to be taken away from
the folk, just as Voltaire wanted them taken away from
tragedy. Möser, however, disagreed with this idea:
"Even in ancient popular customs there are comic and
grotesque elements; therefore, it cannot be allowed,
as Enlightenment rules would have it, that the rude
buffoon be taken from the scene, where he has always
had a place of honor." But beyond such premises, his
Harlekin offers the categorical assertion that by res-
cuing the life of peasants from rationalism (whatever
and wherever it be) one also saves all the values
associated with a spontaneous life lived in harmony
with nature.

Möser's defense of mask-characters was a defense
of the folk. The folk (as he went on to say in
another work of his, *Schreiben an den Herrn Vicar in*

Savoyen, addressed to Rousseau in 1765) needs to be
approached with the intention of understanding it, for
there are reasons behind each custom. Möser realized
that the folk needs religion; in fact, each founder of
a society had "to get assistance from a god, fornicate
with a goddess, suggest that he was fathered by Hercu-
les and that his laws fell from heaven, and slaughter
rebels with lightning bolts." It almost seems as if
we are hearing the voice of Voltaire. Immediately
after, however, he says, "Religion is a 'policy,' the
policy of God in his kingdom among men." Most importantly, he observes that if we judge religion in this
way, it becomes necessary to accept popular superstitions, miracles, and ghosts. He was not attempting to
be a theologian (and he said so expressly); he was
attempting to be a jurist who defended his people and
their superstitions, miracles, and ghosts. This task
often led him to consider the customs of distant countries, and, putting the accounts of old chroniclers or
travelers to advantage, he did not hesitate to justify
the most atrocious punishments, like the sack drownings
to which infanticides were sentenced "by our forefathers, who judged according to experience rather than
theory."

This last point explains the relativity of institutions. In *Harlekin* Möser observes that "nature gener-
ates innumerable enchanting forms for greedy eyes, and
there are as many customs and passions as there are
different faces of men." In "Patriotische phantasien,"
which was first published in 1766 in the *Intelligenz-
blätter* of his city and then published in book form by
his daughter in 1784, he adds (almost as if to exempli-
fy) that "since Voltaire thought it ridiculous that
someone had lost a lawsuit according to the law of one
village while he had won it according to the law of a
neighboring one," from then on he gave a free hand "to
the despotism that wants everything regulated by a few
rules." We should also note that in "Phantasien,"
which was very much admired by Goethe, there is a
description of Westphalian houses that is one of the
most important folkloristic documents of the time.

Defense of customs is at the heart of Möser's work.

One could object, of course, that in combating rationalism he did not realize that giving a reason for all
irrational forces restricted their actual function in
historical development. Nevertheless, the important
contribution of his work as a folklorist and ethnographer is that he discovered a unity in the rich variety
of popular traditions.

7. Johannes Müller and Local Color

Quite different from Bodmer and Möser, who had many
points in common although they differed in their concept of nation, was a Swiss historian, Johannes Müller.
He focused on what Bodmer and Möser overlooked: the
appeal of folk literature. One could say that everything that Bodmer and Möser saw as a function of the
epic or epopee Müller saw as a function of the epico-
lyric. His *Die Geschichten der Schweizer* (the first
edition was published in 1780 and the second completely
revised edition appeared in additional volumes between
1786 and 1808) is the exaltation of his land, a picturesque reinvocation, a rustic fresco of the life of
knights and peasants of the fourteenth and fifteenth
centuries. Indeed, it seems that here a perceptive
observation by Möser was given concrete form--the
observation that in medieval times the Swiss had fused
the knight and the peasant. We are also confronted
here with a rustic who is a small landowner or artisan
living in the freedom of landed-property communities.
But while Möser was consistently like a jurist in his
picturesque recollections, one who always used legal
language in treating questions of aesthetics, Müller
was a poet passionately reliving his country's traditions.
     Müller picturesquely reinvoked Swiss liberty and
focused on the validity of popular traditions and their
preservation (despite the changes that can take place
in the passage of time). He saw the unity of Switzerland in the development of its individual cantons, with
perhaps the following qualification: the Swiss have
passed through the world of Mallet in order to return

to being what Muralt imagined them--Swiss savages (but
"savages" in the sense that missionaries and travelers
had given the term). From Müller's pages, which synthesized these concepts, come the most graphic tales
and adventurous legends. His historiography is based
solely on legend, but legend treated as an index of
truth. We sometimes even forget that he is a historian, discovering instead a writer who presents us with
the local color of his archaic Switzerland, vividly
bringing it back to life. This is precisely the secret
of his "sublime poetic antiquarianism," as Schlegel
defined it in *Athenaeum*.

In his *Gespräche mit Goethe*, Eckermann recalls what
Goethe told him after visiting Switzerland:

> I visited . . . the villages around the lake of the
> Four Cantons, and the nature there, full of enchant-
> ment and magnificence and grandeur, made such an
> impression on me that I became captivated by the
> idea of representing the truth and richness of this
> incomparable country in a poem. But to bring more
> attractiveness, interest, and life to my representa-
> tion, I thought it best to people this highly sig-
> nificant background and this soil with human figures
> of another significance, and I realized that the
> legend of William Tell was precisely what I wanted.
> I imagined Tell as a human hero--innately strong,
> tranquil, and boyishly naive--who, as a tradesman,
> goes from one canton to another, everywhere known,
> everywhere helpful and loved, everywhere affection-
> ate to wife and child, without in the least distin-
> guishing between master and servant.

This was the Switzerland of Müller, whose *Antiquitates*
were saturated with the scent and flavor of a legend in
which, as in real life, it was necessary "to live and
die free, with honor." We know that the drama planned
by Goethe was completed by Johann von Schiller, who, as
he remembered it, made use of Müller's work for his
drama. That drama was a specific representation,
Francesco de Sanctis tells us (perhaps reminding us of
what Goethe had said of Switzerland), in which "every-

thing is Switzerland, everything is local color," while
"the plot is not in one thing alone but in all; and
Tell is not a simple conspirator but an expression of
the folk," because "what he wants, everyone wants."
What Sanctis says of Schiller's *William Tell* can also
be said of the *Geschichten schweizerischer Eidgenos-
senschaft* (that is, the second edition of *Die
Geschichten der Schweizer*), in which the romantic
school discovered an awesome array of inspiring deeds.

8. *The Influence of Swiss Historiography on the
    History of European Folklore*

We can see, then, that between 1726 and 1780 a position
was taken in Germany *and* Switzerland (French and German), a position that is of interest because of the
values that it introduces into the history of historiography and especially because of the importance that
it assumes in the history of folklore. The concepts
that we have seen emerging from England found lively,
impassioned interpreters in Muralt, Bodmer, Möser, and
Müller. But a contrastive point must be made: although these men perceived the power of national virtues just as the English had, they brought such virtues
to life in the name of traditional ethnic beliefs,
which they attempted, in one way or the other, to
introduce into history. With their work, moreover, we
pass from studies dedicated to popular poetry or consecrated with the scholarly taste of the *Antiquitates*
to a genuine historical inquiry equal to the highly
ingenious ones of Voltaire, Hume, and William Robertson. This is why the intercession of England does not
serve merely as an element of contrast to Switzerland.
The Swiss and Möser were opposed to a set of ethical
values, the ethic connected with the French *esprit*,
which consisted, as Muralt said, in the art of making
much of *bagatelles*; but they were also opposed to an
aesthetic creed, the creed of Boileau and Gottsched,
which had been created precisely to give esteem to a
stultifying academism.
    In 1739 Gottsched wrote to Bodmer, "It seems that

the English are for chasing the French from Germany.
Perhaps this is so because they are not afflicted with
the blind self-esteem that dominates the best of all
our courtiers and great men." We know for a fact that
in peaceful eighteenth-century Germany, where numerous
princely courts were ruled by the style of Versailles,
the edicts that came from Switzerland shook the German
youth. We know, furthermore, that the king of Prussia,
Frederick II, wrote a famous essay, published in 1780
and entitled *De la litterature allemande*, which altogether omitted the names of Friedrich Klopstock and
Gotthold Lessing, men who nevertheless were much esteemed by Bodmer. In the name of German art, however,
Möser descended into the field against him. Goethe
had greeted Haller as the first national poet. Almost
at the end of his life, Bodmer had written in a letter
to Gleim, "In the bloom of my youth there was no
poetry! Then it was like being on an isthmus in the
Age of Saturn! Hagedorn, Gleim, and Klopstock came,
and with them the Silver Age; then the spring of a
Golden Age!" And now here was Möser: "We had almost
entirely no poetic language, and we never would have
had it if the valiant Swiss had not conquered
Gottsched." Haller, he continued, was the first German poet, and beside him he placed Gleim, Klopstock,
and Wieland, the disciples of Bodmer.

While Bodmer turned to Milton, Möser looked more
to Cervantes and Shakespeare--and Homer gave him the
impression of "going to the tavern," as he himself had
done in London. But whatever his preferences, he, like
Bodmer, felt that national sentiment was most important.
Through his efforts German literature became national,
and through the efforts of Muralt, Bodmer, Möser, and
Müller, folklore too--including popular tradition and
folklife recognized in its own right, in all its characteristics and particulars--became national.

During this time when the "national" voices of
Klopstock, Lessing, and Wieland resounded and Germany
became linguistically unified, the formulation of the
concept of a consciously national popular spirit became
increasingly more urgent and imperative. Contemporaneously, the need to examine thoroughly (and to safe-

guard) the customs of one's own country was becoming
more consciously recognized. It is said that this
sentimental idea had in fact consolidated German
regionalism. This is an unsupportable thesis, however,
because popular tradition is a vital, prolific element
in history and therefore is a vital, valid part of
history. It is said, moreover, that although such
traditionalism went so far as to recognize the importance of traditions, it did so because it found them
to be dead already. This thesis also is untenable,
however, because although the Swiss historians and
Möser looked nostalgically to the traditions of the
past in which they saw their origins, they did not
forget that these traditions had their own existence,
one that engaged the heart, feelings, and imagination
of man. Nor, finally, can we accept the thesis that
the Swiss historians and Möser considered the peasant
civilization only as a "receptive," passive civilization. Möser was very clear on this point. He maintained that "the peasant grasps useful innovations
rapidly enough, and one accuses him wrongly in saying
he prefers long years of experience to proposed bad
risks. Potato profits spread more rapidly than mul-
berries, and until the cultivation of flax gives him
good bread, he will not desire to produce silk in
order to eat chestnuts."

In a period when the Enlightenment considered
popular traditions as errors of the human spirit, the
Swiss historians and Möser saw them as the very stuff
of humanity, which explains the necessity of placing
traditions in a historical context and making them the
foundation of the original, fundamental character of
each nation. We should note that whereas Enlightenment philosophers thought the masses were basically a
multitude condemned to ignorance and fanaticism, the
Swiss and Möser were opposed, like the English, to the
rules and restrictions of all precepts, asking instead
for inspiration from nature and life; furthermore,
they developed a love for the folk (which has both a
"nature" and a "life") that already had been evidenced
in such philosophers as Vico and Rousseau.

In the works of the Swiss and Möser, the folk or

"popular" spirit was identified with the nation, and
this nation was identified with a civilization of peasants, basically those of Switzerland and Westphalia.
It has been said, especially by Meinecke, that earlier
in Germany the word *nation* was quite distinct from the
word *folk*, used ordinarily for the most humble members
of the lower class (which was also the case in France,
England, and Italy). This distinction, which became
even clearer and more precise after the French Enlightenment, would serve as a starting point for Herder's
efforts to elaborate on the concept of *Volk* (folk, the
peasant class) as an ethico-sentimental life expressed
in songs, legends, and customs. But above all, as
Meinecke has noted, this distinction served as the
starting point for Herder's efforts to join the national spirit of his people with something simple and
original, the life of the *Volk* itself. And here, in
the skies of Germany, is the *Sturm und Drang*.

CHAPTER X

HERDER: A CONCERN FOR HUMANITY

1. *The Concept of the Spirit of Nations*

Although influenced by earlier movements, the *Sturm und
Drang*, as has been observed, was inspired by a new,
powerful, provocative love of life, although it was
also nourished by old hopes, such as pietism. Meinecke
the one who made this observation, went on to say that
this was why Germany continued to examine periods and
peoples that seemed to reflect a completely fresh, natu
ral, and indomitable humanity. Herder was at the cente
of this new revolt. His battle developed on two fronts
since it was inspired by two goals: (1) to combat the
Enlightenment, which regarded tradition as a symbol of
ignorance and fanaticism, and (2) to combat the art of
his time, which followed foreign (especially French)
models that were then quite at home in Germany.
     In regard to the first battle, Herder was obviously
following in the steps of Vico and Rousseau, the English from Macpherson to Percy, from Blackwell to Wood,
and the Swiss historians from Bodmer to Müller. In
regard to the record battle, he opposed his countryman,
Johann Winckelmann, a new and increasingly influential
scholar whose vision and understanding were confined to
Greece. Herder, however, argued that there is only one
way to reach the Greeks; instead of imitating them (it
was customary to compare Klopstock to Homer and Gleim
to Anacreon), one must be as original as they. It has
been said that Herder's battle was a revolt against
classicism, particularly against an inhumane Rome whose
extensive rule had consumed and desiccated all the
then-known world. Actually, this was the same battle

fought by French Enlightenment thinkers, the English,
Bodmer, and Möser. Beyond such controversy, however,
Herder's message was that Germans should not imitate
Greeks and Romans; rather--and here Bodmer and Möser
introduced pietism--Germans should return to their own
genuine primitive origins. This is the central message
in his *Fragmente über die neuere deutsche Literatur*,
published in 1766-1767, in which he denounced the imitation of the classics and the French as an obstacle to
the development of true German art and language.

For quite a while in the eighteenth century, as
Antoni perceptively observes, "one spoke of the spirits
and genies of the folk, but no one had posed the problem of analyzing them. The Swiss had proclaimed the
duty of being faithful to the ways of national thinking,
but they had understood such fidelity, in a politico-
moral sense, as fidelity to a virtuous, free humanity.
Herder perceived national duty as a duty toward a 'natural fact,' toward a particularity that virtually negated
the presuppositions of the Christian and stoic ethic,
and therefore of Western Civilization." Moreover, as
Herder himself said, one must recognize that the national
spirit reflects the spirit of all people. Antoni correctly concludes that Herder thus came to embrace the
concept of the "spirit of nations," as opposed to the
Enlightenment doctrine of national characteristics. In
Herder's view national characteristics were primarily
composed of forces that the Enlightenment had inexorably
rejected. His bold, exuberant work, which was done for
a release and outlet, attempted to determine these characteristics, which he considered from two different perspectives, one national and the other cosmopolitan. But
what was the link uniting these two perspectives? What
procedure did he adopt for his work? And were his attitudes always consistent?

2. Herder's "Primitivism"

One certainly can say of Herder's work what Johann Peter
Hebel said of one of Goethe's most provocative works,
Aus meinem Leben, Dictung und Wahrheit: "In the begin-

ning it is a point that slowly and surely makes a
circle, but it gradually widens until it finally encompasses the entire world." In *Dichtung und Wahrheit*
Goethe remembers the Herder who had held him spellbound
in his youth and with whom he collaborated: "Suddenly
Herder felt compelled to understand all modern stress
and strain and all the forms it seemed to take." This
is precisely what was in Herder's work: modern stress
and strain, to be understood as change coming about
through palingenesis. As Goethe himself said in a
letter to Herder in May of 1775, the residue of history
in a living organism requires not "simply extracting
gold from the residue but making a living seed grow
from the residue itself."

In this palingenesis the "point that slowly and
surely makes a circle" is first centered in the world o
primitives and savages. This world fascinated Herder, as
did everything to which the prefix *Ur* could be applied,
and he considered this world as an ideal reference
point, as did Rousseau and Vico. In his own country,
Winckelmann, Lessing, and even Schiller had no interest
in such a world, one to which J. G. Hamann, Herder's
friend and teacher, had appealed as early as 1762.
Hamann was of the opinion that original man, the primitive, possessed only the five senses, and, were it not
for pictures, the primitive would not have comprehended
anything (a thesis that reconciles Vico with Locke).
Herder was well informed about all the work that had
been done in the field of ethnography. An admirer of
Montaigne, he was quite aware that the so-called savage
folk must be considered with the same impartiality that
Europeans were. But what meaning did he give to the
term *savage* when he applied it to artistic phenomena?

In the *Journal meiner Reise im Jahre 1769* Herder
said, "From small savage nations, as once the Greeks
themselves were, a civilized nation will be born. . . .
Here he was combining the sentiments of the Jesuits wit
the attitudes of Lafitau. In 1773, in his essay "Ossian" (which, along with his essay "Shakespeare," was
published in the miscellany *Von deutscher Art and Kunst*
with writings of Möser and Goethe), he went on to say
that "the poems of a people must be as savage, alive,

and free as the people themselves." Here, once again,
the concept of the noble savage was converted into the
concept of popular poetry--in the sense that the term
savage would come to be used as the basis of an aesthetic concept, even though the term had derived earlier
from ethnographic roots. Herder began by proposing the
premise that the original character of art is to be
recognized in barbarity. But this "barbarity," in his
view, was not merely an ethnological term: he identified
the primitive with all that is beautiful and sincere,
and he identified the popular with all that is pure and
true. Gerbi says, "A powerful belief in nature is obviously behind these two equations." But is it a question
of two equations? Isn't the idolization of poetry an
aspect of the idolization of the primitive, which, as
Muralt demonstrated, was formerly sought at home?

Clearly, one hears in Herder the echo of Rousseau;
but, as Venturi has observed, "Herder's primitives did
not have the revolutionary importance of Rousseau's
savage" because "he naturally tended, with increasing
awareness, to operate at a level that was more aesthetic
[or philosophical] than social, his investigation of *Ur*
aiming at sentimental or poetic emotion rather than at
social purity." The fact is that Herder was captivated
by Rousseau's *Discours* and especially by his *Considérations*, but the Rousseau of the *Contrat* did not appeal
to him; indeed, this Rousseau frightened Herder. The
proof of this is implied in Herder's idea of liberty:
as early as 1765, in his document *Haben wir noch jetzt
das Publikum und Vaterland der Alten?*, he professed to
want only "to be an honest man, owning his own hut and
vineyard in the peaceful shade of the throne, and re-
joicing in the rewards of his own labor, the source of
one's happiness and comfort."

In Herder's work Rousseau's "mighty drama" dis-
solved into a tranquil dream. But to this idyllic
dream (which, unlike the famous *Sturm und Drang*,
bloomed as a petit bourgeois expression) Herder gave
a strong foundation: the *Volk*. The folk, which he
regarded as an elemental and original concept, was
called to reconcile art and history; and the primitive and savage elements of art and history gained a

new importance, in his view, because these elements
were the keys to the national characteristics contained in both history and art. This explains the
great importance that he gave to religion, customs,
and songs. Most important for him, however, was
language, through which he related nation to mankind
and in whose manifestations he saw both nation and
mankind realized.

3. Language and Nation

Believing that language was the key to man, Herder
began by posing the question "what is language?"--
a question that consumed him throughout his life. In
his *Über den Fleiss in mehreren gelehrten Sprachen*
(1764), there is an outline of a theory of linguistic monogenism, along with a proposal for studying
the national characteristics of language. His ideas
about language were more concretely organized, however, in *Abhandlung über den Ursprung der Sprache*,
published in 1772 in a contest on this topic announced by the Berlin Academy. In this work Herder
examined the problem of the origin of language,
proposing that language issued from men as a necessity compelled by the deepest recesses of his nature.
As he says, human language

> is not effected as an organization of the mouth,
> because, as reflection will remind us, even he who
> is mute all his life has language within himself;
> it is not a cry of sensation, because it was not
> discovered by a breathing machine but by a thinking
> creature; it is not a matter of imitation, because
> the imitation of nature is a means while here it
> is a question of explaining the end; and even less
> is it an arbitrary convention. *The savage in the
> solitude of the wood must have been able to create
> language for himself* even though he might not have
> spoken it. Language is the harmonious expression
> of the human spirit, as much a necessity as it is
> that man be man.

This was a period when the problem of language constituted, as it has been said, a πολυθρύλητον of European culture. Previously, some general grammars had emphasized the idea that language was mechanical. Discussions about the formation of language (found in the works of Vico, Lafitau, Rousseau, and Brosses) and the argument about the human or divine origin of language (from Rousseau to James Monboddo) had been lively issues. In entering this argument, Herder provided a concrete basis for philology; one certainly cannot say, however, that he succeeded in defining a new mode of language. If we take a look at Vico, we can see that he and Herder had essentially similar ideas. But Vico considered human language as already formed, an aesthetic creation; in his view, therefore, language and poetry arose simultaneously. In Herder's view on the other hand, language arose from a spiritual exigency, the need that man has for concretizing his thought in expressions.

Unlike Herder, Hamann believed language to be of divine origin, and he did not hesitate in *Aesthetics in nuce* to relate language to poetry (however close he might have been to Goguet in this identification). It was his view that "poetry is the mother language of man, just as gardening is the most ancient form of agriculture, the picture the most ancient form of writing, the song the most ancient form of declamation, the parable the most ancient form of deduction, and barter the most ancient form of commerce." In Herder's view, however, man creates poetry only after creating language. Thus, poetry is an expression that grows within man. This did not prevent Herder from believing that language in primitive peoples is the poetic force *par excellence*, an idea that puts him close to Vico (even though Blackwell may have been his guide); furthermore, he believed that this "force" is found in poetry and song, the two often merging. But to be *truly* "poetry," shouldn't poetry be "popular" in the sense that, as the full expression of man (who is both an individual and a member of the folk), it reveals what is primitive and savage in human nature? For the first time, then, the idea of a "collective spirit," here used to explain poetic development, was raised. And the most genuine expression of this collective spirit is popular poetry.

4. Poetry as Popular Poetry

As early as his *Fragmente* (1767), Herder had maintained that popular poetry was the most precise and loftiest expression of a people's "character." He proposed this idea again in his essay on *Ossian*. At this time *Ossian* had begun to conquer the world. Herder's opinion was that *Ossian* represented the most typical expression of popular poetry, as opposed to artificial poetry. He said that Ossian spoke in a "natural" voice, a notion that the English already had pursued, but in Herder's view this "voice" takes on an apocalyptic significance. Further, he was convinced that only *Ossian*, songs of savages and bards, romances, and lieder had the potential to lead German poets "to a better way."

It certainly is not insignificant, then, that Bürger's *Lenore* was published in the same year. Hoping for a national poetry, Herder aligned himself with the folk, for the folk was "the most genuine and unblemished part of the nation and therefore should be the authentic interpreter of the national spirit." Bürger held the same opinion. In his comments on *Ossian*, moreover, Herder suggested that Homer was a ballad poet (that is, a folk poet) and, following François Hédelin, Abbot of Aubignac, whom he had read, he believed that Homeric songs had been improvised. Similarly, Bürger believed that both the *Iliad* and the *Odyssey* derived from popular poems based on the accounts of old ballads, a thesis later reasserted by Friedrich Wolf in his *Prolegomena ad Homerum* and by Karl Lachmann in his *Über die ursprüngliche Gestalt des Gedichts von der Nibelungen Noth*.

Lenore was intended to provide the first step in the discovery of a new national poetic world and, at the same time, the first example of a German poetry conceived of as popular poetry. *Lenore* comes from a saga widespread among Germanic and Slavic peoples, of

which Bürger had heard some verses. He changed the
original lied, a form of genuine popular poetry, to
epos. His hope, like Herder's, was that a national
epopee might arise from romances and ballads. This
obviously required precision, for it is the *presentation*, rather than the subject, that constitutes art;
indeed, this particular art form will never be popular
because of its subjects. Popular poetry, then, can be
an inspiration to the artist, as the English believed,
but this inspiration is a starting point rather than
an end in itself.

These various propositions were established (and
confused) in Bürger's work, as they were in Herder's.
True enough, their works transformed the concept of
poetry into the concept of popular poetry, with the
result that Homer, Dante, and Shakespeare became popular poets because they were creators of a poetry that
corresponded to the spirit of the people to which they
belonged. But didn't this concept raise the necessity
of finding scattered motifs of national and popular
literature (an invitation, that is, to study the literature itself), which would lead to a disruption of the
cultural unity that had once been sustained by the
classical tradition? On the basis of this concept of
poetry (here understood to be popular poetry), one
came not merely to distinguish poetry from non-poetry;
popular poetry itself, *legitimate* popular poetry, was
placed on the same level as the poetry of Homer, Dante,
and Shakespeare. Such poetry, then, took on an aesthetic validity. Furthermore, such poetry came to be
thought of as a heritage belonging to the world and
its peoples, not as a hereditary and private privilege
of the cultured and refined few (a point made by Goethe,
and no one could make it any better than he). The
poetic revolt was thus transformed into a widespread
revolution, and the example of Percy and his predecessors became a battle cry.

5. *Voices of the Folk*

Collecting lieder became a national duty. Bürger, who

much esteemed Percy's collection, had recommended to
his fellow countrymen the obligation of saving the most
sincere heritage that they possessed. Two years later,
in a collection of his poems, he included (translated)
some English ballads published by Percy. Goethe, who
later praised Ossian (who had taken the place of Homer
in his heart) in *Werther*, sent a letter in November of
1777 to Charlotte von Stein, in which he was quite enthusiastic about the quiet virtue of the citizens of
Harz, a "class of men called 'lower' but certainly most
high in the eyes of God." Later, in fact, he actually
collected folksongs of Alsatia personally.

But above this and other voices Herder's voice
could be heard. More than anyone else, Herder understood the importance of the folk poem, the lied. His
observations on the nature and office of folk literature in his *Von Ähnlichkeit der mittleren englischen
und deutschen Dichtkunst* (1777) are still fresh and
original:

> Folksongs, fables, and legends . . . are in certain
> respects the result of a nation's beliefs, feelings,
> perceptions, and strengths. One believes because
> one does not know, one imagines because one does
> not see, one is excited by his own humanity, honest
> and simple and still undeveloped. This is indeed a
> grand subject for the historian, the poet, the
> critic, the philologist. Ancient Germanic mythol-
> ogy--to the degree that it still exists in tradi-
> tion and in folksongs, is accepted with simplicity,
> and is contemplated with serene heart--will really
> be a treasure for the poet and defender of one's
> own people, for the moralist and the philosopher.
> . . . All uncivilized people sing and work; their
> songs are the archives of the folk, the treasury
> of its science and religion, of its theogony and
> cosmogony, of the deeds of its forefathers and the
> events of its own history, an echo of its heart,
> the mirror of its domestic life in joy and in
> sorrow, from the cradle to the grave. . . . A
> small collection of such songs, taken from the
> lips of each people in their own language, is--

when inclusive, well stated, and *accompanied with music*--exactly what would give us a better idea of the nations mentioned in the idle chatter of travelers.

As we know, Herder constantly tried to give Germany a work like Percy's *Reliques*, a task in which he was assisted by Bürger, Goethe, and Lessing. His project failed because lieder collections were few and thus did not justify the work he had proposed completing. On the other hand, Herder did produce a two-volume collection of popular poems from different nations and places. The nations best represented were England, with its *Reliques* collections of Ramsay and Percy, and Spain, with its romances, especially those in the *Cancionero de romances*. He included many poets who certainly are not, to our minds, "popular"--for example, Gabriello Chiabrera and Giovanni Meli, who combined popular Italian poetry with an ancient religious anthem; and in addition to *Ossian*, there are several passages from the *Edda*. In *Volkslieder*, which came out between 1778 and 1779, Herder held to the idea of popular poetry as "national" poetry. As he himself said, "It is beyond doubt that such poetry, especially the lied, has been absolutely 'popular' in tone; it is light and simple, containing all the qualities and expressions found in the language of the common multitude, the rich, and anyone sensitive to nature." He saw such "nature" in artistic poetry too, when it gave a fresh rendition of folklife.

Thus, Herder came to regard poetry as the true, authentic voice of man. He ignored no voice; all entered into his heart and issued forth as a symphony. We all know what translations are: commentaries, exercises, exfoliations; but Herder's translations are beautiful because he almost always found the right tone. Even "Chevy Chase" put on "foreign clothes," and it wore them well. *Volkslieder* are *Stimmen der Völker,* as Johannes von Müller later called them (he published some in 1807 with this just-mentioned title), which is precisely what Herder had understood them to be. This meant that the poems had a common human basis, but they also had their

own specific characteristics. Here, in *Volkslieder*,
Herder's anxieties seemed to be appeased because the
concepts of "nation" and "cosmopolitanism" both demonstrated the same origin, and Herder saw nations in much
the same way that he saw popular songs; that is, he saw
nations as countries united by the human sentiment that
comprises them all. This is certainly the key to understanding Herder's work. In giving importance to popular
poetry as a voice that is universal in its basics and
national in its various articulations, Herder employed
the same idea that had guided him in the study of language; thus, he considered language, poetry, and nation
as a unity that was actualized, to use Cassirer's expression, in the totality of multiplicity.

6. Voices of God

In his "Romantische Schule," Heinrich Heine observed
that Herder regarded all mankind as a great harp in
the hand of the Grand Maestro (God), while he saw
each nation as a string of that gigantic harp, each
having a particular note. Here, however, we must distinguish two Herders: the first was the forceful
Herder who championed the cause of the masses, the
Herder who argued for the human origin of language;
the other, the second, was the Herder who rejected (or
who, I would say, was actually frightened by) the idea
that had been at the center of his own speculation.
As early as 1774, in his essay *Auch eine Philosophie
der Geschichte zur Bildung der Menscheit*, he expressed
the feeling that his theory on the origin of language
was only a sin of pride. He therefore withdrew into
himself--and in this withdrawal he met God.
     Of great importance in this conversion are two
other essays of his. The first is entitled *Briefe, das
Studium der Theologie betreffend*, published in 1780;
the other, broader but incomplete, bears the title *Vom
Geist der Ebräischen Poesie*, published in 1783. As we
know, Madame de Staël considered the latter essay to be
Herder's happiest and most impassioned work because it
fulfills his attempt to provide a national literary

history of Hebraic poetry. To Herder (and here we are
always referring to the first Herder) the Bible was
not a ponderous theological tract but a collection of
sagas capturing the religious spirit of a people.
Herder knew and appreciated the work of Bishop Lowth,
who had detected a healthy primitivism in these sagas.
But whereas Lowth held to a rigid interpretation of
the Bible, Herder did not hesitate to see imaginative
fables. He saw the vicissitudes of Adam and Eve, for
example, as "the dearest story for children about the
origin of the human race."

In *Studium der Theologie* Herder attempted to create
"an archeology of the Orient," basically analogous, of
course, to the science of classical antiquity created
by his friend, Christian Heyne, who pursued the study
of this antiquity among the savages of Father Lafitau
and the missionaries in order to understand the life
of ancient Greeks. Herder had essentially the same aim
as Heyne: he wanted the Bible, that divine work, to be
studied as a book written by and for men. In other
words, he saw the Bible, as Antoni has said, as a
national poetic history, and, we must add, he came to
see religion itself as a poetic language. To prevent
such a reduction from being a profanation, the history
of nations must acquire the dignity of sacred history,
raised with the highest of divine content to the level
of the Revelation, and the nation, as a single unit,
must be included in a universal order. It is precisely
at this point that we encounter the second Herder. He
had previously been attracted by Shaftesbury's pantheism, but now he was moving close to Bossuet. It was
in this spirit that he would write his *Ideen zur Philosophie der Geschichte der Menscheit*, which was intended to complement the theories previously proposed
in *Auch eine Philosophie*.

7. *"Ideen" and Its Significance*

In Herder's *Ideen*, however, what dominates is not the
individual who creates himself and his history; rather,
man is definitively replaced by God. Herder felt that

his new work had given a foundation to all human knowledge, and in this respect his *Ideen* often reminds us of
Voltaire's *Essai*. But his work was a new, broad *Essai*,
in which the ideas of Voltaire (and the Enlightenment)
were generally refuted. In Herder's view, a nation is
not an accumulation of separate individuals but rather
a spiritual unity within which its components exist; at
the same time, each civilization is not an abstract
unity but rather "a fine particular that is always organic, the product of climate, traditions, and customs."
    We need to be more precise about this concept. In
Ideen, Herder maintained that religion is the oldest,
holiest tradition on earth and that civilization and
science are not at the origin of religious tradition;
furthermore, he maintained that religious sentiment is
anterior to logic and reason. He saw the history of
man as a "pure natural history" of forces and human
tendencies operating according to place and time, and
he gave a traditional character not only to religion
but also to language, poetry, and the arts. If we wish
to understand the "second" Herder, however, we must see
the meaning that he gave to the word *nature*. No one,
he himself says, confuses the use that he makes of the
word *nature*. Nature is not an entity; rather, it is
God, omnipresent in His works. He adds that although
some may believe that the word *nature* has been diluted
and stripped of all meaning by many contemporary writers, he himself associates the word with omnipotence,
excellence, and wisdom, and he says that within his
spirit is the name of the invisible being that no
terrestrial language can express.
    Herder saw God everywhere, in all the world--not
only in men who create their civilization and their
history but also, as he himself says, in *Hommes de
Dieu*. For this reason he considered the history of
man as a lesson to which man must return, and he believed in a progressive development, to which man is
subjected according to place and time. He was influenced by Montesquieu to the extent that he did not
disregard the effect that climate can have on tradition, but his ideal is not an Enlightenment ideal.
His concept of progressive development is not perme-

ated with mathematical, abstract reason but rather with
a genuinely historical value, however it might be conceived (which associates him with Lessing, who believed
that the destination toward which the historical process tends is exactly the same as man's).

In *Ideen* Herder had no preconceived ideas about the
"people of nature," which he considered to be equal
with all other peoples. He believed that the savage,
with his own language and his own system of organization, had a civilization just as we do, and he regarded
the legislation of the savage as a work of art. Further, he did not hesitate to place the savage "above
the modern European with his foul heart and cosmopolitan face"--yet another allusion to the old social controversy of the savage in contrast to civilized man.
Nor did he give the slightest weight to men's color.
In his view, all peoples are made brothers in the name
of tradition, as he conceived it. He transformed the
cosmopolitanism of Enlightenment philosophers into a
serene humanitarianism, and he sought humanity itself
in the sentiment of man. In the panoramas that he
painted (taking us among widely different peoples, whom
he was always more eager to justify than to condemn),
he vindicated the force of tradition, which has its own
significance but changes with the passage of time.
Finally, he brought tradition into history, making it
a part *of* history.

In one of his works, which was proposed for presentation to Catherine of Russia, Herder attempted to
determine the basic elements of civilization. Therein
he had written, "For the love of heaven, let not all
become written law; rather, let it be living emotion,
custom, nature." In these words was the echo of
Möser's message. Such messages, however, resound
throughout *Ideen*, where, perhaps for the first time,
customs were called to make men brothers. In his work
theology was transformed into an instructive anthropology. Unfortunately, however, this philosopher who
refused to recognize the superiority of any one particular nation fell into the idolization of the German
mission. The voice of the people became the voice of
God, but (and this is Herder's limitation) God was to

be conceived of as German. One of Herder's theories
was that the ancient world was to be rejuvenated in
the work of Germanic peoples because they possess
untapped potential and "savage, strong, and good" customs. Thus, he arrived at nationalism (a word that he
himself had coined)--a nationalism that lived in and
for its own past, cloaked in an exoticism that made
it more fascinating and more savage. The harp, then,
had let fall its teutonic chord. This chord was
itself transformed into the harp, despite the fact
that Herder had clearly warned that a country, whatever it may be, must live pure of all political sins
because peace, not war, is the state of man--a state
that does not permit "the bloody struggle of country
against country."

8. *Humanity in Revolt*

Herder's *Ideen* was published between 1784 and 1791.
Meanwhile, the French Revolution had begun. Herder
had predicted some years before, "Liberty, Community,
and Equality will sprout everywhere, and the lower
class will rise to the place now occupied by withered,
useless, proud aristocrats." But when directly confronted with a revolution ushering the lower class
into politics and history, a class to whom had gone
all of the Revolution's concern, he was terrified.
In 1794, in his *Briefe zu Beförderung der Humanität*,
he asserted that he was now at the edge of an abyss,
and he cursed the horrors of a revolution that had
seemed to Kant, Hegel, and Goethe to be the advent of
a new era.

Just as Herder had not understood the revolutionary
spirit of Rousseau, he did not now understand the spirit of the Revolution, or, at the most, he understood
only its negative aspects. Indeed, the importance that
the declaration of human rights assumed in the history
of European civilization altogether escaped him. Nor
could he see the relationship between the new spirit of
the Revolution and the "voices of peoples" that he had
so loved. It is true, of course, that the French

Revolution was permeated with foolish charges against
the Catholic religion, which frightened Herder the
theologian, and it is true that before its altars the
vestments of the church fell. But what was the spirit
in which this destruction was carried out? A decree
of the Committee of Public Safety explicitly said that
the people must at last destroy its practices and prejudices that were related to religious activities. This
was the moment when Catholicism was placed in the same
position in which theologians had placed beliefs, acts,
and customs regarded as remnants of paganism. The
Revolution had its religion, myths, and symbols too,
but didn't these myths and symbols represent a return
to the cults and myths of the folk? During the Revolution, for example, William Tell became the precursor of
the immortal leaders of 1789. And, beginning a year
later, wasn't the tree of liberty derived from that
very maypole around which happy springtime revelers
danced?

One day in that same year, 1790, a bizarre procession appeared before the Assembly, containing representatives of all nations: a Chinaman, a Spaniard, an
Englishman, an Austrian, a Negro, and even a Chaldean,
with the Alsatian baron Anacharsis Cloots at its head.
It has been called a masquerade--but what was this procession intended to be if not the very symbol of mankind, of humanity, which came to France to participate
in the celebration of liberty and brotherhood? Even
the savage, born free but enslaved by colonial con-
quests, could at last return to what he had once been.
In the name of Rousseau, then, the chains were broken
--and religion itself was tempered in the beliefs of
the Revolution!

It should be pointed out, however, that in a document of the Revolution, reported by Groethuysen, one
can read the following: "Listen to what the worthy
pastors say to their parishioners: 'Alas, brothers,
you are resentful, and no longer is there faith or religion in the city; we must strive, then, to conserve
in our countryside the sacred trust given to us by
God.'" The Catholic religion was no longer an instrument for dominating the feudal classes, for such

classes had been destroyed. It returned, then, to its
origins. And what had the Revolution itself been,
anyway, if not an undertaking that, in the name of
human principles, had adopted the moral teachings of
the Church, destroying feudal law and creating universal suffrage?

The French Revolution had united the bourgeoisie
and the folk. In this union, which allowed for a common civil and political equality, the bourgeoisie no
longer could assume the attitude of a Voltaire towards
the folk. Indeed, the folk, a class of peasants and
workers, had achieved the Revolution with the aid of
the bourgeoisie. The Revolution had been launched in
the front line, where it had demonstrated that irrational forces succeed as much as those of reason,
because both forces exist in the "whole" man. This
concept gives a new significance to man's traditions
but does not remove them from man's mind, given the
fact that they are a part of his very humanity. Reason functions to control the impulses underlying our
beliefs and dreams; the French Revolution, however,
had demonstrated that it is *also* necessary to believe
what one dreams.

The anxieties and aspirations of the heretofore
scorned classes were appeased by the Revolution--one
of its greatest merits. The Revolution carried more
than the currents of the Enlightenment, for in it the
streams of proto-Romanticism flowed powerfully, even
if indirectly. Here, then, was a new age in which the
folk would continue to be a politico-social symbol
while its life would become the object of a new and
most productive study. At last, it was no longer
necessary to approach the folk as an inferior class
whose heritage was to be considered only as a by-
product. The way was now open. The *bon sauvage* had
finally become the *bon peuple*.

PART THREE

FOLKLORE AS AN INSTRUMENT OF POLITICS AND
NATIONAL DIGNITY IN THE ROMANTIC PERIOD

CHAPTER XI

"MANKIND" IN GERMANY

1. The "Treasure of Mankind"

Increasingly transformed into a cultural and political force, the concept of the *bon peuple*, now joined to the concept of national origins, assumed a particular aspect in Germany during the age of Romanticism. It is often argued that the first generation of romantics in Germany--Novalis, Tieck, and the Schlegel brothers-- contributed less to the development of Herderian folk- loristic thought than did the second generation, start- ing with Arnim and Brentano. But can we altogether accept this thesis?

We must first observe that German Romanticism was the antithesis of the Enlightenment. In distinguishing these two movements, Cassirer says that they differed greatly in their attitudes toward history. Romantics, according to Cassirer, loved the past in and for itself, not simply as a "fact" but as one of their highest ideals. Everything became understandable as soon as they could go back to the origins, an attitude that was completely foreign to eighteenth-century thinkers; in- deed, those eighteenth-century thinkers who were con- cerned with the advent of man and the birth of a new order considered the study of history as a necessity rather than as an end in itself.

For romantics, history and art were permeated with significant concepts that the Enlightenment had spurned, and they therefore turned anew to the places (the Orient, Greece) and periods (Christianity, Middle Ages) that Enlightenment philosophers had already investigated. But what were the real reasons for their interests?

Basically, romantics loved what Enlightenment thinkers
had hated, at least before the French Revolution.
But if the past was the peak of a mountain from which
romantics affectionately viewed the world, the mountain itself was their own past, which they saw as an
ideal refuge of universal importance. For romantics,
then, the past was not only a contemplation of remote
times but also a lesson for the future, and the romantics' interest in mankind was for the sake of that
future. In seeking their own origins, moreover,
romantics could not fail to encounter deeply embedded
beliefs found in the popular traditions that previously had much interested pre-romantics.

English pre-romantics, discovered and admired
by Herder, Goethe, and Bürger, had given particular
attention to popular poetry, in which they rediscovered their own Middle Ages. German romantics
asked themselves, "Aren't *Märchen* popular poetry, as
even Herder himself had said?" This view of poetry,
when more generally applied to art, generated a new,
clear-cut reaction against traditional aesthetics,
whose last exponent was Nicolai. Indeed, *Volkspoesie*
constituted (and this is a step forward in regard to
the pre-romantics) the major discovery that German
romantics made about the modern temper; in this
poetry they recognized a sense of the infinite pervaded by mystery, which distinguishes it from the
classical world of the finite. Buried within this
discovery was the necessity of accounting for *Lieder*
and *Märchen* that circulated among the folk, the genuine voice of man.

The early romantics hoped for a better world
for man with the same urgency as the Enlightenment
had. But what part was Germany to play in this new
world? Wasn't Germanism, already *in nuce* in the
work of Lessing and Herder, in the process of taking
shape in the minds of the early romantics? And,
however literary it was intended to be, didn't this
concept incorporate a national spirit that, as maintained by contemporary philosophers (one thinks
especially of the youthful Hegel), was the treasure
of all mankind?

2. Novalis, the German Middle Ages, and "Märchen"

Noteworthy on this subject was the attitude of one of
the earliest romantics, Novalis, who was convinced
that Germanism, like the Greek, Roman, and Anglican
spirits, was not limited to a specific state because
it included special universal features. In a letter
written in 1797 to A. W. Schlegel, he observed,
"Germanism is cosmopolitanism combined with the most
marked individuality." This suggests that Novalis,
like Herder, brought the concept of "humanity" to
both Germanism and cosmopolitanism. This was precisely the opinion of a group that included Schiller
and Wilhelm von Humboldt--except, as Meinecke observes, Novalis gave the idea a new romantic coloration.

Novalis was equally romantic in his picture of
the Middle Ages, as is proved by his essay published
in 1799, "Die Christenheit oder Europa." This essay
contains a brief but perceptive sketch of the Christian culture of Europe, which was, by design, a
"program" for the future. In this program, Novalis,
in opposition to Lutheran reforms, spoke emotionally
about the Christian religion and Christianity. I
would say that although he took pleasure in mythic
and aesthetic values, his major hope was that Christianity would prepare a new era in which a Catholic
Middle Ages would return in new forms, portending
the perpetual peace Herder had desired. Finally,
Novalis was obviously quite interested in the Orient,
especially India, which he regarded as the flame that
would illuminate the romantic.

For Novalis, then, a love for the past, particularly the medieval Christian past, was not an end in
itself. In his work the Enlightenment position on
the importance of the Christian tradition was clearly
inverted, casting the history of Christianity in a
new light; but in reassessing the Middle Ages by
emphasizing those noble characteristics that the
Enlightenment had denied, wasn't he following in the
footsteps of the pre-romantics?

In considering the Middle Ages as a Christian

period, the *ideal* Christian period that had reached
its splendor in Germany, Novalis quite obviously had
a "romantic conception" (to use Oskar Walzel's phrase)
of the Middle Ages and Germanism. In conceiving this
fusion, he was inspired by Friedrich Schleiermacher
and Wilhelm Wackenroder. The former, especially in
his *Über die Religion*, had taught him that religion
is a universal feeling man discovers and accepts when
he discovers and accepts the infinite in himself.
This concept helped him discover the symbolic aspects
of Christianity, which, among Protestants, only Jakob
Böhme (whom Novalis greatly admired) had understood.
Schleiermacher, along with Schiller and Johann Fichte,
had also taught him that "from primitive monotonous
Harmony we proceed to Disharmony, and then finally to
Totality," a "harmony" that was at that time usually
sought for in Greece. For Greece, however, Novalis
substituted the German Middle Ages, whose disgregation
was necessary for the development of civilization.
Wackenroder, on the other hand, had compared it to the
Gothic (explored in Germany by Goethe) and to ancient
German literature.

On the basis of these teachings Novalis attempted
to formulate principles for the new art and poetry
that romantics should produce. He saw this art and
poetry as a language consisting of symbols, hiero-
glyphs, and rites--and *Märchen* represented, in his
view, the most typical expression of such language:
"It is like a vision in an insubstantial dream, a mixture of extraordinary events and happenings like a
musical fantasy, the harmonic chords of an aeolian
harp, or nature itself. . . . All nature must have
been marvelously mixed with the worldly spirit in the
age of general anarchy, lawlessness, and liberty in
the untouched state of nature before the world
existed. . . . The world of fable is completely
opposite to the world of fact, as similar to it as
chaos is to perfect creation" (*Fragmente*, nos. 414-
415). It is significant that Novalis enriched the
plots of such romances as *Heinrich von Ofterdingen*
and *Die Lehrlinge zu Sais* by adding *Märchen*, many
of which he skillfully reworked. Recall, for example,

"The Little Rose Flower": "Once upon a time in the
West, there lived a young lad who was very good but
quite mysterious." Thus does the world of *Märchen*
return as a dream actually lived.

3. Tieck and Ancient German Literature

Novalis' interests were fully shared by another sensitive poet, Ludwig Tieck, who contributed to Novalis'
appreciation of Wackenroder. From Wackenroder Tieck
gained an appreciation of the ancient German literature
that had previously influenced Herder, whose interest
in *Lieder* and *Märchen* is well known. "In a region of
Harz lived a knight named Blonde Eckbert." Thus begins
"Der blonde Eckbert." After recounting an ancient lied
about the noble Duke of Burgundy, he says, "The voice
of an old peasant echoed among the rocks as he told
this story." It is the enchanted world of *Märchen* and
Lied, presented in an atmosphere of ecstasy and dream.
Tieck nicely reworked ancient motifs of popular literature, the sources of his own poetry, as Basile and
Perrault had done previously, although for different
reasons; still, one finds in their work the same romantic idea about life that one finds in the works of
Tieck. This idea, observes Walzel, can be expressed
by the following propositions, to which he consistently
held: "Between man and nature there is no insuperable
dividing wall; a sentimental activity predominates in
nature and in man; a part of nature, then, survives in
man." Thus, *Märchen* became poetry, the essence of
poetic contemplation.
    In order to satisfy his poetic interests, Tieck
planned to publish some ancient German texts, and his
first thought was to modernize the *Nibelungenlied*. Of
these projects, however, we only have his *Minnelieder
aus dem schwäbischen Zeitalter*, which he published in
1803. Bodmer and Breitinger had previously provided
a paleographic edition of these *Minnelieder*, but their
edition, which was intended only for scholars, was not
very readable. Tieck wanted to give his contemporaries
a modernized text, simply a selection of *Minnelieder*,

which in his opinion reflected "one of the most serene,
noble moments of the entire Middle Ages." He made an
attempt to prove this in his extensive introduction,
one of the most interesting parts of the book, in which
he argued that poetry is the highest expression of the
human spirit and medieval poetry is the most romantic.

4. *"Minnelieder" as Poetry*

Tieck regarded *Minnelieder*, set against the backdrop of
medieval literature, as poetry congenial to public life,
where nobility and the folk are one and the same.
Minnelieder, he went on to say, had indeed drawn from
provincial models; but just as the pre-romantics had
saved such poets as Shakespeare and Milton from oblivion, giving them back to the heritage of mankind, was
it not worthwhile now to do the same for ancient German
epopees, of which the *Nibelungenlied* is one of the most
perfect examples? He compared the *Nibelungenlied* with
the *Iliad* and the *Odyssey*. He believed (perhaps under
the influence of F. A. Wolf) that one author surely did
not write all the poems in the *Nibelungenlied*. He compared heroic epopees with chivalric poems about King
Arthur, which he considered to be a later-adapted form.
Still, he concluded that both have the same background.
This "background," he argued, had given rise to a great
organic poetry that spread through Europe, fusing Norse
mythology and Oriental fables. Chivalry, he said,

> . . . united all the nations of Europe. Knights
> traveled from remote Northern countries down to
> Spain and Italy. The crusades made this union
> stronger and created admirable relationships be-
> tween East and West. From North and East came
> legends that would mix with local ones: great
> events of war, splendid courts, princes and em-
> perors who found pleasure in poetry, a triumphant
> church that canonized heroes. All these favorable
> circumstances combined to create a marvelous life
> for free and independent nobles and the rich middle
> class, a life in which reawakened aspirations spon-

taneously united with poetry to produce a pure,
clear expression of the surrounding reality reflected in it. Believers sang about faith and
miracles, lovers sang of love, and knights told
stories of adventurous fights and struggles, to
which other faithful knights patiently listened.

Tieck, then, not only gave a new meaning to the
national epopee of Germany, which he saw as the source
of national language, but also created his own medieval
age. The German Middle Ages certainly were very much
different from what he described, but it was typical
of romantics to transfigure all that was remote in time.
But he did not introduce *Minnelieder* merely to praise
the German Middle Ages; the purpose of Tieck's poetic
work, we should not forget, was to reassess the poetry
and values (Middle Ages, Christianity, folklore) of
ancient Germany. Indeed, his *Genoveva*, taken from a
folk legend, was a dramatic work containing his dream
of the return to the beginning of Christianity, an
idea that came to him from thinking about the works
of Böhme and Schleiermacher and from reading Spanish
playwrights. Christianity and the Middle Ages, then,
became for him what they had been for Novalis. And
although this apotheosis of the German Middle Ages
was not overtly political, it certainly contained the
implicit recognition of Germany's greatness.

5. Romanticism and Classical Antiquity

Unlike Novalis and Tieck, Friedrich Schlegel was
interested in classical antiquity from the very start.
He was certainly more philological than Novalis, but,
like Novalis and Tieck, he understood the importance
and pleasure of learning. In some commentary written
between 1795 and 1798, Schlegel demonstrated his keen
interest in training himself in the field of philology.
This commentary was entitled *Zur Philologie*. Here he
spoke admiringly of Herder: "Herder's love for the
ancients is primarily a love for civilization, whether
progressive or classical or barbaric or even childishly

naive." He praised F. A. Wolf, who had been his master: "Wolf's *Prolegomena* are unique in their kind,
thanks to the historical spirit that inspired them."
Inspired as he himself was by this spirit, he observed,
"It is necessary to insist on natural philology."
This suggested that he altogether accepted the concept
of philology then being promulgated by Christian Heyne
and Wolf himself, through whose efforts abstract philology had become the concrete science of antiquity.
He went on to say that "the existence of a true philology is the proof of a nation's civilization," and he
concluded that "if the end of philology is history, the
historian must 'philologize.'"

This contention is the central thesis of his
Geschichte der Poesie der Griechen und Römer (1798),
in which he declared that a nation comes to have a personality only "when it moves toward universality and
the completion of its development in a cosmopolitan
sense, without refusing to admit external elements
likely to transform it." In light of this contention,
it is understandable that he came to see Greece as the
ideal of national life. In this respect he accepted
the teachings of Herder, who had observed as early as
his *Fragmente über die neuere deutsche Literatur* that
just as ancient Greece and Rome had founded their art
and theater on their own traditions and beliefs, so did
these have to become the essence of the new German literature. We know that the pre-romantics and Herder
despised classicism, but they certainly did not despise
the classics, whose ideals they accepted. This was
precisely the opinion of Humboldt, who also moved from
a great interest in Greece to an understanding of
nationality.

Schlegel followed the same path. As had been the
case for Herder and Humboldt before him, it was only
through the study of the Greek people that his hopes
and ideals for his own country arose. These hopes and
ideals led to his yearning for an individual state pervaded by a national life and a political universality,
although his concept of "universality," more than is
the case in Novalis' theocratic medievalism, attempted
to incorporate the cosmopolitan ideas of the French

Revolution. The political situation after 1801 carried
him toward a political theory fully corresponding to
the ecclesiastical rigidity of the Catholic system.
This admirer and student of Böhme and Schleiermacher
thus followed the example of Novalis: he constructed
the romantic ideal of a universal empire--one to which
Germany, quite naturally, belonged. As Schlegel said
in one of his *Ideen*, "The spirit of the ancient heroes
of German art and science must remain ours as long as
we remain German. The German artist either has no
character at all, or he has the character of an
Albrecht Dürer, a Kepler, a Hans Sachs, a Luther, a
Jakob Böhme. This character is direct, open, solid,
clear, and profound, although occasionally naive and
a little awkward. *Only Germans have the national characteristic of giving divine veneration to art and science simply because of their love for art and science.*"
     It is, then, a national characteristic to venerate
art and science--especially when they are German. But
in a passage in the *Lyceum* Schlegel goes on to say,
"We simply must despise the false premise in the model
of the German state that some great German discoverers
have built. The German state lies not behind but before
us." It was like saying, "Germany, arise with your
epopees, your songs, your *Lieder*, your *Märchen*, and make
them become flesh of your flesh!" Nor is it without
significance that in his essay on Goethe he considered
lieder to be the richest heritage of national poetry.

6. *Friedrich Schlegel: Between East and West*

We know that Schlegel was one of the first Germans to
study the Orient, which had so interested Herder. But
how did Schlegel view the Orient, and what values did
it contribute to the spirit of his country? In
"Gespräch über die Poesie," first published in the
Athenaeum of 1800, Schlegel had spoken emotionally
about the German epic and the influence exerted on it
by the Orient: "With the Germans a pure source of a
new heroic epopee spread through Europe, and when the
rough Gothic poetry met, under Arab influence, with an

echo of delicate Oriental tales on the southern coast
that gives onto the Mediterranean, a gay art of delicate songs and mysterious stories bloomed; in one form
or the other, along with the sacred Latin legend, the
secular romance that sang of love and war was spread."
This idea was later resumed by Tieck, but Schlegel did
not stop here. Believing that poetry and mythology
are one and the same, he hoped for the advent of a new
mythology that would join the ancient with the modern:

> The new mythology must be forged from the deepest
> spiritual resources, and it should be the most
> artful of all works of art because it must encom-
> pass all the others, a new bed and vessel for the
> eternal, ancient, original fountainhead of poetry.
> . . . What is mythology, if not a hieroglyphic
> expression of nature transfigured by imagination
> and love? . . . Why won't you arise and renew
> these splendid figures of great antiquity? . . .
> But to hasten the birth of the new mythology,
> other mythologies too must be reawakened according
> to the measure of their significance, beauty, and
> form. Oh, if only the treasures of the Orient
> were as accessible as those of ancient times!
> What new source of poetry could then flow from
> India if some German artists, with their deep
> universal sentiment and their own genius for
> translation, had the opportunity that an increas-
> ingly more dull and brutal nation little profits
> from. We must search the Orient for what is most
> sublimely romantic; and when we get to the source,
> perhaps the southern ardor that we find so charming
> in Spanish poetry will seem western and modest.

Although Schlegel saw the revelation of nature in
mythology, he, like Novalis, looked upon the Orient as
a romantic poetical ideal. We must wait for the
program that he urged later in the introduction to his
Europa, however, to see his treatment of the East--
especially India, which he also discussed in his essay
Über die Sprache und Weisheit der Indier (1808). This
essay was not only a manifesto of Orientalism, to which

the research of Antoine Silvestre de Sacy and Sir William Jones had already opened new inroads, but also a manifesto in which historical linguistics, through the auspices of Sanskrit, was announced. But leaving this essay aside (the study of which concerns problems different from ours), it is in the program of *Europa* that he relates classical antiquity to the modern romantic period.

Enlightenment philosophers had considered the Orient and India as an ensemble of forces to oppose Christianity. But, Schlegel observed, wasn't the self-denial typical of Christianity, along with the materialism of Greek religion, also to be found in India? Thus, says Walzel, Schlegel rejected a division between "classic" and "romantic," which at first he had accepted, and, in fact, he came to believe that a union of the classical with the romantic was quite possible. He concluded that only the Catholic religion had taken possession of the splendor, truth, and poetic beauty of Greek mythology and traditions, and that a revolution was to come from the Orient. As he said, "We cannot forget that the common elements joining all religions and mythologies involve the principles of life, the origins of all ideas." But where had German heroism and the Roman church been fused (and here again is Novalis), if not in the German Middle Ages?

7. *A. W. Schlegel and Folk Poetry*

The theories of Novalis, Tieck, and Friedrich Schlegel were resumed by August Wilhelm Schlegel, who is correctly credited with perpetuating such theories. This points to the importance of his *Vorlesungen über schöne Literatur und Kunst*. This work is a collection of his lectures given at Berlin between 1801 and 1804, and it should be integrated with *Vorlesungen über dramatische Kunst und Literatur*, delivered at Vienna between 1806 and 1808.

Schlegel understood the importance of history, which he saw as a perpetual progress. Like Herder, Schlegel saw history as the philosophy of mankind, in

which the individual always feels a universal presence.
Because he was concerned in his first *Vorlesungen* with
establishing whether or not a history of art is possible, he formulated the following premises: "in the
creation of individuals" we must recognize "the secret
that nature has reserved"; nevertheless, "each genius
reflects the genius of mankind," which is the source
of "the magic power of history." It is clear that
Schlegel adopted the famous genius theory (about which
there had been much discussion in the eighteenth century), but it is equally clear that he acknowledged
the pantheistic idea that man's awareness produces
self-trust, which consequently produces creative
energy.

Schlegel used these theories to provide a historical context for romantic poetry. As early as the first
Vorlesungen, and more precisely in a lecture he gave in
1803, he argued that romantic poetry coincided with the
romantic spirit of the Middle Ages, which obviously
suggests the influence of Novalis and Tieck. Thus, he
viewed romantic poetry as being clearly distinct from
classic poetry, an idea that was resumed and developed
in the second *Vorlesungen*. In his view, this distinction arises from the fact that romantic poetry originated in the Middle Ages under the influence of Christianity, and therefore the "quality of the romantic
springs from the union of the Nordic and Christian
spirits." In neither the first nor the second
Vorlesungen did he alter, as is thought, Novalis' and
Tieck's picture of the Middle Ages as the greatest
period of history. He rejected the idea that German
migrations were the result of a barbaric invasion, however, and in his view the term *barbarian* had a meaning
greatly different from the one provided by historical
studies and earlier critics.

In this poetic resurrection of the German Middle
Ages we find Schlegel's opinion of popular poetry,
which included only "those poems created especially
for the lower social classes or produced among them."
Ernest Tonnelat says this idea should remind us of
Tieck--but had Tieck's *Märchen* ever been popular?
Wasn't his work the perfect example of a refined

literature that was anything but popular? It is evident, however, that at least here Schlegel was not
interested in giving too much importance to his own
speculations, although he established an essential
point: folk poetry may be created either *by* the folk
or *for* the folk. His only concern was to prove that
Germany had no literature (if with this term we mean
not a catalogue but an ensemble of works reflecting a
national spirit) and that only the folk possessed such
a literature. It would be sufficient, he concludes,
for *Lieder* and *Märchen* to be treated by a real poet;
then they would appear in all their magnificence.

It is certainly significant that in his second
Vorlesungen Schlegel recognized that just as German
poetry had been refreshed and reinvigorated by Oriental
influences in the past, so it should now draw new
strength from popular poetry. This had been the task
that Herder, Bürger, Novalis, and Tieck had entrusted
to the new poetry of Germany, and this was now the task
that Schlegel entrusted to it--the Schlegel who, in
searching for a new definition of Romanticism, indirectly offered us a brilliant definition of Germanism.

8. Romanticism and Germanism

What importance did the German "spirit" have in contemporary culture, and what are its relationships with
Romanticism, with which it basically coincides (even
though Romanticism naturally has a broader significance)? Although the early romantics always spoke in
the name of mankind and Europe, the land of their lives
and dreams was implicitly Germany, in whose civilization they discovered, ultimately, the very essence of
Romanticism. As we know, Romanticism continually
exalted the individual, individuality, man, genius.
But above single personalities (and here we move to
Germanism), isn't there the personality of one's race,
which has its own language, traditions, and customs?
Rather than abstractions, we are here speaking of spontaneous and creative movements of the spirit. Romanticism, moreover, provided a new way of understanding

life in whatever it has of inquietude, mystery, nostalgia, and the absolute, and it fused science, religion, satire, and art to produce a clearer vision of
life. In this "vision," Germanism embraced the values
of German life, the *Urmensch*, and from the fusion it
drew new inspirations and new dreams.

Romanticism inspired a great nostalgic interest in
the Orient, the land of magic, dreams, and marvelous
tales. Germanism sought for this magic, these dreams,
and these tales in its ancient literature, which, like
classic literature, was based on personal traditions
and beliefs. Such literature offers us a pure vision
of a Christian medieval age as "marvelous" as a
resplendent Gothic cathedral. In this fact is the
significance of the love that Tieck and the Schlegels
had for romance literatures, in which they saw a poetic
dream come true. Romantics viewed poetry as the highest manifestation of the human spirit, and they
attempted to describe the essence of romantic poetry,
which they discovered in the Christian Middle Ages
(with the exclusion of Friedrich Schlegel, who later
came to see romantic poetry as an eternal attitude of
the spirit). In Herder's opinion, the medieval romantic who produced *Naturpoesie* was the antithesis of the
classical poet, an antithesis in which early romantics
saw much significance. And what poetry is more romantic than folk poetry, the poetry that lives even now in
Märchen, *Lieder*, and the spirit of the folk?

Through the auspices of Germanism, Romanticism in
Germany focused all its attention on medieval literature, which it hoped to revive, and on *Lieder* and
Märchen, which are its direct continuation. The study
of self-origins always depends directly on living folk
traditions, and these--to which Vico, Rousseau, and
Möser had previously paid attention--now came to be
considered not only as historical forms of art or
thought but also as elements of national dignity. The
Napoleonic invasion and the defeat of Jena would soon
come to transform them into instruments of political
attack.

CHAPTER XII

FROM COSMOPOLITANISM TO NATIONALISM

1. *The Political "Nation"*

For Germany, the Napoleonic invasion and the defeat of
Jena were not only political events but also the beginning of a new Renaissance. Early romantics (that is,
romantics who lived between 1796 and 1805) delighted
in elevating culture on the pillars of universal
ideals, although in these ideals a concern with acquiring an awareness of one's own past was equally present.
But when Napoleon extinguished their ideals with his
invasion, making the survival of those various nation-
alisms that Herder had hoped for impossible, the German
romantics felt that it was time to take a stronger,
more realistic stand about the concept of nationality.
The first to move from the idea of universal citizenship to the idea of the political nation were the
Schlegel brothers, who refused to accept the cultural
and political "levelling" implicit in Napoleonic expansion. What force could and therefore would be opposed
to such levelling, if not the concept of "nation"? But
what did this idea of "nation" come to represent in the
thought of the second-generation romantics, and what
were its specific elements?

In one of his *Philosophische Vorlesungen*, delivered
at Vienna between 1804 and 1806, Friedrich Schlegel
said that the greatness of a nation is measured by the
degree of its attachment to its language, religion,
usages, customs, thought, and life, because, as he
himself said, "the older and purer the stock, the
older and purer the customs; and the older and purer
the customs, the greater and truer one's attachment is

to them, and so much greater the nation will be" (Ed.
Windischmann, p. 385). The idea was not new: attachment to one's traditions (whose historical character
was identified by Vico) had been announced as a symbol
of nationality by Rousseau, the Swiss historians,
Möser, and by Herder himself, who observed in his *Ideen*
that each nation derives its national spirit from its
sense of individuality. But now this admonition rever-
berated in the thought of the romantics of the new
generation as a cultural and political ideal. Whether
or not these romantics had a folkloristic concept of
nation, they agreed that if a nation is the sanctuary
where man can find a freedom that allows for individuality, it is also a living symbol of folk traditions.
Indeed, these traditions, in the best sense of the
word, converge and cohere in such a nation, actually
creating it. Strengthening the force of tradition,
then, contributes to self-awareness, an awareness of
one's own past as a concrete historical reality.

The necessity of studying all aspects of folklife
in an increasingly more detailed way developed into the
Rettungsgedanke that Lessing, Herder, and the Schlegels
had hoped for, the saving of a folk heritage that
seemed to be sinking from sight. It was precisely
this concern that brought about the publication of
Des Knaben Wunderhorn by Ludwig Achim von Arnim and
Clemens Brentano.

2. Arnim, Brentano, and the "Wunderhorn"

There is no doubt that Arnim and Brentano began to
compile *Des Knaben Wunderhorn* in order to reach a
determination that not even Herder had achieved. In
collecting folksongs, they were ruled by the one guiding premise of staying exclusively in their own linguistic and cultural sphere. The object of their research was not *Volkslieder* of the world but *Volkslieder*
of their own country.

Brentano was interested in *Volkspoesie* for the same
reasons that had motivated Novalis and Tieck, in that
he thought of using ancient tales and lieder for his

own artistic works. Previously (as early as 1802) he had inserted some lieder, of which he had managed to make an important collection, into the second part of *Godwi*, and it is probable that August Wilhelm Schlegel had him in mind when, in his *Vorlesungen* (1803-04), he predicted a Percy for Germany. Actually, Brentano hoped to be quite different from Percy: he hoped to be, and certainly was, an artist. We do know, however, that he drew inspiration for his works not only from *Lieder* and *Märchen* of his own country but also (and we should remember that his father was Italian) from Basile's *Pentamerone* and Carlo Gozzi's *Favole*. His *Märchen*, whose protagonists frequently were animals, express the most delicate and refined human feelings and are among the most beautiful of romantic works. Italo Maione comments, "Brentano is clearly the king of romantic fabulists. In his poems and *Märchen* he touches the spirit of the child, becoming a child again himself, which offers him a moment of happiness. His Romanticism consists in the dream-like quality to which he abandons himself--as if he were in his own kingdom, where he creates an atmosphere that is larger than life, his own unique reality."

Arnim encouraged Brentano to use his lieder collection and compiled an anthology with him that included materials taken from just about everywhere, from the living oral tradition as well as from ancient prints. At first Arnim and Brentano had thought of doing a broader work. The proof of this is an announcement from Arnim published in 1805, in which, in the name of the fatherland, he invited "men of good will" to collect "the literary traces of their own past" before it was too late. This announcement said:

> In choosing what he wants to communicate, each must be guided by his own personal taste, and, in re-organizing my publication, I find that my taste compels me to understand and serve all. I become increasingly eager when I see my reserves increase each day; to the collections that will follow we will add melodies, drawings (particularly reproductions of ancient wood-prints or landscapes), and

ancient orally-transmitted legends and tales.
Thus, we will be able to gather many threads of
the vast cloth on which our history is embroidered
and which it is our duty to continue to embellish.

In collecting his country's folk traditions, then,
Arnim was conscious of accomplishing a historical and
patriotic work. But when he helped Brentano reorganize
the extensive material of *Des Knaben Wunderhorn*, which
is limited to lieder, was he always faithful to the
collected texts? The two collaborators wanted to do
the work not of scholars or restorers but of "vivi-
fiers," a point that they themselves clearly stated
and obviously the motive behind their clever adaptations. The first volume of *Des Knaben Wunderhorn* was
published in 1806, while the other two volumes appeared
in 1808. This highly successful work was viewed by an
entire generation as a fresh, pure fountain, and from
it much inspiration would be drawn by poets (Eichendorff, Uhland, Hoffmann von Fallersleben, Mörike),
musicians (Schubert, Schumann, Brahms), and painters
(primarily Moritz von Schwind). It seemed as though
someone had unburied a new fountain of youth for lyric
and music.

Des Knaben Wunderhorn was dedicated to Goethe--one
who well understood the importance of folksongs, having
used them himself for his *Lieder*--and Goethe was one of
the first to greet this book with sympathy. "In these
Lieder," he observed, "Germans should find comfort beyond the miasma of the present by seeing the kind of
nature existing during the time when they were composed,
a nature that is characteristic of all time." Equally
positive was the judgment given a few years later by
Heinrich Heine, who certainly did not have much affec-
tion for his country's romantics: "I cannot praise
this book enough. It contains the most delicate flowers of the German spirit, and whoever would hope to
understand the German people from a very amiable viewpoint must read these folk poems. At this very moment
I have the book on my table, and I have the impression
of smelling the perfume of German lime trees. . . .
The lime tree represents an important part of these

poems; in its shadow lovers caress at evening; and it is their favorite tree, perhaps because its leaf has the shape of a human heart." But while lime trees and lovers intrigued Brentano (although his patriotism ran strong and deep), they left Arnim cold; he drew *his* concept of German nationality from German history, which he tried to reconstruct with the threads of oral and folk traditions.

3. Bases for an Educational Folk Literature

Even today the scholarly interest of *Des Knaben Wunderhorn* consists primarily in Arnim's dissertation entitled "Von Volksliedern," which concludes the first volume of the collection. Here we are presented with a discussion of the concept of folk poetry; here we find, perhaps for the first time, the term *Volkskunde* (which Wilhelm Riehl later used to indicate the name of the science of German antiquity)--a term that meant in Germany what the term *folklore* came to mean elsewhere, although both terms sometimes have different meanings; and here, finally, we most clearly see the importance that Arnim gave to folk poetry and the folk as a means to an educational literature.

Following the lead of Herder and the early romantics, Arnim contrasted folk poetry to the poetry of the highest social classes. In his view, the folk was a healthy instinctive force, unlike the enfeebled modern middle class. In his view, the folk is the poet, while the middle class has poor, completely "unpoetic" tastes. He thought of the folk as a sociological concept, a specific class (peasants and artisans), which, as a vital, integral part of the nation, possessed the gift of poetry. Although he felt that this poetry, unlike the poetry of cultured classes, is anonymous, we should note that he did not equate "anonymous" with "impersonal." As he went on to say, even the anonymous folk poet always has an artistic awareness of his own.

This is but one of the aspects of *Volkslied*, which he felt was distinguished, like everything that is popular, by its form and internal beauty. A. W. Schlegel

had distinguished the poetry made *by* the folk from
poetry made *for* the folk, but Arnim wished to be
clearer and more precise about this matter. He
thought that a poetry adopted, loved, and sung by the
folk becomes popular *whoever* the author. It follows,
then, that everything diffused and living among the
folk becomes popular regardless of the source from
which it was taken. For this reason, he says, we must
consider Goethe's *Die Fischerin* as popular, because it
is a work that the folk accepted, repeated, and sang,
even though they did not pay the slightest attention
to the identity of the author. In other words, a lied
diffused among the folk is popular if the folk is unaware of the author who created it. Obviously, this
was merely a speculation, one suggesting that folk
poetry is not to be identified by its origins but by
its characteristics. Indeed, Arnim even considered
Lorenzo de' Medici and Luther as "popular" (which
clearly suggests the influence of Herder and Bürger).
At the heart of this speculation, however, didn't he
feel that he himself was one of those poets whose
words, inspired by the folk, could become the voice
of the entire folk?

Arnim's readaptations of lieder were attempts to
create genuine folk literature. Herder had already
admonished: Educate and form your mind in the mentality of the folk; imitate its attitudes. A. W. Schlegel
added: Let a poet imaginatively rework folk poetry,
and he himself will become the best poet. Arnim's
task, then, was to educate himself about the attitudes
of the folk so that he himself could become a folk poet
--and the songs of the folk were to become the songs of
the whole nation. Arnim believed that a folksong, a
Lied, is always elastic, always a continually regener-
ating form. This was a clear, sharp perception of the
idea that folk poetry is subject to continual reworking.
Now, if the folk continually transforms its songs,
wasn't it up to the collector of folksongs to establish
a definite form and thus create a folk literature?

In the same year that the first volume of *Des
Knaben Wunderhorn* appeared, Ernst Arndt published his
Geist der Zeit, in which he defined the secret spirit

of the folk as an immutable primitive force that, in
civilized societies, appears only in exceptional people. But doesn't this thesis ultimately coincide with
the literary idea that A. W. Schlegel and Arnim proposed when they entrusted to "exceptional" men the
power of expressing the folk spirit in lieder or, we
should say, in readaptions of lieder?

In any event, Arnim was clearly conscious of sacri-
ficing philology to the folk spirit, which accounts for
the major difference between *Des Knaben Wunderhorn* and
the works of Novalis, Tieck, and Brentano himself. In
reworking *Märchen* of their land (or even of other
lands), these men had used the folk and its literature
to produce "good" literature, a literature that certainly could not circulate in the midst of the folk.
In this respect, says Leonello Vincenti, they were
following the English pre-romantics, who often went
back to the past for sources of poetry and literature.
But even though *Des Knaben Wunderhorn* tended to argue
for the aesthetic and mythic values of folk poetry, it
was primarily meant to be a text of educational folk
literature.

Education was indeed the central aim of the skillful readaptions of Brentano and Arnim, for they believed that *all* the folk, the entire nation, could gain an
awareness of its own nationality from such literature.
The Prussian minister Heinrich Stein realized as much
when he recommended "this book of poems, unique in its
importance, as likely to provoke in the *Volk* the patriotism necessary for liberation from the French." This
aim was also at the center of Arnim's *Zeitung für
Einsiedler*, a journal that emphasized the importance of
inspiring love for everything having to do with relationships between the individual and the folk.

4. Görres and Folk Poetry

Collaborating on Arnim's *Zeitung* was Joseph Görres, who,
like Arnim and Brentano, venerated the German Middle
Ages and its literature. Precisely because of this
veneration, Görres did a critical study of those

Deutsche Volksbücher that had so pleased Tieck and
Brentano. In this work, published in 1807, he celebrated folk literature as an instrument of German
nationality.

Before studying folk poetry, Görres had been primarily concerned with mythological studies, and he had
come under the influence of romantic and Oriental
theories. A complicated but interesting and skillful
work of his, *Glauben und Wissen*, was published in 1805.
Here he argued that myths and legends derived from a
single myth and that this myth was first revealed to
the people of India, from which it spread like a sacred
fire to all other populations, including Germany.
Basically, this thesis attempted to restrict only to
India the ideas previously expressed on this subject
by Pierre Huet as early as 1700. Five years later,
Görres returned to the problem of the origins of
mythology and religion in his *Mythengeschichte der
asiatischen Welt*. After providing an extensive examination of the history of religions, he observed that
in its main features each religion is identical to a
single religion (characterized by nature worship and
reflected in traces or "survivals" in all modern peoples). Görres then concluded by stating that all of
man's intellectual activity derives from the relationship between the divine and the human, an opinion that
had been previously asserted by Johann Arnold Kanne in
his *Pantheum der aeltesten Naturphilosophie* (1811).
This is a conclusion that was also reached by another
mythologist of the period, Friedrich Creuzer; in his
*Symbolik und Mythologie der alten Völker, besonders
der Griechen*, published in four substantial volumes
between 1810 and 1812, he said (thus associating himself with Lafitau) that pagan mythology is nothing
other than a distortion of God's revelation to the
people.

Görres's work on the *Deutsche Volksbücher* was published in the period between the compilations of
Glauben und Wissen and *Mythengeschichte*. He believed
that the *Volksbücher* were one of the greatest treasures
of German literature and that they should therefore be
brought to light and studied as a symbol of Germany's

aspirations. In the introduction to *Die teutschen
Volksbücher* Görres, like Herder, distinguished *Naturpoesie* from *Kunstpoesie*, observing that folksongs are
works of nature rather than works of art. This statement, however, contradicted what he said when he conducted a more comprehensive study of popular poetry.

Like A. W. Schlegel and Arnim, Görres believed that
folk poetry (in connection with the "folk booklets" or
Volksbücher) is composed either by or for the folk; in
both cases, however, the popularity of folk poetry depends on the degree to which it has been disseminated
among the folk, whose qualities it witnesses. It is
important to notice that in his view the folk is composed of those who have pure hearts and noble spirits.
This premise led him to state that even the *Volksbücher*
are works of poets and therefore were composed by specific individuals. Although, as Tonnelat says, his
opinions on folk poetry were often fluctuating and
contradictory, he nevertheless was quite firm on one
point: folk poetry is sacred. Tonnelat adds that
Görres's conception of folk poetry had precisely the
same meaning as the one given by romantics like Novalis
and Tieck, who considered nature to be the supreme
creator of poetry, art, and beauty.

Görres defended his view of folk poetry in various
articles in the *Rheinischer Merkur*, defined by Napoleon
as the "fifth great power" of his enemies. In the
preface and notes of his major work, he commented on
the forty-nine *Volksbücher* that he examined, energetically arguing for Germany's necessary interest in folk
poetry, which, however simple and naive, was not therefore to be considered inferior to *Kunstpoesie*. He also
argued that even "cultured" literature acquires a different character and greater vitality when it descends
from "restricted upper-class circles down into the folk,
becoming one with it," which is precisely what gives a
special quality to folk literature. Thus, he adds,
"the great republic of literature has its own houses of
parliament, wherein the nation is directly represented."
Like Arnim, he perceived the vigor that new literature
could gain from such poetry--literature that then had
to be national, patriotic, and therefore contrary to

all that was French (yet another link between poetry
and politics). Just as the low folk (here the term
low has a distinguishing rather than a pejorative
meaning) is necessary to a nation, so too, according
to Görres, is a literature expressing the aims of that
folk. By this time the nation was no longer seen as
a mixture of quite different classes but as a union
of classes that merge with and complement each other,
creating a single national character.

5. Father Jahn: Between Rousseau and Fichte

This same idea was expressed or, to use a more exact
phrase, literally "shouted" by Friedrich L. Jahn, who,
in his book *Deutsches Volkstum*, substituted the terms
Volk and *Volkstum* for two terms often found in the
works of Arnim and Görres, *Nation* and *Nationalität*.
Jahn said that the *Volk* is a mixture of all social
classes while the *Volkstum*, a word that he coined, is
the popular thought and sentiment of the common faith
of a folk, the "folk spirit." This concept generated
another term, *Volkstumskunde*, "the science of nationality," to which Jahn wanted to give a very firm foundation.

    Deutsches Volkstum was published in 1810. In
1807-08 Fichte had begun his *Reden an die deutsche
Nation*. But given the abstruseness of Fichte's metaphysics, his work, as Peter Viereck observes, reached
only a limited number of people, while Jahn's book
offered a more practical program in such a colorful
demagogical style that General Blücher, one of the conquerors of Napoleon, called it "the most verbal German
cannon." Although these two books were indeed created
for the same purpose, what was the actual relationship
between them?

    In his *Reden* Fichte was primarily concerned with
formulating the idea of a national organization. But
should this organization be based on the concept of
the "nation-state," a concept implicit in the French
Revolution, which he had initially supported? Or
should it be based on the concept of the "German

people," the original people *par excellence* (the *Urvolk*), with a native, original language (*Ursprache*) --a concept that defined corruption as the acceptance of anything from outside and the failure of the state to maintain its social function?

The first-generation romantics, along with Görres, had recognized how much their original literature had been assisted by "borrowings," one of their most significant insights. Fichte, however, had altogether different concerns; he was interested in the original people, a people with no attributes, in whose midst lives the man who bases his faith on a certain order of things. As he himself states, "This order is the special spiritual nature of man that indeed exists although it certainly cannot be comprehended in any fixed notion--the nature, I mean, from which man himself has proceeded with his actions, his thought, and his faith in eternity, specifically the people from which he is descended and among which he was educated and grew up to be what he now is" (*Reden*, VIII).

Fichte had the same strong interest in the German Middle Ages that Novalis, Tieck, the Schlegels, Arnim, and Görres had. Taking inspiration from the group of romantics led by Schiller and Humboldt, he expressed the idea of the German nation's universal mission, which he extended beyond all measure to extreme and dangerous consequences. But shouldn't the folk to whom he entrusts this mission be offered an education that will raise it to the throne of reason and give it domain over the liberty of the whole world?

This, in essence, is the thesis of Fichte's *Reden*. In this work, nationalism assumes the characteristics of cosmopolitanism, and his analysis of nationalism and cosmopolitanism, introduced to support the new social organization, led him to rediscover in the national spirit the *humus* of a spiritual society that gives meaning to our acts. This thesis concerning the mission of Germany influenced Jahn, who hoped that the German people would unite and expand so that the Slavs and others would become Christian. But Jahn was not a philosopher; he was an agitator who completely disagreed with Fichte about the kind of education a nation needs

in order for it to perceive nationality in the right
way. His concept was, I would say, essentially folkloristic. A derivative thinker and an assimilator,
very rarely did he express personal ideas, but when he
did he expressed them with the conviction that they
were altogether his own. And, after all, wasn't his
coarseness, as Heinrich von Treitschke observes, actually the skillful technique of one who knew how to
hypnotize and persuade?

A declared enemy of France and the French, Jahn was
the archetypal Jacobin, dressed in German clothes. But
while his *Deutsche Volkstum* was to some extent influenced by the ideals of the French Revolution, it was
more strongly influenced by Rousseau's *Considérations
sur le gouvernement de Pologne*. As a youthful student
Jahn had retired to live in a cave, despising the soft,
"Frenchified" society of his times. In doing so, he
obviously intended, ingenuously, to actualize the myth
of the noble savage postulated by Rousseau. When Napoleon invaded his country, however, he immediately presented himself as a volunteer in the crusade against
the French. And so he remained, crusading for German
independence and liberty in the period between 1806 and
1813--a period during which he, as an enemy of all cosmopolitanism, promoted the most intense Prussian
nationalism and formed some athletic societies, which
were merely simplified popular assemblies. But hadn't
these already been announced by Rousseau in his *Considérations*? Moreover, Jahn's athletes all had the same
costume so that they all would appear equal and be
equal. Indeed, Jahn later thought that a national costume, a German costume, was the purest symbol of German
nationality.

Jahn's credo is based primarily on the folk that
creates all of its history. Isn't the folk, he asks,
the creator of the characteristic manifestations that
form it? And aren't we required to preserve the purity
of the folk because (as Friedrich Schlegel suggested)
the purer the people the better they are? "Only the
union of the public masses with the State," Jahn said,
"can dress the skeleton of the State with the warm
flesh and blood of the folk." And, as a good German

Jacobin, he did not hesitate to proclaim the abolishment of feudal classes and their privileges, advocating instead the free ownership of land and a public elementary education for children of all social classes--ideas that Stein partially adopted and liberally applied to the Prussian State. To unify the State and the folk, Jahn argued for the nationalizing of art. During athletic meetings he praised the young people, reading them the *Nibelungenlied*, and he consistently held to the opinion that anthologies aimed at young people certainly should contain German *Lieder*, *Märchen*, and legends of German heroes, since all were products of popular wisdom.

A perceptive German folklorist, Adolf Spamer, has recently said that Jahn was the first to realize that the surest means for the "renovation, investigation, and strengthening of the life of a population" were to be found in usages and popular customs, in songs, language, games, and art. This is not quite accurate, however; as we know, Arnim and Görres had previously considered folk literature as an appropriate instrument for spreading national sentiment, and Jahn, in broadening this idea by extending it to all traditions, was basically going back to Möser. While Arnim, Görres, and A. W. Schlegel viewed folk productions as individual in their creation and collective in their diffusion, Jahn viewed such productions as important expressions of a collective spirit, through which the *Volk* might be educated. It is the folk, then, that educates itself with itself. But here Jahn was adopting Arnim's and Görres's position, inasmuch as he perceived the folk as an instrument of an education in which tradition is not delimited by reason, as Fichte thought, but by the collective and instinctive forces within the folk.

6. Savigny and the "Making of Laws"

In 1814, a few years after Jahn had begun to be known, Friedrich K. von Savigny made quite a different appeal to instinctive and popular forces. At that time Anton Thibaut had thought of unifying German law and creating a civil code, which he believed would save the liberal

institutions that Napoleon had introduced into Germany.
But, Savigny replied, wasn't the creating of a code to
equalize all regions--without taking into consideration
their life and thought--tantamount to recognizing the
validity of the Napoleonic code, which was a monument
of pride and a result of philosophical and ideological
abstruseness?

Savigny believed, as he said as early as 1803 in
his *Das Recht des Besitzes*, that laws should not remain
immutable and that legislators must not be creators but
intelligent scribes attuned to understanding the contemporary spirit. This conviction explains the importance that he attributed (as Möser had previously) to
traditions and therefore implicitly to popular laws.
Although influenced by legal traditions, popular law,
he believed, exists in various ritual forms or habits
expressed by acts, proverbs, maxims, and songs, and
it includes family rights, ownership, contracts, and
punishments. This, he said, is the language of folk
institutions, which locally--here we have Möser as
opposed to Voltaire--are maintained in certain habits
and therefore in acts that serve to determine law.
In Italy Vincenzo Cuoco, a disciple of Vico, had said
that what is right in Paris is wrong in Naples. Similarly, can we expect that what is legally right for
Westphalia is legally right for Asia? In Germany there
were many specific investigations of popular law (for
example, those of Reitemeier, Biener, and Martens, who
had studied various German folk traditions), which were
completed and improved later by one of Savigny's faithful disciples, Georg Friedrich Puchta.

An incomparable scholar of Roman law--everyone has
heard of his *Geschichte des römischen Rechts im
Mittelalter*--Savigny knew that in ancient Rome there
existed next to the *jus scriptum* a *jus non scriptum*, or
what we might call a traditional law. He also understood the significance this traditional law had, not
only among the ancient Germans but also, for example,
in Italy, where statutes had codified some traditional
principles. Savigny not only turned to this tradition
but also romanticized it. From Friedrich Schelling,
Savigny (Brentano's brother-in-law) had learned that a

work of art, like a principle of law, is always the
work of an unconscious, impersonal intelligence. Such
a maxim had guided Barthold Niebuhr when he maintained
in his *Römische Geschichte* (1811-12) that the Roman
nation was the result of the "popular" genius (while,
on the other hand, he went back to Möser and his concept of agrarian communities to establish Rome's primitive history, which he saw in the light of a national
epos conceived according to the theories of Wolf).

Holding firmly to these cultural ideas, Savigny,
as Meinecke observes, justified and sanctioned "all
traditional institutions and sponteneously created
forms of life related to the popular genius, and he
consequently condemned any arbitrary interference in
the life of states as a violation of a naturally
created order." But is this conviction actually,
as we may think, a condemnation of the present, in
the sense that Savigny only hoped for a return to the
old Germanic law--or does its significance rest in
the fact that it brooks no interference with the continuation of developments basic to law itself?

7. *The Significance of Consuetudinary Law and the
   Consuetudinary School*

In his famous essay *Vom beruf unserer Zeit für
Gesetzgebung und Rechtswissenschaft* (1814), Savigny
announced that "each law is created because of internal
forces that silently act, rather than because of the
arbitrary act of a legislator." This was the same view
of law that he later expressed in the journal *Zeitschrift für geschichtliche Rechtswissenschaft*, where he
said that the historical school supposes the substance
of law to be determined by the nation's past. The substance could be of any kind, so long as it derives from
the innermost workings of a nation. There is not, then,
any isolated moment in human existence, for history and
humanity converge in every man. In his own words:

If this is true, an age does not arbitrarily create
its world but rather creates it within the context

of an indissoluble relationship with the past.
Each age, then, must recognize something already
determined, which is both necessary and free--
necessary because it does not depend on the arbitrary acts of the present, free because it does
not derive from outside forces but rather from the
highest nature of the nation as a developing totality. The present age, too, is a part of this
totality, so much so that whatever is given by the
latter can also be freely produced by the former.
History is, then, not a collection of examples,
but rather the only true means of understanding
our present condition.

This appeal to the nation's past, however, should
not invite us to identify an exclusive worship of the
past in Savigny's work. Albert Sorel says that there
is no place for future law in the historical school,
but opposing this thesis is the opinion that Savigny
had of traditional law; he compared traditional law
with all other institutions, which are always in a
state of continuous transformation precisely because
they are institutions. The evolution of law is no
different, then, from the evolution of lieder as viewed
by Arnim; or, as Savigny said, it is no different from
the evolution of language. Because law is a "moment"
of history, it is *in* history that we must discover the
reasons for its necessity: law exists in human experience, in tradition, which is the immediate expression
of popular juridical awareness.

It was then [observes Jhering in commenting on
Savigny's theory] the romantic period for our
poetry. Whoever is scandalized by this application of the romantic concept to jurisprudence and
whoever takes pains to compare the indirect relationships (in two fields) between them will perhaps
agree that I am correct in saying that the historical school could be called, with the same right,
romantic. It indeed offered a truly romantic
representation; that is, it was based on a false
idealization of the teachings of the past,

according to which law took shape without difficulty, effort, or action, like a mushroom in a
field. Harsh reality teaches us precisely the
opposite.

Actually, we cannot draw any lesson from Savigny's
theory unless we consider it in two different respects:
the origin of law and the application of law. Now, in
regard to the origins and sources of law, what importance does folk awareness have? Isn't the answer to
this question mysterious and elusive, inasmuch as a law
thus conceived--a law, namely, that derives from the
juridical awareness of a people--creates not a historical problem but a psychological one? The origins of
law are to be found in its development, and the awareness of a nation is but the awareness of each single
person. There undoubtedly is opposition to law, but
there is also an adherence to law, which is a result
of tradition; this describes not only our past but also
our future, with all its innovations. Savigny's merit
consists in his calling the attention of scholars to
*Gemeinsames Bewusstsein als gemeinsame Überzeugung des
Volks* as a source of law--an effective protest, then,
against all arbitrary legislation and therefore against
the static positions of *jus naturae.* He must also be
credited with postulating the thesis that it is impossible to make laws without considering popular traditions, which are the "life" of the law. Discovering
the origin of law is a philosophical problem, as it is
for all origins. But the historical school (and this
is why it is historical as well as romantic) felt it
was important to promote the study of the historical
facts of law, considering its evolution in relation to
the particular conditions of each population.
Today the problem of traditional law is viewed as
a separate problem, in which law is generally seen as
a unit expressing both a universal and particular will.
That is why traditions, when they remain fluid, often
have the weight of a normative fact to which the legislator addresses himself and about which each nation has
the duty of being aware. But mustn't we be grateful to
Savigny for this insight?

8. The "Volk" as a Human and Humanitarian Organism

The second-generation romantics, of whom Savigny was
so fond, obviously saw the *Volk*, the entire nation (of
which the lower class is a living part), as an organism
in which all classes and cultures meet under the same
laws. Capable of national awareness because it preserves pure, uncontaminated forms of the creative
spirit presiding over the race, the *Volk*, a repository
of conservative forces, was to be called to an eminent-
ly revolutionary function. It would assume the character of Rousseau's *bon sauvage*, with one major difference, which has been strongly underlined by Walzel:
German Romanticism would renounce the hope of guiding
man to an uncertain happiness in an ignorant world,
preferring instead to guide him to a unique, superior
spiritual and *cultural* perfection. The *Volk*, in other
words, would be called to give life to the concept of
nation--and, through nation, to the State--but it would
also be asked to contribute the results of its intellectual heritage to a national education. In addition
to philosophy, literature, law, and folklore, music too
would attempt to "educate"; consider, for example,
Albrecht Weber, whose works generally offered an interpretation of nature (or of the German spirit, to be
even more precise) and whose influence, in certain
respects, would last until Wagner or, as Massimo Mila
says, at least until his *Tannhäuser*.
     Precisely because this was so, the *Volk* became not
merely a cultural concept, although literature is the
principal field of its being, but also a human concept;
indeed, expressions such as "folk genius" and "folk
spirit," which recur in the works of the second-
generation romantics, would be meaningless if we sought
to reduce them to their naturalistic terms.
     When Hegel tried to clarify these expressions,
especially the last one (which had been used by Arnim,
Arndt, and Savigny), he did not hesitate to consider
the State as a force intimately connected with art,
religion, and philosophy, subjects that he called upon
in order to define the *Volksgeist*. In the spirit of a
people, he said, there is a singular principle that is

uniformly realized in all its manifestations and
aspirations. We know that Hegel considered the spirit
as something that "is" only because it "becomes," and
he believed that history itself is everything about
the spirit that is collected in "perfect dignity."
As he says in his *Vorlesungen über die Philosophie der
Geschichte*, "The very essence of Spirit is activity:
it realizes its potentiality and makes itself its own
deed, its own work. This is also true of the spirit
of a people. This Spirit erects itself into an objective world, one that exists and persists in a particular form of religious worship, morality, customs, constitution, and political laws--the whole complex of
its institutions--in the events and transactions that
make up its history. That is its work--and that is
what a people *is*" (IX, § 44).

This "Spirit," which finds its incarnation in the
Prussian State, is, as Meinecke believes, similar but
not identical to that of the romantics and Savigny.
In both, people are what their works and their spiritual inheritances are. And among these works, those
produced by folklife and folklore were considered to
be the consequence of a renewed spiritual heritage,
one that produced customs, cults, *Lieder*, *Märchen*--in
a word, popular traditions reflecting the best part
of each nation. In this the romantics had perhaps
exaggerated; but, following the lead of the pre-
romantics, they attached an importance to the concept
of folklore that gave a new, provocative impulse to
German literature. This literature, now intimately
related to the concept of the *Volksgeist*, was to have
its strongest advocates in the brothers Grimm.

CHAPTER XIII

THE BROTHERS GRIMM

1. Folk Poetry as "Miracle"

We can say with some confidence that the literature of
the brothers Grimm is primarily based on the concept
of folk poetry. But is this concept the one that their
predecessors had forged under pre-romantic influences,
or did it take on a new aspect and function in their
work? Their conviction that folk poetry must be considered as a factor of national life aligned the brothers
Grimm with Brentano, Herder, Arnim, and Görres, who
maintained that, while the community is important, folk
poetry is produced by specific poetic individuals. The
Grimms, however, had a quite different thesis. They
argued that folk poetry is anonymous, impersonal, and
collective; moreover, they argued that folk poetry, like
the language in which it is expressed and the mythology
to which it is related, has essentially divine origins.
In his famous 1808 essay published in Arnim's magazine, the *Zeitung für Einsiedler*, the elder brother,
Jacob, vigorously supported this thesis, one that
denigrated previous romantic achievements in the realm
of folk poetry. In distinguishing *Naturpoesie* from
Kunstpoesie, he observed that the latter is a "contemplated" poetry and therefore of human origins, produced
by educated people. This is not to say, he adds, that
in later stages folk poetry does not have its own
authors, but such authors remain anonymous in the
community that provides them with interests and
aspirations; and even if these authors did appear, we
would see that they belonged to a class of simple,
uneducated people.

"We would like to have proof for these facts,"
Arnim commented in a note that followed Jacob's article. Arnim did not regard himself as the least bit
ignorant, and yet in his *Des Knaben Wunderhorn* he
attempted to prove that even a learned poet could produce folk poetry when he put himself in the state of
grace proper to the folk poet. But couldn't his comment be extended to the considerations that, in 1808,
Wilhelm Grimm had offered about the *Nibelungenlied* in
the *Studien*, directed by Karl Daub and Friedrich
Creuzer? Less dogmatic than his brother but equally
concerned with the question of origins, Wilhelm believed that folk poetry was born with its poets, which
apparently put him at odds with his brother. But while
he seems here to accept opinions that other romantics
had on this subject, immediately thereafter he takes
back his words and concludes that these poets are in-
voluntarily such, their works having been neither conscious nor contemplated.

In reviewing Rasmus Nyerup's work a few years
later, in 1811, Wilhelm again maintained that a folksong is produced unconsciously; furthermore, he associated this "unconsciousness" with a "mystic form."
In other words, folk poetry is a human manifestation
of the divine. "It is naked," he said in 1811, in
his introduction to the *Altdänische Heldenlieder*, "and
it reflects the very image of God." In saying this
he was not categorizing poetry, for despite its fundamental unity it nevertheless has its own national
character: "The divine, the spirit of poetry, is the
same for all peoples and has but one source, which is
why in different places we may see some apparent
resemblances, an earlier correspondence, a secret
relationship that suggests a common ancestor although
the generating principle has been lost. There is an
analogous development but the external conditions are
different, which is why we find, along with this intimate accord, a difference in external structure."

Folk poetry, then, was regarded by the two brothers
as the product of a collective spirit, which explains
its anonymity. They did not worry about distinguishing
the creation of such poetry (which is always an indi-

vidual act) from its diffusion (which makes the poetry
anonymous). In their view, only the "poetry-making
folk," the opposite of the artist, exists: it is not
"the sum or aggregate of individuals" but rather the
"growth and interpenetration of their spirit." The
folk, for the Grimms, thus acquired "specific physical
characteristics," and, as such, it is the poet, the
creator of *Naturpoesie*.

"I have often supposed the difference between
Naturpoesie and *Kunstpoesie* to be quite clear," Jacob
said later in the preface to his *Über den altdeutschen
Meistergesang*, published in 1811. This is because the
distinction was for him, as for his brother, a given
and intuitively known fact, a dogmatic truth. Jacob
did not really try to answer Arnim's sensible observation that there can be no poetry without a poet and
that even an anonymous poet must have a spark of art
in his soul; rather, he replied to Arnim by switching
roles and preaching a sermon. In answering Arnim's
letters, Jacob re-emphasized his interest in ancient
German epics, which he believed to be of supernatural
origin, and he argued that only ancient poetry (whose
living past is preserved in *Lieder* and *Märchen*) is
totally innocent and pure because it was created
spontaneously. He delighted in images taken directly
from nature; for example, he compared the song of the
folk to the song of a bird, while the mystery of communal poetry reminded him of the mystery of streams
converging in a river. Later, however, when he was
forced to confront the problem that Arnim had put to
him, he placed his interlocutor before his own conscience. In a letter dated 1811, he admonished Arnim:
"If you share my belief that religion springs from a
divine relation, that language too has a wholly miraculous origin, and that it has not been created by
human invention, you must also believe that ancient
poetry and its forms, the source of rhyme and alliteration, probably appeared in an instant. . . ."

Thus, folk poetry took on the characteristics of
a miracle--and one must either accept or reject a
miracle, not discuss it. This is the limitation of
the Grimms' theory about folk poetry, a theory to which

honors and merits have been awarded. The brothers
Grimm placed folk poetry on altars. Like constitu-
tional kings, it was invested with divine grace.

2. Poetry, Epopee, and History

The brothers Grimm had a similar theory about the origin of the epopee, which they believed to have originated in the same way that folk poetry did (a point
that Herder and Bürger had also made). But why did
they feel compelled to say that originally a nation's
epopee was simply its folk poetry? It was no longer
a matter of asserting, as the pre-romantics had, that
folk poetry was a form of national epopee; nor was it
a matter of perceiving great poets like Homer and
Dante as "popular," as Herder had. In their appraisal
of *Naturpoesie* the brothers Grimm agreed with the opinion of Vico, who thought of poetry as the first voice
of man. Nor were they far from Herder, who had considered *Naturpoesie* as a poetry that is totally "natural."
But how does this poetry made from nature--"divine
nature," they say, as if complementing Herder--become
realized in the epopee first forged by each nation?
     The Grimms' theory about this subject is based on
the following propositions: (1) the primitive form of
poetry is the epopee, which sings of the enterprises
of gods and heroes, expressing the community's thoughts
and hopes; (2) the epopee is to be partly identified
with mythology; (3) both myth and epopee are forms of
folk poetry. It is difficult to say what part each of
the two brothers had in the formulation of this theory,
although Jacob was much more inclined than Wilhelm
to generalize. As early as 1808, in the previously
cited *Studien*, Wilhelm demonstrated an interest in the
Nibelungenlied, and he had maintained that the epopee
springs spontaneously not from man but from the collective spirit of the folk. Moreover, he was especially
interested in applying Wolf's theory to the *Nibelungenlied*, a task performed later by Karl Lachmann. More
dogmatic even here, Jacob, in the introduction to his
Meistergesang, reiterated what he had written in the

Zeitung für Einsiedler: he maintained that the epopee contains the most ancient history of the past and that this history, often expressed in myth, is identified with the poetry of that past.

The brothers Grimm, then, not only identified poetry with the epopee, which in their view was initially created in short poems, but they also saw a relationship between poetry and history in such identifications. Thus, they ultimately reduced the epopee to an internal necessary force emanating not from the individual artist but rather from the "poetry-making folk." Or we might say that in their view the vital, active genius of the nation returns personified in the work of the race considered as a single individual, an idea later developed in Schelling's *Zur Philosophie der Kunst*. But this "genius" was now illuminated by its divine origin; and because it is the folk that creates the epopee, it was obvious to the Grimms that the epopee must be not only the epitome of innocence and purity but also the expression of historical truth.

Even at that time there were many critics of this theory, which the Grimms had colored with a certain charm. For example, A. W. Schlegel, who had proclaimed the importance of the individual in folk poetry in the *Heidelbergische Jahrbücher* of 1815, rejected the thesis that an epopee can spring forth spontaneously (even before it has been created, to use Ernest Renan's expression), however much it might be related to the origins. It is true, he observed, that the actual origin of many poems, growing from a small seed and developing only in the course of centuries, is lost in the obscurity of time. But does this mean that an epic poem has no author? Let us even allow, he added, that folk poems and legends, the bases of the epopee, are the common property of many ages and nations. But can the works of the spirit be generated by a common creation without there being specific individual creations? Nor was he persuaded by the argument about there being a relationship between history and epopee, although he admitted that "oral tradition, once it becomes poetic tradition, may prove to have some features that historical truth omits."

Schlegel's observations about the origins of the epopee, which complemented Arnim's, naturally did not convince the brothers Grimm. Here too they stood up for the "miracle," which, in their view, necessarily had to have two aspects, given the identity between poetry and epopee that they proposed. Once again we see the limitation of the Grimms. Schlegel, however, must be credited, as Tonnelat observes, with making sure that the Grimms would purify the quality of their own works, in which, along with metaphysical abstractions (easily eliminated today but then most important), we find some attitudes demonstrating their comprehensive critical awareness.

3. *"Kinder- und Hausmärchen" and the Tone of Folk Literature*

To their credit, the brothers Grimm clearly understood the simple, elementary character of folk poetry (or *Naturpoesie*) as opposed to *Kunstpoesie*: it permits the human heart to express itself fully. Ideas such as these did not go unobserved by their contemporaries. Friedrich Diez, in his early essay *Die Poesie der Troubadours* (1826), argued that the basic characteristic of folk poetry is its simplicity in content and metrical form. Later, in 1838, Hegel, in his *Vorlesungen über die Aesthetik*, re-emphasized the individual character of folk poetry (which he identified with songs) but maintained that it does not need "much content or inner greatness and loftiness, for dignity, nobility, and purity of thought would actually be obstacles to the pleasure of immediate expression." For the Grimms this "immediate expression" was not at all in contrast to the "inner greatness" of *Naturpoesie*. But didn't their premise inevitably imply a methodological principle, the necessity of an absolute fidelity to the folkloristic text?

In recently commenting on this aspect of the Grimms' most famous work, however, Lutz Mackensen had these observations to make:

A lucky event has recently revealed an early version of *Kinder- und Hausmärchen*, the Oelenberg
manuscript, which was named for the place where
it was discovered. We are in a good position,
then, to follow the origin and development of this
very important collection. Begun originally by
Jacob Grimm, who hoped to produce new material
for the history and interpretation of German myth,
the work then passed to the artistically expert
hands of Wilhelm. Although Jacob was primarily
interested in the subject of these tales, Wilhelm
wanted to emphasize their poetic elements. Lacking immediate models, he combined what he had heard
with what he had selected, giving his own fairy-
tale style to his work; that is, he put the tales
in the form in which he thought they should be
told. To reconstruct the original story, he often
combined different versions of the same tale taken
from both folk tradition and books, thus forming a
new story. He used a variety of formulas from
past and present times to obtain a smooth style.
The result was a particular "fairy-tale-like" style
that, from the Grimms onwards, has prevailed in all
our fairy tales.

Kinder- und Hausmärchen is now universally considered
to be one of the greatest of children's books. But
does this work put the brothers Grimm in a class with
Basile and Perrault? Or were they motivated by the
same considerations that had spurred Arnim and Brentano
in their reworking of the literature in *Des Knaben
Wunderhorn*?
     Actually, the discovery of the Oelenberg manuscript
was not necessary for determining the methodology followed by the Grimms in the collecting and reworking of
their materials. It is sufficient to read the introductions and notes in the seven editions of their volumes. Besides, Tonnelat had performed such a minute,
precise investigation of the Grimms' method even before
the discovery of the Oelenberg manuscript, and he had
come to the same conclusions as Lutz Mackensen. But we
have to be more specific.

First of all, we must observe that the Grimms had
not initially intended to write a children's book;
furthermore, they certainly were not influenced by *Des
Knaben Wunderhorn*, for which Jacob had collected the
first tales (later omitted because this work came to
be limited to folk poetry alone). With *Kinder- und
Hausmärchen*, the brothers Grimm hoped to provide an
authentic, genuine work of folk literature. Because
of this, as they expressly said, their concern in
gathering the tales was accuracy and truth: "We have
not added anything. We have not embellished any motif
nor taken away anything from these tales." But even
then, Arnim, who was himself an expert in readaption,
wrote to Jacob: "You will not make me believe, Wilhelm
and you, that you have copied the tales as you have
heard them, even if you believe so yourselves." As a
matter of fact, the Grimms did believe they had collected their texts very faithfully. The important
question, however, is what they meant by fidelity to
a text.

4. A Work of Art Born from a Methodological Error

In collecting *Kinder- und Hausmärchen*, whose various
editions increasingly grew in number, the brothers
Grimm primarily used oral traditions, the traditions
of folk narrators. They vividly remembered, for example, a peasant woman of Niederzwehren who greatly contributed to enriching their materials: "We have had
the fortune of knowing, in the village of Niederzwehren,
near Cassel, a peasant woman whom we must thank for the
most beautiful stories of our second volume. She was
the wife of a poor animal breeder; she was still vigorous and not older than fifty. . . . She carried these
ancient tales in her memory, a gift that nature offers
to few people indeed. She told her stories with great
pleasure, and, if we preferred, in a way that could
easily be taken by dictation."
The brothers Grimm, as they said, used dictation
to secure the stories they had collected. Once they
had the tales in hand, however, their methodological

doubts began. In the introduction to *Kinder- und Hausmärchen*, the Grimms insisted on their fidelity to the texts, but they immediately added:

> We have given the substance of these tales just as we have received it. Understandably, however, the way of telling the details is chiefly due to us. Still, we have made every effort to report anything we have judged characteristic so that we can offer this collection in its natural, true form. Anyone who takes interest in a work of this kind knows that it is impossible to occupy oneself with such matters using the method of an indifferent or insensitive collector; on the contrary, one needs to pay great attention to distinguishing the simplest, purest, and most complete version of a tale from a false version. Wherever we have found that the variations in different versions complement one another, we have given them as one story. But when two versions differ sharply, we have given preference to the better one and given the other in the notes.

Thus, not only was the narrator's personality, which makes a tale popular, lost to the Grimms, but they also missed the very character of variants, each of which is always an original creation. Once again Arnim requested Jacob to notice that a folktale is always in perpetual transformation and that not only is it adapted very slowly in successive periods but it also tends to alter from speaker to speaker; in fact, even a child will never repeat the story that his mother has told him in quite the same way. The Grimms did not deny the narrator's personal contribution to the story; they argued, however, that even if a story does tend to change, its basis is immutable, and the significance of the variants consists in the fact that each conserves some essential elements. Only the literary expression of the story, then, changes from century to century (or from author to author, to be more precise). But do we have the right to change this expression, with variants in hand, so that the original basis remains in each account?

The Grimms sought for a common, impersonal basis
in the folktale, which they regarded as the tale's
"essence." From this premise came the concept of
elaboration, which in their view was merely a textual
restoration. But how one could ever hope to make a
work impersonal with this restoration, which was their
aim, is certainly a mystery. Their "personal" work
resulted in an innocent and elementary narration of
German tales that corresponded to the language of the
folk. This style did not satisfy Brentano, who considered it childish, but the Schlegels, Arnim, and
especially Goethe liked it; Goethe, in fact, recommended *Kinder- und Hausmärchen* to Charlotte Stein as
a book made to please children.

On the one hand, then, interest in folklore has
given to children's literature (and not only to children's literature) one of the most beautiful books in
the history of literature; on the other hand, a philological interest in textual restoration created the
artistic elaboration responsible for the charm of
Kinder- und Hausmärchen. These tales are certainly
in the same class as the *Wunderhorn,* and because they
maintain the tone typical of folk poetry, they are
even closer to the folk spirit. But although the
brothers Grimm were convinced that they had discovered
folk language, they had actually discovered their *own*
language. From a philological interest and a methodological error, a work of art was born.

5. Folktales as National Epopee

Kinder- und Hausmärchen was not intended to be only a
work of art. The two volumes of the first edition,
published in 1812 and 1815 respectively, contain some
notes in which the brothers Grimm talk about the relationship between folk story and epic legend, between
folktale and myth. But as new editions of these volumes followed, beginning with the 1819 edition (which
is the second), tales were presented to the reader in
new and increasingly refined versions credited to
Wilhelm but always with Jacob's consent. This is to

be explained by the success of their work, which had moved from the scientific field for which it was intended and into the hands of children.

The Grimms decided to provide a more scientific third volume containing bibliography, notes, and observations. This volume, entrusted to Wilhelm, was published in 1822, after they had edited *Deutsche Sagen*, published in two volumes, the first in 1816 and the second in 1818. In this second collection the brothers Grimm again followed their procedure of eliminating individual inventions, restoring each legend's original text, and conserving folk language. "The legends we have collected," Jacob wrote to Arnim in 1815, when he and his brother were collecting *Deutsche Sagen*, "contain fragments of German heroic legends." But wasn't this legend *in nuce* in *Kinder- und Hausmärchen*?

In the various notes in the first edition of this work, and especially in the introduction to the second edition, the Grimms had argued for the idea that fairy tales should not be considered simply as imaginative works but also as important historical documents. In their view history was not--and this is in answer to A. W. Schlegel--the relating of chronological facts but rather the reporting of everything the folk thinks and dreams of, whatever it may be. Folktales tell us about a Golden Age when nature was full of life, when plants and birds talked, nymphs slept in the waters, and the moon and stars mingled with man. This enchanted world reveals a universal spirit that has felt the magic touch of the country that embraces it.

In the third volume of *Kinder- und Hausmärchen*, observations such as these were collected and discussed. Wilhelm began by quickly tracing the history of the genre of the fairy tale, which is only a simple, elementary story, and he made some perceptive observations about the *Pentamerone* (which the brothers Grimm thought of translating but which was actually translated later by Felix Liebrecht in 1846), about Perrault, and about the famous *Cabinet des fées*, demonstrating an extensive knowledge of Oriental, Arabic, Germanic, and Hindu stories. But the importance of his

book is not in this *excursus*; rather, its chief importance is in its having established a relationship
between tale and myth. He outlines the relationship
clearly, with the result that all the German world,
the world of myth, is found to reside in the folktale:
Sleeping Beauty becomes Brunhild; in many tales one
often finds Siegfried in the personage of a hunter who,
after eating the heart of a fabulous bird, possesses
the faculty of understanding the language of animals;
Cinderella is the same mythological personage that
Gudrun symbolizes--and so on. In this world Wilhelm
discovered the deepest beliefs of his ancestors--their
myths, which had been thought forgotten and lost, and
their religion, a living and spirited paganism fused
and confused with Christianity.

    Kinder- und Hausmärchen, then, is important because
it preserves the beliefs of ancient Germanic peoples
and transforms them into poetry, with the result that
the tales often appear to be fragments of primitive
poetry. In this study, which used the "survivals"
method previously followed by Fontenelle and Lafitau,
Wilhelm attempted to explain as a scholar what he had
perceived as an artist. But in this explanation he,
like his brother, demonstrated that *Naturpoesie* must
be considered from an ethnographical as well as an
aesthetic perspective. In short, the folktale, like
the folksong, is (or can be) an aesthetic work. Such
a work, however, contains beliefs and superstitions
that must be studied if we want to approach the essential structure of the story. This approach not only
takes nothing away from the aesthetic value of the
stories but also serves to explain meanings that otherwise are not always clear.

6. Poetry, Law, and Mythology

This was also the path traveled by Jacob Grimm, to whom
we are indebted for a truly imposing work, the *Deutsche
Rechtsalterthümer*, published in 1828. In several essays
the brothers Grimm had considered law in the same way as
myth and myth in the same way as language. The folk, in

their opinion, dimly perceives the sanctified character
of traditional laws. This explains why there is something irreducible in consuetudinary rights, an element
that the folk spirit could have produced because it is
obviously a contribution of a superior will. Thus, law
and poetry appear to have the same origins. The study
of juridical fragments, which are found in the document
of traditional law (usually hidden within rites and cus
toms), should make ancient German wisdom evident. It i
precisely on these bases that Jacob established his
Deutsche Rechtsalterthümer. In his essay *Poesie im
Recht*, Jacob had previously observed, "For a long time
now we have recognized an attachment to our fathers'
customs, as well as a repugnance for destroying them, a
one of our nation's most important principles. Were
this not so, we would not today possess a poetry whose
antiquity and value are comparable to ancient Greek
poetry; even today customs, speech, and peasant habits
are not entirely unrelated to ancient legends and laws.

This heritage was given the greatest blessing in
another of Jacob's works, *Deutsche Mythologie*, publishe
in 1835. The *Edda* and the *Nibelungenlied*, two great
poems that the brothers had examined closely, were thei
major reference points, but this study was not limited
to these poems or to the beliefs that they cited to
document the idea of an "ancient" Germany. Jacob also
availed himself of medieval chronicles, hagiographies,
and studies of German antiquity in order to identify
survivals that folklore conserves in all its manifestations (rites, customs, proverbs, dialects, songs,
legends). This is the important contribution of his
Mythologie, a work which, like his *Deutsche Rechtsalter
thümer*, gives a broad treatment of folklore issues,
especially because Jacob did not limit himself to comparisons between myths and rites, tales and beliefs, an
so on; rather, he always attempted to delve into the
significance of such manifestations, critically examining and interpreting them.

Today it is obvious that in these works Grimm attributed to a remote antiquity manifestations actually
having nothing to do with it, producing comparisons
that, although often bold and ingenius, were purely

casual and fallacious. The result, as Iǔriǐ Sokolov observes, was that he confused the identical with the similar. But leaving aside this observation, can we deny Jacob credit for providing the first scientific systemization of folklore in his works? And can we deny him credit for providing a picturesque reinvocation of paganism and German Christianity, which previously had been cleverly concealed in *Kinder- und Hausmärchen* and *Deutsche Sagen*. We should add that Jacob was a prolific, imaginative writer, his language creating an atmosphere in which the reader often remains dazed and dazzled, which explains his success. Like his brother, Jacob loved to wander among the clouds, just like the characters in his fairy tales, and he loved to fly back to Germany's ancient past, riding on a broom; but how often did he descend from the clouds to *terra firma*, where he could walk with sure steps?

7. The "Grammatik"

To walk on the *terra firma* of his specific field of study meant that Jacob had to confront the question of language, the language in which songs, fables, stories, and myths are expressed. In the *Heidelbergische Jahrbücher*, A. W. Schlegel had invited the brothers Grimm to the study of German grammar for a more exact interpretation of folkloristic texts. This question assailed them increasingly as they treated ancient German literature.

The most important work in this area was taken up by Jacob. In 1819 he had published the *Deutsche Grammatik*, in which he traced the formation and development of the German language, comparing dialects of the same base. In his *Grammatik* Jacob followed the teachings of Savigny (to whom the *Grammatik* is dedicated), who believed language and law to be the specific functions of nations, contributing to their individuality. Although Jacob was convinced (as Hamann and the "second" Herder had been) of language's divine origins, he also believed that there was a profound similarity between language and law, in that both are simultaneously old and young and both have a history.

In a well-known essay of his, published in 1812, Humboldt had considered mankind as a giant plant whose branches embraced all the earth. The time had come, he said, to study the multiple relationships between natio and their influences, and he suggested that the difference between nations was to be found in language. This essay did not, however, identify the principles underlying the relationship between various languages, which had previously been hinted at by Sir William Jones and Friedrich Schlegel. These principles would be clearly identified some years later by Franz Bopp, author of the famous *Über das Conjugationssystem der Sanskritsprache in Vergleichung mit jenem der griechischen, lateinischen, persischen und germanischen Sprache*, a work that amply demonstrated the relationship of Sanskrit to Greek, Latin, and other Indo-European languages Thus, comparative linguistics and Indo-European glottology came into being, followed closely by the baptism of Jacob's *Grammatik*. On the one hand, Jacob accepted theories suggesting a common origin for all Indo-European languages, and on the other hand he argued for the existence of a primitive Germanic language, an argu ment deriving from his study of the dialectal varieties in which the German language is articulated. "No peopl on the earth," he said, "possesses a language whose his tory can be compared to that of the Germans."

We should observe that the Grimms were fascinated by the romantic idea of an "original" and "primitive" civilization, in the sense that Herder gave to these two terms. Beginning with their first works, they witnessed that fascination in the folkloristic heritage of their country--in the vehicle, that is, of their own national traditions.

8. The Patriotism of the Brothers Grimm

The work of the brothers Grimm specifically attempted to illustrate national traditions. The result was that they continued a national movement that believed the liberty of the present resided in the past. Educated in and disciples of Savigny's historical school, the

brothers Grimm agreed with their teacher's idea that
"each historical process does not spring from conscious
individual intention but rather carries in itself its
own organic life, which develops through the effect of
a force inaccessible to reason."

Sensitive to romantic influences and friends of the
Schlegels, Arnim, Brentano, and Görres, the brothers
Grimm were brought to the study of folklore by their
interest in the Middle Ages. Ever since their philological and literary apprenticeship, they had viewed
this period as their country's age of liberty, as the
essential stage of its civilization--an original and
primitive civilization on which the concepts of folk
and nation are based. We know about the trepidation
with which the elder of the brothers, Jacob, approached
Bodmer's collection of *Minnelieder* while still a youth;
he found this work in Savigny's well-stocked library,
and he read it twenty times from beginning to end. We
also know how impressed he was with the introduction
that Tieck had written for a selection from this col-
lection--and Wilhelm's initial interests were quite the
same. It is natural, then, that the two brothers perceived the past in national terms, idealized it, and
even deified it. Their patriotism was energetic, fervent, and aggressive, as is demonstrated by the enthusiasm (spurred by the *Rettungsgedanke* that was becoming
increasingly more popular in their country) with which
they applied themselves to the collecting of tales,
legends, myths, proverbs, and beliefs, which they regarded as emanations of the German Spirit.

As we know, the first volume of *Kinder- und Hausmärchen* was published on the eve of the battle of
Leipzig, when the Grimms felt humiliated, Jacob later
said, to be in the grip of such a proud and scornful
enemy. It is significant that, a year before, Wilhelm
observed in his *Altdänische Heldenlieder, Balladen und
Märchen*: "Folktales deserve greater attention than
they have had so far, not only because of their poetic
form, whose charm has provided a precious lesson and
sweet remembrance for whoever has understood it in his
childhood, *but also because they are part of our
national poetry*." Despite its stern composure, their

work had the quality of a national challenge, a political attitude that marked the brothers Grimm throughout
their lives.

Liberal spirits that they were, the Grimms did not
hesitate in 1837 to sign the famous protest drawn up
by the historian Friedrich Christoph Dahlmann against
the government of Hanover for its having violated the
constitution. As a result, Jacob, who had taught at
the University of Göttingen for seven years, was ex-
pelled. His expulsion, however, allowed him to dedi-
cate himself more intensely to studying the language
and dialects of his Germany, an activity that now
interested him more than anything else he had ever
done. The work that the brothers Grimm accomplished
after 1837 was extensive. In 1854 they began the
compilation of their *Deutsches Wörterbuch*, while previously in 1848 Jacob published, as an appendix to
his grammar, the two volumes of the *Geschichte der
deutschen Sprache*. In a sense, these works grew out
of the *Deutsche Grammatik*, which was, as Benvenuto
Terracini comments, a gospel of glottology composed
in the heat of the German revolt; on the other hand,
in examining the linguistic prehistory of Germanism,
the *Geschichte der deutschen Sprache* expressed the
concerns and national sentiments of the 1848 German.
This can also be said of the *Wörterbuch*, which is a
gold mine of folkloristic information and the apex of
the studies undertaken between 1812 and 1848.

The brothers Grimm did everything in their power
to complement Stein's *Monumenta Germaniae Historica* by
providing Germany with a *corpus* wherein the past fuses
with the present to give a precise, unified view of
the German nation. It was the desire of the brothers
Grimm to produce or to reproduce conveniently illustrated texts of the ancient German literature that had
so greatly excited their predecessors; but their major
interest was to rebuild, with elements offered them by
living folklore, everything that tradition had conserved of the most sacred. Their work developed on
two fronts: on one front, specific studies involving
the collection and publication of texts and, on the
other front, broad syntheses involving general theories

about language, law, tales, mythology, and epopee.
The two brothers, as we have seen, did not always
collaborate, but even when they did so, they always
had the sole aim of elevating the Germanic world to a
self-contained poetical and political organism, which
increasingly took on the eternal value of a symbol of
the very folk who inspired it. The folk, Wilhelm had
expressly declared, "is a concept in which the power
of the Spirit is perfectly epitomized." Precisely
because of this, the work of the brothers Grimm dominated German culture, instilling a national concept
with scientific research. Meanwhile, however, what
was the attitude of Romanticism toward folklore in
other European nations--and what influence did the
brothers Grimm and their predecessors have on these
nations?

CHAPTER XIV

RETURN TO THE ORIGINS

1. Aspects of English Romanticism: Wordsworth and Coleridge

It is generally believed that the central documents of Western European Romanticism are *Lyrical Ballads* (England), the *Allemagne* (France), and *Lettera semiseria di Grisostomo* (Italy), a proposition that we are certainly willing to accept. But did Romanticism, we must immediately ask, emerge in other Western European countries in the same way and with the same characteristics as in Germany? Whatever might have been the European experiences from which it took its ideals, German Romanticism was always based on its own particular philosophical substratum and thus was a powerful organism in which those previous experiences converged. This helps to explain the particular condition in which Germany found herself during those years. Romanticism, however congenial it might have been to each country in which it developed, was inevitably a result of earlier pre-romantic movements, which was the case for the value system on which German Romanticism was built.

This too was the case in England, where *Lyrical Ballads* proposed, as is expressly stated in the preface a return to the popular traditions previously promoted by *Ossian*, the *Reliques*, and other pre-romantic works. But we must be precise. Written by William Wordsworth and Samuel Taylor Coleridge (whose travel in Germany provided insight and inspiration), *Lyrical Ballads*, as the authors declare, attempted "to give the charm of novelty to things of every day, and to excite a feeling

analogous to the supernatural" (Wordsworth's purpose)
and to treat "persons and characters supernatural, or
at least romantic; yet so as to transfer from our
inward nature a human interest and a semblance of
truth. . ." (Coleridge's purpose).[1] But despite this
observation, *Lyrical Ballads* actually followed a national tradition that had been expressed in the works
of James Thomson and Thomas Gray. Coleridge and Wordsworth searched for a new language, their own language,
one free from the rules of poetic diction, which is
why Coleridge used archaisms to create an atmosphere
of the past and Wordsworth used expressions that we
commonly find in the language of children and the folk.
   Given their intentions, it is understandable that
Wordsworth would cite the precepts of the *Reliques*,
which he contrasted to *Ossian*:

> Contrast, in this respect, the effect of Macpher-
> son's publication with the *Reliques* of Percy, so
> unassuming, so modest in their pretensions!--I
> have already stated how much Germany is indebted
> to this latter work; and for our own country, its
> poetry has been absolutely redeemed by it. I do
> not think that there is an able writer in verse
> of the present day who would not be proud to
> acknowledge his obligations to the *Reliques*; I
> know that it is so with my friends; and, for my-
> self, I am happy in this occasion to make a public
> avowal of my own.[2]

Wordsworth was especially fond of Norse ballads, which
he had heard when he was a child (a point that brings
The Prelude to mind). His preference for such ballads
coincided with his love of nature, particularly rustic
life, where everything is simple and natural and one

[1]Samuel Taylor Coleridge, *Biographia Literaria*
(London: J. M. Dent and Sons, 1906), p. 161.
   [2]"Essay, Supplementary to the Preface," in *The
Prose Works of William Wordsworth*, ed. W. J. B. Owen
and Jane Worthington Smyser (Oxford: Clarendon Press,
1974), III, 78.

can hear the voice of God. This love of nature explains his interest in children, beggars, and reapers,
where individual feelings give way to the affirmation
of collective values. This is also why Coleridge (who
was quite interested in the lower classes and ballads)
regarded the folk as a primary subject for artistic
treatment. For Wordsworth, moreover, the folk was the
expression of all men's desire to join in nature's
infinite embrace.

"In Wordsworth," observes Christopher Caudwell,
"the revolt takes the form of a return to the natural
man, just as it does in Shelley. Wordsworth, like
Shelley profoundly influenced by French Rousseauism,
seeks freedom, beauty--all that is not now in man
because of his social relations--in 'Nature.'"[3] This
is true in the sense that a child and a peasant, both
being close to nature, reminded Wordsworth of the
divinity of their origins. Wordsworth, in other
words, did not think of a liberty that comes from
rebellion. Liberty, in his view, is the result of a
union between nature, man, and God.

This idea of a better humanity, however, cannot
be separated from the idea of liberty. Shortly after
the publication of *Lyrical Ballads*, didn't the English
call the fight against Napoleon a fight for liberty?
Napoleon was outside the country's borders, but he was
a threat. Thus, while evangelicals and Methodists
argued that this was no time to be thinking of social
equality, Wordsworth's ideas increasingly turned into
a didactic-social morality. His morality was imbued
with a severe Puritanism (against which Byron later
rebelled), but it was still sensitive to the values of
emotional and traditional life, the source of one's
being and one's becoming.

2. Scott: Folklorist and Novelist

The attitude of Walter Scott was quite the same as

[3]*Illusion and Reality* (1937; rpt. New York: International Publishers, 1947), p. 92.

Wordsworth's, and on him, as on Wordsworth, the impact
of Percy's *Reliques* was profound. He himself says in
his *Autobiography*:

> But above all, I then first became acquainted with
> Bishop Percy's *Reliques of Ancient Poetry*. . . .
> I remember well the spot where I read these volumes
> for the first time. It was beneath a huge platanus-
> tree. . . . The summer day sped onward so fast,
> that notwithstanding the sharp appetite of thirteen,
> I forgot the hour of dinner, was sought for with
> anxiety, and was still found entranced in my intel-
> lectual banquet. To read and to remember was in
> this instance the same thing, and henceforth I over-
> whelmed my schoolfellows, and all who would hearken
> to me, with tragical recitations from the ballads
> of Bishop Percy. The first time, too, I could
> scrape a few shillings together, which were not
> common occurrences with me, I bought unto myself a
> copy of these beloved volumes, nor do I believe I
> ever read a book half so frequently, or with half
> the enthusiasm.[4]

This enthusiasm led him, at the age of thirty, to compile a collection of Scottish ballads, which, four years
after the appearance of *Lyrical Ballads*, was published
with the title *Minstrelsy of the Scottish Border*. His
biographer, John Gibson Lockhart, tells us that Scott
wandered among the ruins of the castles near the Scottish border for seven consecutive years, studying all
the manifestation of folklife in that region. Scott
already was looking upon folklore with the interest of
an antiquarian, historian, and artist. In the *Minstrelsy* these interests of his coalesced. On the one hand,
he collected (although sometimes changing) historical
and romantic ballads, thus contributing to preserving
interest in the Middle Ages and local and national folk
traditions; on the other hand, he created some ballads
of his own.

[4]*Memoirs of the Life of Sir Walter Scott, bart.*, ed.
J. G. Lockhart, I (Edinburgh: Robert Cadell, 1837), 38-39.

Scott used many of these collected ballads in his
novels, in which he popularized the "local color"
theory implicit in all Romanticism and warmly endorsed
by Müller. Scott's novels were historical romances--
but what concept of history do they reveal? Scott was
certainly concerned with historical reality and all
its problems. Indeed, one of his admirers, Maurice de
Guérin, says that "it is through his works that one
must study history." Guérin goes on to say that Scott
"will teach history better than all the historians,
because they recount only general facts and public acts
while he enters into life's particulars, capturing all
social classes and all contemporary customs in his
natural, ingenuous dialogues." But if we observe well,
we will notice that everything in Scott's view of his-
tory--the details, dialogues, and so on--seems to give
life to an imaginative and romantic fairy tale. This
is in fact the secret of his work, which often reminds
us of those German romantics whom he had admired and
translated.

The German romantics tried to envision the exigen-
cies from which various conditions of civilization had
originated and therefore the different kinds of customs
they could go back to for national-educational material.
Scott did not have these interests, as is illustrated,
for example, by comparing a Scott novel with one by
Tieck. In Scott's work, historical-national-educational
material became a picturesque contemplation of the past,
or else it was directly transformed into his "ideal
construction," which was only superficially historical.
We must acknowledge, however, that Scott's extensive
work has provided us with a picturesque gallery of folk
antiquities, in which the life of the Scottish people
shines forth in its own particular light. These pictures complement those previously presented by Brand,
Bourne, and Browne, providing us, it would seem, with
an outline of an ideal folklore of all Great Britain.
Scott's antiquities took on the coloration of those
Tales of a Grandfather that he told his grandchildren.
Understandably, Wilhelm Grimm singled out Scott in his
notes to *Kinder- und Hausmärchen* as one who knew how
to reap the inheritance of *Ossian* and the *Reliques*.

3. Aspects of French Romanticism: A Return to Nature and to Natural Man

But what inheritance was reaped by French Romanticism? England had *Ossian* and the *Reliques*. France, on the other hand, had Rousseau. Rousseau was undoubtedly the herald of French Romanticism, which nevertheless had a very clear document in Sébastian Mercier's *Du theatre; ou, Nouvel essai sur l'art dramatique*, published in 1773. In this work, which in many respects is related to Möser's *Harlekin* and Rousseau's *Lettres sur les spectacles*, Mercier, referring generally to contemporary literature but particularly to drama, accused the latter of not reflecting life as it actually unfolds before our eyes. He said that this is so for two reasons: we have not learned how to shake loose from a servile imitation of the ancients, and we have held to the belief that only the world's great people are worthy of being represented on the stage. But because life is neither entirely tragic nor entirely comic, it is impossible to derive the material for a tragedy or a comedy without reducing everything to traditional genres. We must, then, create a new dramatic form that is both tragic and comic at the same time, in greater conformity to present conditions--a drama unregulated by established rules and free to draw its inspiration from the folk and the lowest social classes.

It is easy to see that in this unjustly forgotten and neglected work we have, along with ideas that had been common to the *querelle* between the ancients and the moderns, embryonic ideas that would become the fundamental presuppositions of the romantic program, particularly the idea concerning the need for an art that does not turn to traditional and academic sources. The grotesque, which Victor Hugo later proposed in his famous introduction to *Cromwell* as the essential feature of the greater complexity of Christian art in comparison to pagan art, was implicitly predicted by Mercier. As Hugo said later, even the ugly and horrid can have its own beauty. But aren't we here made to see the need for a more truthful literature, one that is therefore nearer the folk--a literature, in other words, that has more intimate contact with nature?

This nature, considered and contemplated in the eternally various miracle of all created things (from the flower to the mountain, from the simplest to the most complicated beings, including man himself), is well illustrated in the work of Buffon [Georges Louis Leclerc], a naturalist, and the *Études de la nature* and *Harmonies de la nature* of Bernardin de Saint-Pierre, a poet and scientist. It is generally known that Saint-Pierre's exaltation of the state of nature and primitive man, which provides the backdrop for his *Paul et Virginie*, was influenced by Rousseau, whom Saint-Pierre admired, followed, and wrote a long essay about. And it is also generally agreed that he was a transitional figure between Rousseau and François René Chateaubriand.

In his *Essai historique, politique et moral sur les révolutions anciennes et modernes*, published a year before *Lyrical Ballads*, Chateaubriand, after praising *Ossian* as one of the most powerful "voices" of modern poetry, nostalgically recalled those American Indians so beloved by the French, exclaiming, "When I feel bored with life and my heart is saddened by the touch of men, I hang my head in sorrow. Enchanted meditations! Secret and ineffable fascination of a self-contented spirit! It is in the middle of the great plains of America that I can fully enjoy you." Later, when these meditations were transformed into such works as *Atala, René,* and *Les Natchez,* he said, "In the first volume of *Les Natchez,* you will find wonders of all kinds: Christian wonders, mythological wonders, Indian wonders. Too, you will find muses, angels, demons, genies, combats, and personifications such as Fame, Time, Night, and Friendship. This volume offers invocations, sacrifices, wonders, and comparisons, some short, some long, in the manner of Homer. . . ." It would have been more correct to say in the manner of a Homer dressed as Ossian, for Chateaubriand's American savages actually talk and act like the heroes of the Scottish bard. Indeed, we sometimes have the impression that Ossian and Fingal have taken the names of Sciactas and Outougamiz.

But whatever his style, it is certain that in Chateaubriand's work fascination with distant unknown countries was transformed not only into a desire for a better world but also into the sentiments of a simple, naive life, the joy of the eternal and primitive moment found in all mankind. It was precisely this joy that he felt in confronting Christian cults, which he praised for their social and aesthetic value; it was with this joy that he remembered the forests of ancient Gaul, which he compared to the Gothic architecture of his country; and it was this joy that he felt for the various manifestations of folklife, in which the past of France was often to be glimpsed.

4. *From Madame de Staël to Fauriel*

After the attempts of Thiers and Le Brun, the search for this past had been encouraged by Napoleon himself. A minister of his, Emmanuel Cretet, was the first to attempt to save documents that conserved folk idioms. In this same period, the Celtic Academy, founded in 1804 and later renamed the Society of Antiquarians, was also very active. In his inaugural address the secretary general, Éloi Johanneau, emphasized the importance of folk traditions, which had been "generally neglected" in France, and recommended the collecting of romances and songs. He also recommended that the members consult the folk, "whose knowledge is traditional and whose expressions are sacred." These traditions would prove to the French that certain ancient Gallic features still survived; more importantly, however, they could teach the French to be neither Greek nor Roman.

This appeal did not become a dead issue. The Celtic Academy, through the efforts of Jacques Dulaure and Michel Mangourit, sent a questionnaire--the first ever constructed--to its members and to provincial prefects a few years later in order to make a list of holidays, ceremonies, superstitious practices, and all the documents of the folk's spiritual and material life. The third paragraph of the four-paragraph ques-

tionnaire begins: "What are the specific games, songs,
and melodies of each village? Are they sad or gay?
What are the dances and musical instruments? Are there
any songs that seem to have very ancient origins?"

In 1805, Dulaure, taking advantage of the experiences of Lafitau and especially Brosses, had published
a volume entitled *Des divinités génératrices, ou Du
culte du phallus chez les anciens et les modernes*,
which contains a systemization of folkloristic facts
(for example, facts about phallic rites in modern
Italy). Thus, no one knew the importance of gathering
these materials better than he. But in 1810 Claude
Girault, a scholar who was attempting to find etymologies of words related to customs in Burgundy, wrote
to the secretary general of the Academy: "I confess
that I am amazed to see how many people just limit
themselves to a simple enumeration of customs, without
examining their concealed meaning, without searching
for their causes, and without attempting to discover
their origins."

In that same year Napoleon ordered that *De l'Allemagne*, a beautiful book that Madame de Staël had
written about Germany (more specifically, German
Romanticism), be burned because it was not considered
French. Ten years before, in her essay entitled *De la
littérature, considérée dans ses rapports avec les
institutions sociales*, Madame de Staël had noted that.
one must study a nation's literature in relation to the
nation's most intimate and secret features and that
this literature is always the expression of a certain
historical period. *De l'Allemagne*, republished in
1814, gave greater strength to this idea. Madame de
Staël emphasized the national characteristics of German
poetry and contrasted it to the French, which, although
the most classical of all modern poetries, was the only
poetry not diffused among the folk. This, she said,
was precisely because it was not national. Citing
Bürger's *Lenore*, Madame de Staël observed that "folk
superstitions always have something in common with the
dominant religion"; hence, "there is no reason that one
should disdain to use them." Shakespeare, she went on
to say, "obtained marvelous effects with spirits and

magic." Art, she concluded, "could not be popular if
it ignored what is most important in the imagination
of the multitude." This was just like saying: let us
return, we French people, we who are attacked in the
name of Napoleon and literature, to those spontaneous
and immediate sources to which the Germans and English
have already returned--for the concept of folk poetry
is the origin of their new poetics and their new poetry.

The importance of French folk poetry had been suggested earlier by Montaigne, whom Herder mentioned at
the beginning of his *Volkslieder*, and by Rousseau himself. But we must thank Claude Fauriel for underscoring the importance of folk poetry with the publication
of his *Chants populaires de la Grèce moderne*, which
came to be of great interest to folklore scholars.
The first volume of this work was published in 1824,
the same year that Byron died fighting for Greek
independence. The *Chants* not only represented the
voice of that nation but also the voice of a new epopee
and a new poetry (which reminds us of the influence of
folk poetry on Dionysios Solōmos, the initiator of neo-
Hellenic poetry). In presenting his *Chants populaires
de la Grèce*, Fauriel said that these songs were the
Iliad of modern Greece since they were the result of
an epopee-in-progress. Fauriel believed that this
epopee was the direct result of the "folk genius."
He immediately added that "the unlearned genius of
man is one of the phenomena, one of the products, of
nature."

Three years later, in translating Herder's *Ideen*,
Edgar Quinet arrived at similar conclusions. After
giving Herder credit for linking "forgotten monuments"
to the "genius of history," he cited a number of songs
"forming a link between the people and the past." Both
Quinet and Fauriel were familiar with the main works of
the German romantics, which Madame de Staël had previously popularized. Indeed, Fauriel's introduction to
the *Chants* is much indebted to his familiarity with
such works. But Fauriel went further: in a series of
lectures given at the Sorbonne and partly collected in
his *Histoire de la poésie provençale*, he applied the
theories of Wolf, Lachmann, and the brothers Grimm to

the epico-heroic poetry of all peoples. The *Ramayana* and the *Mahabharata* also entered into his examination, as did folk poems of different nations, all of them "little *Iliads.*"

In 1812 in Germany, a philologist and poet by the name of Ludwig Uhland (whom we must thank for one of the most beautiful examples of German folk poetry) observed that the heroic life of Charlemagne had surely inspired poetry, and that legends, romances, and war songs developed gradually until, in more amplified form, they were collected by clergymen in the compositions now in our possession. Naturally, this idea fascinated Fauriel, who, after mentioning it in the introduction to the *Chants*, developed it very persuasively. In 1837 the most poetic of these compositions, the *Chanson de Roland*, was published for the first time in its entirety by Francisque Michel, who had taken it from a codex in Oxford's Bodleian library. France, which had only a vague notion of its epopee, perceived the full signifi-cance of this discovery. Some few years before, the lullaby "Le Chant des Escualdunacs" had come to light, and Michel himself gave it a place of honor at the be-ginning of the appendices to his main edition of the *Chanson*. Fauriel had, or so it seemed, the best of it all. The *Chanson de Roland*, then, has its basis in "brief" songs, folk lullabies in which everything is fresh, innocent, and pure.

5. *France and Its "Romancero"*

In the atmosphere created by these studies, folksongs assumed a great importance. This accounts for the suc-cess achieved by an 1839 collection of folksongs of Brittany entitled *Barzaz-Breiz*, the result of the re-search of Hersart de La Villemarqué. From a begging singer he had collected songs of the *Derniers Bretons*, whose customs and habits Émile Souvestre, for "caprice amoureux," had described three years before. La Villemarqué's motive, however, was quite different: he knew the works of Wolf, the brothers Grimm, Scott, and Fauriel, and he wanted to offer his fellow country-

men the vestiges of the Breton epopee. In the introduction to his collection, he immediately acknowledged
that his texts were primarily the result of personal
adaption, in the sense that when he found an unpoetic
expression in a text, he substituted a poetic expression discovered in another text. "This was the method
of Walter Scott," he said, "and I cannot do other than
follow the best method." He could have added that this
had been the method of the brothers Grimm in *Kinder-
und Hausmärchen*. But he did not have Scott's or the
Grimms' taste, nor did he have Macpherson's stylistic
skill.

By very cleverly interpolating some verses, La
Villemarqué managed to relate his poems to events having absolutely nothing to do with the original poems.
Essentially, then, his work is merely an adulteration
like Prosper Mérimée's 1827 text, *La Guzla, ou Choix
de poésies illyriques, recueillies dans la Dalmatie,
la Bosnie, la Croatie et l'Herzegowine*. Another sensitive poet of the time, Gérard de Nerval, was certainly
right when, in 1842, in commenting on *Les vieilles
ballades françaises*, he observed: "Before writing,
each nation has sung. All poetry is inspired by these
original sources, and Spain, England, Germany, each
with pride, have their own *romancero*. Why doesn't
France have one also?"

A year later, however, France had its own *romancero*,
for in 1843 one of the greatest collections of French
folk poetry appeared, the three volumes (with musical
accompaniment) by Dumersan and Colet entitled *Chants
et chansons populaires de la France* (3rd ed., 1858-59).
In 1852, on the order of the new French emperor, Napoleon III, some intelligent and valuable *Instructions
relatives aux poésies populaires de la France*, by J. J.
Ampère, were sent out--but these *Instructions* (used
later by scholars such as Rolland, Tiersot, Doncieux,
and Coirault) had been partly anticipated by Dumersan
and Colet.

Folk poetry was now to the French what it had been
to Herder: the voice of nationality. At this point
in time, with these new and renewed interests, couldn't
we say that the recently revived literature and histori-

ography of France and Germany were developing at the
same pace? Conservative writers such as Joseph de
Maistre and Louis de Bonald (who deified the noble
savage) had asserted during the Restoration that the
bourgeoisie was an abstraction of Encyclopedism, while
the folk was living history--a premise that did not,
however, alter their belief in the divine right of
kings. George Sand commented later, "We could say
that the folk is the only historian of prehistoric
times that we have." In Sand's work the folk indeed
lived almost ideally with the bourgeoisie, which had
been the wish of Saint-Simon. The folk entered more
emphatically into the writings of Victor Hugo, and
the works published during this period by Augustin
Thierry, Jules Michelet, and François Guizot certainly
cannot be explained without considering the influence
of Chateaubriand and Scott. Nor can they be explained
without the concept of the *Volksgeist*, which took shape
in Germany and which the brothers Grimm, much more than
Hegel, had made familiar to many French scholars, from
whom Italian romantics later drew inspiration. Interest in folklife was established in their works as they
attempted to awaken national awareness.

6. *Aspects of Romanticism in Italy: From the
   "Lettera semiseria di Grisostomo" to "Vecchie
   romanze spagnuole"*

Italian Romanticism began with Vico. Muratori taught
Italians how necessary it was to collect *Antiquitates*,
as had Michel Angelo Carmeli and Giacomo Leopardi (the
former had written, under the influence of Thiers,
*Storia di vari costumi sacri e profani dagli antichi
fino a noi pervenuti*, published in 1750, while the
latter, under the influence of Browne, had written
Saggio sopra gli errori popolari degli antichi in 1815).
And at the time of Napoleon there had also been other
attempts to provide an organically unified collection
of the manifestations of living folklore--for instance,
Michele Placucci's *Usi e pregiudizj dei contadini di
Romagna*, which illustrated the results of Napoleon's

inquiry, between 1809 and 1811, into Italian customs and dialects.

We must, however, thank Giovanni Berchet for promoting interest in folk poetry in Italy with his *Lettera semiseria di Grisostomo* (1816). Berchet refers to Vico (whom he interprets in his own way, however), and he also mentions Cuoco's *Platone in Italia*, besides such foreign writers as Burke, Lessing, Schiller, Friedrich Bouterwek, and Madame de Staël. Through this ideal filiation extending from Vico to Cuoco to Berchet, we can clearly see the development of Italian Romanticism.

In what sense can we speak about the "popularity" of poetry? In Berchet's view, whatever conforms to nature is "popular." But his definition of *nature* and *natural* derived more from a consideration of what is common to most men than from a particular category of sentiments, images, and spiritual conditions considered more poetic than others because more naive and rough. According to Berchet, each of us has an inborn poetic faculty, which in most people remains passive or receptive; only in a chosen few, in poets, is it manifested as poetic creativity. There are those whom he calls Hottentots, who cannot understand poetry because of their natural deficiency, but there is also another category of people, the Parisians, who have become cold and frivolous as a result of extreme refinement and sophistication. The folk, the *true* folk, is a category between Parisians and Hottentots and thus represents the "middle" and common category of readers.

In these examples the essence of Italian Romanticism is evident. It would be better defined later as common sense or Manzonian humor. Italy could not accept the bold exaggerations of the Northern school. In a letter published in the *Biblioteca italiana* and then in *Zibaldone di pensieri* and *Discorso di un italiano intorno alla poesia romantica*, Giacomo Leopardi accused the romantics of "leading poetry away from the business of the senses." "Natural," for the great poet, is whatever can be represented to the senses. Intellect is the great enemy of poetry, men having "an indisputable inclination towards primitive, pure,

unadulterated nature." In this respect, then, the
Parisian's "coldness" and Leopardi's "intellect" coincided.

In the *Lettera*, however, Berchet said that the new
Italian poetry would have to reflect actual beliefs and
feelings if it hoped to evoke the concreteness of reality. Significantly, it was precisely at this time
that, in homage to such reality, those who had taken a
minor part in comedy--the poor, the folk--entered into
the history of Italian literature. Renzo and Lucia, as
it has been observed, romantically broke into the kingdom of poetry, while their common story was "redeemed
by the educative undertaking they were called to serve."
Alessandro Manzoni brought back Walter Scott. Thus,
dialectal poetry bloomed in Italy, for although it had
nothing in common with folk poetry (because it was "conscious" artistic poetry), it was the most suitable for
expressing the feelings of the folk.

Berchet transformed the concept of folk poetry
formulated by the German romantics into a different
concept, one that had been suggested by the German
romantics, particularly Arnim: folk poetry must serve
as a means of education for the folk. But Arnim
regarded the folk as the teacher, while Berchet, as
Benedetto Croce has observed, regarded the folk as the
pupil. In taking this stand, however, did Berchet
deny the importance of folk poetry, as some believed?
Berchet gave an answer to this question in the introduction to his *Vecchie romanze spagnuole*, published in
1837 when he was away from Italy and in more direct
contact with certain foreign romantic atmospheres.
Under these conditions he was able to develop and
clarify his own thinking:

> Folk poetry--and by this I mean the poetry that
> is entirely produced, not just liked, by the folk
> --does not materially produce fixed works in the
> way that artistic poetry does. Unlike artistic
> poetry, folk poetry is not suited to producing
> written works, for folk poetry entrusts its works
> to the fleeting song and the passing word. It
> strolls along, free and alive. With each step

that it takes, it drops one charm only to pick up
a new one, but while doing so it does not cease to
be what it was nor do its original features change.
One person rises and finds a song; a hundred listen
to and then repeat it. The mother repeats to her
children the rhymes heard from her parents, which
are then taught to the grandchildren. When the man
of letters comes, has them repeated to him, and
then fixes them in written forms, who knows how
many mouths these songs have previously passed
through? Who can recognize all the modifications
that they have taken on?

In translating these romances, Berchet was performing a task previously undertaken by Percy, Herder,
Cesarotti, and Diez. Even Jacob Grimm had collected a
Silva de romances viejos. After fighting against
French and Napoleonic imperialism with the aid of
"popular" forces, Spain began to discover its romances,
which later, in 1849, were immortalized in Agustin
Duran's *Romancero general*. These romances, in Berchet's view, constituted the ideal of national
patriotic-popular poetry--an ideal to which he, as a
poet of a language that was anything but popular,
aspired. But in presenting them to Italian readers
(to whom he also planned to offer a translation of
Danish folk poetry), he again was far from accepting
the concept of folk poetry held by the brothers Grimm.
Although he adopted the concept of folk elaboration
previously suggested by A. W. Schlegel and Arnim, he
differed from them in considering folk poetry to be
only that poetry directly produced by the folk, a
specific social class. Folk poetry, he said, is a
greenhouse containing very simple flowers that the
readers can enjoy. But in saying this, didn't Berchet
single out the elementary nature of folk poetry that
the German romantics had discovered?

7. *Tommaseo and Italian Folklore*

Folk poetry was "simple poetry," but it was national

poetry as well. Eight years before the publication of
Vecchie ballate spagnuole, which Berchet had recreated
through his translation, an Italian archeologist,
P. E. Visconti, observed in an essay entitled *Saggio
de'canti popolari della provincia di Marittima e
Campagna* (an assessment of the best collection of
Italian folk poetry made by Italians or by foreigners):

> Folksongs, which are strictly bound by national
> characteristics, geographical conditions, customs,
> and levels of civilization, deserve the attention
> of the philosopher, for they contain the ancient
> secrets of the human heart. As the expression of
> what spontaneously comes to whoever is truly emo-
> tional, they offer a fascinating mixture of the
> common and uncommon, the ordinary and the new.
> Inspired entirely by the heart, they reveal two
> powerful sentiments, love and anger. They express
> these sentiments with an energy that makes feeling
> and expression one and the same. . . . Whoever
> would attempt a collection of these songs would
> not be disappointed. They contain dear and pre-
> cious manners, phrases, and words, along with
> genuinely pure and beautiful verses--and these
> works created in our language would be the objects
> of most satisfying research. Perhaps this sweet
> mother of ours, privileged nurse of all beauty,
> will be crowned with a new garland worthy of her.

Visconti's wish was not to remain unanswered. In
1841 Niccolò Tommaseo published a collection entitled
Canti popolari toscani, one of the most unadulterated
documents of Italian folk poetry and one of the most
famous collections offered by the philology of the
time. Tommaseo unconditionally admired these songs,
in which he joyfully discovered "dear and precious
manners and phrases" created "in our own language."
He did not hesitate to consider them "greenhouse
flowers," produced by "agrestic, unfettered minds."
Tommaseo admonished, "He who does not venerate the
folk as the poet and inspirer of poets must not cast
his eyes upon this collection." And because he

considered the folk to be the source of poetry, his
collection was not limited to Tuscan songs. A second
volume was dedicated to *Canti del popolo corso*, in
which he also demonstrated a great ethnographical
interest in the people of Corsica and their habits.
A third volume, following the lead of Fauriel, was
dedicated to *Canti del popolo greco*. Finally, a fourth
was dedicated to *Canti popolari illirici*. His translations are in excellent taste. He addressed himself
to poets so that they could have "new sources of poetry" at their disposal, while he recognized that folksongs are an aspect of one's own national awareness.

8. *Nationalisms, Supremacies, and Missions*

Without doubt, the study of folk traditions in Western
Europe drew new impetus and new ideas from German
Romanticism, which must be credited with placing this
study on national and historical bases. When Germany,
without denying the universality of romantic ideals,
began to consider the nation as the means through which
such universality is expressed, two great nation-states,
England and France, were in a position to manifest an
ideal that came to be identified with their culture and
civilization—indeed, with their own historical awareness. It was therefore natural that for them folklore
was called not to create this awareness but to strength-
en it, we could say, by "recreating" it.

It has been said that the nation in its modern form
originated in England as early as the Tudors. But England was able to specify its own national characteristics with greater clarity in *Ossian* and the *Reliques*.
For France, on the other hand, we are told that we
should look to the Revolution's defense against the
king. But hadn't France made a laic religion out of
the worship of nation and fatherland, a religion that
Napoleonic domination created and sustained not only
in the countries that it invaded but also in those
that it hoped to invade? And didn't this "religion"
dominate all the following movements of national inde-

pendence in Europe, movements expressing in various ways the desire for a nationality already rooted in each country's past?

On this "past" François Guizot constructed the ideals of a new French supremacy, which resulted from the cultural tradition that expressed France's ever-present desire to be mistress of Europe. In Italy, Vincenzo Gioberti referred to the historical importance of the past in the same way, but he placed the civil and religious mission of the papacy at the center of his conception. Here we should also remember Giuseppe Mazzini, who called upon the greatness of Italian civilization down through the ages, the glories of ancient Rome, the Renaissance, and so on. There was, then, a new note struck by all these thinkers, to whom the primacy or the mission of their own countries was an active and fertile reality. And in their work and thought the Nation became what it had become for the German romantics: not a naturalistic but rather a historical "fact."

CHAPTER XV

TEACHINGS OF FOLKLORE

1. *Aspects of Romanticism in Russia*

England, France, Italy, and Spain--countries with
well developed cultural traditions--cast off the
arrogance that led some of their representatives
during the age of Romanticism to consider folklore
as a "plebeian science." On this subject the comments
of Scott, Fauriel, Tommaseo, and Berchet are quite
significant. Still, we must acknowledge that although
folklore contributed to changing the literature and
culture of those countries, it did not have the
political-national (or national-"popular") thrust that
it had in Germany. Antonio Gramsci notes that in
France the term *national* had a meaning in which the
term *popular* was "politically prepared for because it
was linked to the concept of sovereignty"; that in
Italy this term had a very narrow ideological meaning,
which never coincided with that of *popular*; and that,
on the other hand, the relationship between these two
terms was completely different in Russian and other
Slavic languages in general, in which *national* and
popular were synonyms.

There is another factor, though, that seems to
associate Russia with Germany. We remember that in
Russia, where there had been no kind of national sentiment since the beginning of the reign of Alexander I,
such sentiment was awakened by Napoleon. "Napoleon
brought about an eruption in Russia," said one of the
revolutionaries of the time, A. A. Bestuzhev; "then a
feeling of independence arose in everyone's heart."

To the people Alexander I seemed to be the messiah in
the fight against Napoleonic domination. Later "the
flames of Moscow" would appear to Benjamin Constant as
"the dawn of the world's freedom." But didn't these
flames also illuminate the entrance of Russia into
Europe?

In contrast to what had happened in Germany, folklore in Russia encountered great difficulties in becoming established after the conquest of Napoleon. But
when it did become established, it became something
more than merely a cultural event, as it had been in
England, France, and even Italy. The Italians, English, and French could boast of Dante, Petrarch,
Boccaccio, Chaucer, Shakespeare, Milton, Corneille,
Racine, and so on. But for the Russians, given their
still quite modest literary heritage, folk literature
was a rich intellectual, moral, and social fortune,
both the document of their traditions and the monument
of their language.

Thus, one can explain the reaction caused in 1836
by Petr Chaadaev's celebrated *Lettres philosophiques*.
On the one hand, he appealed to the values of the
Catholic Church, into whose bosom, he argued, the
Orthodox Church must enter for a better future for the
Slavic world (a point Novalis should have considered);
on the other hand, he strongly argued that Russians,
enclosed as they were in their "little huts made of
logs and twigs," had not given a single thought to the
treasure-house of human ideas and had no literature
that could speak to their hearts. The brothers
Kireevskiĭ, Petr and Ivan, two great Slavic scholars
educated in Germany and enthusiastic admirers of the
brothers Grimm, decided to prove how completely wrong
Chaadaev was. They believed that a great literature,
folk literature, had spoken and was still speaking to
the hearts of Russians. The brothers Kireevskiĭ had
much justification for saying so, particularly in regard to folk poetry, to which a Cossack scholar,
Kirsha Danilov, had given dignity a few years earlier.
Indeed, it was through Danilov's efforts that Russian
folk poetry emerged from the museum of beautiful curiosities to which it had been relegated.

2. The Lesson of Danilov

As we know, there is much evidence of the existence
of folksongs and folk singers in Russia as early as
the twelfth century. We also know that the famous
Song of Igor, believed to belong to the twelfth century but discovered during the time of the publication
of *Ossian*, is replete with echoes of folk poetry. The
first transcriptions of this poetry--excluding those
made by two Englishmen, Richard James and Samuel Collins, in the seventeenth century--took place in the
second half of the eighteenth century and the first
ten years of the following century. Until then, folk
poetry had a very low standing in Russian culture,
which initially had been dominated by religious traditions and later, during the times of Peter the Great,
by French classicism. Now, however, although faithfully guarded in the hearts of peasants, merchants,
and pilgrims, folk poems and accompanying music began
to reach the halls of the aristocracy and the palace
of the czar. This helps to explain the emergence of
the songbooks and collections of Chulkov (1770-76),
L'vov (1790), Popov (1792), and Sakharov (1830), in
which the transcribed texts were purified, corrected,
and reworked.

Danilov had contributed to this trend with a
collection of Russian songs published in 1804. The
Napoleonic invasion certainly did not inspire Danilov
in the way that it had Arnim and Brentano, and he perceived the folk to whom those songs belonged quite
differently than his predecessors had. The fight
against Napoleon had already brought officers and
soldiers, the aristocracy and the folk, into closer
accord. At the very moment that the spirit of the
peasant and the national significance of his personality were discovered, Danilov began his work. He
understood that each folksong is a product of this
personality, and in pursuit of this idea he made a
collection of Russian folksongs in 1818. This collection was the best of the period, a precise documentation of what actually was the epic or, to be
more precise, the epopee of the Russian folk.

Folksongs, which in Danilov's view documented the
development of national civilization, therefore
deserved to be placed next to the epopees of other
nations, next to the *Iliad*, the *Odyssey*, and the
Nibelungenlied.

This epopee was accepted in Russia, but only on
the condition that it in no way touch the official
church and the political government, which, after the
victory over Napoleon, were against any reform. When
Pushkin became interested in folksongs reinvoking the
epic figure of Stenka Razin and thought of making a
collection of them, Count Benkendorf, a friend of his,
wrote in an attempt to dissuade him: "The songs about
Stenka Razin, whatever their poetic importance, contain a subject that makes them inappropriate for publication. The church damned Razin." The events
inspiring these songs were the sufferings of Russian
peasants, their struggles against feudatories, exac-
tions, and abuses of power. Razin, who fought against
all injustices, was the voice of the rebellion: he
spoke against injustice and for a trust in justice and
life. For the same reason V. I. Dal was not permitted
to publish, under Nicholas II, a collection of proverbs that would later open new horizons to the study
of paroemiology.

These restrictions or "purgings" did not prevent
a just appreciation of the importance of folklife, a
goal that the brothers Kireevskiĭ did everything they
could to achieve. Even the controversy with Chaadaev
was an encouragement for one of the brothers, Petr,
to intensify his work on a collection of stariny (or,
as they then began to be called, byliny), which was
published posthumously, between 1862 and 1874. This
collection, together with Danilov's collection, was
the nucleus of the Russian people's *chansons de geste*,
initially made known through some essays he had published here and there.

We should add that a great writer of the time,
N. M. Karamzin, had asked for proposals and suggestions for a renewal of literary language. Ever since
the reign of Catherine II, Russia had demonstrated
much interest in linguistic problems, and we know that

Catherine herself was interested in Antoine Court de
Gebelin's *Monde primitif, analysé et comparé avec le
monde moderne*, a work much loved by the French romantics, particularly Sénancour. Many language studies
had been attempted after Catherine's reign, but here
too there was a restriction: the language of Russians
and of Russian literature could only be the Slavo-
ecclesiastical one. Folksong anthologies revealed,
however, that side-by-side with this language was a
simpler, more immediate one. It was Karamzin who
realized this, and, in proposing language reform, he
included a careful study not only of ancient documents
but also of folksongs. In these folksongs, he said,
one finds the language most suited to conveying a
tender simplicity, the expression of the feelings and
the heart. Karamzin used this same language in
romances, ballads, and tales, in which he often praised
the life of country people and their ancestors. As he
said in *Natalia, "Who of us does not love those times
when Russians were real Russians, when they dressed in
their own styles*, followed their own paths, lived
according to their own traditions, and talked in their
own language, in accord with their feelings, saying
exactly what they meant? I, for one, love those times.
I also love to take imaginative journeys back to *ancient times*, under the shadow of old bending elms, to
discover my ancestors and talk with them about ancient
events and the character of the glorious Russian
people."

I. A. Krylov, one of Russia's greatest fabulists,
also contributed to illustrating and clarifying this
"character" of the Russian people. Krylov (like
Karamzin, a lover of the great ancestral past) had no
hesitations about brightening up his prose with different forms of folk language. Indeed, his animals,
although they are the ones typical of fables (the wolf,
the crow, the monkey, the eagle), offer us the essential
spirit of the Russian folk, which was to speak "with
one's own language and one's own heart."

These same goals were also present, in the first
twenty years of the nineteenth century, in the works
of V. A. Zhukovskiĭ, a poet sensitive to the "refresh-

ingness" of European Romanticism. He translated
Bürger's *Lenore*, the inspiration for two famous ballads of his in which he tried to use folk language to
the utmost. Like Gray, he was a singer of bards (in
his case Russian bards), and he translated fragments
from the *Mahabharata*, episodes from the *Iliad*, and
passages from the *Odyssey*.

3. From Pushkin to Glinka

Karamzin's reform was accepted by Pushkin, a poet who
investigated Russian folk language and folklore as no
one had ever done before. It seems that there was no
Western poetic experience that he did not make his own
(from Shakespeare to Macpherson and Byron)--or, rather,
that he did not make Russian. As Ettore Lo Gatto observes, he found the solution by "introducing folk
language into poetic creations to which little notice
had been paid in the eighteenth century." Lo Gatto
goes on to say that "along with the language, other
folk elements entered his art, transformed it, and
unified it; consider, for example, his physical descriptions of Russian nature as opposed to descriptions
in the style of pseudo-classical, sentimental, and
romantic writers, and, on a deeper level, his charac-
terization of the Russian temperament, or, more generi-
cally, the Russian soul."
    Pushkin used many folkloristic elements and motifs
in his works. He partly reworked the readaptions that
Mérimée had made of Serbian songs, on which he impressed his very strong poetic personality. Where he most
effectively used popular elements, however, was in his
tales. Remembering stories that his nurse, Arina
Rodiȯnovna, had told him when he was a child, he exclaimed, "What enchantment they contain! Each of them
is a poem." M. D. Chulkov had previously made an extensive collection of such tales (1766-83), but none
of them had been registered in their authentic form.
Later, A. N. Afanas'ev also reworked collected romances.
He was led to this undertaking, as he declared, by the
example of the brothers Grimm, and he concurred in their

opinion that what really counts are remnants of ancient mythology. Unlike the brothers Grimm, however, Afanas'ev, whose collection was published between 1855 and 1866, had a very rare, refined taste. He reworked (that is, he obviated) the personality of the authors whose texts he collected, but he knew how to give a human warmth to the new elaborations. Chulkov (like Bronnitsyn and Sakharov, who followed him) had not done so. But this, we should observe, does not vitiate the importance of such collections, which document story motifs and themes then most common among the Russian folk.

It was logical that Pushkin, rather than Chulkov, would remember his nurse, she herself being a reworker of tales, aided by her ingenuous imagination. Obviously, though, he did not have scholarly requirements to satisfy. In his view a tale was a subject for art, as it had been for such German romantics as Novalis, Tieck, Brentano, and the brothers Grimm. The tale contained a sentiment that he revived and adopted, turning it into a kind of language. This is why the tales of Pushkin, who had also used folkloristic motifs and elements in earlier works, create a fusion between the artist and the folk (or the spirit of the folk), a fusion accomplished later by such Russian poets and writers as Lermontov, Gogol', Turgenev, Tolstoĭ, and Dostoevskiĭ. Significantly, a few years later even music drew inspiration from the folk, a type of artistic work initiated by Glinka.

But we can go further still. Just as the early Russian folklorists had indicated new horizons for artists, now artists would help the folklore movement. From a cultural viewpoint, the folk now shook loose the shackles of servitude. The folk was no longer the student, an inferior being, but rather the teacher (as it had been for the German romantics). Gogol', who gave us an exquisite revised collection of Ukrainian legends, declared, "My life, my joy, oh beautiful songs, how much I love you!" These songs, like the tales and proverbs, would become the call to sincerity and spontaneity, turning the folk into artists.

Meanwhile, an archeologist and latinist, I. M.

Snegirev, had committed himself to collecting proverbs,
which Pushkin had regarded as a linguistic gold mine.
Later, in 1838, Snegirev provided an extensive synthesis in which he described the festivals of the Russian
people. Accustomed to scientific research, Snegirev
went further than mere description, and his reflections
on the paganism enveloping peasant life are very perceptive. In 1848 another Slav, Aleksandr Tereschenko,
continued in these studies. But at that time the work
of F. I. Buslaev, a devoted disciple of the brothers
Grimm, was especially influential. After giving extensive study to Russian folk literature and art, he said
that the folk alone possesses the moral basis of
nationality in its language and mythology, both of
which are closely related to poetry, law, and custom,
and that all the moral ideas possessed by the folk
since primitive times constitute a sacred tradition,
a venerable antiquity, the sublime inheritance of the
past.

4. Czechoslovakian and Polish Folklorists

This inheritance was appealed to by the Czechs of
Bohemia and Moravia, as well as the Slovaks, who were
the most outspoken advocates of the Slavic mission
that Mazzini later predicted would be fatal for Austria as well as Turkey. In 1781 the Czechs had obtained from Austria the abolishment of serfdom. In
return, they were required to accept German as the
official language. This proved to be the first sign
of battle. The fight broke out when Romanticism
raised the issue of a national spirit. Here we witness a movement aimed at determining the common characteristics of Slavic peoples, as they were reported
by archeology, ethnography, and especially linguistics.
The Czechs, too, wanted their own "monuments." And
they were to have them in the work of Josef Dobrovský,
who provided, in Latin, an incomparable reconstruction
of the primitive Slavic world; in the work of Josef
Jungmann, who brought the history of Czech literature
into this "world"; and in the work of František

Palacký, who, in tracing the history of Bohemia, launched a manifesto of national independence.

Along with these and similar studies, there was a concern for creating a national poetry, an original poetry capable of awakening national awareness in the people. This was precisely the intention not only of Jungmann but also of Jan Kollár and of F. L. Čelakovský. Čelakovský made a collection of Czech folksongs in which the philological interests of the collector were often sacrificed to the taste of the poet. In these songs was to be found the well-spring in which ancestral language lived and relived, a language against which certain parties had attempted to conspire; but we also find here a documentation of the legendary past that had been the basis of the poetry of Jungmann, Kollár, and Čelakovský himself. Precisely here, in the name of this legendary past, Kollár, a Slovak, raised the hope in one of his poems that Russia would one day form a single country, not only with the Poles but also with the Serbs and the Croats. It goes without saying that Kollár's wish was well received some years later, in 1848, by August Ciezkowski, who, like a new Slavic Fichte, gave mystical treatment to the idea of a Slavic mission, but on one condition: the Slavs were to be guided in this mission by the Poles, who themselves had lived all the literary experiences of the West and were in a position to make all Slavic peoples brothers.

The truth of the matter, however, was quite different. We must remember that Poland, after having been largely incorporated by Russia after the Congress of Vienna, was always kept in a state of dependence by Russia. The Polish insurrections of 1830 and 1863 only had the effect of enticing the czar to make the Polish provinces more Russianized, although not everyone in Russia approved of the czar's politics. In his famous *Russkaîa pravda*, P. I. Pestel', chief of the Southern Association (which was politically quite active between 1821 and 1825), had declared himself to be against the right of nationality for the smallest countries, such as Finland, Estonia, and Latvia, but he believed it necessary to recognize Poland as nationally independent.

This hoped-for independence pervaded all the Polish
poetry of the time, as is demonstrated by the works of
Julian Niemcewicz and Teofil Lenartowicz, and it is in
the name of this independence that collections of folk
poetry would be made. Consider, for example, the collections of Lipiński and Muzzbach, whose texts educa-
tors later used to inculcate a love for the fatherland.
Oskar Kolberg, however, was the first to study Polish
folklife in a series of volumes, and he was the first
to emphasize an art of which little had been said until
then: folk art, popular art, that quite distinctive
art expressed in engravings, embroideries, hand-made
artifacts, and so on. On this subject it should be
noted that a Polish patriot, Chopin, while in Paris,
revived the popular and national voice of his distant
country in his *mazurkas* and *polonaises*, thus giving
support to a musical nationalism that is, as has been
observed, the very perfection of Romanticism.

5. *Karadžić and Serbo-Croatian Poetry*

The Poles, whose spirit perhaps has been captured by
no one as by Chopin, did not actually have an epic
poetry comparable to that of the Russians, Czechs, or
Slovaks. There were epic seeds in their poetry, but
there was no epic. This could not be said, however,
of the Southern Slavs, who were troubled by many wars
during the romantic period. Subject to the Turkish
Empire until 1830, the Serbians finally saw their
dream come true in that year: they became a princi-
pality under Russian protection. Croatia, especially
while under Napoleonic domination from 1803 to 1813,
had initiated a movement for Slavo-national revival.
We know that it was the Serbian defeat of 1813 that
caused Vuk Stefanović Karadžić to emigrate to Vienna,
where he met Bartholomäus Kopitar, a Slovenian philologist who encouraged him to publish the Serbo-Croatian
songs.
     Karadžić followed his advice. His first collec-
tion of Serbo-Croatian songs was published between
1814 and 1815 and was much admired by the brothers

Grimm, who saw it as the affirmation and confirmation
of their own theories about folk poetry. Karadžić
himself did not hesitate to compare these songs to the
Odyssey and *Ossian*, and his attitude towards them was
of one who devotedly and unconditionally loves everything sung by the folk. He collected the songs of
original singers, but these singers (philology would
later be based on their tradition) did not raise any
particular problems for him. Like the brothers Grimm,
he believed that whoever says "poetry" also says "folk."
It is the folk that creates.

Karadžić, however, did not stop with this first
work; rather, he continued with the task of collecting
songs of peoples to whom he felt tied. Between 1823
and 1824 he republished his collection with many additions, and some years later, between 1841 and 1846, his
Srpske narodne pjesme was published in six volumes
(which, with all the additions, became nine volumes in
the national edition published between 1891 and 1902).
Reorganized and falsified by Mérimée (followed not only
by Pushkin but also by the English Sir John Bowring and
the German Eduard Gerhard, this collection found a good
translator in Élise Voiart, who published *Chants populaires des Serviens, recueillis par Wuk Stephanowitch
et traduits, d'aprés Talvy* in Paris in 1834. Talvy (a
pseudonym) translated these songs not only into French
but into German as well. The translations made by
Tommaseo in his volume *Canti illirici*, however, had an
altogether different tone. In light of these translations, the songs of the Serbo-Croatian people appeared
to scholars to be a pure, powerful national voice.
Arturo Cronia observes that not only Goethe, Herder,
the brothers Grimm, Talvy, and Tommaseo, but also
Eckermann, Humboldt, Staël, Nodier, and Scott looked
at Serbo-Croatian folk poetry through the eyes of
Karadžić. These songs constituted the most important
element of Serbo-Croatian national literature--the only
modern form, in fact, of this literature.

In collecting these songs, Karadžić well understood
the task involved. Of course he was concerned with
providing scholars with authentic poetic texts, but he
was also aware that these texts served to place a new

national language in high esteem. Nevertheless, his
intense love for authentic texts did not prevent him
from occasionally reworking and correcting them in
order to produce metrical perfection. This arbitrariness was followed in 1852 in Rumania by a good poet,
Vasile Alecsandri, who, in reworking his country's
poems so that they might better be accepted by contemporary *literati* and serve as a "classical source,"
appealed to the authority of Karadžić. Leaving aside
this question of arbitrariness (however important it
might be in the literary field), it is to Karadžić's
credit that he did not isolate the collected documents;
rather, he considered them as an aspect of eastern
Europe's poetic tradition. The epic that Karadžić had
collected was indeed a national voice, but this voice
was just a part of a chorus that was impossible to
disregard. In fact, Karadžić asked himself if his
collection did not illuminate Greek folk poetry as
well as the folk poetry of Bulgaria, Rumania, and
Albania. The Greeks replied that it was also possible
to reverse this proposition. Obviously, the problem
was not posed in this way merely to determine the
tradition of a specific group of songs; nonetheless,
we must recognize that Karadžić was a European folklorist with a broad vision--one who perceived folk
poetry as an essential aspect of national culture and
life.

6. *The Birth of the "Kalevala"*

The same enthusiasm that Karadžić expressed for Serbo-
Croatian folk poetry, which he collected with the
faithfulness of a missionary and apostle, was expressed
for the folk poetry of Finland by an unassuming doctor,
Elias Lönnrot. Finland was then under Russian domination. In 1809 Finland's autonomy had been guaranteed
by the czar, who had become Grand Duke of Finland; but
in Finland, as previously in Poland, this guarantee of
freedom was accompanied by an energetic political movement to make the country as Russian as possible. It
was natural, then, that Finland, which had nothing in

common with the Slavs, increasingly sought refuge in
the spiritual world of its traditions. From 1776 to
1788, following the example of Macpherson, a learned
Finnish philologist, H. G. Porthan, collected some
fragments of his people's ancient poetry. But it was
Topelius, father of the poet of the same name, who
revealed the treasure that the Finnish people possessed
in their ancient runes. The Society of Finnish Literature, founded in 1831, assisted the research of a young
man who had well understood the importance of the message left by Topelius: Lönnrot had demonstrated considerable interest in the folk medicine of Finland
while he was still a student, and later he made an
excellent investigation of this subject. Basically,
such medicine was merely a recipe book of magical
rules. But didn't those rules come to life again in
runes, the epico-lyrical songs that the Finnish folk
handed down from generation to generation?

Dressed as a peasant, Lönnrot began his collection
of runes. In his hands, runes multiplied: each of
them had variants, and each variant was like a different poem. Lönnrot, however, did not set about to publish this material, as his predecessors had. What were
these runes, he asked himself, if not the epopee of the
Finnish folk? Thus, he decided to offer the Finns
their own poem, the *Kalevala.* Lönnrot had tried to
reconstruct a poem by bringing runes together, unifying
them with the help of variants--a work, as he himself
maintained, in which there was nothing of his own because everything belonged to the folk. It has been
said that he was like one who attempts to reconstruct
a vase from its broken fragments. But if we consider
the various pieces once forming that vase, we see that
this is not a very precise image--for here the problem
consisted in building a new vase with the fragments of
different vases. This is why the twenty-two thousand
verses of the poem do not come close to forming an
organic work. One rune says:

> The cold told me verses
> And the rain long songs:
> The wind brought me strophes,

> As did the ocean waves;
> The birds added voices,
> And the trees added songs.
> I collected them together. . . .

The *Kalevala* is the collection the author speaks of;
as such, it is the work of an educated man with a
refined poetic taste--of a Wolf who imitates Macpherson, using an uncertain poetic folk heritage,
in this case the heritage of Finnish singers, the
laulajat. But is the *Kalevala* only the result of a
love for the epic, or is it, rather, the result of a
love for one's country and one's literature, a national
literature that is at once a new conquest and a new
affirmation?

Left to themselves, these runes would have been of
interest only to specialists; collected in a single
poem, they conquered Europe. In fact, the *Kalevala*
was translated into all European languages, creating
new and renewed interest in folk poetry. The runes
have the distinction of offering us a fresh, ingenuous
poetry in which, as has been noted, the domestic elegy
mixes with a respect for everything that is gentle and
kind. In the *Kalevala* those things loved by the poets
who recited them, even the "sad lands" and "poor
regions," are transfigured so that they might be offered to us in a sweet atmosphere of twilight, which accounts for the *Kalevala*'s enchantment. Following this
example, the Estonians attempted to create their
Kalewipoeg, containing nineteen thousand verses. The
Kalewipoeg is the work of another doctor, Friedrich
Kreutzwald, who used more than twenty thousand songs
collected not only by him but also by Fahlmann and
Neus. Because of its lack of freshness, however, this
work is quite different from the *Kalevala*.

7. *Folklore in Scandinavian Countries*

Meanwhile, the work done in Scandinavian countries to
preserve and emphasize their folkloristic heritage was
equally intense. These Scandinavian countries were

geographically close to the Slavic countries, but
their cultural ties were with Germany. Scandinavia's
medieval mythology, along with the literature in which
it is expressed, had previously been spread throughout
Europe by Paul Henri Mallet during the same period that
Ossian and the *Reliques* were published. The credit for
making this an object of critical and historical investigation, however, goes to the German romantics, especially the brothers Grimm.

In an article published in 1808 in the *Studien*,
Jacob Grimm had emphatically stated that the "medieval
poetry of the Scandinavian peoples is neither generated
by nor dependent upon medieval German poetry"; therefore, "both originated in the same period under the
influence of the same events, and they have developed
in parallel fashion without interfering with each
other." Although he recognized that the oldest populations of Germany came from Scandinavia, he was here
holding to his idea of the "common base" to which he
appealed in the name of folk poetry. Wilhelm's attitude was quite similar (he translated a collection of
Danish heroic poems, previously published in Denmark
as early as 1591 and divided into four different
groups). In his *Altdänische Heldenlieder, Balladen
und Märchen*, containing this translation and preceded
by an important introduction, Wilhelm divided the material into two groups: on one hand, heroic poems and,
on the other, songs and ballads. He did so because in
his opinion the heroic poems were anterior to the
Nibelungenlied, and were authentic remnants of ancient
primitive songs, and thus belonged to the pagan period,
while the songs and ballads were permeated with Christian ideas. But his main point was that both were folk
poetry.

The *Altdänische Heldenlieder* was published in 1811.
Three years later the publication of a vast four-volume
work entitled *Svenska folk-visor*, collected by E. I.
Geijer and A. A. Afzelius, was begun. Geijer, a poet
and historian, undertook this work with the devotion of
the great folklorists of the time, an effort in which
he had been assisted by Afzelius. Of noteworthy interest in this collection are the musical motifs accom-

panying many songs. Geijer was convinced that the
more poets a language possesses, the less the folk
sings, and for the Swedish folk, as W. P. Ker observes,
the ballad was national poetry. Geijer had arrived at
this thesis because of the importance of the ballad in
his country. But isn't his thesis also correct in
suggesting that folk poetry ends up in second place in
a country that has many learned poets? Ker adds that
in Denmark, as in Sweden, "the imaginative life" is
"all of the kind which is called 'popular.'"[1] This
points to the essence of Hans Christian Andersen's
work. Although Andersen did not collect popular tales,
he used them, following the example of the brothers
Grimm, to make some exquisite creations of his own.

In the field of folklore, however, the most imposing work to come to us from Scandinavian countries was
that of Svend Grundtvig, who collected *Danmarks gamle
folkeviser* in seven volumes between 1853 and 1899.
Collections of this kind had previously been made in
Denmark by Anders Vedel (1591), Peder Syv (1695), and
Knud Rahbek (1812-14). However, Grundtvig's collection
of popular songs (completed by Axel Olrik) was of a
different nature. It has been defined as a work most
noteworthy for its sound methodology and rich erudition.
With this collection Grundtvig initiated a methodology
that would become much used in the field of folkloristic philology, and certainly the experiences of earlier
collectors influenced his work. The German romantics
clearly must be credited with identifying the importance of variants, and Karadžić and especially Lönnrot
had followed their example. But for Grundtvig--as
later for Sophus Bugge, who collected Norwegian folksongs (*Gamle norske folkeviser*, Christiana, 1858) in
accord with the same criteria--variants were used not
only to determine the song's popularity but also to
specify its tradition. It was a matter of designating
the lines of development of a song or a group of songs
to see how a heritage combining the Norse saga with
Germanic heroic material came to life again. This

[1]"On the History of the Ballads, 1100-1500," in
Proceedings of the British Academy (1909-10), p. 198.

approach was obviously Grundtvig's major contribution,
but in addition to philologically perfect collections
we are also indebted to him for some sagas, *Danske
folkesagen* (1854-61), and some folktales, *Danske
folkeaeventyr* (1876-84).

*8. The Romantic Lesson of Folklore: "Think in
     European"*

We can certainly say that when the modern concept of
nationality was asserted in Slavic and Scandinavian
countries, contact with the folk assisted the discovery
of new treasures of life and art. Germany offered its
philological, folkloristic, and national weapons to
Russia and to Poland as well, in a curious succession
of "supremacies and missions." Thus, pan-Germanism
created and sustained pan-Slavism. In a letter to
Strauss, Ernest Renan had written: "The comparative
philology that you have wrongly transported to political ground will perhaps play you some wicked tricks;
the Slavs will love it." This was true enough. But
if philology had not been placed on political and
social ground, would it have given us the rich rewards
that it has, in the name of fatherland, independence,
and national rights? Burke said that whoever does not
love his ancestors does not love his descendants. And
folklore, the study of various manifestations and the
assessment and reassessment of values, was the bridge
between past and future.
     No one can deny that the study of folklore always
advances toward a transcendence of the spiritual and
cultural confines of each individual nation for the
purpose of arriving at the recognition of a broader
community, one which unites all peoples. Indeed, it
seemed that Herder's wish, picked up in Russia by
Chaadaev, might be realized in the field of folklore--
the wish that each nation might live harmoniously with
other nations in the name of the national voice, the
voice of mankind itself. Briefly put, nations that
were politically divided were called to the study of
their own individuality, the major factor in historical

knowledge, but they were not called to suffocate in
it. The open competition (of which we have given only
a sample) to save the most intimate aspects of each
people and each nation was certainly promoted by
nationalistic sentiment; but wasn't this sentiment the
product of a common national and European mission?
The concept of Europe, the *new* concept of Europe, was
empty and meaningless when not imbedded in the cultural and moral forces that folklore had helped to
create. Folklore compelled scholars to think in
German, English, French, Russian, or some other language, but at the same time it also compelled them,
to use Madame de Staël's phrase, to "think in European."

PART FOUR

FOLKLORE BETWEEN PHILOLOGY AND HISTORY
DURING THE AGE OF POSITIVISM

CHAPTER XVI

IN THE "WORKSHOP" OF MAX MÜLLER

1. *The Importance of the Aryan World*

Through the auspices of philology, Romanticism taught
us to think not only in European but also in Indo-
European. Hegel, as we know, considered the discovery
of the linguistic relationship of Sanskrit to Greek,
Latin, and other languages to be the discovery of a
new world. We also know that such a discovery spurred
the investigation of a common Indo-European culture.
The principle of the unity of languages extended from
grammatical considerations to considerations of the
mythology and religion common to all Aryan tribes
before their diffusion and recognizable in the literature of their descendants.

    This principle had previously been suggested in
Jacob Grimm's interesting 1834 preface to *Reinhart
Fuchs*. Transferring linguistic matters to the field
of short stories, Jacob maintained that the relationship between some ancient German lieder and Aesopian
fables supported the theory of a common Indo-European
origin. We should also remember that Wilhelm, as if
continuing his brother's discourse, emphatically stated
in the third volume of *Kinder- und Hausmärchen* that
"the Aryans, emigrating from primitive places to new
ones in Asia and Europe, carried the seeds of stories
and fables with them; these later took shape and
developed independently in each new ethnic center."
He believed that this was why the motifs in *Kinder-
und Hausmärchen* went all the way back to the dispersion
of Aryan peoples--peoples who were cited to explain not

only the eventual connection between languages and folklore but also the hypothetical connection between language and race.

It inevitably followed that in studying this genetic unity, which had transformed Germanism in Germany into the purest expression of Aryanism, scholars replaced the primitive of ethnology (who had been the basis of the noble savage concept) not with the Aryan of linguistics, who was a historical Aryan, but rather with the primitive Aryan, on whom the myth of our origins was to be based. All of this was taking place in the Age of Positivism, an age that, in synthesizing the ideas of the Pre-Enlightenment, the Enlightenment, and Romanticism, was greatly concerned with experimental sciences, social problems, and especially phenomenology relating to primitive peoples.

In 1830 one of the founders of Positivism, Auguste Comte, in initiating the publication of *Cours de philosophie positive*, observed that the history of man can be divided into three stages of development, the first of which, the theological, was dominated by the intervention of supernatural forces or beings. Under the influence of Brosses, Comte believed that fetishism must be considered as the first stage of religion. He also thought that man's history surely began with the history of primitive peoples.

But were primitives (or savages, as they were then called) more than creatures belonging to the animal world? This is the question that Arthur de Gobineau raised a few years later in France in his *Essai sur l'inégalité des races humaines*. Although he regarded himself as an ethnologist, he obviously did not have the slightest idea of what primitive peoples really were. Nor did Gobineau try to understand those peoples (although he adopted some theories popularized by the Society of Ethnology, which William Edwards had established in Paris in 1839). In his view man's history began with the advent of the Aryans or, more specifically, with the advent of the original Aryan race; before them, all was darkness. Gobineau thought that this hypothetical race, endowed with the best qualities, was the original nucleus of all succeeding

civilizations, the leaven of ancient classical civilizations like the Greek and the Roman. The cradle of
this pure, uncontaminated race was central Asia. The
Aryans, branching out from this single trunk, had then
dispersed, acquiring new characteristics in various
places, which gave rise not only to different languages
but also to different civilizations (treated in Adolfe
Pictet's perceptive but hurried investigations some
years later).

Gobineau believed (and this is another example of
Aryanism turning into Germanism) that the most immediate and genuine representatives of this ancient trunk
were the Germans, whose race, like that of their
fathers, was free of any impurities. Germanism thus
received its blood-baptism, while through a confusing
mixture of relationships and languages history was
reduced to a simple naturalistic process. But in the
midst of such naturalism the Aryan (that is, the primitive Aryan) remained as a shining light. This light
would fall upon Friedrich Max Müller, a champion of
the pure Aryan race who was far removed from Gobineau's
racism.

2. Müller's Positivism

A pupil of Schelling and Bopp, Max Müller had gone to
Oxford in 1848 to attend to the publication of the oldest monument of the ancient Aryans that we have, the
Vedas, which had previously been presented in Europe
by Antoine de Polier, a friend of William Jones. Oxford was Müller's stronghold, the citadel from which
he launched his theories in a series of lively, clear,
well-written essays on a variety of topics.

Collected in volumes that became quite popular,
some of these essays appeared under the title *Chips
from a German Workshop*. His essays were indeed "chips"
as well as being from a "German workshop." This is
also an appropriate term to apply to his various lectures and contributions, in which he always proceeded
in "bits and pieces" in addressing various issues
related to "the science of language," the "science of

myth," and the "science of religion." More organic is
his *A History of Ancient Sanskrit Literature*, published
in 1859, which was followed by a collection of sacred
Oriental texts in English translation, entitled *Sacred
Books of the East*.

In these volumes, which appeared under various
titles in innumerable European translations, Müller
demonstrated that he possessed the linguistic, religious, and folkloristic knowledge of his predecessors.
Too, he participated in the contemporary movement known
as Positivism. Positivists claimed for themselves, as
did Müller, the right to reduce facts to a system of
classification, with the result that history took on
the characteristics of a naturalistic science. Furthermore, it was typical of positivists to proceed from
the observation of a single case to the consideration
of the whole--as did Müller. We must also note, however, that Müller and the positivists continually combined earlier Enlightenment ideas with romantic ideas.
But what was Müller's view of the relationships
between language and myth? What surviving elements
has myth left to folklore?

3. *Linguistic-Methodological Interpretations of Myth*

Study of the *Vedas* had convinced Müller that it was
impossible to study myth as an isolated phenomenon and
that it was impossible to interpret myth apart from
language. But hadn't this parallel been identified by
Vico even before the *Vedas* were discovered? Vico considered myth to be an expression of language; moreover,
he found the (theoretical) origin of religion in the
thundering sky that caused amazed and terrified human
"beasts" to form the first idea of God. This "beast"
(the primitive of ethnology, the primitive of Lafitau
and Rousseau) was totally absorbed, Vico believed, in
a personal dream that he projected into natural objects. In the rustling of the leaves he perceived a
sure sign of the will of the gods; in the clear, tranquil flow of the brook he saw reflections of nymphs;
and in the continual change of the seasons was to be

found the sad story of Proserpina and Ceres.

When the *Scienza Nuova* had been out a few years, two works by a Frenchman, Charles François Dupuis, appeared: *Mémoire sur l'origine des constellations et sur l'explication de la Fable par l'astronomie* (1781) and *Origine de tous les cultes* (1795). Although not opposing the euhemeristic trend then predominant, Vico had said that fables based on myths were not modifications of real stories but rather *were* real stories, in the sense that their alleged modification is actually the truth. Dupuis later searched for this "truth" in the worship of nature, which he regarded as the universal impulse from which languages, laws, and the arts originate. In his opinion, such worship must be seen as the basis of primitive religion. He added that, since there are two fundamental elements of nature, light and dark, the common basis of all myths is to be found in the rising and setting of the sun; Christ, for example, represents the sun, and the Christian myth is merely a solar myth.

Dupuis considered myth as a projection of a people's historical life. In Germany, this principle was adopted by Friedrich Creuzer, who maintained in his *Symbolik* that the first religious concept was the result of the animation of nature, which had led to a language permeated with symbolic personifications. We should not forget that Creuzer used etymologies to demonstrate this assumption, even though he used them in an altogether arbitrary fashion. Görres had followed this method, for the most part, as had K. O. Müller in an even more intelligent way. Although K. O. Müller's research dealt only with Greece, he had promoted the historical understanding of myth to which Vico, in particular, had appealed. In a certain sense the brothers Grimm complemented this process, inasmuch as they accepted Vico's idea that myths are poetic images expressing natural phenomena (although their concept of poetry differed from Vico's). The brothers Grimm can be considered as the strongest advocates of comparative mythology, because their comparisons always tended to make myth coincide with language. In the second edition of *Mythologie*, for example, Jacob

expressed the idea that divine mythological beings are
prototypes of an original unity, just as the sounds of
different languages derive from a *unicum*. Differences
between mythologies, then, would correspond to dialectal differences.

But the Grimms--who were especially interested in
seeing how the seeds of tales (which are the survivals
of myths) developed in a special ethnic center, Ger-
many--did not have access to the *Vedas*, a crucial
source. This work was later used by one of their
admirers, Adalbert Kuhn. Combining his linguistic
interest with his interest in the history of religions,
he not only substituted the primitive of philology for
the primitive of ethnology but also asserted that the
basic nature of the gods--specifically, Aryan gods--
is related to such transitory phenomena as clouds and
tempests, a thesis later followed by Wilhelm Schwartz.
The characteristics of the "beast" were thus transferred to the historical Aryan, and Kuhn constructed
his principal works, such as *Die Herabkunft des Feuers
und des Göttertranks* (1859) and *Über Entwicklungsstufen
der Mythenbildung* (1873), precisely on these characteristics.

In his essay entitled *Comparative Mythology*, Max
Müller said that Kuhn was one of his most direct
sources of inspiration. In fact, Müller followed Kuhn
in bringing the names of various Aryan divinities back
to an Indo-European base, reconstructing their hypothetical primitive meaning and therefore their original significance. The significance that Müller gave
to these divinities reminds us of Dupuis, but a Dupuis
corrected and modernized by German philology. Kuhn
had substituted the storm, the tempest, and the hurri-
cane for the sun (or perhaps we should say the rising
and the setting of the sun) as the source of inspiration for mythology. Müller put the sun back in its
rightful place. In doing so, he combined Vico's ideas
with Dupuis' ideas and Creuzer's ideas with Kuhn's.
In contrast to Kuhn, however, he was not content to
examine only the historical Aryans. He extended his
examination to primitive Aryans, those early fathers
whom the diaspora had scattered to the winds.

4. The Generative Language of Myths

This was the origin of Müller's philologico-linguistic theory, which attempted to clarify relationships between language and myth. In his *Comparative Mythology* Müller said that comparative philology offered him a "telescope of such power"[1] that he could see the distinct forms and outlines of what had previously been seen as nebulous clouds. Comparative philology took him back to a time when Sanskrit and Greek did not even exist, because both of them, like other Aryan languages, were contained in one common language. Comparative philology helped him understand extant linguistic evidence that this period had left behind, and at the same time it gave him the opportunity to consider the primogenitive state of thought, religion, and civilization.

Comparative philology, Müller said, not only gives us proof of the existence of this primitive Aryan period, but it also gives us data on the intellectual state of the Aryan family before its dispersion. Moreover, he went to the romance languages for the magic formula that would open the archives of the most ancient history of the Aryan race. For example, if we find in all the romance dialects a word like *pont* (in Italian *ponte*, in Spanish *puente*, in Wallachian *pod*), we have the right, after taking account of national particularities, to say that the word *pont* was known before languages separated.

During this period before the formation of distinct nationalities, each word was, according to Müller, a myth. Each name in the original Aryan language, he therefore said, was an image; each substantive was a person; each sentence was a little drama. But those names lost their original vitality through phonetic decay and became names of people, to whom were attributed all the dramatic actions that reproduce life, death, and the daily renewal of nature. This is why many pagan, Indic, and Greek gods are

[1]*Comparative Mythology* (1856; rpt. London: George Routledge and Sons, Ltd., 1909), p. 21.

merely poetical names assuming a divine personality never contemplated by their inventors: *nomina, numina*. These *nomina-numina* would subsequently become the subject of a mythology dominated by the rising and setting of the sun and the battle between light and dark, a genuine drama manifested in all of its particulars every day, every month, every year.

Thus, Müller completely changed the relationship between myth and language proposed by Vico and the German philologists. For Müller myth was no longer a powerful "felt" reality; rather, it was a philological deception. On this subject Cassirer says, "Certainly Müller did not see a simple, arbitrary invention, a deception by an astute social class, in the making of myth. But he did believe that ultimately myth is merely a great illusion, an unwitting and unconscious deception." He came to regard myth, the most suggestive and most powerful expression of language, as a "disease of language." He considered language as a naturalistic science whose nature, origin, and development he wished to vindicate. And he came to see religion, at least in some respects, in much the same way as he saw myth.

5. The Sources of Religion

In 1873 in his *Introduction to the Science of Religion*, Müller, paraphrasing Goethe's statement that "he who knows one language knows none," said of religion, "He who knows one, knows none."[2] However, the religions that he preferred and that he used as reference points for constructing the history of religions were the Indic ones. In this respect the *Vedas* were very important to him. In an essay later collected in *Lectures on the Science of Language*, Müller, in clarifying the "drama" which he saw at work in mythology, observed, "I consider that the very idea of divine powers sprang from the wonderment with which the forefathers of the

[2]*Introduction to the Science of Religion* (1873; rpt. Varansi, India: Bharata Manisha, 1972), p. 13.

Aryan family stared at the bright (deva) powers that
came and went no one knew whence or whither, that never
failed, never faded, never died, and were called immortal, i.e., unfading, as compared with the feeble and
decaying race of man. I consider the regular recur-
rence of phenomena an almost indispensable condition of
their being raised, through the charms of mythological
phraseology, to the rank of immortals. . . ."[3]

Although Müller did not argue that there once was a
historical revelation, he did believe in an indeterminate internal revelation, an influence of the infinite
on the soul. According to him, perception of the
infinite gave the first impulse to "thought" or to the
"language" of religion, since initially men were fascinated not by the objects in their environment but by
the spectacle of nature as a whole. Thus, while sub-
scribing to romantic and symbolic theories about the
earliest times, he rejected the theory of fetishism
then in vogue in the Age of Positivism. He did so
because this theory contradicted the *Vedas*.

In the famous *Hibbert Lectures*, initiated at Oxford in 1878, Müller distinguished three types of
religious objects: (1) tangible ones, such as rocks
and shells; (2) semi-tangible ones, such as trees,
rivers, and mountains; (3) intangible ones, such as
the sky, the sun, and the stars. He concluded that
the hymns of the most ancient poets had been dedicated
to the last two types but not to the first type, which
is the object of a "physical" religion. Man's social
relationships led to anthropological religion, which
led to the worship of God. But man also had a conscience, an "inner voice" that would lead him to
natural religion.

Müller was convinced that language and thought are
inseparable, with the result that a "disease of language" is also a disease of thought:

To represent the supreme God as committing every
kind of crime, as being deceived by men, as being

[3]*Lectures on the Science of Language*, 6th ed.
(London: Longmans, Green, and Co., 1871), pp. 565-66.

angry with his wife and violent with his children,
is surely proof of a disease, of an unusual condition of thought, or, to speak more clearly, of
real madness. . . . These cases form a very small
section of mythologic pathology, and they owe
their popularity chiefly to the fact that they are
amusing and easily intelligible. But I meant much
more by a disease of language. . . . The cases of
diseased language due to a mere misunderstanding,
to false etymology, to wrong pronunciation, and
similar accidents, are curious no doubt, but they
are very slight complaints, and do not touch the
deepest springs of mythology.[4]

In erroneously leading us to the worship of objects
conceived of as persons, language thus brings about a
misunderstanding of religion. And now that Romanticism
had been swept away, Müller returned to the point from
which he had begun in explaining the relationship between language and myth; he returned, that is, to
rationalism and intellectualism.

6. *In the Enchanted World of Folklore*

This theory was not unrelated to the field of folklore,
a study to which Müller had always been particularly
attracted. As if to complement what Wilhelm Grimm had
written on the subject, he professed that the nation
was strongly attached to its *Märchen*, whose origins
belong to the period preceding the dispersion of the
Aryan race. He was also of the opinion that "the same
people who, in their migrations to the North and the
South carried along with them the names of the Sun and
the Dawn, and their belief in the bright gods of Heaven,
possessed in their very language, in their mythological
and proverbial phraseology, the more or less developed
germs that were sure to grow into the same or very

[4]*Contributions to the Science of Mythology* (London:
Longmans, Green, and Co., 1897), I, 69.

similar plants on every soil and under every sky."[5]

To undertake the scientific study of folk narrative, the first task, according to Müller, is to trace
each modern account back to an old legend, and each
legend back to a primitive myth. We must realize, however, that although our tales were originally reproductions of older legends, a pleasure in the marvelous
developed with the passing of time, with the result
that new tales were invented by our grandmothers and
our nurses. But in such purely imaginative tales, we
can discover similarities with more primitive tales.
We must therefore trace each tale back to its most
primitive form, which is its simplest form; we must
examine and analyze this form, rigorously observing
the rules of comparative philology; and, finally, when
we have discovered the simple and original conception
of the myth, we must see how the conception and the
myth have gradually developed and how they have taken
on different forms under the brilliant sky of India
and in the forests of Germany.

In considering existing *Märchen* as a mass of fragments left to us by primitive mythology, Müller obviously came to regard the *Vedas* as the *deus ex machina*
for their interpretation. Angelo de Gubernatis, the
greatest proponent of Müller's thought, has this to say
on the subject:

> The *Rig-Veda* offers us pure myths: *man views and
> notes celestial events, and yet he does not narrate
> them.* After collecting these various myths apper-
> taining to the dawn cycle, however, I cannot help
> but see a beautiful legend, an entire series of
> legends, which can easily be compared to other
> epopees and legends. . . . What is dawn in the
> Vedic hymns? *It is a young maiden who appears on
> the peak of the mountain; she has a brilliant
> dress, a glowing body, and is the guardian of the
> herds.* She has a sister, darkness, who is ugly,

[5]*Chips from a German Workshop* (London: Longmans,
Green, and Co., 1867), II, 226.

while dawn is splendid and beautiful. She is the
good sister who disperses the *darkness of her
sister and removes her.* She kills the black monster, the daughter of darkness. . . . Let us collect these myths and explicate them. If we do so,
the following story will emerge: Once upon a time
there was an ugly, monstrous woman, a witch, who
had two daughters. One was like her, ugly and
evil; the other was different, for she was beautiful and good. The woman loved the ugly daughter
as her own child, but she hated the beautiful
daughter, who was only a step-child. She sent the
beautiful girl to guard the herds, but when she
returned at dawn, a great splendor surrounded her
on the mountain top. She found herself adorned
with a golden dress, while on her forehead was a
splendid star. (*Le novelline di S. Stefano*,
Torino, 1869, pp. 6-7)

It was precisely in images like this that Psyche comes
to symbolize the dawn that disappears when the sun
shines; Cinderella symbolizes the break of day among
the clouds; the imprisoned beauties freed by a prince
symbolize spring freed from winter; and the monster-
killer who frees the golden-haired princess symbolizes
the solar hero.

Müller did not take recourse to the *Vedas* only to
explain *Märchen*; they are also the source for various
customs: "If we find the same custom in India and in
Greece, we are apt to suppose that it must have sprung
from a common source, and we are inclined to ascribe
its origin to the times preceding the Aryan separation.
. . . It is one of the principal charms in the study
of customs to watch their growth and their extraordinary tenacity."[6] In his essays Müller traced the
development of some customs which also interested his
greatest interpreter, Angelo de Gubernatis. Gubernatis produced such works as *Zoological Mythology* and
La mythologie des plantes, and he also wrote a series
of comparative histories about funeral customs and

[6]*Chips from a German Workshop*, II, 262, 281.

Christmas traditions, for the purpose of "reconstructing traditional logic as completely as possible, at
least for the Indo-European race; although it might
not conform precisely to the logical systems of philosophers, it is of more interest to the observer than
the latter systems are, and it is perhaps less capricious and disorganized" (*Storia comparata degli usi
funebri in Italia e presso gli altri popoli Indo-
Europei*, Milano, 1875, p. 6). Despite this purpose,
however, Gubernatis' works are merely catalogues of
Müller's ideas, for Müller had greatly influenced his
study of mythology and customs. In fact, Müller had
many followers in both his adopted and his original
country, as well as in Italy, France, and especially
Russia. Comparative philology broke forth everywhere,
just as the sun breaks from behind the clouds. And
with the sun--when it was not, alas, replaced by fire
or water--Müller traveled the road of folklore,
accounting for such aspects as customs, myths, tales,
legends, fables, and lieder.

7. Criticisms and Controversies Surrounding Müller

Philology was not concerned only with Müller and his
immediate followers. While Müller constructed his
theory gradually, the Indo-European myth had quickly
undergone changes and adaptions in regard to its center
of diffusion. We are especially reminded of Paul
Geiger's work, which placed the center of the primitive
Aryan world in the middle of Germany. Too, we are
reminded of Theodor Poesche, who dogmatically proposed
the assimilation of blond Nordics with Aryans, in the
hope of finding conditions favorable to the origin and
development of this ethnic type in western Russia.
But despite changes and adaptions in the Indo-European
myth, the original Aryan civilization imagined and
constructed by Müller remained hypothetical--particu-
larly in light of geological evidence that Europe had
been inhabited since earliest times. The *Vedas*, the
basis for Müller's concept of folk poetry (a concept
constructed by the brothers Grimm), were viewed by

scholars for what they actually were, sacerdotal hymns
having nothing to do with folk poetry. We must also
remember that Egyptian or Assyrian-Babylonian tales
did not appear to be any less ancient than the Indic
tales contained in the *Vedas*. Furthermore, comparative philology was forced to acknowledge that the
derivation of mythology from gender terminations cannot be dogmatically asserted because mythology is also
the expression of peoples unfamiliar with grammatical
genders. Comparative philology was therefore forced
to admit that Müller's theory about grammatical endings
(*nomina-numina*) had validity only in some identifications.

In addition to the accusation that he did not account for particularities of myths or similarities
between myths of different languages, Müller was also
charged with mistakenly basing his system on the
uncertain ground of grammatical terminations without
then saying that one could not help but derive uniform
interpretations from narrow etymological explanations.
Georges Dumézil says, "We must recognize that the comparative philology [of Müller] brought about its own
disgrace." In 1900, the same year in which Müller
died, one of his severest critics, Marinus de Visser,
declared that he had learned nothing from mythologists
like Müller because they did not actually compare anything.

Visser also observed that to reduce mythology to a
simple lyrical paraphrase or an epic of celestial
phenomena was to pose the problem of religion badly,
inasmuch as God is certainly more than a mere personi-
fication of a celestial phenomenon--which was Vico's
point, we might add. For any name to become a numen,
the object to which it was first applied must appear
to the folk consciousness as being endowed with divine
virtue, and, despite its development from a primitive
concept, it remains as only a vague sign of certain
ideal notions that are generally lofty, refined, and
rational. Without taking account of religious intuition, observes Michele Kerbaker (who generally favored
Müller's school of thought), one cannot understand how
simple observations could have been transformed into a

poetic tale inspiring the enthusiasm of singers, exciting folk admiration, and appearing to subsequent
generations as the ultimate in human knowledge.

We must not forget that before these and other
critical attacks there were satirical attacks, the
most terrible weapon with which a system, a theory,
or a man can be blasted. Müller suffered the same fate
in England that Dupuis had in France a century before.
Comme quoi Napoléon n'a jamais existé, a humorous pamphlet that went into thirteen editions, was very popular in France between 1836 and 1840. Relying on
Dupuis's theories, this work maintained the "incontestable" truth that Napoleon had never existed and
that he was only the reflection and survival of a solar
myth. In 1870, when Müller was in vogue, Oxford students published a pamphlet about a follower of his,
George William Cox. In this pamphlet the students
demonstrated, with the help of the *Vedas*, that Max
Müller was also a solar myth (a notion that was applied
to Caesar and Gladstone in England a few years later).

In recalling these controversies Henri Gaidoz
remembers some verses by Victor Hugo:

> *O temps évanouis!   O splendeurs eclipsées!*
> *O soleil descendu derrière l'horizon!*

Müller's sun had also been eclipsed; but, critics and
controversies aside, can we fairly reduce his works to
a formula and then judge them only in terms of that
formula? Sokolov says, quite rightly, "It would be
very erroneous to define under this term [specifically,
the term "solar" given to his mythology] the whole complex, exceedingly erudite system of scientific views
established by Max Müller."[7] Terracini observes that
Müller had "the kind of scientific imagination that
very much complicates the results obtained," confusing
"the working hypotheses with what is actually proved."

[7] *Russian Folklore*, trans. Catherine Ruth Smith,
with an Introduction and Bibliography by Felix Oinas
(1950; rpt. Hatboro, Pa.: Folklore Associates, 1966),
p. 60.

His hypotheses, however, were not useless or insignificant, and, although his solar theory is perhaps only
an interesting episode in the history of mythological
studies, the stance that he took in facing many aspects
of mythology, religion, and folklore is certainly *not*
an "episode." Some aspects of his extensive work are
still of great interest. In this work the theorist is
no longer important, but the incomparable Orientalist,
the keen researcher, the elegant writer remains.

8. *The Validity of Müller's Precepts*

One of Müller's contributions is in his having arranged
his work in such a way that ethnic manifestations were
considered in relation to specific groups of peoples.
Another contribution is his declaration that knowledge
of the Aryan world was not useless, for it mirrored the
"story of our own race, of our own family--nay, of our
own selves."[8] Finally, it is to his credit that, after
exploring the Aryan world, he maintained that an ethnologist who would speak of the Aryan race, Aryan blood,
Aryan eyes and hair would commit the enormous error of
a linguist who spoke of a dolichocephalic vocabulary or
a brachycephalic grammar.[9] In this respect his philology, although positivistic, clearly had a historical
slant. Raffaele Pettazzoni comments on this subject:

> The linguistic factor with which it [Müller's
> school] explained the mythico-religious act was
> best suited for presenting comparisons of tempera-
> mental differences between one people and another,
> and therefore it was best suited for presenting the
> characteristics of individual peoples and nations.
> This is of great importance for the understanding
> of history (and thus it is also important for the
> understanding of religious history). . . . On the
> other hand, philology was more than just the

[8]*Comparative Mythology*, p. 7.
[9]See *Introduction to the Science of Religion*,
p. 238.

science of language and the science of myth founded
on language (*vergleichende Mythologie*). The text
that was brought to the attention of the scholar,
whether literary or documentary, was, in its concreteness and historical precision, more than
simply a phonetic datum of semasiological abstraction.

The imaginative poetic reconstruction that Müller
gave to various folkloristic manifestations was a new
and potent stimulus because such manifestations, now
invested with dignity, began to be collected more carefully everywhere. In a letter that Müller wrote to
Giuseppe Pitrè, which served as the introduction to the
Archivio per lo studio delle tradizioni popolari, one
finds these words:

> . . . You ask me again to send you a preface to a
> journal which you intend to publish with some
> friends of yours, and which is to form an *Archive
> for popular traditions in Europe*, and I confess I
> feel again the same difficulty. The study of
> popular traditions of Europe and of the whole
> world has made such gigantic strides during the
> last twenty years that I have only been able, not
> possessing myself a pair of those famous
> *Meilenstiefeln*, to watch it from a very respectful
> distance. Years ago, when that study was, if not
> despised, at least ignored, I spoke out as strongly
> as I could against its detractors. Now that I
> begin to feel old and tired, I find the trees which
> I helped to plant growing into such forests that I
> often feel tempted to cry out, enough, enough![10]

[10]*Archivio per lo studio delle tradizioni popolari*,
I (Palermo: Luigi Pedone Lauriel, 1882), 5-6. The
letter appears in Italian in the *Archivio*, but I am
quoting from the original letter (written in English),
which has been made available to me by Professor Gaetano
Falzone, director of the Pitrè Ethnographic Museum in
Palermo. *Translator.*

In his research he established the rules of the method
that he had given to Pitrè for collecting tales, which,
of all the products of folklore, he had most loved and
cared for:

> To collect popular stories is either a most
> difficult or most easy task. . . . First of all,
> not every story that an old woman may tell deserves
> to be written down and printed. There is a pecu-
> liar earthy flavour about the genuine home grown,
> or, if I may say so, autochthonic *Märchen* . . .
> which we must learn to appreciate before we can
> tell whether a story is old or new, genuine or made
> up, whether it comes in fact from the forest or the
> hot-house. This is a matter of taste. . . .
> Secondly, the same story should, whenever that
> is possible, be collected from different sources
> and in different localities, and the elements which
> are common to all versions should be carefully dis-
> tinguished from those that are peculiar to one or
> more only.
> Thirdly, each collector should acquaint himself
> with the results already obtained in the classifi-
> cation of stories, in order to see and to say at
> once to what cluster each new story belongs. . . .
> Fourthly, whenever it is possible, the story
> ought to be given in the *ipsissima verba* of the
> story teller. This would be a safe-guard against
> that dishonesty of collectors of stories from
> which we have suffered so much. It is quite true
> that a collector who trims and embellishes a story
> ought to be whipped. . . .[11]

It seems, then, that Müller would not have hesitated to whip even the brothers Grimm, whom he had always admired; but the brothers Grimm, as Müller knew,
had undertaken a personal work of art while Müller was
interested in the texts of true, authentic folklore.
Nor is his warning to collect tales in the narrator's
ipsissima verba without significance, when we consider

[11]Ibid., pp. 6-7.

that only tales so collected can document the richness of dialects: "That study of dialects, I feel certain, is full of promise, and I still hold as strongly as ever that, in order to know what language is, we must study it in dialects, which can represent the real natural life of language."[12]

With this wish the master, "old and tired," as he himself said, left his spiritual testament to the scholars of folk tradition; meanwhile, an idea that had much interested pre-romantics and romantics was strengthened by his teaching and by all his work--the idea that individual philologies are valuable because they capture the histories of individual countries.

CHAPTER XVII

IN THE FOOTSTEPS OF BENFEY

1. India as Dogma

While Müller and his followers coupled comparative
grammar to the sun, dawn, and the sunset, Theodor
Benfey, another German Orientalist educated in Bopp's
school, gave folktale study his own particular systemization, one that descended from the clouds to the
earth, as he liked to say. Unlike Müller, Benfey did
not attempt to explain the origin of mythology and
therefore of folk narrative. In his view, the study
of folk narrative should be based primarily on an examination of the popular or literary vehicles through
which a short story, fable, or tale is propagated.

Although Müller and Benfey both looked to India,
Benfey's India had nothing in common with the India
of the ancient Aryans, whose "distant migrations" he
viewed with some skepticism. Benfey's India was the
historical India, the India that could be placed in
time and space. We know that the *Vedas* were the *deus
ex machina* with which Müller began in order to create
an idyllic primitive (Aryan) world, which he then
gradually came to see in the contemporary world.
Benfey, on the other hand, appealed to another Indic
text, the *Panchatantra*, which he regarded as one of
the principal sources of European popular narrative.
This is the nucleus of the extensive introduction or,
rather, treatise (it contains some six hundred pages)
that accompanied his German translation of the *Panchatantra* in 1859.

In this treatise, which is as important for the
study of folk narrative as the third volume of *Kinder-
und Hausmärchen*, Benfey not only demonstrated the

measure of his interests but also demonstrated that
his temperament was completely opposite to Müller's.
Müller was ingenious and brilliant while Benfey was
rigid and "blockish"; Müller was an artist who gave a
distinct warmth to his researches and syntheses, whatever they were, while Benfey had neither style nor
charm; the *Vedas* were the forge of Müller's imagination,
while the *Panchatantra*, for Benfey, was the source from
which theorems, axioms, and equations could be drawn;
finally, Müller was clear while Benfey was complicated
--a fact that caused Keller, one of Benfey's major
critics, to say that we cannot find a clearly expressed
principle anywhere in Benfey's work. But this does not
alter the fact, Francesco Ribezzo observes, that although Benfey "occasionally makes contradictory observations and judgments," one "can organize and assemble
them more organically by gleaning various passages and
by passing over partial contradictions."

2. The "Panchatantra" and the Indic Origin of Tales

In order to come to grips with this "organization,"
we must refer to a French scholar, Auguste Loiseleur-
Deslongchamps, who had published his *Essai sur les
fables indiennes et sur leur introduction en Europe*
in Paris in 1838. In attempting to amplify the
researches of his teacher, Antoine Silvestre de Sacy,
Loiseleur-Deslongchamps had worked on a collateral
readaption of the *Panchatantra*, the romance *Calila et
Dimna*. Silvestre de Sacy's memoirs, published in
1816, carried the title *Calila et Dimna, ou les Fables
de Bidpai en arabe*. This title clearly indicates that
Silvestre de Sacy intended to study folktales in terms
of their propagation. He was not concerned with establishing a common remote Aryan source from which popular
tales, stories, and fables might have emerged like
Venus from the sea; rather, his work consisted in
establishing the tales' propagation with the help of
presumably concrete facts. Nor was this the full
extent of Silvestre de Sacy's research. In treating
sacred Buddhist literature, he also considered the

enormous number of tales, maxims, and proverbs that
helped preachers reach the souls of the people. After
the fall of Buddhism, the Brahmans took on this inheritance, one of whose fruits was the *Panchatantra*. As
the preface indicates, the *Panchatantra* was composed
by a sage named Visnusarma to educate the three sons
of Amarasacti, King of Mihiralopia:

> Gathering from the world the entire essence
> Of all moral doctrine, in five parts
> This book of doctrine that the heart
> Touches and enraptures, Visnusarma wrote.

We know nothing about this sage, who skillfully
combined his moral precepts with superb tales, stories,
and apologues. We do know, however, that the first
translation of the text was made in the sixth century
by an educated man, Buzurcimihr, who lived at court in
Persia; later, in the eighth century, 'Abd Allāh Ibn
al-Muqaffa', a Persian who had just been converted to
the Mohammedan religion and who used the language of
the conquerors, provided an Arabic translation known
under the name of *Calila and Dimna*. In publishing the
Arabic text of this prodigious book ('Abd Allāh himself
mentioned the Pahlavian translation, now lost), Silvestre de Sacy had undertaken the study of its diffusion and its ramifications, but he had limited his
research to the Oriental world; Loiseleur-Deslongchamps
extended it to the Western world. He presented Huet's
and La Fontaine's ideas about the diffusion of Indic
tales in Europe, but in a significantly different way.
With text in hand and using formal philological research, he posed the question of the Indic origin of
each type of apologue.

Studies of this type were continued some years
later by Augúste Wagener in his "Essai sur les rapports
qui existent entre les apologues de l'Inde et les
apologues de la Grèce," published in 1852. In this
essay he formulated a detailed theory about the historical propagation of fables, and he argued for the
thesis that the fable is diffused through collective
rather than individual effort. This explains his con-

viction that Aesop did not exist and that the tradition
credited to him "as to a central ideal" is explained by
the propagation of fables from the interior of Asia to
the Ionian colonies and Greece.

After comparing some Greek fables with some Indic
ones (taken in part from the *Panchatantra*), Wagener
came to believe that he had discovered this fact: "As
one goes back from the most recent versions to the most
primitive myths in these two types of tales, the similarity of detail steadily increases"; therefore, it
must follow that Greece had received its fables from
India in one block. Wagener's thesis proved the opposite of what it had intended to demonstrate although,
as Albrecht Weber says, "the proofs that he adopted to
demonstrate that the fable was not of Greek origin did
indeed contain data demonstrating that the fables were
extremely old." On this basis Weber, one of the sharpest of contemporary critics and philologists, argued,
in some essays published in the *Indische Studien* of
1856, that it was most improbable that Indic fables
had been introduced into Greece.

Wagener based the documenting of his thesis not
only on the antiquity of the *Panchatantra*, which in
his view went back to the fourth century, but also on
the localization of Greek fables, which refer to places
ranging all the way from the Orient to Europe. In
light of the given facts, Weber clearly had the upper
hand--for although the supposed antiquity of the *Panchatantra* had not been proved, the antiquity of the
Aesopian fables had; they had been cited by authors
living in a period anterior to the one in which Wagener
supposed the transmission of this book had taken place
(200-150 B.C.). Besides, the reference to a specific
place that one occasionally finds in a tale could be a
device of its creator. Was Weber perhaps on more solid
ground than Wagener? And what inspiration did Benfey
draw from his predecessors?

3. Benfey's Historical-Oriental Theory

There is no doubt that Benfey, as he himself said, was

influenced by Silvestre de Sacy's studies, and he was
particularly interested in the origin and development
of various translations of the *Panchatantra*. But in
his minute and precise examination, a masterpiece of
Orientalist philology, could he neglect the diffusion
of the *Panchatantra* tales in folk literature? Taking
up Loiseleur-Deslongchamps's thesis about the Indic
origin of the apologue, Benfey formulated a comprehensive theory that went beyond determining the origin of
the apologue, inasmuch as it included a variety of
narrative forms, including short stories, tales, and
riddles. Benfey himself said, "My research has brought
me to the conclusion that a large number of *Märchen* and
other folktales have traveled from India to all the
world." He believed that this diffusion had begun in
the tenth century, A.D., with fables and apologues that
had become known through readaptions and translations
of the *Panchatantra* (familiar to travelers and merchants who had gone to the Orient).

Obviously, then, in Benfey's view the first vehicle
for the propagation of these tales from India to Europe
was the oral tradition. But after this came another
tradition, the literary one. Benfey described its
advent in the following way:

> In the tenth century an awareness of India began
> with the attacks and conquests of India's Moslems.
> From that moment on, the oral tradition became
> less important than the written one. India's
> narrative works began to be translated into
> Persian and Arabic, and in a relatively short
> time they were spread--and by this I do not mean
> only their content or narrative plot--to lands
> occupied by the Moslems in Asia, Africa, and
> Europe. Because of the frequent association of
> these peoples with Christians, the narratives
> also spread throughout the entire Christian West.
> In the Christian West, the principal points of
> contact were the Byzantine Empire, Spain, and
> Italy.

In addition to Buddhist literature, he said, fables,

parables, and legends had migrated into China and then Tibet, beginning in the first century, A.D. Nor did their journey stop there: "From Tibet those compositions [fables, parables, and so on] came, with Buddhism, to the Mongolians, and we know with the greatest certainty that they translated Indic tales into their own language. Obviously these translations contained many modifications and changes in details. . . . The Mongolians, as we know, dominated Europe for two hundred years; therefore, they also contributed to the diffusion of Indic tales in Europe."

Benfey documented this diffusion by pointing to various translations and adaptions that had been made of the *Panchatantra*. After having been translated from ancient Persian into Arabic (twelfth century), it was translated from Arabic into Hebrew (twelfth century), from Hebrew into Latin (thirteenth century), and finally from Latin into French, German, Italian, and other languages. As if to complete the picture, he identified a reciprocal relationship between the oral tradition and the literary tradition, or at least what he believed to be the literary tradition: "In European literature the tales appeared primarily in Boccaccio and in Straparola's *Märchen*. They were taken from literature by the folk, and, *after having been changed by the folk*, they again entered literature; then they were again taken up by the folk. Through this alternating activity of nations and individuals, many tales took on qualities of national truth and individual unity that give them a great poetic value" (*Panchatantra*, I, 150).

Benfey, then, emphasized one fact: the European folk had indeed reproduced some themes and motifs coming from India, but, through its own reworkings, it had also created some new, truly artistic tales. Although he was concerned with studying the propagation of tales, he understood, however vaguely, that the philologist must go further than earlier literary scholars by also considering the aesthetic genesis of a tale, the creative moment when an old tale is reworked into a new one.

4. *The Propagation and Creation of Folktales*

In taking account of Wagener's and Weber's theories
on the origin of the folk narrative, Benfey quickly
admitted that although many fables derive from the
inventive genius of India, many others derive from
the inventive genius of Greece. In recognizing this,
he obviously reconciled Wagener with Weber. But was
his position taken only to express a conciliatory
thesis? Benfey himself said, "It is clear that in
general most fables about animals originated in the
West and are basically transformations of Aesopian
fables. Nevertheless, some of them appear to have
originated in India. . . . The difference between
Indic and Aesopian fables generally consists in the
fact that while the Aesopian writer made his animals
act with their own characteristics, the Indic fables
treated animals without regard to their special
nature, as if they actually were men masked in the
shape of animals" (*Panchatantra*, I, 250).

Here again Benfey obviously was concerned not
only with the propagation of tales but also with
their artistic genesis. Weber was convinced that to
find the original version of a narrative, one must
find its most artistically valid form. But to this
aesthetic criterion Benfey opposed another one:

> The beauty, the perfect congruity of idea and
> form, is the result of a long, continual and,
> in a certain sense, reflective and critical
> transformation, in which the folk takes part
> more in judging than in creating. If we could
> trace the history of all fables back to their
> origin, we would find that our most beautiful
> creations have come from crude, shapeless
> beginnings. We would discover that they have
> taken on a homogeneous form only through a long
> process of reworking by the folk and that they
> have attained their highest perfection only
> through this process. In this process some of
> them, *as living expressions of the folk spirit*,
> came into the hands of some genius and were

stamped with a high degree of individuality.
(*Panchatantra*, I, 325)

Certainly no one will contest Benfey's principle
that in "the hands of some genius" a tale can become
a work of art--but Weber had approached this problem
for an altogether different angle. Weber had wrongly
considered the *original* form of a tale as its best
version. Benfey, following Wolf's teaching, had been
quick to right this wrong. Although he contradicted
himself and although his language was not always clear,
Benfey indeed recognized that India was in fact the
great reservoir of European tales; but this did not
exclude *a priori* the fact that such tales could be
influenced by the imagination of whoever took up those
themes and motifs.

5. *Köhler, Landau, and Cosquin*

Benfey's Oriental-historical theory about the origin
of folktales is less inflexible than is generally
believed, or at least it is less inflexible than its
proponents have made it appear to be. One of these
proponents, Reinhold Köhler, was extremely popular in
Germany. In his extensive essay *Über die europäischen
Volksmärchen* (1865), he followed the lead of his
teacher by saying that "*most important folktales*, as
well as many of the stories that had come into Western
literatures in the late Middle Ages, are either directly Indic or suggested by Indic literature." Immediately after, without considering the importance of
the preceding sentence, he added, "Benfey's opinion
about the origin and propagation of European folktales
is, as he himself says, a question that will be completely resolved only when all or almost all tales
have been traced back to the original Indic ones."
    This viewpoint explains Köhler's long catalogues,
patiently taken from folktale collections that were
then being published in Europe. Without exception,
these catalogues led him back to a single source:
India. In this respect Marcus Landau, who published

an extensive essay in 1869 entitled *Die quellen des
Dakameron*, was equally orthodox. But unlike Köhler
(whose studies were in catalogue form), Landau did not
deal only with simple checklists. He was (or attempted
to be) more flexible. For example, in examining
Boccaccio's tale "Federigo degli Alberighi," he first
mentions a Buddhist legend in which Buddha transforms
himself into a dove and allows the hungry family of a
fowler to roast him, and then he cites a similar tale
from the *Panchatantra*, in which a dove throws itself
into the fire in order to serve as food for a hunter.
He concludes, "In Boccaccio, Federigo degli Alberighi
has nothing to give to the beloved woman who comes to
visit him. Thus, he finds himself in the same situation as the dove of the *Panchatantra*. He sacrifices
not his own body but rather his dearest treasure, his
only falcon; he receives, in exchange, the greatest
gift, the love of the woman he loves."

In France, Landau had a faithful disciple in
Eugène Lévêque. The latter, in an 1880 work entitled
Les mythes et les légendes de l'Inde et de la Perse,
examined myths and legends in the works of Aristophanes,
Plato, Ovid, Livy, Dante, Boccaccio, Ariosto, Rabelais,
Perrault, and La Fontaine. Naturally, he did this with
the greatest ingenuity. But the French scholar who
most contributed to dogmatizing Benfey's Orientalistic
thesis was Emmanuel Cosquin, a famous collector of his
country's folktales. His *Contes populaires de Lorraine*
(1886), each of which is told by an archetypal Indian,
has a long introduction dealing with the origin and
propagation of European folktales. His innumerable
"little monographs" hinge on this origin-propagation
thesis. Beginning in 1886, these monographs were published in various periodicals, and they were collected
in 1922 in *Les contes indiens et l'Occident* and *Études
folkloriques*.

Cosquin dogmatically regarded India as the indisputable source of all tales, and he often referred to
Indic beliefs and institutions to explain the origin
of folktales diffused in Europe. He was convinced,
for example, that belief in metempsychosis had contributed much to the rise and diffusion of fables and

tales, but he was also convinced that metempsychosis was solely an Indic characteristic. In contrast to Benfey but in line with Köhler and Landau, he did not hesitate to say that a tale was of Indic origin if a tale with the same theme had later been found in India.

Another French scholar, Henri Gaidoz, suggested quite logically that Cosquin should observe that belief in metempsychosis is African, American, and Oceanic as well as Indic, and a folktale found in our own time proves nothing about its antiquity. It goes without saying that a similarity of theme does not necessarily mean a similarity of artistic form--which is what is most important in a tale. Ignoring Gaidoz and other critics in his treatment of the origin of European tales, Cosquin posed the problem even more categorically than his teacher had, and he amassed some arbitrarily selected parallels to demonstrate that India was an Eden in which the fountain of all tales gushed, fresh and eternal.

6. Genesis of the Russian Historical School: Miller and Veselovskiĭ

Later, other scholars added fables as well as other folk productions, such as Russian byliny. It is a well known fact that Russia had fully adhered (initially, at least) to the Orientalist theory, particularly because Benfey had reinforced A. N. Pypin's earlier studies on the subject. We must add that around the time that Benfey's translation of *Panchatantra* was published, some Russian scholars (Schiefner and Radlov, for example) published some collections of folk productions from the eastern part of the country, and they were struck by the amazing similarity between Mongolian and Turkic songs.

In 1868 a well educated philologist, V. V. Stasov, published an essay on the origin of Russian byliny entitled *Proiskhoźhdenie russkikh bylin*. After rejecting all the theories of the mythological school (such a rejection being an indispensable premise

for the followers of the Orientalist theory), he demonstrated (or believed he demonstrated) that all Russian
byliny clearly had an Oriental origin. For example, he
related the Russian story "The Firebird" to the Hindu
narratives of Somadeva, and he related the legend of
Yeruslan Lazarevich to an episode recounted in
Ferdowsi's *Shāh-namāh*.

But another great contemporary philologist, O. F.
Miller, asked if this were an acceptable thesis. In a
work of his on Elijah of Murom, published in 1869,
Miller had proposed the thesis that the importance of
a production is not determined by its subject. In his
view the Grimms' and Müller's mythical theory was a
valid one. This theory maintains that there is no
borrowing without re-elaboration and that this re-
elaboration makes a literature national, whatever its
sources. He added that this is why the poem of Elijah
of Murom must be considered national, as must the entire Russian epopee.

Other scholars concerned with discovering the reflection of contemporary ideas in folk productions
participated in the controversy raised by Stasov's
essay. Noteworthy is the activity of another Miller,
Vsevolod, who gave vigor and strength to a critical
movement that attempted to identify characters and
accounts in byliny in order to establish a "historical base" for the epopee. In fact, it is to him that
we attribute the beginning of the historical school
in Russia, a school that A. N. Veselovskiĭ revived by
providing the aesthetic criteria that it had generally
lacked.

Interested in Slavic and Western problems,
Veselovskiĭ was primarily a humanist who was attracted
to both European and Oriental national literatures,
which in his opinion included folkloristic productions.
Veselovskiĭ combined the enthusiasm of Herder and the
brothers Grimm with the erudition of Müller and Benfey.
This brilliant, indefatigable scholar, who was receptive to all contemporary intellectual movements, was
initially influenced by Benfey; he was unable, however,
to accept Benfey's Orientalist thesis, which had been
so dogmatized by his disciples.

In his doctoral dissertation, published in 1872, Veselovskiĭ examined the relationships between the Slavic legends of Solomon and Kitovras, arguing that although the Orient had influenced the West, the West had also exercised an influence on the Orient--and not only through Greek fables or scattered circumstances, as Benfey allowed. He was convinced that Byzantium had exerted an influence on Russian folk literature, but the latter, endowed with variety and its own unmistakable characteristics, had been the link between the Orient and the West. In these detailed and precise investigations, which were never reduced to catalogues, Veselovskiĭ proposed a unique thesis that demonstrated his balance and good sense.

In the following editions Veselovskiĭ's thesis became a veritable treatise on the relationship between the Orient and the West, which are treated in equal proportion. Veselovskiĭ followed this thesis with a series of monographs on the history and development of the Chinese legend, Russian religious poetry, byliny, and tales about Ivan the Terrible. As Sokolov says, these and countless other essays "established the national and foreign, the oral and written sources of the works" in order to explain "the connections of literary phenomena with other manifestations of spiritual culture--with philosophical, religious, and social-journalistic currents."[1] In his work the traditions of Benfeyism met with principles that Hippolyte Taine was applying to his studies in France.

Veselovskiĭ, however, did not limit himself to these positions. As if to summarize his studies, he spoke of the usefulness of his work, which had given him detailed knowledge of poetic genres (epopee, poetry, lyric, drama) whose external characteristics are revealed in their various forms; further, he recognized that the literary history of a nation, and

[1]*Russian Folklore*, trans. Catherine Ruth Smith, with an Introduction and Bibliography by Felix Oinas (1950; rpt. Hatboro, Pa.: Folklore Associates, 1966), p. 103.

therefore the literary history of the folk, is in continuous development. But precisely because of this
last point, he concluded by emphatically asserting that
if the philologist wishes to judge a work of art--a
great romance, a bylina, a story by an author, or a
folktale--he must not merely consider its themes; he
must also consider its social ideas and artistic forms.

As a scholar, Veselovskiĭ gave his sources a purely
documentary value. What for Benfey had been a question
of detail (that is, a question of artistic creation)
became for Veselovskiĭ a historical and an aesthetic
issue. On the other hand, one remembers that there had
been virtually a revolution in Russian folklore, beginning in 1871; by that time A. F. Gil'ferding had published more than three hundred byliny, no longer by
genres but by authors, thus inaugurating a research
method that tended to emphasize the importance of the
personality of the folk poet (singer, narrator, and so
on). Veselovskiĭ maintained that the importance of a
folk production, like that of an artistic production,
is not to be measured by its subject. Besides, does
any subject exist that has never been repeated? And
is it legitimate to give exclusive importance to the
similarity of themes when what counts in a national
literature is the established work of art? Thus, it
was not a matter of denying the importance of sources
but of giving them a correct value. In the light of
this premise, Veselovskiĭ considered folk poetry as
the first phase of all literary evolution; moreover,
in eliminating the hypothesis of a collective origin
of folksongs, he came to recognize byliny and other
productions as poetic works formed in the "environment" of folk singers. He believed, then, that folk
traditions can indeed diffuse from a specific center
but that they always represent the continual work of
the imagination, in all times and places.

7. *The Finnish School and the Historical-
     Geographical Method*

It is with this last premise that the founder of the

Finnish school, Julius Krohn, began his work, and his method was perfected by his son, Kaarle. Although he was a poet and short-story writer, Julius Krohn undertook a scholarly study of the *Kalevala*, whose composition had intrigued him even in his youth. Nor should we forget that as early as 1884 he had observed in his interesting work on the genesis of the *Kalevala*, "Before coming to any conclusion about the genesis of a song, I put the readaptions in geographical and chronological order; this is the only way that one can distinguish original from added elements."

This is precisely the method that Krohn applied, with excellent results, in his scholarly *Kalevalan toisinnot*, published in 1888. In this work, he stressed the importance of variants, which contribute to the popularity of a folk text, and he presented the poets and singers entrusted with renewing the epopee of the *Kalevala*. He arranged the variants of this poem according to content, but he also arranged the variants according to place of derivation. Although Julius Krohn died prematurely, he left much material demonstrating the importance of his thesis. It was on this material that his son labored, publishing some works in the name of his father that are still basic to folklore studies. Included in these are some volumes on pagan worship in Finland and some even more interesting ones on the *Kanteletar*, the Finnish folk lyric.

In applying the geographico-historical method to his works, Julius Krohn had followed Grundtvig's research, while making use of a hypothesis that Wilhelm Heinrich Riehl had stated in Germany as early as 1854. Riehl had proposed the binomial of "*Land und Leute*" as a basis for the natural history of the German people. In the field of mythology, this thesis was strongly supported by Wilhelm Schwartz, who studied pagan traditions surviving in country regions, particularly their historical and geographical diffusion. But what was Krohn's attitude toward Benfey?

Krohn was quick to admit that his own method rejected everything that is absolute and exclusive in the theories proposed by Benfey and his followers. He asserted that although many tales came into the West from India, many

others traveled into India from the West, and that one
also had to consider other creative areas such as Asia
Minor and central Europe. He believed, then, that
everything was possible (*cum grano salis*). But he felt
that Benfey and Veselovskiĭ (in his first works) erred
in giving primary importance to the readaptions of a
literary text and a clearly secondary importance to
more recent popular texts. True, Benfey and Veselovskiĭ recognized the significance of the oral tradition.
It was necessary to go a step further, however, by
putting the oral tradition on an equal footing with the
literary one. Besides, it is obvious, he added, that
a song's variants--an expression of the trustworthy,
"conserving" memory of the folk--often reveal the oldest forms, a point that can be applied with equal
validity to tales. But in studying those forms, wasn't
Krohn concerned with the same problem that assailed
Benfey, the problem of discovering the original text
of a specific poetic production?

On this subject it is helpful to read what his son
Kaarle said at a meeting of the International Congress
of Folklore held in Paris in 1889. At this gathering
Kaarle called the attention of his audience to his
father's work: "My father's main work is the comparative study of the *Kalevala*, which constitutes the first
part of his history of Finnish literature. . . . Studies on the *Kalevala* are of great importance for understanding the links between Finnish epic poems, on the
one hand, and old Lithuanian, Russian, and Scandinavian
songs, on the other hand. . . . But probably of even
greater importance is my father's work on the interpretation of Finnish songs in the context of similar traditions in all countries of the world, a work that I have
continued."

After paying homage to his father's work, Kaarle
added these points: (1) the international quality of
a tale (as well as of a song) consists not only in a
common general idea but also in the complication and
development in plot and theme; (2) themes are expressed
in specific motifs; (3) in order to find the primitive
form of an "adventure," one must collect all the variants; (4) these variants should be arranged according

to a historical criterion if the literary sources
allow, or according to a geographical criterion if the
variants are taken from the "living voice" of the folk;
(5) in order to perform this last task, one must have
the variants of each country, province, and community.
Knowing about these variants, whether unpublished or
published (Marian Cox gave us three hundred and fifty
versions of *Cinderella* for the first time in 1893),
leads us to believe in the existence of original
tales, each having its own author. But who can deny
--and here we have Benfey and the early Veselovskii--
that some variants in northern Europe have been preserved in a form older than, say, the legend of Polyphemus? Thus, the oldest text should be identified
as the most natural one. Julius Krohn observed that
this was Keller's concept of simplicity, but it would
be more exact to say that this was the concept of the
origin of the epopee that was conceived by the romantics and applied by Weber to narratives. In Krohn's
view, the original text has the simplest but most perfect form. Krohn's son, however, thought that the
discovery of the original form of a legend or tale was
certainly not "the most interesting thing" offered by
the geographico-historical study of these productions;
rather, it is most important to see what changes that
first form had immediately undergone and how it has
been expressed in variants in different times and
places. This, however, did not preclude his considering all variants in the same way and with the same
criteria.

These principles, found in Krohn's various works
on comparative literature and particularly in his
investigations of fables about the man and the fox,
were also applied by Kaarle in his studies on the
Kalevala and Estonian folksongs. Nor is it without
significance that the work to which Kaarle entrusted
his belief (actually, his father's belief, which he
updated), *Die folkloristische Arbeitsmethode* (1926),
was fundamentally a reflection of his *Kalevalanky-
symyksiä*, which was published in 1910. Another
excellent work is his *Kalevalan kertomarunojen opas*,
published in 1932.

8. *Tools of Scholarship*

The Finnish method has received some strong, sharp
criticism. For example, the Krohns were reproached
with the fact that although their method can indeed
be called geographical, it is in no way historical,
since their groupings result in arbitrary or mechanical and static classifications. Recently a Swedish
scholar, Carl von Sydow, who began his works according to this method, observed that the Finnish school
is often based on premises that are unverifiable if
not absolutely false. We must recognize, however,
that the Finnish school has made one great contribution: it has offered us several critical tools that
are indispensable to anyone who intends to undertake
the study of folktales.

We are here reminded of the work of a disciple of
the Krohns, Antti Aarne. In 1910 he published an
important volume, *Verzeichnis der Märchentypen*, the
first work to provide a catalogue of tale motifs and
themes, with related bibliography. This volume is the
third of a collection (*Folklore Fellows Communications*)
that was begun in 1907 by Krohn, Sydow, and Olrik,
through the auspices of the International Federation
of Folklorists.

Some years before, the French folklorist Henri
Gaidoz had said that if a courageous scholar would one
day compile an index of tales (including themes and
motifs), the study of tales would make rapid progress.
The above-cited collection (whose volumes contained
more than one hundred works) accepted catalogues and
indexes that, following Aarne's example, had been made
for various European countries; it also accepted important monographs on the study of particular folktale
problems. Along with the founders of the Folklore
Fellows Federation, others who contributed monographs
included Václav Tille, R. T. Christiansen, Walter
Anderson, and N. P. Andreev. What is most important
is that they established an international collaboration that was extremely productive for European and
American folklorists. Another indispensable critical
tool, owed in great part to the example of Köhler but

also to the influence of the Finnish school, is
*Anmerkungen zu den Kinder- und Hausmärchen der Brüder
Grimm* by Johannes Bolte and Jiří Polívka, published
in five volumes between 1913 and 1932. Bolte, one of
Germany's greatest folklore scholars, followed F. A.
Weinhold as director of the *Zeitschrift für Volkskunde*,
to which he gave significant impulse. Polívka, one of
Russia's most experienced folklorists, indeed followed
in the footsteps of Benfey, but he believed that one
must distinguish national characteristics in folktales.
From their collaboration came a thesaurus of comparative tales initiated and completed in the name of the
brothers Grimm, a thesaurus in which each tale told by
the Grimms is brought back to life.

Although the Finnish school was particularly concerned with developing investigations in the specific
field of folk literature, in the last analysis it
actually restricted folklore research in this field.
When the two Krohns examined tales and songs for
vestiges of the past--vestiges of mythology and magic
--they were taking a historical approach. However,
the school that took its name from its country was
tied to a kind of work that we might best call
geographico-cartographical. For example, it is a
well known fact that the Finnish school deliberately
excluded folk music from the field of folklore, an
obvious self-contradiction. In regard to Finland
itself, some extremely valuable work on folk music has
been left to us by another of Julius Krohn's sons,
Ilmari Krohn (while one of his daughters, Aino Kallas,
used Finnish folklore in her work on Finnish storytellers). But whatever its defects, the Finnish
school deserves credit for having justified the worth
of a method that, within limits, is indisputably
valuable; furthermore, the Finnish school must be
credited with considering the question of folk literature not as a minor literary question but as one of
great significance for the history of civilization.

CHAPTER XVIII

IN THE WORLD OF ROMANCE

1. The Birth of Romance Philology: From Diez to Paris

Whatever its particular developments, the Aryan-European synthesis provided a broad perspective of the historical community, its ethnic origins and literatures. These literatures genuinely seemed worthy of being studied, inasmuch as they could be followed from their origin. Even though the boundaries of research had never stretched beyond the Aryan world, this community continued to put forth the concept of the primitive as it had been formulated by Herder. Both Müller and Benfey had viewed India (prehistoric and historic) as being endowed with an ancientness that clearly gave it a primitive quality. As had already. happened in German and Slavic studies, this quality would be enhanced by a new, young discipline that appeared on the cultural horizon of the nineteenth century: romance philology.

With an aim of defining and characterizing a specific field of studies, romance philology (leaving aside the fact that its beginnings boast a Vico and a Muratori) became a genuine scientific system through the efforts of a German, Friedrich Diez, the author of two fundamental works, *Grammatik der romanischen Sprachen*, published between 1836 and 1844, and *Etymologisches Wörterbuch der romanischen Sprachen*. With these works Diez brought the romance realm into the broader Aryan world. Focusing on the romance realm, however, did not mean enclosing that realm in itself, making it a separate world. "Borrowings" did

not alarm Diez; in fact, they were a stimulus because
he could infuse them with a national character. As
had been the case for the brothers Grimm and Müller,
he was particularly attracted to the problem of folk
poetry. Like the romantics, he believed that folk
poetry included all the oral productions found among
the folk and that it was necessary to elucidate such
productions in order to see their relationship to
"cultured" literature and poetry.

In some of his early works, particularly in *Die
Poesie der Troubadours*, Diez had formulated a principle that was, at least in intent, both historical
and aesthetic; specifically, he said that in France,
more precisely in Provence, the origins of lyrical
poetry are to be found in the popular poets before
William IX and that a new element, chivalry, had
made these wandering poets into genuine troubadours.
When the minstrel (the true maker of popular poetry,
in Diez's view) was no longer enough for the nobles,
then an aristocratic, more cultured poetry, the court
lyric, was created. Thus, two contrasting types or
genres of poetry came about: the poetry of the minstrels, which was folk poetry, and the poetry of the
troubadours, which was a cultured and refined poetry.
Furthermore, he argued that an ascending process
existed between the former and the latter. The romantics, particularly the German romantics, although
allowing a categorical distinction between *Volkspoesie*
or *Naturpoesie* and *Kunstpoesie*, could not allow that
the first could be refined, inasmuch as it was poetry
par excellence. Diez, however, had two theses in common with the German romantics: folk poetry was always
the initial source of poetry, and the first poetry to
make itself heard was folk poetry.

With these theses in hand, one of Diez's first
disciples, Gaston Paris, went into action in France.
In his extensive work one often finds ideas that are
related to Romanticism, although, as has been noted,
only a superficial critic finds a mere repetition of
ideas credited to Wolf, the brothers Grimm, and
Fauriel. In his younger days, Paris was opposed to
the mythical interpretation of the *Chanson de Roland*,

which became for romance philology what the *Vedas* were
for Müller and the *Panchatantra* was for Benfey.
Paris' sympathies went more to Benfey, to his method
of research and his theory of migrations, than to
Müller. Nevertheless, he agreed with Müller's idea
that a tale can also be the translation of a myth.
This, in fact, is the nucleus of his essay *Le petit
Poucet et la Grand Ourse*, published in 1875. But
despite the influence exercised on him by contemporary
intellectual movements, the fact is that Paris, a
romantic in his preference of themes, imprinted the
mark of a strong and unmistakable personality on his
research.

2. French Literature and Nationality

In his research Paris was much intrigued by the folk,
whom he regarded as a reservoir of literary and cultural interests. He was also intrigued by folk poetry
(which he related to *chansons de geste*), *fabliaux*, and
Lives of the Saints (created for the folk by the
clergy). As far as he was concerned, studies of early
French literature were incomplete if they did not treat
such works. His interest in folk productions came from
his father, who had inspired him with the joy of exploration that often infects the investigator of medieval
texts. But, unlike his father, his interest in the
ancient literary monuments of *la belle France* was not
merely a love for the national sources of its literature, for in them he also perceived the threads of a
"life" and a developing history--matters of great
moment for all mankind. "We French have not had anyone like the brothers Grimm," he lamented in the first
years of his work. But Paris had Jacob's diligence
and knowledge, along with Wilhelm's artistic taste and
polished expository style. In reading his work, one
discovers that Paris was actually the artist not of
learning but of the *pleasure* of learning. There is
an entire world that takes shape in his simple, clear,
straightforward prose--the world of gallant knights
for whom each act is an act of faith.

The work of Paris, too, was an act of faith, one that he approached diligently--and in his work the artist becomes worldly-wise, while the nationalist becomes cosmopolitan in the name of his science. We know that in a memorable lecture of his held on December 8, 1870, at the Sorbonne, when the city of Paris was under fire and sword, he had chosen the *Chanson de Roland* for his topic. In this lecture, Ernesto Monaci recalls, he

> attempted to demonstrate how much national interest and practicality were in this subject. He explained how the study of similar literary works leads us into the history of a nation, helps us to analyze its spirit, and reveals its secrets. He explained that such a study is necessary so that the nation's awareness is not obfuscated nor its importance extinguished when proofs of its mortality appear. By studying this old epopee, the French could go back to the origins of their own nationality, distinguish the various elements, recognize the great role of poetry in its formation, see what distinguishes the vital organism of a nation from the lifeless mechanism of the empire, and rediscover what is most indestructible in a nation--that which raises its "life" above the events and strokes of fortune and allows for the regaining of the country even when the native land is lost.

Two years later, as if to take up that discourse again, Paris, along with Paul Meyer, founded *Romania*, a journal that became the greenhouse of romance philology. The verses of an old Norman trouveur accompanied it:

> *Pur remebrerer des ancessurs*
> *Les dits et les faiz et les murs.*

In the prospectus, published a bit earlier, Paris acknowledged that the idea for such a journal was not new and that it had not been initiated because of his country's misfortunes. Nevertheless, he intended for his

journal to be national in character because he and
Meyer fully believed that "France's too abrupt and
radical break with its past, an ignorance of our true
traditions, and the general indifference of our country
must be considered as the cause of our disaster." He
immediately added, however, that he "did not want to
produce a tendentious work" and that the purpose of his
journal was primarily scientific. He concluded, "For
nations and individuals the first motto of wisdom, the
first condition of all national activity, and the basis
of true dignity is still the ancient saying, 'Know
thyself.'"

Paris, as we see, here pointed out the link uniting
all of his own work: the link between literary history
and civilized man. It has been said that as long as
romance philology was restricted to Germany, it was a
lifeless statue; however, if ever there was a scholar
who gave life to that statue in Latin lands, it was
Paris. Paris *did* have a great love for France, and he
did give it the same romantic character that had directed German and Slavic studies--for he believed that
a nation's traditions are the innermost life of its
history. However, he did not isolate this history.
For example, Paris pointed out the Indic origin of many
medieval French folk productions, particularly *fabliaux*,
as is evidenced in some of his most provocative essays,
later collected under the titles *La poésie du moyen âge*
and *Poèmes et légendes du moyen âge*, and in his valuable
manual entitled *La littérature française au moyen âge*.
The Indic origin of the themes and motifs of some French
productions certainly did not cloud his awareness of the
fact that literature taken to a foreign soil acquires
foreign characteristics. For him the nationality of
French literature was an act of faith--his faith.

3. *The Origin of the French Epopee and the Theory of
     Singsongs*

In light of this concept, Paris' greatest work, *Histoire
poétique de Charlemagne*, first published in 1865, is
quite clear. He did not consider such literatures as

the German, Scandinavian, Spanish, and Italian ones
because he was primarily concerned with explaining the
origins of the French epopee. He was not content, however, to explain those origins with vague explanations
of primitive ages; rather, he wished to supply some
specific facts, dates, and, we could even say, an area
of diffusion.

Paris accepted the Germanic theory that singsongs
were antecedents of *chansons de geste*, a theory that
had been revived in France by Fauriel, but in his view
these singsongs were not the product of the creative
instinct of the throng; rather, they were the product
of specific authors who wrote between the seventh and
tenth centuries. But although in this respect he
adopted the concept of folk poetry, Paris (like Diez)
did not adopt the concept of the brothers Grimm but
rather the one proposed by Görres, Arnim, and the
Schlegels, who were convinced that there was a poet
behind each poem.

But let us return to France. In *Cahiers de
jeunesse* (1845-46, p. 133 of the 1906 edition), Renan
said that we must look for the spirit and genius of
the French nation in the *Chanson de Roland*. (After
attending a lecture by Ozanam, Renan began to consider
primitivism as the greatest discovery of the nineteenth
century.) But didn't Renan immediately add that the
poet is the harmonious echo, the one who writes under
the dictation of the folk and tells its dreams? It
should be added that such dreams were regarded by Vico
and the brothers Grimm as the very truth of history.

This, too, was the concept of Ampère and Monin,
who were the first to mine the field of romance philology in France. In their view (as in the view of earlier
romantics who disagreed with the brothers Grimm), the
folk has a voice that is expressed by the individual,
by the poet. Calling the poet a "folk poet" signifies
that he expresses everyone's sentiments with a voice
and spirit shared by all. Renan, then, sacrificed
Turoldus to the folk spirit. But let us give a more
literal meaning to these metaphorical words. Despite
his metaphoric expressions, Renan in no way intended
to deny the *Chanson de Roland* its poet; rather, he

wanted to assert categorically that behind the poet one
finds the nation, the family, and the civilized life of
France. This is the meaning of Paris' statement that
the author of the *Chanson* is called legion.

Paris argued that an unknown poet celebrated
Roland's courage in a poem in order to console
Roland's companions (a point clarified in his famous
essay, "Roncevaux"). Paris adds:

> France was then in full epic swing. The events and
> characters that struck the imagination of those
> belonging to the warrior class immediately became
> the topic of songs. These songs were quickly dif-
> fused, thanks to minstrels (court singers of the
> Middle Ages), from the point of origin to the en-
> tire world. They were adapted in different dia-
> lects, and they increased like the waves produced
> in ever-increasing number by an impact at the
> center. . . . The new songs that continually ap-
> peared did not cause old ones to be forgotten, if
> these for some particular reason deserved to sur-
> vive. Generations transmitted these old songs to
> following generations, which modified and amplified
> them more or less successfully. The poem about
> Roland spans the entire Carolingian Age. In the
> eleventh century it still existed in different
> forms--all of them, naturally, a far cry from the
> first one. (*Revue de Paris,* September 15, 1901)

In saying that a poetic text diffused among the folk is
always being continually reworked, Paris perceived the
idea of folk elaboration, which makes a poetic production truly "popular." Although he believed that folk
poetry is the source of all true poetry, he also believed that it was absurd to establish a relationship
between folk poetry and "clerical" poetry, because the
former had no influence on the latter, and the clergy
had nothing but disdain for folk poetry.

Paris was convinced that the folk either immediately sings about a historical event or it does not sing
about it at all, and that the oral tradition receives
this heritage, which is continually transformed through

the work of poets. With this conviction in mind, Paris maintained that the first singsongs must have been contemporary with the events that they described. It is here that his investigation took on some subtlety, because he attempted to establish that although primitive singsongs about Charlemagne had been sung by his warriors as early as the end of the eighth century, these isolated songs later came to be grouped around a single idea and a single hero.

After Paris' thesis about folk poetry had been applied to the origins of the epopee (which he considered to be an expression of folk poetry), it was then applied to other literary genres. For example, in 1889 Alfred Jeanroy wrote *Les origines de la poésie lyrique en France au moyen âge*, using refrains as his basis; and in the same year Julien Tiersot compiled his *Histoire de la chanson populaire en France*, in which he maintained that the *laisse* for assonance in *chansons de geste* had been based on the model of the melodic formulas of the day. Along the same lines, in 1894 Giovanni Cesareo composed an important short work, *Le origini della poesia lirica in Italia*, in which he argued for the existence of a Sicilian folk poetry anterior to the Norman-Swabian school of poetry, with the Norman-Swabian school following after Sicilian folk poetry. And if we go from the field of poetry to the field of the narrative, we will find that these principles were applied in 1904 by Hippolyte Delehaye in his *Les légendes hagiographiques*.

Paris was accustomed to giving reviews of important new books, later turning these reviews into monographs. In the *Journal des Savants* of 1891 he advanced the theory, inspired by Jeanroy's *Origines*, of an uninterrupted Latin folk tradition, independent of the literary tradition. In this hypothesis he maintained that a Roman folk poetry composed of springtime poems is necessarily antecedent to the Provençal court lyric, and this Roman folk poetry itself derives from May Day folksongs.

Thus, the world of minstrels and the world of clerics were clearly separated. In the meantime, however, an Italian philologist, Pio Rajna, entered the field of romance philology and took up some of Paris'

major theses, illuminating them with his criticism and
keen judgment.

4. *Rajna: Investigator of Origins*

Pio Rajna, also a romantic in his choice of themes,
focused on the French epopee as his specific area of
interest. The difference between his work and Paris'
is the same as the difference between Müller and Benfey.
Both Paris and Rajna venerated the text, the document,
the codex, as their critical editions demonstrate.
These texts, documents, and codices did not exhaust
their interests, however, for they are only an introduction to and the basis of their work. It was the
interpretation of the documents that attracted them.
These two philologists lived during a time when science
was considered to be virtually a religion. In 1870, as
a prelude to his essay "Rinaldo di Montalbano," Rajna
emphatically stated:

> The nineteenth century, which has done and con-
> tinues to do so much for the progress of experi-
> mental sciences, has also provided new impetus
> to literary studies, putting them on untraveled
> roads. To the nineteenth century alone belongs
> the glory of having established the basis for a
> genuine science of literature. To as great an
> extent as is possible, this frees the documents
> of the past from the prejudice of research,
> studies, and schools of thought; the science of
> literature extends its vision to all places and
> all times in order to compare all similar phe-
> nomena, with the result that such phenomena
> illustrate and clarify one another. This science
> takes particular delight in investigating the
> origins of individual works as well as the ori-
> gins of various literary forms. Patiently fol-
> lowing the course of the work through peoples and
> countries, it observes differences with an intel-
> ligent eye in order to discover rules and reasons
> for gradual transformations.

This was Rajna's scientific credo, in homage to which he studied *Reali di Francia* in 1872, in a methodical investigation of the passage of the French chivalric epopee into Italy. In his *Histoire poétique* Paris had maintained that *Reali di Francia* was a collection of different Franco-Italian poems later translated into Tuscan prose. These Franco-Italian poems, he argued, surely gave a unique quality to the chivalric subject matter, which was Italy's chief contribution to this kind of composition. But, Rajna asked himself, of what other tales is the *Reali* composed? These are his premises:

> As I look back, I am amazed at the number of texts that the author must have used. I now well understand the force of those words at the beginning of the Modenese edition: "According to the many legends that I have discovered and gathered together." If anyone deserves the name of compiler, it is he who composed the *Reali*. His sources can be divided into five categories: (1) French *chansons de geste*; (2) Franco-Italian songs; (3) Venetian songs; (4) Italian prose romances; (5) *cantari* in ottava rima.

Among these categories the third and fifth are the most numerous, according to Rajna.

Rajna argued that, as Paris had said, the compiler of the *Reali* must be recognized as an individual author whose compilation adheres perfectly to the folk spirit. This man was also, according to Rajna, the author of *Aspromonte*, the author who even in the *Reali* had debased subject matter that originally had quite a different attraction:

> Many beautiful narratives--the adventures of Fiorio and Fioravante, the long adventures of Drusiana and Berta, the loves of Mainetto, the childhood of Roland--lose much of their attractiveness in our compilation. They were highly poetic legends, *the spontaneous product of the folk imagination*, and they only needed a suitable form. Our author

stripped them of verse, reduced them to prolix and feeble prose, and removed all personal sentiment so that they might be taken for true history; but in making them acceptable to the intellect, he violated the holy rights of the imagination.

However, in his 1876 study, *Le fonte dell' Orlando furioso*, Rajna, who had distinguished literary forms from individual works, was guilty himself of altogether overlooking the "holy rights of the imagination." He said that if "Ludovico alone had invented all that he took from others, more than one laurel leaf would have to be added to the crown of his glory." This was an assertion that only the worst disciple of Benfey would have made and that Paris would never have made, since he was convinced that the raw material the artist uses is one thing while the work of art the artist produces is quite another.

Significantly, the first to protest against such an assumption was Cesareo, himself an investigator of origins. Rajna, on the other hand, was convinced that the sources have a greater artistic importance than the work itself, a conviction derived from the implied idea that original poetry is gradually extinguished in successive works and that the best text is therefore the first one. This was Wagener's thesis, which was applied by Manuel Milá y Fontanals to Spanish romances and adopted later by the Finnish school. This explains why, in his valuable *Le origini dell' epopea francese* (1884), Rajna proposed some germinal songs as the basis of the French epopee. These songs are perfect in their kind, real *chansons de geste*; furthermore, they were generally contemporary with the events that they described, and they were in the German language.

Actually, this was not a new idea. Ludwig Uhland had expressed a similar thesis as early as 1812 when, following the lead of A. W. Schlegel, he said that the French epopee is the Germanic spirit in romance form--an idea also proposed by Léon Gautier, one of the greatest scholars of the French epopee. On the other hand, Paul Meyer believed that "our epopee completely appertains to our literature." But although

Paris was disposed to concede a certain Germanic influence on the French epopee, he could not explain to himself how German songs could become romance songs. Rajna did everything he could to account for this occurrence, speculating that there was a period of bilingualism in which the poets who recited at the courts of French lords and princes addressed themselves to two different groups of people, the Germanic aristocracy and the "romance population." As for the dates, he later acknowledged that the themes found in the narratives of Gregory of Tours were identical to those found in *chansons de geste.* He also acknowledged that *chansons de geste* of the twelfth century were survivals of the Merovingian epopee, heiress of the French epopee.

Although Rajna did not accept many of Paris' hypotheses and would not acknowledge that Charlemagne's warriors had recounted their adventures before a real poet put them into verse, he did acknowledge and reaffirm the antiquity of *chansons de geste.* And although Paris held to his theory about singsongs, he ended up in accepting Rajna's thesis. Paris was convinced, as Uhland had been, that the Germanic origin of *chansons de geste* in no way detracted from the originality of French poems.

5. *Bédier and Eleventh-Century France*

Despite the efforts of Paris and Rajna, it was a disciple of Paris, Joseph Bédier, who managed to put the study of the French epopee on another level. Bédier wrote as elegantly as Paris and reasoned as convincingly as Rajna. He undertook the study of the French epopee in the two thousand pages of his *Les légendes épiques*, published between 1908 and 1913. This work attempted to dismantle and destroy what Paris and Rajna had patiently constructed--a construction that Bédier had initially accepted. We can say with assurance that he took distinct pleasure in overturning the theories maintained by these two famous scholars. They had often declared that their reconstruction of the French epopee was merely an attempt to represent the facts of

the epopee as they had developed, but Bédier, at least
in theory, did not give the "right of citizenship" to
such attempts. Did brief, rough singsongs contemporaneous with the facts that they describe actually exist
as Paris had imagined them? And did *chansons de geste*
exist as Rajna had imagined them? No text of either
remains. Paris and Rajna had imagined their existence
in order to give a past to twelfth-century *chansons de
geste*. Thus, they loved the documents that we have for
the sake of all the ones we have lost, and they drew
pertinent deductions and inferences from the former.
In Bédier's opinion, however, the absence of a document
is itself a document. With this essentially anti-
historical premise he hoped to destroy the links joining the defeat of Roncesvalles with *chansons de geste*
describing this defeat; he hoped, that is, to refute
the thesis that the French epopee is coeval with the
events that it narrates.

To strengthen this thesis, Rajna and Paris had
based their theory primarily on oral tradition
(recognized as valid by all the folklorists of the
time), which was used to reconcile history and poetry.
Bédier hoped to eradicate the initial impression that
this theory had aroused, because no coeval written
source seriously supported it; so he began with
another premise, no less anti-historical than the
one about the absence of documents: the premise
that the oral tradition never comments on historical
events.

This assumption had previously been expressed in
his *Les fabliaux*, published in 1893. In this work he
had said that historical legends, which were created
for a certain period and a certain people, did not
interest subsequent generations. Later, in his *Les
légendes épiques* (III, 127 ff.), he added that if
nations have historical traditions, they do so because such traditions have been conserved in writing;
when the recollection of a fact or person is related
to battlefields, invasions, changes of dynasties, and
so on, such events turn into shapeless residue in the
folk memory. In short, folklore never conserves historical traditions, as far as he was concerned; it

conserves only "marvelous" songs, fabliaux, cosmogonic
fables, and other such works.

6. "Fabliaux" and "Légendes épiques"

It is difficult to imagine what sources Bédier drew
from. Actually, he appealed to collections of folk
traditions compiled in all countries in the last century; but since those accounts would have told him just
the contrary (consider, for example, Spanish romances,
eastern European epico-lyrical songs, and Russian
byliny), he was careful not to mention any one source.
Similarly, he took no account of what the pre-romantics,
the great folklorists of the romantic period, and especially the folklorists of his own time had written
about the memory of the folk in regard to wars, invasions, and historical characters.
     Bédier denied the importance of the oral tradition
in relation to historical events on the basis of a
purely imaginary folklore. One could argue, of course,
that these historical events can indeed be transmitted
by the folk, even over great periods of time. But even
here, isn't there an "ideal" contemporaneity contained
in the oral traditions, in the folk memory? Besides,
Bédier was faced with the specter of the French epopee
contaminated by German influences. It has been said
that in transporting the origin of the French epopee
to the twelfth century, Bédier hoped to suggest that
France did not have national heroes, let alone a
national epopee. This is the remark that Robert
Fawtier made about him--and, following the example of
Ferdinando Gabotto and Ferdinand Lot, Fawtier proved
once again how valid the relationships between history
and *chansons de geste* can be. The truth of the matter,
however, is quite different. As Luigi Foscolo Benedetto (who has recently given new life to the old
theoretical presuppositions of the eighteenth century)
observes, Bédier hoped to prove that "the French epic
is a French product that originated after there had
been a France in the modern sense of the word, therefore not before the eleventh century." Precisely for

this reason his studies "all conclude in the beautiful
myth--a melodic motif often found in his works--of the
great miracle of the eleventh century: France suddenly asserts herself as the brilliant creator in all
areas of human endeavor and places herself at the head
of the civilized world. This miracle is to remain
only a French one."

Although supported by elaborate investigation,
Bédier's thesis was a nationalistic one. The same can
be said of Paris' thesis. But while the nationalism
of Paris' thesis was based on a humanistic concept,
Bédier's nationalism was ultimately self-enclosed,
even though it is presented to us as an aesthetic and
a historical-cultural study.

7. *Does a "Folk Memory" Exist?*

In his *Les fabliaux*, which was published about the
same time as Benedetto Croce's first works on aesthetics, Bédier rightly called attention to the concept
of art as the representation of the individual, and
he attempted to reduce Benfey's theory about the
origins of tales to the correct limits. Of a hundred
and forty-seven *fabliaux*, only eleven could possibly
be compared to Indic tales. But didn't these similarities, he asked himself, concern only the established and generic elements of the tale? And is a
tale's motherland the one in which it is found or the
one in which it is created, in the sense that its true
reality consists in the act of creation or "recrea-
tion"? Considered from this point of view, the
monogenesis of tales obviously has to be resolved in
a polygenesis, and it therefore becomes a legitimate
aesthetic problem. But beyond this problem, isn't
there a rich cultural history in which the migration
of a tale is to be considered in terms of the civilization to which it has adhered? And didn't Bédier
become a prisoner of his theory about sources, the
theory found in his *Les légendes épiques*?

Bédier certainly did not fail to study these
legends in accordance with aesthetic criteria. In

one of the most famous passages of his *Légendes* (III, 149 ff.), he said that "a work of art begins and ends with its author"--which is precisely the way that he considered the *Chanson de Roland*, in a poetic, brilliant study. He immediately added that it was therefore useless to appeal "to theories that always attempt to substitute collective forces for individual ones." Bédier concluded that it was ridiculous to suppose that centuries were needed to shape the legend of Roland or that innumerable singers followed each other. One moment was sufficient, "the sacred moment when the poet, perhaps taking advantage of some romance, a rough outline of his theme, conceived the idea of a conflict between Oliver and Roland."

Of *course* that "moment" is sufficient. But didn't all of Bédier's studies aim at understanding how the romance is formed, which means that those studies have nothing to do with the aesthetic validity of the work as it has been formed by the individual poet? His major argument was that this romance was formed in the eleventh century; only on this point was Bédier (who played with his subjects as though they were pieces in a chess game) disposed to make all possible concessions --which he would then withdraw, as if he regretted what he had done.

Although it is very difficult to find a straight line of thought in Bédier's work, Bédier was obviously providing two different perspectives in both *Les fabliaux* and *Les légendes épiques*: the perspective of aesthetics and the perspective of cultural history. It is true that Rajna confused one with the other in regard to Ariosto. But it is also true that Bédier himself often became confused, even though his works proved that studies of cultural history (and therefore of the history of origins), in which sources are important for explaining the poetic text, are just as legitimate as aesthetic studies.

8. *Bédier: Between Romanticism and Anti-Romanticism*

After destroying (at least to his own satisfaction) the

links between history and legend--or, to be more accurate, after removing the "romantic value" from the
origins of the epopee--Bédier immediately began to
reconstruct the legend of Roland, which he believed
took place in the eleventh century. He attacked the
thesis that an epopee emerges at the same time as the
historical facts, transforms these facts into poetry,
and preserves these facts through *chansons de geste*.
After tearing apart this thesis, Bédier again took up
the thesis that had been discussed by Philipp Becker
some years before. Specifically, this thesis maintains that twelfth-century *chansons de geste* cannot be
explained unless we consider pilgrimages and pilgrims
as vehicles of propagation for epic subject matter,
including the legend of Roland. Rajna had already
admitted that "the epopee was taken along the roads
of pilgrimages." But Bédier developed this thesis in
such great detail and with so many sharp postulates
that he wins the reader's admiration, if nothing else.
He believed that "laymen and clergymen, merchants,
burghers, poets, and members of the folk and of the
church" had contributed to the formation of the oldest
and most beautiful epic legends. He immediately went
on to say, however, that these legends were "formed
in the church and were about the church," obviously in
preparation for the Oriental crusades, and it is "impossible to discern the contribution of each person."
   This basically seems to be a return to the traditional criticism offered by Paris and Rajna. But while
these two scholars had considered the French epopee as
a document deriving from the affirmation of the laic
and folk spirituality that had developed outside of the
Latin tradition, Bédier considered it as a cultural
product resulting from a clerico-popular collaboration.
In the beginning there was folk poetry, Paris and Rajna
had said; in the beginning there was the road dotted
with sanctuaries, Bédier exclaimed. After mentioning
medieval itinerancy, he then proceeded to make an inventory of the most famous and most frequented roads
of the eleventh century, on which merchants, knights,
clergymen, and pilgrims traveled and on which famous
sanctuaries were to be found. All *chansons de geste*

"were quite familiar with the paths of pilgrimage and only them," while the churches scattered along those paths conserved tombs and reliques of the epic heroes. This is why a knowledge of these paths clarifies the spiritual climate from which and in which twelfth-century *chansons de geste* arose.

In Bédier's view, then, the legend--the local or church legend--was formed before the *chansons de geste*, with the monks acting as the minstrels' informants. From this information (and this explains the miracle) *chansons de geste* originated in the twelfth century. Thus, Bédier himself recognized that *chansons de geste* poets were not very literate because only with great difficulty could they extract themes from literary and Latin sources, which they found in the sanctuaries; but he also believed that such material had entered into the literary and scholastic tradition, with the help of the clergy. Obviously, then, it is impossible to conceive of *chansons de geste* poets without this distinction, as far as he was concerned.

In a work of his entitled *Les plus anciennes danses françaises* (1906), Bédier said that the folk has never created anything, that it has only accepted and imitated creations arising from centers of civilization, and that folksongs are, for the most part, modified imitations of literary forms. Bédier thus created a theory that was as artificial as those of his predecessors. This is particularly true when we consider (and this was Lot's criticism) the absurdity of thinking that the genesis of a song needs a sanctuary, monks, and the passing of many years, and it is equally absurd to presuppose that *chansons de geste* derive only from religious sources. Bédier demonstrated, then, that he had no real feel for folk poetry, which, whatever its relationship to *chansons de geste*, had been a prolific stimulus in the history of poetry. Furthermore, he denied the humble people the greatest gift that they possess--the gift of being able to create their own poetry.

CHAPTER XIX

THE LIFE OF LITERARY FOLKLORE

1. *From Child to Nigra*

The problem of folk elaboration had been perceived by
Arnim and gradually studied by the Finnish, Russian,
and Swedish folklorists; in addition, this problem
stirred considerable interest in the field of romance
philology. Because of its concern with clarifying
the origins of the epic and lyric, romance philology
not only utilized contemporary folkloristic studies
but also contributed to enriching and extending them.
We should add that in advancing with the general advancement of philology, romance philology sustained
a lively interest in neo-latin folk literature, which
was beginning to be more highly valued and better
understood, and increasingly called the attention of
folklorists to methodological problems.

In this respect the studies and contributions of
Italian philologists and folklorists are significant.
Among such scholars we must first cite Constantino
Nigra, whose cultural theory coincided with the basic
theory of romance philology. Nigra, Camillo Cavour's
friend and collaborator, was a truly European man.
Although he had other political concerns, his philological training helped him to illuminate and clarify
the difficult problems treated in his study of literary folklore. He revised the method of collecting
folksongs, although he certainly did not restrict his
activity to this task--and his methodology gave validity to his *Canti popolari del Piemonte*. This work did
not come out in a complete edition until 1888, but,

beginning in 1854, he had published many essays about these particular songs.

It has been said that Nigra was the first to draw historical deductions about the folksong's area of diffusion. Certainly this is true in the field of romance or Celto-romance, which was the field he preferred. In the brief preface to his *Canti popolari del Piemonte*, Nigra himself said, "Now that the songs are collected, honestly collected, it is time that we try to find out how they came about, where they came from, and what they mean." But he immediately added that "outside the Celto-romance domain, investigations [of folk poetry] have been undertaken with unceasing alacrity and success"; proof of this is the fact that "the efforts of Grundtvig, Bugge, Child, and others demonstrate that now studies on the genesis of folk poetry are not only possible but indeed profitable, even when they are not successful." Nigra (like the Krohns and Veselovskiĭ) followed in the tradition of Svend Grundtvig and Sophus Bugge, from whom, in the field of English philology, Francis James Child directly descended. Between 1882 and 1898 Child published his *The English and Scottish Popular Ballads*, a work that continues to serve as a model for studies on folk poetry. We could even say that all the philological work that almost two centuries of scholars from all of Europe had dedicated to folk poetry culminated in the work of Child. Consider, for example, the bibliography of folk ballads found in his last volume, as exact and precise a bibliography as one could hope to find. The index of various European ballad titles also demonstrates his absolute command in this particular field of research.

Child was well prepared to undertake the study of English and Scottish ballads, each of which he studied within the context of the tradition in which it developed. Child's *corpus* is in a certain sense the complement of Percy's *Reliques*. As Sergio Baldi correctly notes, Child's great contribution lies in the fact that "he collected and organized virtually inaccessible documents: original manuscripts; he explored old collections of broadsides (the loose-leaf printings of the

sixteenth and seventeenth centuries); he published
extant manuscripts with philological exactness, from
the famous Percy manuscript to others by Herd, Mother-
well, Buchan, and Scott; and he selected, coordinated,
and annotated the entire work with a learning and love
that has had no equal in this kind of study."

Child's "learning and love" were actually the
learning and love of Grundtvig and Bugge. The same
can be said of Nigra, who recognized not only a philological and aesthetic problem in the study of folk
poetry but also a problem of civil history.

2. The "Canti popolari del Piemonte"

The primary purpose of *Canti popolari del Piemonte* was
to determine the geographical area of diffusion of
folksongs in Italy. To this end, Nigra divided Italy
into two large zones. One zone is northern Italy,
whose particular kind of poetry is the lyrico-narrative
songs (Child's ballads), and the other zone is middle
and lower Italy, whose folk poetry is made up of
strambotti and *stornelli*. In 1876, after he had made
great progress in his comparative study in *Canti popolari del Piemonte*, Nigra wrote an essay entitled "La
poesia popolare italiana" for Paris' *Romania* journal.
This essay was "meant to serve as an introduction to a
collection of folksongs of Piedmont." In this essay
he acknowledged that lyrico-narrative songs are "sometimes found in non-Italian romance nations," but he
also proposed the thesis that *strambotti* and *stornelli*
constitute "an original poetry that is clearly Italian."

To strengthen this thesis, Nigra began with the
principle that "in folk poetry, as in all other manifestations of art, the form is a part, a major part,
of the thing itself":

> A given poetical theme and a given poetical subject
> can easily pass from one country to another, sub-
> sequently being transmitted to peoples of different
> languages and races. . . . This happened, for ex-
> ample, to a considerable number of fables, apo-

logues, tales, and stories that came to Europe from
the Orient or went from Europe to the Orient. From
earliest times these works were transmitted in different forms. But when the poetical material became fixed in verse, strophe, or composition, when
it was fashioned in a specific mold or shaped in a
fairly precise form, the *novum opus* was no longer
transmitted in this form, as a general rule, except
to people speaking the same or very similar language; in such cases the work could be understood
by everyone without much difficulty.

After establishing this principle, which was obviously
inspired by Benfey, Nigra went on to investigate the
formation period of songs: "The genetic period always
has something of the mysterious, perhaps because there
was a continual genesis even in those early times when
there was no writing or literature to express human
feelings. *Many songs were born and then died, while
those that have come to us have undergone numerous,
profound, and continual modifications.* . . ." Hence,
Nigra believed that one can trace the threads of the
tradition through the variants and that the best text
is the result of many reworkings:

When our peasants compose a song, they begin by
establishing the melody, which is usually taken
from an earlier song. *The melody determines the
meter.* Entire phrases, verses, and often the
beginning of the composition depend on already-
existing songs. Added innovations are often incorrect, rough, and therefore confused. As it
passes through many mouths, the song is gradually
modified, purified, and completed. New ideas are
added, while incorrect expressions are eliminated
or replaced by more correct ones. These, in passing through other mouths and finding themselves
in less propitious surroundings, again become corrupt and obscure, only to be revised later. . . .
In transmitting the song from mouth to mouth, the
folk constantly revises and modifies it in dialectal forms, in content, and partly in meter and

melody. Continual modifications such as these
actually constitute *a perpetual creation of folk
poetry*. These creations pass through many different phases, and their "conditions" of vitality and
perfection or of degeneration and oblivion are
intimately connected with those of the folk author
and conserver.

In the preceding is the erroneous notion that a
song must be slowly perfected if it is to have aesthetic validity. Still, we do find here a very precise
concept about the nature of folk elaboration, which
not only conserves and transmits but also creates.
Fundamental to Nigra's concept of elaboration is his
conviction that many epico-lyrical songs are exclusively Piedmontese, while others are common to the Celto-
romance peoples of France, Provence, and Catalonia.
When *Canti popolari del Piemonte* (which exemplified these relationships) was published, Paris objected
that Portugal had to be separated from the Celto-
romance group and reunited with Castile, and he compared the epico-lyrical songs of France, Piedmont, and
Catalonia with the epico-lyrical songs of Spain, Germanic countries, Greece, Slavic countries, and Hungary.
It was, then, a matter of determining a tradition of
plots and forms, the historical and geographical "life"
of a genre. Nigra had assigned the song "Donna Lombarda" to the sixth century because he was convinced
that a song is almost always coeval with the narrative
fact; Paris, however, while supporting this thesis in
regard to the origin of the French epopee, reminded
Nigra that songs of the "Donna Lombarda" type were
identical to French narrative songs whose origins could
not go back further than the fifteenth century. But
whatever the nature of these elaborate theories, Nigra
was undeniably the first in Italy to understand that
the tradition of folksongs is extremely important,
inasmuch as it determines the temper, design, and diffusion of poetry.

3. Areas of Diffusion and Centers of Irradiation

In dividing Italy into two specific "poetical zones,"
Nigra began with an assumption to which he always
held: epico-lyrical songs, *strambotti* and *stornelli*,
corresponded "to the different natures of the dialects
of the two parts of Italy" and therefore to the "substrata of two distinct races." In other terms, as he
himself said:

> The lexical base and the grammatical forms of the
> dialects of northern and southern Italy (as is
> true for all romance languages) substantially
> derive from the Latin language and therefore have
> essentially the same base. But although the lexi-
> cal and grammatical parts are essentially identical
> in the two dialectal branches of the peninsula, the
> phonology and syntax, on the contrary, are notice-
> ably different. The reason for this fact is to be
> found in the original diversity of the two races
> that prevailed in the two parts of the peninsula.
> The populations living in southern Italy during the
> period of Roman domination primarily belonged to
> the large Italian block, of which the Latins had
> been the strongest branch. In contrast, northern
> Italy had been populated by Gauls and other Celtic
> races, or races very similar to the Celtic, who
> spoke their own languages before coming under Roman
> domination.

Returning to the central thesis of his studies, he went
on to make the following observation:

> But folk poetry, like language, is a spontaneous,
> essentially ethnic creation. Race, language, and
> folk poetry are three successive forms of the same
> idea and follow an analogous course in their gene-
> sis and development. In saying this, we do not
> mean to exclude the possibility of the passage of
> folk poetry from one nation to another. What
> happened to language could have happened to folk
> poetry. In this case it will be the task of

history to find reasons for this fact and to distinguish the originally borrowed part from the
part that was added by the nation that adopted
and assimilated it. As a rule, however, one can
say that folk poetry is a spontaneous creation
of the race that expresses it, it corresponds to
the poetic and aesthetic sentiment of this race,
and it reflects an ethnic character particular to
the race. Now, to apply this rule to Italy: just
as we find the substrata of two distinct races and
two different dialectal trunks in the two parts of
the peninsula, so we ought to find, and indeed do
find, two perfectly corresponding and clearly distinct species of folk poetry.

These observations are particularly applicable to
"sung" and secular poetry because, in Nigra's opinion,
recited poetry (games, riddles, nursery rhymes, lullabies, proverbs) and religious poetry (prayers, ejacu-
lations, legends) have a less ethnic and more general
character, and from their beginning they generally
follow a separate line of development. His intention,
then, was to demonstrate the character, especially the
ethnic character, of folk poetry. Now, there is no
doubt that Nigra followed Carlo Cattaneo in this regard.
Cattaneo had believed that languages "can be created
and undone" and that "none of them is necessary" since
they all are "human and social products like customs,
laws, and cities." But in relating poetry to a specific substratum, Nigra was pronouncing a false
naturalistic concept, one essentially the same as
Gobineau's. The error lies in the fact that the distinction of two zones with particular ethnic strata
presupposes the idea of two pure and uncontaminated
races.
　　In Nigra's work, this naturalistic concept ended
up by being permeated with natural history. Although
Nigra linked the concept of poetry with the concept of
race, he believed that the concept of race was concerned exclusively with the natural, moral, intellectual, and artistic attitudes of the people--which gives
validity to his assumption. Despite his essentially

naturalistic premises, he recognized that folk poetry, like folk narrative, is always a creation of the people reciting it, and such poetry reflects their poetic and aesthetic sentiment. Here he was following a tradition of studies that passed from the Grimms to Müller and that is echoed in the Russian and Finnish historical schools. Nigra saw the necessity of classifying, but he was also an attentive and scrupulous researcher who clearly understood the importance that cultural verification can and does have in the study of poetry; that is, he understood the diffusion of a song or cluster of songs in a specific area, from which the song or cluster of songs can pass into other areas, establishing a circle of borrowings and reworkings. The fact of re-elaboration is the reason that a revised folksong must be judged as an *opus novum*.

4. Rubieri and "Storia della poesia popolare italiana"

Nigra had admitted in the preface to his *Canti popolari del Piemonte* that his study would have been "less incomplete" if he could have examined "the aesthetic and moral values of the two great branches of folk poetry in Italy." But such an examination had already been made or at least initiated in Italy by another *Risorgimento* scholar, Ermolao Rubieri, author of *Storia della poesia popolare italiana*, published in 1877. In this work Rubieri used the many collections of oral traditions that had been gathered throughout Italy. It was then thought that one had to go to libraries and archives to "breathe new air," and from such libraries and archives many folksongs had been unearthed. One of the first, if not the first, to set this example was a poet, Giosuè Carducci. Although he had only a vague understanding of folk poetry, he had the merit of publishing a collection entitled *Di alcune poesie popolari bolognesi del secolo XIII* in 1866, and in 1871 he compiled a tasteful anthology, *Cantilene e ballate, strambotti e madrigali nei secoli XIII e XIV*. This latter work was an imposing collection of folksongs of ancient origin.

In examining folksongs that had been previously
unearthed and collected, Rubieri proved to be a good
philologist--but the purpose for which he wrote his
book (which was primarily a message to the Italian
people, who had just then gained their unity) was not
merely philological. In contrast to Nigra, Rubieri
avoided appealing to racial criteria, which reminded
him of Vincenzo Gioberti, whom he had always despised.
In his view, there was only the *Italian* folk, which
expressed its characteristics, tendencies, and moods
in song in each of its regions. Rubieri was convinced
that among human creations poetry is the "first" and
"most elect"; he believed, then, that folk poetry preceded literary poetry--nor did he neglect to explain
the relationships between these two forms of poetry:

> In the fifteenth and sixteenth centuries, literary
> poetry, following the lead of Dante, tried unsuc-
> cessfully to separate itself from folk poetry.
> The older sister always exercised a powerful at-
> traction on the younger sister, and the younger,
> unable to detach herself, started to imitate the
> older. The younger thought of making fun of the
> older but concluded by honoring her. In fact, all
> the great poets of the fifteenth century (Medici,
> Pulci, Poliziano) and some of the sixteenth century
> (Machiavelli, Bronzino, Berni) took the most comic
> part and exaggerated it. Some, like Poliziano,
> touched on the most delicate part and refined it.
> A very few, like Bronzino, reproduced it as it was.
> But in one way or another they all salvaged suffi-
> cient material to allow them to reconstruct a
> beautiful monument.

This is not to say, however, that Rubieri stood in
front of folk poetry in the prayerful posture of absolute devotion, for he often exposed the lack of artist-
ry in certain folk compositions. Nevertheless, he
suggested that even non-artistic folk literature was a
social, psychological, and historical document because
a people that sings is always a people that confesses
itself: "If one attends to the ideas and sentiments

most commonly revealed by a people's words and observes
that these may be either chaste or licentious, frivolous or wise, innocent or evil, mild or angry, generous
or cowardly, patriotic or treasonous, he will find it
difficult to ignore the inference that the nature of
the state of that people corresponds to the virtues or
the vices appearing in its songs. A people whose songs
convey not merely domestic or public virtues but public
and domestic virtue together is a happy but rare people
indeed. . . ."

5. Rubieri's View of Folk Poetry and Traditional Poetry

Rubieri believed that although Italian folksongs reflected the characteristics of various regions, these
songs actually should be considered, despite dialectal
variations, as the expression of both linguistic and
political unity. He treated three different aspects
of Italian poetry--the rhythmical, the psychological,
and the moral--in order to depict the national life of
a people that would come to draw strength from such
unity. But although Rubieri performed skillful philological examinations of these aspects in both Italian
and non-Italian folk poetry, he often became entangled
in naturalistic formulas, concluding, for example, that
the mechanical qualities of meter were a natural consequence of physiological qualities. But we must also
recognize that through folk poetry he provided a picture of the ideal values of the Italian folk spirit.
In other words, he depicted the values of what Nigra
had called the ethnic spirit. Rubieri appreciated the
brilliant work of Nigra, who by then was well known to
both Italian and non-Italian scholars. Rubieri said,
"Nigra divided the songs of his collection [extracts
of which appeared in the journal *Rivista Contemporanea*]
into two series, historical and romance, which logically corresponded to the two genres of folk poetry most
common among the subalpine people because most suitable
to this people's chivalrous and serious nature."

Rubieri agreed with Nigra that the Piedmontese
held supremacy in narrative poetry while the Sicilians
reigned supreme in the madrigal. He immediately added,
however, that the supremacy of the Piedmontese "is not
total and absolute." He took this point into consideration in his excellent study of the diffusion of the
epico-lyrical song in Italy. The problem relating to
strambotti and *stornelli* (types of poetry predominant
in Sicily but diffused everywhere) was handled in the
same way with the same excellent results. Rubieri
basically held to the "two-zone" thesis maintained by
Nigra, but, in contrast to Nigra, he believed that
folk reworking also had a very modest function in
poetry that he considered to be traditional: "The
term *traditional* characterizes the kind of popular
poetry that tends to transmit some folk composition
through long periods of time--from generation to
generation and from century to century--*with no or
few alterations*, whatever the folk composition. . . .
This poetry had been invented and sometimes improvised
by the folk."

In Rubieri's view, then, traditional poetry is
poetry that is widely diffused, establishing migrations
and contacts in different regions. In essence, folk
poetry, according to Rubieri, is characterized by its
stability. Thus, his limitation largely derived from
the nature of his investigation: he studied the folksong only as a document of art or custom.

6. Ancona

A year after the publication of *Storia della poesia
popolare italiana*, some studies by Alessandro d'Ancona
were published under the title *La poesia popolare
italiana*. Ancona, also a *Risorgimento* man, certainly
had a scholarly orientation that was completely different from Rubieri's. As a philologist, literary historian, and textual scholar, he was incomparably precise
and exact in his studies. These characteristics linked
him to the scholarly tradition of the Italian eighteenth
century and to the more recent tradition of Benfey and

Veselovskiĭ, the latter a friend whom he much admired.

In his *La poesia popolare italiana* Ancona, like Rubieri, maintained that the unity of Italian popular poetry was to be recognized in its variety. But while Rubieri attempted to delineate a completely internal history of Italian popular poetry, Ancona searched for the origins of external forms or genres. In 1906 when he republished his *La poesia popolare italiana* he himself observed, "In the first edition I wrote a preface in which I asserted that my studies owed nothing to Ermolao Rubieri's *Storia della poesia popolare italiana*, which was published after everything I had written and consigned to the editor, a good part of my work, had been printed; there was, then, no plagiarism on my part where we agreed nor confutation where we disagreed. . . . But now, as the reader will see, I have used the work of my now deceased friend, citing it whenever his authoritative view conforms or disagrees with mine."

In his studies Ancona was especially interested in investigating relationships between folk poetry and cultured poetry. He recognized a clear difference between "poetry imitating ancient or recent foreign models and a completely popular and ingenuous kind of poetry"; too, he was convinced that even if all the poems he cited could not be "absolutely said to have originated among the folk or to have been adopted by the folk, it is certain that their birth must have been brought about by feelings quite different from those that inspired the poetry of educated men and courtiers. . . ." Thus, he did not hesitate to adopt Nigra's thesis; that is, he saw the importance of establishing the origin and diffusion of songs, a subject about which he was quite clear:

> We believe, and the kind and attentive reader must have already glimpsed the truth of what we say, that the Italian folksong is native to Sicily. In saying this we do not mean to imply that the populaces of other provinces lack a poetic faculty or that there are not other types of folk poetry in other Italian regions that have developed there

and diffused outward. But we believe that in most
cases the Italian folksong has the island of Sicily
for its country of origin and Tuscany for its country of adoption; we believe that it originated in
the Sicilian dialect, assumed its illustrious and
common form in Tuscany, and with these new embel-
lishments migrated to other provinces. But, although this is the general case, there certainly
are exceptions.

Obviously this theory is incorrect, inasmuch as
Ancona limited the Italian folksong to *strambotti*,
stornelli, and lyrical poetry in general, with Sicily
proposed as the country of origin. And what of narrative poetry? He immediately adds: "Coming further
north, we encounter a more cultured people, in whom
the poetic impulse is almost dead or is now expressed
only in crude improvisations or in simple rearrange-
ments of traditional folksongs. . . . And whoever
would go even further north to the countries of Celto-
Roman populations would find the Sicilian stanzas to
be few in number. . . . Here indigenous and traditional poetry is related not to southern Italy but to
other peoples and idioms stretching as far as Provence,
France, Catalonia, and Portugal. . . ." But in regard
to the distinction posed by Nigra (specifically, that
there is a lyrical form agreeing with the temperament
of southern Italy and a different narrative form consonant with northern Italy), Ancona always held to
what he had written in his review of *Canti popolari
del Piemonte* (later collected in his *Saggi di letteratura popolare*); in that review he said that Nigra's
distinction was "an ingenious hypothesis perhaps containing some truth, but one that needs to be accompanied by stronger proofs."
Ancona was not interested only in popular poetry,
which gained him the kind of prestige in Italy that
Berchet and Tommaseo had previously gained; he was
also interested in popular printed literature. Such
interest led to his *Poemetti popolari italiani* (1898),
which is an example of the kind of comparative literature that gives folklore its particular charm. This

volume explored the diffusion of "Storia di San Giovanni Boccadoro," "Trattato della Superbia e morte di
Senso," "Attila Flagellum Dei," and "Storia di
Ottinello e Guilia." He thought that these originated
in the Orient, but he was always cautious and prudent
about this idea. Finally, we must not overlook
Ancona's work on the folk theater in his *Origini del
teatro italiano*; here he discusses May Day celebra-
tions, Epiphany ceremonies, gypsy activities, and all
those folk productions that he saw with the eyes of a
romantic, convinced as he was that of all the poets
the folk is always the best.

A student of Italian literature, an investigator
of sources, and a proposer of daring hypotheses,
Ancona intended to demonstrate, through his work and
with his efforts, that in addition to the so-called
"cultured" literature there is another kind of literature, one that deserves to be studied and evaluated
with the same seriousness as the first. Although the
worship of cultured literature in Italy was such as
not to facilitate the consideration and advent of the
other kind of literature, his studies did open the way
for a group of skilled and seasoned disciples, especially Francesco Novati. Novati contributed much to
the study of popular poetry and related iconography,
and his work was characterized by a rare sensitivity.

7. Comparetti

In Pisa, more precisely in the Normal School, Ancona
found an excellent collaborator in his colleague,
Domenico Comparetti. A student of Weber, Comparetti
believed, despite his thorough preparation in classical
and modern literatures, that a love for the "popular"
was an integral part of these literatures. In regard
to the second volume of his *Virgilio nel medio evo* (the
first edition of which was published in 1872), Comparetti's biographer, Giorgio Pasquali, said that there
one could see the influence of Ancona, "with whom
Comparetti had a great friendship." He adds:

His romantic and folkloristic works on romance
philology, his studies on neo-Grecian dialects of
southern Italy, his treatise *Edipo e la mitologia
comparata* (in which he argued that the Greek imagination worked moral concepts into tale motifs),
and other works fall into the period of those first
years at Pisa. Previously, in 1862, in his first
work on Greek epigraphy, Comparetti formulated the
problem of Greco-Oriental religious syncretism.
The collaboration with Ancona is also externally
evident: he worked with Ancona for thirteen years
on the laborious publication of an ancient collection of Italian rhymes contained in a Vatican
codex. Ancona published an Italian adaption of
the Book of Sindibad, the book of the Seven Sages
of Rome. Comparetti traced the tradition, particularly . . . the Greek one, although he also published an ancient Spanish adaption in the appendix.
In 1875 Comparetti published a collection entitled
Novelline popolari italiane in a series directed by
Ancona.

The series cited by Pasquali is the collection entitled *Canti e racconti del popolo italiano*, which
Ancona founded and directed with the collaboration of
Comparetti, in hopes of producing a national work that
would unify and elevate "the thought of the commoners
in various Italian provinces." But in addition to this
purpose the collection had the specific aim of providing scholars of Italian folklore with some authentic
documents. The first volume of the collection was published in 1871. Ten years later two collections were
initiated in Paris, *Collection des chansons et des
contes populaires* and *Les littératures populaires de
toutes les nations* (which attempted to present a
hundred volumes of great documentary interest). *Novelline popolari italiane*, published in the collection
that Comparetti directed with Ancona, was meant to be
a contribution to the Italian narrative. But how did
Comparetti consider this narrative? In a letter dated
April 24, 1870, Comparetti wrote to Giuseppe Pitrè:

As you well know, Italian folk poetry varies greatly in certain areas of our country, as is demonstrated by different characteristics and forms. In regard to folksongs, then, there is no doubt that one can and should put the songs of each province or even more restricted localities in separate volumes. This, however, does not apply to tales. Now, everyone knows that some of those tales that the Germans call *Märchen* have been diffused among all European (to say nothing of non-European) countries, and they have certainly or probably been equally diffused among the Italian people. As you well understand, one who wishes to publish local tales, as has been done for the songs, clearly runs the risk of producing many volumes containing narrative materials that are for the most part identical. . . . It would be best, then, to produce a general collection entitled *Conti* (or *novelline*) *popolari italiani*, giving the text of the best and most complete version of each tale among those collected in various parts of Italy by each collaborator and supplying the most important variants in notes. This is what the brothers Grimm did with German tales and what Afanas'ev did with Russian tales.

Three years later, on January 1, 1873, Comparetti reasserted his conviction about his *Novelline popolari italiane* in another letter to Pitrè: "My collection will begin publication next month. The tales will all be reduced to a common language except one or two for each province, which will be published in dialect. I will give illustrations at the end of the collection in the last volume, including information on each tale and comparisons with corresponding Italian and foreign tales, and I will also provide a bibliography of tales published in various countries. This collection of Italian tales has been achieved with a method and intent that must distinguish it from partial collections of tales of Lombardy, Venice, and Sicily."

8. *Folk Narrative and Folk Poetry*

Only the first volume of Comparetti's projected collection was published. But did Comparetti actually
follow the method of the brothers Grimm and Afanas'ev?
The Grimms and Afanas'ev reconstructed the text of a
tale on the basis of its variants, while Comparetti
provided variants that he considered the best. He was,
then, faithful to the text. But, like Ancona, who
naively reproved Vittorio Imbriani (one of Italy's most
serious and scrupulous collectors of folk poetry) for
his having stenographically transcribed the tales in
his *La novellaja milanese*, he did not understand that
the narrative material of different regions can be
identical in themes and motifs but quite different in
its expressive form, and that at times it can be an
opus novum; rather, he believed that this was the case
only for folk poetry. In his work entitled *Il Kalevala;
o, La poesia tradizionale dei Finni*, published in 1891,
Comparetti characterized such poetry, which is folk
poetry *par excellence*, in the following way:

> *The singer, the "laulaja," repeats and creates at
> the same moment. He feels that the large group
> of songs that he has in his mind belongs to him
> and to everyone.* This constitutes his knowledge,
> his model, his means, and, at the same time, the
> technique of his work. He interweaves verses of
> a song that we would call lyrical with a song that
> we would call epical or magical, and he also does
> the reverse. In this interweaving, he freely pro-
> ceeds like one who on various occasions uses the
> words, phrases, and combinations of a language
> belonging to and understood by everyone. Because
> of this right that the singers feel they have (and
> often use) and because of the natural evolution
> that poetry committed to memory and propagated
> only orally must undergo, the number of variants
> that each song has is very great. A song not only
> differs from singer to singer but also a singer
> himself never repeats the same song twice in
> exactly the same way, today combining into one

song what yesterday had been two or more separate
and distinct songs. Thus, the sum total of all
the songs collected until now, together with their
infinite variations, appears as a mass of verses
of poetical-imaginative creations, fluctuating and
in a state of perpetual transformation, decomposi-
tion, and recomposition. This is the true, natural
condition of folk poetry. . . .

It is obvious here to observe that generally he adopted
the ideas of Julius Krohn, a close friend of his, and
he was the first to make Krohn's works known in Italy.
But isn't the natural condition of folk poetry the same
as that of the narrative, which he studied according to
the theory of migrations and borrowings?
    A precise philologist and an open-minded, refined
writer, Comparetti was also inspired by his interest in
following a folktale from country to country in order
to discover it in a Sanskrit text, in a Persian readaption, or in a Syrian or Greco-Byzantine translation.
His *Ricerche intorno al libro di Sindibad*, published in
1870, resulted from this interest. In this work he outlined the tradition of the book of Sindibad and also
studied the Western and Oriental adaptions, which he
traced back to a tenth-century Arabic text. While
acknowledging the influence that those adaptions had on
folk narrative, Comparetti strongly argued that the
popular tradition can change the content of any book.
Nor should we forget that in another work published
some years before, *Edipo e la mitologia comparata*, he
had opposed the mythological theories of one of
Müller's disciples, Michel Bréal: "To say that in expressing these moral concepts the folk imagination is
limited to modifying myths originating from the sensible world, remodeling them in a moral sense and *expressly creating nothing*, is an absurdity opposed by
fact and good sense. The power of the human imagination, particularly in periods of little culture, is
far from being condemned to the miserable parsimony of
production to which many mythologists reduce the wonderful faculty of man, which Goethe has justly called
eternally changing and ever new."

Although these were intelligent premises, Comparetti said in the first edition of his *Virgilio nel medio evo* that Italy lacked imaginative productions, a thesis later expressed in Arturo Graf's folkloristic essays and in Letterio di Francia's *Novellistica*; thus, Comparetti forgot, as Ferdinando Neri observed, that he himself had said that the legend of Virgil "was born in Naples" and from there "had spread throughout Europe." This investigation by Comparetti was also marred by a fundamental defect: he presupposed a Neapolitan legend whose existence he believed to be documented as early as the twelfth century, when in fact it seems that this legend was an invention of English and German clerics of the fourteenth century who had brought widely diffused narrative motifs to Naples and Rome. But whatever its sources, can we deny that this legend, wherever or however invented, also belongs to Neapolitan folklore? Comparetti was fully convinced that "the popular is distinguished from the literary primarily by its nature, character, and various elements, regardless of the condition of the one who relates, believes, or conceives it"; further, he argued that a legend "will be popular even when we can prove that it derives from the imagination of a clergyman who has written it." Won't everything that the folk accepts be popular, then, just so long as they accept it?

In Comparetti we find doubts, uncertainties, and errors of perspective. But the fact is that in both his minor and major works (his *Virgilio* and *Kalevala* are great frescoes depicting Italian and Finnish folklife, respectively, against the background of the epopee) he approached folklore with the ardor of a great maestro. The result was that he, along with Nigra, Rubieri, and Ancona, synthesized Italian and European culture, thus realizing the romantic ideal.

CHAPTER XX

THE LESSON OF PITRÈ

1. *Faith in the Folk*

In the same period in which the work of Nigra, Rubieri,
and Comparetti was developing, when folkloristic studies
were being revolutionized by the contributions of
Müller, Benfey, and Paris, one Italian scholar, whose
name we have already encountered several times, Giuseppe
Pitrè, not only participated in but also became the
master craftsman of such studies. In him (a *Risorgimento* man like Nigra, Rubieri, and Ancona) we find a
fervent belief in the *vox populi*, as we find in Percy,
Herder, and Arnim; in him we also find the historical
awareness of a Bodmer and a Möser in regard to those
"spiritual" formations that we call folk traditions; and
in him we find the patriotic and humanitarian impulse
with which the brothers Grimm undertook the study of
folklore in their own country, a study characterized by
a sharp historical awareness and deep faith. Although
the historical conditions of the respective countries
were different, Pitrè, like the brothers Grimm, was
dominated by the same *Rettungsgedanke* that Herder had
proposed as a program of work for the following generations.

The result of this *Rettungsgedanke* was Pitrè's
principal work, *Biblioteca delle tradizoni popolari
siciliane*, which demonstrates that he knew how to be
both Sicilian and Italian, both Italian and European.
This had happened in other fields as well: many writers
and scholars contemporary with Pitrè had made the folk
of different regions the subject of their art, thus
becoming simultaneously Sicilian and Italian, Pied-

montese and Italian, Tuscan and Italian, and, most
importantly, Italian and European.

In 1879, after the publication of Rubieri's and
Ancona's histories of folk poetry, Francesco de
Sanctis said in his lecture on Zola and *L'assommoir*:
"The learned languages, the languages commonly used
and almost exhausted by art, need to be retempered in
the languages of the people closest to nature, a people
that has the liveliest passions, the most immediate
impressions, and that derives its language not from
rules but from those impressions. The artist should
search for and wholly appropriate this treasure-trove
of images, attitudes, proverbs, and phrases in their
lively, quick, free, and easy dialectal style." In a
sense, this is the literary manifesto and prophecy of
the art of Giovanni Verga and his followers. But is
there anything in this manifesto (whose ideas are expressed by de Sanctis in one of the chapters of his
Giovinezza) that differs from what Herder had said in
Germany, Madame de Staël in France, Karamzin in Russia,
and Berchet in Italy? It had been the romantics who
had introduced the folk into narrative and poetry as
the hero of history. It had been the romantics, from
the brothers Grimm to Pushkin and from Wordsworth to
Glinka, who had used the language, literature, and
music of the folk to create and give life to their own
language. And although in Italy such literature (which
had not been thoroughly documented) was not taken into
consideration by Manzoni, now we find--and this is not
happenstance--that it dominates Verga's narrative, his
epopee, in which the folk is, as in Pitrè's *Biblioteca
delle tradizioni popolari siciliane*, the choral protagonist of his faith and despair.

Even Zola's naturalism (to which Verga's realism
is incorrectly linked) is to be explained in the light
of Romanticism, supported in some of its deepest beliefs by Positivism. The low centers of urban life,
the "bowels" of the great cities, had been brought on
the scene by the second Romanticism. In his work Zola
was as precise in searching for his sources as Paris
had been in the field of ancient literature. On the
one hand, he added the humble tragedy of the crude

plebeian of the large cities to the French epopee, and,
on the other, he proposed to elevate the plebeian to
the true dignity of the folk. Verga's sources were
quite different. Yet didn't these two very different
writers (as Luigi Russo has defined them, the first
was clinically prosaic while the second was epico-
lyrical) share the same convictions? Just as Zola's
naturalism and Verga's realism continued the worship
of truth professed by romantics, so did the concepts
asserted in political and social struggles reflect
the need for a radical renovation of man, for a better
humanity--the same faith in man and his perfectability
that one can see in the most enthusiastic apostles of
the romantic period. In this respect, what does
socialism, even the socialism of Marx (one remembers
the insistent motif of money in Zola's work and of
material things in Verga's work), propose to give us
if not what derives from its scientific presuppositions?

Romantic historiography made its influence felt in
all fields, even in music. One thinks of Wagner, who
made music, song, and poetry of myths beloved by the
Schlegels, the brothers Grimm, Müller, and Benfey. In
a letter to a painter friend in June, 1875, the Russian
musician Musorgskiĭ exclaimed, "The folk is what I want
to represent." And, in fact, he did represent and sing
about the folk with the zeal of Pushkin, renewing the
message of Glinka, just as Wagner renewed the message
of Weber, Schubert, and Schumann. Nor should we forget
that in Italy, not to mention other countries, we often
encounter themes in the works of Vincenzo Bellini and
Giuseppe Verdi that, while bearing the typically original stamp of their genius, show a clearly popular
origin.

In other words, a belief in the folk continued to
be a faith, a continuation of what had been the fundamentally anti-literary, anti-rhetorical demand of
Romanticism. The folk was always, in contrast to the
old and abused conventionalisms, the symbol of truth
and virtue, work and progress--a concept that completely informed the course of the eighteenth and nineteenth
centuries. But we must observe that as the concept of

the folk and everything understood as popular were
reassessed, the world enclosed by the boundaries of
the province or in the more restricted limits of a
remote or distant tradition actually faded in the minds
of most people, faded in the light of a new culture
with different social, political, and economic needs.

This world was regarded with the nostalgia, regret,
and mournful love of one who wished it better luck, in
that he now felt such a world to be so different and
distant from the large movements of culture and life
that were committed to proceeding in one particular
way, a way unlike the past. In a certain sense, then,
the "myth" of the province constitutes an overcoming
of the province, which is why Verga, like Pitrè, can
be understood only in a culture that is not Sicilian
but rather Italian and European.

2. *Pitrè's Main Works:* The *"Biblioteca,"* the *"Archivio,"* and the *"Curiosità"*

The *Biblioteca delle tradizioni popolari siciliane*,
a twenty-five volume work of nostalgia and faith, was
published between 1871 and 1913, a half-century of
work. Pitrè was not a literary man even though while
a youth he wrote a series, *Profili biografici di
contemporanei italiani*, about famous personalities of
the time. He was not a philologist coming from a
strict academic discipline; rather, like Zola, he was
a doctor. Yet this doctor, who had begun his profes-
sion in the folk quarters of Palermo during a cholera
epidemic, had the qualities of a litterateur and a
philologist. Giovanni Verga, for example, did not
hesitate to praise his works on Sicilian folklife,
while Ernesto Monaci placed him among the greatest
Italian philologists of the day.

In his *Biblioteca* Pitrè was scholarly in collecting
his materials. His classifications are careful and his
field of investigation is broad. The *Biblioteca*, which
has the merit of preserving many of the traditional
hereditary riches of the folk, is, however, more than
merely a collection: it is the meeting point where the

experiences and achievements of European folklore
coalesce. In beginning his project, Pitrè wanted to
know what had been and was being done in Europe on all
the subjects of his own collection. His prefaces,
however, are not limited to tracing the actual state
of these studies; rather, he goes on to discuss various problems that these studies involve. Taken as a
whole, his prefaces constitute a treatise in which
many folkloristic problems are subjected to his
judgment and good sense.

To accompany his work on the *Biblioteca*, Pitrè
had begun to supervise, with Salvatore Salomone-Marino,
the *Archivio per lo studio delle tradizioni popolari*
in 1882. The prospectus says:

> Recent progress in comparative mythology and demo-
> psychology and the evergrowing interest in folk
> traditions now make us aware of the need for a
> magazine in which scholars of various nations can
> meet and have a means of communicating and dis-
> seminating their studies and collections. Modest
> in its aims, the *Archivio* proposes to illustrate
> and present various forms of folk literature and
> many manifestations of the physical and moral
> life of nations in general and of Italy in particu-
> lar. . . . A magazine and a bibliographic bulletin
> will take account of new publications on the sub-
> ject, and nothing will be neglected so that readers
> can be fully informed of present movements in the
> studies of folk traditions.

To be honest, however, the *Archivio* was in fact anything but modest. In bringing scholars together for
the probing of common concerns, it constituted an
active palaestra where all the controversial problems
of folklore could be found. We must add that, on the
one hand, Pitrè's bibliographic bulletins complemented
the prefaces of his *Biblioteca*; on the other hand, they
served as a critical introduction to the history of
European folklore.

To give his studies maximum development, Pitrè
founded the collection *Curiosità popolari tradizionali*,

with the collaboration of another Sicilian folklorist,
Gaetano di Giovanni, in 1885. This work covers sixteen
volumes, each of which makes a significant contribution
to the study of folk traditions. The *Biblioteca,* the
Archivio, and the *Curiosità* (leaving aside such other
works as *Novelle popolari toscane* and *Bibliografia
delle tradizioni popolari d'Italia*) are like the
columns of a temple from which Pitrè, with the voice of
the folk, put forth his teaching, a teaching intended
to give us a clear vision of the nature of folklore.

3. Folklore as History in Pitrè's Thought

The starting point for Pitrè's teaching is Sicily, its
folklore, and especially the concept that Pitrè had
about history. When Pitrè wrote *Profile biografici
contemporanei* in 1864, while still a young man, he had
observed, "History should not be simply a list of men
and the dates of their significant actions; rather, it
should be a revelation of ideas, passions, customs,
and civil interests. In short, it should be the revelation of a people, the life of a nation." A few years
later, in his *Sui canti popolari siciliani*, he added:

> The history of a nation is confused with the his-
> tory of its rulers. . . . We often attempt to
> make a nation's history correspond to the history
> of its government, without considering that it has
> memories quite different from those that are often
> attributed to it, in regard to its institutions
> and the powerful forces with which it supports its
> rights. The time for exploring those memories,
> studying them patiently and nurturing them loving-
> ly, has now arrived. The philosopher, the legis-
> lator, and the historian who attempt to know every-
> thing about a nation now recognize the necessity
> of observing its songs, proverbs, and tales as well
> as its phrases, mottos, and words. Next to the
> word is always its meaning, and behind the literal
> sense is the allegorical and mystical sense; under
> the strange and different trappings of the tale

one will find the history and the religion of
peoples and nations adumbrated.

It is evident that here Pitrè picks up the concept of
history previously expressed by Voltaire and advanced
in the specific field of folklore by Bodmer, Möser,
Herder, and especially the brothers Grimm. Indeed,
each volume of the *Biblioteca* lives in the light of
this concept.

Having concluded this work, Pitrè did not hesitate
to claim the title of historian, which he had proposed
for himself. In the last volume of the *Biblioteca* (*La
famiglia, la casa, la vita del popolo siciliano*), he
warmly exclaims:

> Consider a country that until yesterday lived in
> and for itself, under foreign domination, in con-
> tact only with often unpleasant nations, each of
> which left strong traces of its passage and its
> stay; a country where civilization followed civili-
> zation (if indeed they were always worthy of this
> name) and where, like so many layers of tradition,
> spoken rather than written history was formed:
> such a country offers *rare material for investiga-
> tion and criticism.* Whoever will take the time to
> follow, one by one, the subjects here treated will
> surely notice certain forms that otherwise would
> remain isolated and mute. *To one who observes
> well, they are so many rings of a chain of customs,
> practices, and beliefs in which spirit and matter
> mutually develop.*

In compiling his *Biblioteca*, Pitrè had the single aim of
searching for the history of folklore where no one had
yet searched. It was necessary to save in Sicily--and
this is the essence of his *Rettungsgedanke*--a whole heritage that was disappearing, the heritage of the folk.
At the moment that Sicily was entering into the broader
confines of Italy, this heritage served to demonstrate
Sicily's historical individuality. In this respect,
there is no doubt that Pitrè was Sicily's most enthusiastic philologist; in particular, he was Sicily's histo-

rian, the clever illustrator of an entire world in which
the echoes of the most ancient civilizations are heard.

Still, it seems strange that almost at the end of
his career Pitrè concluded with baptizing his discipline with a term that we have already encountered in
the prospectus of his *Archivio*: demopsychology. But,
after all, was demopsychology, as Pitrè conceived it,
in any way different from what we call the history of
folk traditions?

4. *Folk Poetry as a Problem*

Having clarified the historical nature of Sicilian
folklore--which was the taking of a position for the
purpose of understanding the material of folklore,
wherever it is--Pitrè, slowly proceeding in his work,
took on the task of clarifying the creative capacity
of individuals who make up the folk and who are, in
essence, the true creators of folklore. It is here
that his research, while apparently moving along the
same lines as the research of Nigra, Ancona, and
Comparetti, nevertheless managed to illuminate more
vividly many problems relating to folk literature.
In regard to the birth and diffusion of the folksong,
for example, he says:

> The most common opinion is that folksongs are
> created by this or that rustic poet, poets who
> are often found in villages and country places;
> but we do not have their names nor the when,
> where, or why of the song. This obscurity, which
> seems a defect, is actually the reason that the
> folksong becomes popular. If the folk knew the
> author of a song, perhaps the folk would not learn
> the song, particularly if it is by a learned per-
> son. The time and place of a song's origin, if
> not deduced from some allusion, cannot be guessed.
> *The song of one person becomes the song of all*
> because we find that it originates in conditions
> most favorable to a long existence; it lasts be-
> cause it responds to the natural feelings, customs,

and traditions of the folk. One fine morning, in
the middle of a square or at the end of a dark
alley or in an open field, a beautiful song, never
before heard, is raised. Who has created it? Who
could have created it? No one knows and no one
attempts to know. The author willingly does without the fame of a poet; the folk, respecting his
modesty, rewards him by keeping his songs for
itself, transmitting similar songs to others.
(*Sui canti popolari siciliani*, p. 113)

After posing the problem in this way, Pitrè was
interested in examining the origin of folk poetry as
it had been conceived by Ancona. Ancona's theory on
the origin of Italian folk poetry seemed premature to
him. Pitrè did not deny that such lines of communica-
tion as wars, pilgrimages, and festivals had explained
the diffusion of a large number of songs. But while
acknowledging that it was very useful to determine
whether a song has come to Sicily from Tuscany or the
reverse, he suggested that it was even more useful to
see if the song corresponds to the feelings of Sicilians or Tuscans. "Transplanted outside their native
soil," Pitrè poetically says, folksongs "are guests
invited to the hearth of the family after having been
dressed in other clothes."
In the same way and for the same reasons, Pitrè
put little stock in the literary origin of folksongs.
In his view, as he says in his *Studi di poesia popolare*,
"the folksong, born among the folk, carries the mark of
the absolute ignorance of the author; its form has no
controlling idea, no verse, no phrase, no word; it
issues from the mind, rhythm, and vocabulary of low and
unlearned people, and it is anonymous and traditional."
After making a quick comparison between Sicilian *strambotti* and the poetry of Antonio Veneziano, he adds:

According to what we can gather from more than
eight hundred printed Sicilian octavos, Veneziano's
love poetry is most notable for its greatness of
style, sharpness of conception, sweet expression
of feeling, and the nobility and novelty of its

images. It is rich with profound philosophical
thoughts, and with rare artistic ability he presents them to the shadowy and gentle graces of the
imagination. . . . I think that I have said everything about the extrinsic form of his work in saying that it is lofty in conception, there being no
Sicilian words that point to the commonplace or
plebeian. . . .

How poetry could be considered a source of popular
Sicilian *strambotti*, he concludes, is indeed a mystery.
In his *Sui canti popolari siciliani*, he says that since
authentic folksongs are poetry, "the product of virgin
imagination, which the schools disdain looking at but
which the schools cannot produce, they are a gold mine
of sentiments, thoughts, and images, from which any
scholar capable of imitating them, from the clumsiest
versifier to the most inspired poet, could draw inestimable beauties. . . . Sincere language in love, in
jealousy, in spite, in domestic joy, under a foreign
roof, in the midst of prison and in whatever state of
fortune or spirit or condition of life: the folksong
is the truest, most heartfelt expression of the character of the folk. . . ."
     In Pitrè's words one certainly hears the echoes of
romantic and pre-romantic theories. Nevertheless, Pitrè
attempted (as did Ancona, Rubieri, and Comparetti) to
define the difference, which he considered essential,
between the two forms of poetry, by using a criterion
that we could call psychological. In his opinion, folk
poetry, whatever its origins, is a form of literature in
which everything acquires and keeps a particular character.

5. *"Bearers" and Creators of Folklore*

Pitrè thought the problem of folk poetry, as well as
the problem of folktales, was essentially an aesthetic
one, which places him in clear contrast to both Ancona
and Comparetti. In a letter sent to Ernesto Monaci in
December of 1873, it almost seemed that he wished to

respond specifically to his illustrious fellow workers.
His assertions leave no doubts:

> Now I find myself with other, no less precious
> materials of Sicilian tales. . . . What beauty,
> my friend! One must know and feel the Sicilian
> dialect in order to know and feel the exquisiteness
> of the tales that I have succeeded in gathering
> from one of my many narrators. Her name is
> Agatuzza, one of those types one rarely encounters:
> I feel humble before her. Her phraseology is the
> ideal Sicilian phraseology, and her words are so
> rich and personal that there is no art of craft or
> condition of life that she cannot represent with
> appropriate voice. All this makes me admire her
> greatly, but it much embarrasses me to be con-
> fronted at every moment with words and phrases
> that are completely new to our vocabulary. . . .

In the preface to *Fiabe novelle e racconti popolari
siciliani*, he adds, always in honor of the messiah
(Agatuzza), "The miming of narrations . . . must be
taken into account, for without it the narration loses
half of its force and effectiveness. It is fortunate
when language remains so full of natural inspiration
and images wholly taken from actual events, with the
result that abstract things become concrete, super-
sensible things become corporal, and things that had
no or only one life live and speak." The important
contribution of women in narrative reworkings was also
acknowledged by an indefatigable scholar of French
folklore, Paul Sébillot. In 1892 in an essay published in *Revue des Traditions Populaires*, which he
directed, he asserted:

> In passing through the mouths of women, oral
> literature takes on a fascination, ingenuousness,
> and at times an effective form that few men are
> able to attain. Almost all the great collectors
> of tales observe that women have provided them
> with the best and most beautiful versions: the
> brothers Grimm and F. Luzel, for example,

acknowledge that the most complete and finest tales
come from peasant women and that the sureness of
their memory, as well as the form of their narration, is superior to men's. A long experience with
women narrators of Great Britain confirms the
above.

The difference between the brothers Grimm and Pitrè
is that Pitrè did not limit himself to the recognition
of this contribution; following the system previously
inaugurated in Russia by Gil'ferding, he transcribed
and published the dialectal text with the greatest
exactness. Besides, it seemed to Pitrè that in translating the dialectal text of tales, as Comparetti
wished, one eliminates or at least changes the personality of the narrator. He clearly understood that if
a tale is popular it is so because, although developing
in a traditional context and in ordinary places, it
reveals the folk personality of the narrator who has
transformed his sources.

6. The Origin of Folktales and Riddles

Pitrè undertook the examination of these sources with
exceedingly clear judgment. In the *Discorso* preceding
his collection of folktales, he observes that "our
folktales are documents of the relationship among the
Indo-European races and their offspring, documents
that many centuries, nations, and generations have not
been able to destroy; indeed, the passing of time has
made them more solid and durable. It is a remarkable
fact in the history of mankind that, while peoples and
nations have almost completely disappeared . . . and
the cold wings of time have caused the memory of the
most famous deeds to be lost, these childish tales
live to testify to an incalculable antiquity." Here
he was following Müller, on the one hand, and Benfey,
on the other. It is true, he immediately adds, that
we find primitive myths in many folktales, but this
does not mean that there must be a continuation of a
myth in each folktale, if we consider that "the desire

to recognize everywhere what careful studies could
prove only for a number of folktales is a fatal error
to these studies, which should proceed without pre-
occupations and preconceptions."

Pitrè believed that a certain number of folktales
originated in the Orient. In this respect, one must
recognize that Mohammedans and Buddhists spread Indic
tales in Africa, Asia, and Europe; one must also recognize that the cause of this propagation is owed not
only to books but also to the oral tradition; finally,
one must recognize that the tales, after having
appeared in European literature, passed to the folk
and from this transformation again passed into literature, and then again to the folk, like a flood whose
violent and tempestuous course can never be checked.
Because of its geographical position, Sicily clearly
must have collected tales and legends from Persia,
Greece, and Arabia and transmitted them to the European
continent; but, we must ask ourselves, does this obviate the fact that in Sicily, as elsewhere, these
tales and legends have received something from narrators' imaginations? And isn't this "something"--here
is the concept of folk re-elaboration, which was continually running through Pitrè's mind--precisely what
gives folksongs their own particular character, their
own historical concreteness?

The same problem exists in regard to proverbs. In
the introduction to the first volume of *Proverbi e
canti popolari siciliani*, Pitrè began by observing that
the observable characteristics of such compositions are
brevity, popularity, meter, rhyme, and alliteration.
He neglected no previous investigation in order to
establish characteristics found in classical and modern
civilizations. But his studies assumed a new and original character when he examined the meter and rhyme of
proverbs, for this was an investigation that led him to
consider the forms of proverbs as aesthetically valid.
After considering the rhyme of the proverb, Pitrè observed, "The inclination towards rhyme sometimes concludes in a simple assonance, as in Portuguese and
Spanish proverbs." Although his language is not very
precise, he maintained that "the poetic expression,

characterized by ellipsis and conciseness, is a rela-
tively artistic form, which the folk spirit found and
substituted for ordinary expressions on certain
naturally exalted occasions."

In divining these forms, Pitrè was moving toward
an increasingly clear understanding of the origin of
folk productions. He observes, for example, that the
"primitive expression" that "led to the proverb" was
individual and "not from that collective entity called
folk, which is not by nature an inventor." Remembering a Greek proverb that the word issues from one
mouth and arrives at a thousand, he concludes, "Only
those individuals more endowed than others are creators, inventors, and initiators--but the names of these
authors of proverbs have been lost because the folk
takes less account of the maker of a proverb than
learned people do of the maker of a maxim."

We find these concepts expressed, or rather, impressed, in Pitrè's *Indovinelli, dubbi scioglilingua
del popolo siciliano.* "The origin of certain riddles,"
he wrote in this volume, "is itself a riddle that does
not have its Oedipus, although perhaps it one day will;
this is so because the ways in which riddles traveled
through different peoples and races, through hidden
and unknown passages, can still be investigated and,
if investigated, they can be retraced and collected."
But while looking forward to this new work, he said
that it was "not a question of scientific curiosity
pure and simple, let alone a pastime for busy people.
It is, if you will pardon the expression, a question
of 'archaeological monuments' of the folk mind; these
are also documents of contemporary social history and
literature because they belong to a living tradition."

It was the first time in Italy that proverbs and
riddles were considered to be more than simple linguistic documents. They are indeed literary documents,
but let us not forget, Pitrè immediately adds, that
they are also documents of social history--a characteristic shared by folksongs *and* folktales. Folk literature thus becomes an integral part of the ethnic tradition.

7. Unity of Folklore

In studying various kinds of folk literature, Pitrè
immediately perceived that this study was not an end
in itself. The work done in this field by Nigra,
Rubieri, and Ancona, so rich in teachings and achievements, had its limitations inasmuch as it remained
circumscribed by the confines of folk literature that,
in one way or the other, had been investigated as a
function of mythology, comparative literature, and
philology. It is true that Nigra and Rubieri had
given a certain autonomy to literary folklore, and it
is also true that Ancona and Comparetti clearly recognized the ineliminable values that folklore declares.
But in following the path of Diez, Paris, and Rajna,
they were moving away from the tradition of folklore
studies best exemplified by the brothers Grimm. In
the Grimms' work, folklore had indeed been posed as a
philological problem that was to be resolved in the
literature and history of the specific country, but
they also saw folklore as a unitary phenomenon in which
folk literature and the ethnic tradition were integrated, a point they made to clarify many aspects of
this literature and to provide a complete picture of
its history.

It is this new tradition that Pitrè followed in
Italy. His merit consists not only in his having emphasized the historical and poetic nature of folk compositions but also in his having understood that songs,
stories, proverbs, and riddles remain as lifeless
organisms, philological pieces, branches broken from a
tree, if they are not placed within the context of the
custom that harmonizes and enlivens them all. Pitrè
himself, in his *Sui canti popolari siciliani*, had
explicitly said:

> I begin with the principle that each kind of folk
> poetry ought to be taken as a revelation, on the
> one hand, of the special feeling of an individual
> member of the folk and, on the other hand, of the
> refinement of the individual and of the folk that
> reveals it. Herder said that folksongs are the

archives of the folk, the treasury of its knowledge
of its religion, of its theogony and its cosmogony,
of the life of its fathers and the glorious deeds
of its history. Folksongs are the expression of
its heart, the image of its soul, in joy and in
grief, from the cradle to the grave. Thus, one
should not be surprised if Diodorus Siculus and
Plutarch cite the verses of rhapsodic poets as a
witness of ancient habits and customs or if Paulus
Diaconus uses the traditions of his countrymen for
the primitive history of the Lombards; nor should
we blame those who, in setting forth history, try
to illustrate each fact and event with the history
of folklife--the laws, usages, dialects, and
proverbs of the nation.

In the second edition (1891) of *Sui canti popolari
siciliani*, he was even more precise: "By carefully
observing songs, we find inestimable hidden treasures.
The folksong is another source of traditions, revealing, in the strict sense of the word, specific customs
and usages."
    Pitrè's specific methodology was always the same:
he never considered folk literature in itself. Moreover (and his *Biblioteca* is ample evidence of this),
he understood that to tell the history and civilization of the Sicilian folk it was necessary not only to
study its poetico-literary productions but also to
embrace its entire life. Along with its songs the folk
has its customs, along with its tales it has its
festivals, and along with its proverbs it has its
beliefs. These are links that hold it together, leaves
of a tree that sinks its roots into the past to absorb
the vital fluids of its future.
    The "spoken history" of Sicily would remain "incom-
plete," as Pitrè said in the introduction to his
Spettacoli e feste popolari siciliane, "if not supported and enriched by the Sicilian tradition, which was
gathered in past centuries and whose continuity can be
proved by going back to its origins in antiquity." In
this volume Pitrè tells us that the sources from which
he had drawn his "sacred representations" are tradi-

tions, books, and manuscripts, while for the festivals
he had drawn once again from the oral traditions "in
every sense of the word: legends, folktales, songs,
proverbs, usages, beliefs, superstitions. For whoever
considers them, all of these are elements and manifestations of folklife."

Pitrè was careful and scrupulous in the study of
all these documents. In oral texts and archive researches he had complete mastery of the historical-
philological method. But did all of his work end here?
Actually, the historical-philological method in
Pitrè's research was a means rather than an end. For
example, he was not much interested in such studies
as Ancona's investigation of the theater, which established schemes of an evolutionistic character. In
Pitrè's view the "sacred representation," other than
as a poetic or literary document, was interesting as
an observed act, an objective tradition. This is why
he used festivals and spectacles as a prelude to his
"sacred representation"; through them he attempted to
penetrate the spirit of his people, clarifying and
delving into all of its aspects.

Pitrè clearly saw the unity of folk traditions.
In the first volume of *Usi e costumi, credenze e
pregiudizi del popolo siciliano*, he says, "It is not
easy to make a distinction between usages and customs,
between beliefs and prejudices, when one wishes to
illustrate the physical and moral life of the folk, as
I have proposed. The usage is often confused and lost
in the belief, and the superstition is often the ultimate result of a custom. Try to describe birth,
marriage, and funeral customs, and you will find your-
self confronted with superstitions that you cannot
detach from these customs without believing them to
be mutilated and disfigured." Thus, the study of folk
tradition was stripped of the particular characteristics, or at least the particularities, in which it had
been contained. Until then, each folk production had
basically been studied on its own. Pitrè showed us
the error. And it was with his work that in Italy the
study of folk traditions, *all* the folk traditions,
attained a totally organic systemization.

8. *Pitrè and the Comparative Method*

In his study, based on a historical methodology that
established the personality of the "bearers" of folklore, Pitrè demonstrated the great importance of the
comparative method. An insistent premise in his
writings is that Sicilian traditions are the echo of
ancient civilizations, "archaeological monuments" of
thought, relics of the past. But when he moved from
these assertions to actual comparisons in order to see
the degree to which folk traditions are relics, what
was his attitude?

In undertaking the investigation of Sicilian folk
literature, particularly stories, proverbs, and riddles, Pitrè often put in evidence, although very carefully, the values of folk traditions in the ancient
world; thus, he instituted a cautious parallelism
between ancient folklife and modern folklife. The
pagan world was revealed to him primarily when he
confronted objective traditions. But are the comparisons instituted by Pitrè really effective, or do
they remain as sketches, as they are in his *Fiabe*,
his *Proverbi*, and his *Indovinelli*? In a letter dated
July, 1876, a famous mythologist, Hermann Usener, had
written to Pitrè: "Given the fact that you are the
uncontested master in collecting everything from all
fields and in drawing everything into your circle of
observation, I do not know how to recommend warmly
enough those things that you could easily put aside
because they are surface elements of the folk--for
example, the different manifestations of superstitions and the local forms of religious worship. In
this regard, one can understand that the significant
instructive rites of paganism are conserved in almost
all localities." Pitrè, who collected and continued
collecting everything, renewed this discourse in his
Spettacoli e feste:

> It has been often said that the greater part of
> today's folk usages and beliefs are merely ancient
> beliefs and usages that have come to us through
> the Greek and Roman religions. . . . It is common

opinion that the festival of the Circumcision coincides with the Latin festival in honor of Janus,
which opens the month of January; it is also believed that Candlemas is related to Lupercalia, a
Roman ceremony at the beginning of February, some
of whose Roman usages passed directly into those
of the Carnevale, although there are those who
consider it a continuation of the festival of
Proserpina. . . . We carry around the old witch,
the old *Befana*, the *Carcavecchia*, the Old Christmas
Woman, and we follow her; during the Ides the
Romans carried Mamurio Veturio, Old Winter, in the
form of a human covered with furs, through the city
of Rome, driving him outside the walls of the city.

Pitrè took up the same issues some years later in
his volume entitled *Giuochi fanciulleschi siciliani*.
"It is no wonder," he observed, "that many traditional
games of our children are relics of ancient customs,
ceremonies, and rites now lost or disappearing from
the memory of the common people; in general, these are
connected to the three great happenings of life: birth,
marriage, and death." Yet "it is not always easy--in
fact, it is often extremely difficult--to read into
those events and get the innermost meaning in order to
connect them to their original significance," because
"modifications have developed as the tradition passes
from nation to nation, and the meanings of the words
of the game have become submerged after so many centuries." In the preface to the book entitled *Medicina
popolare siciliana*, he added:

Folk medicine is a complex of curious and diverse
facts, which in their totality appear as an aberra-
tion of the human spirit and in their particulars
as relics of dead civilizations and peoples. Everything is represented in folk medicine, from the
sacred and mysterious practices of ancient priests
to the impious practices of today's witches, from
the theurgical medicine of the Persians, Assyrians,
and Egyptians to the iatrophysical medicine of the
last fifty years of the past century.

He concluded by saying, "These are remnants of dead
rites, forgotten ceremonies, and cast-off practices.
What strikes us about these is the simultaneous surviving of different usages, which for us are equivalent
to geological layers revealing various periods."

In clarifying the character of these remnants,
Pitrè did not hesitate to consider primitive peoples,
to whom his Italian predecessors had given little or
no importance. In this, however, he did not go further than Lescarbot, Lafitau, and Voltaire. For
example, he referred to an English ethnologist, John
Lubbock, author of the superficial *Origin of Civilisation*, according to whom "savages closely resemble
children in their character." Lubbock believed that
"the development of the individual is an epitome of
that of the species," that "the young states of each
species and group resemble older forms of the same
group," and that "regarded from this point of view,
the similarity existing between savages and children
assumes a singular importance."[1] But this theory,
Pitrè said, is not to be accepted without great
reservation and with due regard to the observations
of Max Müller about the similarities between savages
and children.[2]

In his comparisons Pitrè often returned to the
savages or primitives. It is clear, however, that
these comparisons, even though he did not get very
involved in them, indicated to him that a new road
had been opened to the studies of folklore. In the
last volume of *Biblioteca* he said that to understand
the analogies offered by the various manifestations
of folklore one must consider not only classical
antiquity but also "modern savages, in whom the past
has been crystalized," although "no one will conclude
that the origins and source of certain Sicilian

[1]*The Origin of Civilisation and the Primitive
Condition of Man*, 7th ed. (London: Longmans, Green,
and Co., 1912), pp. 426-31.
[2]See Müller's *Contributions to the Science of
Mythology* (London: Longmans, Green, and Co., 1897),
I, 291-95.

beliefs and superstitions are to be found in primitive peoples."

The study of these analogies, however and wherever made, did not enclose Pitrè within the boundaries of a self-contained past. "The past," he said, "is not dead. It lives in and with us." He was particularly interested in emphasizing the fact that this past is in many respects the contemporary history of Sicily. Pitrè believed, then, that folk traditions are the result of the past but that they live because the present, in renewing them, has taken them as its own. Further, he was convinced that ethnology must meet with folklore in order to give folklore a more solid historical foundation. In the introduction to his *Biblioteca* and in the bulletins of the *Archivio*, he had attentively followed the work produced by Tylor, Frazer, Lang, Hartland, and the Gommes. And now, satisfied with the part he had played, he indicated to his successors the new methodology from which folklore studies were to draw new vigor and impulse.

PART FIVE

THE ENGLISH ANTHROPOLOGICAL SCHOOL
AND ITS INFLUENCE ON STUDIES
OF FOLK TRADITIONS

CHAPTER XXI

TYLOR AND "PRIMITIVE CULTURE"

1. *Anthropology as the "Study of Man"*

In 1871, when Müller's and Benfey's theories reigned
supreme in folklore studies, *Primitive Culture,* a book
that has become fundamental to the study of folklore,
was published in England. In this book the author,
Edward B. Tylor, reconsidered the relationship between
ethnology and folklore, two disciplines to which, we
could say, he gave a new scientific systemization. In
joining folklore to ethnology, Tylor clearly followed
a tradition that had been given impetus by the concept
of the noble savage. In his work we return to ideas
proposed previously, although in different ways, in the
works of Montaigne, Lescarbot, Baron Lahontan, Fontenelle, Vico, Rousseau, Goguet, Brosses, and Boulanger.
In Tylor's work, however, the comparison between primitive peoples and the commoners of civilized peoples was
supported by a more robust and skillful philological
investigation, one that avoided the politico-social
controversy raised by the concept of the noble savage.

At this time ethnological and folkloristic studies
went under the generic name of anthropology, a discipline that, while professing to undertake a comprehensive study of all mankind, actually sank its roots
into naturalistic soil. The term *anthropology*, initially adopted from Aristotle in the literal sense of
"study of man," now came to mean "the natural history
of mankind." This "history" contributed to a dangerous
confusion between nation, race, and linguistic group,
a confusion into which Gobineau and Müller (at first)
had fallen.

As early as his *Researches into the Early History of Mankind* (1865), Tylor had reasoned that one must study *homo sapiens* from an intellectual rather than from a zoological viewpoint; it is in this respect that anthropology assumed the adjectives *cultural* and *social*. But did Tylor, the great pioneer of this anthropology, remain immune to the naturalistic procedures that his predecessors had introduced to the study of man and that the theory of evolution later carried to extremes, or is there a historical aspect in his works that redeems such procedures? Is anthropology the mother science in which the ethnology of folklore is rooted, in Tylor's view, or is it history, without any adjectives?

2. *Premises of the English Anthropological School*

First of all, one must observe that the English anthropological school, which had its official birth certificate in *Primitive Culture*, was based on a much-used method in European scholarship: the comparative method. In applying this method, Tylor viewed the Aryan world as *a* province of knowledge but not the *only* province of knowledge. For the most part, he was led to the main roads of ethnology by his dissatisfaction with studies of the Aryan world. He conceived man's history as the history of humanity, all humanity, including not only the civilized world but also the savage world, that world from which the brothers Grimm, Müller, and their followers had come away with a renewed national pride.

We should add that it was easy enough for a German to consider the religion, mythology, and folklore of Aryan populations, but such was not the case for an Englishman, who would not be particularly interested in the study of savages who populated vast colonial territories. *Primitive Culture*, which was begun in Oxford, Müller's beloved citadel, explores the savages' world in order to illustrate related aspects; further, this work attempts to make us see that such a world is not self-enclosed, for it persists in folk traditions, usages, customs--everything that constitutes a nation's heritage. In this examination Tylor certainly did not neglect either classical peoples or ancient and modern Oriental civilizations. His specific intent, however, was to identify some laws that, in his opinion, guide the history of man and to explore the links uniting past and present.

Clearly, Tylor wanted to place his ethnologico-folkloristic studies within a historical context. The fact that he considered the complex of manifestations of the material and spiritual life of savage peoples and commoners of civilized people as "primitive culture" obviously suggests that he was compelled by the same interests that had led Enlightenment writers, especially Montesquieu and Voltaire, to emphasize the sentiments, beliefs, and institutions not only of various European social classes but also of primitive nations. Additionally, we should note that for Tylor the term *culture* had the same meaning that the term *civilization* had for Vico. As Tylor says in *Primitive Culture,* "Culture or Civilization, taken in its wide ethnographic sense, is that complex whole which includes knowledge, belief, art, morals, law, custom and any other capabilities and habits acquired by man as a member of society."[1] This "complex whole" is, of course, the domain of both culture and civilization, two terms deriving from the eighteenth century. Their identification, in Tylor's understanding of the words, is owed to English terminology, which, like the German, mixes the terms *civilization* and *culture*--while for us *culture* is an aspect of civilization denoting the total spirituality of a period or of all mankind (as opposed to *civilization,* which is the "act of becoming civilized").

In *Primitive Culture,* Tylor says that the best way to study the laws of human action and thought is to study the degrees of civilization of different human groups. He goes on to say, "On the one hand, the uniformity which so largely pervades civilization may be ascribed, in great measure, to the uniform action of

[1]*The Origin of Culture* (1871; rpt. New York: Harper and Row, 1958), p. 1.

uniform causes: while on the other hand its various
grades may be regarded as stages of development or
evolution, each the outcome of previous history, and
about to do its proper part in shaping the history of
the future. To the investigation of these two great
principles in several departments of ethnography, with
special consideration of the civilization of the lower
tribes as related to the civilization of the higher
nations, the present volumes are devoted."[2] But what
were the premises underlying this task, which in his
view required comparisons between the civilization of
"lower" nations and the civilization of more advanced
nations, and how did he differ from his predecessors?

3. *"Homo Sapiens" as Nature*

It has been correctly observed that although Tylor was
influenced by eighteenth-century rationalism, he was
molded by evolutionary and natural science, under the
influence of Comte's positivism. In the preface to his
Primitive Culture, he cites two works that contributed
to his studies. One is Theodor Waitz's *Anthropologie
der Naturvölker* (1859), regarded as the first ethnological treatise to judge and evaluate primitive mentality
in all its complexity; the other is *Der Mensch in der
Geschichte*, published by Adolf Bastian in the same
year, which rigorously applied the theory of evolution
to that mentality. Waitz provided Tylor with a broad
and detailed understanding of all that had been done
in the field of ethnography, not only from a philological perspective (that is, collection of materials) but
also from a historical perspective (that is, interpretation of those materials). Bastian provided him even
more, giving him the key that he believed would open
the door of the primitive world so that it could become
an interpretative criterion of some particular aspects
still conserved by Western Civilization.
     In the eighteenth century the belief that human
mentality was universally the same was in fashion (from

[2]Ibid.

Fontenelle to Helvétius, from Voltaire to Buffon).
Bastian accepted this idea. On the one hand, he maintained that "nations possess the same elementary ideas,
which is the primitive psychological basis of their
culture"; on the other hand, he believed that "in a
later stage of development differences show up--
apparitional reflections of ideas originally belonging
to individual nations." These premises generated a
conclusion that Tylor fully accepted: the savage,
after all, is no different from civilized man. According to Tylor (and to Bastian) there is no essential
difference between the mind of the savage and the mind
of civilized man, although the thoughts of the former
initially seem a bit strange. This accounts for the
relationship between the commoners of savage and
civilized nations and, hence, for the possibility of
comparing them.

    In Tylor's work, however, the comparison went
beyond this legitimate assumption. After recognizing
the similarity between the thought of savage and
modern nations, he revealed his conviction that similarities existing between different customs are not
to be attributed to contacts among various civilizations but rather to the similarity of human minds:
"The character and habit of mankind at once display
[a] similarity and consistency of phenomena. . . .
To general likeness in human nature on the one hand,
and to general likeness in the circumstances of life
on the other, this similarity and consistency may no
doubt be traced. . . . For the present purpose it
appears both possible and desirable to eliminate considerations of hereditary varieties of races of man,
and to treat mankind as homogeneous in nature, though
placed in different grades of civilization."[3] There
is, however, an absolute chronological beginning to
the history of these "grades": the primitive world.
In this Tylor followed Lafitau, who regarded the primitives as our ancestors and asserted that the primordial phases of man's development are still conserved
in primitive peoples of today. Like Brosses and Comte

[3]Ibid., pp. 6-7.

before him, Tylor extended this thesis in order to
ascertain the degree to which the opinions and acts
of modern nations rested on the solid ground of clearly determined modern systems of knowledge and the
degree to which they rested on imperfect systems of
knowledge, the only ones existing in primitive phases
of civilization.

Tylor believed that "history within its proper
field and ethnography over a wider range"[4] combine to
show us that the institutions best suited to survive
in the world have replaced less durable ones, the
result of this incessant conflict being the general
course of culture. He recognized that in the broad
domain of human customs and ideas civilization always
ultimately triumphs, although it is obliged to combat
the persistent vestiges of an inferior state and the
degenerations it produces. But did Tylor view the
vestiges of this lower state in the same way that
Enlightenment thinkers did? And, in his view, wasn't
ethnography (a term he adopted to denote the discipline
that we today call ethnology) resolved in a history of
civilization?

4. *Superstition as a "Survival"*

After quickly outlining the progress of civilization,
Tylor confronted a problem that had previously been
confronted by Fontenelle, the problem of "survivals."
As he himself says:

> When a custom, an art, or an opinion is fairly
> started in the world, disturbing influences may
> long affect it so slightly that it may keep its
> course from generation to generation, as a stream
> once settled in its bed will flow on for ages.
> This is mere permanence of culture; and the special
> wonder about it is that the change and revolution
> of human affairs should have left so many of its
> feeblest rivulets to run so long. On the Tartar

[4]Ibid., p. 69.

steppes, six hundred years ago, it was an offence
to tread on the threshold or touch the ropes in
entering a tent, and so it appears to be still.
Eighteen centuries ago Ovid mentions the vulgar
Roman objection to marriages in May, which he not
unreasonably explains by the occurrence in that
month of the funeral rites of the Lemuralia. . . .
The saying that marriages in May are unlucky survives to this day in England, a striking example
how an idea, the meaning of which has perished for
ages, may continue to exist simply because it has
existed.

    Now there are thousands of cases of the kind
which have become, so to speak, landmarks in the
course of culture. When in the process of time
there has come general change in the condition of
a people, it is usual, notwithstanding, to find
much that manifestly had not its origin in the new
state of things, but has simply lasted on into it.
On the strength of these survivals, it becomes
possible to declare that the civilization of the
people they are observed among must have been
derived from an earlier state, in which the proper
home and meaning of these things are to be found;
and thus collections of such facts are to be
worked as mines of historic knowledge.[5]

This is the passage that opens the second chapter of
Primitive Culture, one of the most discussed and most
fundamental chapters--and it is significant that Tylor
here considered survivals as documents of historical
knowledge, which means that they can be handled only
with the historical method. History cannot absolve or
condemn them, as Tylor himself half wished; rather, it
considers them as phenomena on which a conception of
life and the world is based. In considering survivals,
Tylor occasionally leaves the impression of indiscriminately posing the theory of (savage) origins of culture
as the basis of the science of folklore; moreover, he
thought of survivals as static facts that remain among

[5]*Ibid.*, p. 70.

the commoners of civilized peoples by dint of inertia,
thus documenting primordial phases of savage life and
thought. They are, then, documents that make historians
ask whether a nation's civilization is itself derived
from a "lower" condition.

Tylor argued that many superstitions still existing
today among the commoners of civilized nations are simply facts transported from one environment to another;
as a result of such migration, these "facts" lost their
original meaning, but they remain as proof and example
of an older cultural state from which the new one has
developed. This, in his view, is the essence of the
survival, which often is merely a superstition. But
didn't Tylor acknowledge the validity of survivals in
considering them in an environment that was no longer
their own? And what importance could this validity
have if the environment that assimilates survivals does
so only with the attitude of the geologist who collects
fossils? The truth is that a fact is never the same as
its predecessor, because what counts in a fact is not
only its origin but also its adaption. The task of the
folklorist, then, must be to search for differences as
well as similarities--differences *within* apparent uniformity.

5. Survivals and Revivals

Tylor said that one often sees old ideas and abandoned
practices come back into use in a society that had
believed them dead. In this case, he says, there is a
"revival," not a "survival." In certain respects this
can be true, but only on the condition that one regards
these two expressions (whose terminology can only have
an empirical justification) as the result of a concrete, ever-changing folklife. Basically, these are
merely variations of folkloristic philology. In studying these revivals, Tylor asked himself about the
degree to which we are creators or at least modifiers
of the inheritance of past centuries. In his own words:

As men's minds change in progressing culture, old

customs and opinions fade gradually in a new and uncongenial atmosphere, or pass into states more congruous with the new life around them. But this is so far from being a law without exception, that a narrow view of history may often make it seem to be no law at all. For the stream of civilization winds and turns upon itself, and what seems the bright onward current of one age may in the next spin round in a whirling eddy, or spread into a dull and pestilential swamp. Studying with a wide view the course of human opinion, we may now and then trace on from the very turning-point the change from passive survival into active revival.[6]

As an evolutionist who believed in the history of civilization as a "marching forward," Tylor was perplexed by these phenomena. At this point the historian in him awakened, and he became concerned primarily with seeing the probable genetic chain of phenomena in facts (whether they be survivals or revivals). Precisely because of this, Tylor's historical diligence must be sought in his comparative examination of the beliefs and customs of savage and civilized nations, an examination revealing the limitations of Tylor as sociologist. Although his studies were characterized by a great historical *pietas*, which provided him with a sympathetic view of the primitive world, he nevertheless was bound to empirical and psychological ideas that, as such, are not legitimate historical criteria. It is true that Tylor constantly attempted to transform these vague ideas into concepts, but when we view such concepts in the light of the fundamental thesis supporting them (the thesis that all mankind is subject to the laws of development and that all mankind has passed through analogous stages of evolution), we see that Tylor overlooked the fact that man, whether he lives among primitives or the commoners of civilized peoples or wherever, is never the product of nature; rather, he is the product of the civilization in which he has been and continues to be shaped.

[6]Ibid., pp. 136-37.

Whatever his premises, Tylor provided a brilliant, lively picture of historical developments in which various cultures resemble one another, and he then proceeded to a precise delineation of what appeared to him to be the original culture, the culture of primitives or (as he called them) savages. His major concern was to join the "barbarian" of civilization (the world of survivals and revivals, which is the same as saying the world of folklore) to the civilization of the barbarians--the uneliminable moment in which civilization comes into being. Since there is no civilization without religion, he attempted to analyze the religion of the primitives--for he believed that without such knowledge mythology, usages, and customs could never be explained.

6. *Mythology and Religion*

In one of the most interesting chapters of *Primitive Culture*, Tylor says that mythology, in contrast to what Müller had believed, began when man was in his savage state; therefore, its earliest developments belong to the primordial phase of man's life. It was here that the concept of animism appeared in his work, a concept that would meet with the same success as his theory about survivals. In a certain sense one could say that Tylor took an idea from Müller that had previously been asserted by Fontenelle: man narrates what he sees. But for Tylor, what man sees (more specifically, what primitive man sees) is completely different from what Müller's ancient Aryan saw. Myths, in Tylor's view, are indeed the projections of specific daily experiences in which the life of the primitive or savage is concretized. But his savage believes in the animation of all of nature as it presents itself to him with its spirits and genies. This is why metaphors, which we regard merely as imaginative flights of fancy, were a reality for our ancestors.

To clarify this reality, Tylor examined the origin of religion, an issue of great importance and interest. Comte, following Brosses, had characterized the evolu-

tion of the history of religions in three stages:
fetishism, polytheism, and monotheism. Tylor accepted
this scheme, with the exception that in his view the
first stage of evolution is not to be discovered in
fetishism but in animism, which is precisely where
religion begins. This idea underlies his definition
of religion:

> The first requisite in a systematic study of the
> religions of the lower races is to lay down a
> rudimentary definition of religion. By requiring
> in this definition the belief in a supreme deity
> or of judgment after death, the adoration of idols
> or the practice of sacrifice, or other partially-
> diffused doctrines or rites, no doubt many tribes
> may be excluded from the category of religions.
> But such narrow definition has the fault of identi-
> fying religion rather with particular developments
> than with the deeper motive which underlies them.
> It seems best to fall back at once on this essen-
> tial source, and simply to claim, as a minimum
> definition of religion, the belief in Spiritual
> Beings.[7]

Immediately after, he proposes a "minimum definition"
of animism: "I propose here, under the name of Animism,
to investigate the deep-lying doctrine of Spiritual
Beings, which embodies the very essence of Spiritualistic as opposed to Materialistic philosophy. . . .
From its special relation to the doctrine of the soul,
it will be seen to have a peculiar appropriateness to
the view here taken of the mode in which theological
ideas have been developed among mankind. The word
Spiritualism, though it may be, and sometimes is, used
in a general sense, has this obvious defect to us, that
it has become the designation of a particular modern
sect, who indeed hold extreme spiritualistic views, but
cannot be taken as typical representatives of these
views in the world at large. The sense of Spiritualism

[7]*Religion in Primitive Culture* (1871; rpt. New
York: Harper and Row, 1958), p. 8.

in its wider acceptation, the general belief in spiritual beings, is here given to Animism."[8]

Tylor was convinced--and this is the premise with
which he began and on which he based his theory--that
from the very start the savage obtained the concept
of soul from a misunderstood vision of life, which
came to him in states of wakefulness and sleep. When
the savage dreams of being in a distant country, he
believes that he is actually there. This is so because
two beings exist in him: one, the corporal being,
stays asleep, so that when the savage awakens, he
finds that his body has not moved; during the same
period of time, however, the other "being" has moved
through space. These two beings are clearly different
because the soul is much more mobile; indeed, it can
cover great distances in an instant. But, Tylor asks,
is the soul a spirit? Because it is attached to a
body from which it rarely departs, the soul can become
spirit only if it is transformed. The simple application of the preceding ideas to the phenomenon of death
produces a metamorphosis such as this.

To the rudimentary mind, death is the same as a
long sleep. Death appears to involve a separation of
the soul from the body, similar to what can happen during the night. When we realize, however, that the body
can no longer be reanimated, we first glimpse the idea
of a physical separation. When the body is destroyed
(and funeral rites serve to accelerate this destruction), the separation is final. Thus, spirits are de-
tached from their bodies and left free in space. Their
number increases with time, so that a population of
spirits, in the sense of a "living" population with
human needs and passions, is formed. Given their extreme fluidity, these spirits can enter a human body
and cause all kinds of disorder (possessions, diseases)
or, on the other hand, bring it vitality. In this way
is the soul transformed. From a simple vital principle
animating the human body, it becomes a spirit, a good
or bad genius, or a divinity, according to the kind of
effects attributed to it. But since death is what has

[8]Ibid., pp. 9-10.

brought about this metamorphosis, it is the dead, the souls of ancestors, that man first worshiped; in fact, the first sacrifices were merely simple offerings to the dead.

Tylor's dogmatic thesis did not stop here, for it applied the idea of pure spirits to nature. Believing that spirits animated individual elements of nature, savages worshiped rivers, trees, and forests. In the beginning, then, a life and a feeling were attributed to all inanimate objects. If a river flowed, a fountain gushed, or a tree rustled, it happened because these phenomena were animated by invisible beings. The same was true of clouds, rain, and wind. Only later (and we are now moving toward monotheism) were natural phenomena attributed to a god (of rain, of water, or of the wind). In Tylor's opinion, the idea of divinity was the clear and logical result of animism in primitive populations, along with being the clear and logical complement of polytheistic religion.

But, Tylor asked himself, is animism only a religious manifestation, the first that we encounter in the primitive world? Or does this manifestation, although in the form of superstition and therefore a survival, still dominate the life of the commoners of civilized nations? Consider, for example, the innumerable superstitions that are still associated with genies, spirits, ghosts, or the many beings from the regions of the air, the water, the forests, and the underground that exert their influence on the sky, the land, men, animals, and plants; fix your gaze on their origins and there you will find animism, once the religion of primitive peoples and now a superstition for the commoners of civilized nations. The link between the two worlds was now powerfully forged--and animism should therefore be considered not only for what it once was but also for what it now is.

7. Animism: The Infancy of Religion?

Although this thesis is supported by a deep, perceptive analysis, by a very appealing comparison, and by a rich,

elegant writing style, it nevertheless raises an intellectual concept that invalidates it. In Tylor's thesis
French positivism and English empiricism are fused and
confused. In the beginning was primitive man--but
isn't that man pictured as a philosopher, a man of perfect reason, a thinker who deduces accurate conclusions
from all the premises that life puts to him? Now, I do
not mean to deny that there are elements of truth in
Tylor's animistic theory. Even in the wide variety of
forms in which it is articulated, animism is undoubtedly an expression of the life of primitive peoples, as
is the case among the commoners of civilized nations.
But how can we say that it truly begins the history of
civilization? And is it actually as universal among
the primitive peoples as Tylor thought?

It has been said that Tylor, who was interested in
savages for what they are and not for what they were,
wished to write the history of man's religion without
writing an introduction to such a study--the kind of
"introduction" that was written by Spencer a few years
after the publication of *Primitive Culture*. Spencer
theorized that the roots of religion were to be found
in ancestor-worship, a term that he used in the broadest sense in order to include all forms of veneration
for the dead, whether consanguineous or not. Both
Tylor and Spencer, however, like Brosses and Comte
before them, began with a particular premise--specifi-
cally, as Wilhelm Schmidt observed, that the chronological succession and reciprocal relation of facts are
based solely on the imagined psychological possibility
of such a succession or relation; as a rule, this possibility appears to be justified by the axiom that simple
things precede complicated things. Of course, animism
is anything but simple, and the same can also be said
of Spencer's manism. But in attempting to give an evolutionistic definition to the basics of religion, Tylor
and Spencer assumed that the *most* basic form was the
beginning of religion. This assumption is the gravest
error of the two theories, an error which led to a dis-
torted treatment of ethnological documents.

In light of such documents, it is difficult to
understand why Tylor regarded as universal fact the

notion that the idea of soul derives from a dream.
It is also difficult to understand how Tylor could
have thought that the soul can always change its nature
after death. Too, we must consider his third thesis,
the transformation of spirits in the worship of nature.
Can we acknowledge the universality of a transformation
based on the supposition that spirit-worship clearly
precedes ancestor-worship (or just the opposite, as
Spencer believed)?

Ethnology has demonstrated that worship of the
spirits of the dead is not as primitive as Tylor and
Spencer believed and that religious anthropomorphism
is anything but primitive. Furthermore, animism (and
the same can be said for manism) certainly does not
have the universal diffusion that Tylor attributed to
it in constructing one savage from all savages and one
commoner from all commoners of civilized nations, both
of whom think in the same way. Thus animism, rejected
by many because it was constructed on a variety of dogmatic principles, is of use only when it is restricted
by an evaluation of its specific forms, each of which
is always the result of a spiritual rather than a biological fact. As such, it can be effectively applied
to savages and to commoners of civilized nations. This
obviously does not exclude the possibility that in the
traditions of savages and "civilized" commoners the
spirits of the land, sea, wind, and fire can also be
directly personified without being obliged to travel
down the road of animism.

8. *Tylor's Naturalism and Historicism*

This, then, is the panorama that Tylor provided in his
Primitive Culture. In this work, as we have seen,
there are naturalistic difficulties, errors of perspective, and aprioristic procedures. Tylor wanted to construct an anthropology in the aristocratic sense of the
word, but his anthropology refers to man's "being"
rather than to his "becoming." One can object that his
causal determinism always remained outside history,
where the only actor is the will of man. One could

also object that a universal history does not and cannot exist--for such a history is unable to isolate historical individuality, which is the most important aspect of a nation. Finally, one could object that his comparisons are made without time-space restrictions. In fact, we know that for Tylor the similarity was an end in itself. And if this is the case, would not the similarity lose the particular quality Tylor assigned to it, in that he, like Vico, was convinced that each similarity must find its true correspondence in our mind?

Tylor's principal merit, however, is that, despite his naturalistic premises, he related folklore to ethnology and made ethnology a contemporary history, in which he included the history of folklore. For this reason much of his text--which is still important and which takes on the flavor of Vico's writings--is not burdened with the formulations that he himself utilized to construct his history of culture (animism as the first form of religion, religion as the first accomplishment of human thought, the thought of primitives as the first page of universal history, and so on). Read his minute analyses of proverbs, childhood games, and folk customs and beliefs. Observe how he relates the song to the usage, the proverb to the custom, the tale to the belief. In other words, observe how he gives vigor and impulse to the study of folklore as a whole. He demonstrates the interest and the inspiration of Herder, the brothers Grimm, and Pitrè, who perceived in nature profound subjects for the philosopher. In this regard, Tylor, himself a philosopher about such matters, had the single aim of seeing, apart from chronological determinations, what of the primitive still remains in us.

It has been observed that the good historian is similar to the ogre of the fairy tale: wherever he smells human flesh, there is his game. We should add that when an awareness of the primitive arises or is renewed in history, there is reason to believe that it is a constant spur to historical thought. It is with this awareness that Tylor entered the world of primitives and the world of civilization's commoners.

The result was that he, as a positivist and evolutionist, sometimes unknowingly found his redemption in a historicism that Vico himself had previously conceived.

CHAPTER XXII

UNDER THE BANNER OF ANIMISM

1. *Classical Philology, Ethnology, and Folklore*

Successfully garnered from the specific arena of the
history of religions, Tylor's theory of animism dominated that arena virtually undisputed for more than
thirty years. Animism then seemed to be the very "seed
of religion," and it appeared as such in various works
on the science of religion and the history of ancient
civilizations. Along with this theory, however, Tylor
had also proposed a methodology that, through the study
of survivals, would join the history of religions (and
therefore the history of mythology) to the history of
folklore by means of his implicit principle that the
religion of one generation was bound to become the
"superstition-survival" of the next generation.

Tylor's theory of animism and folkloristic methodology found immediate and open acceptance in one country, Germany, where an interest in natural mythology
had been predominant. Germany was the first country to
give Tylor his official "consecration," and in Germany
Tylor's *Primitive Culture* served as an inspiration to
those who worshiped such mythology. On this subject
Schmidt remarks, "In the growing current of Tylor's
animism there developed, by strange coincidence, a
minor current as well, one already followed by advocates of the theory of Germany's natural mythology and
the theory of Indo-Germanic peoples. These advocates
now wished to apply the results of linguistic research
about Indo-Germanic peoples to ethnological discoveries
about the 'people of nature.'" But was it in fact a
"minor current" that utilized Tylor's theory and

methodology in Germany by applying them to the study
of German folklore and, when appropriate, to both the
history of ethnology and the history of classical
civilizations? And was this utilization altogether
coincidental? The fact of the matter is that Tylor's
work did not generate merely a minor current in Germany, either in respect to animism (a theory which
this "current" attempted to complement) or in respect
to folklore (about which this "current" raised new
questions and issues). Moreover, this "current" was
not so much the result of a "strange coincidence" as
of a developing critical awareness.

The proof of what I am saying is offered by Wilhelm
Mannhardt, the mythologist who, more than anyone else,
possessed such a critical awareness. His first works
did not derive from the "double tracks" of the Grimms
and Müller--an obvious point when we recall that his
Germanische Mythen was published in 1858 and his *Die
Götterwelt der deutschen und nordischen Völker* was
published in 1860. As Mannhardt admitted, he was
forced to change his ideas about mythology when he
saw the shape of such ideas in the conceptions of the
people themselves--that is, in their traditions, particularly their customs, beliefs, and childhood games.
Of great help here were Danzica's studies of Austrian,
Danish, and French prisoners, which Mannhardt had
completed. And in his 1865 and 1867 works, *Roggenwolf
und Roggenhund* and *Die Korndämonen*, we can clearly see
that he was already under the influence of Wilhelm
Schwartz, who believed in identifying the most perma-
nent elements of mythology and folklore. However, his
broadest work, *Der Baumkultus der Germanen*, was published in 1875, followed two years later by *Wald- und
Feldkulte* (with *Der baumkultus* serving as the first
part). It is here that the distinction between Mannhardt and Müller is clear, sharp, and conclusive.
This distinction is sharper still in *Mythologische
Forschungen aus dem Nachlasse* (edited by Hermann
Patzig in 1884, with scholarly introductions by Karl
Müllenhoff and Wilhelm Scherer); this volume, published
four years after his death, may be considered as the
third part of *Wald- und Feldkulte.* In these works,

particularly in *Mythologische Forschungen*, Mannhardt
only occasionally quoted Tylor. Clearly, however, he
was very much under the direct influence of Tylor,
inasmuch as *Wald- und Feldkulte* reproposed Tylor's
mythology in a variety of ways and applied the theory
of animism to a number of vegetation cults and rites
to which Tylor himself had given great importance.

2. Mannhardt and "Monumenta mythica Germaniae"

In Mannhardt's opinion, the starting point for such
investigations was the myth. But how did he come to
view myth, which in his first works seemed to be only
a projection and explanation of the brilliant phenomena
of nature? In the "Vorwort" to *Wald- und Feldkulte*,
Mannhardt observed, first of all, that mythologies are
much more elaborate and irregular than linguistic phenomena. Müller's mythological school, he went on to
say, "attempted to shape Indo-European myths into a
model built upon Indic conceptions, without investigating the environmental context in which they originated." For this reason, he continued, mythology must
develop its own naturalistic method of classifying and
collecting various phenomena, which will then serve to
establish types.
     Mannhardt had already given evidence of such
naturalistic work in the third issue of his *Zeitschrift
für deutsche Mythologie und Sittenkunde*, which he published between 1853 and 1859. It was in this issue,
in fact, that "regular demological inquiries" first
appeared. We should add that it was then his intention
to publish a collection entitled *Monumenta mythica
Germaniae*, a collection and illustration not only of
the mythical and magical lieder of his own country but
also of popular customs about holidays, agrarian customs and superstitions, and wedding ceremonies. It
was for this reason that, following through on his own
assumptions, he attempted to support his personal research with a questionnaire, 150,000 copies of which
he succeeded in printing a few years later. This questionnaire, which concerned German harvest customs, was

composed of twenty-three questions on four small pages.
These questions, however, referred not only to Germanic
customs but to those of other countries as well. In a
lecture given in 1865, the same year that his questionnaire was published, Mannhardt expressed the point he
wished to make to his collaborators:

> The only way to proceed is to distribute handbills
> containing an example of the desired information,
> with all the materials under examination condensed
> into a certain number of specific accurate ques-
> tions. These questions have to be skillfully for-
> mulated with a sure knowledge of the material, in
> such a way that a hint will immediately call to the
> respondent's mind everything that we want to know
> from him; furthermore, the questions should prevent
> the one being questioned from answering with a cate-
> gorical "yes" or "no" or with vague and superficial
> responses. Instead, *the questions should invite im-*
> *portant personal distinctions and specific details.*
> As the work proceeds, we can search for ways to im-
> prove and modify the questions from time to time,
> not on the basis of a more profound knowledge of
> the material as the material increases but on the
> basis of psychological experience and observations
> made about the effect these questions have on who-
> ever is being questioned. The content of the
> questions has to remain the same for the entire
> geographical area included in the research; but it
> is also necessary to give the research different
> specific forms for different specific zones.

Obviously, Mannhardt was intent on giving his future
collaborators a well-established norm: he who asks
must first know what to ask. As Erich Röhr correctly
says, Mannhardt not only wanted to procure much-needed
materials for German folklore, but he also planned to
discriminate between haphazard facts and homogeneous
and equivalent ones--because it was known even then
that without such discrimination one would stand help-
less in front of the collected materials. In the same
lecture in which he emphasized the importance of ques-

tionnaires, he cautioned, "The collected materials must be systematized in ethnographically and geographically distinct series for each region--stressing, first of all, the most prevailing aspect and principal form of the tradition, with an indication of where it has been attested. *Then all the variations of the tradition being studied are to be registered, with a precise indication of where these too have been observed.*"

Notwithstanding the two thousand responses that were returned to Mannhardt, *Monumenta mythica Germaniae* remained as an uncompleted project. From this project, however, came *Wald- und Feldkulte*, in which Mannhardt resumed the thesis he had previously proposed in 1865. Here Mannhardt observed that, given the desire to grasp the essence of collected material, the study of folklore must be based on comparison. He quickly added, however, that one must never proceed with a pre-arranged method (an obvious allusion to Tylor); rather, one must distinguish simple analogies from genuine congruencies. In other words, as he himself says, "every tradition is explained primarily by itself and by its most proximate environment. Only when it does not conclude in this environment can it be progressively traced in an ever deepening and widening field. . . . Where a popular tradition will most probably travel is a chronological determination, and a reconstruction of the original form puts us on the correct path of analysis; here we are assisted by analogy, which we can examine very carefully according to its content and value."

It has been observed that Mannhardt's idea of looking for the explanation of a specific folkloristic phenomenon was based on a crude evolutionism. But isn't the "environment," as Mannhardt conceived it, the civilization in which a tradition lives? And is it possible to discover the real meaning of a tradition without relating the tradition and its variations (which keep it alive) to the civilization within which it exists?

In a letter of November, 1876, Mannhardt told Pitrè of his intentions in *Wald- und Feldkulte*:

"Taking the popular tradition of northern Europe as a
reference point, I attempted to illuminate a number
of similarities between the ideas and customs of the
ancient world and those of the peoples of northern
Europe. . . . As you will see in my recent treatises,
central to my intent is a lengthy collection and explanation of customs arising from the agricultural
myth." But how did Mannhardt view this "agriculture,"
and what place did he assign it in the history of
civilization?

3. Agrarian Rites and Cults

In the first volume of *Wald- und Feldkulte* (that is,
in *Der Baumkultus der Germanen*), Mannhardt began his
examination by studying the tree-worship found among
Germans and neighboring nations. At this point he
posed the problem of seeing how agriculture revealed
the mystery of vegetive regeneration through rites
and cults. Mannhardt proposed that the foundation of
such rites and cults was the belief (still persistent
in folklore) that man lives in the plant (which has a
"soul," as does nature) and that plant and man are
united by a secret sympathetic bond. This explains
the natural affinity between man and plant, each
endowed with its own spirit.

To clarify this affinity, Mannhardt proceeded to
illustrate the idea that Germans had about the soul
of the tree. From this idea he went on to note the
emergence of forest spirits and their various types,
pointing out that the "soul" of the tree was like the
"spirit" of vegetation. Particularly revealing here
are the common customs related to such a belief--the
springtime festivities in modern Europe, for example,
in which the spirit of vegetation is represented by
May and by men dressed in green leaves. As Mannhardt
says, "this spirit gives life to the tree and to
plants. . . . Understandably, it is also presumed
that this spirit manifests its presence in the first
flower of spring, and it is revealed as such in a girl
representing a rose as well as in the messenger in

Walber. The procession of these representatives of
divinity was supposed to produce the beneficial effects of the presence of the divinities themselves on
the chickens, fruit trees, and harvest. In other
words, the mask was considered to be not an image but
the representational actuality of the spirit of vegetation."

The existence of a tree spirit, the nucleus of
Mannhardt's animistic theory, is based on four factors,
which Mircea Eliade recently summarized in the following way: (1) the general tendency of the myth to
compare the world and man to a tree; (2) the custom of
relating the life of man to the life of a tree; (3) the
primitive belief that the tree is the dwelling place
not only of the forest spirit but also of other malign
or benign gods, some of whose lives are organically
joined to the life of the tree; (4) the custom of punishing criminals on a tree.

In his investigations, then, Mannhardt clearly saw,
in contrast to the "high" gods who especially pleased
his predecessors, the clear outline of the figures of
another mythology, a mythology that, not without irony,
he called "low"; it is a mythology in which fates,
genii, and spirits rule. He asked himself, however,
if this mythology was indeed the detritus of a higher
mythology, as his predecessors had argued. Was it,
rather, the very nucleus from which the higher mythology derived? It is to this second hypothesis that
Mannhardt was inclined. In the beginning is the people, he said romantically. But in taking his research
beyond this assertion, he began to believe that the
vegetation myths and cults abounding in northern and
central Europe had been influenced by southern Europe,
with the ancient Romans (who offer us a more precise
idea of ancient times) serving as intermediaries
between the two stages of civilization. The "low"
mythology of the Germans thus could be (if not wholly,
at least in part) an imported product. This underscores the usefulness of comparing the agrarian myths
and cults of Europe with those of classical periods,
inasmuch as they mutually illuminate each other, revealing their origins to us.

The above idea is the central thesis developed in
Der Baumkultus der Germanen. In *Wald- und Feldkulte*
Mannhardt extended his examination to cults found in
classical antiquity, comparing them to agrarian cults
and beliefs in northern European folklore, and he compared dryads, centaurs, Cyclopes, and satyrs with corresponding German, French, Scandinavian, and Russian
forms. Mannhardt was the master of classical mythology, reigning supreme. After studying Greco-Roman
legends, he went on to examine classical holidays in
relation to vegetation spirits, personal gods of vegetation (Adonis, Attis) appearing in the annual holidays, and so forth. Mannhardt's study was detailed,
precise, and philologically sound--with vegetation
cults and rites receiving an essential systemization
against the backdrop of the powerful drama of vegetation and fertility, expressed in alternating cycles:
"Annually, vegetation dies; annually, its death is
followed by the renewal of fruitful life. In agrarian
religion, the periodic disappearance and reappearance
of vegetive life correspond to the death, burial, and
resurrection of the agrarian god." Plants, animals,
and men are therefore invested with the same life-
giving, fertile power. We might think here, for example, of the "stimulating" action trees are credited
with in marriage ceremonies. Vegetive power thus
passes, or at least has the potential to pass, from
one place to another. This is why a sacrificial animal
can be an incarnation of God, and the parts of this
animal-God, when scattered throughout the countryside,
can operate as a power that profits both the partici-
pants in the rite and the earth itself. But God returns again, like the months, seasons, and years, all
of which are united in the very rhythm of agriculture.

4. *Mannhardt's Naturalism and Historicism*

It is clear that in his reconstruction of agrarian
society, one page in the history of civilization,
Mannhardt was often responding to intellectual attitudes of the period. In inserting agrarian rites into

nature worship (which Tylor had fully identified),
Mannhardt had presupposed the existence of tree and
forest spirits. In Tylor's view, the concept of soul
produces the concept of spirit. Similarly, in Mannhardt's view the tree spirit gives rise to the concept
of a forest spirit, which then leads to the more general concept of the spirit of vegetation.

As Waldemar Liungman correctly observes, however,
there is not a single fact that allows us to establish
such a "totality of individual spirits." Moreover,
Mannhardt stated that the vegetive "genius," a demon
incarnated in a tree, is transformed into personifications of spring and summer--but can these structures
be analytically deduced from each other? Or does each
of them depend, rather, on a specific ritual? As a
substitute for what Mannhardt called a "vegetation
demon," Liungman proposed a holy power in vegetation
itself. And in regard to sacrifices made to vegetation, Liungman asked if it were possible to forget
Egypt, where one finds the oldest evidence of such
matters.

Because of these limitations, Mannhardt's theory
is often quite inflexible, and many of his conclusions
seem hasty. Still, he remained faithful to his sense
of "mission," his desire to historicize material containing the ring of truth. Of course Mannhardt occasionally used, as he himself says, "research methods
that one's own age requires for investigations of
nature," but, like Tylor, didn't he also attempt to
transform folklore into a significant history of
civilization, one in which collected material is
assessed in order to reveal the needs, affections,
and dreams of men?

Despite the attempts of Boulanger, Dulaure, and
the Grimms, this was the first time that vegetation
myths and rites (Mannhardt also provided an important
study of phallic rites) attained a place in history.
Particularly is this so when we consider that Mannhardt did not engage in an arbitrary comparison of
cults and rites, attributing such comparisons to a
common "primitive mentality"; rather, he attempted to
understand how and why a cult is born, how and where

it is dispersed, and under what conditions it operates.
In his investigations, he occasionally lost sight of
the concept of "environment" to which his theory appealed; on other occasions, however, his study of
"environment" was of great importance for understanding
the variety and significance of agricultural traditions,
even though these traditions cannot always be explained
by comparing them with ancient fertility cults.

Wilhelm Scherer has said of Mannhardt, "One of the
most curious and significant facts of contemporary science is that ethnology has arrived at the point of
overthrowing classical philology. The initiator of
this revolution was Mannhardt, who died in virtual
anonymity in 1880." In truth, the revolution hinted
at by Scherer had been initiated by a group of scholars
ranging from Lafitau to Tylor. Mannhardt, however,
gave the movement an impulse and vitality that was rich
in productive results.

5. From "Cité antique" to "Psyche"

An example of such productive results is found in the
work of Erwin Rohde, whose volume entitled *Psyche* shows
the influence of Tylor and Mannhardt. He did no more
than cite the works of these two scholars in some marginal notes, but when we read his work closely we immediately perceive that Tylor's animistic theory and
Mannhardt's concern with the ties between world and
underworld dominate the background against which
Rohde's rich and suggestive theories were constructed.

These influences explain the sharp difference
between *Psyche* and an earlier work, Numa Fustel de
Coulanges' *La cité antique*. Fustel de Coulanges said
in 1864, "Even in the latest ages of Greek and Roman
history a set of ideas and usages persisted among the
populace that certainly dated back to the distant past,
by means of which we can discern man's early attitude
toward nature, the soul, and death." Revealing
Müller's influence, he added: "However far one goes
back into the history of the Indo-European race (of
which the Greeks and Italians are two branches), one

never finds the thought that after death everything is
finished for man." We see, then, that in historical-
philosophical studies there is an emphasis not only on
great poets and philosophers but also on the common
folk--their customs, ideas, and thoughts.

Rohde, whose book was published between 1891 and
1894, almost appears to be continuing this discourse
when he states that "the popular belief about the
perdurability of the spirit of the dead, a belief
based on spirit-worship and abetted by some ready beliefs in the Homeric doctrine about souls, remained
substantially unchanged in strength throughout all the
centuries of Greek life." But despite these shared
interests, Rohde proceeded on a course that was quite
different from the one followed by Fustel de Coulanges.
In one of his notes Rohde said, "Here I should mention
an ingenious book rich in ideas, Fustel de Coulanges'
La cité antique, which attempts to *demonstrate that
ancestor-worship is the basis of the highest forms of
Greek religion.* It in no way disparages the richness
of the book's thesis when I say that the fundamental
idea, as far as it concerns Greece, must remain as only
a conjecture which cannot be demonstrated, even though
it may be perfectly true."

In suggesting ancestor-worship as the primogenitive
religious element in Greek society, Fustel de Coulanges
had, in a sense, anticipated Herbert Spencer, who later
placed such worship at the origin of civilization--and
Rohde cited Spencer in discussing the subject of man's
duality: "Naturally, it seems peculiar that one can
conceive of a fully alive, flesh-and-bone man as one
who has within him a strange guest, a more shadowy
duplicate, another 'I,' as a psyche. But this is exactly what is believed by all the world's so-called
'primitive people,' as Herbert Spencer, more than anyone else, has perceptively demonstrated. It is not
altogether surprising to see that the Greeks, too,
shared in a way of thinking that has been so natural
to primitive man." It is precisely this "primitive
man" that he often referred to as a kind of touchstone.
For example, on another occasion he observed, "Primitive

people attribute great power to disembodied souls,
which are more awesome because invisible; moreover, all
occult powers derive, in a sense, from these souls--
powers which are anxiously and continually employed to
earn the blessings of these spirits." But is it Spencer who is behind this idea, or is this actually an
idea conceived by Tylor? Rohde also said, "Homer did
not know of any influence exerted by spirits on the
visible world, and therefore he was unaware of spirit-
worship." Nevertheless, he asked himself, aren't there
some rudiments in Homer's poetry that indirectly bear
witness to such influence? English scholars, he says,
have called these rudiments "survivals"--which again
brings us back to Tylor.

It is true that Rohde believed that primitive people do not have a history even though they have a past.
But despite this idea, it is clear that, in beginning
with primitives, he came to see the ancient world of
the Greeks from a new perspective. The result is that
Rohde, while operating in an area devoted to specific
methods (we know, for example, about the argument that
he had with Ulrich von Wilamowitz-Moellendorff in
defense of Nietzsche's *Die Geburt der Tragödie*), succeeded in illuminating the existence of a spiritual
world, one that is undeniably less obvious in literary
sources but not less worthy of study because of that.
We could criticize Rohde for not including modern
Greek folklore in his study of the folklore of ancient
Greece (an area that John Lawson later researched).
But despite studies on this subject, Rohde's book
clearly remains as a basic work.

6. Usener

No less basic--to return to issues of more immediate
interest to mythology--is Hermann Usener's *Götternamen*,
an 1896 work that attempted to reconcile the demands
of comparative mythology with those of folkloristic-
ethnological methodology. In this book, Usener primarily aimed at reconstructing the origin and development
of religious concepts contained in the names of gods.

In essence, he turned to a study of language in order
to investigate the formation of myths. Unlike Müller,
he utilized myth in a unique way, as it has been said
--in that he saw myth as the only means of entrance
into the cultural world to which the mythology of a
given people belongs. In identifying the parallel
between language and myth, Usener arrived at the
following conclusion: from the beginning, man believed
in an endless number of spontaneous and momentary gods,
born in single moments during daily activities (*Augen-*
blicksgötter). These are simply a special class of
Sondergötter, which preside over specific facts and
phenomena. It is only after the creation of these gods
that one finally arrives at the idea of more general
and personal gods, with the *Sondergötter* then becoming
appellatives. In Usener's view, then, primitive man
receives, in a single moment of individual sensations,
that which is changed into individual representations
(for example, in these representations what predominates is not the idea of *the* tree but the idea of *a*
tree); next, the initial representation acquires perma-
nent significance; finally, "this potent concept leads
toward more general conceptions."

Agrarian rites and cults over which a specific
divinity presides are of great importance in Usener's
ingenious theory. Here Usener was employing Mannhardt,
but unlike Mannhardt, he was often guided by etymologies that produced totally arbitrary results. Like
Mannhardt, however, he concerned himself with the mysteries of classical mythology, the most interesting
part of his study. Also of interest are his investigations of the mythology of southern slavs and his fre-
quent references to Italian folklore. For example, he
tells us, "In Rocca Pia, in the Abruzzi, the following
custom is practiced: when the grain is dry, the farm-
ers make a straw puppet that is placed on top of a cart
full of grain sacks; with songs and great shouts of
glee, this puppet is carried to the house and put in
the kitchen where it is offered food and drink." We
are in the presence, to use Mannhardt's phrase, of the
grain demon, but in Usener's view this demon protects
only one specific field, not all fields.

On the subject of Usener's view of mythology,
Raffaele Pettazzoni offers the following comment:

> With his law about the development of divinities'
> names, a discovery intended to make mythology the
> "science of myth," Usener's thought basically cor-
> responded with the evolutionistic theory, which,
> without the aid of any linguistic investigation,
> had come to conceive the evolutionary idea of God
> developing through the three stages of animism,
> polytheism, and monotheism. In fact, the immense
> number of "instantaneous" deities (*Augenblicks-
> götter*) corresponds to the immense number of
> spirits in the animistic faith; the plurality of
> *Sondergötter* corresponds to a more limited animism,
> or polytheism; and the formation of personal gods,
> with an implicit reduction in the number of divini-
> ties, describes a polytheism destined to become a
> monotheism.

Pettazzoni goes on to say that when Usener wished to
explain personal gods such as the various ancient gods
(where the name has become an unusual proper name for
purely extrinsic reasons), he did not consider the
spiritual (or "poetic") factor that was at work. But
one finds the vitality of his study in the details he
collected and in his numerous discussions of the folklife of ancients and moderns, rather than in his reconstruction of the origins of religion.
    Also of interest is a series of essays (almost
always concerning the origin of a myth motif) which
Usener wrote on various occasions and collected in his
Kleine Schriften. Many of these essays could have
carried the title of a book that was then very popular
in Germany: *Ethnographische Parallelen und Vergleiche*,
by Richard Andree. In addition to the similarity in
the titles of these two scholars' works, there is a
great similarity in writing style. Directly or indirectly, both Usener and Andree were influenced by Tylor
as well as by Mannhardt--and they both were convinced
that although the history of religion (and therefore
the history of mythology) must extend to all ancient

peoples, such a history was still incomplete if not integrated with the documents offered by actual, living folklore.

7. *Dieterich*

Another German philologist who moved in this direction was Albrecht Dieterich. Dieterich, Usener's grandson, provided a series of works in which collected materials were submitted to a close analytical examination. An indefatigable scholar, he produced two much-discussed books, *Eine Mithrasliturgie* and *Nekyia*, as well as his noteworthy *Studien zur Religionsgeschichte*. But the work to which he was most committed and which is most interesting for the study of folklore is his *Mutter Erde*, published in 1905.

In this book (a complete and revised edition of which has been recently provided by a German scholar, Eugen Fehrle), Dieterich studied ancient rites and beliefs in a world conceived of as the Earth-Mother. Unlike Usener, he did not undertake an examination of all divinities; rather, he examined only one divinity, which naturally gave him an advantage over his grandfather, Usener. Dieterich, too, followed the path outlined by Tylor, and animism is certainly at the very center of his reconstructions. In these reconstructions, however, one can also perceive the influence of Mannhardt, inasmuch as Dieterich's investigations of the origin and development of the idea that the earth is a "Mother" (the Mother of all) center on representations of soil fertility and animal reproduction, which he considered to be parallel and analogous to human generation.

In his examination, Dieterich first considered three customs found in classical antiquity: (1) the placing of the new-born child on the ground, (2) the inhumation of infants, and (3) the placing of the sick and dying on the ground, so that contact with the bare earth will promote healing. He did not investigate the innumerable correspondences among primitive peoples. He used these (although the

procedure occasionally seemed otherwise) to give a
historical aura to his reconstructions as he examined
German folklore in particular and European and non-
European folklore in general. For example, after
citing the Abruzzi custom of placing the baby on the
ground, he maintained that such a custom must be regarded as a survival of an ancient rite, according to
which the child was consecrated by the Earth-Mother.
From this came the belief that babies come from the
earth (or from trees or rocks, which are permanently
bound to the earth).

Dieterich, then, regarded the earth as a living
creature, a "soul" containing many souls. The earth
is living because "she" is fertile. This idea is the
source of the binomial *homo-humus*, to which popular
beliefs appeal, and it also explains the strong parallel existing between the fertility of the field and
the fertility of woman, which gave rise to another set
of beliefs and permitted the drawing of a parallel
between agricultural work and the reproductive act
(for example, the parallel between the plough and the
phallus).

Many of Dieterich's theses were attacked by Emil
Goldmann in his *Cartam levare* and by Martin Nilsson
in his recent *Geschichte der griechischen Religion*.
But we must recognize, as Eliade correctly says, that,
along with Rohde's *Psyche*, *Mutter Erde* is still a truly
classic book.

8. *Custom as a Religious Worship of Life*

A French scholar, Henry Pinard de la Boullaye, defined
scholars who followed the lead of Tylor and Mannhardt
and revived studies of classical philology as "ethnological philologists" or, if you prefer, "philological
ethnologists." On the one hand, he continued, they
joined the philological school, which attempted to
evaluate the meanings of myth, with the anthropological school, which in studying those meanings had enlarged its own research; on the other hand, they
employed a new research methodology, which was of

great service to the anthropological school. Thus, there came about an exchange of ideas that was not only of mutual benefit to the two schools but to folklore as well, which received an invigorating exposure and a breath of fresh air from this exchange. Actually, it was no easy matter to disturb such a settled, hallowed and even "holy" field as that of classical philology with those lively and provocative suggestions that excited students of ethnology and folklore. Yet, in the light of this new research, didn't classical texts often acquire a new meaning that illuminated them?

The *Archiv für Religionswissenschaft*, first directed by Edmund Hardy, was of great importance in underscoring the benefit of these studies. The directorship of this journal was taken over by Dieterich, who, in describing the new program, emphatically stated that although ethnologists had much to learn from philologists, philologists should also avail themselves of help from ethnologists. He added that the ethnic tradition was very old ground indeed, but it was also eternal and contemporary with all historical events.

This awareness led to Dieterich's adoption of the comparative method, with which he achieved results previously specified by Mannhardt and, in a sense, by Usener and Rohde as well. We recall that the comparative method had begun to be used indiscriminately in Germany by a new discipline, judicial ethnology; this discipline, particularly in Albert Post's work, attempted to discover the ultimate, deepest origin of law through a study of primitive peoples, which, as has been observed, was obviously a gnosiological error. However, the comparative method as used by Dieterich (and this was its task in judicial ethnology) served to extend historical knowledge of institutions, the objects of his examination. We also recall that Wilhelm Wundt was of the same persuasion as Post. In his *Mythus und Religion*, which appeared in three volumes between 1905 and 1909, Wundt gave a radical reshaping to Tylor's animism. Wundt's version, unsurprisingly, was influenced by Mannhardt, a fact that becomes apparent when one remembers that in Wundt's view the soul and the spirit create the demon, who possesses the superhuman power to help or harm. Hampered by a dry naturalism, Wundt accumulated facts from all civilizations without perceiving the concatenation of these facts in each civilization. Furthermore, he forgot that a fact could have different explanations because of differences in the environments in which that fact was revealed, a point that Dieterich had made.

This last point suggests Dieterich's reason for including many of the best German ethnologists and folklorists in his *Archiv*. As Adolf Spamer says, "When Paul Sartori decided a quarter-century ago to publish his great treatise on German folk customs and usages, an important step was taken for studies of folk usages. In three extensive sections dealing with birth, weddings, and death, with life and work inside and outside the home, and with the seasons and holidays (along with general observations about terminology, considerations of the origin and development of usages and customs, and interpretive analyses), Sartori collected, arranged, and precisely documented material of remarkable richness." Spamer goes on to say, "In recognizing that most usages are rooted in religion, Sartori, who suggests that custom is the religious worship of everyday life, demonstrates the strong influence of the comparative history of religion, which, ever since 1898, had found an important center in the *Archiv für Religionswissenschaft*." Furthermore, we should remember that these studies were now achieving the same results that, after Tylor, were being achieved by the English anthropological school. In Dieterich's work, animism had already begun to be replaced by "magical moments." And from behind those "moments" appeared the strong personality of an English scholar, James G. Frazer--who gave due consideration to Mannhardt's theories in his *The Golden Bough*.

CHAPTER XXIII

FRAZER: THE DEVIL'S ADVOCATE

1. *Frazer's Work*

It has often been said that James George Frazer's work
in ethnology and folklore is comparable to the histori-
ographical work done in Italy by Lodovico Muratori.
Certainly Frazer and Muratori are comparable in their
extraordinary capacity for work, their indefatigable
alacrity in research, and the richness of their texts;
the difference, however, is that Muratori's investigations were restricted to Italy, while Frazer's province
was the world. In this world he viewed the most mysterious and disquieting aspects--the superstitions and
beliefs that are at the heart of institutions, myths,
and legends.

As was the case for Tylor, Frazer used the comparative method to enter into this world. He was operating
in the midst of a culture dominated by Positivism, and
one senses his ease with this approach. Like Fontenelle, Lafitau, Tylor, and Mannhardt, he was much
attracted to classical literature. He was quite interested in various aspects of the world of "savages,"
which is what he, like Tylor, called the primitives.
And, following Tylor's lead, he was particularly interested in these savages' spiritual life, which exists
or survives among the folk of today. In this respect,
moreover, he not only complemented Tylor (from whom he
had taken the concept of survivals), but he also gave
his material, and folklore itself, a more methodical
organization than Tylor had. His model was given him
by Mannhardt.

Using beliefs, institutions, and superstitions,

410

Frazer compared classical civilizations to primitive
peoples and primitive peoples to the common folk within civilizations; thus, his connections result in a
kind of ladder: the first step is primitive peoples,
the second step is classical civilizations, and the
last step is folklore. But Frazer did not merely
collect various scholarly evidence. His real concern
was not to "embalm" such evidence but to keep it alive
and suggestive, so that his work could be articulated
in a uniform, compact document. After reading his
texts, one could say that all of Europe's ethnologists
and folklorists worked for him, a favor he returned by
transforming even the most careless and dogmatic of
ethnologists and folklorists into genteel men of
letters. Frazer combined quotations from scholars
with evocative passages from classical and Oriental
literature, and he took pleasure in citing excerpts
from learned writers and poets. Thus, his work illustrates the blending of a profoundly humanistic tradition with the refined sensibilities of modern culture.
Nevertheless, his pages (and he has written thousands
of them) are never tiresome or boring; indeed, they
compel the reader to continue reading, even when the
author integrates his own descriptive analyses with
interpretations of various constituent elements of a
tradition, usage, or rite.

We should add that almost all of Frazer's works
are the result of a single and continuous effort, a
single obligation that he always felt he had only
partially satisfied--which suggests the power of his
energetic temperament. For example, Frazer's first-
published ethnological work, entitled *Totemism*, appeared in 1884, and he returned to totemism again in
1892; but we have to wait until 1910 to see this
particular topic developed fully in *Totemism and
Exogamy*, a four-volume work. Equally taxing was the
compilation of *The Golden Bough*, Frazer's most popular work. Published in two volumes in 1890, this
work was reprinted in 1900, with an additional volume.
But his investigations, so nicely begun in those first
editions, were continually developing in an increasing
number of directions, culminating finally in his

twelve-volume edition of *The Golden Bough*, which was published between 1911 and 1915.

It is in this most provocative of his works that one finds a coalescence of Frazer's mutually illuminating interests. The English have called this work the Bible of modern times. Here the man of letters is coupled with the ethnologist and the ethnologist is coupled with the folklorist--and here both ethnologists and folklorist have the greatest admiration for culture and classical civilization. Culture and classical civilization were precisely the areas that Frazer (who, as a young man, had edited Sallustius Crispus' *Bellum Jugurthinum* in 1884) confronted even more directly in the remarkable six-volume *Pausanias's Description of Greece* and the five-volume *Fasti of Ovid*, in which the holidays, beliefs, institutions, and superstitions of ancient Greece and Rome are explained, clarified, and illuminated by the contributions of ethnology and folklore.

On an equal level with these ground-breaking syntheses of ethnology, classical philology, and folklore is Frazer's three-volume *Folk-lore in the Old Testament*--but this is not the last of Frazer's work. We should note that, not even counting his more literary works, he published the three-volume *The Belief in Immortality and the Worship of the Dead*, a work predominantly of ethnological interest, between 1913 and 1924; in 1926, the two-volume *The Worship of Nature*; in 1930, the long essay *Myths of the Origin of Fire*; and in 1933, when he was eighty years old, *The Fear of the Dead in Primitive Religion*. Also of interest, despite the lack of commentary on the materials, is the three-volume *Anthologia Anthropologica*, published in 1938-39.

To continue in considering some conclusions which he had already reached in his wide-ranging work, Frazer published until 1908 a series of essays that initially bore the title *Psyche's Task*. In republishing these in 1927--the same year that he produced *Man, God and Immortality*, a lively anthology of some of his works--Frazer decided to change the title. He called it, significantly, *The Devil's Advocate*. This lawyer,

this "devil's advocate," would indeed defend his clients throughout the long course of his life, but his
"clients," as he himself states in his book, would be
beliefs, institutions, and legends. Especially would
he defend his most "dangerous" client, superstitions--
which certainly involves a part if not all of the history of man.

2. In Search of the King of the Wood

It was with this "defense" in mind that Frazer began
his compilation of *The Golden Bough*, which was his
attempt to discover the first stage of human thought.
Although he (like Tylor) was convinced that ethnology
is an interpretative criterion for folklore, he believed that to apply this principle one first had to
reject Tylor's concept of animism. Tylor said that
in the beginning was animism. Frazer replied that
in the beginning was magic--and *The Golden Bough*
itself carries the subtitle *A Study in Magic and
Religion.*
     Like a pilgrim and poet, Frazer leaves from Nemi
(more precisely, from the Sanctuary of Diana
Nemorensis) for the streets of the world. In ancient
times this sanctuary observed one inexorable law, the
law of the King of the Wood. The King of the Wood
was both priest and murderer, for only he who killed
his predecessor could aspire to that office. In investigating the genesis of this custom, Frazer immediately noticed that even in primitive societies the
king is often both priest and magician, one who gains
supremacy through his supposed skill in the art of
magic. Like the Nemian King of the Wood, the primitive king had to yield to a series of prohibitions on
which his office and his life depended. The fact that
the law of the King of the Wood was unacknowledged in
classical antiquity compelled Frazer to travel to more
distant lands, among the savages. As he himself says,
"In order to understand the evolution of the kingship
and the sacred character with which the office has
commonly been invested in the eyes of savage or

barbarous peoples, it is essential to have some acquaintance with the principles of magic. . . ."[1]

In this apparent digression, Frazer confronted one of the most difficult problems associated with the history of primitive thought--and this "digression" indicated his angle of approach. As an admirer and student of Tylor, Frazer could have based his approach on animism. But as early as his slim volume entitled *Totemism*, he had found himself face-to-face with the magic beliefs that shackled savage life. He then asked himself about the character, nature, and purpose of these beliefs. In the first edition of *The Golden Bough* (1890), Frazer restricted himself to contending that to the savage the world appeared to be endowed with and directed by personal beings and impersonal forces (i.e., natural laws), in the midst of which magic developed. In the second edition in 1900, however, he gave these ideas greater emphasis. And in the first volume of the third edition of *The Golden Bough*, in which he attempted to determine the origins of magic and to classify magical methods and principles, he gave his ideas the most emphatic treatment of all, although the emphasis came more from his great diligence than from a clever dialectical argument.

In 1892, in the interval between the first and second editions of *The Golden Bough*, a work examining various questions about the magic of the primitives appeared in England. This work, written by John H. King, was entitled *The Supernatural: Its Origin, Nature and Evolution.* In essence, King was much like the Frazer who appears to us *after* the first edition of *The Golden Bough.* King seemed to be wholly convinced that magic was the result of specific forces unrelated to animism; furthermore, he suggested that "magical" customs were formed when the natural course of events was interrupted by an extraordinary happening, identified by the savage as a good or evil force bringing fortune or misfortune, which provoked love

[1]*The Magic Art*, 2nd ed., Vol. I of *The Golden Bough* (1900; rpt. New York: The Macmillan Company, 1935), p. 51.

or fear. In King's view, then, magic could be best understood and explained when one realized that it derived
from the vision of things new, extraordinary, and supernatural, in the context of the known world. It is at
this point, according to King, that the savage's mind
was struck by an excitement that aroused an accidental
association of ideas, which led to placing the object in
relation to other things as cause, effect, or both cause
and effect. It was precisely in this "association of
ideas" that Frazer, beginning with the second edition of
The Golden Bough, found the origin of magic. Frazer
never cited King's work, and we cannot say with any
assurance that he was even aware of it. We do know,
however, how Frazer came to define magical beliefs:
judgments produced by an "accidental" impulse.

3. The Principles of Magic Formulated by Frazer

Frazer believed that magic, a "false" science and art,
derived from two basic principles: (1) likes produce
likes, or the effect resembles the cause; (2) things that
were once in contact continue to affect each other at a
distance after physical contact has ended. The first
principle, he says, could be called the law of similarity, and the second could be called the law of contact
or contagion. He stresses that these two principles are
themselves merely two different erroneous applications
of an association of ideas. Homoeopathic (or imitative)
magic is based on an association of ideas generated by
the principle of similarity, while contagious magic is
based on an association of ideas generated by the principle of contiguity. In practice, however,

> the two branches are often combined; or, to be
> more exact, while homoeopathic or imitative magic
> may be practised by itself, contagious magic will
> generally be found to involve an application of
> the homoeopathic or imitative principle. Thus
> generally stated the two things may be a little
> difficult to grasp, but they will readily become
> intelligible when they are illustrated by particu-

lar examples. Both trains of thought are in fact
extremely simple and elementary. It could hardly
be otherwise, since they are familiar in the concrete, though certainly not in the abstract, to
the crude intelligence not only of the savage, but
of ignorant and dull-witted people everywhere.
Both branches of magic, the homoeopathic and the
contagious, may conveniently be comprehended under
the general name of Sympathetic Magic, since both
assume that things act on each other at a distance
through a secret sympathy, the impulse being transmitted from one to the other by means of what we
may conceive as a kind of invisible ether, not
unlike that which is postulated by modern science
for a precisely similar purpose, namely, to explain
how things can physically affect each other through
space which appears to be empty.[2]

The most familiar application of the first princi-
ple--"like produces like"--is found in the belief that
one can destroy or damage an enemy by destroying or
damaging the enemy's image, or in the belief that one
can cure or prevent sickness by transferring the malady
to the earth, a tree, a rock, and so on. The principle
is also found in the belief that things of the same
species are drawn to one another by their common spirit
as well as in the belief that one can help or even
insure abundant crops, fishing, and hunting by partici-
pating in appropriate ceremonies. The system of sympathetic magic is not made up only of positive precepts,
however; it also includes a large number of negative
precepts or prohibitions. Thus, this system of magic

> tells you not merely what to do, but also what to
> leave undone. The positive precepts are charms:
> the negative precepts are taboos. In fact the
> whole doctrine of taboo, or at all events a large
> part of it, would seem to be only a special appli-
> cation of sympathetic magic, with its two great
> laws of similarity and contact. . . . Positive

[2]Ibid., p. 54.

magic or sorcery says, "Do this in order that so
and so may happen." Negative magic or taboo says,
"Do not do this, lest so and so should happen."
The aim of positive magic or sorcery is to produce
a desired event; the aim of negative magic or
taboo is to avoid an undesirable one. But both
consequences, the desirable and the undesirable,
are supposed to be brought about in accordance with
the laws of similarity and contact. . . . The two
things are merely opposite sides or poles of one
great disastrous fallacy, a mistaken conception of
the association of ideas. Of that fallacy, sorcery
is the positive, and taboo the negative pole.[3]

The most familiar example of contagious magic, says
Frazer, is the magical sympathy believed to exist
between a man and those parts of his body that may be
cut from it, such as hair and nails; thus, it is believed that anyone who comes in possession of these
nails and hair can do whatever he wishes to the person
from whom they were cut, regardless of the distance
between them. Another example is the sympathetic connection between a wounded man and the weapon that has
wounded him--and contagious magic could be exercised
on a man even through imprints his body has left on
the sand or ground.
  Despite their continuous interplay, both of these
forms could be practiced not only for the benefit of
individuals but of the community as well--and it is
in this latter case that the magician becomes a public
functionary, a "personality." Frazer says:

The development of such a class of functionaries
is of great importance for the political as well
as the religious evolution of society. For when
the welfare of the tribe is supposed to depend on
the performance of these magical rites, the magician rises into a position of much influence and
repute, and may readily acquire the rank and
authority of a chief or king. . . . The general

[3]Ibid., pp. 111-12.

result is that at this stage of social evolution
the supreme power tends to fall into the hands of
men of the keenest intelligence. . . .[4]

This is a key point for Frazer. In the first volume
of *The Golden Bough* (appropriately entitled *The Magic
Art and the Evolution of Kings*), he made a clear distinction between magic, which he saw as an elementary
form of thought (in fact the most elementary and
therefore, according to the dictates of evolution, the
oldest), and religion, which represents a more complex
form of that thought. It is not only a matter of complexity, however; the god of magic is an impersonal
force, while the god of religion is a personal agent
to whose will the believer submits himself (which is
not the case with the god of magic, who imposes his
will). In *The Magic Art* Frazer synthesizes his ideas
in the following way:

> In the first place a consideration of the funda-
> mental notions of magic and religion may incline
> us to surmise that magic is older than religion
> in the history of humanity. We have seen that on
> the one hand magic is nothing but a mistaken
> application of the very simplest and most elemen-
> tary processes of the mind, namely the association
> of ideas by virtue of resemblance or contiguity;
> and that on the other hand religion assumes the
> operation of conscious or personal agents, superior
> to man, behind the visible screen of nature. Ob-
> viously the conception of personal agents is more
> complex than a simple recognition of the similarity
> of contiguity of ideas; and a theory which assumes
> that the course of nature is determined by con-
> scious agents is more abstruse and recondite, and
> requires for its apprehension a far higher degree
> of intelligence and reflection, than the view that
> things succeed each other simply by reason of their
> contiguity or resemblance.[5]

[4]Ibid., pp. 215-16.
[5]Ibid., pp. 233-34.

Frazer never divorced himself from these principles, which became the "protagonists" of his works;
however, the same cannot be said of another phenomenon,
totemism, with which he was finished after he identified the characteristics of magic contained within it.

4. Totemism As Magic

Doubtless the first scholar to work with the scientific
criteria of totemism was John Ferguson McLennan. He
was also the first to identify the structure of the
esogamia, the prohibition preventing members of a clan
from marrying with each other. As early as 1866,
McLennan had published an essay entitled *Primitive
Marriage*, which was later included, along with other
essays of a similar kind, in *Studies in Ancient History*
(1876). McLennan is one to whom Frazer often referred,
beginning with references in his *Totemism*.

In his studies McLennan undertook research in the
field of religion, and this research, initiated in a
specific area (the family), led him to the discovery of
totemism. Up until that time, there had been only rare
and sporadic reports about totemism, but it had already
been presented as a system of belief influencing the
development of human relations, inasmuch as totemic
beliefs consisted of attributing a relationship between
families and particular species of animals and plants.
But the social nature of totemism did not prevent
McLennan from seeing a religious element in it, an
ancestor-worship associated with animal and plant worship. It was, in any event, a form of religion that
he traced back to zoolatrous and phytolatrous cults
existing among peoples of classical antiquity.

This thesis was rejected by Tylor, who (while
recognizing their importance) held that totemic facts
must be associated with animism. In Tylor's view
totemism was a form of ancestor-worship, but one connected to the doctrine of reincarnation, the transition point between ancestor-worship and totemism. Nor
was this thesis accepted by Spencer, who saw totemism
as a specific form of ancestor-worship. Thus, it is

evident that both Tylor and Spencer brought totemism
into their religious systems.

At this point, one of McLennan's disciples, William Robertson Smith, intervened in order to develop
McLennan's vague hypothesis. In 1889, in his wide-ranging *Lectures on the Religion of Semites*, he maintained that totemism must be considered as the basis
of both the Semitic and Arabic religions because (1)
among peoples who practice these religions, certain
tribes bear the name of an animal, and (2) in these
religions one rediscovers the worship of nature (stars,
rocks, fountains, and so on), along with dietary prohibitions and the use of animal images on war flags.
The most important proof, however--and this is at the
heart of his theory--is the sacrifice, which he considered not as a peace offering to a divinity but as
a social act of communion between the god and his
faithful followers. As Smith saw it, the sacrificial
animal was originally the totemic animal.

In broad outline, this was the state of totemistic
studies at the time that Frazer resumed the topic in his
Totemism and Exogamy. In his first work, *Totemism*, he
expressed the belief that totemism was partially a
religious phenomenon (which is suggested by the relation
between man and totem) and partially a social one (which
is suggested by the obligations imposed on members of
the same clan). But this definition, which was proposed
in 1887, no longer satisfied him in 1910--for he had now
come to consider totemism as only a form of social
organization. In this new conclusion one sees the influence of his theory about the origin of magic, which
chronologically preceded religion--a theory previously
formulated in the second edition of *The Golden Bough*.
In *The Magic Art* volume of *The Golden Bough*, Frazer
offers this clarification:

> Nowhere is the theory of sympathetic magic more
> systematically carried into practice for the maintenance of the food supply than in the barren
> regions of Central Australia. Here the tribes are
> divided into a number of totem clans, each of which
> is charged with the duty of propagating and multi-

plying their totem for the good of the community
by means of magical ceremonies and incantations.
The great majority of the totems are edible animals and plants, and the general result supposed
to be accomplished by these magical totemic ceremonies . . . is that of supplying the tribe with
food and other necessaries. Often the rites con-
sist of an imitation of the effect which the
people desire to produce; in other words, their
magic is of the homoeopathic or imitative sort.[6]

We can also observe the ceremonies that totemism
allows. Here we discover a reinvocation of the past,
including the history of the clan and the family
spirit. But is this past revived in a utilitarian
sense, or is it largely a set of gestures reproducing
the ancestors' deeds? "Do this so that something else
will happen" is the guiding rule of these ceremonies,
which presuppose the presence of the totem. This
"presence" also produces the other magical precept:
"Don't do this so that something else will not happen
--and not only to you as an individual but to every
clan of which you are a part." We also can observe
myths and legends related to totemism, which always
tell of relationships between clan and totem, details
of the origin of the totem group, and the totem's
miraculous metamorphosis into a man. In other words,
primitive man "believes," and, as in magic, rites and
cults are the "operative" forms of his thought, while
myths and legends are the corresponding "spoken" forms.
Between these two forms, however, there are no gulfs
or separations--only transitions.

5. *Folklore in Frazer's Thought*

Frazer came to see magic (dominated by an error-ridden
totemism) as an interpretative criterion for clarifying
and elucidating cults, myths, and ancient classical
rites. In this respect his notes were at times "quick,"

[6]*Ibid.*, p. 85.

as Lafitau would say. For example, in talking about
contagious magic, he observed, "We can now understand
why it was a maxim with the Pythagoreans that in rising
from bed you should smooth away the impression left by
your body on the bed-clothes. The rule was simply an
old precaution against magic, forming part of a whole
code of superstitious maxims which antiquity fathered
on Pythagoras, though doubtless they were familiar to
the barbarous forefathers of the Greeks long before the
time of that philosopher."[7] At other times, however,
his comments on classical civilization are legitimate
assessments, with magic providing the general framework. Instructive here, in addition to the King of the
Wood (which is both the chorus and the dominant voice
of *The Golden Bough*), are *Folk-lore in the Old Testament* and the commentaries on Ovid and Pausanias. It
seems that, like Lafitau, Frazer wished to say that
Greeks and Romans were not much removed from thinking
like the barbarian. Too, Frazer's assessments are
partially supported by folklore, by the survivals that
still remain at the center of our civilization. It
could be said, then, that he used folklore to verify
his assertions, but (in contrast to Tylor) he concluded
by turning to man himself. Frazer did not ignore any
cults, myths, or ancient classical beliefs in his extensive work, which presented almost all those expressions that, to Herder, appeared to be (and were) voices
of humanity. Indeed, European folklore is reassembled
in his work as a precise expression of man--a rich,
imaginative, lively, warm humanity effusive in its
beliefs, pulsatingly alive in its spectacles, expressive in its tales and legends.

In *The Golden Bough* Frazer felt obliged to include
a study of tree-worship, a field of investigation that
had already been extensively ploughed by Mannhardt.
It has been rightly said that Frazer popularized the
theories proposed in *Wald- und Feldkulte* (which had
been an inspiration to so many other scholars). But
although Frazer acknowledged his debt to Mannhardt,
was he actually following the same path? In the

[7]Ibid., pp. 213-14.

preface to the abridged edition of *The Golden Bough*,
he admitted:

> If in the present work I have dwelt at some length
> on the worship of trees, it is not, I trust, be-
> cause I exaggerate its importance in the history of
> religion, still less because I would deduce from it
> a whole system of mythology; it is simply because
> I could not ignore the subject in attempting to ex-
> plain the significance of a priest who bore the
> title of King of the Wood, and one of whose titles
> to office was the plucking of a bough--the Golden
> Bough--from a tree in the sacred grove. But I am
> so far from regarding the reverence for trees as of
> supreme importance for the evolution of religion
> that I consider it to have been altogether subordi-
> nate to other factors. . . .[8]

Here he was obviously putting Mannhardt's theory in its
proper perspective. There is no doubt, however, that
when he did focus on this cult he basically accepted
many of Mannhardt's premises. Consider, for example,
his examination of a highly poetic aspect of folklore,
the vestiges of tree-worship in modern Europe: in
stating that the spirit of vegetation is often represented by a tree, he was clearly adopting Mannhardt's
convictions. Or consider his treatment of the killing
of the tree-spirit, in which he appealed to Mannhardt
for support. In *The Golden Bough*, one senses Mannhardt's presence everywhere, with the following qualification: although Frazer accepted Mannhardt, he subordinated Mannhardt to his own system. In Frazer's
system tree-worship is merely one aspect of magic, which
even today reigns supreme in the life of the folk.

6. *Magic and Religion*

Frazer reduced every tradition extant among the folk

[8]*The Golden Bough,* Abridged ed. (1922; rpt. New
York: The Macmillan Company, 1951), pp. vi-vii.

into a rite, the rite into a belief, and the belief
into a system of ideas. Folklore itself, then, becomes a surging stream that no civilization can stem
since it is ultimately a part of that civilization.
This, at any rate, was Frazer's conclusion. What path
did he follow and what labor did he expend in arriving
at this conclusion?

In pursuing various avenues of approach, the first
avenue Frazer perceived was that of primitive peoples.
Thus, Comte is always present in Frazer's work. Furthermore, Frazer, like Tylor, was convinced that today's savages are savages in a relative rather than in
an absolute sense. Still, his "first age" was there,
among the savages. In clarifying the relationships
between ethnology and folklore, Frazer observed that
"to our predecessors we are indebted for much of what
we thought most our own."[9] On this subject he says:

> Contempt and ridicule or abhorrence and denuncia-
> tion are too often the only recognition vouchsafed
> to the savage and his ways. Yet of the benefactors
> whom we are bound thankfully to commemorate, many,
> perhaps most, were savages. For when all is said
> and done our resemblances to the savage are still
> far more numerous than our differences from him;
> and what we have in common with him, and deliber-
> ately retain as true and useful, we owe to our
> savage forefathers who slowly acquired by experi-
> ence and transmitted to us by inheritance those
> seemingly fundamental ideas which we are apt to
> regard as original and intuitive. We are like
> heirs to a fortune which has been handed down for
> so many ages that the memory of those who built it
> up is lost, and its possessors for the time being
> regard it as having been an original and unalter-
> able possession of their race since the beginning
> of the world.[10]

[9]*Taboo and the Perils of the Soul*, Vol. III of
The Golden Bough (1911; rpt. New York: The Macmillan
Company, 1935), p. 422.
    [10]Ibid., pp. 421-22.

Frazer wished to evoke this memory. Thus, the
world in which he saw the past became the world of the
savages, which had been exalted by Enlightenment theorists. Here magic assumed importance, though it was
but one aspect of ages past. But how did Frazer view
this magic? He saw it, as we have already noted, as a
web of errors, as a false association of ideas resulting from ignorance. This was an inductive conclusion
based on the premise that magic is an elementary form
of religion, which is a "superior" form. He was, then,
like an Enlightenment thinker who had converted to
religion. However, in assessing magic in the world of
the savage, didn't he place himself in the position of
the scholars whom he wished to condemn?

Although magic appears to us to be made up of error
and superstition, it obviously was not so to savages,
for whom it was a historical form of thought characterized by an alternation of ideas, fears, anxieties, con-
frontations, and escapes. Frazer understood magic as
an attempt to extend the confines of one's power to
perform or produce. But how could he then reconcile
that attempt (the work of a conscious and intelligent
being) with his condemnation of it, as conveyed in his
judgment that the savage could only make use of the
contiguous category of magic? Holding true to evolutionistic principles (which maintain that whatever is
simplest is earliest), Frazer placed magic at the beginning of human thought. But who can say whether the
idea of a God or of magical power was the simpler idea
for the truly primitive man? And if there were a psychological cause operating in man's mind in the evolution of magic into religion (which Frazer supposed),
wouldn't all those exquisite magical beliefs found in
history and folklore still exist today in our own
societies?

The fact is that magic cannot be placed as a "first
cause," for that leads to an arbitrary assumption about
one moment or one aspect in the course of history; furthermore, magic cannot be regarded as a "necessary
condition" (the *only* necessary condition); and least of
all can it be viewed, as Frazer argued, as a "consequence." We can immediately acknowledge that magic is

clearly distinct from religion, but the two are not
and cannot be other than two *degrees* of thought, and,
as such, only two degrees of *historical* thought. It
is therefore useless to try to find in them a lesser
(magical) or greater (religious) intelligence, a
lesser or greater simplicity of mind. In such cases,
magic and religion are empirical concepts, classifications indicating degrees of respect toward a specific conception of the world and its relationship to
man. Religion involves a divinity that is completely
free from the control of man. Magic, on the other
hand, is a force that can be subjected to man's con-
structive action. Both magic and religion originated
and developed in the experience of the primitive as a
spiritual attitude that, according to specific historical conditions, is dominated by magic or religion.

Truth can originate from an error, but only on the
condition that the error comes to be considered as a
logical act. History, too, can originate from an
illusion, but only on the condition that the illusion
is the result of human experience. From the negative,
obviously, history cannot be made.

7. To "Demand Others Earlier"

Although he considered magic as a web of errors,
Frazer also thought of magic as "historical"--indeed,
the starting point of history. A good lawyer must
know how to attack his own client in order that he
might conduct a defense with more credibility and
skill. The essence of Frazer's defense was that although magic is indeed a web of erroneous and absurd
ideas, a form of superstition, these errors, conceptions, and superstitions are of great use to man.
In *The Devil's Advocate* Frazer reconsidered concepts
that he had proposed in various works, concluding (1)
that among certain races and peoples superstition had
strengthened respect for government, contributing to
social stability; (2) that among certain races and in
certain periods superstition had strengthened respect
for private property, contributing to the guarantee

of its enjoyment; (3) that among certain races and
in certain periods superstition had strengthened
respect for the institution of marriage, contributing
to a greater observance of the rules of sexual morality; and (4) that among certain races and peoples
superstition had strengthened respect for human life.

Frazer added that these institutions (government,
property, marriage, and respect for human life) are
the very pillars of human society. If these supporting columns are destroyed, society falls. Here,
apparently, Frazer was much like Vico, who, as is
well known, saw civilization as having been built
on three human institutions. But while Vico related
these institutions to the cyclical alternations of
the historical process, Frazer identified the process
with the postulate of the theory of organic evolution
that maintains that a knowledge of man first requires
a knowledge of his origin--as if man's origin were
not inherent in the development of his institutions.
Vico, however, sought the genesis of facts in the
"intimacy" of their nature, which is the only factor
that provides us with even the "semblance of knowledge." He said that "it doesn't matter who made the
world of nations: it was made by men with intelligence. It was not fate, for they made it by choice;
not chance, for the results of their always so acting
are perpetually the same." Given this view of the
eternal nature of things, we can see why Vico argued
that it is "an idle curiosity to demand others
earlier." Frazer, on the other hand, was on a desperate search for these past and present "earlier
people" among the primitives, to whom he attributed
an undifferentiated mentality that also applies to
the folk in civilized nations.

Just as Frazer believed in unlimited progress, so
did he believe in a comparison completely derived
from a concept of human uniformity. In establishing
these premises, he hoped to open the door to a universal history of man. This was the ambitious aim of
his work, which is flawed by a false concept of a
philosophy of history (specifically, evolutionism),
by a sociology that connects Comte with Tylor *via*

Bastian, and by a universal history based as much on the philosophy of history as on sociology.

8. *Suggestions and Inspirations in Frazer's Work*

Notwithstanding these and other faults, we can say of Frazer's work what he himself said of magic: from its errors comes much utility. Separate his descriptions from the context of his theories about "now and then"; consider the institutions that he describes in terms of their own natural "life," their historical nature; examine his discussions within the highly charged atmosphere in which they were created--and here you will find a naturalistic Frazer who provided comment of strictly historical interest. Indeed, it could even be said that Frazer became historical only when he forgot to be so.

In Frazer's work there are many successful interpretations of various ethnological problems--penetrating proposals and approaches that, although placed on naturalistic ground, actually reveal historical qualities. As in the case with the works of Tylor and Mannhardt, those parts of Frazer's work of a profound historical interest are the ones in which he joins (in an ideal sense) the beliefs of civilization's "folk" with the beliefs of primitive peoples, transforming ethnology and folklore into truly contemporary history. It is then that those traditions are revived, becoming the very life of history. True enough, he believed that popular traditions were fossils because of the primitive ideas that they retained. But then with what great care he investigated their nature! Moreover, Frazer observed the changes, the similarities, and the differences in such traditions.

We must be impressed by the skill with which Frazer handled material to determine cultural relationships and especially by the almost poetic style with which he illuminated those relationships. In this regard, Frazer not only had a more refined sensibility than his predecessors but also, it seems to me, the kind of appealing intelligence that makes a poet of a scholar.

Although Frazer did not always successfully complete
the historian's mission of discovering the history of
man, he consistently demonstrated the exceptional
qualities of the author, the artist, the poet. Too,
he came to understand in the last years of his life
(and this is said in his honor) that we have been
given the documents of man's history by the change
itself in that history: "If my writings should survive the writer, they will do so, I believe, less for
the sake of the theories which they propound than for
the sake of the facts which they record. They will
live, if they live at all, as a picture or moving
panorama of the vanished life of primitive man all
over the world. . . ."[11]

This is not, in fact, Frazer's epitaph. In those
works of his that confront the problems afflicting
mankind--problems that at the same time illuminate
mankind, providing purpose and dignity--he succeeded
in giving us useful lessons for the study of ethnology
and folklore, and he constructed a tightly-woven net
of cultural interests involving all historical and
moral disciplines. Briefly put, Frazer combined the
work of Lafitau, Fontenelle, and Rousseau with the
work of Herder, the brothers Grimm, and Pitrè. All
of his theories may well fade and die, as has been the
case already for some of them (or at least those that
he had regarded as fundamental). But this waning does
not mitigate the evocative force that strikes the mind
of whoever pauses to ponder these theories. And precisely because this is so, the advocate has won his
case.

[11]*Aftermath: A Supplement to The Golden Bough*
(New York: The Macmillan Company, 1937), p. v.

CHAPTER XXIV

THE PRIMITIVE IN US

1. Lang and the Method of Folklore

Primitive Culture and *The Golden Bough* may be regarded
as the fundamental pillars supporting the English
anthropological school. In addition to its influence
on all European countries, the English anthropological
school should be credited with promoting a broader,
deeper view of culture, which it achieved by combining
ethnology and folklore. We should add that Mannhardt's
work gave new impulse to this school. Just as Frazer
profited from the methodology (if not the problematical
aspects) of Tylor's work, invigorating this methodology
with Mannhardt's new ideas, so do we see that these
scholars influenced the works of their associates and
successors, who were quite prepared to put their convictions and efforts at the service of a discipline
they called social anthropology, one of many fields of
possible historical research.

Consider, for example, the case of Andrew Lang,
whose apprenticeship developed under the influence of
Tylor, in sharp contrast to Müller. A refined poet,
a scholar and translator of Aristotle and Homer, and
a historian of his Scotland, Lang had a specific aim
in his apprenticeship: to study mythology. Mythology,
along with its attendant problems, was the nucleus of
his studies, in which he combined his interest in
classical civilizations with his interest in ethnology
and folklore.

In discussing folklore in an important essay, "The
Method of Folklore" (which was later included in his
1884 volume entitled *Custom and Myth*), Lang expressed

430

his creed, which is the following: (1) if one wishes
to study folklore, he needs to use the anthropological
method; (2) folklore encompasses not only beliefs and
customs but also legends and songs, inasmuch as legends
and songs contain "survivals"; (3) for self-study,
folklore needs ethnology; (4) we establish comparisons
by applying ethnological studies to the study of folklore; (5) such comparisons reveal the great similarities the folk of civilized peoples share with classical
or Aryan civilizations and with all the world's peoples
and therefore with primitives (or savages, as he called
them); and (6) we can understand these comparisons and
similarities without there being any necessity that the
peoples among whom the similarities are established be
of the same origin or in touch with each other, because
similar mentalities produce similar beliefs and practices; the folklorist does not have to accept this explanation indiscriminately, however, for he is at
liberty to see if a people has in fact imported an
ethnic theme.

In approaching the study of myths (and therefore
fables), Lang particularly wanted to determine the
ethnological nature of such products. Like Tylor, he
wanted to know if there was a mentality that actually
considered myths credible and natural, and, like Tylor,
he responded that if there is such a mentality, it is
to be found only among the savages. This response,
however, did not satisfy him. In another essay (later
collected in his first volume of work, *Myth, Ritual and
Religion*, in 1887), Lang acknowledged that today's
savage, the savage of whom we have historical and philological evidence, is anything but the true primitive.
In his view, however, it doesn't really matter whether
we know about the actual primitive condition of man
(an attitude reminiscent of Rousseau). What matters
is the establishing of the law that all the ancestors
of present races came from a state analogous to the
savage state. The savage state, he adds, is one
through which all societies have passed, or at least
it is a social state from which all societies have borrowed. It is therefore obvious, he continues, that
savages must hold the key to the interpretation of

myths, an obvious confutation of Müller's theory of
mythology. To destroy Müller's theory, all he needed
was Mannhardt, and to create his own theory, all he
needed was Tylor (or perhaps it would be better to say
that he needed Fontenelle as revised by Tylor).

Myth and fable merely provided the framework for
Tylor's treatment, while in Lang's portrayal they became the picture itself. Lang collected scattered
threads of myths and fables, revived them, and wove
them into a unified, homogeneous design. Within this
embroidery is the myth--which, however, is not self-
explanatory, and even less is it explained by its
words or by the etymological roots of its words;
rather, the explanation is to be found in the comparative study of institutions, laws, and customs, which
are found among today's savages and which are based
on specific beliefs. Now, for the savage, myth is
merely the projection of these beliefs, and thus myth
is a credible and natural thing, related to a "public
motive" for truth. We could say that in this respect
Lang adopted a maxim from Vico: uniform ideas found
among peoples unknown to each other must have an element of truth in them. But while Vico saw these
uniform ideas as indicative of the universal tendencies of the human spirit, Lang saw them as indicative
of the uniformity of primitive life; Lang, then, converted Vico's *ideal* "first" into a *chronological*
"first"--which is precisely what happened in the works
of Comte, Tylor, and Frazer.

2. Fables, Myths, and Customs

After composing his picture, Lang proceeded to exem-
plification, which is the personal contribution that
he made to the study of myth and fable. Here his
starting point was Tylor, or perhaps it would be
better to say Tylor's animism, a theory he accepted.
Like Tylor (but also with the aid of Mannhardt), he
applied this theory to fairies, witches, and talking
animals. Lang was quite impressed by the fascinating
world of fable. In 1888, for example, he initiated

the publication of those Christmas "gifts" that he supplemented each year with new fairy tales and romances.
We also know how much care he gave to the translation
of Perrault's *Contes* and the Grimms' *Märchen*. In
essays in his *Custom and Myth* and in even more numerous
essays in *Myth, Ritual and Religion*, he revived the
characters of these tales and *Märchen*, placing them in
their own fantasy world, while at the same time he took
these characters far back into time and space, analyzing them at the very moment of their presumed birth.

At the center of this "birth" is the world of the
primitives, their belief, faith, and hope. To cite a
classic example, it has been said that Psyche symbol-
ized dawn, which hides at the appearance of the sun.
But what is the major theme of this tale, which is
found in various forms just about everywhere? It is
the theme of the bride guilty of having seen the groom
undressed. But isn't it more logical, Lang asked, to
see this as the projection of a taboo common to many
primitive peoples as well as to ancient Spartans and
Malaysians? According to this taboo, newlyweds were
prohibited from seeing each other naked. Conclusion:
the theme originates in the taboo. Our fables, like
our myths, are full of talking objects, inexplicable
phenomena that we dismiss as purely imaginative devices. But given their animistic conceptions, argued
Lang, didn't savages believe that objects *could* talk?
In our fables we encounter humans who are transformed
into animals and animals that are transformed into
humans. This too is, in our view, the imagination at
work. But among primitives, weren't such transformations the result of totemic beliefs? On the basis of
such examples as these, Lang concluded that the background (or the "common ground," we would say) for these
fables is to be found in an ancient usage or belief
that, unlike the primitives, we no longer understand.
The concept of the survival, in Lang's view, is also
valid for studying the tale, since the tale expresses
the specific "phase of thought" in which it originated.
In the process of migration, however, it lost the meaning that brought it into existence, particularly during
the classical age, and it therefore follows that the

meaning will be even more obscure among today's folk.
But Lang asked if we could even say that, for example,
the Artemis of savage peoples is the same as the Artemis of the classical age.

It certainly cannot be denied that tales and myths
contain some themes and motifs that are also found in
savage beliefs. Since this is so, such research is
valid, provided it stays within legitimate confines,
with no artistic elements being added to or taken from
the myth or the tale. But notwithstanding the last
article of his folkloristic creed, Lang clearly over-
played his hand in searching among savages for the
origins of myths and beliefs. As he himself said in
his preface to Cox's *Cinderella*, there are a number of
genealogically different popular tales: (1) fairy
tale or myth, probably of savage origin; (2) folktales
circulating among the lower classes of today; (3)
heroic myths of ancient literature; and (4) versions
of modern literary tales. It is a question, then, of
a source, not *the* source, of a tale. As a poet and
man of letters, Lang certainly did not attempt to
minimize the personal contribution that the poet who
recounts the myths or reworks the tales can bring to
themes or motifs. The intent of this researcher of
sources, as had been the case for Benfey, Paris, and
Rajna, was to examine the evolution of ideas from the
barbarous to the civilized in myths and rites (although he should have limited himself to the study of
those ideas). He also hoped to establish the polygenesis of myth and fairy tale, which points to the
validity of his research. Basically, Lang reached
the same conclusions in ethnography that Bédier reached in aesthetics; and, significantly, Bédier subscrib-
ed to the anthropological theory about interpretative
possibilities in the popular narrative.

3. Research in Primitive Faith

It is clear that these interpretative possibilities
were linked to the interpretation of ethnological
facts. But did Lang's thought truly embrace these

facts? In presenting the French translation of *Myth,
Ritual and Religion,* Léon Marillier, a noted religious-
history scholar, observed that this work "carried the
stamp of the age in which it was written, as did Lang's
temperament." He went on to say that "the author has
written not only to determine the laws to which ceremonies and myths are subjected in their origin and
development, but also to demonstrate the fragility of
the bases of a theory that he justifiably considered
to be fallacious. He did not study savage beliefs in
and for themselves; rather, he studied them for analogies between various legends and some of the great
ancient myths. And when he compared the two sets of
facts, it was not so much to render them more intelligible as it was to prove the futility of one method of
interpretation."

One could argue with Marillier's observation,
inasmuch as the strength of Lang's work *was* his making
the origin and development of tales intelligible (although these findings were colored by rhetoric that,
though lively, was overly insistent). Certainly, however, he availed himself of savage beliefs appearing
in travelers' descriptions and ethnologists' speculations. It was not long after Marillier's 1896 preface
that Lang descended into the field in order to study
"savage beliefs, in and for themselves," as is evidenced by *The Making of Religion* (1898), *Magic and
Religion* (1901), *Social Origins* (1903), and *The Secret
of the Totem* (1905). In his first works, during his
apprenticeship period, Lang concerned himself with
non-Aryan myths about the origin of the world and man
in order to examine those origins--an endeavor that
takes up the major part of his *Myth, Ritual and
Religion.* Simply look at some of the chapter titles
themselves: "Greek Myths of the Origin of the World
and Man," "Greek Cosmogonic Myths," "Savage Divine
Myths," "Gods of the Lowest Races," "American Divine
Myths." At first he had been satisfied with the idea
that religion had developed from animism. Later, however (and this is at the center of *The Making of
Religion*), he placed himself in distinct opposition
to this theory, but not in the direct manner of Müller

or the indirect manner of Benfey and Cosquin. For
him, Tylor was always the master and *Primitive Culture*
his gospel.

In this "gospel," however, there were many pages
that Lang did not hesitate to tear out and destroy.
Primitive Culture was guided by the spirit of animism,
a theory whose importance he well knew. The question,
however, was how one could reconcile this theory with
the ever-growing number of proofs collected by ethnographers giving verifiable evidence that primitives
possessed the idea of a supreme being, which Tylor had
considered to be the result of missionary influence.

4. Theological Ethnology

Lang observed in *The Making of Religion* that the animistic theory suggests that the idea of "spirit" arose
from phenomena of sleep, dream, and death. But in the
supreme being, as he appeared to the primitives, can
one truly recognize a spirit--or simply a being? To
support this latter point, he says:

> As soon as man had the idea of "making" things,
> he might conjecture as to a Maker of things which
> he himself had not made, and could not make. He
> would regard this unknown Maker as a "magnified
> non-natural man" . . . . This conception of a
> magnified non-natural man, who is a Maker, being
> given; his Power would be recognized, and fancy
> would clothe one who had made such useful things
> with certain other moral attributes, as of Father-
> hood, goodness, and regard for the ethics of his
> children. . . . In all this there is nothing
> "mystical," nor anything, as far as I can see,
> beyond the limited mental powers of any beings
> that deserve to be called human.[1]

According to Lang, then, there is no *sensus numinis*,

[1]*The Making of Religion*, 3rd ed. (London: Longmans, Green, and Co., 1909), p. xii.

no divine revelation, in such a concept. However,
as Raffaele Pettazzoni says, "There was indeed a connection here with theological doctrines, which should
have been quite obvious; it was precisely this feature
that was first captured in Lang's new hypothesis,
accounting for his success. It must be said that
Lang himself offered some deliberate contributions to
make this feature more notable and emphatic; perhaps
yielding to his literary tendencies and his romantic
inclinations, he did not hesitate to apply evangelical terminology to savage beliefs, citing St. Paul
and the Church Fathers and comparing (for example)
the Ten Commandments with tribal precepts practiced
by Australian societies and promulgated, it was
believed, by a supreme being."

On the other hand, Lang never proposed giving a
definitive answer to the question of the origin of
religion. In this the age of evolutionary theory,
it was enough, in his view, to establish the fact
that one need not develop a new concept about religion, as Tylor had done, to find religion among
primitives. He felt it was sufficient to affirm
the principle that, among primitives, belief in a
supreme being is as old as animism itself. This led
him to reject the idea that magic was anterior to
religion; furthermore, he considered magic as an
"extra-normal" force, an area ignored by Tylor and
Frazer.

In the light of these new ideas, Lang greatly
revised his old works. He polished them, softening
the polemical aspects and providing a more imposing
ethnological framework. *Myth, Ritual and Religion*
was republished in 1901, and *Custom and Myth* was
republished in 1904. His new view of religion,
however, did not alter some of his old beliefs,
particularly the belief that mythological tales
had originated at a specific stage of human life,
had traveled through all nations, and, for the most
part, still lived among primitive peoples; it was
a stage of life wherein those things that may seem
miraculous to us were the result of a touching,
sincere faith.

5. *Hartland and His Studies of Narrative*

A quite similar attitude about this "stage" was assumed
by another representative of the English anthropological school, E. S. Hartland, whose interests coincided
with Lang's: for Hartland, too, the world of folklore
was bedecked with myth and fable; for Hartland, too,
the comparative method was the valid method for studying myth and fable; and for Hartland, too, such a
method presupposes a detailed knowledge of ethnology
in all of its aspects. On the other hand, Hartland
(who, without much examination, had rejected the idea
of God as early as 1898) finally came to recognize
later, between 1905 and 1908, that animism could not
stand as a general theory, inasmuch as a sense of wonder is what sustained the primitive, and magic and
religion are merely two sides of the same coin. We
should observe, however, that his broadest works
always move within the context of Tylorian animism
and especially within the context of magic as Frazer
had conceived it.

These theories of animism and magic were Hartland's
guides in the world of fairy tales. *The Science of
Fairy Tales*, first published in 1891, attempts to
provide a firmer, more organic foundation to the (ethnological) problem of folk narrative. But how did he
pose this problem, and what was his procedure? In *The
Science of Fairy Tales* he demonstrated that he was a
skillful philologist with an exceptionally comprehensive view of the narrative, although he was plagued by
some uncertainties. He asserted that the issue of
folk narrative concerned tradition, not literature.
Thus, he supported a principle that led some to the
erroneous conclusion that just as the English anthropological school ignored the issue of migration in the
study of tale construction, so it ignored the issue of
a marvelous individual originality.

One could object that although this may be one
aspect of the English anthropological school, it is
certainly not the only aspect. To see this, all we
need do is to continue to read Hartland himself, for
it is at this point that he suddenly remembers the

contribution given, for example, to Sicilian tales by
the "messiah," Agatuzza, of whom he draws a touching
portrait. Later on, he takes up different ways of
telling stories about fairies, which vary from country
to country, and he examines themes and motifs that lead
back to animistic, magical, and totemic beliefs. Thus,
the fairies become the protagonists of his colloquy.
In this colloquy, conducted in the manner of Lang and
Frazer, we are shown not only gift-giving fairies but
also those that steal or exchange babies. The fairy,
then, is a spirit that can be either good or malicious.
A product of animism, the fairy lives a life of magic.
And at the center of this life we see a reflection of
our oldest customs, the beliefs of our ancestors, and
our own world itself--a world now not lived but dreamed.

6. *Narrative as Tradition*

To complete his picture of popular narrative, Hartland
wrote two other books. The first, *The Legend of Perseus*, was published between 1894 and 1896; the second,
Primitive Paternity, which was published in 1909-10,
illustrated the myth of supernatural birth in relation
to the history of the family. In these works Hartland
demonstrated his competence not only in ethnology and
folklore but also in classical philology; too, his
comparisons became more persuasive, and he attempted
to exert more critical control over the treated material. In introducing the first work, which contains
three substantial volumes, he said:

> In these volumes I have attempted an examination
> of the myth upon scientific principles [that is,
> the principles of the anthropological school].
> The first three chapters of the present volume
> are devoted to an account of the story, as given
> by the poets and historians of antiquity, and in
> modern folklore. Taking, then, the four chief in-
> cidents in order, the remaining chapters comprise
> an inquiry into analogous forms of the Supernatural
> Birth, alike in tale and custom, throughout the

world. They will be followed by similar inquiries
into the incidents of the Life-Token, the rescue
of Andromeda, and the Quest of the Gorgon's Head.
Having thus analysed the incidents, and determined,
so far as the means at my command will permit,
their foundation in belief and custom, and the
large part played by some of the conceptions in
savage life, I shall return to the story as a
whole, and, treating it as an artistic work, I
shall inquire whether it be possible to ascertain
what was its primitive form, where it originated,
and how it became diffused over the Eastern continent.[2]

Hartland followed this same method--which later
became the method of *The Golden Bough*--in his second
work, *Primitive Paternity*. He began by providing an
ample illustration of conception and its origin--and
therefore of incarnation. In this respect, too, he
was like Frazer. But later in *Primitive Paternity* he
turned to a subject involving complex research: he
examined legends about supernatural births and studied
primitive magical practices in regard to conception.
Thus, he enlarged his picture by attempting to illustrate the problems of family, paternity, and descent,
which are found in the primitive world in all their
complexity. Of particular interest here is his two-
volume investigation of marriage rites and different
forms of conjugal union, subjects that had been treated
as early as 1891 by Edvard Westermarck in his *The History of Human Marriage* and later (but from a quite
different angle) by Alfred Crawley in his evocative
1902 work, *The Mystic Rose*. Westermarck, a Finn who
had grown up under the influence of the English anthropological school, nevertheless concluded by tracing all
moral ideas associated with these institutions to emotional states. This idea is the nucleus of his *The
Origin and Development of the Moral Ideas* (1906-08),
a work that is rich in collected materials (classified

[2]*The Legend of Perseus* (London: David Nutt, 1894),
pp. v-vi.

in a very useful way) but that has been criticized for
its psychology, which far exceeds the limits proposed
by the English anthropological school. This cannot be
said of Crawley, who maintained in another work, *The
Idea of the Soul*, that animism was too difficult an
idea for primitive peoples.

Knowledge of marriage rites and various forms of
conjugal union (with related taboos), which can be
inferred to be at the very center of the life of these
peoples, clarifies one of the most characteristic
aspects of popular law--which has been given able
treatment by Baltasar Bogišič, a Russian, and especially by Emilio Costa, a Spaniard. In Hartland's
work, however, it is evident that nuptial customs and
rites are resolved in many ethnic themes, from which
many tale motifs result. For Hartland, then, as for
his predecessors, myth and fairy tale became vehicles
for entering the primitive world. Perhaps we could
also say that although he acknowledged the importance
of narrators, he ultimately forgot the true (artistic)
nature of the myth or tale, which, as a work of art,
derives only from the mind and heart of whoever re-
creates it. But when he restricted his studies to
themes as such--that is, themes as reflected in usages
and customs--didn't he give strength to theories previously forged by Lang and Frazer?

It is also true that Hartland was rather dogmatic.
Nevertheless, the picture that he drew of the popular
narrative was delineated neatly, precisely, persuasively. Not far removed from this picture was his
colleague, J. A. Macculloch, to whom we are indebted
for the brilliant and picturesque *The Childhood of
Fiction*, published in 1905. This work arranged into
fifteen groups (according to such themes as the disembodied soul and the sacrifice of the youngest son)
those characteristic features of tales that could be
related to primitive customs and beliefs.

7. *A. B. Gomme and Childhood Games*

In studying the world of fable (a children's world

where one finds grown-ups), the English anthropologists
agreed that man generally narrates what he sees. They
believed that this was also true for children's games
and rhymes, although narrating, in this case, also includes performing. Man appears to be just barely at
the dawn of life, yet don't his games often seem to
carry us back to primitive society, while his rhymes
document primitive ideals and beliefs? Tylor himself
considered the ethnological aspect of children's games
in *Primitive Culture* and wrote a substantial essay
entitled "The History of Games" (published in *The Fort-
nightly Review*) in order to clarify this aspect, a ven-
ture later undertaken by Lang and Hartland. There were
others who addressed this topic, too. In 1869 Louis
Becq de Fouquiéres wrote *Les jeux des anciens*, in which
he demonstrated how many children's games still found
in folklore (as had been previously illustrated by
Claudius and Arwidson) could be traced back to classical antiquity; and some years later, in 1889, a Frenchman, Édouard Fournier, wrote *Histoire des jouets et des
jeux d'enfants*, in which he reasserted that one could
not write a complete history of civilization without
including a chapter on games and toys.

The credit for outlining this chapter must go to
Alice B. Gomme. On the one hand, she demonstrated an
intelligent, precise philology in collecting the texts,
and on the other hand she enlivened those texts, studying them in light of the principles of the English
anthropological school. Her *Traditional Games of England, Scotland, and Ireland*, published between 1894 and
1898, was primarily a collection of texts. This collection has a rational classification, a clear description of games, an imposing number of variants (whose
importance the author well understood), and an accurate
transcription of the musical motifs accompanying the
lullabies and rhymes. She could be faulted, as Pitrè
said, for limiting her collection to the British Isles,
which undermined the book's intent to discover the
games' origins, relationships, analogies, and deepest
meanings. As Pitrè said, "The analysis of a game,
fairy tale, or riddle cannot be definitively made by
the efforts of only two or three people." But Gomme

attempted to paint a panorama into which one could then introduce specific perspectives, and she was most interested in seeing what the ethnological origin of the games was or might be.

In these childhood games we can see the reconstruction of the drama of life itself as it appeared to the peoples of ancient classical civilizations and, even more importantly, to primitive peoples. Games originate from cults, are the projections of certain customs, and reinvoke the mysteries of matrimony, death, and so on. Consider, for example, the child innocently playing with his spinning top. A Shakespearean critic, George Steevens, said that this toy, once of considerable dimension, was used in the villages "to be whipt in frosty weather, that the peasants might be kept warm by exercise, and out of mischief, while they could not work."[3] Thus, it was an instrument of public usefulness. But isn't it possible, asked Gomme, that the spinning of the top was actually the revival of magical or religious practices? In her opinion "the Totem is really only a top to spin by hand," and "it is not improbable that the tee-totem is the earliest form of top. . . . As its use is for gambling [for example, in *roulette*], it is probable that this and the top were formerly used for purposes of divination."[4] Actually, the first hypothesis does not necessarily exclude the second hypothesis. But now we find, in another village, a group of boys playing *fare il mulinello*, a game in which a lighted match is passed around until it goes out in the hands of one of the children, who then must pay a forfeit. Tylor thought that he recognized a "Manichean atrocity" in this childhood practice. Tylor quotes John of Osun, who said of one Manichean sect, "When they have slain by the worst of deaths a boy, the first-born of his mother, thrown from hand to hand among them by turns, they venerate him in whose hand the child expires as having attained the first dignity

---

[3]Quoted in A. B. Gomme's *The Traditional Games of England, Scotland, and Ireland* (1898; rpt. New York: Dover, 1964), II, 302.
[4]Ibid., p. 303.

of the sect."[5] Gomme, however, is quick to cite "the
old tribal custom of carrying the fiery cross to rouse
the clans. . . . The detention of the fiery cross
through neglect or other impediment was regarded with
much dread by the inhabitants of the place in which it
should occur."[6] Nor is it improbable, she adds, that
the forfeit in this and other games reflects the idea
of ancient ceremonial rites, in which every infraction
of faithfully executed traditional rites was punished.

Research into these comparisons between ancient
customs and modern games was of great interest to
scholars of other countries. For example, in 1897
F. Magnus Böhme produced a comprehensive study,
Deutsches Kinderlied und Kinderspiel, in which the
conclusions of the anthropological school were somewhat tempered (although here, as in his *Geschichte des
Tanzes in Deutschland*, Böhme tended to trace everything
back to the period of German origins). More persuasive
and complete was the work of a Finnish scholar, Yrjö
Hirn, who authored a fine book, *Barnlek*, which was published in 1916 and translated into Italian with the
title *I giuochi dei bimbi*. In this text Hirn attempted
to expand the investigations initiated by Gomme by providing "some chapters on songs, dances, and pageants."
Hirn had a more subtle sensibility than Gomme, and he
was also better prepared, given the enormous amount of
literature at his disposal; he was in a much better
position, then, to shed light on the derivation of
particular games from ancient forms of cults. However,
only in part did he follow the English anthropological
school, to which he referred for the pedagogical concept of games.

Without minimizing the importance of pedagogical
games introduced in kindergartens and nursery schools,
Hirn deplored the fact that these new creations contributed to the demise of older games. Didn't these
games, as Gomme observed, reflect the greatest sim-

[5]*The Origins of Culture* (1871; rpt. New York:
Harper and Row, 1958), p. 77.
[6]*The Traditional Games of England, Scotland, and
Ireland* (1894; rpt. New York: Dover, 1964), I, 259.

plicity of human nature? In those old games children
were able to recapture something of the primitive that
is still in us all. It was because of this that Gomme
published the important two-volume work entitled *Children's Singing Games* in 1894; and it was because of
this that a few years later Edith Harwood extracted
from *Traditional Games* a series of *Old English Singing
Games* to educate Nordic children.

8. *George Laurence Gomme: Folklore Theorist*

Alice Gomme's *Traditional Games of British Children*
provided the first two volumes in a projected "grammar"
of British folklore with which her husband, George
Laurence Gomme, hoped to crown his efforts as organizer
of folklore studies in England. He was not, however,
simply an organizer. Ever since 1878, Gomme, a devoted
disciple of the English anthropological school, was
what we might call the guiding spirit of the Folklore
Society, which attracted, along with Tylor, Frazer,
Lang, and Hartland, a host of scholars who were then
turning to folklore studies in England (although members such as Edward Clodd, Alfred Nutt, and W. R. S.
Ralston did not break into publication). The organ of
this society was the *Folklore Record*, which became the
Folklore Journal in 1883 and then *Folklore* (still in
existence) in 1890. The society compiled a manual
entitled *The Handbook of Folklore*, which Gomme published in 1887, while another manual with the same
title and format was produced by Charlotte Burne some
years later.
     In essence, Gomme and Burne shared in the belief
of the first English folklore theorist, William Thoms,
who had the traditional culture of European peasants
in mind when he coined the term *folklore* in 1846,
after having read the second edition of Grimm's *Mythologie*. Unlike Thoms, however, Gomme and Burne related
this culture to the primitive world (which was and is
the intention of *Folklore*, too). Gomme clarifies this
point by saying that the science of folklore is "the
comparison and identification of the survivals of

archaic beliefs, customs, and traditions in modern ages."[7]

In this clarification is the limitation of the English anthropological school. In light of this definition, the English anthropological school obviously could not include a belief developed in our own times or a song or story spontaneously arising in a present-day peasant as a part of folklore. It was as if to say, let us examine a custom, let us see if it is a survival--and if it is, we can then say that it appertains to folklore. But if it is not, does a folk custom cease to be such? Gomme did not pose this question. His concern was with the peasant's "past," a concern illustrated in his lively little *Ethnology in Folklore*, published in 1892, and in his more celebrated *Folklore as an Historical Science*, published in 1908.

In this latter book Gomme attempted to demonstrate that folklore is "a definite section of historical material"; following a traditional line running from Voltaire to Pitrè, he argued that "pure history was intimately related to folklore at many stages."[8] Although Gomme did not draw all the conclusions embedded in his premise, and although his conception of history was distinctly positivistic, his book intentionally offered a clear admonition: Folklore *as* an Historical Science. This was not merely a matter of saying that folklore is a part of history; rather, it was to say that folklore must be studied with the historical *method*.

[7]*The Handbook of Folklore* (London: David Nutt, 1890), p. 5.

[8]*Folklore as an Historical Science* (London: Methuen, 1908), p. xii.

CHAPTER XXV

THE IMMORTALITY OF FOLKLORE

1. *England and Its Ethnologists of Classical*
   Philology

To complete the picture of the English anthropological
school, we must now cite the work produced by scholars
whose interest was in the specific field of classical
civilizations. These scholars are important because
they advanced the research accomplished or begun in
this field by Tylor, Frazer, Lang, Hartland, and the
Gommes in England and by Mannhardt, Rohde, Usener, and
Dieterich in Germany.

In 1903, a lively and intelligent scholar, Jane
Ellen Harrison, asserted in her *Prolegomena to the*
Study of Greek Religion:

> Greek religion, as set forth in popular handbooks
> and even in more ambitious treatises, is an affair
> mainly of mythology as seen through the medium of
> literature. . . . No serious attempt has been
> made to examine Greek ritual. Yet the facts of
> ritual are more easy definitely to ascertain, more
> permanent, and at least equally significant. What
> a people *does* in relation to its gods must always
> be one clue, and perhaps the safest, to what it
> *thinks*. The first preliminary to any scientific
> understanding of Greek religion is a minute exami-
> nation of its ritual.[1]

[1]*Prolegomena to the Study of Greek Religion*
(Cambridge, England: University Press, 1903),
p. vii.

This was the aim of *Prolegomena*, along with such other works by Harrison as *Themis* (1912) and *Ancient Art and Ritual* (1913). This was also the aim of Lewis Richard Farnell and Arthur Bernard Cook; to the former we owe *The Cults of the Greek States* (published between 1896 and 1909), and to the latter we owe *Zeus* (published between 1914 and 1919). Both Farnell and Cook undertook an examination of Greek cults and rites as if these were concrete facts produced in a specific civilization. Both, however, attempted to clarify cults and rites by means of comparison. Thus, we see that comparison becomes a critical method not only in the field of ethnology but also in the field of folklore.

We could say much the same of a less extensive but more ingenious work than the foregoing, William Ridgeway's *The Origin of Tragedy*, which was published in 1910 with an extensive appendix (published separately some years later as *The Dramas and Dramatic Dances of Non-European Races*). Rohde and Dieterich had advanced the hypothesis (in contrast to Aristotle's opinion) that Greek tragedy could be traced back to the Mysteries. Ridgeway went even further; in his view, the origin of tragedy is related to mimetic dances held in honor of heroes (the illustrious dead, deified people), verified by dances of the same type going on among primitive peoples and by survivals remaining in the modern carnivals of France and Thessaly. Briefly put, the celebration of a death, the death of a deified hero, initially created tragedy, and only later was it linked to the cult of Dionysus. Ridgeway's thesis can be summarized by saying that this cult constituted one aspect of the origin of tragedy, but it was not *the* origin. Arthur Pickard-Cambridge, author of the well-known 1927 work entitled *Dithyramb, Tragedy and Comedy*, correctly identified this thesis as a milestone in the field of classical philology, benefiting ethnology and folklore, especially the folklore of modern Greece.

It was precisely from this scholastic trend that the work of a French scholar, Salomon Reinach, emerged. But whereas the new philological ethnologists turned

to totems and taboos ably and carefully, always staying within the confines of comparison to illustrate
particular institutions under examination, Reinach
made totems and taboos of all that he touched, often
finding them where in fact they did not exist. We
should also add that whereas the new philological
ethnologists reinvoked the past not only for itself
but for what it could add to an understanding of the
present age, Reinach reinvoked the past as if it were
a motionless, fearful shadow.

2. Reinach and Religions

An energetic and impulsive writer, Reinach had published, beginning in 1903, a series of essays in the
Revue Archéologique that attempted to demonstrate
that totemism, taboo, and magic were phenomena found
in all religions. Collected in six volumes entitled
Cultes, mythes et religions (the same title given to
Lang's *Myth, Ritual and Religion* when it was translated into French) and published between 1905 and
1920, these essays were given an appendix in *Orpheus*.
The material treated in these essays was quite varied,
but the very best parts discussed such great pioneers
of folklore as Tylor, Mannhardt, Frazer, and Lang,
whose works Reinach praised and evaluated in a comprehensive, clear-minded, non-prejudicial way. Yet
despite this he had a specific purpose that placed
him at odds with those predecessors whom he had so
highly praised: his purpose was to put to scorn and
ridicule (echoing a phrase from Frazer) all religions,
all cults, all traditions, even though he acknowledged
their validity in certain historical periods.

Believing that man's history is the history of a
progressive secularization, Reinach essentially proposed to conclude this secular progress, announcing
the "good word" of revealed religions: "I am deeply
conscious of the moral responsibility I assume in
giving, for the first time, a picture of all religions
considered purely and simply as natural phenomena.
If I do so, it is because I believe that the times are

ripe for such an essay and that in this, as in other
fields, secular reason must exercise its rights."
Reinach wished, then, to deal with these religions as
a historian. But is it possible for a historian to
consider religions as natural phenomena? After defining religion as a set of scruples hindering the free
exercise of our minds, Reinach adds:

> I have tried to show that animism, on the one hand,
> and taboo, on the other, can be regarded as the
> principal elements of religion and mythology. But
> they are not the only ones: there are some others
> that, although less primitive, have not been any
> less general in their action. . . . The social
> instinct of primitive man, like that of the child,
> readily transcends the limits of species and even
> those of the organic world to which he belongs.
> The illusion of animism makes him recognize every-
> where spirits that are like his own; he makes
> friends and allies of them, and he enters into
> communication with them. This universal tendency
> of the human mind is manifested in fetishism, but
> it is not, as Brosses believed, the worship of
> material objects; rather, it is the friendly com-
> merce of man with those spirits that he believes
> to live within those objects. As a child, before
> I had heard of fetishism, I had a bright blue sea-
> shell that was a veritable fetish to me because I
> thought it contained a protecting spirit. . . .
> Thus, once primitive man has yielded to the ten-
> dency to enlarge almost indefinitely his circle of
> relationships, whether they be real or imagined,
> it is quite natural that he should include within
> it certain animals and vegetables. . . . Soon
> enough a similar scruple protects men and totems
> against caprice and violence, and it seems, to
> those who observe it, to attest their common origin.

Here Reinach was attempting to reconcile Brosses with
Tylor while joining Tylor to Frazer. This "reconcilia-
tion," however, is more apparent than real. Consider,
for example, that Frazer clearly distinguished magic

from religion and regarded taboo as a specific aspect
of magic. Moreover, Reinach wandered from his premise
that taboo is an unmotivated scruple. As Alfred Loisy
reminded him, wasn't taboo quite the opposite? And
with what right could one consider magic as a secondary
phenomenon in respect to the taboo itself?

Just as animism, magic, and taboo do not sufficiently explain the religions that Reinach studied, so
these phenomena--anything but universal--in no way
sufficiently explain superstitions and survivals. We
should grant, however, that he did admit in *Orpheus*,
"Although the system of taboos and totems explains many
things about ancient and modern religions and mythologies, we must guard against believing that it explains
everything." But if we then read the essays collected
in *Cultes, mythes et religions*, we find that he saw
totems and taboos everywhere.

In France the theories of the English anthropological school had found ample application in the works of
Henri Gaidoz and Laurent Bérenger-Féraud. In the first
volume· of the latter's *Superstitions et survivances*,
published in Paris in 1896, one finds the following
definition of a survival: "When a practice, idea, or
formula is introduced into the human community, it
undergoes a continual and infinite modification although it never completely disappears." Reinach, however, consistently embraced a diametrically opposite
attitude. In his view, modifications essentially do
not matter. Now, it is obvious that some criminal
practices are so ingrained in civilization that only
the most intense effort can eradicate them; there are
other practices, however, that serve as a source of
eternal youth and universal poetry--and that, too, is
obvious. All of this had been clearly recognized by
rationalists whom Reinach admired, but (as one who
wished to be a Voltaire but who lacked the stature)
he did not understand or appreciate the point. For
him, all tradition is placed within the same temple,
where everything is then sacrificed in the name of
mankind--even popular traditions, which he basically
regarded as so much worthless trash. Just as Bédier
had dismissed popular literature by saying that he

knew nothing of it, so did Reinach attempt to dismiss
the ethnic tradition by saying that he knew it all too
well. But wasn't he here going beyond the province of
the English anthropological school? And didn't his
evaluative study of survivals follow the principles of
that school?

3. Reinach and the English Anthropological School

There is no doubt that Reinach accepted the narrow
definition of survivals formulated by Tylor, with the
exception that he gave no weight to what the great
English anthropologists called a "revival." Moreover,
his guides, particularly in mythological study, were
Frazer, Lang, and Hartland. Unlike these scholars,
however, he was dogmatic: rather than discussing, he
passed judgment. In a passage in *Orpheus*, for example,
he categorically asserted:

> The worship of animals, like the worship of trees
> and plants, is found in all ancient societies in
> the form of survivals. This is the origin . . .
> of fables that are called *metamorphoses*. When the
> Greeks tell us that Jupiter-Zeus transformed him-
> self into an eagle or a swan, we must recognize an
> inverted myth. The divine eagle and the divine
> swan gave way to Zeus when the Greek gods began to
> be worshipped in human form. Discounting the fact
> that sacred animals remained as attributes or com-
> panions of gods, who sometimes disguised themselves
> in animal form, the metamorphosis of the gods is
> merely a return to their primitive state. Thus,
> the myth of the transformation of Zeus into a swan
> to charm Leda means that at a very remote period a
> Greek tribe had a sacred swan for a god, and they
> believed that this swan had intercourse with mor-
> tals. Later this swan came to be replaced by a
> god in human form, Zeus; but the fable was not for-
> gotten, and it was believed that Zeus turned into
> a swan in order to beget Helen, Castor, and Pollux,
> the children of the divine swan and Leda.

Reinach assumed a similar attitude in the essays in *Cultes*, where he was quick to recognize totemic vestiges in the legends of Orpheus, Athena, Marsyas, Hippolytus, Phaeton, and Adonis and in cults such as the cult of Dionysus. Connections like these had been used by the English anthropological school, of course. Reinach's error, however, was in holding that survivals were bereft of modifications, which amounts to saying they were bereft of life. On the basis of this assumption he went on to explore not only the Greeks and Romans but also the Semites, Hebrews, and Celts. His last stop was Christianity, which in his view is a combination of totems and taboos, two phenomena to which he attributed the origin of sacraments and Christian mysteries (the Eucharist, Baptism, holy water).

But should a historian propose assumptions like these? Rather than seeing whether there are totemic or magic elements in the religions under examination, the historian should characterize the connection between the totemic or magic element and the total conception of the universe to ascertain whether or not the totemic or magical element in such religions stays in a role subordinate to the conception (not a totemic or magic one) of the universe. Reinach was quite removed from these issues, which in one way or the other had plagued all the English anthropologists.

Popular traditions did not have any better luck; in these Reinach saw (and in this respect he was close to G. L. Gomme) only totemism, magic, taboo. He never evaluated these comparisons, never saw the necessity of these phenomena, never caught even a fleeting glimpse of the reason behind their perpetuation. Thus, it is useless to search for a controlling idea in the connections that he did make. In the English anthropological school such comparisons, even when they became merely ethnographical parallels, were inspired by two interests: an interest in the primordial that is within each of us and an interest in all human things, wherever they may be found. In vain does one search in his works for any effort to understand why the primitive within us may be an ever-living ideal.

It has been said that if Reinach had done what the

English anthropologists did--if he had tried to understand the primitive mentality operating in the primitive's incessant search for the truth, *his* truth--he
would have seen the intimate workings of a will, a
deep reason, in totems and taboos. Reinach, however,
was miles away from even imagining such a spiritual
reconstruction, which is the only thing that will let
us understand the mentality of primitive peoples in
relation to the mentality of Western civilizations.
He accumulated curiosities, anecdotes, facts upon
facts--an extensive bibliography of ever-so-deceptive
details. In the last analysis, the English anthropological school could not have had a worse disciple.

4.   *The Last Classicist of the English Anthropological School: Marett*

The previous point was aptly made by one of the most
perceptive members of the English anthropological
school, R. R. Marett. On the one hand, Marett's work
offers the most open condemnation of Reinach's "castles in the air"; on the other hand, his work provides
the legitimate conclusion to an entire movement of
studies that attempted to rise from the labyrinth of
naturalism to a profitable and productive historicism.
In a touching commemoration to Andrew Lang,
Marett lets us know the nature and extent of the inspiration he received from his reading of *Custom and
Myth*. This work argued for the anthropological trend
that Tylor had introduced to the scholarly world, and
Tylor would become one of Marett's spiritual guides.
What most appealed to Marett were Lang's polemics,
his impetuousness, his practice of thinking about
ethnology and folklore as characters of a drama in
which he himself directly participated in order to
become contemporaneous with antiquity.
Although Marett's first interests were primarily
ethnological, these initial sympathies opened the
door to ethnology and folklore. When Marett went on
to folklore, then, he had already served his apprenticeship, in addition to having studied ancient,

modern, and contemporary philosophy. In his work,
written in the composed style of a classicist, we hear
echoes of this preparation and perceive his motivation
as a search for truth provided, as he said, by the
litterae humaniores.

Unlike his predecessors, Marett did not write any
monumental works. His volumes (books which seem to
suggest he could only write *Anthropology*) are simply
collections of essays. As an essayist--and in this
respect he was very similar to Lang--he belongs to the
same English tradition that produced Thomas Browne.
His 1909 volume, *The Threshold of Religion*, is an important ethnological text containing three now-famous
essays: the first is "Pre-Animistic Religion," originally published in *Folklore* in 1900; the second is
"From Spell to Prayer," originally published in *Folklore* in 1904; and the third is entitled "Is Taboo a
Negative Magic?" which appeared in the *Anthropological
Essays* presented to E. B. Tylor in honor of his seventy-
fifth birthday. Basic to the study of folklore is his
Psychology and Folklore, published in 1920; this collection includes a 1914 essay, "The Interpretation of
Survivals," which is the very heart of the book. Other
collections of essays that are of interest to folklore
and ethnology include *Faith, Hope and Charity in Primitive Religion* (1932), *Sacraments of Simple Folk* (1933),
and *Head, Heart and Hands in Human Evolution* (1935).

In these works Marett is fairly close to what I
would call a traditional concept of social anthropology,
"the whole history of man as fired and pervaded by the
idea of evolution"[2]--even though obviously the "whole
history" of man is not a matter of evolution but of an
unfolding of life in all its vicissitudes. Nevertheless, he was convinced that anthropology "is science
in whatever way history is science; that it is not
philosophy, though it must conform to its needs."[3]
In comparison with his predecessors, this was a notable
step forward, when we consider that, influenced as he

[2]*Anthropology* (London: Williams and Norgate,
n.d.), p. 1.
[3]Ibid., p. 12.

was by the concept of history previously reasoned out
by Hegel--of a history that is at one with philosophy
--Marett did not confuse philosophy with the evolutionistic history of man. Indeed, the difference between
Marett and his predecessors consists precisely in the
fact that he viewed the theory of evolution as merely
a working hypothesis. We should add that he believed
there was no such thing as different *kinds* of history:
the history of religion, ethnology, and folklore needed
no other aim than the pursuit of truth. He asserted
that the anthropologist must be a historian, although
the meaning he gave to the word *anthropologist* is somewhat misleading. Caught in the midst of these issues,
Marett was trapped in the ambiguities of scientific
terminology in his attempts to restore lines of connection between history and science. It was then fashionable to debate whether science was the basis of history
or history the basis of science, and it was forgotten
that only when science is understood as "philosophy" is
it the basis of history and therefore ethnology. This
"forgetfulness" was Marett's failing, at least in the
history of religion, his preferred field of study.

5. The Concept of Preanimism

Marett's name is linked to the theory of preanimism.
According to this theory, there was in the primitive
mentality something more indeterminate than and psy-
chologically anterior to animism: "Here we seem to
have a case of that very wide-spread notion of which
the most famous representatives are the *mana* . . .
and the *orenda*. . . . It would appear that the root-
idea is that of power . . . tending to be conceived
as a psychic energy, almost, in fact, as what we would
call 'will power.'"[4] Here we obviously find ourselves
confronted with an attitude similar to that of Tylor,
Frazer, and Lang. Marett was also concerned with discovering which phenomena preceded which, and like

[4]*The Threshold of Religion,* 3rd ed. (London:
Metheun and Co., 1913), p. 86.

Tylor (as well as Brosses, Comte, and Spencer), he
wished to provide at least a minimum definition of
religion.

Although Marett did not deny the vitality of animism, his desire to provide a minimum definition of
religion was his motive for relating *mana* to taboo,
and he explained this latter term not with the mechanical concept of negative magic but rather with the
concept of *mana*. His point was that magic is not a
web of illusion, nor is it merely an association of
ideas; rather, it is a creation of a mind strongly
engaged by the will to believe or to act. This blow
was aimed at Frazer, but he was not the only one in
this battle; contemporaneously the French anthropological school, founded by Émile Durkheim, was committed both to bringing about the downfall of Tylor's
theory of animism and to crushing the thesis that
primitive mentality is imbued only with illusory
associations, an idea that Frazer had sustained
throughout the course of his work.

Durkheim had initiated the publication of the
Année Sociologique in 1892. But it was in his 1912
volume, the substantial *Les formes élémentaires de la
vie religieuse*, that he formulated his own concept of
the origin of religion, which was based on many ethnological sources. The origin of religion, he said,
coincides with man's first involvement with totemism.
Actually, this was not a new idea, nor was the idea of
a blend of totemism, religion, and magic, which he had
placed in the sphere of preanimism (considered by
Marett as a blend of religion and magic). Durkheim,
however, had rooted this concept in the first social
phase of man's history. Both Marett and Durkheim,
then, placed magic and religion on the same intellectual level, regardless of which came first, and both
agreed that an institution could not be built on a
lie. But wasn't this another blow aimed at Frazer
(even though Frazer had perceived elements of truth
in that lie)?

In posing the problem of the origin of religion,
both Marett and Durkheim unfortunately relapsed into
research about what comes first and what comes later,

a trap they had avoided in treating magic in respect
to religion and *vice versa*. Because of this, their
research concluded in abstractions and classifications,
nor did their work become speculative and historio-
graphical, as they had intended. In the final analysis, the essence of religion eluded them both. Needless to say (as Hegel warned), he who goes in search
of the irreducible by turning to mankind's past ends
up by abandoning the human world itself. Marett's and
Durkheim's error was in elevating psychological and
sociological research, respectively, to historical
phases. Durkheim followed the false trail of a sociology that excluded the contribution of psychology,
whatever it might have been. Marett, on the other
hand, started along the path of a psychology that he
tended to confuse with philosophy. But if psychology
(rather than philosophy and therefore history) led him
to pose the problem of religion in an anti-historical
fashion, psychology also helped him understand the
concept of survivals.

6. *The "Survival" in the Light of Historical
    Judgment*

The English had made the concept of the survival a
veritable tool of research. We should not forget, of
course, that when Tylor contrasted the "revival" (as
he called it) to the "survival," he intended to under-
score the immortal character of folklore. Still,
Tylor and his successors often failed to evaluate the
nature of the survival in its modern form. Now understand, no one wishes to deny that folklore has many
survivals which are in effect the residue or, to use
a linguistic term, the "detritus" of a world lost to
us, or at least distant from us. But does the fact
that survivals are the detritus of a lost world dis-
qualify them from being a relevant part of the modern
world in which we live? If this were the case, we
might as well say that the dream, religion, and
morality of contemporary man are not his but the ones
of his ancestors.

Marett entered the field of battle precisely for
the purpose of defending this concept, and if his
voice was not a new one in the field of social anthropology, it was certainly an imposing force   The English anthropologists were moving to a study of dead
things, fossils--and in doing so they discovered things
that were full of life. We should add that as early
as 1900 two authoritative representatives of the
French sociological school, Henri Hubert and Marcel
Mauss, in their *Étude sommaire de la représentation du
temps dans la religion et la magie*, had sustained the
thesis that although some folkloristic traditions do
indeed die, others are, to use their term, rejuvenated.
This rejuvenation makes folklore immortal--as immortal
as the life of which it is an eternal and universal
expression.

Perhaps because they were primarily engaged in
ethnological research, the French sociologists regarded
folklore as merely an appendix to ethnography or, to be
more precise, ethnology. It was against this idea that
Marett particularly rebelled. In a passage in his *Psychology and Folklore*, he observed:

We go about collecting odd bits of contemporary
culture which seem to us to be more or less out of
place in a so-called civilized world, and are exceedingly apt to overlook the truth that for old-
fashioned minds the old fashions are as ever new.
Now, of course, I am not against the study of
origins. By all means let us try, so far as we
can, to refer back this or that obsolescent institution or belief to some more or less remote
past, reconstituted by means of the supposed
analogies provided by backward peoples of to-day,
among whom similar institutions or beliefs are
seen to exist in full working order. But to make
this the sole concern of folk-lore is to subordinate it as a mere appendix to the anthropology of
savages. . . . But this unequal state of things
can assuredly be remedied, if we folk-lorists will
only realize our opportunities. I am convinced
that folk-lore, if developed along the right lines,

can teach the anthropology of savages as much as
the anthropology of savages can teach folk-lore.[5]

This idea had previously been expressed by Mannhardt
and discussed by Frazer. But this is not why folklore
is not an appendix to ethnography or ethnology. The
object of a folklorist's investigation, the object of
his critical discernment, is a specific folkloristic
fact, which is his starting point. In other words, he
begins with an interest in present life, which spurs
him to investigate a past fact that in his own mind is
still regarded as being present. The same is true for
the ethnologist, who begins with an ethnological fact
that then becomes a living part of his own consciousness. Could we therefore say that both folklore and
ethnology are to be considered as appendices to history? Obviously not, for history is the mirror, we
could say, of all "mental" life, in which there are no
appendices but only living, mutually integrated parts.
The folklorist only studies one part of this mental
life. But in undertaking the study of a custom,
belief, or superstition, the folklorist must first see
what the new life *is* that these customs, beliefs, and
superstitions have created.

The task of the folklorist, Marett adds, is not
only to examine the old, which had been the intent of
his predecessors and the doctrine of G. L. Gomme and
Burne, but also to integrate the old with the new.
The demand that the folklorist must make of himself
is not that of considering the survival as merely an
aspect of the past, since the past is contained within
the present, and even the most contemporary present
recedes into the past; rather, the folklorist must
come to see where and how a survival exists. Marett
adds that no historical judgment can stand on the
principle of analogy, because the mind that receives
present facts exists in present conditions, which in
effect causes each survival to be a revival. Of
course a fact can also have its precedents in the

[5]*Psychology and Folklore* (London: Methuen and Co.,
1920), pp. 13-14.

ancient mind in which that fact once lived; but in
order to continue living, the fact must find an adaption (and therefore a legitimate existence) in the mind
of whoever revives it.

On the other hand, it is obvious that, in the field
of folklore, everything that dies comes back to life in
a different form, thus completing the cycle. When a
superstition (or survival) has lost its original meaning, it assumes a new one, or else it would not indeed
survive. It is vain to delude oneself, as did G. L.
Gomme, with the thought that a man acquires a specific
"habit" through a custom that is itself an unconscious
survival of a totemic cult. It will become a survival,
we must repeat, only if man *believes* in that habitual
action, only if he has faith in it. It is this faith
that must most certainly count.

7. The Importance of the Individual in Ethnology

Starting from the viewpoint of psychology, Marett
arrived at one of the most important principles controlling the life of folklore, one that the folklorist
cannot overlook in interpreting and evaluating folklore
itself. Nor was this the extent of Marett's historical
interest in folklore. In its incessant labor, the
French sociological school had emphasized the collective forces governing society. In Germany, Moritz
Lazarus and Heymann Steinthal had energetically argued
(1) that it is useless to assert the dependency of the
individual on his environment if one has no knowledge
of that environment; (2) that because this is so, one
must obtain information about all fields of human endeavor; (3) and that if one wishes to understand art,
literature, language, and religion, one must consider
these as collective manifestations. It was with these
premises that Wundt later began his work; he restricted
his *Völkerpsychologie* to the study of language, myth,
and custom, and he linked Bastian and Waitz with Lazarus and Steinthal in order to construct a collective
psychology that would explain historical and social
developments. Wundt excluded any possibility that

the individual could be the truly operative cause of
social evolution. Durkheim went even further; he was
convinced that psychological induction was insufficient
to explain such social "facts" as art and custom, whose
specialized characteristics result from a combination
of objective elements rather than a combination of contributions by individuals. This was the basis of
Lucien Lévy-Bruhl's study of primitive mentality, to
which French sociologists referred in their studies of
religion and magic (Hubert, Mauss, Hertz), law (Davy,
Huvelin), and art (Guyau).

In contrast to the conclusions drawn by the French
sociologists, who salvaged and restored the remains of
Comtian philosophy in light of a revised *Volksgeist*,
the English anthropological school had essentially
worked on the basis of an individual psychology, implicitly accepting Western Civilization's Christian and
humanistic tradition and its emphasis on the spirit of
individualism. Tylor and Frazer never denied the contribution that the individual savage made to his society through his inventions, creations, and influence.
Moreover, Frazer maintained that one must never exclude
a priori the explanation that a peasant can provide
about a custom, which is always the result of a personal interpretation. This was not to deny, after all,
the importance of society in the field of ethnology or
folklore; rather, it was to assert that the collective
consciousness and the individual consciousness are
inherently related.

It was to this principle that Marett returned. In
his *Anthropology* he said:

> The man of high individuality, then, the excep-
> tional man, the man of genius, be he man of thought,
> man of feeling, or man of action, is no accident
> that can be overlooked by history. On the contrary,
> he is in no small part the history-maker; and, as
> such, should be treated with due respect by the
> history-compiler. The "dry bones" of history, its
> statistical averages, and so on, are all very well
> in their way; but they correspond to the superfi-
> cial truth that history repeats itself. . . .

Anthropology, then, should not disdain what might
be termed the method of the historical novel. To
study the plot without studying the characters
will never make sense of the drama of human life.[6]

The concept that Marett had formulated about survivals
did not exclude society, but neither did it exclude the
individual. His attitude here paralleled that of philologists who rightly claimed that the origin of songs,
tales, and stories belonged to specific individuals.
Too, he believed that the individual contribution to
the ethnic tradition gave that tradition a sense of
perennial creativity--and in this respect European
peasants are comparable to primitives. Perhaps this
is one of the reasons that he refuted the conclusions
reached by Lévy-Bruhl, who, unlike the English anthropological school and the French sociological school,
questioned the uniformity of logical thought in cultured and primitive man.

8. Marett vs. Reinach

The conclusions reached by Marett constitute the positive aspects of the English anthropological school,
just as Reinach's conclusions represent the negative.
This suggests that, despite similar initial premises,
the theories of the English anthropological school and
its followers cannot be reduced to a common denominator.
   In his *Naturalismo e storiasmo nell' etnologia*,
Ernesto de Martino has correctly observed:

   The old ethnology, inspired by the Lucretian
   "Tantum religio potuit suadere malorum," contained
   a fairly obvious argument directed against the
   aberrations of superstitions and intended to
   accomplish, for those concerned, a dissipation of
   mental fog by bringing in the light of "science."
   At times it is possible to catch the newly en-

[6]*Anthropology*, p. 242.

lightened advocates of positivism in the posture
of a Dantean navigator who "gazes at the perilous
water" from a safe shore or, to switch metaphors,
in the posture of a worshipper of *Raison*, one
scornful of the web of illusion and error in the
succession of pathological mental attitudes characterizing primitive man.

This, as we have seen, was precisely Reinach's posture.
But while other anthropologists such as Tylor, Frazer,
Lang, the Gommes, and Marett may have begun with similar premises, they reached an altogether opposite conclusion: although considering animism, magic, or
preanimism as the basis of religion or as the source
of specific powers, they concluded by seeing the well-
spring of morality, law, and art in peoples' traditions.
We might say, using Vico's phrase, that they came to
see the (historical) process through which the sons of
Polyphemus became *Scipiones Africani* (magicians became
king, magic became science, and totemism became art).
 Thus, the anthropological school offered folklore,
the *history* of folklore, the most valid chart for navigation. And if it is true (as it partially is) that
the English anthropologists did not justly value the
poetic nature of popular literature, it is equally
true that they clearly viewed the most troublesome
problems of folklore from a broad, comprehensive perspective. Humanists by education and Enlightenment
thinkers by inclination, they unintentionally romanticized primitive peoples, classical civilizations, the
"multitude" found within civilized nations. In their
enthusiasm for embracing not merely Europe but the
world, not merely Aryan civilizations but those of
primitive peoples--always in the name of our own
civilization, in which they placed all their faith--
these citizens of a colonial empire believed it
possible to realize the founding of a true inter-
nationalism in which, regardless of race and color,
each nation was called to participate, in the name of
man.

PART SIX

ASPECTS OF FOLKLORE IN THE LAST FIFTY YEARS

CHAPTER XXVI

THE STRUGGLE OF HISTORY

1. *The Historical-Cultural School*

Despite its evolutionistic schemes, the English anthropological school clearly tried (at times successfully)
to historicize both ethnology and folklore. This task
was assumed with even greater zeal by another school,
now known as the historical-cultural school. An
Italian folklorist, Giuseppe Vidossi, recently noted:

> This school, whose precursors and masters include
> Fr. Ratzel, L. Frobenius, W. Foy, and F. Graebner,
> author of the highly significant *Essay on Ethno-
> logical Methodology*, operates on the concept of
> the single origin and successive propagation of
> cultural elements through cultural *relationships*,
> from which it deduces the necessity of establish-
> ing the geographical area of each element in order
> to recognize objectively the stratification which
> appertains and to discover, therefore, the chron-
> ology. Cases of polygenesis, of consequences
> independent of cultural contacts, are possible,
> sometimes even probable. But the hypothesis of
> multiple origins of phenomena, which is in con-
> trast to historical experience, as a rule lacks
> demonstrability that it can ever become a method-
> ological principle, nor is it in any sense exempt
> from the obligations of historico-geographical
> research. What is valid in the ethnological field
> is even more valid in the demological field, where
> presumedly primitive elements variously intertwine
> with others of literary derivation, with the

result that in all cases research is absolutely
indispensable for disentangling them.

Vidossi was here referring to Willy Foy's introduction
to Fritz Graebner's *Methode der Ethnologie* (1911),
wherein one finds the essential guidelines for the
historical-cultural school. In this introduction, Foy
maintained that the norms of the historical-cultural
school were valid for the ethnologist and the folklorist, a point that he had occasion to insist upon
when he reviewed Samter's *Geburt, Hochzeit und Tod*
a year later.

In believing that *Kulturgeschichte* (the concept
that he was so insistent on) embraces all forms of
the nation's spiritual and institutional life, Foy
essentially adopted the teachings of Johann Droysen,
even though he always remained trapped in the network
of a single universal history. Droysen had asserted
that the historian, in doing his spade-work, must
account for discovered remains, including usages and
customs, which are merely the products of history.
His admonition was that we must study folklore with
the method of ethnology--with, that is, the historical
method. But, we should ask, to what degree can the
historical-cultural school be useful to the folklorist? And to what degree can the science of folklore
travel along the pathways traced by this school?

2. *The Precursor of the Historical-Cultural School: Ratzel*

The historical-cultural school is based on two essential postulates: (1) the resolution of history in the
spatial, temporal, and causal order of facts and (2)
the overthrow of the old evolutionistic ethnology,
thanks to the elaboration of a research method that is
accurate in all details. The first step in the formulation of these postulates was provided by a humanistic
geographer, Friedrich Ratzel. In his famous *Anthropo-
geographie* he proposed revising the direction of ethnography, "leading it to consider man's movements on

the face of the earth." He then underscored an important fact: environmental influences on man should not
make us forget that man also influences the environment.

This was the central idea of one of Ratzel's most
important essays, "Geschichte, Völkerkunde und historische Perspektive." Convinced that man is always
a part of the land and that geography must always guide
us in ethnographical and folkloristic research, Ratzel
rebelled against the criteria of the English anthropological school in this essay, vigorously arguing that
in ethnology, too, one needs to search for historical
links among various civilizations, since modifications
are explained only by areas of propagation. However,
he did agree with the English anthropological school
on the essential point that it is absurd to consider
primitives outside of history, a point that had been
made by both Bastian and Hegel. Granting this principle, Ratzel combined geography with history in such a
way that ethnographical research would proceed along
these two parallel lines. This was basically the
method that had previously entered into the folkloristic philology of Schwartz and Krohn by way of Riehl.
Nor should we forget that in the field of ethnic
studies Mannhardt had come close to this method in his
Wald- und Feldkulte.

In ethnic studies, the most effective exponent of
this method was Wilhelm Pessler, who published a still-
fundamental work, *Das altsächsische Bauernhaus in
seiner geographischen Verbreitung*, in 1906. In studying the rustic architecture of lower Germany, he complemented geographical research by using maps to indicate diffusion. Pessler also sustained and applied
this method in a series of interesting volumes,
including *Beiträge zur vergleichenden Volkskunde
Niedersachsens* (1910) and *Plattdeutscher Wortatlas
von Nordwestdeutschland* (1928).

But what were the results of Pessler's efforts?
Erich Röhr, one of the most authoritative critics in
German folklore, said of him, "Pessler has revealed
his ideas in the essay 'Deutsche Volkstumsgeographie';
however, he is mostly concerned with the profit we can

extract from maps for a knowledge of the facts of 'life,' if we must say so, by means of the cartograph- ical representation of broad collections of materials. But only from a knowledge of such 'life' is it possible to extract the methodological presuppositions and the necessary guarantees for a full interpretation of demo- logical maps." In other words, the importance of cartography and areas of diffusion cannot be denied, but the historian must go further. To hold that this should be the actual field of study rather than simply one of the methods facilitating that study is to for- get, as Röhr rightly points out, that geography is not and can never be history.

3. *Graebner's "Methode"*

In his effort to link geography to history, Ratzel had criticized the limitations of Bastian's theory, which maintained that elementary ideas are the primitive psychological base of all cultures. Does it necessar- ily follow, Ratzel asked, that differentiations and interventions are manifestations only of a later stage of development? Or do such differentiations and inter- ventions also exist among primitives, which Bastian held to be outside history? It may be true, moreover, that written sources do not exist in the materialistic primitive culture, but this culture itself deserves examination. In his 1887 study of African bows, Ratzel came to the conclusion that similar objects found in quite distant territorial zones suggest a historical-genetic connection. This led to his cri- terion of "quality," which was later complemented with the criterion of "form" by a disciple of his, Leo Frobenius, while investigating the origin of African civilization, his area of specialization, in 1898. Ratzel himself was quite interested in studying the ways in which different ideas were related to a common source. Frobenius believed that such a relation is extended to an entire complex of cultural phenomena, as expressed in material, social, and mythological elements.

It was precisely with these sources that Fritz
Graebner began his work. Considering ethnology as a
"study of the human spirit," he, as a good historian,
acknowledged the importance of the individual in this
study, while he attempted to maintain a distinction
between history and natural sciences. On this subject
Schmidt observes:

> If ethnology is the science of the human spirit,
> its method must also be that of the science of the
> human spirit, not the method of the natural sci-
> ences. It should have the effect of accounting
> for and appraising the person, the individual,
> free will--elements that too often appear to be
> submerged in the masses, even though talents and
> geniuses actually work effectively within the
> "content" of the masses in much the same way that
> leaders do in "form." This method must be able
> to comprehend the single person, the individual,
> along with the collective, and it must not concern
> itself with only the typical or the average; it
> must be ideographic, and it must be conceived and
> equipped to understand and appreciate the indi-
> vidual.

Graebner thus completely rejected the problematical
approach that had been worked out by the French sociological school in opposition to the English anthropological school. In his opinion the individual is not
only the maker of society (in this case, primitive
society) but also of history. This premise would
become the insignia of the historical-cultural school,
which, we should add, openly opposed the English
anthropological school, or at least its evolutionistic
principles.
     In Graebner's view, it was absurd to maintain that
the development of mankind proceeds from the lower to
the higher in all fields and that human development
always follows an ascending line; judgments of whether
something is lower or higher are largely value judgments so subjective as to invalidate the historian's
knowledge. Although there is perhaps a confusion of

terms here, there is no doubt that we are also hearing
the last gasp of the historian who considers history
to be the sole form of knowledge. As a matter of fact,
the English anthropological school *did* use such schemes
(or such philosophy, it would perhaps be better to say)
to establish such ascendant processes as monotheism
(which arises from humanism) and religion (which arises
from magic). However, it would be equally absurd, as
we have seen, to lock the English anthropological
school within those schemes, which merely served to
spur their very productive labors.

Although we cannot indiscriminately attribute to
the anthropological school all the defects that Graebner attributed to it, the English anthropological
school certainly did construct its theories on the
basis of an undifferentiated primitive mentality.
But, Graebner insistently asked, was primitive man
really like that? Or was the culture of primitive
peoples (who can be found living in the world even
today) characterized by different strata or cycles of
civilization?

4. *Ethnological Philology*

To determine the variety of primitive life and to
clarify the problem of cultural cycles previously
posed by Ratzel and Frobenius, Graebner took the
stance of a precept-maker; he offered ethnology the
tools, the working hypotheses, for examining the savages' world, in which one could establish various cultural cycles, the developmental phases of a specific
element within these cycles, and the oldest forms of
an object or belief relative to other forms. This
precept-maker was comprehensive and complex in his
formulation and in his details. Graebner's first step
was to set down criteria of verification for cultural
areas co-existing in time and place:

> When two cultural zones of different character
> meet, they may be superimposed upon one another
> in the contact-zone, thus creating some mixed

forms, or they may only enter into marginal relationships, creating phenomena of contact. . . .
At times single cultural elements form a very
homogeneous organic combination in a particular
determined zone, which makes it easy to recognize
similarities with other particular zones. . . .
At other times certain cultural elements that do
not seem to be closely related nevertheless appear
constantly, even in different zones, in more or
less intimate union. It is then a matter of cultural cycles of more ancient date.

It is with this last criterion that one can proceed
to an examination of geographically co-existing cultural cycles. Briefly put, Graebner attempted to create a genuine philology to replace the written documents
of history. As Ernesto de Martino correctly says, the
reason that

the historical-cultural school has deserved well of
ethnology is primarily because of the great philological exactness that it has established in such
research. Although philological exactness may not
be history, it *is* a precious commodity, a solid
guarantee against tricks of the imagination and the
intrusion of sentiment. No one can contest that in
this area the exactness of ethnological information
is now much more advanced than it used to be. To
restore the exact words of a text, to specify
interpolations, to establish attributions and origins, to reconstruct genealogies, to distinguish
successive editions of a work, to determine the
chronological order of succession of a series of
texts--in a word, to exercise with alacrity a
rigorous, objective textual criticism--is a
fatiguing yet indispensable heuristic necessity.

5. *Ethnological Interpretations*

Although folkloristic philology had nothing to learn
from Graebner, in many respects ethnological philology

continued his approach. Unlike the ethnologist, however, the folklorist operates in clearly established
historical environments, and he certainly has many
other tools at his disposal. The ascertaining of
cycles or areas of diffusion is used to establish a
fact already illustrated by the science of folklore--
the fact that a custom can assume an animistic character in one civilization, a totemic character in a
second civilization, a magical character in a third,
or none of these in a fourth.

A second point should be made. There is no real
justification, Graebner argued, for assuming that
"equal phenomena must have equal meanings." On this
point he categorically asserted that the task of the
historian (and therefore, we could say with Foy, the
task of the ethnologist and folklorist) must be to
interpret without any preconceptions, which, as
Droysen says, is a good way to understand research.
As Droysen explains, "Each interpretation generally
allows for prudent, sharp criticism. First, the
evidence for the explanation must be ascertained in
all its critical fullness; secondly, the fact thus
proved must be so formally or ideally analogous to
the one under interpretation that a false step would
be impossible or at least improbable; lastly, points
of comparison must be clear. . . . Most facts reach
the highest degree of capacity for interpretation
only when they belong to a cultural unity of time
and place."

This was yet another blow aimed at the English
anthropological school. But despite his criticism
of Frazer, Graebner himself loyally acknowledged
that when Frazer's explanations "are consciously or
unconsciously restricted to a specific cultural
context, the results rightfully deserve to be accepted with some degree of confidence." But can't
what he says of Frazer be extended, within limits,
to all the representatives of the English anthropological school? And is it always necessary to
explain all analogies with their reciprocal influences, giving no acknowledgment to the fact that they
can also arise spontaneously?

6. *"Father" Schmidt: Ethnologist and Historian of Folklore*

The ideas of Graebner, a solid but difficult writer, were resumed in a minor, speculative way by Wilhelm Schmidt, who was to become the major representative of the historical-cultural school. As one of the best ethnologists Europe has ever had, he energetically confronted the problems of cultural cycles--their ascertainment and their historical validity according to criteria of time and place. Nor did he overlook the problematical nature of folklore in his investigations, as is demonstrated in his essay "Die kulturhistorische Methode in der Ethnologie," published in 1911 in *Anthropos* (a journal that has significantly advanced ethnological and folkloristic studies) and even more especially in his *Handbuch der Methode der kulturhistorischen Ethnologie*, published in 1937 (but preceded by a 1924 work, *Völker und Kulturen*, which he wrote in collaboration with Wilhelm Koppers).

In these essentially theoretical works, Schmidt consistently claimed that the historical-cultural school is the sister or, better still, the daughter of history, its principal end being historical certainty and its methodology being the historical method. These categorical assertions, however, did not prevent his making distinctions among sources, which he believed could be immediate or derived in respect to origins, while they could be quite alive and actual in respect to their gnoseological value. Nor did it prevent him from asserting that ethnology indeed has its own characteristics: "As Graebner has said, few sciences have as perfect a method at their disposal as history. Now, naturally, this is also to the benefit of ethnology; *however, as a special branch of all historical science, ethnology certainly has its own characteristics*, which require special consideration in regard to method. . . ."

Schmidt was convinced that the method for learning about philosophy must be distinguished from the method for learning about historical knowledge. His reason was that philosophy proceeds from the facts of experi-

ence as furnished by nature and history, but it prefers
to find causality in the remote and general rather than
in the concrete and near-at-hand. Marett had taken
this approach to the extreme, as had other English
anthropologists before him; for them philosophy, specifically the history of philosophy rather than evolutionistic philosophy, had taught that theory is most
important for telling us what is "thought"--and thought
cannot exist outside philosophy.

After battling with the anthropological school
(although he did not really go any further than Graebner in this battle), Schmidt took aim at Mannhardt.
In his *Volkskunde und Völkerkunde*, Arthur Haberlandt,
a serious and well trained Austrian historian and
scholar, had asserted that Mannhardt had anticipated
"a good part of the methodological foundation of folklore and comparative ethnology--that is, the ethnological method of Graebner." Schmidt, who usually was very
polite in judging the theories of others, responded
indignantly, "It would be extraordinary indeed if folklore had so quickly apprehended the historical-cultural
method." Continuing in his indignation, he pointed to
the works of Spamer, Maurer, and Schier, which were
published under Spamer's general editorship in an
extensive collection entitled *Die deutsche Volkskunde*,
to which Spamer added the following note: "The
geographical-cultural branch with the excellent application of cartography was primarily created by W.
Pessler." It is true that Pessler's activity began
in 1906, before Graebner's *Methode* was published.
However, Ratzel's essay "Geschichte, Völkerkunde und
historische Perspektive" had been published in 1893,
and Pessler was therefore only a part of the picture.
Despite all of this, Schmidt was quick to acknowledge:

> Historical investigation has so rapidly reached
> such height because of particularly favorable
> conditions. This fruit matured in Finnish schol-
> ars' research into the origins of their national
> epopee, the *Kalevala*. While such older scholars
> as Lönnrot, J. Krohn and others inherited an
> evolutionistic-naturalistic viewpoint for explain-

ing these origins, research then came to be perfected under J. Krohn and, later still, K. Krohn
in a fully historical investigation that traveled
the transitional path from a geographical approach
to a purely historical one. Thus, they could
demonstrate that the *Kalevala* in its present form
did not originate in prehistoric pagan times but
in the transitional period between paganism and
Christianity.

It is curious that Schmidt did not have the same
reservations about Julius Krohn that he had about
Mannhardt, which suggests that one detail had eluded
him: although the historical-cultural school used the
historical method, it did not necessarily follow that
it came from the historical-cultural school, because
history itself had provided the criterion of interpretation for folklore. This is precisely why history
and the historical method had given such life and vigor
to the works of the Grimms, Pitrè, Mannhardt, and
Dieterich.

In the final analysis, Schmidt was convinced that
"the lower strata of folk correspond generally to
primitive peoples," the basis of his implied principle
that ethnology, as an interpretive criterion for folklore, can legitimately be taken to its own level of
historical thought. If the methodology of folklore is
historical and if ethnology is pure history, can we
disregard results in the specific field of ethnology
given to us by the historical-cultural school?

7. *Belief in God*

No one could now deny that through its ethnological
findings the historical-cultural school provided what
was, in effect, a new vision of the primitive world.
One thinks of Schmidt's great work, *Der Ursprung der
Gottesidee*, the true "Bible" of primitive peoples,
about whom he reached the following conclusions:
today there are some primitive peoples whose culture
documents the most remote antiquity of man, truly

primitive man, on earth; belief in God exists among
these people, and therefore we have a belief in God
at our very origins. This was the conclusion to which
ethnology, which Schmidt had contrasted to history,
inevitably led.

As we can see, we here have a theory that rejected
earlier theories about the origin of religion, aligned
itself with theistic positions that Tylor, Frazer, and
Durkheim had refused to accept, and posed a purely
religious and religiously pure belief at our origins:
the belief in God. But can we actually say that an
isolatable belief in God existed at our origins? And
is God indeed the product of causal logical thought,
as Schmidt imagined?

In this respect, Schmidt was complementing the
"second" Lang. Actually, Lang had hesitated to define
deities as Supreme Beings. Schmidt, however, offered
precisely this definition, observing that even among
the most ethnologically ancient peoples God was regarded as the creator, omnipotent and all-seeing. Nor
should we forget that in Schmidt's view, as in Lang's,
the most ancient form of religion, with its fundamental
belief in God, is essentially different from myth because of its association with the world of rational
thought; the God of the "ultra-primitives," that is,
answers to a rational conception of cause. "The need
for a rational cause," Schmidt observes, "is fulfilled
by the certainty of a Supreme Creator of the world and
man."

Now, it is clearly to Schmidt's credit that he
ascertained a belief in God among the primitives, a
line of thought that the historical-cultural school
followed with excellent results. Besides, no one
could doubt that the religious moment appears, in one
way or the other, in the human consciousness in all
times and places. But the exact aspect that this
moment had assumed in the beginning is and will continue to be hypothetical--or an act of faith. This
is so because it is impossible to submit any thesis
about a "first age" to historical judgment, since this
thesis leads one arbitrarily to assume one moment or
aspect in the course of history as the necessary

condition (the *only* necessary condition) of all else.
It is one thing to establish that a concept may be
disseminated throughout the world, but it is quite
another matter to assert that this concept rests at
the base of the institution with which it is associated.

In placing a belief in God instead of fetishism,
animism, or preanimism at the origins of religion,
Schmidt fell into the same evolutionistic thinking that
he had opposed. His, however, is an evolutionism in
reverse. To strengthen his findings, he started with
the premise that there are some "chronologically"
primitive cultures in the world. Obviously, however,
the lowest and most rudimentary civilization, when
considered historically, can only be seen as a product
of successive transformations.

The historical-cultural school studied specific
cycles, illuminating them in much the same way that
one could illuminate the Egyptian, Hebrew, or Mohammedan civilizations. But then it went on to assign
these cycles chronological priority and necessity in
much the same way that the historian could for the
Egyptian, Hebraic, or Mohammedan civilizations if he
wished to consider one of these civilizations as the
world's first. No one can tell us, though, that a
culture that is ethnologically older is the one that
is chronologically older.

8. *The English Anthropological School and the*
    Historical-Cultural School

Clearly, an ethnology so conceived remains on a par
with the ethnology that earlier served anthropologists
in their interpretations. It is an ethnology, that is,
permeated from beginning to end with the persistent
concept of universal history, a history that becomes
psychology. When the devotees of the historical-
cultural school entered into the world of chronological
sequence, they usually departed from historicism in
order to arrive at a more categorical naturalism. This
is not to deny that they had good reason to criticize

the English anthropological school. However, they
made one error: they failed to recognize that what
happened to the representatives of this school was
generally just the opposite of what happened to them;
that is, starting from a more categorical naturalism,
the anthropologists then arrived at a historicism that
redeemed them, putting them in the vanguard of this
field of studies.

The English anthropologists arrived at a healthy
historicism when they freed themselves from their evolutionistic theories and came to regard the primitive
world as a page of contemporary history in which survivals are resolved--when, that is, they assigned this
world the task of illuminating an aspect of Western
Civilization and, along with it, our awareness of our
own existence. The historical-cultural school, on the
other hand, restricted its view to the primitives, and
thus its scholars ultimately were lacking in such intentions. It is true that the importance of time and
place occasionally eluded the English anthropological
school, and it is also true that the historical-
cultural school hoped to make such concepts very concrete. It is a fact, however, that the historical-
cultural school made the error, as Martino says, of
considering time and place not as practical contexts
of humanistic importance but as categories of the
historical process. Additionally, in taking facts
back to their cause, they followed a procedure that
was inverse to that of historiography.

The merit of the historical-cultural school, however, is that it provided us with precise norms for
establishing the area of diffusion of identical traditions, and it revitalized scholarly philological
awareness of the ethnic tradition. Although we cannot
say with Schmidt that one must recommence a new history
of folklore with such a school, we certainly can say
that Ratzel, Graebner, and Schmidt deserve all due
credit for having effectively proposed that the historical method is the method to be used by folklore.

CHAPTER XXVII

BETWEEN HISTORY AND SOCIOLOGY

1. *The Work of Arnold van Gennep*

Standing between the English anthropological school
and the historical-cultural school, at a time when the
historical method was increasingly becoming the method
of folklore, was a French scholar, Arnold van Gennep.
When he viewed the matter from a theoretical vantage
point, he was opposed to this methodology. After
setting about to study the popular traditions in
France, however, he ended up by following it.

Educated in the English anthropological school and
an enthusiastic, intelligent worker of exceptional
temperament, Gennep has been called, not incorrectly,
the Pitrè of France. His apprenticeship began with
some ethnological works that suggested he was an
ingenious, scrupulous, attentive scholar: *Tabou et
totémisme à Madagascar* (1904), *Mythes et légendes d'
Australie* (1906), and *Les rites de passage* (1909).
His wide-ranging discussion of classical philology,
La question d'Homere (1909), was followed a year later
by *La formation des légendes*, a popular work that
nevertheless revealed its author's good sense. Five
volumes entitled *Religions, mœurs et légendes* came
out between 1908 and 1914; these included studies,
reviews, and position papers of contemporary interest
to ethnology and folklore. His *Études d'ethnographie
algérienne*, published between 1911 and 1914 and con-
densed in a smaller volume entitled *En Algérie*, was
about ethnology, and two years later, in 1916, he
brought out one of his volumes on French folklore, *En
Savoie: du berceau à la tombe*. Thereafter, French

folklore was his preferred area of studies, as is indicated by the works he published between 1932 and 1936:
Le folklore du Dauphiné, *Le folklore de la Bourgogne*,
Le folklore de la Flandre et du Hainaut français, and
Le folklore de l'Auvergne et du Velay. These were
followed by his most comprehensive and extensive compilation, the *Manuel de folklore français contemporain*,
a multi-volumed work that is truly a library of French
popular traditions.[1]

As an ethnologist and folklorist, Gennep was in
line with the English anthropologists, with whom he
shared an interest in classical civilizations. We
should add that Gennep proceeded to ethnological
studies of medieval history, which associates him with
Graebner. Unlike the English anthropologists and
Graebner, however, Gennep wished to bring the science
of folklore within the realm of biology, as is first
evidenced in his essay on the historical development
of ethnology, published in the second volume of *Religions, mœurs et légendes*. In this essay he began by
distinguishing the historical method from the comparative method. The first method, in his opinion, considers phenomena in their chronological order and
employs written documents, while the second method
disregards conditions of time and place and employs
oral documents. The legitimacy of both methods, he
said, is supported by the fact that the object of
study is quite different in the two approaches. Now
there is no doubt, he continued, that the phenomena
with which the folklorist is concerned are living
phenomena, while those with which the historian is
concerned are dead. Thus, he appealed to biology as
the science that must renovate the study of folklore.

As we know, Karl Lamprecht had argued that historiography needed to be reduced to an exact science
through an application of biological laws. Gennep
went beyond that proposition. Convinced that most
folklorists are not very good observers because they
are content to impose the historical (or at least the

[1]Cocchiara is here alluding to Pitrè's *Biblioteca
delle tradizioni popolari siciliane*.

psychological) method on folklore, he argued that the
entire science of folklore now needed the new method
of direct observation.

2. *Folklore and Biology*

In his little volume entitled *Le folklore* (1924), Gennep
attempted to clarify these ideas. Essentially, however,
he held firm to his initial point:

> In the first place, folklore uses the method of
> observation because . . . it is concerned with
> living, present facts. Secondly, a present fact
> has antecedents that cannot be explained with the
> historical method. . . . This theory is well
> known. . . . But one fact needs to be insisted
> upon: folklore is not solely historical, nor is
> it a section of history. Folklore has gradually
> begun to recover from a nineteenth century malady
> that could be called historical mania, according
> to which nothing current counts except in relation
> to the past, or, as is suggested by the theme of
> a famous romance work, the Living only count in
> relation to the Dead. . . . This psychical and
> methodological malady is so wide-spread that most
> educated people, when in the presence of an object
> or event, appraise only its archeological or his-
> torical importance. . . . He who wishes to become
> involved in folklore must abandon the historical
> attitude, adopting instead the attitude of zoolo-
> gists and botanists, who study the lives of animals
> and plants in their actual environment; one must,
> then, substitute the biological method for the
> historical method.

In the general introduction to the first volume of the
Manuel de folklore français contemporain, Gennep set
forth the rule that he felt each folklorist should obey
in collecting material:

> Since folklore is a biological science, collections

of materials can only be made with the exact and
methodical technique of observation worked out by
the natural sciences. . . . This technique is here
subject to certain amplifications, on the one hand,
and to certain restrictions, on the other. The
amplification is that *no fact can be taken in isolation, because it is a part of a complex, ever-
changing whole.* At the same time the scholar is
forced to notice that a good many factual details
are grouped around a central nucleus; but each of
these details can also serve, under other conditions, as a central nucleus. Initially, this
difficulty discourages beginners, who willingly
confess their confusion and despair of remaining
forever submerged in facts. The solution is that
one must proceed from the easiest to the most
difficult, from the outward manifestations to the
beliefs. . . . In folkloristic practice, it is
not necessary to subject the witnesses to a
methodical interrogation, as a judge would do;
but it is necessary to let them make headway and
to make them give themselves up to their recollections.

The advice that Gennep gives to folklorists in his
various works is always useful. But was it necessary
to take recourse to biology to justify such advice?
In the previously cited introduction, Gennep did not
change his attitude toward history, but he did modify
his attitude toward biology:

I do not here take the term *biology* in the trans-
formistic or evolutionistic sense that some critics
seem to have had, but in the precise sense of "that
which concerns life." This is not a metaphor for
representing the state of society as a living
organism subject to the natural laws of growth,
maturity, old age, and death, laws upon which all
organisms depend. I am only saying--and this seems
to me to be an irrefutable fact--that since men are
living beings who are free to make decisions, free
to move heaven and earth and to yield (within

certain self-imposed limits) to their own feelings
and passions, their relationships must be examined
and evaluated as living biological relationships
and not as relationships of inanimate objects or
dead beings. It is not a matter here of theory
or a system but of an angle of vision that reveals
folkloristic and ethnographic facts in a way
altogether different from what is revealed by a
mechanistic or historical angle of vision--a way
that permits the subordination of thousands upon
thousands of apparent morphological details to
the study of living agents and social functions.

3. Folklore Without History

In light of these assertions, one can clearly see that
Gennep had a totally erroneous conception of history.
It suffices here to criticize that unfortunate combination of terms in his phrase "mechanistic or
historical." Gennep was convinced that history was
only "erudition," a superficial summary, a schematic,
anagraphic, chronological catalogue of facts. Convinced as he is of this, he immediately adds:

The best definition of folklore, the one that, all
things considered, is most satisfactory, is *the
methodical study, and therefore science, of usages
and customs.* It is useless to add *popular*, because
usages and customs are general communal phenomena,
which can be discerned independent of race, type
of civilization, social class or, in certain countries, professional caste. *Usages* means: ways of
living, without political or ethical evaluation.
Customs means: ways of living, in conformity with
written or unwritten rules acknowledged by the
general consent of all, spontaneously and without
the coercion of state or government; depending on
the periods and countries, and notwithstanding or
in opposition to such coercion, customs are often
justified, not initially but afterwards, by one or
more laws, which are necessarily always late in the

progressive or regressive evolution of customs
themselves. . . .

Gennep was obviously indulging himself here in a
strictly positivistic attitude: as an "angle of
vision," biology must allow the folklorist to formulate some general laws for the chaotic mass of details
surrounding him. Indeed, it is in the name of these
laws that we are given his concept of folklore, which
in his view is only a methodical catalogue of facts,
each of which is related to a law. Given his unitary
concept of folklore, Gennep certainly did not mean to
exclude songs, tales, legends, and proverbs from folklore; his definition of folklore, however, actually
excludes those productions. Additionally, he quickly
acknowledged a seafaring folklore, a rural folklore,
a workmen's folklore, and so on. But how is it then
possible not to specify whether the usages are popular?
In defining folklore and proposing its methodology,
Gennep began, as we have said, with the premise that
folklore is the study of living and present facts, as
opposed to history, which is the study of dead facts.
Obviously, however, living and present facts are also
a part of history, nor can one exclude from the folklorist's area of investigation those usages and customs
that belong strictly to times past. For example,
doesn't the scholar who concerns himself with, say,
folklore of the Renaissance period have a perfect right
to call himself a folklorist? The historian, moreover,
does not weigh facts according to whether they are
written or oral, but only according to the thought they
contain. And although the comparative method that
Gennep contrasts to the historical method is occasionally guilty of naturalistic procedures, it should be
considered as heuristic research that the historian
must raise to the level of history through appropriate
modification.

4.   *Individuality and Communality in Gennep's Thought*

The formulation of general laws did not prevent Gennep

from recognizing individual contributions to traditions or "communal phenomena," as he called them. As
he himself observes in the introduction to his *Manuel*,
"Each individual has many social relationships, and he
is always free, within the fixed limits of tradition,
to act within these established relationships. In the
family, he has the choice of spouse and number of
children; as a soldier, he can perform acts of heroism;
as a constituent, he can use the vote. In other words,
to understand the workings of global social life, one
must begin with the individual, not with the community,
the latter being merely an abstraction or, at most, a
a perspective such as is offered by an aerial photo-
graph." In this respect, Gennep is in line with those
folklorists who have emphasized the human element as
the very source of folklore. While he is here linked
to A. W. Schlegel and Pitrè, it is clear that he is
contradicting himself. The recognition that he gives
to the individual in folkloristic theory actually
negates the general laws that he had championed.
Moreover, as he himself says, although there are individuals A and B who may submit to a specific environment, there is also individual C who rebels against
it. It is then that this person can become the modi-
fier or inventor of specific folkloristic facts.

5. Rites and Sequences

Before estimating the importance of the individual in
folklore, Gennep had attempted a similar estimation
in the field of ethnology. In referring to the modifications to which Australian tribes are subjected, he
observed in the introduction to his *Mythes et légendes
d'Australie* that "the agents of these modifications
are, in very well-known cases, specific individuals or
a very small group of individuals. This individual
element, which Durkheim overlooks, plays an important
part in Australian societies. At times an individual
endowed with a very lively imagination is favored by
gods who tell him what change to introduce."
This historical attitude is at the center of

Gennep's *La formation des légendes;* although Gennep
here accepts the anthropological theory of the origin
of fables, he does not ignore the contribution that
each narrator gives to each fable. In *Rites de
passage*, however, he indulges in social schemata,
laws, and values (much like Boulanger, with whom he
shared similar ideas on the subject)--while the individual life, whatever it may be, is biologically
reduced to the passage from one age to another or from
one occupation to another:

> Each change in an individual's situation involves
> actions and reactions between sacred and profane,
> actions and reactions that must be regulated and
> supervised so that general society will not suffer
> discomfort or harm. Various and successive transi-
> tions from one particular society to another and
> from one social situation to another are implicit
> in the very fact of existence, so that a man's
> life comes to be made up of a succession of stages
> with similar beginnings and ends: birth, social
> puberty, marriage, fatherhood, social advancement,
> occupational specialization, and death. For every
> one of these events there are ceremonies that have
> the one essential goal of helping the individual
> pass from one defined situation to another that is
> equally well defined. Since the goal is the same,
> it necessarily follows that the means for obtaining
> the purpose be, if not identical in detail, at
> least analogous, because the individual too is
> slowly undergoing modification, since he has quite
> a few stages behind him and quite a few ahead of
> him, on the frontier. This explains the general
> resemblance among ceremonies of birth, childhood,
> social puberty, betrothal, marriage, pregnancy,
> fatherhood, initiation into religious societies,
> and funerals. Moreover, neither the individual nor
> society operates independently of nature or the
> universe, which is itself governed by a periodicity
> that has repercussions on human life. In the uni-
> verse, too, there are stages and transitions, for-
> ward surges and states of relative inactivity, of

pause. Thus, we should also include among ceremonies of human passage those rites occasioned by
celestial changes: for example, the passage from
one month to another (plenilunar ceremonies), from
one season to another (ceremonies related to sol-
stices of equinoxes), and from one year to another
(New Year's Day, etc.). It seems logical to me,
then, to group all these ceremonies together
according to a scheme whose details, nonetheless,
cannot be worked out as yet.

As we can see, it is a matter of a mechanical grouping
whose limitation Gennep himself perceived. Moreover,
he knew that it was impossible to put everything that,
by his own definition, is living and therefore natural
within a rigid scheme. This is why he put the emphasis
on sequences in his own *Rites de passage*:

The sequential pattern [of rites of passage] has
hardly been examined, although the study of certain
modern rituals known in great detail (for Australia
and the Pueblo Indians) . . . shows that, in large
outline and sometimes in the smallest detail, the
order in which the rites proceed and must be performed is a magico-religious element of fundamental
significance. The principal aim of this book is
precisely to react against the "folkloristic" or
"anthropological" procedure, which consists of
extracting various rites--whether positive or
negative--from a sequence, then considering them
in isolation, thus depriving them of their chief
raison d'être and their logical placement within
a contextual whole.

Gennep perceived and expressed this same exigency
in the first volume of his *Manuel* when, in examining
folkloristic institutions grouped under the title *Du
berceau à la tombe*, he felt compelled to return to the
phenomenology of rites of passage. In this volume,
however, as in the ones that follow it, the schemes
are only a tool, a means for grouping facts that are
then examined from a historical perspective.

6. Gennep and the Cartographical Method

From his first monographs on French folklore to his
Manuel, the *summa* of all his research, Gennep proved
to be an incomparable collector. The questionnaires
he distributed to collect his many materials are perfect models. With the aid of these questionnaires, he
was able to avoid vagueness and approximation by documenting the confines of a living or lost usage, which
is why he always insisted on the great usefulness the
folklorist can extract from even a negative response.
Furthermore, Gennep never began a collection without
first constructing an exact bibliography of the subject with which he was dealing. A considerable part
of his *Manuel* (vols. 3 and 4) is a bibliography of
studies on French popular traditions, and this bibli-
ography--as exemplary as Pitrè's bibliography of
Italian popular traditions--accompanies his classification and presentation of newly collected facts.

For the presentation of more of these facts in the
best possible way, Gennep argued for the usefulness of
the cartographical method. In his extensive 1904
review of the first volume of Sébillot's *Le folklore
de France*, he asked, "Why didn't Sébillot add some
maps indicating the geographical areas of specific
beliefs or customs for those places where specific
inquiries have not yet been initiated?" Indeed, what
Sébillot ignored or treated only minimally was to become Gennep's chief area of interest. After delineat-
ing the history of the cartographical method from
Ratzel to Pessler in his programmatic essay "Contribution à la méthodologie du folklore" (also published in
Lares in 1934), Gennep went on to assert categorically
that such a method, along with his training in biology,
had given him a much more precise scientific preparation than that demanded by historical, linguistic,
economic, and political studies.

The cartographical method, Gennep said, is valid
because it allows us to account for all elements determining the continuation or disappearance of the phenomena under study. He added that he had never proposed
to use this method to perpetuate the survival of super-

stition; rather, his purpose was to identify bonds
determining the cohesion of local communities, which,
after all, make up the nation. The cartographical
method is heuristic research, and as such it certainly
has its usefulness; but it is not and cannot be more
than that, as is demonstrated by Gennep's works. In
these works he indeed utilized all of his folkloristic
experiences--precisely because behind *those* experiences
was the experienced student of historical, linguistic,
economic, and political studies.

It is true that a cartographical representation
accompanies Gennep's explanation of material in the
Manuel, and the regional and local variations in which
he delighted certainly give his groupings liveliness
and color. But for Gennep (and this can be said not
only of the *Manuel* but also of his other works on
French folklore) collecting was never an end in itself.
He did indeed collect folklore facts, but only so that
he could interpret them. It is at this point that the
uneasy folklore theorist usually becomes the French
folklore historian, concerned with only one goal and
with only one methodology: the displaying of folkloristic facts in specific historical forms. In fact, he
himself says that if one wishes to study the folklore
of France, one must contemplate the complex factors
that have produced the very formation of this nation.
Then, it could be added, isn't it the task of the folklorist to specify a nation's traditions, which follow
a course that is itself engendered by history?

7. *Gennep: Historian of French Folklore*

Gennep, then, was not content merely to examine a folkloristic fact just as he found it; he "contemplated"
it (to repeat his word), making it the object of his
scrutiny; furthermore, he attempted to see this fact--
whatever it was--in the various aspects it had assumed
through the ages. With this investigation he came to
a better understanding of the fact, because he distinguished new motifs and new meanings that had enriched
or impoverished it. In other words, he went beyond

his own theoretical definition of folklore in his
research, investigating not biological facts but documents of the human spirit. Read, for example, his
investigations of baptismal or marriage rites or his
essays (in the second part, which bears the title *Du*
berceau à la tombe) on marriages and funerals. Or
read the other parts of the first volume of *Cérémonies*
periodiques cycliques, including ceremonies related to
the carnival season, Lent, Easter, May Day festivities,
and St. John's fire, as well as agricultural and rural
summer ceremonies. Once again the theorist ultimately
vanishes, leaving us with the confident, attentive,
perceptive historian of French folklore.

Consider the following example. In the first part
of the first volume, Gennep examines the custom of
baptismal godfathers, which in many areas of France
are chosen from among the grandparents. Now, as he
adds, one must observe

> . . . that this juridical-folkloristic pattern
> cannot be explained with the theory of survivals;
> rather, it must be considered as an autonomous
> invention that formed and slowly developed in the
> medieval ages or, to be more exact, when the bap-
> tism of adults gave way to the baptism of children,
> which did not happen simultaneously everywhere in
> Europe. Christianity was not established through-
> out France until the end of the Merovingian period,
> with a rapidity that depended on the pressure
> applied by missionaries and bishops. It was
> necessary, then, to replace the godfathers of adult
> catechumens, whose civil obligations were limited,
> with other guarantors with greater responsibility
> in matters of liturgy and custom. It was exactly
> at this point that the conventions of honors and
> their rewards, the obligation of consanguinity and
> close kinship, entered into play in an increasingly
> generalized fashion, and innumerable magico-
> religious beliefs were devised--beliefs whose basic
> aim was and is to provide psychological, social,
> and economic support for the very personification
> of weakness, the newborn babe.

He wrote in his Contribution à la méthodologie du

Here again the explanation of present facts is based on "dead" facts that actually cannot be considered to be dead, in that they have only become modified and adapted. It goes without saying, then, that in this examination the biologist has become a historian. Finally, Gennep could not undertake this examination without referring to the concept of the survival, the concept that he had excluded in his abstract definition of folklore.

8. Merits and Defects of Gennep's Theories

All of Gennep's works reveal a total revision of the theories with which ethnology attempted to explain folklore. The starting point is a specific belief, a particular custom, some rite that he had previously collected and classified; the destination is the revision of a specific theory explaining that fact.

Gennep certainly had some preconceptions that put him on the wrong track. "I do not have the right," he wrote in his *Contribution à la méthodologie du folklore*, "to reconstruct the past by using theories, like the theory of survivals, based on an evaluation of what is called the primitive." He overlooked the fact that it is not a question of reconstructing the past, as he understood it, but of illuminating and explaining the present. It is true that he avoided talking about primitives in his *Manuel*, although they much intrigued him in his younger days. But it is also true that all of the problematical issues generated by the primitive world were before his very eyes. For example, he did not deny the magical function of bonfires. But without the ethnological interpretation of bonfires, which implies their magical function, could we ever arrive at such a concept? And didn't magic, which had been codified by Frazer, guide him in his interpretations? He sometimes rebelled against theories that had been "done to a turn"--but when he asserted that one comes to see a sexual reflex rather than a survival of a tree-cult or grain-cult in May Day ceremonies developed in France, wasn't he following the very method of the English anthropological school?

In Gennep's "rebellions" (which were not really rebellions, after all), one does find some persuasive observations. Often, though, he is peremptory. On this subject Paolo Toschi makes some penetrating remarks:

> Gennep's "rebellion" is useful and necessary, but more than once we observe the danger that this rebellion exaggerates. If it is difficult to document the relationship and prolongation of pagan festivals in medieval and present folklore to explain the May-cycle, it is even more difficult, at least in regard to Italy, to allow that there is a clear separation between the floral festivals and festivals in honor of the goddess Maja, on the one hand, and, on the other, our May Day celebrations, which are found as early as the medieval ages. Changes due to the natural evolving of usages, to change of religion, to invasions of barbarians, yes; but a genuine separation, no-- particularly because the dedication of the month of May to the Virgin Mary is a relatively recent happening. The existence (in the belief of that time) of mythical personages in northern European countries, such as Balder in Norway, Ligo in Latvia, Kupalo in Russia, and related customs in specific regions (Baltic customs, for example), where Christianity arrived late and did not have a profound effect, remind us--as do similar ceremonies associated with St. John--of a great pre-Christian seasonal festival. One must take account of the large area in which the most important of these customs take place. In short, we must guard against confusing a lack of documents with a lack of facts.

In such cases, Gennep the folklorist adopted basically the same historical concept that had been expressed by Gennep the theorist, although it was mostly a matter of introductory comments, digressions, and brief suggestions. This is not, however, to take

anything away from his *Manuel*; although much of this
work is restricted by sociological limitations, it is,
taken altogether, an example of a historical methodology wherein we find the very historian that he himself
wished to expel from his work. Gennep's error was in
believing that it was possible to consider the biological method, and therefore observation, as something
that was or could be exterior and anterior to thought.
Thus, his collection of material preceded his interpretation, when in fact both could take place simultaneously. To his credit, however, he showed us that
for him--and this is Gennep at his best--observation
was merely a spur to thought. This last point suggests
why he can be considered as one of the most representative figures of European folkloristic scholarship.

CHAPTER XXVIII

APOLOGIA OF FOLKLORE

1. *In the Wake of Saintyves: Modernism*

Along with Gennep, another French scholar, Pierre
Saintyves, has dominated the science of folklore in
the last fifty years. As a faithful disciple of the
teachings of the English anthropological school, he
addressed the ethnological problem of folklore with
ever-increasing command. Directly or indirectly his
interests were always associated with traditions that
were magico-religious in nature. Those who shared in
these interests of his included not only Tylor, Frazer,
Lang, and Hartland, but also the major representatives
of an entire current of studies baptized with the name
Modernism. In the late nineteenth and early twentieth
centuries, this school attempted to apply the most
rigorous principles of the historical method to the
Church and its traditional doctrine.

An English modernist, George Tyrrell, emphasized
the dangers of this approach:

> I see how the vigorous historical investigation of
> the origin and development of Christianity must
> undermine many of our most fundamental assumptions
> in regard to dogmas and institutions. I see how
> the sphere of the miraculous is daily limited by
> the growing difficulty in verifying such facts,
> and the growing facility of reducing either them
> or the belief in them to natural and recognized
> causes. I see and feel moreover how these and like
> objections would be as nothing could we point
> triumphantly to the Christian ethos of the Church,

to the religious spirit developed by her system
as by no other; and were there not in the approved writings of her ascetical teachers, and
her moralists; in the prevailing practices of
her confessors and directors; in the liturgical
biographies of her canonized saints . . . much
that revolts the very same moral and religious
sense to which in the first instance her claims
to our submission must appeal.[1]

And yet he went on to say, with conviction, "Catholicism is not primarily a theology, or at most a
system of practical observances regulated by that
theology. No, Catholicism is primarily a life, and
the Church a spiritual organism in whose life we
participate. . . ."[2]
       This is the nucleus of Tyrrell's *A Much-Abused
Letter*, which was addressed, we should note, "to a
professor of anthropology." Anthropology (that is,
the English anthropological school) had given impetus
to Modernism, or at least to some of its representatives. Typical of this is the case of Alfred Loisy,
who made use of ethnology and, to a lesser degree,
folklore in many of his works. It was Loisy that
Saintyves followed, as friend and editor--and after
Saintyves came none other than Émile Nourry and the
Parisian "Critical Library," one of the most active
centers of Modernism.[3]
       Saintyves was clearly the most experienced lay
representative of this movement. In fact, he could
be called the modernist of folklore or, better still,
the folklorist of Modernism. As a folklorist, he did
indeed make use of the advances Modernism had made in
the field of ethnology, but he always had just one
aim: to penetrate the thicket of popular traditions

[1]*A Much-Abused Letter* (London: Longmans, Green,
and Co., 1907), pp. 3-4.
       [2]Ibid., p. 4.
       [3]Saintyves, that is, used his real name, Émile
Nourry, in connection with his *Bibliothèque de
Critique religieuse* (1901-14).

with the same attitude that dominated the research of
Tyrrell and Loisy. In 1887, when he was scarcely
seventeen, he wrote in his diary, "I hope I can always
practice the following rules: to follow my heart and
my love for things of the spirit; to educate myself
so that I can be useful in increasingly effective
ways; and to strive to produce useful works for
science." His science was folklore, to which he gave
(to use his expression) his heart and his love.

An able writer, Saintyves had a lively intellectual curiosity that allowed him to attack various
subjects, which he handled with sympathy and dispatch.
This is why his books always make for interesting
reading, even when they are on topics that are anything but easy. In this respect he might be called
the "Frazer of France"--and, like Frazer, he turned
out a large number of scholarly works, all of which
were based on his concept of the nature of folklore.

2. *Folklore Between Naturalism and Historicism*

Convinced that the folklorist must have the qualities
of the naturalist and the historian, Saintyves was
miles away from considering folklore as a biological
science. In his extensive *L'astrologie populaire*
(1937), he observed, in contrast to Gennep:

> There has been much talk of applying the "bio-
> logical method" to folklore. It has been said
> that folklorists must place all of their atten-
> tion on the living fact, on the present fact,
> as if the analysis of the living fact would
> surely reveal its causes. But we must note that
> folklore essentially derives from tradition, and
> tradition, properly speaking, is a psychological
> and social fact rather than a biological one.
> Thus, we have an equivocation here, an unfor-
> tunate confusion. Although intelligence and its
> manifestations appear in living beings, it does
> not follow that there are no facts to be dis-
> tinguished from biological ones. Such facts

belong essentially to general or social psychology. As far as I know, introspection and interrogation are not within the province of biology,
but folklore almost always rests on investigations
that are products of direct or indirect interrogation. . . . Since the living fact that we study
is a traditional fact, it derives from a hundred
previous facts that can only be studied with historical methods. This is not to say that popular
life never offers anything original; rather, it
is to suggest that the intellectual life of the
folk always evolves within the context of tradition. The very nature of a folkloric fact, its
traditional nature, simply will not allow us to
forget that it is almost always deeply rooted in
the past.

This is also his stance in his *Manuel de folklore*, the
first volume of which was published in 1936; this volume is rather like a spiritual testament, particularly
when one adds some fragments from the second volume
(parts of which had been previously published in the
first issue of *Cahiers Pierre Saintyves*). It has been
said that one seldom finds in this work what one
usually looks for in a manual: clear ideas seriously
expressed in a way that makes them accessible to everyone. Although it is certainly true that the *Manuel*--
whose title can indeed deceive the reader--was written
for beginners, as he himself suggests at the end of his
discussion of questionnaires (a subject that Gennep had
thoroughly discussed), the *Manuel* is actually a treatise in which Saintyves tackled the theoretical issues
of folklore (at least as he understood them) as a
scholar, certainly not as a popularizer.

Saintyves' *Manuel* reflects both his work and the
criteria guiding that work. In his *Manuel*, as in his
work, Saintyves proved to be a truly great folklorist
when he acted as a historian. Like Gennep, however,
he sometimes gave himself up to sociology, which
explains why his *Manuel de folklore* and his work
reveal a facile naturalism combined with an informed
historicism.

3. *Folkloric Facts and Comparison*

We can infer from Saintyves' definition of folklore
that, like Gennep, he embraced the concept of historical causality. This led him to establish laws with
which he believed one could explain the existence of
popular traditions. Although he acknowledged, for
example, that tradition includes both past and present,
he believed tradition could be transmitted involuntar-
ily, and he therefore stressed the importance of contagion and suggestion in the diffusion of popular
traditions. These laws led him to consider folklore
as a psychological science, a natural history of man,
which in turn led to his confusing the historical
method with the sociological method. But didn't
psychology essentially serve (as biology served
Gennep) as an angle of vision? And even though he
reduced folklore to sociology, didn't he also engage
in a constant attempt to reduce sociology to history?

Although Saintyves gave historical science a character it could not have, he was convinced that historical science and natural sciences have a common touchstone in the comparative method. He quickly cautioned,
however, that the task of the folklorist is primarily
to explain the nature of folkloric facts. As he says
in one of the fragments in the second volume of the
*Manuel, "the comparison must illuminate not only simi-
larities but differences,* and one must not forget that
the key to the explanation may be offered by some particularity. . . . The comparison can only be made by
establishing a systematic series while also taking the
essential circumstances of time and place into account.
It is not a matter of simply raking in an immense collection of notecards on all the ancient and modern
sources . . . , but of proceeding by means of a
methodical collection appropriate for facilitating a
truly scientific comparison."

Despite a certain imprecision in terminology, we
glimpse here the historical awareness of one who
intends to deal with popular traditions by considering
them not as biological expressions but as facts of the
human spirit, facts that tradition conveys and renews.

As Saintyves himself says in another of his fragments
(as if attempting to finish the definition of folklore), "Folklore studies tradition, and, after collecting and ordering the facts composing that tradition, it must furnish some explanation of their nature
and traditional essence. . . . Popular tradition cannot be compared to buried treasure: it is a flow of
all kinds of riches, an endless transmission of thousands and thousands of human inventions from which the
folk of civilized nations benefits. *The golden chain
of tradition does not rest, unmoving, in a sealed
case; rather, like the stars, it achieves the miracle
of perpetual motion.*"
     It was now evident that the nature of traditional
facts had to be investigated with the methodology of
history, and it was to Saintyves' credit that he
singled out historical research in the study of different ethnic traditions. He made the mistake, however, of believing that psychological and sociological
schemes could help the historian understand the dialectic of the spirit, when, in fact, these schemes
only provide the historian with an intellectual
orientation.

4. *"Pagan-itis"*

As a matter of fact, Saintyves' first works did not
range beyond the confines of his own intellectual
orientation. In compiling his works, Saintyves was
always guided by one clear concept: a tradition must
first be studied in the moment of its formation, then
in the course of its existence, and finally in the
moment of its disappearance. In his study, however,
these "moments" became separated from each other.
Gennep was essentially correct when he called
Saintyves' volumes "collections of materials," but
his collected materials are always unified by a central idea. For example, Saintyves proposed to demonstrate in his *Les saints, successeurs des dieux*
(1907) that the veneration of the saints is a continuation of the pagan worship of the dead. This is

why many legends attributed to saints are based on
interpretations of epitaphs and inscriptions. Moreover, the religious calendar, in his view, must be
considered not as a simple list of holidays but as a
ritual and cyclical systemization of legends essential
to each cult.

This thesis incorporated the one proposed by
Hippolyte Delehaye three years before in his *Les
légendes hagiographiques*; although Delehaye identified
an echo of pagan survivals in the worship of saints
(a point that had already been extensively demonstrated
by Usener, Frazer, Dieterich, Lang, and others), he
maintained that the worship of saints derived from the
worship of martyrs. In reality, however, the historian's inquiry cannot be restricted to establishing that
the worship of a pagan god survives in the worship of
a saint; rather, it is a matter of seeing what kinds
of mentality operate in these two cults, which are
not and cannot be identical. It is precisely this
kind of investigation that is missing in Saintyves'
inquiry--and in subsequent essays he went even further
into the nature of pagan survivals in the worship of
saints, as is exemplified in his essay "Saint Chris-
tophe, d'Hermes et d'Héracles," published in 1935 in
the *Revue d'Anthropologie* (where he published some of
his best essays).

An ample outline of some matters not treated in *Les
saints, successeurs des dieux* is provided by Saintyves'
thin volume entitled *Les vierges meres et les naissances
miraculeuses* (1908), which seems to be a chapter added
to Hartland's *The Legend of Perseus*. Here Saintyves
was concerned with the worship of fertility stones,
aquatic theogonies and the worship of water, vegetable
totems, miraculous births caused by the simultaneous
actions of plants and holy water, meteorological
fecundations, and solar theogonies. His comparisons
were cautious and effective, and, as was the case for
the English anthropologists, he related his study of
primitives to his study of classical civilizations and
the folk of civilized nations. Nor is it insignificant
that he began his last chapter (on the idealization of
the birth of Christ) with two passages from Loisy.

Saintyves also referred to Loisy in such other
works as *Le discernement du miracle, Les reliques et
les images legendaires*, and *La simulation du marveil-
leux*, published between 1909 and 1912. In these works
Saintyves examined doll-like figures that could open
and close their eyes, corporal relics of Christ, talis-
mans and relics that have fallen from the sky, and
miraculous cures in an effort to determine the derivation of such practices and cults from mankind's oldest
beliefs. Too, he used recent discoveries of both
ethnology and Biblical criticism.

5. *Religion as Magic*

To be honest, Saintyves' first works did not often
give extensive treatment to the ethnological facts
used for his comparative approach. As his examinations began to go deeper, however, he came to feel
that he should re-examine many problems that had already been thoroughly examined by his predecessors,
as is indicated by the following volumes, published
between 1914 and 1915: *La guérison des verrues, La
force magique, Les origines de la médicine*, and
*L'éternuement et la bâillement dans la magie, l'eth-
nographie et le folklore médical*. In these works
Saintyves was primarily interested in seeing how the
medical magic of primitive peoples had led man to
psychotherapy and how these peoples' concept of *mana*
contained a nucleus that paved the way for science.
In this respect, Saintyves was adopting Frazer's
thesis that magic is a false science that nonetheless
contains truth. Saintyves complemented and integrated
this thesis, however, inasmuch as he considered magic
as something more than a false science.

In addition to his interest in the relationships
between magic and religion (about which he made some
extremely perceptive comments), Saintyves was also
interested in the magical character of religion--and
here again he and Loisy were on similar paths. In
his little volume entitled *A propos d'histoire des
religions* Loisy had written:

We can conjecture a most imperfect social state in
which magic and religion are still confused in something that cannot actually be called either magic or
religion but that takes the place of both. . . . What
produced (simultaneously but not suddenly) both religion and magic was the process of differentiation at
work among primitive peoples, a result of the social
intellectual, and moral development within the first
human societies. . . . The distinguishing of magic
from religion, the choosing of their respective
practices, and their increasing conflict revolve
around a social principle: religion is an official
and public worship, while magic is a kind of private ritual, often unpopular and even forbidden.

Loisy believed that while magic ingeniously took short-
cuts, religion completed its journey in a more sophis-
ticated and experienced fashion. This "identification"
(let us call it), which echoed the preanimistic thesis,
was for Loisy simply a conjecture or a working hypothesis. Saintyves was on the same path. In his view, the
world of magic was a means for better understanding religion, for seeing how both magic and religion co-exist
in cults, traditional practices, and the popular ethnic
tradition. It is here that one finds his constant
pledge to clarify questions about magic and religion,
the two constant guides in his folkloristic work.

6. *Biblical Folklore*

In his folkloristic work Saintyves also used another
tool, Biblical criticism, which by then had become an
aspect of scholarship. Indeed, he was forever referring
to the Old and New Testaments, an impulse that took full
control in his *Essais de folklore biblique* (1922), which
is often regarded as a completion of Frazer's *Folk-lore
in the Old Testament*. Actually, however, his *Essais*
began coming out as early as 1909, well before they were
collected, while Frazer's *Folk-lore in the Old Testament*
did not appear until 1918. Nor should we forget that
these essays are the culmination of Saintyves' work.

In these essays Saintyves examined a related series
of themes, some of which he had treated in earlier
books: fire that descends from the sky, the broken
bough that again becomes green, the miracle of water
changed to wine, the miracle of the multiplication of
loaves, walking on water. As we can see, these are
compelling themes, and in taking them on he was confronted with the Bible, on the one hand, and with popular practices and beliefs, on the other. The result
was that comparison was no longer an end in itself, as
had sometimes been the case in his earlier works;
rather, comparison was used to illuminate the specific
historical fact under examination. The *Essais* carried
the subtitle "Magic, Myth, and Miracle in the Old and
New Testaments"--and in a prefatory note Saintyves
himself said:

We have not treated a New Testament theme without
carefully researching everything that anticipated
it in the Old Testament, and conversely we have
not treated a theme from the sacred history of
Israel without indicating the answers of applications furnished by the New Testament. Reimarus
anticipated the task of Tradition when he saw
Daniel's dream as an imitation of Joseph's dream
and the star of the Magi as an adaption of the
Mosaic account of the pillar of fire and cloud.
This sort of chain, then, was not broken in passing
from one account to the other, and thus we have not
believed it possible, for example, to treat Christ's
walking on water without discussing the crossing of
the Red Sea. The two facts are related not only
because of the admissions of the authors of the New
Testament (particularly Paul) but because obviously
they are merely two variations of one traditional
Jewish theme. As a matter of fact, this theme is
also found in the miracles that took place in the
lives of Joshua, Elijah, and Elisha and in the
poetry of the Psalms and the Prophets.

After noting that Biblical themes are often related to
myths, he comments on his methodology:

Knowing the origins of a folkloric theme is certainly an important ingredient for apprehending
the primitive meaning of what could be called the
"magical sense." But this is not enough. In the
fact that a theme is used in a religious book is
the presumption that to a degree it must have been
included consciously to reinforce a spiritual message, which gives it one or more symbolic meanings.
The changing of water into wine at the marriage in
Cana prefigures or symbolizes the Eucharist, and
the song in Psalms that shows us all of nature
troubled by the approach of Yahweh tends not only
to glorify His power but also to make that power
understood as a demiurge or even as the world-
spirit. . . . Creuzer's school . . . has fallen
into total disrepute today, an unfortunate over-
statement to have to make. Symbolic mythology was
much closer to the truth than pure rationalism,
which has desiccated and misrepresented certain
aspects of religious history. Naturally, magic
and elementary religions are permeated with symbolism. The principle of similarity, which explains the miracle of the transformation of water
into wine and the magic rite intended to procure
an abundance of grapes, is also at the heart of
spiritual transformations and consequently their
symbolic explanations. For primitives, the spiritual world is not distinct from the material
world: the same magical operations that insure
the transformation of water into wine also insure
spiritual sentiments.[4] The initiate has participated in cosmic life, and it is thanks to this
participation that the transformation is brought
about. *For them, a distinction is to be made
between evil magical influence and divine influence, a distinction which explains both the sun's
effect on the plants and the effect of the world-
spirit on the hearts of men.* There may well be
a time when we will no longer believe in the power

[4]This is a reference to rites insuring rainfall
(water) for the growth of productive vineyards (wine).

of the magical principle in the material world even
though we continue to accept the power of an analogous principle in the spiritual world.

In pushing hard for his magico-religious identification, going beyond even the confines posed by Loisy,
Saintyves certainly revealed one of the basic interests
of the modernists; but, like other modernists, he also
revealed an interest in using the historical method to
explain those folkloristic facts whose well-spring was
to be found in the Bible. One could criticize his
symbolic conception of myth as often being superficial;
however, no one should overlook the importance of
Saintyves' constant promise to relate myths to rites,
associating them with the emotions that produced them:
myths and rites thus become historical facts that the
historian is called to interpret. Precisely because of
this, the *Essais* reveal a Saintyves who is more experienced in historical investigation, one whose research
aimed at determining the dialectics of the traditions
he examined. And we encounter these accomplishments
once again in one of his most celebrated and discussed
books, *Les contes de Perrault*.

7. *"Les contes de Perrault"*: Saintyves' Most Fascinating Book

In examining the themes in Perrault's tales (which
obviously serve only as reference points), Saintyves
complemented studies in this field previously undertaken by Lang, Hartland, and Macculloch. As in the
Essais, moreover, he attempted to reconcile the symbolic theory and the euhemeristic theory (although he
remained within the confines of the English anthropological school) because he was convinced that popular
tales are often compendia of and commentaries on
primitive rituals, whose echo still lingers in the
practices and beliefs of the low commoners of civilized
peoples.

Previously, in a 1919 work entitled *Rondes en-
fantines et quêtes saisonnières*, Saintyves had empha-

sized the importance of ancient popular liturgies,
which are related to childhood dances. These liturgies were for the most part merely seasonal ceremonies,
which served as the basis of such Perrault tales as
"The Fairies," "Sleeping Beauty," "Cinderella,"
"Donkey-skin," and "Little Red Riding Hood." The
first tale, in Saintyves' opinion, is the projection
of the belief that one should give fairies food and
drink. The second tale is concerned with the prohibition against spinning, which applied to the period
around New Year's Day. The other three comment on
customs that precede and prepare for the new year:
Cinderella is the Queen of Ashes, Donkey-skin is the
Carnival Queen, and Little Red Riding Hood is the
May-Queen.

In Saintyves' view, initiation ceremonies are
related to such other tales told by Perrault as
"Little Thumbling," "Blue Beard," "Riquet with the
Tuft," and "Puss in Boots." Saintyves observes that
such stories require a sensitive, subtle interpretation. One can nevertheless say that "Little Thumbling" suggests the rite through which the child
becomes initiated into the secrets of the adult
world; "Blue Beard" suggests another aspect of this
rite, the initiation of the woman into married life.
"Riquet with the Tuft" illustrates the importance of
learning wedding laws; and "Puss in Boots" provides
a conclusion that bears this moral: the one who comes
to know himself--to know himself, that is, as a *man*--
confirms his manhood with marriage.

Finally, a third group of tales, which Saintyves
calls *Fabliaux* or *Apologues*, reflects religious precepts whose moral lesson is a part of sacred ceremonies. This, for example, is the case in "Griselda."
Significantly, Saintyves concludes his comments on this
group by stating in the preface of his book, "The feeling of holiness that presides over the birth of all our
moral and religious ideas cannot fail to provide a
source for tales and fables; indeed, we have admirable
evidence of this in the marvelous parables that illuminate and perfume the entire Gospel with their freshness." In this respect his *Les contes de Perrault* is

a continuation of his *Essais*, both of which contain
many abstract generalizations. Nonetheless, he always
used ethnological parallels subtly and tastefully, and,
although some of his hypotheses are overly bold, others
are quite persuasive. Vladimir Propp, a Russian folklorist who has recently identified the echo of initiation rites in many folktales, used Saintyves' *Les
contes de Perrault* as a constant reference point for
his research, as can also be said of Henri Jeanmaire,
a Belgian scholar who has investigated initiation rites
in relation to ancient classical myths.

8. Folklore and the Doctrine of Human Brotherhood

Taken altogether, Saintyves' work certainly has its
weaknesses, which is one of the reasons that his work
has been subjected to harsh but often fair criticism.
On the other hand, it also has its merits, which is
why it was and is a source of provocative possibilities
for folklore studies. His work gains our attention not
only because of his fascinating themes but also because
of the conclusions he reached in treating those themes.
    In light of its merits and defects, Saintyves' work
evidences the powerful personality of a scholar who
confronted his themes with a broad vision, a serious
purpose, and the conscience of one who seeks only
truth. At times we seem to hear in him the voice of a
Thiers or a Le Brun, both of whom were intent on discovering pagan survivals. But there is one difference:
although, as an advocate of Modernism, Saintyves proposed to strip popular incrustations from, say, the
worship of saints, he did so not to condemn but rather
to understand and explain them. As a loyal modernist,
he emphasized the historical base of miracles, with all
due respect to the natural and physical sciences and
the results of scientific progress; in the ethno-
graphico-religious sphere, however, nothing could
detract from the validity of the miracle, the miracle
that reflects the hopes and aspirations of the folk.
    Although anxious (like all modernists) to transform
doctrines into living forces that could be extended

and adapted to the needs of the modern temperament,
Saintyves himself embraced only one such doctrine:
human brotherhood. He believed that, in light of
this doctrine, one might call the science of folklore
"the discipline of love," which teaches that "the
understanding of the human heart is impossible without spiritual friendship." In an essay entitled
"Apologie du Folklore," Saintyves had written that the
method of folklore obliges folklorists to bring the
doctrine of human brotherhood to light. This doctrine,
which had previously been formulated in the name of
folklore by Herder, grew stronger as it passed through
the English anthropological school and Modernism into
Saintyves. Indeed, it became the major note, both
human and humanistic, in Saintyves' work.

CHAPTER XXIX

POETICS IN A STATE OF CRISIS

1. The Apprenticeship of Benedetto Croce

During the same period that folklore's ethnological
problem was becoming increasingly clearer and more
insistent, new aesthetic and philological trends began
to take effect, particularly in the field of literary
folklore. The result was that literary folklore began
to be assisted by alternating (or, in the best cases,
synthesized) applications of aesthetics and philology.

In the field of aesthetics, the work of Benedetto
Croce--who, as is well known, always demonstrated a
lively, profound interest in the Neapolitan people--
is of great importance. Croce later became a student
of Vico (who served as the starting point for his
philosophical and aesthetic discoveries), but he
actually began his historical-cultural inquiries by
collaborating on the magazine of Molinaro del Chiaro,
a modest Neapolitan folklorist who produced a collection of Neapolitan songs, among other things. Between 1883 and 1895 we often encounter Croce's name
in this magazine, which was entitled *Giambattista
Basile*. Croce contributed some proverbs and popular
poems that he had come across in old manuscripts,
along with transcriptions of songs and tales that he
had personally collected from the "living voice" of
the folk. Praiseworthy in this regard is a little
collection of folksongs of Vomero, which he considered "quite common, or at least variations and repe-
titions of known songs," although they had "a certain
merit that should not be disregarded." One such song
has these two lines:

Caru Cupidu fammi 'nu favuri
Caru Cupidu ca me lo può fari.[1]

He comments, "Now Cupid has become a character in the folk world, and his being named in songs is not always an indication of literary origin. And why is that? Because the folk devoutly believes that Cupid was a talented composer of songs. The commoner who told me the song provided the proof of this, for when this young girl bungled the songs, her mother scolded her by saying, 'Eh! Cupid has worked so hard to make them, and you ruin them.'"

The "life" of the folksong indeed rests precisely in such renewal, which is not always, as that Vomerese woman believed, a ruination. But Croce was obviously most concerned with clarifying previous relationships between the literary world and the folk world, and he was most pleased that the folk world was a living fact. "Taken from a 'folk-woman' of Vomero," he wrote in the margin of the tale "L'uorco e'l'orca." In such a world he came to feel the vibrant life of his Naples and its history, which, as he said in the introduction to his *La rivoluzione napoletana del 1799*, is the history of rulers *and* the ruled (although in his later historical work he emphasized only the rulers).

From the collecting of these materials, which satisfied his desires for research, he immediately proceeded to the study of various folk manifestations. In this respect, his investigation of the *Leggenda di Cola Pesce* was his first attempt at contributing to scholarly research. When Arturo Graf suggested that he had little information on certain sources relating to this legend, Croce responded, "Although Graf has softened the impact of my assertions, he has not been able to catch me in an error of judgment or reason; my weakness is that I hold very tightly to logic and a bit less so to the knowledge of Gervase of Tilbury." In effect, however, his works on popular literature and folk manifestations revealed philological as well

[1]Dear Cupid, give me your favor,
Dear Cupid, give me your help.

as logical precision. Nor is it insignificant that he
says of such works in his *Contributo alla critica di
me stesso,* "I now perceive some positive aspects;
first, in the pleasure with which I evoked these images
of the past there was an outlet for a youthful imagination thirsting for poetic dreams and literary exercise;
second, in the assiduous and fatiguing research there
was a formal discipline that came to me in my labors in
the service of science."

In all of Croce's work, his research was like a
peaceful oasis, a place of rest. One could call it
Croce's *otium.* And it is the folk--the Neapolitan
folk, with its legends, *lazzari,* masks, games, bandits,
and customs--that is the leading or supporting actor
in his *I teatri di Napoli, Storie e leggende napoletane, La Spagna nelle vita italiana durante la
Rinascenza,* in many investigations in his *Aneddoti di
vita letteraria,* in some of his first and second *Saggi
sulla letteratura italiana del Seicento,* and in some
discussions in *Uomini e cose della vecchia Italia.*

2. Croce as Folklorist

We are also indebted to Croce for an excellent edition
of Basile's *Pentamerone*; he published the first two
"days" in 1892, and the entire work came out in 1925.
In the prefaces to both of these editions, he returns
with pleasure but skepticism to the problems of folk
narrative. For example, in the preface to the 1925
edition, later collected in *Storia della età barocca
in Italia,* Croce maintained that traditional tales,
"as they are ordinarily narrated by the folk, have
lost what they indeed once had in their original
poetic life: the breath of inspiration provided by
the one who first imagined and composed them; they now
resemble those pale and superficial plot summaries of
the 'facts' of a novel or a romance. This explains
the usual insipidness of tales stenographically collected by folklorists or demopsychologists--*documents
of dialects, customs and, if you will, myths,* but seldom works of poetry; and, after all, these collections

never become books that one would read unless they have been reworked or retouched by an artist's hand."

Croce's words echo, however faintly, the old claims of Benfey's followers, who held that the popular tale was merely the patching up of a text that originally came from a "cultured" source but that was now without artistic interest--a thesis that had been subsequently sustained by André Jolles in his volume *Einfache Formen* (1930) and by Albert Wesselski in his essay *Versuch einer Theorie des Märchens* (1931). But although there are some average and mediocre artists in popular art, one could say, in opposition to this thesis, that there are some great ones as well. On the other hand, Croce recognized that the question of the folktale's origin was now being replaced with the question of its history. Well and good--but in that case, can't the poetic quality also return, as it often does, in one who had not first imagined the tale?

In the essay prefaced to the completed translation of the *Pentamerone*, Croce said:

> I have altogether omitted a comparativistic illustration of the tales although I could have easily completed the table of comparisons that accompanied the first two "days" in my 1892 edition. This kind of illustration would transfer attention to abstract matters in Basile's book, transforming it from an artistic work with its own intrinsic character into a demopsychological document. How could it be important for the reader to whom I address this translation to know, for example, that Basile's *Mortella* corresponds to *Rosmarina* in Pitrè's Sicilian tales, to *Mela* in his Tuscan tales, and to *Die Nelke* in the Grimms' collection? . . . It has absolutely no importance, and it would only serve to distract him.

Here it was not really a matter of measuring the *Pentamerone* with the reader's inclinations. He had a different point: the *Pentamerone* is unquestionably a work of art. But isn't it at the same time, to use

Croce's phrase, a demopsychological document? Croce's
merit is in his clearly showing that the external
origins of a work of art have nothing to do with the
already-formed work and that it would be absurd to draw
aesthetic judgments from source research. But when he
moved into the field of cultural history, didn't Croce
himself admit that the comparative method helps us
specify the development of the *epos* or religious drama
within a given nation? Why wouldn't this also apply
to the narrative? Leaving aside the new creations that
occasionally arise, can't one, in giving the history
of a narrative, specify what happens to themes, motifs,
even (to use Croce's very words) customs and, if you
will, myths?

Although these uncertainties always plagued Croce
in his study of folk narrative, they did not dampen
his interest in all things popular. A sufficient
example is one of the most beautiful passages in his
Poesia e non poesia--a passage by Fernán Caballero,
who, in the words of Croce, responded to the innova-
tors, liberals, and free-thinkers who defied the
sacred past:

> You, the enlightened enemies of superstitions, you
> who mock popular customs, sanctuaries, miraculous
> paintings, ex-votos, sacred tattooings and the
> like, have you ever grasped the spirit of such
> practices, have you ever understood them for what
> they are, symbols of the moral life that restrain,
> menace, console, and inspire kind feelings and good
> deeds? You scorn the clumsy Spanish churches,
> where the images of the saints are incrusted with
> silver plating and with other ornaments in bad
> taste: do you think, perhaps, that those churches
> are museums for artists rather than houses of God,
> to which only devout simpletons go to pray?

This response to folklore's detractors is not so much
Caballero's as it is Croce's. He always maintained
his own special brand of love for the popular, especially what in a strict sense is called popular poetry,
admiring the "immediacy with which it captures an

ambience, gives character to a locale, and breathes
life into works that remain as testaments of the past."
The result of this love (so true is it that one returns
in his maturity to what he dearly loved in his youth!)
was the extensive essay "Poesia popolare e poesia
d'arte," which appeared in *La Critica* in 1929 and was
then published separately in 1933.

3. *Popular Poetry and Artistic Poetry*

In this essay, Croce begins with the premise that the
tone of popular poetry is simple and elementary, in
contrast to the mediate and reflective tone of artistic poetry. This, as we have seen, is an essentially
romantic premise. Croce does not cite what the Grimms,
Arnim, and Diez had said on this subject, but he does
cite Hegel. Casting his mind back to the thought of
Hegel (and Paris and Pitrè), he argued that popular
poetry expresses spiritual stirrings that have not been
prompted immediately beforehand by any great intellectual effort. In Croce's view, then, "popular poetry
reaches its destination not by traveling the broad,
sweeping turns of wide avenues but by going the
shortest and quickest way. The words and rhythms in
which it is incarnated are quite adequate for its
motifs, just as the words and rhythms of artistic
poetry are quite adequate for its own motifs--and each
of these two types is rife with implications lacking
in the other."
    But does the fact that popular poetry is charac-
terized by a particular tone or by a specific expressive attitude necessarily lead to the conclusion that
it cannot be artistic? Croce made a real contribution
by emphasizing the distinction between artistic and
popular poetry. Nevertheless, he understood this distinction in an altogether different way from the
romantics. The romantics also contrasted artistic
poetry to popular poetry, regarding the latter as
poetry *par excellence*. For Croce, however, the distinction was a psychological rather than an aesthetic
one. There is, observes Croce,

a popular poetry that is beautiful and one ("non-poetry") that is ugly, as is the case in artistic poetry. This is not to say that there are any fewer ugly, awkward, cold, mechanical productions in the first group, where one will find, as he will in the other group, much and various gnomic, parenthetic, anecdotal, humorous versification that is not and does not pretend to be true poetry. *But when popular poetry is true poetry, it is no different from artistic poetry, and in its own way it enchants and delights.* The difference to look for, then, and the corresponding definition, will be only . . . psychological, a matter of tendency or prevalence rather than of essence. Within limits this distinction is useful for the purposes of criticism.

4. *Folk Elaboration, Once Again*

While acknowledging the special identity of each poetic act, Croce observed that folk poetry must have an appropriate touchstone, which is or should be aesthetics. In his view, this is why it is useful to translate the term *primitive*, which is generally applied to popular poetry, into a genuinely poetic term. Croce recognized, however, that artistic poetry can itself be "popular" and that popular poetry can therefore bloom everywhere. He says that "although popular poetry usually blooms in the popular sphere, it is not necessarily restricted to this sphere; indeed, its tone can be heard wherever there are ears disposed to hear, and thus it can be created in 'non-popular' spheres and by 'non-popular' men. . . . For this tone to be heard, all that is necessary is that some men, even cultured ones, stay in or return to an attitude of simplicity or ingenuousness of feeling about life, at least in some of its aspects."

In allowing that popular poetry too can be artistic poetry, Croce restored dignity to the former. As has been observed, he no longer aspired to illustrate how popular poetry was made or how it derived from literary

or cultured poetry. He was now concerned with extracting the most characteristic accent or tone from the
intrinsic aspects of popular poetry--that which always
remains as it is, whatever its origin. His concept of
tone, then, placed the relationship between popular
poetry and artistic poetry on a radically different
basis, which is to his credit.

But as clear as the concept of popular poetry is
in an aesthetic sense, can we then forget that, as
popular poetry, it subsists because of a continual reworking at the hands of the people? As a matter of
fact, in re-opening the old question about the origin
of popular poetry, Croce asserted the following:

> Without denying that new folksongs can arise here
> and there among the common folk of Italy, and with-
> out denying those that came by different routes
> and others that were composed after the sixteenth
> century and remained in the tradition, and espe-
> cially *without denying that many others were com-*
> *posed by means of imitation or by following old*
> *schemes*--for to deny all this would be to deny the
> obvious--it seems to me that the most substantially
> valid theory is the one that traces the origin of
> a great original mass of *strambotti* or octaves, the
> respected collections of the nineteenth century, to
> fourteenth- and fifteenth-century Tuscany, and then
> through Tuscany to Sicily, the cradle of the new
> popular poetry.

In saying this, Croce unquestionably joined ranks, however cautiously, with Ancona. But despite the undeniable clarifications offered by his investigation, he
neglected the importance of elaboration in popular
poetry.

5. Barbi as Folklorist

As we have seen, this problem, which had been undertaken previously in European countries by folkloristic
philology, was one to which Constantino Nigra had made

an important contribution in Italy. Nigra's work
served as the starting point for one of the major
representatives of modern philology, Michele Barbi.
A disciple of Ancona, Barbi spent his younger days in
the same historical climate in which Croce matured.
     As early as 1895 in his essay "Poesia popolare
pistoiese," which was published in Pitrè's *Archivio*,
Barbi, after reviewing regional collections, proposed
substituting for such collections, "imperfect in one
way or the other, a collection made with more extensive criteria and more continued patience in research;
this would allow the procuring of various readings of
the same song, which are necessary for distinguishing
the essential lines of the primitive text from among
the adulterations caused by oral transmission, as well
as the procuring of factual data illustrating the
song's origin, form, and content in relation to those
of other Italian regions and, occasionally, of neighboring nations." In 1911, in another of his proposals,
"Per la storia della poesia popolare italiana" (which
was published in a miscellany dedicated to Pio Rajna),
Barbi returned to this topic, but this time with
greater critical insight:

> Popular poetry is always alive: it receives,
> transforms, and relinquishes; there are forms that
> one finds at certain moments but not at others;
> some remain local, others migrate from one region
> to another, and often, depending on their adaption
> to different customs, they receive significant
> modification. Our study must constantly focus on
> recognizing true forms within all of this variety,
> noting the characteristics, the relationships, and
> the extension in time and place; but all forms are
> equally legitimate. Although the primitive form
> of a given song can be researched, such is not the
> case for the primitive and genuine form of popular
> poetry, which must be considered in its entirety
> as being in a perpetual state of transmission.

In his view, moreover, "the history of popular poetry
is not merely the history of the rustic *strambotto* and

the epico-lyric: *everything is popular that the peo-*
ple adopts in forms that it has come to accept and
prefer. Some forms are more popular than others, and
some songs endure longer than others in the tradition;
nevertheless, each of these forms and each of these
songs, according to its degree of popularity, deserves
to enter into the history of popular poetry." In a
clarifying note he adds:

> One can certainly say that the *strambotto*, the
> *stornello*, the epico-lyrical song, nursery rhymes,
> and iterative and enumerative songs are all popu-
> lar poetry *par excellence*. Such works were long
> entrusted almost exclusively to memory, their
> brevity and form easily allowed for variants, and
> the process of reworking took place slowly but
> continually over a long period of time. But all
> of the individual songs and the most noteworthy
> variants always have their own authors, whether
> a literary poet or a rustic one. All songs that
> have become popular have variants, and the dif-
> fusion has been as significant as it has been
> great.

In defining "popular" as whatever has received a
degree of popularity, Barbi was going back to the idea
that A. W. Schlegel had proposed on the subject.
Barbi's concern, however, was with documenting this
"degree" of popularity. While Nigra, as Santoli has
correctly said, "had focused on understanding the
diversity of the principal forms of neo-Latin songs
and their wide distribution," now we find that for
Barbi "popular songs were to be studied from the viewpoint of a most rigorous formal philology, emphasizing
individual texts and traditions, which were to be reconstructed with the largest possible number of versions." Barbi was more interested in the popularity
of the song, the documentation of variants serving as
the documentation of its popularity, than he was in
research into the primogenitive text.

We might well conclude, then, that a song is truly
popular when it has two basic elements: tone, which

Croce discussed, and variants, which Barbi stressed.
Yet Barbi did not even come close to drawing this conclusion. On the contrary, he admonished in one of the
essays in his little 1939 volume entitled *Poesia popolare italiana*, "We must develop a more exact concept
of popular poetry, a concept that is more in keeping
with the truth of its history. It is not a matter of
securing a new, more appropriate theoretical concept
of popular poetry, as Benedetto Croce tried to do some
years earlier; until now a given empirical concept has
prevailed, and one cannot suddenly change the names of
things."

In this admonition one finds Barbi's limitation,
even though it was one that he consciously chose: he
disregarded the fact that such concepts are always
just that--namely, pseudo-concepts--and such concepts
do not suggest that "changing the names of things" is
typical of scientific work and its progress.

6. *Philology without Aesthetics*

In his volume *La nuova filologia e l'edizione dei
nostri scrittori da Dante al Manzoni,* Barbi observed,
"Today too much is said of different kinds of criticism.
Instead of making distinctions between aesthetic criticism and other kinds of criticism, we should distinguish
between useless and good criticism, between stupid improvisations and thoughtful new research, regardless of
what kind it is. . . . When one stands in front of aesthetic and philological criticism, he feels an impulse
to repeat the words of Manzoni: 'Why does one need to
choose? Both are here at last. . . . These two things
are like legs: we can move better on two than on one.'"
There is no doubt that Barbi himself has given us the
proof of this in his work on literary criticism. He
also recognized that the Italian folksong is a part of
"our art and our national spirit," as he explicitly
states in the preface to his *Poesia popolare italiana*.
This is clearly his reason for preparing a monumental
collection of Tuscan folksongs (and not only Tuscan),
which is still awaiting a critical edition.

We should add that Barbi fully appreciated the
importance of music in the study of popular poetry:

> The fact that popular poetry has always been con-
> sidered apart from its melodies has done grave
> harm to its study and evaluation. Genuinely
> "popular" poetry does not exist without song, and
> more strictly philological questions, such as the
> structure of the strophe, often cannot be answered
> without taking the musical part into account. The
> study of music is one that presents the gravest
> difficulties. . . . The sad condition of this
> part of our studies has been accurately noted by
> two *maestri* who have recently treated folk music:
> Giulio Fara in his *L'anima musicale d'Italia* and
> Francesco Balilla Pratella in his *Saggio di gridi,
> canzoni, cori e danze del popolo italiano*.

In addition, he underscored the ethnographic importance
of popular poetry:

> We have sung in our youth:
>
>> --Here are the messengers. . . .
>> --What do you want? . . .
>> --We want your daughter. . . .
>> --What will you give? . . .
>
> But how many know that the game and the childish
> song conserve evidence of an actual marriage-
> proposal ceremony practiced in certain regions of
> France (and, perhaps, in other places), of which
> there is also a very detailed description in
> George Sand's *La mare au diable*? In addition to
> being in Berry, this song is found throughout
> Nivernais, and Tiersot gives us the melody.

In this rapid but evocative and synthesizing way,
Barbi proceeds to outline the development of the history of Italian popular poetry. He also indicates,
if only in passing, what is useful and productive in
this field of studies. But we may then ask why Barbi

gave no weight to his conviction that popular poetry
can be art, even though he had no preconceptions about
aesthetic criticism.

Barbi's desire to give emphasis, even absolute
domain, to the philological rather than the aesthetic
aspects of popular poetry was essentially a polemical
matter, in the sense that he preferred the cold investigation of song to the more mellow judgmental consideration of popular poetry. This led him to overlook
the fact that the philological does not exclude the
aesthetic in the study of popular poetry. It is also
a fact that aesthetic questions cannot and should not
be set apart from a song's tradition--a proper rejoin-
der to Croce. On the other hand (and this is Croce's
point), a song's life is not merely the mechanical
life of common places, common formulae, and common
areas--for the life of a song is or can be quite
"poetic."

7. *Menéndez Pidal*

This was the assumption adopted by Ramón Menéndez
Pidal, a Spanish scholar who seemed to combine the
interests of Croce and Barbi. Just as Croce and Barbi
emerged from the tradition of Nigra, Ancona, and Comparetti, Menéndez Pidal emerged from the tradition of
Paris, Rajna, and Bédier.

In his work, however, Menéndez Pidal proposed the
"people/popular poetry" symbiosis in very precise
terms, and he also reconsidered problems relating to
the epopee with the verve of a scholar-become-poet.
First and foremost, in his view, was the Spanish people
as it had been represented, for example, by Fernán
Caballero: Catholic and warlike, pragmatic and wise.
For Menéndez Pidal, as for Fernán Caballero, it is a
people because it is distinguished by specific characteristics.

This belief provides the fundamental note of
national enthusiasm heard in all of the work of Menéndez Pidal. From his *La leyenda de los Infantes de
Lara* (1896) to his *España del Cid* (1929), he attempted

to demonstrate that Spanish epic poetry is basically
historical poetry of a realistic character; furthermore, he attempted to emphasize the special historical
conditions of the Spanish people. He did not deny
borrowings or residues. However, he felt that Arabic
influence on the Spanish epopee was limited merely to
reflections of customs; he minimized the French influence in the making of that epopee; and although he
accepted the thesis about German influence, he did so
very cautiously, because he was convinced that each
poetic nature is always quite different from all
others.

Menéndez Pidal has been accused of thinking only
in national terms. But wasn't it this kind of thinking that led him to his great theories, ones that
remind Leo Spitzer (who made the accusation in the
first place) of the work of the brothers Grimm? A
better comparison, we could add, would be to the works
of Bédier, inasmuch as *España del Cid*, like *Légendes
épiques*, is a work towards which the entire history of
a people moves; it is precisely for this reason that
the Cid becomes the model hero of a nation.

Menéndez Pidal collated chronicles and romances,
both of which were, in his view, living documents of
national life. He traced chronicles and romances to
a common source of interests and inspirations. He was
convinced that romances were not the oldest epico-
lyrical songs and therefore anterior to the *cantares*;
rather, he believed that the romances derived from such
songs. Romances originated, he said, when the old
chivalric poetry sung in castles and pervaded with a
warlike spirit was followed, within the context of
Spain's changing historical conditions, by a more "ag-
ile" poetry that "could recapture old legends in the
beat of a few verses." Menéndez Pidal did not deny
that these romances were sometimes retouched by "cultured" poets, but he maintained that in such cases the
poets adopted the forms and rhythms in which *recitadores* and peasants expressed themselves.

It has been rightly said that there was no temperament more disposed than Menéndez Pidal's to welcome and
revive the quintessential power of such poetry. In

this respect, one should see his anthology *Flor nueva de romances viejos*, in which he fused ancient romances with romances conserved by the oral tradition. He did so not to become the Villemarqué of Spain but to fulfill the desire of becoming one of the *recitadores* of his people, those who in so many ways "receive, refine, repay." Before he discovered these romances in indexes and prepared critical editions that are indeed philological miracles, he had heard them in the midst of the people, from the mouths of peasants and *recitadores*. In similar fashion he had heard various forms of the popular lyric, which he reinvoked movingly in his lecture *Poesía arabe y poesía europea*, delivered in 1937: "The modern Andalusian dancers--who, to the sharp click of castanets, throw little strophes of *sevillanas, malagueñas, rondeñas, peteneras*, and I do not know how many others, to the four winds--appear to be ethico-cultural descendants of the young girls of Cadiz (*puellae gaditanae*); shaking lascivious hips and bronze rattles (as Juvenal said of them), they carried the graceful strophes of Cadiz (*cantica gaditana*) into far places, into the Rome of Tito and Trajan, and fashionable young Romans never tired of repeating them." In this rather oleographic picture, one finds the love that Menéndez Pidal had for his people, a love that provided incentive to his work.

Menéndez Pidal concerned himself with clarifying the concept of popular poetry, which he considered to be the result of reworkings, and he distinguished it from traditional poetry. The former includes creations accorded great public favor, which the public repeats without altering, while the latter exists through its variants. In other words, he proposed calling popular poetry traditional, in contrast to what Rubieri had written on the subject. For example, he says of minstrel songs in his lucid essay *La primitiva poesía lírica española* (1919), "These songs are clearly popular, but they are not traditional. Most are the work of cultured, well-known poets; *notwithstanding their fundamental simplicity*, they smack of artifice, nor do they suggest a genuinely popular reworking. Some of them, however, do come to us in variants suggesting the work of elaboration, inasmuch as the subject matter of poetry lives its life in the voice of the people."

8. Popular Poetry and Traditional Poetry in the Concept of Menéndez Pidal

Menéndez Pidal did not hesitate to propose that such poetry be studied through the application of the historical-geographical method, which had previously produced excellent results in literary folklore, ethnic traditions, and particularly linguistics (for example, Gilliéron's and Edmont's *Atlas linguistique de la France*, published between 1902 and 1910). His interest in this method culminated in his essay "Sobre geografía folklórica," which he published in 1920 in his *Revista de Filología Española* (a veritable storehouse of folkloric contributions), with the subtitle "Ensayo de un método." This method consists in determining regional variations and stylistic particularities of a folksong or a group of songs found in the oral tradition of today; in tracing the geographical areas where such tradition, through its variants, has remained or waned; in locating centers of irradiation and currents of expansion; and, finally, in providing an exact idea of the historical development accounting for the actual differentiation.

It has been noted that in giving a philological definition to the term *popular*, Menéndez Pidal dismissed the question of *popular* as meaning "originated by the people," preferring instead to understand that adjective as meaning "reworked by the people." True enough—but in the aesthetic sense isn't the notion of "created" (or, if you prefer, "recreated") implicit in the concept of "reworkings"? Menéndez Pidal acknowledged that the people "reproduces" in traditional poetry too, but in such cases, he asked, how often are the reproductions actual acts of creation in which the imagination and emotion of individual poets operate? In *Romancero*, the 1927 collection of some of his most important theoretical works, he was totally explicit and clear about the subject of popular elaboration:

In contrast to the modern assertion that traditional poetry is anonymous simply because the
author's name has been forgotten, one must recognize that it is anonymous because it is the result
of multiple individual creations that intersect and
combine. The author cannot have a specific name:
his name is legion. But there is nothing of the
habitual, the insurmountable, or the mysterious in
this collective poetic creation. The mystery of
communal poetization is fully and simply explained
by recognizing that variants are not useless artistic accidents; rather, they are part of poetic
invention. *The pinnacle of beauty, of aesthetic
worth, may be conquered not only by the first
singer but also by some other reciter of the song.*

Through these affirmations Menéndez Pidal reconciled theories about the importance of the primogenitive text held by Wagener, Benfey, and the Krohns, and,
with a spirit as romantic as that of his people, he
joined ranks with Paris, who had appealed precisely to
this idea of folk elaboration in his study of the
epopee. Menéndez Pidal has indeed been accused of considering such reworking as a mechanical process, which
undoubtedly was the case in some of his specific investigations. But when he explicitly stated that a
song's highest pinnacle of beauty can be conquered not
only by its first but also by its last singer, he was
obviously embracing the belief that the imitative process was not executed as an act of the anthologist but
as the act of poetic creation. This obviously dispels
the mystery of poetry's birth by identifying it as an
eternal fact found in a particular form of life, one
that is forever renewed.

Menéndez Pidal, like Croce, thus contributed to
putting the poetics of primitivism, which was coupled
with a fertile aesthetico-sentimental tendency in
studies of popular poetry, into a state of crisis.
It is precisely in that crisis, however, that we find
the revival of studies of popular literature.

CHAPTER XXX

POETICS OF A MYTH

1. Meier and His "Rezeptionstheorie"

Croce's thesis about folk poetry was formulated at a
time when the relationship between popular and artistic
poetry and the principal characteristics of folk elaboration were being enthusiastically restudied throughout Europe, as is evidenced, for example, in the work
of Menéndez Pidal. In addition to Menéndez Pidal,
however, there was an entire group of scholars who
approached and complemented Croce's concept, although
traveling different avenues.

First and foremost in this group was John Meier,
one of the sharpest German folklore scholars of recent
times. To him we are indebted for two significant
treatises, *Kunstlied und Volkslied in Deutschland*
(1898) and *Kunstlieder im Volksmunde* (1906). In these
essays, along with others that were published after
1928 in the *Jahrbuch für Volksliedforschung,* Meier
attempted to illustrate the evolving process, the so-
called "literary tradition," of folk poetry. This
attempt initiated his careful and detailed examination
of more than a thousand lieder, which he completed
with rare erudition. Essentially an anti-romantic,
he integrated the Benfeyian method of researching
sources with the demands imposed by Bédier's philology.
In contrast to Bédier, however, Meier did not under-
estimate the importance of popular poetry; rather, he
gave such poetry significant weight in both civil and
cultural history. This was logical enough, given the
different intellectual environments of the two scholars.

In his essays, Meier concluded that most folksongs
derive from "cultured" poetry, whose specific themes

528

are preserved by the songs. This is the very center
of his now-famous *Rezeptionstheorie*. This theory,
which is based on a comparison of themes rather than
songs, often falls into the same errors made by Benfey
and, more particularly, by Benfey's disciples. But
unlike Benfey's disciples, Meier acknowledged a receptive capacity *and* a creative faculty in popular forces
--that is, in specific individuals.

In his more recent works, especially in his extensive *Deutsche Volkslieder mit ihren Melodien* (1935-36),
Meier attempted to explain how this faculty is manifested in the folk, while the relationship between
artistic and popular poetry came to assume a different
value in his view of things. The conclusions reached
in this work were given additional treatment in his
extensive essay "L'organizzazione, i compiti, i mezzi,
gli scopi degli studi sul canto popolare," written for
a special issue on German folklore in *Lares* (1939).
After reviewing the philological and critical work done
on various collections of folksongs in Germany, he
emphasized the individuality of folk poetry, attributing folksongs (as did Croce) to a single poetic personality. In short, he believed that the author of the
folksong is individual rather than collective, as the
Grimms had maintained. Nor did he believe it important
to find out what social class the author belonged to or
whether he was a "non-poet," a folk composer, or a poet
and musician educated in the arts. As he himself said,
"The only essential point is that the individual's song
became a communal one by taking root among the folk,
so that it becomes (to use the German term) *volkläufig*;
the indications of this, in both the text and the
melody, are certain stylistic forms proper to the folksong, which derive from the 'oral style.'"

2. The Essence of Folk Poetry

In this respect, Meier was obviously going further than
Croce. Meier believed, in other words, that a genuine
folksong must become communal. But what was this
"community," in his view--and with what attributes did
he invest it?

In reconsidering the problem of artistic and popular poetry in his *Kunstlied und Volkslied in Deutschland*, Meier acknowledged that if a peasant woman recited the lied "In einem kühlen Grunde" fully knowing that it is a lied by Eichendorff, then that lied must be considered to be artistic poetry; but if this knowledge is lacking, the same lied must be considered to be popular poetry. Here he was merely echoing Arnim, who, as we have seen, made precisely the same point about a Goethe lied. But is the text of a Goethe or Eichendorff lied as it appears in artistic poetry preserved when it reaches the mouth of that peasant woman or the folk, or does it undergo the changes, adaptions, or (we could even say) corruptions characteristic of popular poetry? Popular "tone," which Croce had proposed as a psychological criterion distinguishing folk poetry from artistic poetry, is clearly an important factor, one not considered by Meier's thesis. We must observe, however, that while Croce identified the importance of tone, he overlooked the fact that what truly counts in folk poetry is popular circulation, precisely the point that Meier made. Croce, for example, considered Berchet to be a popular poet. But whether or not this is so, does Berchet's poetry remain in the midst of the folk in the way that authentic popular poetry does? Or does his poetry only have the kind of popularity characteristic of other "cultured" texts that are catchy or popular in tone?

On the other hand, Meier emphasized the importance of folk elaboration, a clear advantage in respect to Croce's thesis; furthermore, he did not confuse this reworking, as did Croce, with simple transmission, which is altogether different from the "re-touching" or "re-doing" characteristic of artistic poetry. According to Meier, the folk participates in this elaboration through its poets. As he himself observed:

> . . . When we succeed in discovering the original version of a folksong, it occurs to us that we have discovered not *the* folksong but the "individual" song from which the folksong has developed. At the close of fifteenth-century and sixteenth-century

songs, one often finds hints about their authors
("a bold young knight," "the son of a rich farmer,"
"a young collier," "two brave lancers, one young
and one old"); generally, however, these are fictions, with no factual foundation. Almost always
these presumed authors have merely "sung anew"
those songs actually belonging to their heritage.

Thus, themes that could have international characteristics are continually transformed in songs, and the
folksong, the individual work which serves as the
vehicle for the migration of these themes, becomes
communal:

> Each time a song is sung, it takes on new atti-
> tudes, which explains why the same song, like the
> same phrase in language, will never be sung or
> recited in quite the same way, no matter how brief
> the interval and even though there be no conscious
> intention to introduce changes. Everything influ-
> ences the text, the melody and rhythmical form of
> the song, and its execution: one's state of mind,
> whether one is rested or weary, influences exerted
> by a happy companion or by the song's manner of
> composition (by men only or by men and women, or
> only by women), and the place where it is sung (a
> private dwelling or a public inn).

Popular poetry, we might say, reminded Meier of
those thin, cobweb-like threads that the folk calls
"della Madonna"; borne by the autumn winds, they settle
here and there and then easily float away to someplace
else, forever forming new and different patterns. In
characterizing these interlacing patterns, Meier was
appealing to a specific style whose forms corresponded
to a singer's needs, apparently assisting him in his
task. But were the forms revealed by Meier's examination totally external? He believed that there is
always a song "which must be called popular because of
its innermost essence and its very nature of existence."
If we translate "essence" to mean "popular tone" and if
we translate "nature of existence" to mean "folk elabo-

ration" then we will see that ultimately Meier is in
line with Croce as revised by Menéndez Pidal.

3. Naumann and Abased Cultural Values

Meier's *Rezeptionstheorie* was strengthened and transferred from studies of lieder to studies of all folk
productions by another German scholar, Hans Naumann.
Naumann's two major works are *Primitive Gemeinschafts-
kultur* (1921) and *Grundzüge der deutschen Volkskunde*
(1922).

In reconsidering problems about the origins of
folklore, Naumann began by establishing three phases
through which mankind must pass: he called the first
the primordial phase, in which man is an unconscious
"fragment" of nature; the second he called the communal phase, in which man participates in social life;
and the third he called the individual phase, in which
man has his own personality. In light of his sociological basis, which allowed him to imagine a tightly
compartmentalized *anthropos*, Naumann was far from
giving primordial man the kind of nature Vico had
given him; moreover, his distinction between the
individual and the communal is extremely fragile,
inasmuch as the individual always reflects the communal just as the communal reflects the individual.
In any event, his sociological basis led him to formulate two principles that were, in his view, the very
foundation of folklore. The first principle concerns
primitive culture, the culture of agricultural and
farming societies; lacking in real differences, these
societies have their own heritage, and each manifestation in that heritage begins with a single individual.
The second principle concerns abased cultural values
or impoverished cultural material, which, according to
Naumann, transforms a nation into a powerful receptive
force that accepts everything produced by the ruling
classes. The folklorist's task, then, is to see how
these two worlds blend into each other, distinguishing
original elements from those imported or borrowed by
the folk.

In his theory Naumann made use of a concept previously reasoned out by Eduard Hoffmann-Krayer, a
Swiss folklorist. Hoffmann-Krayer initiated the publication of the periodical *Schweizerisches Archiv für
Volkskunde*, founded the *Volkskundliche Bibliographie*
(continued by Paul Geiger, who also succeeded him as
editor of the journal), and organized the *Handwörterbuch des deutschen Aberglaubens*, now an indispensable
tool in the study of ethnic traditions, which he
directed with the assistance of Hanns Bächtold-
Stäubli. Now, ever since 1932 Hoffmann-Krayer had
given the strictest attention to the "folk spirit" as
it had been conceived by W. H. Riehl. In his *Die
Volkskunde als Wissenschaft* Hoffmann-Krayer had proposed an idea to which he always remained faithful:
the lower class, the folk, is less differentiated than
the upper class, which explains the uniformity of the
folk personality. This, in turn, was the source of
Naumann's principle that in genuine communal folklore
whatever is created by one could also be created by
another. In essence, what Naumann here describes is
what other folklorists call a "common spirit" or,
better still, "traditional commonplaces." But does
tradition exist only in these commonplaces? And is it
these commonplaces that determine the various processes
of popular poetry?

4. *Sources of Hoffmann-Krayer's "System"*

Hoffmann-Krayer answered this question--one that had
become even more compelling after Naumann's research--
in his essay "Individuelle Triebkräfte im Volksleben,"
published in 1930 in *Archives Suisses des Traditions
Populaires*, a journal he edited, which was supported
by an interesting collection of folkloristic studies.
Although his first works had sustained the idea that
the folk reproduces more than it creates, Hoffmann-
Krayer broadened his conception of folklore in this
essay (a conception that had initially been restricted
to the formula *vulgus in populo*), and he also provided
a broad-based examination of folk individuality as it

should be understood. His conception of folklore is
fairly similar to Barbi's, inasmuch as he argued that
(1) everything is popular that consciously or unconsciously circulates among the folk, and that (2) it
is essential to see that folklore is not only what the
folk accepts but especially what it uses. Here, then,
is the "renewal" of folklore, in which it becomes difficult, he says, to discriminate between higher and
lower elements by appealing to individual impulses
that should characterize the former and to communal
impulses that should characterize the latter. An
obvious response, he says with a clear historiographic
and aesthetic awareness, is to argue that in both
manifestations the principal actor is not the folk but
a more learned individual. Giuseppe Vidossi, however,
distinguishes Hoffmann-Krayer's position from Croce's
position:

> When Croce says of popular poetry, "no poetry is
> communal in origin because it requires the person
> of a poet to be created, and it does or can diffuse
> to a greater or lesser degree in the society in
> which it originated," he passes over the fact of
> this diffusion; this may be extraneous to aesthetic
> considerations, but for the student of popular
> traditions the question of diffusion has perhaps
> never been of such capital interest as it is today.
> In Hoffmann-Krayer's view, diffusion is achieved
> through assimilation, which he feels is the govern-
> ing principle in all social groups. At the center
> of this assimilation . . . one always finds the
> strongest individual work, which provides the tone
> for weaker ones.

5. Confutations

Assimilated material does not remain as such, according
to Hoffmann-Krayer; rather, it is modified and adapted
by the prevailing taste. Although Hoffmann-Krayer did
not have interpretative criteria for approaching what
Croce had previously conceived as the "two worlds" of

cultured and popular literature, he certainly made
himself the guarantor of an experience that was also
maturing in the minds of many other scholars who were
restudying relationships between popular and artistic
poetry.

In the field of folk poetry, for example, there
were many scholars who attempted to reconcile Meier's
early positions with Naumann's theories. Among these
scholars we must certainly cite Renata Dessauer, who
wrote an interesting monograph entitled *Das Zersingen*
(1926), and Emma Funk, who wrote a work entitled *Die
Rolle der künstlichen Bearbeitung in der Textgeschichte
der alten deutschen Volksballaden* (1931). These works
examined the "layers" built up around some German folksongs. There is no doubt that the authors succeeded
in demonstrating that many literary songs become corrupted in passing into the folk, and these studies are
certainly legitimate. But can we draw general conclusions from such specific and special cases?

In this regard, an ingenious French folklorist,
Patrice Coirault, clearly took a proper stance. In his
*Recherches sur notre ancienne chanson populaire tradi-
tionnelle*, published between 1927 and 1932, he demonstrated (1) that it is absurd to pose the problem of
relationships between popular and artistic poetry in a
series of "descents" and "degradations," (2) that between the two degrees of culture there are also some
altogether intermediate degrees, without "solution of
continuity," and (3) that folk creation is always tied
to folk elaboration.

Especially important is Coirault's analysis of
creation and *elaboration* as these terms had come to be
understood in both popular and artistic poetry. His
thesis, as Paolo Toschi has nicely summarized it, is
that the two terms are not nearly as distinct as they
appear to be in Crocian aesthetics, because just as
a creation in cultured literature exists within a
stylistic tradition so is it impossible to explain
popular poetry without placing it within the context
of its particular tradition.

Convinced that the essential characteristic of
popular poetry is its "inimitable simplicity of form

and basic expression" (which suggested to him, erroneously, the absence of individuality), Coirault maintained that in many cases such characteristics were
acquired rather than innate. Thus, although he was
moving in the right direction in his assessment of the
relationship between popular and artistic poetry, he
reduced popular poetry to a genre in which "inimitable
simplicity" was equated with absence of individuality.
As Toschi observes, however, Coirault perceived the
necessity of having a theory of poetics to go along
with poetry. At many points Coirault's theory corresponds to Croce's, but the concept of folk elaboration
offered Coirault a more extensive criterion for interpreting the problem of folk poetry.

In the field of dance, one of Naumann's pupils,
Paul J. Bloch, attempted to demonstrate in his comprehensive work entitled *Der deutsche Volkstanz* (1926)
that, aside from dances deriving from ancient cults,
"there are no true folk dances" but only "forms derived
from stage and drawing-room dances." Richard Wolfram
answered him, however, in his essay "Lo studio della
danza popolare in Germania," published in the previously cited special issue of *Lares*: "In my *Volkstanz nur
gesunkenes Kulturgut?* I have refuted these errors.
. . . Using studies of 'linguistic islands,' I have
attempted to clarify the typical case of our love-
dances--*Ländler*, *Steirischer*, and *Schuhplattler*--which
Bloch sees as deriving from nineteenth-century stage
dances. Among emigrants who left the Fatherland a
century ago and who therefore had no ties with their
original land, I found *Ländler* that must have been with
them as early as 1730. The connection with medieval
'skipping' dances and the galliard proves the significant antiquity and popular origin of our love-dances."

As for folk art, one of the least-studied areas of
folklore (although ethnographic museums now developing
throughout Europe may become veritable laboratories of
study), Konrad Hahm offered some significant observations in his extensive monograph entitled *Deutsche
Volkskunst*, published in 1928. In his essay "Indagine
dell'arte popolare in Germania," published in *Lares*,
Hahm observed, "Because of their general importance

[in the field of folk art], one must mention the works and studies of Michael and Arthur Haberlandt, Otto Lehmann, and Adolf Spamer. Karl Spiess's *Bauernkunst, ihre Art und ihr Sinn* . . . contains important thoughts that can well serve as a guide for such studies."

All of these authors, we should note, agreed in rejecting Naumann's thesis, although some of them (Spamer, for example) initially had accepted it. This was because folk art, in order to be such, must have precisely that simple and elemental tone that modifies and transforms sources. In other words, what counts in folk poetry also counts in folk art.

6. *Gor'kiĭ's Request*

In contrast to Naumann one must pose Ĩuriĭ Sokolov, the leader of a new generation of Russian folklore scholars. Educated in Veselovskiĭ's historical school, he had a lively and profound interest, as did his teacher, in various problems about folkloristic theory and method- ology that were being debated throughout Europe.

Like Meier and Hoffmann-Krayer in their first works, Sokolov initially accepted the thesis that the folk receives its heritage from others. Even before Naumann's works had come out, this thesis had been sustained in Russia by V. A. Keltuĩala and O. F. Miller, who were much influenced by Bédier. Sokolov himself had argued for this thesis in his essay on byliny, which he published in 1929 in the *Great Soviet Ency- clopedia.* Some years later, however, he posed the problem of "decadent values" quite differently in talking about the narrative. In his essay on the folk narrative he observed, "Tales usually called magical-- for example, the one about Prince Ivan conquering the *Car-devica* [princess] and the ones about the firebird or some other miracle--obviously originated in the age of feudalism and, we must think, not in a peasant environment but rather in that of boyars, princes, and merchants. Only afterwards were they reworked by peas- ants according to their tastes and class."

Thus was the "left wing" (as Hippius and Chicherov

correctly called it) of the historical school created,
one which was best trained to combat the theories of
Naumann, his predecessors, and his followers. The
major representative of this wing was to be Sokolov
himself, who found a tenacious collaborator in his
brother, Boris. The Sokolovs are today the Grimms of
Russia. It is largely to their credit that the problem of individual versus folk creation has been subjected to close criticism aimed at distinguishing
between artistic and non-artistic folklore. Veselovskiĭ had demonstrated how a source comes to be absorbed
by new creators of folklore: the Sokolovs exemplified
this concept. In Russia, Gil'ferding had given importance to the creative individuality of the "bearers"
of folklore--and it was Gil'ferding's system that the
Sokolovs followed when, in 1915, they published an
extensive collection of tales and songs of the White
Sea region.

It was on these bases that Russian folklorists
worked with renewed energy after the Revolution. And
it was then that some genuine poetical personalities,
who belonged to the ranks of the folk and who were
treated in some accurate monographs, emerged from the
anonymity generally characteristic of folklore. The
extensive folkloristic researches presided over, after
the Revolution, by Maksim Gor'kiĭ, with the aid of IUriĭ
Sokolov, especially contributed to the discovery of
these personalities. Gor'kiĭ was an expert in Russian
literary folklore, which he invoked in his many works,
especially those dealing with his own life. In 1934
at the Congress of Soviet Writers, he said, after
emphasizing how folklore harmoniously reconciled reason
and intuition, thought and feeling:

I turn again, with a word of friendly advice,
which may also be understood as a request, to the
representatives of the nationalities of the Caucasus and Central Asia. Upon me--and, I know, not
upon me alone--the *ashug* Suleyman Stalsky has made
a most profound impression. I saw this old man,
illiterate but wise, sitting in the presiding
council, whispering, creating his verses; then he,

the Homer of the twentieth century, recited them
most wonderfully.

Cherish the people who are able to create such
pearls of poetry as Suleyman produces. I repeat:
the beginning of the art of words is in folklore.
Collect your folklore, make a study of it, work
it over. It will yield a great deal of material
both to you and to us, the poets and prose writers
of the Soviet Union.[1]

We also must credit Gor'kiĭ for initiating the
publication of a work bearing the significant title
Creative Works of the Peoples of the USSR. The intent
of these studies, to which the Sokolovs also contributed, was to account not only for rural areas but also
for shipyards, factories, and so forth. This demonstrated the vitality of working-class folklore, and it
especially revealed the fallacy of the theory (a very
productive one, which had been advanced by Herder) that
folklore dies and that it therefore must be immediately
collected and saved. Gor'kiĭ had proposed the thesis
that, rather than dying, folklore follows a path of
continuous development--a thesis that had been fully
anticipated in Russia by Pushkin and N. A. Dobroliŭbov.
However, we must credit Sokolov with giving a scientific foundation to this thesis, which he synthesized
in a straightforward, clear, and decisive way. In his
view, folklore is indeed the voice of the past, but it
is also the powerful voice of the present.

It is the *contemporary* consciousness, then, that
illuminates folklore. This contemporaneity of folklore
(also perceptively investigated by M. K. Azadovskiĭ,
who studied his predecessors, emphasizing the work of
Gil'ferding, Pushkin, and Dobroliŭbov) constituted the
new conception of Russian folklore. According to this
new conception, the central problem was no longer to
research origins of traditional genres but rather to

[1]Quoted in IŬ. M. Sokolov, *Russian Folklore*, trans.
Catherine Ruth Smith, with an Introduction and Bibliog-
raphy by Felix Oinas (1950; rpt. Hatboro, Pa., Folklore
Associates, 1966), p. 25.

see how these genres live today--to see, that is, how
poetry is actually made and how the folk finds its own
educational literature in such poetry. This is essentially a return to Romanticism, but this new Romanticism tends not only to emphasize national values but
also to place these values within a social context.

7. *Sokolov's Concept of Poetic Folklore*

In reasserting the validity of folkloristic research,
Russian scholars of the new generation were not concerned only with seeing the social function served by
the "bearers" of folklore; they were also particularly
interested in investigating the idea of "artistic
personality." The conclusions reached on this subject
by Iûriĭ Sokolov in his book on Russian literary folklore, published in Leningrad in 1938, are especially
significant.

In *Russian Folklore*, Sokolov first emphasizes
that the distinction between artistic and popular
poetry (or, to use his terms, "artificial" and "natural" poetry) is quite mechanical, because both are or
can be authentic "manifestations of one great literary
art."[2] Here he is in agreement with Croce, whom he
did not cite and probably did not know. In contrast
to Croce--and this is a consequence of Russian folkloristic research aimed at determining the personalities that create folklore--Sokolov focuses on and
gives prominence to common people and workers. Croce
had written that popular poetry is largely owed to
literate and semi-literate rather than ignorant people
(an "ignorance" about which there would be much to
distinguish and discuss). Sokolov, however, said that
the common people and workers acquire a creative capacity because of a broad, deep awareness of their own
nation's poetic and narrative folklore, which constitutes their culture. The "ignorance" of common people
and workers, then, does not actually correspond to our
concept of ignorance, inasmuch as we customarily

[2]Ibid., p. 10.

measure everything exclusively in terms of our own
knowledge, despising whatever does not belong to us or
our social class.

Sokolov concludes that folk poets and writers fall
into a variety of schools, which are distinguished by
their subject matter, their style, and the execution
of their work--a thesis fully shared by Sydow and in
some respects by our own scholar, Sergio Baldi, although each arrived at his conclusions independently
of the other. In any event, the best folk compositions
obviously reveal a genuine "artistic skill"; moreover
(and this is another point on which Sokolov and Croce
agree), the process of creation in poetic and narrative
folklore is identical to the process in artistic literature.

After acknowledging that each variant has the
validity of a new production (each variant, he says,
must be considered as an "artistic fact"), Sokolov does
not ignore the power of tradition, in which the work of
the community must be recognized. Agreeing fully with
Coirault, he says:

> Here a question arises concerning *tradition*,
> which also is considered by certain investigators
> as an essential characteristic that distinguishes
> folklore from literature. But again we insist that
> the distinction between folklore and artistic lit-
> erature, in this relationship too, is more of a
> quantitative than of a qualitative kind. Surely,
> apart from poetic tradition, one cannot even con-
> ceive of the development of literature. In folk-
> lore this power of tradition appears to be stronger,
> because the oral creation, not being fixed in any
> outward form, has had to work out, in the course
> of many centuries of practice, such traditional
> mnemonic devices as would preserve in the memory
> sometimes very complicated subjects.

> An analysis of the poetics of folklore will
> have to show how the stylistic and compositional
> devices worked out by tradition, on the one hand,
> contribute to the memorizing of artistic texts,
> and, on the other hand, facilitate their reworking

> or the creation of new texts by means of improvi-
> sation. . . . Folklore cannot be reduced to one
> tradition alone; otherwise it would be necessary
> to acknowledge in it only the source of stagnation,
> sluggishness, and conservatism.[3]

In conclusion, one cannot deny the importance of tradition, which affirms the popularity of a poem. When
the poem achieves aesthetic fulfillment, however, it
is best to separate it from all variants, regarding
it exclusively as an artistic fact.

8. *The Folk and the Clerisy*

Aesthetics has increasingly assisted philology with
the formulation of its principles, while the "poetry-
people" symbiosis at the base of such principles has
come to be formulated in an increasingly detailed and
certainly more persuasive way. It was believed that
the concept of popular poetry was dead. Actually, it
is more alive than ever before.
    In posing relationships between popular and artis-
tic poetry, Romanticism had been clear, consistent,
and categorical, in that it had attributed to the folk
a number of lyrical themes, narrative inventions, and
myths, which came to serve as sources for artistic
literature. Later, as positivistic philology gradually proceeded in investigations, soundings, and
excavations, it acknowledged a current account involving a debit, which has kept Romanticism continu-
ously working, and a credit. This is not a "credit"
in the sense given the term by the Grimms or Müller
and clarified later by Menéndez Pidal--in the sense,
that is, of borrowings that were completely revised
and recreated--but rather in the sense given the term
by Benfey, who, while admitting that artistic and popular literature co-exist, maintained that the latter is
merely a transcription of the former. Better still
is the example of Bédier, who, in posing certain

[3]Ibid., pp. 13-14.

relationships between the folk and the clerisy, had made the folk into an abstraction that was no less arbitrary than the concept of clerisy. But in contrast to Benfey (and before Bédier had formulated his thesis), Paris imposed a clear distinction between popular and artistic literature. This distinction was emphasized by Ancona, Comparetti, and Pitrè, who always remained convinced that these two forms corresponded to two distinct modes of feeling.

It was now a matter of clarifying these two modes with the best choice of terms--of seeing what their nature and essence might be. Menéndez Pidal converted the "national spirit" of the romantics into a "common feeling," attributing this feeling to popular or, as he says, "traditional" poetry. This was obviously in contrast to artistic poetry, which remained in another sphere. In postulating his "folk-clerisy" antithesis, Bédier attributed everything to the clerisy. The colloquy still remained open, and it often seemed to be a matter of a veritable class struggle, either *for* or *against* the folk.

As if to respond to this colloquy, Croce distinguished popular poetry from artistic poetry, but without doing harm to its artistic nature. The concept of folk elaboration, which gradually has become better understood, tells us, however, that a popular tone truly lives in, with, and among the folk. Even the most elementary poetry made by literate men is often difficult; when such poetry reaches the folk, however, we discover that the folk has, to use Sokolov's phrase, its own schools with which and in which to instruct. And if the poetry *does* arrive, it never remains as it came. As Sokolov says, however, the works of poets and poetic personalities, of singers and narrators, must never be studied only to trace a tradition; they must also be studied as artistic facts.

On the other hand, this is not to deny--and it would be absurd to deny it (hence the validity of Meier's studies)--that folk literature can serve as a subterranean well-spring for artistic literature, and *vice versa*. Indeed, it is a great error to consider the folk as a self-enclosed entity. When

cultured literature becomes popular--that is, when
the motifs of the former are revived in the latter--
it forgets its source (a thesis first suggested by
Görres) and becomes a part of a specific literature
that must be justified on its own terms. Just as
artistic poetry must not be viewed as a presumed
refinement of popular poetry (nor is this said to
degrade the former), so is popular poetry no longer
such when it is made into cultured, courtly, "contemplated" poetry--and *vice versa*. It is not a question,
then, of denying one form and favoring the other, but
of giving concrete life to both. Popular poetry and
artistic ("contemplated") poetry--given the fact,
we repeat, that popular poetry can be artistic poetry
--should be viewed as two parallel lines which always
remain separate, even when they seem to converge.

Bédier had taken the gift of poetry from the
humble ones, the folk poets. Philology and aesthetic
criticism are now in agreement that the gift should
be returned. And as this happens, it seems that we
hear the echo of Maksim Gor'kiĭ's request: "Collect
your folklore, make a study of it, work it over." It
is true even today that folklore, an inseparable part
of social and cultural history, has not always been
considered in such history (notwithstanding the example now given us by Huizinga and Bloch). It is also
true that the history of folklore is almost totally
neglected by the history of European historiography,
to which it most certainly belongs. But although
these and other suspicions (if we can call them that)
are bound to diminish, they can only serve, for one
who cultivates these studies, as an inducement to continue the work of his predecessors--those who deserve
credit for having broken ground and built roads, open-
ing a new way for us all.

NOTES AND BIBLIOGRAPHICAL ENTRIES

The notes that follow do not pretend to be a complete
bibliography of my *Storia del folklore in Europa*.
Bibliographies either indiscriminately include everything that has been written on a topic or they follow
a criterion of inclusion that conforms to the method
that the author has followed in his work. It is this
latter criterion that I have followed, to aid those
readers who wish to pursue the subject matter treated
in the individual chapters. [Translator's note:
Entries have been modified to conform to Library of
Congress entries, when possible. The reader will find
bibliographic information in brackets for works cited
by Cocchiara as translations. I have provided such
information only in Cocchiara's initial reference to
a translated work.]

NOTES AND BIBLIOGRAPHICAL ENTRIES

Preface

An extensive history of folklore is provided by A.
Guichot y Sierra in his *Orígines en todos los países
hasta 1890. Desarrollo en España hasta 1921* (Madrid,
1922). This, however, is merely a catalogue of
antique-trade, of no historical or critical interest.
Altogether different, however, is the essay on European folkloristic historiography by IŨ. M. Sokolov,
Russian Folklore (New York, 1950), pp. 3-156; this
work, first published in Russia [*Ruskiǐ fol'lor*,
Leningrad, 1938], has been translated into French in
an abridged version that leaves out, among other
things, the bibliographical notes. For international
folklore bibliographies, manuals and general treatments, comparative collections, etc., see A. van
Gennep, *Manuel de folklore français contemporain*,
III (Paris, 1937-38), 98-113, and IV, 559-60, 596-97,
621-23, 655-60, 717-62, 769-805, 815-18, 853-91,
893-94, 939-49, 1012-16. We will have occasion to
cite some of these works. For other bibliographic
notes of the same type, see A. H. Krappe, *The Science
of Folk-lore* (London, 1930), which is most useful for
the bibliography at the end of each chapter); G.
Jungebauer, *Geschichte der deutschen Volkskunde*
(Praga, 1931); A. Haberlandt, *Die deutsche Volkskunde*
(Halle, 1935); R. Corso, *Folklore*, 2nd ed. (Napoli,
1943); and P. Toschi, *Guida allo studio delle tradizioni popolari*, 2nd ed. (Roma, 1948). On the historical nature of folklore and related issues, see G. Cocchiara, *Storia degli studi delle tradizioni popolari
in Italia* (Palermo, 1947). In regard to the relationship between folklore and ethnology, this work can be

integrated with E. de Martino, *Naturalismo e storicismo nell' etnologia* (Bari, 1941). References: P.
Saintyves, "Les origines de la méthode comparative et
la naissance du folklore," in *Revue de l'Histoire des
Religions* (1932), pp. 45ff; and A. Gramsci, *Letteratura e vita nazionale* (Torino, 1951), pp. 140ff.

PART ONE

Chapter I

1. There is now extensive literature on the origin
and formation of the concept of the noble savage, which
has recently been reviewed in G. Cocchiara, *Il mito del
buon selvaggio* (Messina, 1948). We should also add
N. H. Fairchild, *The Noble Savage* (New York, 1928), and
A. Gerbi, *Viejas polémicas sobre el nuevo mundo* (Lima,
1946). Fueter gave prominence to Martire's work in
Storia della storiografia moderna [*Geschichte der
neueren Historiographie*, 3rd ed., München, 1936],
trans. Spinelli (Napoli, 1944), I, 350. For Léry, however, see R. Allier, *Le non-civilisé et nous* (Paris,
1927). Even today there are differences of opinion
about the activity of Bartolomé de las Casas. On this
point see, for example, J. B. Terán, *La nascita dell'
America spagnuola* [*El nacimiento de la América española,*
n.p., 1927], trans. Doria (Bari, 1931), which gives a
favorable view, and R. Menéndez Pidal, *Poesia arabe e
poesia europea* [*Poesía arabe y poesía europea*, Buenos
Aires, 1941], trans. Ruggero (Bari, 1949), which gives
a quite opposite view.

2-4. The opinion that the concept of the noble savage
coincides with the Golden Age was formulated by Gonnard, *La légende du bon sauvage* (Paris, 1946). In his
"Le voyage de Jean de Léry et la découverte du 'bon
sauvage'" in the *Revue de l'Institut de Sociologie*
(Bruxelles, 1927), Clerc clarified the connections
between Léry and Montaigne; moreover, he argued that
the concept of the noble savage had been formulated by
Léry. But this claim is without foundation, because

Columbus and especially Gonneville (1503-1505) had be-
lieved the American savages to be good and peaceful,
and this concept had been clearly formulated previous-
ly, in the thought of such men as Martire and Casas.
On this subject see the excellent book *Les François en
Amérique pendant le première moitié du XVIe siècle*, ed.
C. A. Julien, R. Herval, and T. Beauchesne (Paris, 1946).
For Montaigne's conception of the savage, see G. Chinard,
*L'exotisme américain dans la littérature française au
XVIe siècle d'après Rabelais* (Paris, 1911), and *L'Amérique et le rêve exotique* (Paris, 1934); G. Atkinson, *Les
nouveaux horizons de la Renaissance Française* (Paris,
1935); G. Toffanin, *Montaigne e l'idea classica* (Bologna, 1942); and G. Lawson, *Les "Essais" de Montaigne*
(Paris, 1948), pp. 150ff. A. Bros provides some rather
harsh comments on Lescarbot in his *L'ethnologie religieuse*, 2nd ed. (Paris, 1938), pp. 129ff.

5. For Baron Lahontan, see the tasteful treatment provided in P. Hazard, *La crisi della coscienza europea*
[*La crise de la conscience européenne*, Paris, 1934-35],
trans. Serini (Torino, 1946), pp. 13ff, and *La pensée
européenne au XVIIIe siècle* (Paris, 1946), II, 126ff.
There is a large body of literature on utopias that has
recently been reviewed in C. Curcio, *Utopisti italiani
del cinquecento, scelti e annotati*, selected and annotated (Roma, 1944), pp. 30-32. There are some good
observations on Thomas More's *Utopia* as a religious
text in M. Petrocchi, *L'uomo e la storia* (Bologna,
1944), pp. 7ff. See also F. Battaglia, *Saggi sull'
"Utopia" di Tommaso Moro* (Bologna, 1949), pp. 43ff.
Finally, see the very perceptive treatment offered by
A. Gramsci, *Il Risorgimento* (Torino, 1949), pp. 217ff.
Gramsci believes that "the technique of attributing to
foreign nations those institutions that would be desirable in one's own country derived from the utopias,"
and he further believes that "all of this literature
has had no little importance in the history of the
diffusion of social and political opinion among specific masses of people and therefore in the history of
culture." References: G. Salvemini, *La rivoluzione
francese*, 6th ed. (Milano, 1947), p. 58.

6-7. For the early missionaries' attitude toward the
religion of primitives, see especially A. Bros, op.
cit., pp. 27ff, and W. Koppers, *La religione dell'uomo
primitivo* ["Urmensch und Urreligion," in *Wissen und
Bekenntnis*, ed. Friedrich Dessauer, Olten, 1944]
(Milano, 1947), pp. 20ff. For Pigafetta see C. Man-
froni in *Pigafetta, Il primo viaggio intorno al mondo*
(Milano, 1939), pp. 117ff. Keep in mind the work by
F. Mazzei, *Recherches historiques et politiques sur les
États-Unis de l'Amérique Septentrionale*, III (Paris,
1788); this volume cites Condorcet's extremely interesting pamphlet entitled *Influence de la revolution de
l'Amérique sur l'Europe*, which intelligently discusses
the advantages and disadvantages that the discovery of
America brought to Europe. References: A. Gerbi, *La
politica del Settecento* (Bari, 1934), p. 50.

8. Clear and penetrating discussions of Europe as a
historical entity are offered in F. Chabod, "L'idea di
Europa," in *Rassegna d'Italia*, 4 (1947), 4ff, and in
C. Morandi, *L'idea dell'unità politica d'Europa nel
XIX e XX secolo* (Milano, 1948). We are familiar with
Eliot's thesis in *Notes Towards the Definition of Culture* (London, 1948), pp. 123-24, which holds that the
bases of European culture are to be found in the modern
idea of man, as well as in the classical world and in
the texts of ancient Revelation.

Chapter II

1. For the importance of Oriental travels in sixteenth-
and seventeenth-century Europe, see G. Dugat, *Histoire
des orientalists de l'Europe du XIIe au XIXe siècle*
(Paris, 1868-70). Always quite useful is P. Martino,
L'Orient dans la littérature française au XVIIe siècle
(Paris, 1906). For whatever use they may give us, let
us also add W. Schubart, *L'Europa e l'anima dell'Oriente*
[*Europa und die Seele des Ostens*, Luzern, 1938], trans.
Gentilli (Roma, 1947), and G. Tucci, *Italia e Oriente*
(Milano, 1949). References: P. Hazard, *La crisi della
coscienza europea*, trans. Serini (Torino, 1946),

pp. 13ff, and F. Gabrieli, *Storia e civiltà musulmana* (Napoli, 1947), pp. 73ff.

2. There is an interesting biographical sketch of Pietro della Valle which G. B. Bellori has prefaced to the 1658-1663 edition of *Viaggi*. There are some good observations on his ethnographic attitudes in G. Pennisi, "Pietro della Valle e i suoi viaggi in Turchia, Persia e India," in *Boll. Soc. Geogr. It.* (Nov.-Dec. 1890); and in L. Bianconi, who has edited P. della Valle's *Viaggio in Levante* (Firenze, 1942). Of the many manuscripts that Valle brought back from the Orient, some were known by Kircher (for example, the first grammar and the first Coptic dictionary), which he used in his *Prodromus Coptus sive Aegyptiacus* (Roma, 1636).

3. Even today Bartoli is primarily regarded as a prose writer, not as an ethnographical writer. On this point, see G. Marzot, "Forward" to D. Bartoli, *Missione al Gran Mogor* (Milano, 1946). See also L. Anceschi, "La poetica di una 'certa beatitudine del gusto,'" in his book *Civiltà delle lettere* (Milano, 1945). For Ricci see H. Cordier, *Histoire générale de la Chine*, III (Paris, 1920), 318ff, and *Opere storiche del P. Matteo Ricci*, ed. P. Tacchi Venturi (Macerata, 1911-1913). For Roberto de Nobili there is Bertrand's always-useful work, *Mémoires historiques sur les missions des ordres religieux*, 2nd ed. (Paris, 1862), pp. 286ff. For the controversy over the Chinese and Malabar rites, see the works of H. Pinard de la Boullaye, *L'étude comparée des religions*, I (Paris, 1922), 184, and V. Pinot, *La Chine et la formation de l'esprit philosophique en France (1640-1740)* (Paris, 1932).

4. An interesting treatment of Marana is provided by P. Toldo in *Giornale storico della letteratura italiana* (1897), pp. 46ff. For Chinard, however, see the recent work of G. L. Van Roosbroeck, *Persian Letters before Montesquieu* (New York, 1932). For additional information, see Dodd's essay, *Les récits de voyages: Sources de l' "Esprit des Lois" de Montesquieu* (Paris, 1929).

5. Egypt's importance in the field of ethnology has been brought to light by Pinard de la Boullaye, op. cit., 232ff. For additional information see Réville, *Les phases successives de l'histoire des religions* (Paris, 1909).

6. A fine book on French fairy tales and their historical antecedents is M. E. Storer's *La mode des contes de fées* (Paris, 1928). For Huet, however, see A. Dupront, *Pierre-Daniel Huet et l'exégèse comparatiste au XVIIe siècle* (Paris, 1930). For Italian tale-writers (Straparola, Basile, etc.), see G. Cocchiara, *Genesi di leggende*, 3rd ed. (Palermo, 1949), pp. 10ff.

7. One of the most lucid essays on *Thousand and One Nights* is F. Gabrieli's *Storia e civiltà musulmana*, pp. 99ff (revised and republished in the first Italian translation of *Thousand and One Nights* [*Mille e una notte*], ed. Gabrieli, Torino, 1949).

8. For various histories of religion originating from the convergence of Oriental studies and studies of primitives (or at least having an affinity with these Oriental studies), see Pinard de la Boullaye, op. cit., I, 170ff. Spencer is considered the founder of the comparative history of religion by Robertson Smith, *Lectures on the Religion of Semites*, 2nd ed. (London, 1894). In opposition to this is W. Schmidt, *Manuale di storia comparata delle religioni* [*Ursprung und Werden der Religion: Theorien und Tatsachen*, Münster, 1930], trans. Bugatto (Brescia, 1934), p. 42. References: A. van Gennep, "L'exotisme dans la littérature française du XVIe au XVIIIe siècle," in *Religions, mœurs et légendes*, V (Paris, 1914), 100.

Chapter III

1. For the struggle against error, which began after the discovery of America, it is always helpful to consult the work of J. L. Castilhon, *Essai sur les erreurs et les superstitions* (Paris, 1765). The problem is

treated from a quite different critical angle by P. Hazard, *La crisi della coscienza europea*, trans. Serini (Torino, 1946), pp. 125-229.

2. Generally we do not find much importance given to the influence of the Reformation in the field of folk-lore. If one wishes to provide the necessary basis for such research, he should by all means use the work of E. Troeltsch, *Il protestantesimo nella formazione del mondo moderno* [*Die Bedeutung des Protestantismus für die Entstehung der modernen Welt*, München-Berlin, 1911], Italian translation (Firenze, 1929). This should be integrated with the essays of F. Battaglia, "Lo spirito politico della Riforma," in *La Cultura* (1928), and of C. Morandi, "Problemi storici della Riforma," in *Civiltà Moderna*, 1 (1929), 668ff, which cites the essential bibliographic information for this subject. For relationships between the Reformation and studies of the histories of religions, see Pinard de la Boullaye, *L'étude comparée des religions*, I (Paris, 1922), 151ff, and W. Schmidt, *Manuale di storia comparata delle religioni*, trans. Bugatto (Brescia, 1934), pp. 42ff (which also alludes to the work of cited humanists). For Vossio see A. Bros, *L'ethnologie religieuse*, 2nd ed. (Paris, 1938), pp. 23-24. It should be noted that Vossio's natural-istic theory was followed by Bossuet's famous adver-sary, Jurieu, author of the curious *Histoire critique des dogmes et des cultes, bons 8. mauvais, qui ont été dans l'eglise depuis Adam jusqu'à Jésus-Christ* (Amsterdam, 1704).

3. For the Counter Reformation see G. Gothein, *L'età della controriforma*, trans. Thiel (Venezia, 1928). This should be integrated with B. Croce, *Storia della età barocca in Italia*, 3rd ed. (Bari, 1941), and, in regard to belief in witches, with S. A. Nulli, *I pro-cessi delle streghe* (Torino, 1939). We have recently been given a good English translation of the *Malleus* (of which there are very few copies, unfortunately) by an English folklore scholar, Montague-Summers (London, 1928). There is additional information on

the *Malleus* in G. Bonomo, "Il Malleus Maleficarum,"
in *Annali del Museo Pitrè*, 1 (Palermo, 1950). References: J. Michelet, *La sorcière*, 2nd ed. (Paris,
1878), p. 31.

4-5. One of the most penetrating studies of Bodin is
A. Garosci's *Jean Bodin* (Milano, 1934). Of particular
interest for Bodin's view of law and natural religion
are G. del Vecchio, *Il concetto della natura e il
principio del diritto*, 2nd ed. (Bologna, 1922), and G.
Radetti, "Il problema della religione nel pensiero di
G. Bodin," in *Giornale critico della filosofia italiana*, 19 (1938), 267-68. As might be imagined, Bodin
appears in all treatments of demonology published after
his *De la démonomanie des sorciers*. Additional information is in G. Santonastaso, "La sovranità del Bodin,"
in *Le dottrine politiche da Lutero a Suarez*, III
Milano, 1946). For Spee, consult S. A. Nulli, op. cit.,
pp. 20ff. For Browne see especially M. Praz, *Studi e
svaghi inglesi* (Firenze, 1937), pp. 3ff. Some curious
and interesting information on belief in fairies is
found in an old book by Maury, *Les fées du moyen-âge*
(Paris, 1843).

6. There are some lively comments on Bekker and
Thomasius in P. Hazard, op. cit., pp. 179ff. For
major details see the brief monograph by W. P. C.
Knuttel, *Balthasar Bekker* (den Haag, 1906), and the
interesting study by F. Battaglia, *Cristiano Thomasio,
filosofo e giurista* (Roma, 1935). For the antecedents
of natural law one can always use G. Montemayor, *Storia
del diritto naturale* (Palermo, 1911). With caution,
see E. Restivo, *La filosofia del diretto di natura*
(Palermo, 1902), and O. Gierke, *Giovanni Althusius e
lo sviluppo storico delle teorie politiche giusnatural-
istiche*, ed. A. Giolitti (Torino, 1943), and A. Corsano,
Ugo Grozio (Bari, 1948).

7. For Cherbury see A. Carlini, "Herbert di Cherbury
e la scuola di Cambridge," in *Rend. Accademia Lincei*
(1917); and G. de Ruggiero, *Storia della filosofia,
parte III: Rinascimento, riforma e controriforma*, 2nd

ed. (Bari, 1937), II, 260ff. On deism see L. Stephen,
History of English Thought in the Eighteenth Century,
2nd ed. (London, 1902), I, 200ff; E. Troeltsch,
"Deismus," in *Ges. Schrif.* 4, 429ff; E. Cassirer, *La
filosofia dell' Illuminismo* [*Die Philosophie der
Aufklärung,* Tübingen, 1932], trans. Pocar, 2nd ed.
(Firenze, 1945), pp. 246ff; and C. Motzo Dentice di
Accadia, "Il preilluminismo," in *Giornale critico della
filosofia italiana* (1928). On anti-deism it is best
to consult Butler's monograph, *The Analogy of Religion,
Natural and Revealed, to the Constitution and Course of
Nature* (London, 1736). M. Petrocchi, in the *Riv.
Storica It.,* 61 (1949), 142, believes that the beginning of deistic solutions is to be found in the respect
that many missionaries, particularly the Jesuits, had
for natural religions (which brings to mind, for him,
the matter of the Malibar rites).

8. For Thiers and Le Brun see A. van Gennep, *Le folklore* (Paris, 1924), pp. 13ff, and his *Manuel de folklore français contemporain,* I (Paris, 1937-38), 6ff.
For English precursors see T. Davidson, "Le folklore
en Angleterre," in *La Tradition* (1890), pp. 4, 5-8,
33-36.

Chapter IV

There is a great deal of literature on Bayle, although
it most often emphasizes what folklore studies owe to
him. Among the most interesting essays are L. Levy-
Bruhl, "Les tendences générales de Bayle et de Fontenelle," in *Revue d'Histoire de la Philosophie* (January-
March, 1927); H. E. Haxo, "Pierre Bayle et Voltaire
avant les lettres philosophiques," in *PMLA* (New York,
1931); and B. Magnino, "Lo scetticismo di Pierre Bayle,"
in *Giornale critico della filosofia italiana* (1941)
(reprinted in part in the book by the same author,
Alle origini della crisi contemporanea, Roma, 1946).
There is an excellent treatment of Bayle's view of
primitive peoples in Devolvé, *Essai sur Pierre Bayle,
religion, critique et philosophie positive* (Paris,

1906), pp. 395ff.   As a matter of curiosity, see H.
Robinson, *The Great Comet of 1680: A Study in the
History of Rationalism*   (Northfield, 1916).

2.   On the concept of superstition as an element of
power, see G. Cocchiara, *Sul concetto di superstizione*
(Palermo, 1945), pp. 20ff.   This subject is also
treated in Robinson, *Bayle the Sceptic* (London, 1931),
pp. 50ff.

3-4.   J. R. Carré has written a lively, scholarly, but
one-sided book on Fontenelle, *La philosophie de Fontenelle* (Paris, 1932), which provides an extensive bibliography on the subject.   The best critical edition
of *Histoire des oracles* is by L. Maigron (Paris, 1908).
The translation that I have used is by G. Falco
(Milano, 1947).   References: L. Maigron, *Fontenelle,
l'homme, l'œuvre, l'influence* (Paris, 1906), pp. 42,
287; and P. Hazard, *La crisi della coscienza europea*,
trans. Serini (Torino, 1946), p. 175.

5-7.   Carré has provided a recent critical edition of
De l'origine des fables (Paris, 1932), which, although
too soft and flabby, is still useful because of its
large number of bibliographical references.   In his
notes Carré attempts to prove that the ideas found in
this essay had been formulated by Fontenelle as early
as 1680.   This then allows him to consider Fontenelle
as the first precursor of Comparativism, preceding
Bayle, Tournemine, and others.   Actually, however,
many earlier scholars (from Léry to Vossio) had anticipated Comparativism.   Carré does give some convincing
consideration to the sources that led Fontenelle to
give a false interpretation of the primitive world,
pp. 52-54.   References: A. Lang, *Myth, Ritual and
Religion*, 2nd ed. (London, 1887), pp. 321ff.

8.   Dilthey, in *Gesammelte Schriften*, 2nd and 3rd eds.
(Tübingen, 1921 and 1927), was the first to call the
anti-historicism of the Enlightenment a *faible con-
venue*.   More cautious is Fueter, *Storia della storiografia moderna*, trans. Spinelli (Napoli, 1944), II,

1ff; and B. Croce, *Teoria e storia della storiografia* (Bari, 1925), pp. 50ff.

Chapter V

1. To the works cited in the last paragraph, one should add M. Roustan, *Les philosophes et la société française au XVIIIe siècle* (Paris, 1911); and C. Seignobos, *Essai d'une histoire comparée des peuples de l'Europe* (Paris, 1925). References: E. Cassirer, *La filosofia dell'- illuminismo*, trans. Pocar, 2nd ed. (Firenze, 1945), pp. 295ff.

2. For the *Lettres Persanes*, see E. Carcassonne's perceptive introduction in the critical edition which he edited (Paris, 1929). On pp. xxxv-xxxvi Carcassonne cites an entire series of letters using a foreigner's "voice" to draw a picture of European customs. Sometimes the foreigner was a savage, but often he was a Turk, a Chinese, an Indian, etc.

3-4. On the *Esprit des lois* see especially the work of Faguet, *La politique comparée de Montesquieu, Rousseau et Voltaire* (Paris, 1902). One of the most provocative books on Montesquieu, however, is still Sorel's *Montesquieu* (Paris, 1887). There is much more than the title promises in E. Carcassonne's *Montesquieu et le problème de la constitution française au XVIIIe siècle* (Paris, 1927). It is common knowledge that Montesquieu is an indispensable reference point for all those concerned with the origins of law and political doctrine. See especially G. Solari, *La scuola del diritto naturale nelle dottrine etico-giuridiche dei secoli XVII e XVIII* (Torino, 1904), and G. Mosca, *Storia delle dottrine politiche* (Bari, 1942), pp. 150ff. We should add the recent and very useful work of Maxime Leroy, *Histoire des idées sociales en France. I: De Montesquieu à Robespierre* (Paris, 1946). References: G. Hervé, *Revue de l'Ecole d'Anthropologie* (1907), p. 337 (summarized by A. van Gennep, "La méthode ethnographique en France au XVIIIe siècle," in *Religions, mœurs et légendes*, V (Paris, 1914), 135-139; and A.

Gerbi, *La politica del Settecento* (Bari, 1934),
p. 150.

5. Even today it is always useful to refer to the
work of G. Desnoiresterres, *Voltaire et la société au
XXVIIIe siècle* (Paris, 1867-76). Other helpful monographs include G. Lanson, *Voltaire* (Paris, 1906), and
R. Aldington, *Voltaire* (London, 1926). References:
R. Craveri, *Voltaire, politico dell'Illuminismo*
(Torino, 1937), p. 163; this work has the most extensive bibliography on Voltaire and includes general
works on the Enlightenment. The passage cited from
Verri is taken from the context of "Commentariolo di
un galantuomo di malumore che ha ragione, sulla mas-
sima l'uomo è un animale ragionevole," originally published in *Caffè* and reprinted in *Scritti vari di
Pietro Verri*, ed. G. Carcano (Firenze, 1854), I, 100ff.

6-7. Hervé's information (loc. cit., pp. 225ff) on
Voltaire's ethnographical tendencies is imprecise and
butchered. Some suggestions are provided in E. Fueter,
Storia della storiografia moderna, trans. Spinelli
(Napoli, 1944), II, 28ff, and in G. Cocchiara, *Il mito
del buon selvaggio* (Messina, 1948), pp. 17ff. References: A. Gerbi, op. cit., p. 134 (on pp. 121ff is a
brief picture of the Enlightenment view of the Orient);
but particularly for Hegel's concept of the Orient,
this work should be integrated with K. Löwith's *Da
Hegel à Nietzsche* [*Von Hegel bis Nietzsche*, Zürich,
1941], Ital. trans. (Torino, 1949), pp. 63ff.

8. For the concept of the "spirit of nations," particularly see F. Meinecke's fine book, *Cosmopolitismo e
stato nazionale* [*Weltbürgertum und Nationalstaat*,
München-Berlin, 1908], trans. Oberdorfer (Firenze,
1930). References: for the references to Saint-
Evremond, see C. Antoni, *La lotta contro la ragione*
(Firenze, 1942), p. 8; and B. Groethuysen, *Origini
dello spirito borghese in Francia* [*Die Entstehung der
bürgerlichen Welt- und Lebensanschauung in Frankreich*,
Halle-Saale, 1927-30], trans. Forti (Torino, 1949),
p. 52.

PART TWO

Chapter VI

1-4. In Fueter, *Storia della storiografia moderna*,
trans. Spinelli (Napoli, 1944), there is no mention of
the work of Lafitau, to whom, however, Meinecke has
given attention in his *Die Entstehung des Historismus*
(Berlin, 1936). Meinecke especially focuses on the
sensation that Lafitau's observations about the primitive world caused in Europe. But it is not here that
one must find the validity of Lafitau's work, which is
amply illustrated by Father W. Schmidt, *Semaine de
l'Ethnologie religieuse* (Paris, 1913), even though he
concentrates on Lafitau's most debatable opinion--
namely, that savages are still today what they were in
times past. See also Bros, *L'ethnologie religieuse*,
2nd ed. (Paris, 1938), pp. 120ff; Saintyves, "Les
origines de la méthode comparative, et la naissance du
folklore," in *Revue de l'Histoire des Religions* (1932),
pp. 57ff; and Pinard de la Boullaye, *L'étude comparée
des religions,* I (Paris, 1922), 182ff. References:
B. de Jouvenel, *Il potere* [*Du pouvoir, histoire natu-
relle de sa croissance,* Genève, 1945], trans. Serini
(Milano, 1947), p. 7; Gerardus van der Leeuw, *La
religion dans son essence et ses manifestations*
[*Phänomenologie der Religion*, Tübingen, 1933], trans.
Marty (Paris, 1948), p. 672; and A. van Gennep, *Religions, mœurs et légendes* (Paris, 1914), V, 130ff.

5-7. Bibliography on Vico has recently been reviewed
by Croce and Nicolini in the two-volume *Bibliografia
vichiana* (Napoli, 1948). It also cites important contributions that Vico has made to ethnology and folklore.
The reader who wishes to look into Vico's contribution
should also see B. Croce, *La filosofia di Giambattista
Vico* (Bari, 1922); A. Corsano, *Umanesimo e religione in
G. B. Vico* (Bari, 1935); E. Paci, *Ingens sylva* (Milano,
1949); and G. Villa, *La filosofia del mito secondo
G. B. Vico* (Milano, 1949). In this last work--which
has been commented on by N. Badaloni in *Società*, 5
(1949), 561-62--there is an essay entitled "Il Problema

filosofico dell'arte popolare con particolare riferi-
mento alla Romania" (pp. 81-107), in which the author,
following in the footsteps of Jorga, clearly distinguishes popular poetry from folklore--an unfounded
opinion. Villa also maintains that popular art exists
outside the boundaries of history, which indicates that
he has no conception of either art or history. References: M. Fubini, *Stile e umanità di Giambattista Vico*
(Bari, 1946), pp. 203ff (reviewed by R. Spongano, *La
prosa di Galileo e altri scritti,* Messina, 1949,
pp. 117ff), and F. Nicolini, *La religiosità di Giambattista Vico* (Bari, 1949), pp. 170ff.

8.   For Muratori's great contribution to studies of
popular traditions, see G. Cocchiara, *Storia degli
studi delle tradizioni popolari in Italia* (Palermo,
1947), pp. 34-41. We should add B. Brunello, *Il pensiero politico italiano del Settecento* (Milano, 1942),
pp. 100ff; L. Salvatorelli, *Il pensiero politico italiana dal 1700 al 1870,* 2nd ed. (Torino, 1941), pp. 90ff;
and G. Bonomo, "Il contributo di L. A. Muratori allo
studio delle tradizioni popolari," in *Miscellanea di
muratoriani* (Modena, 1951).

Chapter VII

1-3.   There is no complete study that illustrates and
documents the importance of Rousseau either for ethnology or for folklore. See, however, the recent works on
him by Schinz, *La pensée de J.-J. Rousseau* (Paris, 1929)
pp. 50ff; and by Wrighter, *The Meaning of Rousseau* (Oxford, 1929). For Rousseau as ethnologist, see G. Cocchiara, *Il mito del buon selvaggio* (Messina, 1948),
pp. 15ff. There are some well-focused passages on the
topic in G. Ferretti, *L'uomo nell'infanzia* (Città di
Castello, n.d.); L. Giusso, *Leopardi, Stendhal, Nietzsche* (Napoli, 1933), pp. 151ff; and C. Dawson, *Progresso e religione* [*Progress and Religion,* London, 1929]
trans. Foà (Milano, 1948). For ethnographic sources,
see A. van Gennep, *Religions, mœurs et légendes,* V
(Paris, 1914), 141-47. References: E. Cassirer, "Das

problem Jean Jacques Rousseau," in *Archiv für
Geschichte der Philosophie*, 42 (1930); and O. Vossler,
L'idea di nazione dal Rousseau al Ranke [*Der National-
gedanke von Rousseau bis Ranke*, München, 1937], trans.
Federici Airoldi (Firenze, 1949), pp. 13-39.

4. A. van Gennep (op. cit., V, 154-56) draws a brilliant profile of Goguet. R. Schmidt, *L'anima dei
primitivi* [*Der Geist der Vorzeit*, Berlin], Italian
trans. (Roma, 1931), p. 12, associates the Condorcet
of the *Esquisse* with Goguet. Sébillot, *Le paganisme
contemporain chez les peuples celtolatins* (Paris, 1908),
p. 50, observed earlier that the encyclopedists had not
included superstitions and "rustic mythology" within
their realm of study. On this, see also A. van Gennep,
Manuel de folklore français contemporain, I (Paris,
1937-38), 12-13. A close examination reveals that
Sébillot's observation is groundless. On this subject
see, for example, F. Venturi, *Le origini dell'Enciclo-
pedia* (Firenze, 1946), pp. 103ff.

5. There is extensive bibliography on Charles de
Brosses, whose name is recorded in all histories of
studies of religions. See, for example, W. Schmidt,
Manuale di storia comparata delle religioni, trans.
Bugatto (Brescia, 1934), pp. 85-91. There is inexact
information in Bros, *L'ethnologie religieuse*, 2nd ed.
(Paris, 1938), p. 149, which maintains that Brosses did
not know Lafitau.

6-8. For Boulanger see, for all matters, the fine book
by F. Venturi, *L'antichità svelata e l'idea del progresso in N. A. Boulanger* (Bari, 1947); see especially
pp. 124-40, where the complete bibliography on the topic
is recorded. We should add A. van Gennep, op. cit., V,
179-201. In this same work, III, 21-32, there is an
essay on Demounier. References: Giovanni Francesco
Finetti, *Difesa dell'autorità della sacra scrittura contro Giambattista Vico,* a 1768 dissertation with an introduction by B. Croce (Bari, 1936), p. 21; and "Lettere
inedite di B. Tanucci a F. Galiani," ed. F. Nicolini, in
Arch. storico per le provincie napoletane, 30, 233ff.

Chapter VIII

1-3. For general aspects of Pre-Romanticism and especially for its literary characteristics, see the three
volumes by P. Van Tieghem, *Le préromantisme; études
d'histoire littéraire européenne* (Paris, 1948). This
should be integrated with the book by H. A. Beers, *A
History of English Romanticism in the Eighteenth Century* (London, 1926), in which the reader will find the
most complete bibliography relating to *Ossian* and the
Reliques up until that time. From the large bibliography generated by Macpherson's work, the fundamental
works are R. Tombo, *Ossian in Germany* (New York, 1901)
and Van Tieghem, *Ossian en France* (Paris, 1917); see,
however, Van Tieghem's important essay (now included
with a modified title in the above-cited *Préromantisme*,
I, 197-277) entitled *Ossian et l'Ossianisme dans la
littérature européenne au XVIIIe siècle* (den Haag,
1920). Also consult, but with great care, A. Farinelli,
Il romanticismo nel mondo latino (Torino, 1927). For
the influence that *Ossian* has had on English poetry,
see the recent and perceptive essay by J. Lindsay in
The Modern Quarterly Miscellany, No. 1 (London, 1948).
For the influence *Ossian* had in Italy, see, in addition
to Marzot, *Il gran Cesarotti* (Firenze, 1949), the insightful volume by W. Binni, *Preromanticismo italiano*
(Napoli, 1948), pp. 40ff.

4. The first collections of popular poetry undertaken
in England are reviewed by Child, *The English and Scottish Popular Ballads* (Boston, 1882-98). Among the most
important critical works are S. B. Hustvedt, *Ballad
Criticism in Scandinavia and Great Britain During the
Eighteenth Century* (New York, 1916); E. B. Reed, "Addison and the Old English Ballads," in *Modern Philology*,
6 (1908-09), 186ff; and E. A. H. Broadus, "Addison's
Influence on the Development of Interest in Folk-Poetry
of the 18th Century," in *Modern Philology*, 8 (1910),
50ff. For collections of Spanish popular poetry, however, see A. Duran, *Romancero general* (Madrid, 1849),
I, lxvii. References: C. de Lollis, *Saggi sulla forma
poetica italiana dell'Ottocento*, ed. B. Croce (Torino,
1929), p. 52.

5-8. There have been many studies on the *Reliques*.
Among the most important are M. Willinsky, *Bischof
Percy's Bearbeitung der Volksballaden und Kunstgedichte
seines Folio-Manuscriptes* (Leipzig, 1932), and C. V. H.
Marwell, *Thomas Percy*, Diss. (Göttingen, 1934). For
major details, however, see the rich bibliography on
the subject that is provided in Baldi, *Studi sulla
poesia popolare d'Inghilterra e di Scozia* (Roma, 1949).
References: S. Baldi, ibid., pp. 42-58, 67; and F.
Meinecke, *Senso storico e significato della storia*
[*Vom geschichtlichen Sinn und vom Sinn der Geschichte*,
Leipzig, 1939], trans. Mandalari (Napoli, 1948), p. 158.
Wordsworth's phrase is taken from the appendix which
follows the preface to the second edition of *Lyrical
Ballads*. The idea of popular poetry's being called to
reinvigorate and refreshen poetry is from Sanctis; his
La giovinezza (Chapter XXV) contains this very significant passage: "you speak of formal poetry and popular
poetry. You demonstrate that the path of formal poetry
is determined by civilization, and it must always move
toward the greatest freedom of design and the greatest
popularity. Thus language, to enrich itself, must increasingly break from its native confines, and it must
become increasingly close to popular forms of dialect.
In precisely this same way, poetry produces with the
greatest freedom in its forms, and it is refreshed and
reinvigorated by the popular imagination."

Chapter IX

1. For Switzerland's mediating function, see, besides
the previously cited works of Van Tieghem, the perceptive essay by F. Ernst, "La tradition médiatrice de la
Suisse au XVIIIe siècle et au XIXe siècle," in *Revue
de Littér. Comp.*, 6 (1926), 549-60. For Muralt, see F.
Meinecke, *Die Entstehung des Historismus* (Berlin, 1936),
I, 2ff; and C. Antoni, *La lottra contro la ragione*
(Firenze, 1942), pp. 7-12. The thesis that Muralt provided the first and most famous example of an exegesis
of a people's characteristics is to be credited to M.
Fubini, *Stile e umanità di Giambattista Vico* (Bari,
1946), p. 171.

2. Farinelli has written an extensive essay on Haller,
"A. v. H.," in *L'opera di un maestro* (Torino, 1920),
pp. 224-25. There is additional information in C.
Antoni, op. cit., pp. 16-19, where one finds an extensive bibliography on the subject. For the fascination
that the Alps have had for poets and writers, we should
add J. Grand-Carteret, *La montagne à travers les âges,
rôle joué par elle* (Grenoble, 1903-04). References:
P. Hazard, *La crisi della coscienza europea*, trans.
Serini (Torino, 1946), p. 438.

3-5. Bodmer is most generally known to us as the precursor of modern aesthetics. See, for all matters, B.
Croce, "L'efficacia dell'estetica italiana sulle origini
dell'estetica tedesca," in *Problemi di estetica*, 2nd ed.
(Bari, 1923), pp. 374-93, and *La poesia di Dante* (Bari,
1929), p. 177. Antoni has recently written a fine
essay on Bodmer as historian, with a very satisfactory
bibliography (op. cit., pp. 19-33). There is additional
information in R. Feller, *Die schweizerische Geschicht-
schreibung im 19. Jahrhundert; Beiträgen von Giuseppe
Zoppi und Jean R. de Salis* (Zürich, 1938), in which one
also finds an extensive discussion of Mallet. There
are some vague suggestions in R. Weiss, *Volkskunde der
Schweiz* (Zürich, 1946), p. 395. Weiss considers R.
Cysat (1545-1614) to be the founder of Swiss folklore.

6. The most recent monograph on Möser is by P. Klassen,
Justus Möser (Frankfurt a.M., 1936), reviewed in Italy
by Antoni, *Considerazioni su Hegel e Marx* (Napoli,
1946), pp. 285ff. Klassen has also provided an accurate
anthology of Möser's writings, *Deutsche Staatskunst und
Nationalerziehung* (Leipzig, 1939), reviewed by A.
Omodeo, *Il senso della storia* (Torino, 1949), pp. 464ff.
There is additional information in A. Gerbi, *La politica
del romanticismo* (Bari, 1932), pp. 20ff. This should
be integrated with C. Antoni, op. cit., pp. 64-97.

7. For Müller, in addition to Feller, op. cit. (which
compares him to Mallet and Sismondi), see especially E.
Fueter, *Storia della storiografia moderna*, trans.
Spinelli (Napoli, 1944), II, 47. Sanctis' assessment

of Schiller is in the *Saggi critici*, particularly the essay on Giambattista Niccolini.

8. For the distinction between "people" and "nation," see, for all matters, F. Meinecke, *Cosmopolitismo e stato nazionale*, trans. Oberdorfer (Firenze, 1930), I, 22ff. On the "spirit of peoples" see E. Restivo, *Il genio dei popoli e il fattore predominante nella loro storia* (Trani, 1910).

Chapter X

1. On the *Sturm und Drang* there is a great deal of literature that was reviewed in 1923 by V. Santoli in an appendix to his translation of O. Walzel, *Il romanticismo tedesco* [*Deutsche Romantik*, 3 vols., Leipzig, 1923-26] (Firenze, 1923). This should be integrated, however, with the more recent bibliography given to us by L. Bate, *J. G. Herder* (Stuttgart, 1948). For Herder see *Sämtliche Werke*, ed. B. Suphan (Berlin, 1877-1910, 32 vols.). The principal works on Herder, which we have to take into account: C. Joret, *Herder et la renaissance litteraire en Allemagne au XVIII*e *siècle* (Paris, 1875); R. Stadelmann, *Der historische Sinn bei Herder* (Halle, 1928); W. Kohlschmidt, *Herder-Studien* (Berlin, 1929); A. Gillies, *Herder und Ossian* (Berlin, 1933). References: F. Meinecke, *Senso storico e significato della storia*, ed. Mandalari (Napoli, 1948), p. 60; and C. Antoni, *La lotta contro la ragione* (Firenze, 1942), p. 152.

2. For Herder's primitivism, see G. Cocchiara, *Il mito del buon selvaggio* (Messina, 1948), pp. 15ff. References: A. Gerbi, *La politica del romanticismo* (Bari, 1932), pp. 158ff; F. Venturi, *L'antichità svelata e l'idea del progresso in N. A. Boulanger* (Bari, 1947), p. 146, in which one also finds a perceptive comparison of Herder and Boulanger. For the connections between Herder and Goethe, see Goethe's own "Poesia e verità" ["Dichtung und Wahrheit"] in *Opere*, ed. L. Mazzucchetti (Firenze, 1943), I, 967-72, and *Colloqui col Goethe*

[*Gespräche mit Goethe*, 3 vols., Leipzig, 1885] by Eckermann, s. v. *Herder*. The cited letter from Goethe to
Herder is in Goethe, *Briefe*, II (ed. Weimar), 262, and
it is quoted in part by Cassirer, *La filosofia dell'-
Illuminismo*, trans. Pocar, 2nd ed. (Firenze, 1945),
p. 187.

3. For Herder as a student of language, see B. Croce,
*Estetica come scienza dell'espressione e linguistica
generale* (Bari, 1941); and A. Pagliaro, *Sommario di
linguistica ario-europea*, I (Roma, 1930), 35ff. For
connections between Herder and Vico, see K. Vossler,
Lingua e nazione in Italia e in Germania (Firenze,
1936), pp. 21ff. G. de Ruggiero, in his *Storia della
filosofia, parte IV: La filosofia moderna, 4: L'età
del romanticismo* (Bari, 1943), 83, does not hesitate
to put Herder before Humboldt, who is considered by
most as the founder of modern linguistics. In contrast, Lupi (in J. G. Hamann, *Scritti e frammenti di
estetica*, intro., trans., and notes, Firenze, 1938)
reserves that claim for Hamann. It is a fact, however,
that the problem of the origin of language posed by
both Herder and Hamann was very much a real issue during their times. Nevertheless, it cannot be denied
that Hamann had posed the problem in a way that was
altogether different from his predecessors, in that
he was not only the first to classify the world's
languages but he was also the first to reduce them to
basic classes. Bibliographical note: see, for all
matters, E. Cassirer, *Saggio sull'uomo* [*An Essay on
Man*, London, 1944], trans. Pavolini (Milano, 1949),
pp. 179ff.

4-5. For Herder's concept of popular poetry and for
collections that preceded his *Volklieder*, see the extremely important introduction by E. Meyer in Herder's
Stimmen der Völker, which Meyer also edited (Stuttgart,
1887). We should add B. Croce, "La forma primitiva
della poesia secondo Hamann e Herder," in *Conversaz-
ioni critiche*, 2nd ed. (Bari, 1924), I, 53-58. For
Croce himself (also for references to Bürger), see
Poesia popolare e poesia d'arte (Bari, 1938), pp. 14ff.

For connections between Herder and Wolf, see the perceptive observations of M. Bréal, *Pour mieux connaître Homère* (Paris, 1906), and P. Levy, *Geschichte des Begriffes Volkslied* (Berlin, 1911). This should be integrated with B. Croce, "Il Vico e la critica omerica," in *Saggio sullo Hegel*, 3rd ed. (Bari, 1927), pp. 263, 76. For other information: A. Galletti's preface to G. Berchet, *Lettera semiseria di Grisostomo* (Lanciano, 1913). References: E. Cassirer, *Philosophie der symbolischen Formen, I: Die Sprache* (Berlin, 1923), pp. 123ff.

6-7. For Herder's concept about tradition, as understood in the religious sense, see, for all matters, G. van der Leeuw, *La religion dans son essence et ses manifestations*, trans. Marty (Paris, 1948), pp. 676ff. On Herderian metamorphosis, C. Antoni (op. cit., pp. 171ff) has some excellent pages. On the relationship between nation and humanity as they were understood by Herder, see A. Farinelli, "Herder e il concetto della razza nella storia dello spirito," in *Franche parole alla mia nazione* (Torino, 1949). For the "mission" of the German people, see R. Mondolfo, "Il primo assertore della missione germanica," in *Riv. d. Nazioni Latine* (June, 1918), which should be integrated with H. O. Ziegler, *Die Moderne Nation* (Tübingen, 1931), pp. 50ff; and P. Viereck, *Dai romantici a Hitler* [*Metapolitics From the Romantics to Hitler*, New York, 1941], trans. Astrologo and Pintor (Torino, 1948), pp. 67ff. Viereck is convinced that without Herder "the Nazi and Wagnerian cult of the organic instinctive *volk* could not have existed," but he adds that Herder "would be jailed as a pacifist and internationalist if he lived in Germany today." The fact is that these kinds of comparisons are always vague and superficial because they ignore the fact that the ideals of one period can degenerate in another period. On this subject, see the observation by G. Barbagallo, "Come si generò il nazismo," in *Nuova Rivista Storica* (1944-45), pp. 2ff. References: H. Heine's *Die romantische Schule* was published in 1836; Italian trans. (Roma, 1927), pp. 41ff. For Christian Heyne, see, for all

matters, A. Bernardini and G. Righi, *Il concetto di
filologia e di cultura classica nel pensiero moderno*
(Bari, 1947), pp. 233ff. We know that as early as
1765 Heyne, in *De studii historici ad omnes disciplinas
utilitate, necessitate ac praestantia*, warned that a
discipline that exists in isolation cannot be illuminated by nor seen in those fertile relationships deriving from its affinity with other disciplines. For
relationships between Herder and Lessing, see N.
Chernyshevskiĭ, "Lessing nella storia del popolo
tedesco," in *Società*, 4 (1948), 40 [first published as
"Lessing, evo uremĭa, evo zhizn i deĭatelnost," *Polnoe
sobranĭe sochineniĭ*, IV (Moscow, 1948)].

8. For the relationship between the French Revolution
and the bourgeoisie's new attitude toward folklore, see
the works of Mathiez, *Les origines des cultes revolu-
tionnaires* (Paris, 1904); Tiersot, *Les fêtes et les
chants de la révolution française* (Paris, 1904); and
Dror, *L'Allemagne et la révolution française* (Paris,
1944). References: B. Groethuysen, *Origini dello
spirito borghese in Francia*, trans. Forti (Torino,
1949), p. 47.

PART THREE

Chapter XI

1. There is an extensive bibliography on German Romanticism in A. Farinelli, *Il romanticismo in Germania*,
2nd ed. (Bari, 1923), pp. 93-185. A fundamental bibliography is provided by Santoli in the appendix to the
translation of O. Walzel, *Il romanticismo tedesco*
(Firenze, 1923). The most recent publications on the
subject (Spirito, Vinciguerra, Croce, etc.) are reviewed
by G. de Ruggiero, *Storia della filosofia, parte IV:
La filosofia moderna, 4: L' età del romanticismo* (Bari,
1933), pp. 413-36. This should be integrated with the
many up-dated bibliographic notes given us by Viereck,
Dai romantici a Hitler, trans. Astrologo and Pintor
(Torino, 1948), p. 34 (footnote I) and p. 56. Refer-

ences: H. Heine, *Die romantische Schule* (Roma, 1927),
p. 52; E. Cassirer, *Il mito dello stato* [*Myth of the
State*, Oxford, 1947], trans. Pellizzi (Milano, 1950),
pp. 270-73.

2. There are bibliographical citations for Novalis
in Walzel-Santoli, p. 203. Monographs include J. E.
Spenlé, *Novalis; essai sur l'idéalisme romantique en
Allemagne* (Paris, 1904), and H. Simon, *Der magische
Idealismus* (Heidelberg, 1906). For the connections
among Novalis, Schleiermacher, and Wackenroder, the
basic treatment is in Dilthey, *Das Erlebnis und die
Dichtung*, 3rd ed. (Leipzig, 1920), pp. 120ff. There
is additional information in S. Lupi, *Il romanticismo
tedesco* (Firenze, 1936), and in A. Van Tieghem, *L'ère
romantique; le romantisme dans la littérature européenne* (Paris, 1948). References: F. Meinecke, *Cosmopolitismo e stato nazionale*, trans. Oberdorfer
(Firenze, 1930), I, 49ff.

3. For Tieck see B. Steiner, *Ludwig Tieck und die
Volksbücher* (Berlin, 1893), and W. Steinert, *Ludwig
Tieck und das Farbenempfinden der romantischen Dichtung*
(Dortmund, 1910). For the connections between Wacken-
roder and Tieck, see L. Mittner, *Wackenroder e Tieck*
(Venezia, 1942). For the influence exercised on Tieck
by Böhme and the Spanish dramatists, see E. Edertheimer,
J. Böhme und die Romantiker (Heidelberg, 1904), and
especially E. Tonnelat, *Les frères Grimm* (Paris, 1923),
pp. 23ff. References: O. Walzel, op. cit., pp. 137-53.

4. It is common knowledge that F. Schlegel's later
work is not as interesting as his early work. On this
subject see, but with reserve, G. de Ruggiero, op. cit.,
pp. 494-502. Further information on F. Schlegel's folkloristic interests is in E. Tonnelat, op. cit. The
quotations that I have used are taken from F. Schlegel,
Frammenti critici e scritti di estetica, introduction
and translation by V. Santoli (Firenze, 1937). Also by
Santoli is *Filologia, storia e filosofia nel pensiero
di F. Schlegel*, in *Civiltà Moderna*, 2 (1930), 18ff. On
this subject see also G. Pasquali, *Filologia e storia*

(Firenze, 1920); and A. Bernardini and G. Righi, *Il concetto di filologia e di cultura classica nel pensiero moderno* (Bari, 1947), pp. 234ff. References: O. Walzel, op. cit., p. 128.

5. There is an excellent edition of the *Vorlesungen über schöne Literatur und Kunst* by Minor (Heilbronn, 1884) (in Vol. 3, p. 18, there is a eulogy on popular poetry). For Schlegel's contribution to folklore studies, see E. Tonnelat, op. cit., pp. 34-35.

6. G. Berchet gives a brilliant assessment of the romantics' attitude toward the classical world in *Lettera semiseria di Grisostomo*, ed. A. Galletti (Lanciano, 1913), pp. 30ff. Fundamental is W. Jaeger in the "Einführung" to his journal *Die Antike*, I (1925). References: H. Heine, op. cit., pp. 91ff.

7. On the early romantics' Orientalism see, above all, P. T. Haffmann, *Der indische und deutsche Geist von Herder bis zur Romantischer* (Tübingen, 1915), pp. 50ff. There is additional information, especially on mythological studies, in Pinard de la Boullaye, *L'étude comparée des religions*, I (Paris, 1922), 260, which cites bibliography on the topic. For linguistic studies see A. Pagliaro, *Sommario di linguistica ario-euɪopea* (Roma, 1930), pp. 1ff; G. Nencioni, *Idealismo e realismo nella scienza del linguaggio* (Firenze, 1946), pp. 108ff; B. Terracini, *Guida allo studio della linguistica storica, 1: Profilo storico-critico* (Roma, 1949), pp. 14ff.

8. The question of relationships between Romanticism and Germanism has been taken up by G. A. Borgese, *Italia e Germania*, 2nd ed. (Milano, 1929); by G. Manacorda, *La selva e il tempio*, 2nd ed. (Firenze, 1933); and especially by L. Mittner, *Romanticismo e germanesimo* (Venezia, 1946). On the patriotism of the early romantics, see F. Meinecke, op. cit., pp. 50ff, and, with some caution, P. Viereck, op. cit., pp. 56ff. For the concept of "romantico-medievalism" and for the evolution of the term "romantic," see M. Praz, *La carne,*

la morte e il diavolo nella letteratura romantica,
2nd ed. (Torino, 1942), pp. 12ff.

Chapter XII

1. The transition from cosmopolitanism to nationalism
in the romantic period has been amply delineated by
Meinecke, *Cosmopolitismo e stato nazionale*, trans.
Oberdorfer (Firenze, 1930), I, 79-263. Many of
Meinecke's conclusions have been rejected by Binder,
La fondazione della filosofia del diritto [*Grundlegung
zur Rechtsphilosophie*, Tübingen, 1935], trans. Giolitti
(Torino, 1934), pp. 51-52. There is additional informa-
tion in G. de Ruggiero, *Storia del liberalismo europeo*,
2nd ed. (Bari, 1945), pp. 223-42 (on pp. 487-88 there
is an extensive bibliography on the subject); in O.
Vossler, *L'idea di nazione dal Rousseau al Ranke*, trans.
Federici-Airoldi (Firenze, 1949), pp. 70ff; and in B.
Russell, *Storia delle idee del secolo XIX* [*Freedom and
Organization*, London, 1934], trans. Maturi-Egidi
(Torino, 1950), pp. 397ff.

2-3. The basic work is R. Steig, *Achim von Arnim und
Clemens Brentano* (Stuttgart, 1894). On *Des Knaben
Wunderhorn* see H. Lohre, *Von Percy zum Wunderhorn*
(Berlin, 1902); F. Riese, *Des Knaben Wunderhorn und
seine Quellen* (Dortmund, 1908); K. Bode, *Die Bearbeitung der Vorlagen in Des Knaben Wunderhorn* (Berlin,
1909); H. Schewe, "Neue Wege zu den Quellen des Wunder-
horns," in *Jahrbuch für Volkliedforschung*, 3 (1932),
120-30; and I. Maione, *Profili della Germania romantica*
(Padova, 1939), pp. 100ff. References: Tieck, Novalis,
Brentano, *Fiabe romantiche*, ed. I. Maione (Torino, 1945)
(on p. ix there is an assessment of Brentano's *Märchen*);
and L. Vincenti, *Brentano* (Torino, 1932), pp. 121ff.
Other references: E. Tonnelat, *Les frères Grimm* (Paris,
1923), p. 90; and H. Heine, *Die romantische Schule*
(Roma, 1927), p. 164. Arnim's "announcement" is in R.
Steig, op. cit., pp. 224ff.

4. For Görres see the excellent monograph by F.

Schultz, *Joseph Görres als Herausgeber, Litterarhis-
toriker Kritiker im Zusammenhange mit der Jüngeren
Romantik* (Berlin, 1902). There is other important
information in E. Tonnelat, op. cit.

5. Jahn's credo (which the Nazis revived and brushed
up--with consequences that we know all too well) has
produced an extremely large bibliography. Viereck
reviews this bibliography in his *Dai romantici a
Hitler*, trans. Astrologo and Pintor (Torino, 1948),
pp. 79-104. It is interesting to see how Jahn's idea
was later picked up by Hauer, *Deutsche Gottschau* (Stuttgart, 1934). But on this, see E. de Martino, "Intorno
a una storia del mondo popolare subalterno," in *Società*,
5 (1949), 417-18. References: H. von Treitschke,
Deutsche Geschichte im 19. Jahrhundert, III (Berlin,
1886-95), 7; and A. Spamer, "Usi e credenze popolari,"
in *Lares*, 10 (1939), 289-90.

6-7. For the precedents of the historical school, the
basic work is Landsberg, *Geschichte der deutschen
Rechtswissenschaft* (Berlin, 1910). Monographs of noteworthy interest include Enneccerus, *Friedrich Carl v.
Savigny und die Richtung der neueren Rechtswissenschaft*
(Marburg, 1879), and A. Stoll, *Friedrich Karl von
Savignys sächsische Studienreise 1799 und 1800* (Cassel,
1890). For the Italian bibliography, which is also
quite extensive, see B. Brugi, *Introduzione enciclo-
pedica alle scienze giuridiche e sociali nel sistema
della giurisprudenza*, 4th ed. (Milano, 1907), pp. 55ff;
and G. del Vecchio, *Lezioni di filosofia del diritto*,
5th ed. (Milano, 1946), pp. 101ff. On the importance
of popular law, see the recent book by E. Sauer, *Grund-
lehre des Völkerrechts*, 2nd ed. (Koln, 1948). On the
importance of consuetude as a "normative fact" of law,
see especially N. Bobbio, *La consuetudine come fatto
normativo* (Padova, 1942). References: G. Sorel, *Les
illusions du progrès* (Paris, 1908), pp. 33ff; R.
Jhering, *La lotta pel diritto* [*Der Kampf ums Recht*,
Leipzig, 1925], trans. Mariano (Bari, 1935), pp. 24ff;
and F. Meinecke, op. cit., p. 265.

8. For the concept of "Volksgeist," see especially the lucid monograph by B. Fazio-Allmayer, "Il concetto di 'Missione dei popoli' nell'interpretazione filosofica della storia," in *G. critico d. filosofia italiana*, 22 (1941), 121-29. References: M. Mila, *Breve storia della musica* (Milano, 1948), p. 187 (this is a work in which the relationships between music and folklore are studied sensitively and fairly).

Chapter XIII

1-2. There are many monographs on the work of the Grimms. Let us mention W. Scherer, *Jacob Grimm*, 2nd ed. (Berlin, 1885); A. Duncker, *Die Brüder Grimm* (Kassel, 1884); and especially E. Tonnelat, *Les frères Grimm* (Paris, 1923), a work limited to the juvenile books of the two brothers. For works of a general nature, particularly see H. Paul, *Grundriss der germanischen Philologie*, I (Strassburg, 1891), 56ff. For the Grimms' concept of popular poetry, there are assessments and information in P. Levy, *Geschichte des Begriffes Volkslied* (Berlin, 1911), pp. 97ff; and in J. Meyer, "L'organizzazione degli studi sul canto popolare tedesco," in *Lares*, 10 (1939), 307ff; along with the bibliography cited therein. For their concept of the epopee, however, see J. Bédier, *Les légendes épiques*, III (Paris, 1912), 217ff. For connections between the Grimms and Arnim, see R. Steig, *Achim von Arnim und Jacob und Wilhelm Grimm* (Stuttgart, 1904). For connections between the Grimms and A. W. Schlegel, see E. Tonnelat, op. cit., pp. 223ff. For Croce's concept about popular poetry, which he expressed in the volume *Poesia popolare e poesia d'arte* (Bari, 1927), see G. Cocchiara, *Il linguaggio della poesia popolare*, 2nd ed. (Palermo, 1951), pp. 7-20.

3-5. The most recent edition of *Kinder- und Hausmärchen* was edited in 1935 by Otto Ubbelohde. The unabridged Italian translation (of the first two volumes) is edited by Clara Bovero (Torino, 1951). Important monographs

include R. Steig, "Zur Entstehungsgeschichte der Märchen und Sagen der Brüder Grimm," in *Arch. f. das
Studium der neueren Sprachen*, 107, pp. 227ff; and,
from the same journal, "Zu Grimms Märchen," ibid., 118,
pp. 17ff. There are additional evaluations and information in E. Tonnelat, *Les contes des frères Grimm;
études sur la composition et le style du recueil des
Kinder- und Hausmärchen* (Paris, 1912); in I. Lefftz,
Märchen der Brüder Grimm (Heidelberg, 1927); and in S.
Thompson, *The Folktale* (New York, 1946), pp. 367ff,
where the most recent bibliography on the topic is recorded. The list of collations initiated by W. Grimm
has been continued, with excellent results, by J. Bolte
and G. Polivka, *Anmerkungen zu den Kinder- und Hausmärchen der Brüder Grimm* (5 vols., Leipzig, 1913-32). We
should also add: L. Mackensen, *Handwörterbuch des
deutschen Märchens, herausgegeben unter besonderer Mit-
wirkung von Johannes Bolte* (Leipzig, 1930-36). References: L. Mackensen, "Gli studi sul patrimonio narra-
tivo," in *Lares*, 10 (1939), 364 (also very useful for
the bibliography cited). For legends see S. Aschner,
Die deutschen Sagen der Brüder Grimm (Berlin, 1909).

6. For J. Grimm's contribution to the study of law,
see H. Hübner, *J. Grimm und das deutsche Recht* (Gottin-
gen, 1895); and E. Landsberg, *Geschichte der deutschen
Rechtswissenschaft* (Berlin, 1910). For J. Grimm's contribution to the study of mythology, see F. Strich, *Die
Mythologie in der deutschen Literatur von Klopstock bis
Wagner* (Halle, 1910).

7. For J. Grimm's theory about language and his relationship to Bopp and Rask, see especially the work of
B. Terracini, *Guida allo studio della linguistica
storica, I: Pofilo storico-critico* (Roma, 1949),
pp. 71-72. The Indo-European theory, which also served
as the basis for the study of narrative, is illustrated,
with a wealth of details, by J. W. Spargo, *Linguistic
Science in the Nineteenth Century* (Cambridge, Mass.,
1931). Additional information and assessments are in
Pagliaro, *Sommario di linguistica ario-europea*, I; see
Bopp, Grimm, etc. (Roma, 1930).

8. For the Grimms' patriotism, see the bibliography cited in § 1. See also the insightful essay by J. Huizinga, "Sviluppo e forme della coscienze nazionale in Europa sino alla fine del secolo decimonono," in *Civiltà e storia*, trans. Chiaruttini (Modena, 1946), pp. 255-56, where J. Grimm's discourse *De desiderio patriae* is examined. References: B. Terracini, op. cit., I, 72.

Chapter XIV

1. On the so-called ethical period of Romanticism, it is very useful to examine D. Busk, *Mythology and the Romantic Tradition in English Poetry* (Oxford, 1926); and B. I. Evans, *Tradition and Romanticism; Studies in English Poetry from Chaucer to Yeats* (London, 1940).

2. For Scott as folklorist, see A. Lang, *Sir Walter Scott and the Border Minstrelsy* (London, 1910). On the validity of his *antiquitates*: B. Croce, *Poesia e non poesia* (Bari, 1916), pp. 59-70. For Scott as historian: E. Fueter, *Storia della storiografia moderna*, trans. Spinelli (Napoli, 1944), II, 131ff. (I do not, however, share in his idea that the first to formulate the "local color" theory was Chateaubriand and that Scott systematically developed the ideas of the French romantic.)

3. There are bibliographical notes and information on French Pre-Romanticism in G. Cocchiara, *Il mito del buon selvaggio* (Messina, 1948), pp. 20ff. We should add A. Pizzorusso, *Senancour* (Messina, 1950). Despite its polemical intent, it will be useful to consult L. Reynaud, *Le romantisme: ses origines anglo-germaniques* (Paris, 1929), which considers French Romanticism as an "infection." For the beginnings of French folklore, see the essay by H. Tronchon, "Quelques notes sur le premier mouvement folkloriste en France," in *Mélanges Baldensperger*, No. 2 (Paris, 1930), pp. 296ff. But especially see A. van Gennep, *Manuel de folklore français contemporain*, I (Paris, 1937-38), 32ff (the Dulaure-Mangourit questionnaire is reproduced in III,

12ff). In *Recueil Centenaire Soc. nationale Antiquaires France, 1804-1904*, there is an important article by Gaidoz, "De l'influence de l'Académie celtique sur les études de folklore," which indicates the influence that the research of the Academy had on J. Grimm when he went to Paris in 1804. There is more information in M.-J. Durry, "L'Académie celtique et la chanson populaire," in *Revue de Littérature Comparée*, 9 (1929), 62-73. For various published contributions throughout the years of the *Mémoires de l'Académie Celtique* (later the *Mém. Soc. Antiquaires France*), see A. van Gennep, op. cit., III, IV (see *Bourquelot, Maury*, etc.).

4. There are notes and judgments on Fauriel in J. Bédier, *Les légendes épiques*, III (Paris, 1912), 201ff.

5. For Villamarqué see F. M. Luzel, *De l'authenticité des chants du Barzaz-Breiz* (Paris, 1872). Extremely useful because it studies the songs, melodies, and popular usages that are found in French poets and romancers is J. Tiersot's *La chanson populaire et les écrivains romantiques* (Paris, 1931). This should be integrated with J. Marsan, *La bataille romantique*, II serie (Paris, n.d.), pp. 125ff. For French romantic historiography, see, for all matters, Fueter, op. cit., under the appropriate entries. References: Gérard de Nerval, "Les vieilles ballades, françaises," in *La Sylphide*, 6 (1842); reprinted by A. Loquin (ed.) under the title *Chansons et ballades populaires du Valois* (Paris, 1885).

6-7. There are notes and critical judgments on Berchet and Tommaseo in G. Cocchiara, *Storia degli studi delle tradizioni popolari in Italia* (Palermo, 1947). References: U. Bosco, "Preromanticismo e romanticismo," in *Questioni e correnti di storia letteraria* (Milano, 1949), pp. 597-657; B. Croce, *Poesia popolare e poesia d'arte* (Bari, 1938), p. 27. For Manzoni's attitude toward the humble folk, see also A. Gramsci, *Letteratura e vita nazionale* (Torino, 1951), pp. 72ff.

8. For all matters see the treatise by C. Morandi, *L'idea dell'unità politica d'Europa nel XIX e XX secolo*

(Milano, 1948), which cites an extensive bibliography, one that should be integrated with B. Russell, *Storia delle idee del secolo XIX*, trans. Maturi-Egidi (Torino, 1950), pp. 393-423. Both Morandi and Russell completely overlook the importance of the concept of popular poetry in the formation of national awareness. This cannot be said of Croce, *Storia d'Europa nel secolo decimonono* (Bari, 1932), pp. 134ff.

Chapter XV

1. For Russia's participation in the European sphere, see the excellent treatment by C. Morandi, *L'idea dell'unità politica d'Europa nel XIX e XX secolo* (Milano, 1948), pp. 42ff; and F. Chabod, "L'idea di Europa," in *La Rassegna d'Italia*, 4 (1947), 28ff. Chaadaev's *Lettres philosophiques* has recently been translated by A. Tomborra (Bari, 1950), preceded by the translator's introduction; bibliography is on pp. 79-80. References: A. Gramsci, *Letteratura e vita nazionale* (Torino, 1951), p. 105.

2-3. For the early Russian folklorists and for Russian authors who have been inspired by folklore, see the extremely interesting work by A. Pypin, *Istoríĭã russkoĭ etnografíĭ* (4 vols., Petersburg, 1890-92). There are more recent bibliographic entries in IŪ. M. Sokolov, *Russian Folklore* (New York, 1950), pp. 20-21, 30-31. This should be integrated with D. Zelenin, *Russische Volkskunde* (Berlin, 1927), pp. 15-50, and, for the literary aspects, with E. Lo Gatto, *Storia della letteratura russa*, 3rd ed. (Firenze, 1944), I, 44ff. References: M. Mila, *Breve storia della musica* (Milano, 1948), p. 264.

4. For the pan-Slavism of the Czechs, see, for all matters, L. Dumont-Wilden, *L'évolution de l'esprit européen* (Paris, 1937), pp. 101-04; and W. Gusti, *Due secoli di pensiero politico russo* (Firenze, 1943), especially for his view of Pestel. For folklore: J. Horach, "Les études ethnographiques en Tchécoslovaquie,"

in *Revue des Études Slaves*, 1 (1921). A useful work
providing an overview of the Polish folklore movement
is G. Maver's *Alle fonti del romanticismo polacco*
(Roma, 1928). There is additional information in M.
de Smirgrodki, "Le folklore en Pologne," in *La Tradition*, 3 (1889), 265ff; but especially see A. Ficher,
Ethnografia słowiánska (Lwow, 1934). For Chopin, consult, for all matters, M. Mila, op. cit., pp. 205ff.

5. For Serbo-Croatian popular poetry, particularly see
M. Murko, *La poésie populaire épique en Yougoslavie au
début du XXe siècle* (Paris, 1929); and A. Cronia,
Poesia popolare serbo-croata (Padova, 1949), which has
an extensive bibliography on Karadžić. For Alecsandri
see O. Densusianu, "Il folklore come deve intendersi,"
trans. from Romanian and introduced with an essay by
I. Onciulescu, in *Folklore*, 3, Nos. 3-4, No. 6 for the
abstract (Napoli, 1949).

6. For the early Finnish folklorists, see K. Krohn,
"Histoire du traditionnisme en Finlande," in *La Tradition*, 4 (1890), 4, 45-49, 72-73, 103-107. The *Kalevala*
was translated into Italian by P. E. Pavolini (Palermo,
1909). We will have occasion to cite studies on this
poem; however, one should note the preliminary remarks
on the subject of Pavolini's translation made by G. A.
Borgese, *La vita e il libro*, serie II (Bologna, 1928),
pp. 175-178.

7. On the ancient poetry and mythology of Scandinavian
countries, see P. Van Tieghem, *Le préromantisme, études
d'histoire littéraire européenne*, I (Paris, 1948), 77-193.
For the early folklorists of Scandinavian countries, see
the excellent book by Paul, *Grundriss der germanischen
Philologie*, II (Strassburg, 1893); and, in particular,
H. Schück, *Histoire de la littérature suédoise* (Paris,
1923). V. Santoli offers an opinion about Grundtvig in
I canti popolari italiani (Firenze, 1940), p. 84.

8. On pan-Slavism, see the works cited in § 4, above.
References: Renan's letter is quoted in L. Dumont-
Wilden, op. cit., p. 102.

PART FOUR

Chapter XVI

1. The richest bibliography on Müller is in H. Pinard de la Boullaye, *L'étude comparée des religions*, I (Paris, 1922), 341-350. For additional information, we should also add the following works: L. Garello, *La morte di Pàn* (Torino, 1908); L. Savatorelli, *Introduzione bibliografica alla scienza delle religioni* (Roma, 1914); and M. Eliade, *Traité d'histoire des religions* (Paris, 1948).

2. On the Aryan issue, see--in addition to Pinard de la Boullaye, op. cit., I, pp. 342, 352--the recent volume by G. Poisson, *Les Aryens* (Paris, 1934), which cites extensive bibliography on the topic. Cassirer has given noteworthy treatment to Gobineau and his recent inauspicious influence in his *Il mito dello stato*, trans. Pellizzi (Milano, 1950), pp. 327ff; and P. Viereck, *Dai romantici a Hitler*, trans. Astrologo and Pintor (Torino, 1948), pp. 108ff.

3-4. For the meteorological interpretation of myth and for the influence exercised on Müller by his predecessors, see, above all, the old but very useful work by Sayce, *The Principles of Comparative Philology* (London, 1874), and R. Pettazzoni, *Nozioni di mitologia* (Roma, 1949). There is additional information in L. Spence, *An Introduction to Mythology* (London, 1921), and in A. H. Krappe, *La genèse des mythes* (Paris, 1938). References: E. Cassirer, op. cit., p. 44.

5. On Müller's place in the history of religions, see R. Pettazzoni, *Svolgimento e carattere della storia delle religioni* (Bari, 1924). There is additional information in J. Reville, *Les phases successives de l'histoire des religions* (Paris, 1909); A. Bros, *L'ethnologie religieuse*, 2nd ed. (Paris, 1928), pp. 48ff; and W. Schmidt, *Manuale di storia comparata delle religioni*, trans. Bugatto (Brescia, 1934), pp. 59-65.

6. In England the most active followers of Müller
were G. W. Cox and S. Baring-Gould. In Germany: W.
Schwartz, W. H. Roescher, and E. H. Meyer. In Italy,
in addition to Gubernatis: S. Prato and G. Ferraro.
In France: M. Bréal, Ch. Ploix, and H. D'Arbois de
Joubainville. In Russia: A. N. Afanas'ev, O. F.
Miller, and A. A. Kotliarevskii. For bibliography
and additional information, see W. A. Clouston,
*Popular Times and Fictions, Their Migrations and
Transformations*, I (Edinburgh, 1887); J. Bédier, *Les
fabliaux* (Paris, 1893), pp. 23-30; A. van Gennep,
Manuel de folklore française contemporain, IV (Paris,
1937-58), 656-658; G. Cocchiara, *Storia degli studi
delle tradizioni popolari in Italia* (Palermo, 1947),
pp. 167-183; and IU. M. Sokolov, *Russian Folklore*
(New York, 1950), pp. 56-75.

7. For the various critical assessments of Müller,
see the fine essay by P. Ehrenreich, *Die allgemeine
Mythologie* (Leipzig, 1910). For additional information and for the return of certain Müllerian attitudes, see R. Grossens, "Notes de mythologie indo-
européenne," in *La nouvelle Clio*, 1 (Bruxelles, 1949),
1-22. For the satire directed against Depuis and
Müller, see H. Gaidoz, "Comme quoi M. Müller n'a
jamais existé," in *Mélusine*, 2 (1884-85), col. 73ff.
The same author wrote "Comme quoi Napoléon n'a jamais
existé," ibid., col. 145ff. References: G. Dumézil,
Le festin d'immortalité (Paris, 1924), p. 5; M. W.
de Visser, *De Graecorum diis non referentibus speciem
humanam* (Lugduni Batavorum, 1900), pp. 22ff; M.
Kerbaker, *Sâvitri ed Alcesti*, in *G. Nap. di Filosofia
e Lettere*, 1 (1871), 1ff; IU. M. Sokolov, op. cit.,
p. 50; B. Terracini, *Guida allo studio della linguistica storica, I: Profilo storico-critico* (Roma,
1949), p. 77.

8. For the connections between Müller and Pitrè, see
G. Cocchiara, *Pitrè, la Sicilia e il folklore* (Messina,
1951), pp. 70-74. References: R. Pettazzoni, *Svolgimento e carattere della storia delle religion*, op.
cit., pp. 12-13.

Chapter XVII

1-4. For relationships between Benfey and Müller, see Müller's essay on the migration of tales, first published in the *Contemporary Review* of July, 1870. On the Orientalist theory (and for the numerous bibliographic references contained therein), see the following works: Bédier, *Les fabliaux* (Paris, 1893), pp. 40-44; A. H. Krappe, *The Science of Folklore* (London, 1930), pp. 10ff; and S. Thompson, *The Folktale* (New York, 1946), pp. 376ff. For the great Oriental collections—it is common knowledge that in Italy the *Panchatantra* was translated by Pizzi (Torino, 1896)—a quick but precise account is provided by S. Battaglia, *Contributi alla storia della novellistica* (Napoli, 1947). References: V. Keller, *Ueber die Geschichte der Griechen Fabeln* (Leipzig, 1870), p. 333; and F. Ribezzo, *Nuovi studi sulla origine e propagazione delle favole indo-elleniche comunemente dette esopiche* (Napoli, 1901), pp. 10-20 (in which the theories of Benfey and his adversaries are discussed).

5. Köhler's numerous essays, in which he demonstrated that he was indeed familiar with all of Europe's treasury of tales, have been collected by a faithful disciple, J. Bolte, and published with the title *Kleinere Schriften* (3 vols., Weimar, 1898-1900). In collaboration with E. Schmidt, Bolte also edited Köhler's work, *Ueber Märchen und Volkslieder* (Berlin, 1894). There is bibliography on Cosquin in A. van Gennep, *Manuel de folklore français contemporain*, IV (Paris, 1937-38).

6. For the contribution of Russian folklorists to the theoretical formulation of folklore, see the clear treatment provided by Sokolov, *Russian Folklore* (New York, 1950), pp. 78-90, 100-123. There is additional information in E. Lo Gatto, *Storia della letteratura russo*, 3rd ed. (Firenze, 1944), I, 46-92.

7-8. For the Finnish school, see especially Krappe, op. cit., pp. 10, 43ff; and Thompson, op. cit.,

pp. 394ff. For the origins of the geographico-
historical method, see F. Krüger, *Géographie des traditions populaires en France* (Mendoza, 1950), pp. 4ff.
For Kaarle Krohn see the moving essay by P. E. Pavolini
in *Lares*, 4 (1933), 3ff. Aarne's index has been perfected by one of America's greatest folklorists, Stith
Thompson (cf. A. Aarne's *The Types of the Folktale*,
trans. and enlarged by Stith Thompson, Folklore Fellows
Communications No. 74, Helsinki, 1928). Moreover, we
are indebted to Thompson today for the richest collection of themes and narrative motifs, *Motif-Index of
Folk-Literature: A Classification of Narrative Elements
in Folk-tales, Ballads, Myths, Fables, Medieval Romances,
Exampla, Fabliaux, Jest Books, and Local Legends* (6 vols.
FFC, Nos. 106-109, 116, 117, Helsinki, 1932-36). For
criticisms directed at this school, see Sokolov, op.
cit., pp. 90ff; and A. van Gennep, op. cit., I, 28ff.
References: K. Krohn, "La métode de M. Jules Krohn,"
Congres International des Traditions Populaires, Paris
1889 (Paris, 1891), pp. 64-68; and E. Morote Best,
Elementos de folklore (Cuzco, 1950), pp. 245ff. See
also the perceptive communique of C. W. von Sydow,
"Circulations des contes populaires," *Travaux du Congre.
Internat. de Folklore* (Tours, 1938), pp. 132ff.

Chapter XVIII

1-3. For the origins of romance philology, it is always
useful to see the old book by G. Gröber, *Grundriss der
romanischen Philologie*, 2nd ed., I (Strassburg, 1904-
06). There is additional information in A. Monteverdi,
Introduzione allo studio della filologia romanza (Roma,
1943). See the essay by the same author, "Neolatine,"
in *Saggi neolatini* (Roma, 1945), pp. 3-22. See also L.
Sorrento, *Medievalia* (Brescia, 1943), and C. Tagliavini
Le origini delle lingue neolatine (Bologna, 1948). For
the contribution of German romantics to the study of
romance philology, see G. Bertoni, *Le origini della
letterature romanze nel pensiero dei romantici tedeschi*
(Leipzig, 1938). For an exact bibliography relating to
various questions about the French epopee, see J.

Bédier, *Les légendes épiques*, III (Paris, 1912), 200-88;
A. Viscardi, *Le origini* (Milano, 1939); and I. Siciliano, *Le origini delle canzoni di gesta* (Padova, 1940).
Also by Viscardi are *Posizioni vecchie e nuove della
storia letteraria romanza* (Milano, 1944), and *Letterature d'oc e d'oil* (Milano, 1952). Still of great interest for Paris are the essays of F. Novati in *Emporium*
(1903) and of P. Rajna in *Atti della R. Accademia della
Crusca* (1904). See also (differences of opinion notwithstanding) J. Bédier, *Hommage à Gaston Paris* (Paris,
1904). References: E. Monaci, "G. Paris," in *Nuova
Antologia* (1 April 1903). On the origin of the romance
lyric, see the extensive bibliography of the topic in
G. Errante, *Sulla lirica romanza delle origini* (New
York, 1943). By the same author: *Marcabru e le fonti
sacre dell'antica lirica romanza* (Firenze, 1948).

4. For Rajna see the excellent essays by M. Casella
in *Marzocco* (7 December 1930) and G. Vandelli in *Atti
Accademia degli Arcadi*, 7 and 8 (Firenze, 1931). An
accurate essay is A. Schiaffini's "Pio Rajna ricerca-
tore di origini," in *Ulisse* (1 May 1947). For additional information on Rajna's folkloristic activity,
see G. Cocchiara, *Storia degli studi delle tradizioni
popolari in Italia* (Palermo, 1947), pp. 185-89.

5-8. There are bibliographies of studies on the French
epopee in *A Critical Bibliography of French Literature,
I: The Medieval Period*, ed. U. T. Holmes, Jr., notes
548-83 (Syracuse, 1947), and more recently in R.
Bossuat, *Manuel bibliographique de la littérature
française du moyen âge* (Melun, 1951). On the folk
"memory"--which is a historical source, in that a document is such not because it is written or spoken but
because it is "thought"--see especially the comments
of M. Bloch, *La società feudale* [*La societé féodale*,
2 vols., Paris, 1939], trans. Cremonesi (Torino, 1949),
pp. 420ff. For Bédier and his attitude about the Germanic origin of the French epopee, see G. Bertoni, *La
"Chanson de Roland"* (Firenze, 1935), pp. 93-95. Bertoni
says that "the epopee of France is certainly French (as
Bédier would have it), but it is the artistic and poetic

expression of the Germanic spirit." For Bédier see the
fine essay by G. Contini, "Ricordo di Bédier," in *Un
anno di letteratura* (Firenze, 1942), pp. 114ff. Contini unconditionally accepts Bédier's viewpoints.
References: R. Fawtier, *La Chanson de Roland* (Paris,
1933), pp. 50ff; and L. Foscolo Benedetto, *L'epopea di
Roncisvalle* (Firenze, 1941), pp. 124, 144, 200 (in whic
Bédier's theories are put into proper perspective).

Chapter XIX

1-2. There are bibliographic entries and information
on Child in S. Baldi, *Studi sulla poesia popolare
d'Inghilterra e di Scozia* (Roma, 1949), pp. 21-37.
Santoli, in *I canti popolari italiani* (Firenze, 1940),
p. 90, observes correctly that "the transition from the
old way of collecting and publishing folksongs to the
new way initiated by Grundtvig and Nigra is in a certai
sense parallel to the transition from empirical, abstract, purist grammar to comparative and historical
linguistics." For Nigra see G. Cocchiara, *Storia degli
studi delle tradizioni popolari in Italia* (Palermo,
1947). To the bibliography therein we can now add V.
Santoli, *Gli studi di letteratura popolare*, in *Cinquant'anni di vita intellettuale italiana 1896-1946:
Scritti in onore di B. Croce*, II (Napoli, 1950).
References: S. Baldi, op. cit., p. 14.

3-8. Bibliographical information on the various author
treated can be found in G. Cocchiara, op. cit., and V.
Santoli, *Gli studi di letteratura popolare*, op. cit.
For the study of area norms and their application in
linguistic atlases, there are bibliographic notes in
V. Santoli, *I canti popolari*, op. cit., p. 54. References: G. Pasquali, in D. Comparetti, *Virgilio nel
medio evo*, ed. G. Pasquali, I (Firenze, 1937), xxi; and
F. Neri, *Storia e poesia* (Torino, 1936), pp. 15ff.

Chapter XX

1-8. For the work of G. Pitrè, see G. Cocchiara, *Pitrè*

la Sicilia e il folklore (Messina, 1951), where the
reader will find an extensive bibliography on the topic.
On the folklore journals that were then coming out just
about everywhere in Europe, supporting and complementing the work developed in Pitrè's *Archivio*, see R.
Corso, *Folklore*, 2nd ed. (Napoli, 1943), pp. 175-179.
References: L. Russo, *Giovanni Verga*, 4th ed. (Bari,
1947), pp. 90ff.

PART FIVE

Chapter XXI

1-8. There are notes and bibliographical information
on Tylor in G. Cocchiara, *Il mito del buon selvaggio*
(Messina, 1948), pp. 61-92. Of particular interest are
P. Radin, *Primitive Man as Philosopher* (London, 1927),
and R. H. Lowie, *The History of Ethnological Theory*
(London, 1937).

Chapter XXII

1-4. The letter that Mannhardt sent to Pitrè is still
unedited and can be found in the Pitrè Library (the
Sicilian Ethnographic Museum, Palermo). There is a
new edition of the work *Wald- und Feldkulte*, ed. W.
Heuschkel (Berlin, 1904-05). There is additional bio-
bibliographic information in M. Eliade, *Traité d'histoire des religions* (Paris, 1948), pp. 309-313, which
is also useful for the extensive bibliography cited
throughout. See the interesting volume by Liungman,
Traditionswanderungen, Euphrat-Rhein, I (Helsinki,
1937), 336ff. This should be integrated with A. W.
Ratansalo, *Der Ackerbau im Volksaberglauben der Finnen
und Esten mit entsprechenden Gebräuchen der Germanen
verglichen* (FFC nos. 30-32, 55, 62, Helsinki, 1919-25).
We should add J. J. Meyer, *Trilogie altindischer Mächte
und Feste der Vegetation* (Leipzig, 1937). Of noteworthy interest is C. W. von Sydow's essay on Mannhardt's theories, which is included in his *Selected
Papers on Folklore* (Copenhagen, 1948). References:

W. Schmidt, *Manuale di storia comparata delle religioni*,
trans. Bugatto (Brescia, 1934), p. 205. By the same
author: *Manuale di metodologia etnologica* [*Handbuch
der Methode der kulturhistorischen Ethnologie*, Münster,
1937], trans. Vannucelli (Milano, 1949), p. 270. Most
useful is E. Röhr's essay "Geografia demologica tedesca," in *Lares*, 10 (1939), pp. 269-88.

5.   For Rohde see the helpful monograph by O. Crusius,
E. Rohde (Tübingen, 1902). For later studies generated
by his researches, see R. Mondolfo's notes in E. Zeller,
La filosofia dei Greci nel suo sviluppo storico
[*Grundriss der Geschichte der griechischen Philosophie*,
Leipzig, 1883], trans. and up-dated by R. Mondolfo
(Firenze, 1932), I, 141ff. Lawson's book is entitled
Modern Greek Folklore and Ancient Greek Religion (Cam-
bridge, 1910). For additional information, see the
notes to chapter XXV, § 1.

6.   For Usener see the essays of Farnell, Wissowa, and
Kroll, cited by H. Pinard de la Boullaye, *L'étude comparée des religions*, I (Paris, 1922), 356. References:
R. Pettazoni, *Nozioni di mitologia* (Roma, 1949),
pp. 37ff.

7.   For Dieterich see M. Eliade, op. cit. There are
some perceptive observations on the aims and limits of
judicial ethnology in F. Battaglia, *Diritto e filosofia
della pratica* (Firenze, 1932), pp. 20ff. For the bibliography cited therein, we should add the important
work of Vinogradoff, *Outlines of Historical Jurisprudence* (Oxford, 1920-22).

8.   Sartori's work is entitled *Sitte und Brauch* (Leipzig, 1910-14), and it is part of the collection *Hand-
bücher zur Volkskunde,* ed. Heims, who also published
the following volumes in the same collection between
1908 and 1909: 1. K. Wehrhan, *Die Sage*; 2. A. Thimme
Das Märchen; 3. O. Schell, *Das Volkslied*; 4. K. Wehrhan, *Kinderlied und Kinderspiel*. Sartori's volumes
correspond to numbers 5-8. Sartori's work was completed
by P. Geiger, *Deutsches Volkstum in Sitte und Brauch*

(Berlin, 1936). References: H. Pinard de la Boullaye, op. cit., I, 356; and A. Spamer, "Usi e credenze popolari," in *Lares*, 10 (1939), 294. Spamer also reviews the research of Lily Weiser-Aall, Otto Hofler, R. Wolfram, L. Rutimeyer, and Karl Meuli--research reflecting the influence of the current of studies we have examined.

Chapter XXIII

1-2. The last edition of *The Golden Bough* contains the following volumes: part I, *The Magic Art and the Evolution of Kings* (2 vols.); part II, *Taboo and the Perils of the Soul* (1 vol.); part III, *The Dying God* (1 vol.); part IV, *Adonis, Attis, Osiris* (2 vols.), first published as a separate work in 1903; part V, *Spirits of the Corn and the Wild* (2 vols.); part VI, *The Scapegoat* (1 vol.); part VII, *Balder the Beautiful: The Fire-Festivals of Europe and the Doctrine of the External Soul* (2 vols.); vol. XII, *Bibliography and General Index*. Before Frazer's abridged edition, *The Golden Bough: A Study in Magic and Religion* (London, 1925), an anthology edited by Lady Frazer, *Leaves from The Golden Bough*, was published. Lauro de Bosis has done an accurate Italian translation of the abridged edition, with a preface by G. Cocchiara (Torino, 1950). See also: J. G. Frazer, *Introduzione all'antropologia sociale*, selected essays, translated and annotated by G. Cocchiara (Palermo, 1945). In 1934, when Frazer was eighty years old, a complete bibliography of his writings, consisting of 266 entries, was published. Among these we must not forget the volume *The Gorgon's Head, and Other Literary Pieces*, with a preface by A. France (London, 1927)--where, along with essays of lively humanistic interest (for example, those on Roman life in the time of Pliny the Younger and the robust essay on London life in the time of Addison), one also finds some of his delicate poetry and translations of French poets.

3-8. For Frazer's theories, see, for all matters, G.

Davy, *Sociologues d'hier et d'aujourd'hui* (Paris, 1931):
R. H. Lowie, *The History of Ethnological Theory* (London,
1937); and G. Cocchiara, *Il mito del buon selvaggio*
(Messina, 1948). We should add, particularly for the
concept of magic, E. de Martino, *Il mondo magico*
(Torino, 1948). An extensive critical review of the
most significant publications in the field of history
of religions concerning arguments for and against Frazer
is found in W. Schmidt, *Der Ursprung der Gottesidee*, I,
(Münster, 1926). By the same author: *Manuale di storia
comparata delle religioni*, trans. Bugatto (Brescia,
1934), pp. 165-280. There is additional information in
Pinard de la Boullaye, *L'étude comparée des religions*
(Paris, 1922), I, 352-89; and in C. Dawson, *Progresso
e religione* [*Progress and Religion*, London, 1929],
trans. Foà (Milano, 1948), pp. 58ff. There is a good
monograph by R. A. Downie, *James George Frazer, The
Portrait of a Scholar* (London, 1940). For the interests
that Frazer's work has provoked in the fields of psychology and philology (from Delacroix to Brunschvicg,
from Freud to Róhein, from Jung to Aldrich, from Bergson
to Boutroux and especially Cassirer), see C. Delacroix,
La mentalité primitive (Paris, 1926), and R. Cantoni,
I primitivi (Milano, 1941). We should add that it
would be impossible to understand the atmosphere created
by some of Eliot's poetry and Mann's and Lawrence's
prose without knowing *The Golden Bough*. Eliot was certainly not wrong when he asserted that *The Golden Bough*
has exercised an extremely significant influence on his
generation. On this subject, see T. S. Eliot, *Collected Poems, 1909-1935*, notes on *The Waste Land* (London, 1936).

Chapter XXIV

1-4. For Lang see the fine essay by R. R. Marett,
"Andrew Lang," in *Folklore*, 23 (1912). We should also
add Salvatorelli, "Andrew Lang," in *Lares*, I (1912).
Also by Salvatorelli is *Introduzione bibliographica
alla scienza delle religioni* (Roma, 1914). For Lang
as a student of folk narrative, see R. Corso, *Folklore*,

2nd ed. (Napoli, 1943), pp. 80ff. A useful work on Lang as a historian of religions is S. Reinach, "Andrew Lang et l'histoire des religions," in *Cultes, mythes et religions* (Paris, 1923), V, 13ff. This should be integrated with W. Schmidt, *Manuale di storia comparata delle religioni*, trans. Bugatto (Brescia, 1934), and, in regard to the study of magic, with E. de Martino, *Il mondo magico* (Torino, 1948), pp. 207ff. References: J. Bédier, *Les fabliaux* (Paris, 1893), pp. 20ff; and R. Pettazzoni, *Dio: Formazione e sviluppo del monoteismo nella storia delle religioni* (Roma, 1922), p. 42.

5-6. For the philosophy of MacCulloch, one of the most perceptive interpreters of the Celtic world (to which Rhys, too, dedicated extensive research), consult the substantial work by O. Dähnhardt, *Natursagen: Eine Sammlung naturdeutender Sagen, Märchen, Fabeln und Legenden* (Leipzig, 1907 ff). Dähnhardt has provided an extensive classification of narrative themes (among the topics: nature, animals, plants); furthermore, he has demonstrated that the tale is an interpretation of present as well as past experiences. Some years later this was reasserted by Friedrich von der Leyen in his fine book *Das Märchen*, 3rd ed. (Leipzig, 1925). Weston is directly linked with MacCulloch and, through him, with Lang and Hartland; to Weston we owe two excellent works, *The Legend of Sir Perceval* (London, 1909) and *From Ritual to Romance* (Cambridge, 1920). Macleod Yearsley's *The Folklore of Fairy-Tale* (London, 1924) has a faulty bibliography and is merely a recapitulation of MacCulloch's position. In looking at wedding customs, we should keep in mind H. Bächtold-Stäubli's *Die Gebräuche bei Verlobung und Hochzeit* (Basel, 1942), and R. Corso's *Patti d'amore e pegni di promessa* (S. Maria Capua Vetere, 1924).

7. For Gomme and her critical work concerning the ethnological aspect of childhood games, of particular interest are the notes, comments, and citations that accompany Hirn's book, *I giuochi dei bimbi* [*Barnlek*, Stockholm, 1916], trans. Faggioli (Venezia, 1929), pp. 227ff. Hirn also deserves to be remembered for *The Origins of Art* (London, 1900). For the study of

relationships among song, dance, and game, there are
some excellent pages in F. B. Gunmere, *The Beginnings
of Poetry* (New York, 1901), pp. 337-46. References:
G. Pitrè, *Archivio per lo studio delle tradizioni popolari*, XVIII (1889), 143.

8. For Gomme's theory about the nature of folklore,
see W. Crooke, "Scientific Aspects of Folklore," in
Folklore, 23 (1912), 14ff; also see various presiden-
tial addresses published in *Folklore* (1895ff). For
opposing comments see K. Knortz, *Was ist Volkskunde
und wie studiert man dieselbe?* (Jena, 1900), pp. 212ff;
G. Pitrè, "Per l'inaugurazione del corso di demopsi-
cologia nella R. Università di Palermo" in *Atti R.
Accad. Sc. Lett. ed Arti*, pp. 7ff of the abstract
(1911); R. Corso, op. cit., pp. 35ff (where the reader
will find other references). There is bibliographical
information on the Folklore Society in A. Guichot y
Sierra, *Historia del folklore* (Madrid, 1922), pp. 35ff.

Chapter XXV

1. For the contribution that studies in folklore and
ethnology have made to studies in classical philology,
there is a very useful work by H. J. Rose, *Modern
Methods in Classical Mythology* (London, 1930). There
are notes and information in the works of A. Gudeman,
Grundriss zur Geschichte der klassischen Philologie,
2nd ed. (Leipzig, 1909), and J. E. Sandys, *History of
Classical Scholarship*, 3rd ed. (Cambridge, 1921). One
must observe, nevertheless, that this contribution is
often overlooked or ignored by historians of classical
philology. For example, in G. Funaioli's "Lineamenti
d'una storia della filologia attraverso i secoli," in
Studi di letteratura antica, I (Bologna, 1946), 185-
365, the names of Mannhardt, Tylor, and Frazer are
nowhere mentioned. This brings to mind Toutain's well-
known essay on Wissowa in the *Revue de l'Histoire des
Religions*, 25 (Paris, 1904), 273, in which he denounced
the position taken by those philologists who, incased
in their ivory towers, did not see or pretended not to

see what was right under their noses. Even today it
is baffling to see the kind of reception often given
to research by scholars of classical philology who well
know the importance of folklore and ethnology--two disciplines that, in fact, not all philologists wish to
study and that, after all, are most convenient to
ignore.

2-3. For Reinach as historian of religions, see W.
Schmidt, *Manuale di storia comparata delle religioni*,
trans. Bugatto (Brescia, 1934); and A. Bros, *L'ethnologie religieuse*, 2nd ed. (Paris, 1938). There is
some disagreement about Reinach's thesis of the survival of a prehistoric totemism and the dawning of
Greek civilization. On this subject see the work of
O. Kern, *Die Religion der Griechen*, I (Berlin, 1926),
11ff. There is additional bibliographic information
in O. Falsirol, *Il totemismo e l'animismo dell'anima*
(Napoli, 1941), and in G. Thomson, *Aeschylus and
Athens* (London: Lawrence and Wishart, 1941).

4-8. For Marett's activity, see the collection of
essays *Custom is King*, presented to him by his friends
in 1936 for his seventieth birthday. In this collection there is an accurate bibliography of all of
Marett's writings, including numerous reviews. For
additional information see G. Cocchiara, in R. R.
Marett, *Introduzione allo studio dell'uomo* [*Man in the
Making: An Introduction to Anthropology*, London,
1927], trans. G. Cocchiara (Palermo, 1944); H. Hubert
and M. Mauss, "Étude sommaire de la représentation du
temps dans la religion et la magie," in *Mélanges d'histoire des religions*, 2nd ed. (Paris, 1929), trans. E.
de Martino, in the volume *Durkheim, Hubert, Mauss, Le
origini dei poteri magici* (Torino, 1951).

PART SIX

Chapter XXVI

1-8. There are notes and information on the historical-

cultural school in H. Pinard de la Boullaye, *L'étude
comparée des religions*, I (Paris, 1922), 397ff, and
II, 254ff. To this, one must add E. de Martino,
Naturalismo e storicismo nell'etnologia (Bari, 1941),
pp. 125-28, 207-23. See also E. Morote Best, *Elementos
de folklore* (Cuzco, 1950), pp. 247ff. References: G.
Vidossi, "Nuovi orientamenti nello studio delle tradizioni popolari," *Atti lll Congr. Arti e Tradizione
popolari* (Roma, 1936), pp. 172-73.

Chapter XXVII

1-8. For Gennep and his system, see R. Corso, *Folklore*, 2nd ed. (Napoli, 1943), pp. 97-180, and the bibliography cited therein. For opposition to Gennep's
biological claims, see also what A. Varagnac has written in *Définition du folklore* (Paris, 1938), p. 18,
note 1. Varagnac also discusses the limitations of
the psychoanalytic method, with which some scholars
(Rhoeim, for example) had sought to unveil the mystery
of popular traditions. Gennep's positions have been
supported by A. Marinus, a Belgian scholar who has asserted, in a small volume entitled *La causalité folk-
lorique* (Bruxelles, 1940), that folklore is essentially
a sociological discipline that must be studied with the
methods of psychology, not the methods of history. He
adds that the science of folklore must free itself of
a "purely historical conception of facts," since it is
required to undertake an analysis of "psychological
strata." Corso, op. cit., p. 100, says that the work
of Marinus (for whom he gives a complete bibliography)
is that of a courageous man in the vanguard of the
Belgian folklore movement, a man whose doctrine deserves the name "neo-folklore." In reality, however,
Marinus had no historical or philosophical training
whatever, and his conclusions about folklore demonstrate only that he failed to delimit the confines of
psychology and history and that he was firmly en-
trenched in what could be called the archeology of history. Of quite different training is S. Erixon, "Ethnologie régionale ou folklore," *Laos*, 1 (Stockholm,

1951), 9ff; while asserting that folklore must account
for certain ethnological and psychological aspects,
he believes that folklore presupposes a historical and
comparative-historical investigation of traditional
culture. Sebillot's review of Gennep's *Folklore*
français is in the *Revue de l'Histoire des Religions*,
25 (1904), 407. References: P. Toschi, review in
Lares, 16 (1950), 129-330.

Chapter XXVIII

1-8. For the history of Modernism, see particularly
A. Houtin, *Histoire du modernisme catholique* (Paris,
1913); and E. Bonaiuti, *Storia del Cristianesimo*
(Milano, 1943), III, 651ff. We should add, especially
for the passages on Loisy, G. Martini, *Storicismo e*
modernismo (Napoli, 1951). Bibliography for Saintyves
is in his own volume, *L'astrologie populaire* (Paris,
1937), pp. 452-457. This should be integrated with
A. van Gennep, *Manuel de folklore français contem-*
porain (Paris, 1937-38) (in IV, 663, the arguments
against the *Contes de Perrault* are recorded). I do
not share Thompson's opinion of Saintyves, offered in
The Folktale (New York, 1946), p. 386. See the evaluations of Saintyves offered by R. Maunier, J. Menand,
A. Marinus, and P. Rivet in the miscellaneous volume
Les Cahiers Pierre Saintyves (Paris, 1940).

Chapter XXIX

1-4. There is bibliographical information on Croce's
folkloristic activity in G. Cocchiara, *Storia degli*
studi delle tradizioni popolari in Italia (Palermo,
1947). We should add the essays of Corsi, "Il pensiero
giovanile di B. Croce," in *Ann. Scuola Normale di Pisa*
(2), 17 (1948), and Navacco, "Appunti su Benedetto
Croce, studioso delle tradizioni popolari napoletane,"
in *Belfagor*, 5 (1950), n. 5. For Croce's concept of
popular poetry, see P. Toschi, *Fenomenologia del canto*
popolare (Bari, 1942), pp. 227ff.

5-6. For Barbi as folklorist, see G. Cocchiara, op.
cit. (and the bibliography cited therein). For his
unedited collection of folksongs, see V. Santoli, *I
canti popolari italiani* (Firenze, 1940), pp. 117-200.
References: V. Santoli, "Gli studi di letteratura
popolare," in the miscellany *Cinquant'anni di vita
intellettuale italiana 1896-1946* (Napoli, 1950), II,
p. 7 of the abstract.

7-8. There is a bibliography of Menéndez Pidal's
writings in H. Serís and G. Arteta y Errasti, *Bibliog-
rafía Hispanica Ramón Menéndez Pidal* (New York, 1935).
We also have the miscellany *Homenaje a Menéndez Pidal*
(Madrid, 1925). The reader who wants an accurate picture of Menéndez Pidal's theories can see the introduction to the *Historia general de las literaturas
hispánicas*, published under the direction of G. Díaz
Plaja (Barcellona, 1949). For some opposition to these
theories, see E. R. Curtius, *Europäische Literatur und
lateinisches Mittelalter* (Bern, 1948), p. 173 et passim.
Baldi, *Studi sulla poesia popolare d'Inghilterra e di
Scozia* (Roma, 1949), p. 51, maintains that Menéndez
Pidal, in his *Romancero* (Madrid, 1927), pp. 28ff, while
illustrating "an excellent case of re-elaboration
through contamination," would seem to "have it supposed
that the re-elaboration is an altogether unconscious
choice." There is additional information in S. Battaglia, *Poema del mio Cid* (Roma, 1943); G. Guerrieri
Crocetti, *L'epopea spagnuola* (Milano, 1944); and E. Li
Gotti, "El cantar de mio Cid, cantar del buen vassalo,"
in *Letterature moderne* (Milano, 1951), which has a
quite extensive bibliography. References: L. Spitzer,
Modern Language Quarterly, 4 (1943), 420-421.

Chapter XXX

1-2. For Meier and the development of German studies on
popular poetry in the last fifty years, see A. Haberlandt, *Die deutsch Volkskunde* (Halle, 1935). There is
additional information in P. Toschi, "Nuovi orientamenti

nello studio della poesia popolare," in *Lares*, 16 (1950), 2ff.

3-4. There is an extremely large bibliography on Naumann's neo-folklorism. See, for all matters, A. H. Krappe, *The Science of Folk-lore* (London, 1930), pp. 105, 189; S. Thompson, *The Folktale* (New York, 1946), pp. 40, 87; R. Corso, *Folklore*, 2nd ed. (Napoli, 1943), pp. 104-107; and G. Vidossi, "Nuovi orientamenti nello studio delle tradizioni popolari," *Atti 111 Congr. Arti e Tradizioni popolari* (Roma, 1936), p. 175. There are numerous criticisms of his system: see, for example, IU. M. Sokolov, *Russian Folklore* (New York, 1950); R. Wolfram, "Lo studio della danza popolare in Germania," and C. Hahm, "L'indagine sull'arte popolare in Germania," in *Lares*, 10 (1939), 341ff and 384ff, respectively.

5. By Hoffmann-Krayer, author of scholarly works on Swiss folklore (among other things), see especially the volume *Kleine Schriften zur Volkskunde*, ed. P. Geiger (Basel, 1946). The term "vulgus in populo" is in *Die Volkskunde als Wissenschaft* (Zürich, 1902). For additional information on his work, see R. Weiss, *Volkskunde der Schweiz* (Zürich, 1946), pp. 7ff. References: G. Vidossi, op. cit., p. 169.

6-8. For developments in Russian folklore, see especially Sokolov, op. cit. pp. 30-92. There is additional information in M. Azadovskiĭ, "Étude du folklore en URSS (1918-32)," in *V.O.K.S.* (1933), pp. 40-65; and in A. Marinus, "Ethnographie, folklore et archéologie en Russie soviétique," in *Bull. Soc. Roy. Belge d'Anthropologie et Préhistoire*, 49 (1934), 177-186. L. Hippius and V. Chicherov have written an extremely informative and accurate essay, "Trent'anni di studi sovietici sul folklore," in *Rassegna della Stampa Sovietica*, Nos. 4 and 5 (1949). This should be integrated with E. de Martino, "Etnologia e folklore nella Unione Sovietica," in *Scienza e cultura nell'URSS* (Roma, 1950). References: P. Toschi, review of the French translation of

Sokolov's *Russian Folklore* in *Lares*, 15 (1949), 105;
C. W. von Sydow, "Circulation des contes populaires,"
Trav. Ier Congr. Internat. de Folklore (Tours, 1938),
pp. 132ff; S. Baldi, *Studi sulla poesia popolare
d'Inghilterra e di Scozia* (Roma, 1949), pp. 55ff.

ANNOTATED LIST OF NAMES

AARNE, Antti Amatus (1867-1925): Major Finnish folklorist. His main works are his index of folktale
types, *Verzeichnis der Märchentypen* (1910), and
his comparative study of folktales, *Leitfaden der
vergleichenden Märchenforschung* (1913), basic works
in the historical-geographical school.
ADDISON, Joseph (1672-1719): English writer and politician who published satirical journals, including
the *Spectator*.
AFANAS'EV, Aleksandr Nikolaevich (1826-1871): Russian
folklorist and ethnographer, follower of the
brothers Grimm and Max Müller. He compiled the
most important collection of Russian folktales in
the nineteenth century.
AFZELIUS, Arvid August (1785-1871): Swedish poet,
folklorist, and historian.
ALCIATI, Andrea (1492-1550): Italian jurist, historian, and poet.
ALECSANDRI, Vasile (1821-1890): Rumanian romantic
poet, founder of Rumanian folklore scholarship.
His works include *Poezii populare ale românilor*,
2 vols. (1852-53), and *Doine și lăcrimioare* (1852).
ALTUSIO, Johann (1557-1638): German jurist who believed in the theory of natural law. According to
him, the people are the true bearers of supreme
power; their representatives elect the ruler.
AMPÈRE, Jean Jacques (1800-1864): Literary historian
and linguist, member of the French Academy. He
deals with folklore in *Discours sur l'ancienne
litérature scandinave* (1832) and *Des Bardes chez
les Gallois et les autres nations celtiques*.
ANCONA, Alessandro d' (1835-1914): Italian philologist, literary historian, professor at Pisa. He
participated in the national liberation movement
and joined the Liberal Party. He also wrote a
work on Italian folk poetry entitled *La poesia
popolare italiana* (1859).

ANDREE, Richard (1835-1912): German ethnographer who
dealt chiefly with the comparative ethnography of
Slavic peoples (especially Czechs and Serbs).
ANDREEV, Nikolaĭ Petrovich (1892-1942): Soviet folklorist. In his first works he followed the Finnish
school, but later he criticized its faulty methodology. He studied Russian and Ukrainian folklore
and the mutual relationship between literature and
folklore. He published Aarne's index of fairy tale
types, adding a reference to Russian tales, in his
Ukasatel' skazochnykh siŭzhetov po sisteme Aarne
(1929).
ANTONI, Carlo (born in 1896): Italian philosopher.
AQUINAS, Saint Thomas (1225-1274): Great scholastic
philosopher and theologian, Dominican monk, professor at the University of Paris.
ARIOSTO, Lodovico (1474-1533): Italian poet of the
late Renaissance. His *Orlando furioso* (1516) was
intended as a continuation of Matteo Bojardo's
Orlando innamorato (1486), although the two works
are quite different in tone and style. In his work
he utilized the motifs of medieval epics, chivalric
romances, and ancient poetry.
ARNAULD, Antoine (1612-1694): French jurist and theologian who believed in Jansenism. As a result of
his pleading a case for the University of Paris
against the Jesuits he was forced to flee to the
Netherlands.
ARNDT, Ernst M. (1769-1860): German poet, historian,
and linguist, opponent of serfdom. His thesis on
"The Mysterious Spirit of the People" is based on
the genius theory.
ARNIM, Ludwig Achim (1781-1831), and BRENTANO, Clemens
(1778-1842): Stirred a great interest in folk
poetry by publishing a collection of folksongs,
Des Knaben Wunderhorn. Viewing the folk as a
homogeneous, classless group, they included
songs by known authors in their collection. They
idealized the Middle Ages and patriarchal social
organization. Brentano eventually converted to
Catholicism, repudiated his former activities, and
became an advocate of asceticism.

ATHENAEUM: Periodical of the Schlegel brothers published in Germany from 1798 to 1800 (during the period of enthusiasm for the Classical Age).

AUBIGNAC, François d' (1604-1676): French abbot, writer, and critic, devoted to classicism.

AUGUSTINE, Saint (354-430): Bishop of Hippo (North Africa), theologian, author of *The City of God* and the *Confessions*.

AZADOVSKIĬ, Mark Konstantinovich (1888-1954): Soviet folklorist, literary historian, and ethnographer. Azadovskiĭ organized the collection of folklore materials in connection with the Second World War. His chief works are his history of Russian folklore, *Istoriĭa russkoĭ fol'kloristiki* (1958), and his collection of articles on history and folklore, *Stat'i o literature i fol'klore* (1960).

BACHOFEN, Johann Jacob (1815-1887): Swiss jurist and historian. He founded the study of family history, stating that ancient peoples lived first in promiscuity and later in a matriarchal society. His work on maternal law, *Das Mutterrecht*, was published in 1861.

BALTUS, Jean François (1667-1743): Jesuit, author of *Réponse a l'histoire des oracles de Fontenelle*, 2 vols. (1707-08).

BANIER, Antoine (1673-1741): French abbot who dealt with mythology in *Explication historique des fables*, 2 vols. (1711).

BARBI, Michele (1867-1941): Italian philologist and Dante scholar, professor at Messina. His emphasis on the importance of collecting and studying ballads and songs according to precise philological criteria led to the large manuscript collection of popular Italian songs known by the title *Raccolta Barbi*. His works on folklore include *Scibilia nobili e la raccolta dei canti popolari* (1929) and *Poesia popolare italiana: studi e proposte* (1939).

BARTOLI, Daniello (1608-1685): Rector of Roman College; his supervisors ordered him to write the history of the order (*Dell'historia della Compagnia di Giesù*,

1653-63). He also wrote works on physics, philology, and other topics.

BASILE, Giovanni Battista (1575-1632): Italian poet and writer of novellas, author of a collection of folktales entitled the *Pentamerone*. The English edition, *The Pentamerone of Giambattista Basile*, trans. Benedetto Croce, 2 vols. (London: John Lane/The Bodley Head, 1932; New York: Dutton, 1932), includes a detailed history of the book.

BASTIAN, Adolf (1826-1905): German ethnographer and traveler, founder of the Ethnographic Museum in Berlin. In the course of his two twenty-five-year journeys, he collected an abundance of material on every continent. He propounded the theory of "basic thought," according to which fundamental ideas are similar throughout the world: cultures having the same prerequisites will establish the same types of technical, societal, and spiritual institutions. Their unique features, he argued, are formed entirely by geographical factors.

BAYLE, Pierre (1647-1706): French thinker, forerunner of the Enlightenment; in 1682 he emigrated to the Netherlands. Bayle believed in tolerance; he even defended atheism and criticized religion and superstition. He compiled ample ethnographic and folklore material, although he himself viewed it as "an accumulation of lies and mistakes." His chief work is the *Dictionnaire historique et critique* (1697).

BECCARIA, Cesare (1738-1794): Italian jurist and publicist of the Enlightenment. In his study on crime and punishment, *Dei delitti et delle pene* (1764), he defended the freedom of the individual. He demanded the reduction of criminal sentences and the abolition of the death penalty.

BECKER, Philipp August (1862-1947): German romantic, expert on medieval and Renaissance French literature.

BÉDIER, Joseph (1864-1937): French literary historian. His most important works--*Le roman de Tristan et Iseult* (1907), *Les légendes épiques* (1908-13), *Les fabliaux* (1893), and *Les chansons de croisade*

(1909)--are concerned with medieval literature.
In his work entitled *Études critiques* (1903), he
elucidated his views on methodology, rejecting the
diffusion theory and the Indic origin of the
fabliau. He attempted to discover links between
medieval works and national poetry. According to
him, medieval legends were written long after the
events they describe, and monks had a great role
in their creation.

BEHN, Aphra (1640-1689): English writer who spent her
youth in the West Indies and became acquainted with
all the miseries of colonial slavery. Her novel
Oroonoko, or the Royal Slave (1686) made European
readers realize the extreme hardships of slaves.
Her novel is often compared with Harriet Beecher
Stowe's *Uncle Tom's Cabin* (1852).

BEKKER, Balthasar (1634-1698): Dutch Cartesian philosopher. He opposed superstitions and witchhunts,
and he demanded an end to "old wives' tales about
the Devil and his plots." In his book entitled *De
betoverde Weereld* (1691), he cited many examples
of small children and old people being charged with
witchcraft and persecuted by the Inquisition and
Protestant courts.

BELLINI, Vincenzo (1801-1835): Italian composer; among
his operas are *La sonnambula* and *Norma*.

BENFEY, Theodor (1809-1881): German philologist, professor at Göttingen, proponent of the diffusion
theory (migrating themes, etc.). Benfey recognized
the primitive source of folklore and attributed its
later stages of development entirely to cultural
and literary influences. He thought Indic literature was the source of "migrating themes": he
edited the *Samaveda Hymns* (1848) and the *Panchatantra* (1859).

BERCHET, Giovanni (1783-1851): Nationalist Italian
poet, one of the founders of the romantic school
called "Young Italy." He worked actively for
Italy's unification.

BERGIER, Nicolas (1718-1790): French theologian, opponent of the followers of the Enlightenment
(especially Voltaire and Holbach).

BERNIER, François (1620-1688): French traveler, physician (not a gem merchant). From 1658 to 1666 he
lived in Delhi, the capital of the Mogul empire;
in 1670 he published a description of his journeys.
BESTUZHEV, Aleksandr Aleksandrovich (1797-1837):
Russian writer and publicist, Ryleev's friend,
active participant in the December uprising of
1825. His pen name was Alexander Marlinskiĭ.
BIDPAI (Bindhapati): The legendary author of old Indic
fables and stories written about 1500-2000 years
ago. These works, which were translated into
Arabic and many other Eastern languages, arrived
in Europe in the thirteenth century. In the fables
attributed to Bidpai the moral is usually voiced by
animals. For the English version of these fables,
see Maude Barrows Dutton, *The Tortoise and the
Geese, and Other Fables of Bidpai*, Boston: Hough-
ton Mifflin, 1908.
BLACKWELL, Thomas (1701-1757): Scottish classical
philologist. His works are *An Enquiry into the
Life and Writings of Homer* (1735) and *Letters Concerning Mythology* (1748).
BLAIR, Hugh (1718-1800): Scottish clergyman, professor
of Rhetoric and Literature at the University of
Edinburgh. In 1763 he published his *Dissertations
on the Poems of Ossian*, in which he argued that the
poems were authentic.
BLÜCHER, Gebhardt Lebrecht (1742-1819): Prussian
general, commander of the German troops in the
battle of Waterloo.
BODIN, Jean (1530-1596): French jurist and politician,
devotee of absolute monarchy. To promote the
development of industry and trade, he attempted to
establish an alliance of the middle class with the
crown. During the civil wars of the sixteenth
century, Bodin worked for the termination of religious fighting. For the sake of his country's
unity, he preached tolerance; nevertheless, he
believed in magic and demanded the extermination
of witches.
BODMER, Johann Jakob (1698-1783): German poet and
critic who opposed French classicism and fought

for the foundation of a German national literature.
He considered medieval German and English poets,
as well as classical authors, worthy of imitation.
He translated Milton and edited many medieval
literary texts.

BÖHME, Franz Magnus (1827-1898): German scholar and
musicologist. His folklore works include his collection of old German songs, *Altdeutsches Lieder-
buch* (1877), and his collection of German children's
songs and games, *Deutsches Kinderlied und Kinderspiel* (1897).

BÖHME, Jakob (1575-1624): German mystical philosopher,
of peasant origin. Böhme saw God as the origin of
both good and evil, and he was therefore persecuted
by the Church. The mysticism of his philosophy
attracted some of the German romantics.

BOILEAU, Nicolas (1636-1711): French poet and classical theorist. His ideas, defended in Germany by
Gottsched, were elucidated in his *L'art poétique*.

BOLTE, Johannes (1858-1937): German folklorist. He
collected and edited texts of sixteenth-century
songs and tales, and, in collaboration with Georg
(Jiři) Polivka, he edited *Anmerkungen zu den
Kinder- und Hausmärchen der Brüder Grimm*, 5 vols.
(1913-31).

BONALD, Louis Gabriel Ambroise de (1753-1840): French
politician, "legitimist" philosopher, writer. Like
Joseph de Maistre, he opposed the principles of the
French Revolution. He fought against revolutionary
France, and during the Restoration he was the
leader of the extreme royalists.

BOPP, Franz (1791-1867): German scholar, founder of
comparative linguistics and Sanskrit studies. His
chief activity was the elaboration of his *Comparative Grammar*, which appeared in six volumes (1833-
52) as *Vergleichende Grammatik des Sanskrit, Zend,
Griechischen, Lateinischen, Litauischen,
Altslawischen, Gothischen und Deutschen*, English
translation by E. B. Eastwick (1856). Bopp's
efforts to discover the common origin of the grammatical forms or inflections of Sanskrit, Persian,
Greek, Latin, and German by means of historical

analysis had never before been attempted, and
those efforts provided the first dependable
material for comparative studies of languages.
BOSSUET, Jacques-Bénigne (1627-1704): French bishop,
writer, and preacher. His *Politique tirée de
l'Ecriture Sainte* is a treatise against anti-
clerical literature and against criticism of the
Bible and Church dogma.
BOULANGER, Nicolas Antoine (1722-1759): Engineer, writer,
and philosopher, one of the Encyclopedists. He dealt
with Oriental languages and religious history.
BOWRING, John (1792-1872): English statesman, traveler,
and writer. He translated and published Russian,
Serbian, Polish, and other folklore material, which
he collected in the course of his journeys.
BRÉAL, Michel (1832-1915): French linguist. He was a
Latin scholar who also studied Indo-European
mythology.
BREITINGER, Johann Jakob (1701-1776): Swiss writer
and literary critic, Bodmer's friend.
BRENTANO: See ARNIM, Ludwig Achim.
BROSSES, Charles de (1709-1777): French historian and
writer, one of the Encyclopedists. On Buffon's
advice, he wrote *Histoire des navigations aux
Terres Australes* (1756). He coined the names
Australia and Polynesia. His study of the worship
of fetish gods, *Du culte des dieux fétiches*
(1760), prepared the way for the scientific study
of "primitive" religions. He also wrote on linguistic problems and Roman history.
BROWNE, Thomas (1605-1682): English physician, writer,
antiquarian, and royalist. His first work, written
in 1635 but not published until 1642, was *Religio
Medici*, wherein one finds Browne's expression of
his belief in the reality of witchcraft. In 1646,
he published *Pseudodoxia Epidemica: or Enquiries
into very many Received Tenents and commonly presumed Truths*, popularly known as *Vulgar Errors*, in
an attempt to confute what he viewed as the unsound
beliefs of the commonalty. His last and perhaps
most famous work, *Hydriotaphia, Urn Burial, or a
Discourse of the Sepulchral Urns lately found in*

Norfolk, together with the Garden of Cyrus (1658), combines his antiquarian and scientific interests with eloquent meditations on life, death, and immortality.

BÜRGER, Gottfried August (1747-1794): Poet who wrote literary German ballads. He translated the satire of the German gentility, *The Adventures of Baron Münnchausen* (1786). His ballads, including *Lenore* (1773) and *Wilde Jäger* (1783), are imbued with mystery and reveal his interest in ghosts, the dead, and werewolves.

BUGGE, Sophus (1833-1907): Norwegian linguist. He published the *Edda* songs under the title *Norroen fornkvaedi* (1867); his other works include *Gamle norske Folkeviser* (1858) and *Norrone skrifter af sagnhistorisk indhold* (1864-65).

BURKE, Edmund (1729-1797): English politician, political philosopher, and member of Parliament. His interest in aesthetic theory led to his *Philosophical Inquiry into the Origin of our Ideas on the Sublime and Beautiful* (1757), which had some influence on later German philosophy. Perhaps his greatest work is *Reflections on the Revolution in France* (1789), in which he argued that the principles and sentiments of the French revolutionists were likely to destroy traditions and institutions, the most valuable "protective" elements that civilization offers to man.

BUSLAEV, Fedor Ivanovich (1818-1897): Russian professor of philology.

CABALLERO, Fernán (1796-1877): Spanish writer whose real name was Cecilia Böhl de Faber. She borrowed much from folk legends and beliefs, and she endeavored to depict everyday life and morals realistically.

CALEPINO, Ambrogio (1435-1511): Italian humanist, Augustinian monk. He wrote a multilingual dictionary which was long considered the best available.

CALVIN: See LUTHER.

CARDUCCI, Giosuè (1835-1907): Italian nationalist poet

who published collections of folk poetry. In
several of his works he was concerned with the
history of Italian literature.

CARMELI, Michel Angelo (1706-1766): Italian Orientalist.

CASAS, Bartolomé de las (1474-1566): Dominican monk.
In 1501 he went to America in one of Columbus's
expeditions, and, while there, he attempted to
ease conditions for the Indians. Later he was
appointed "protector of the Indians" and became
the first to suggest that their work should be
taken over by Negro slaves.

CASSIRER, Ernst (1874-1945): German Neo-Kantian philosopher who was also influenced by Hegel's *Phenomenology of Mind* and Herder's philosophy of history.
His best-known work is his three-volume *Philosophie
der symbolischen Formen* (1923-29), in which he
argued that areas of human culture--language, myth,
science, art, religion--are different "forms of
apprehension" originating in primitive symbols,
images, and acts. He wrote extensively on primitive culture, myth, and language, and his writings
have influenced twentieth-century semantics, cultural and philosophical anthropology, and social
psychology. His works include *Sprache und Mythos*
(1925), *Die Philosophie der Aufklärung* (1932),
Logik der Kulturwissenschaften (1942), *An Essay
on Man* (1944), and *The Myth of the State* (1946).

CATTANEO, Carlo (1801-1869): Italian republican and
revolutionary. He wrote works on philosophy,
economy, politics, literature, and linguistics.

CAUDWELL, Christopher (pseudonym for Christopher St.
John Sprigg) (1907-1937): Marxist English literary
critic who was killed in 1937 while fighting in the
Spanish Civil War.

CAVOUR, Camillo Benso (1810-1861): Italian statesman,
count, leader of the liberal monarchists; he believed in the unification of Italy "from above,"
by divine intervention.

ČELAKOVSKÝ, František Ladislav (1799-1852): Czech
poet, philologist, and folklorist. Among his works
are two studies of slavic folksongs and proverbs,

Slovanské národní písně (1822-27) and *Mudrosloví*
národu slovanského ve příslovích (1852).
CESAROTTI, Melchiorre (1730-1808): Italian scholar
and poet, professor of Greek and Hebrew at Padua.
His translation of *Ossian* marked a significant
change in Italian literature, in which classicism
was prevailing at the time.
CHAADAEV, Petr Iakovlevich (1796-1856): Russian
writer, friend of Pushkin. For a while he was a
member of the Secret Society of the Decembrists.
His political and religious views are revealed in
his *Lettres philosophiques*, only one of which was
published in his lifetime--in 1836 in *The Tele-*
scope. He argued that Russia was historically and
culturally outside the mainstream of civilization,
and he bitterly criticized Russia's isolationist
stance. He thought that only by rejecting Greek
Orthodoxy and embracing Roman Catholicism could
Russia assume its rightful role as a world leader.
His political philosophy was colored by his religious mysticism: he believed that it was the
divine purpose of the Roman Catholic Church to
bring about the kingdom of God on earth by uniting
Eastern and Western Christianity and ultimately
the whole of humanity.
CHARDIN, Sir John (1643-1713): French traveler who
journeyed to the Orient twice to buy precious
stones. He lived in Iran for many years and
visited the Crimean peninsula, the Caucasus, and
India. His several volumes describing his journeys
are a valuable source for the study of countries
and cultures in Asia Minor.
CHARRON, Pierre (1541-1603): Montaigne's follower and
friend who systematized Montaigne's ideas in such
works as *De la sagesse* (1601). He believed that
Nature is the source of man's morality and that
religion is a result of education.
CHATEAUBRIAND, François René de (1768-1848): French
romantic writer. His novels *Atala* (1801), *René*
(1802), and *Les Natchez* (1826) stressed individualism and idealized primitive peoples.
CHIABRERA, Gabriello (1552-1638): Italian lyric poet

who imitated the epics of Homer and Virgil.

CHILD, Francis James (1826-1896): American ballad scholar. As a professor at Harvard University, Child specialized in medieval and Renaissance literature, editing the definitive edition of Edmund Spenser and the American edition of *British Poets*. He is best known, however, for his *The English and Scottish Popular Ballads*, 5 vols. (1882-98), which was modeled after Svend Grundtvig's *Danmarks gamle Folkeviser*. The 305 ballads in Child's collection are among the oldest in the British tradition. Child's arrangement of and commentary on these ballads have made *The English and Scottish Popular Ballads* one of the most influential works in ballad scholarship.

CHULKOV, Mikhail Dmitrievich (1740-1793): Russian writer, folklorist, ethnographer, and economist. Among his works are his collection of songs, *Sobranie raznykh pĩesen*, 4 vols. (1870-74), his lexicon of mythology, *Kratkoĭ mifologicheskoĭ leksikon* (1767), his collection of Russian tales, *Russkĩia skazki* (1780-83), and his dictionary of Russian superstitions, *Slovar' ruskikh suevĩeriĭ* (1782).

CIESZKOWSKI, August (1814-1894): Polish Hegelian philosopher.

CLOOTS, Anacharsis (his given name was Jean Baptiste) (1755-1794): French philosopher of Prussian origin; publicist and politician during the French Revolution. A believer in pantheism and the forceful suppression of Christianity, he was executed with the Hébertists.

COLERIDGE: See WORDSWORTH, William.

COLLINS, Samuel (1619-1670): Tsar Alexeĭ Mikhailovich's physician. He lived in Russia from 1659 to 1666 and recorded some Russian tales.

COMPARETTI, Domenico (1835-1927): Italian writer and philologist. His works were concerned with the study of folklore and dialects: *Edipo e la mitologia comparata* (1867); *Novelline popolari italiane* (1875); and *Il Kalevala e la poesia tradizionale dei Finni* (1891).

COMTE, Auguste (1798-1857): French philosopher and
sociologist, founder of Positivism. His works
include *Cours de philosophie positive*, 6 vols.
(1830-42), and *Système de politique positive*,
4 vols. (1851-54). Comte suggested in his works
that society should embrace a new man-centered
theology based upon science rather than upon
superstition. In Comte's view, man's thinking
passes through three stages: in the theological
stage, man sees the universe as being controlled
by supernatural forces, invisible but anthropomorphic gods; in the metaphysical stage, man
rejects the supernatural for more speculative
concepts of undefined forces operating beneath
observable phenomena; in the positivistic stage,
man confronts natural and social phenomena with
the principles of science. Comte believed that
although the pure sciences had passed through all
three stages, the study of collective man, "sociology" (a term that he coined), had not yet
reached the positivistic stage. In his *Politique
positive* he put forth his utopian view of a society ruled by positivistic philosophers and devoted
to the "Cult of Humanity," and he argued for a
rigorous application of the scientific method to
the study of man's habits and environment.

CONSTANT, Benjamin (1767-1830): French writer, publicist, and politician; he spent a long period of
time in voluntary exile and returned to France
only during the Restoration.

COURT DE GEBELIN, Antoine (1725-1784): French scholar.
In his *Monde primitif, analysé et comparé avec le
monde moderne*, 9 vols. (1773-96), he suggested that
comparative grammars, based on language groups, be
written.

COX, George William (1827-1902): English historian and
philologist. His works are *The Mythology of the
Aryan Nations* (1870) and *An Introduction to the
Science of Comparative Mythology and Folklore*
(1881).

CREUZER, Georg Friedrich (1771-1858): German philologist and professor at Marburg and Heidelberg.

His chief work is his study of the symbolism and
mythology of ancient peoples, *Symbolik und Mythologie der alten Völker, besonders der Griechen*,
4 vols. (1810-12).
CROCE, Benedetto (1866-1952): Italian politician,
philosopher, aesthetician, historian, and literary
critic. His idealistic historicism, derived in
part from Vico, stressed the importance of "indi-
vidualizing history" through a study of unique and
unrepeatable phenomena in order to arrive at an
assessment of the concept of the "spirit" in human
affairs. (On this point see his major philosophical work, *Filosofia come scienza dello spirito*,
4 vols., 1902-17.) As a folklore scholar, he
criticized much of the comparative research of the
nineteenth century as a pseudoscientific "positivistic naturalism." In his studies of popular
poetry and folk narrative (especially the *Pentamerone*, which he first translated into Italian in
1925), he rejected abstract categories involved in
questions of "popularity," "origin," and "narrative
motifs," preferring instead to apply historical and
aesthetic criteria to these genres. His discussion
of popular and artistic poetry appears in his
Poesia popolare e poesia d'arte, first published in
La Critica in 1929, then published as a volume in
1933.
CUOCO, Vincenzo (1770-1823): Italian historian and
politician.

DAHLMANN, Friedrich Christoph (1785-1860): German
historian and politician, professor at Göttingen.
In 1848 he was a representative to the Parliament
of Frankfurt, advocating the unification of Germany
under Prussian hegemony.
DAL', Vladimir Ivanovich (1801-1872): Russian scholar
and writer. His collection of Russian proverbs,
Poslovitsy russkogo naroda, was published in 1861.
He also published his four-volume dictionary of
the Russian language in 1862.
DALE, Antonius van (1638-1708): Dutch physician,
philosopher, and antiquarian scholar. Fontenelle

used Dale's *De oraculis veterum ethnicorum* (1683)
to write *Histoire des oracles*.

DALRYMPLE, Sir David (also known as Lord Hailes) (1726-
1792): Scottish jurist and historian, Commissioner
of Scotland. His chief work is *Annals of Scotland*,
2 vols. (1776).

DEFOE, Daniel (ca. 1660-1731): English journalist,
satirist, author of *Robinson Crusoe*. After an un-
successful career as a London merchant, he turned
to the writing of political pamphlets and satires
aimed against the Tories, the most famous of which
is *The Shortest Way with the Dissenters* (1703). In
1704 he founded the *Review*, a newspaper that was the
forerunner of the *Tatler* and *Spectator*. *Robinson
Crusoe* (1719) was the first in a series of ficti-
tious autobiographies--including *Captain Singleton*
(1720), *Moll Flanders* (1722), *Colonel Jack* (1722),
and *Roxana* (1724)--in which he characterized the
rogues and adventurers of London society.

DEMEUNIER, Jean Nicolas (1741-1814): French politician
and writer.

DIETERICH, Albrecht (1866-1908): German historian of
religion.

DIEZ, Friedrich (1794-1876): German linguist, founder
of comparative romance philology.

DOBROLIÙBOV, Nikolaĭ Aleksandrovich (1836-1861):
Russian folklorist who was particularly concerned
with the methodology of collecting and publishing
folklore materials. He himself collected proverbs
and riddles, folksongs, legends, and folk customs.

DOBROVSKÝ, Josef (1753-1829): Slavist, one of the
leaders of the Czech national movement. He fought
against the Germanization of Slavs and worked on
the development of a Czech literary language.

DUFRESNY, Charles Rivière (1648-1724): French poet,
novelist, playwright, composer, and great-grandson
of Henry IV. Under Louis XIV he was the supervisor
of the gardens of the court and thus had a knowledge of court secrets.

DULAURE, Jacques Antoine (1755-1835): French politician and historian, one of the founders of the
Celtic Academy.

DUPUIS, Charles François (1742-1809): French politician and scholar. In his works he tried to explain
mythological and religious notions as astronomical
symbols.
DURÁN, Agustin (1789-1862): Spanish poet and critic.
He published two editions of his *Romancero general*
(1828-32 and 1851).
DURKHEIM, Emile (1858-1917): French sociologist who
is often regarded as one of the founders of modern
sociological theory. Influenced by such predecessors as Descartes, Rousseau, and Comte, Durkheim
focused his attention on the nature of the social
system and its relation to the personality of the
individual. In his earlier works--*De la division
du travail social* (1893), *Les régles de la méthode
sociologique* (1895), and *Le suicide: étude de
sociologie* (1897)--he examined the dynamics of
group action and the importance of normative values
in what he called the *conscience collective*. In
his later works, particularly *Les formes élémentaires de la vie religieuse, le système totémique
en Australie* (1912), he examined the closeness of
integration between religious systems and the
structure of the society itself, observing that
such integration seems particularly close in primitive societies. He concluded that religion was
the primordial "matrix" from which the chief elements of culture evolved by the process of differentiation, and he believed that totemism was the
most ancient form of religion.

ECKERMANN, Johann Peter (1792-1854): Goethe's secretary (1823-1832), who published a book of memoirs,
*Gespräche mit Goethe in den letzten Jahren seines
Lebens* (1835-47).
THE EDDA: Icelandic collection containing ancient
myths and heroic poems. Its pieces were written
between the seventh and thirteenth centuries; they
were collected in the thirteenth century (ca. 1270)
and discovered in 1643. It is not only a valuable
work of art but also an important source for the
study of the history of ancient Scandinavian

peoples during the period of tribal disintegration.
EDWARDS, William Frédéric (1777-1842): French philologist.
EICHENDORFF, Joseph von (1788-1857): German romantic
lyric poet, member of the Heidelberg circle.
ERASMUS, Desiderius (1469-1536): Dutch theologian,
scholar, humanist, and traveler. Distrustful of
rational theology and scholasticism, he argued for
a simple, practical, ethical Christian conduct and
against prescribed and formal ritual in his well-
known *Enchiridion Militis Christiani* (1503). Although his repeated calls for a purification of
the Church appealed to such reformers as Luther,
Hutten, and Dürer and gave impetus to the Reformation, Erasmus himself was never an advocate of
church separation; rather, he maintained the role
of conciliator among the warring factions of the
Church.
EUHEMERUS (second half of the 4th cent., B.C.): Greek
philosopher who was the first man to try to interpret Greek myths rationally. In his view, the gods
were merely people who took on god-like qualities
in the imagination of later generations.

FAURIEL, Claude Charles (1772-1844): French historian,
philologist, and critic who wrote on the literary
history and folklore of France and Italy. Some of
his works are mentioned in the text; others are
Histoire de la poésie provençale (1846), *Dante et
les origines de la langue et de la littérature
italiennes* (1854), and *Histoire de la croisade
contre les hérétiques albigeois écrite en vers
provençaux par un poète contemporain* (1837).
FÉNELON, François de Salignac de la Mothe (1651-1715):
French writer, educator, and member of the French
Academy, one of the forerunners of the Enlightenment; Bishop of Cambrai and instructor of the crown
prince. His main works are *De l'éducation des
filles* (1687), *Dialogues des morts* (1700-18), and
Les aventures de Télémaque (1699).
FERDOWSI (ca. 935-ca. 1020): Great Persian poet and
author of the *Shāh-namāh*, published in English as

*The Epic of the Kings: Shāh-Nama, The National
Epic of Persia by Ferdowski*, trans. Reuben Levy,
Chicago: Univ. of Chicago Press, 1967.

FICHTE, Johann Gottlieb (1762-1814): German idealist
philosopher who played a substantial role in the
national uprising of 1807-1814. In his early
philosophical works, especially his *Versuch einer
Kritik aller Offenbarung* (1793), he extended
Kantian philosophy by investigating the conditions
under which revealed religion is possible; he concluded that religion ultimately rests upon practical reason and depends upon an adherence to moral
law, which is in itself divine. In his later
works, however, Fichte's philosophy moved from an
ethical and rational emphasis to an emphasis on a
mystical and theological metaphysics, in that he
came to believe--under the influence of Schleiermacher, Schelling, Hegel, and the German romantics
--that religious faith surpasses moral reason.
His intense interest in Germany's efforts for
national independence is best reflected in his
Reden an die deutsche Nation, a series of lectures
delivered at the University of Berlin in 1807-08,
and in his lectures on the idea of true war, *Über
den Begriff eines wahrhaften Krieges* (1813).

FICINO, Marsilio (1433-1499): Italian neo-Platonist
philosopher who was the governor of the Florence
Academy founded by Cosimo de' Medici. His major
philosophical work, *Theologia Platonica de immor-
talitate animorum* (1482), attempted to reconcile
Christian and pagan doctrine about immortality.

FONTENELLE, Bernard de (1657-1757): French thinker,
composer, playwright, poet, satirist; follower of
Descartes. For forty-two years he was Secretary
of the French Academy. Among other works, he
wrote *Histoire des oracles* (1687).

FRAZER, Sir James George (1854-1941): English ethnographer and historian of religion. Like Tylor, he
connected the origin and development of religion
with psychology. His most influential work is
The Golden Bough, 12 vols., 3rd edition, London,
1911-15.

FROBENIUS, Leo (1873-1938): German ethnographer. He
led twelve expeditions to Africa (1904-1935), where
he collected a great deal of material. One of the
originators of the theory of *Kulturkreis*, he regarded culture as an individual organism which
develops according to its own biological laws.
According to Frobenius, the people are not creators, only bearers of culture, which develops independent of them.

FUBINI, Mario (born in 1900): Italian literary critic,
editor of the *Giornale storico della letteratura
italiana*, and author of a book on Vico, *Stile e
umanità di Giambattista Vico* (1946).

FUSTEL DE COULANGES, Numa Denis (1830-1889): French
historian. According to his *La cité antique*
(1864), the early city-state was based on respect
for ancestors, and every change was connected with
religion. Later in his career he studied the
early Middle Ages.

GALATEO (1444-1517): Italian humanist monk, physician,
and philosopher (Antonio de Ferrari was his secular
name). He wrote on medicine, history, geography,
and theology.

GALIANI, Ferdinando (1728-1787): Italian economist,
abbot. From 1759 until 1769 he lived in Paris,
where he was in contact with the Encyclopedists.

GALLAND, Antoine (1646-1715): French Orientalist and
professor of Arabic at the Collège de France. He
traveled through the countries of the Orient and
translated the *Arabian Nights* into French under
the title *Les mille et une nuits* (1704).

GAUTIER, Léon (1832-1897): French medieval philologist.
His works are *Les épopées françaises* (1865-68) and
La Chanson de Roland (1872).

GEIGER, Ludwig Wilhelm (1856-1943): German Orientalist,
scholar of ancient and living languages of India
and Iran. He related the study of language to the
study of culture.

GEIJER, Erik Gustaf (1783-1847): Swedish romantic historian, poet, composer, and politician.

GENNEP, Arnold van (1873-1957): French folklorist,

professor of ethnography at Neuchâtel, and publisher of the *Revue d'Ethnographie et de Sociologie*. Beginning in 1904 with *Tabou et totémisme
à Madagascar*, he published several works on
ethnology and primitive history, including his
well-known *Les rites de passage* (1909). In this
latter book, he systematically compared rites-of-
passage ceremonies that celebrate an individual's
transition from one status to another within specific societies. Instead of applying *a priori*
categories as his predecessors had, he inductively
examined the structure of the ceremonies themselves
concluding that the tripartite phases of such cere-
monies--separation (*séparation*), transition (*marge*)
and incorporation (*agrégation*)--illustrated the
principles of regenerative renewal required by all
societies. He also saw folk literature and practices as aspects of living culture, and he collected and published folklore materials of France
and the French provinces, especially Flanders, Bur-
gandy, and Savoy. His most extensive collection is
the monumental *Manuel de folklore français contemporain* (1937-58).

GENTILI, Aberico (1552-1608): English scholar of civil
law and one of the first theoreticians of interna-
tional law. His works were placed on the *Index
Librorum Prohibitorum*. The most important ones are
De jure belli (1589), *De legationibus* (1585), and
Hispanicae advocationes (1613).

GÉRARD DE NERVAL (also known as Gérard Labrunie) (1808-
1855): French romantic poet and mystic.

GERHARD, Eduard (1795-1867): German scholar of classical archeology and mythology.

GESSNER, Salomon (1730-1788): German author of idyllic
poems.

GIANNONE, Pietro (1676-1748): Italian historian and
publicist, author of *Dell' istoria civile del regno
di Napoli*, 40 vols. (1723). He was persecuted because of his attacks on the papacy, and he died in
prison.

GIBBON, Edward (1734-1794): English historian who is
best known for his *The History of the Decline and*

Fall of the Roman Empire, 6 vols. (1776-88).

GIL'FERDING, Aleksandr Fedorovich (also known as Hil'-ferding) (1831-1872): Russian slavist, historian, and folklorist. In 1871 he led an expedition to the Olonets territory, and in *Onezhskie byliny* (1873) he recorded over three hundred byliny. He was the first to classify material according to the informant, although P. N. Rybnikov (1831-1885) previously suggested this method. He showed that epic works are closely related to natural circumstances, in this case to the social situation of Olonets peasants.

GIOBERTI, Vincenzo (1801-1852): Italian politician and idealist philosopher; in 1848-49, Premier of Piedmont. In his most important philosophical work, *Del primato morale e civile degli Italiani* (1843), he argued that the political and cultural emancipation of Italy could best be brought about by a civic papacy. This argument for a reliance on papal power as a source of political and cultural rejuvenation gave rise to the so-called Neo-Gulphic school. His other works include *Teorica del sovranaturale* (1838), *Il gesuita moderno* (1847), and *Il rinnovamento civile d'Italia* (1851).

GIRAULT, Claude Xavier (1764-1823): French historian and classical philologist.

GLADSTONE, William Ewart (1809-1898): English statesman, leader of the Liberal Party; Prime Minister 1868-74, 1880-85, 1886, 1892-94.

GLEIM, Johann Wilhelm Ludwig (1719-1803): German poet and priest. He founded the Poetic Society of Halle.

GOBINEAU, Joseph-Arthur (1816-1882): French diplomat, writer, and sociologist, one of the originators of the race theory. His theories were adopted by Nietzsche, H. S. Chamberlain, and later by the German Fascists, who considered Gobineau "German" and a "forerunner of Nazism."

GÖRRES, Johann Joseph (1776-1848): German publicist and scholar. Like many other romantics, he gravitated from being sympathetic toward the French

Revolution to being a devout Catholic. He was a
member of the Heidelberg circle of romantics and
one of the founders of the *Zeitung für Einsiedler.*
GOGUET, Antoine (1716-1758): French scholar and
jurist.
GOMME, Sir George Laurence (1853-1916): English folklorist, ethnographer, and historian, founder and
first president of the Folklore Society. He edited
the periodicals *Archeological Review, Antiquary,*
and *Folklore Journal.* His wife, Alice B. Gomme,
also a famous folklore scholar, concentrated on the
folkloristic aspects of children's games.
GÓNGORA Y ARGOTE, Luis de (1561-1627): Spanish poet
who wrote satirical "romances," odes, and sonnets,
as well as "letrillas" (popular poems consisting
of short lines). The collection of his best works
is *Soledades* (1636).
GOSSE, Edmund William (1849-1928): English poet and
literary historian. Among his works are *Seventeenth Century Studies: A Contribution to the
History of English Poetry* (1883) and *A History of
Eighteenth Century Literature* (1889).
GOTTSCHED, Johann Cristoph (1700-1766): German writer
and critic; theoretician of German classicism,
major literary figure of the first half of the
eighteenth century. Lessing and others criticized
him severely for his insistence upon the canons of
classicism.
GOZZI, Carlo (1722-1806): Italian playwright who
endeavored to revive the forms of the *Commedia
dell'arte.* For the fantastic themes of his fables,
he drew upon Basile's *Pentamerone.*
GRAEBNER, Fritz (1877-1934): German ethnographer, head
of the historical-cultural school. Wilhelm Schmidt
was one of his followers.
GRAF, Arturo (1848-1913): Italian poet, literary
critic, folklorist, and ethnographer. He was the
author of a work on the myths of the Middle Ages,
Miti, leggende e superstizioni del medio evo
(1892-93).
GRAMSCI, Antonio (1891-1937): Founder of the Italian
Communist Party. In his work *Lettere dal carcere*

(1947) he analyzed philosophical, political, and literary problems. His essay "Osservazioni sul folclore," written in 1929-30 while he was in prison and published in 1950 in *Letteratura e vita nazionale*, characterized folklore as a concept of the world held by a specific social strata, the "people of subaltern classes." As a Marxist, he came to see the folk as a socially and historically formed "lower class," in opposition to the romantic conception of the folk as the "spirit of the nation."

GRAVINA, Giovanni Vincenzo (1664-1718): Italian historian, jurist, poet, and critic.

GRAY, Thomas (1716-1771): English sentimental poet. In his odes he imitated ancient Greek poets, Old Icelandic poetry (e.g., "The Fatal Sisters"), and Celtic poetry (e.g., "The Bard").

GREUZE, Jean Baptiste (1725-1805): French painter.

GRIMM brothers: Jacob (1785-1863) and Wilhelm (1786-1859): German linguists, professors at the University of Göttingen, later at the University of Berlin; members of the Prussian Academy; collectors of German folktales and legends. The main works of Jacob Grimm are *Deutsche Rechtsalterthümer* (1828), *Deutsche Grammatik* (1819-37), *Deutsche Mythologie* (1835), and *Geschichte der deutschen Sprache* (1848). Wilhelm Grimm's main work is *Die deutsche Heldensage* (1829). Their collaborative works are *Kinder- und Hausmärchen* (1812-14) and *Deutsche Sagen* (1816-18). In 1854 they started publishing their German dictionary, the *Deutsches Wörterbuch*. *Kinder- und Hausmärchen*, loosely known as the *Fairy Tales*, is of course available in many English editions. *Deutsche Sagen* was issued under the title *German Legends* (trans. Donald Ward) as the first volume in the series of which this English translation of Cocchiara's text is a part. For biographical studies, see Ruth Michaelis-Jena, *The Brothers Grimm*, New York: Praeger, 1970; and Murray B. Peppard, *Paths Through the Forest: A Biography of the Brothers Grimm*, New York: Holt, Rinehart and Winston, 1971. An evaluation of their

work and its influence upon folklore scholarship
appeared in a special issue of *Hessische Blätter
für Volkskunde*, 54 (1963), devoted to the centen-
nial anniversary of Jacob Grimm's death.
GROTIUS, Hugo (1583-1645): Dutch jurist, historian,
and statesman; renowned systematizer of international law. He fled to France because of religious persecution. His main work is *De jure belli
et pacis* (1625).
GRUNDTVIG, Svend (1824-1883): Leading nineteenth-
century Danish linguist and folklorist; professor
of Scandinavian linguistics. The principles that
he formulated for ballad scholarship in *Danmarks
gamle Folkeviser*, 5 vols. (Copenhagen, 1855-90),
had a great impact on international folklore
research.
GUBERNATIS, Angelo de (1840-1913): Italian literary
historian, folklorist, and ethnographer. His
research was primarily focused on the relationships between European and Oriental mythology.
He accepted Adalbert Kuhn's and Max Müller's
theories, exaggerating their mythological interpretation. In his book *Zoological Mythology*, 2
vols. (1872), he published ample material on India,
Italy, and the Slavic countries (especially Russia).
His other works include *Storia comparata degli usi
nuziali in Italia e presso gli atri popoli indoeuropei* (1869), *Storia popolare degli usi funebri
indoeuropei* (1873), and *Mitologie comparata* (1880).
GUEUDEVILLE, Pierre-Nicolas (1650-1720): French writer
who moved to the Netherlands in 1671. Author of
Critique générale du Télémaque (1700-01), *L'Utopie
de Thomas Morus* (1715), *Dialogues de Monsieur le
baron de Lahontan et d'un sauvage, dans l'Amérique*
(1704), and *Voyages du baron de La Hontan dans
l'Amérique Septentrionale* (1706).
GUIZOT, François (1787-1874), THIERRY, Augustin (1795-
1856): French historians who developed theories
about the growth and development of the middle
class.

HABERLANDT, Arthur (1889-1964): Austrian folklorist

and ethnographer, director of the Vienna Folklore
Museum. His works are chiefly concerned with the
peoples of the Balkans.

HABERLANDT, Michael (1860-1940): Austrian Indologist,
ethnographer, and folklorist, Arthur Haberlandt's
father.

HAGEDORN, Friedrich (1708-1754): German poet whose
works are permeated with motifs from Anacreon.

HAKLUYT, Richard (ca. 1553-1616): English geographer
and diplomat; collector and publisher of English
maritime exploration accounts. In addition to the
Principal Navigations (1589), his major works include *Divers Voyages Touching the Discoverie of
America and the Islands adjacent unto the same*
(1582) and *A Particular Discourse concerning West-
erne Discoveries* (1877).

HALLER, Albrecht von (1708-1777): Swiss scientist and
poet; professor for seventeen years at the University of Göttingen, where he dealt with botany,
embryology, and physiology. In his poetic works
he was concerned with philosophical problems; the
poem *Die Alpen* describes the Swiss countryside and
the patriarchal way of life among peasants.

HAMANN, Johann Georg (1730-1788): German philosopher
and writer whose mysticism influenced German romantic writers. His major works include *Biblische
Betrachtungen eines Christen* (1758), *Sokratische
Denkwürdigkeiten* (1759), *Kreuzzüge des Philologen*
(1762), *Golgatha und Scheblimini* (1784), and
Metakritik über den Purismus der Vernunft (1800).

HARRISON, Jane Ellen (1850-1928): English classical
scholar, historian of art and religion. Her theories on the ritualistic origin of mythology have
had considerable influence on modern anthropologists. Her first work was *The Mythology and Monuments of Ancient Athens* (1890), but she is best
known for *Prolegomena to the Study of Greek Religion* (1903), in which she studied the actual ritual
of Greek festivals in an attempt to ascertain the
make-up of the Greek theogony. An even broader
work is *Themis* (1912), which used anthropological
theories and findings to explore the entire field

of Greek religion. Her *Epilegomena* (1921) is an
anthropological and psychological study of modern
religion.

HAZARD, Paul (1878-1944): Professor at the Collège
de France, member of the French Academy; expert
on Italian literature and promoter of its spread
in France. His most significant works are *La révolution française et les lettres italiennes* (1910),
Discours sur la langue française (1913), *Giacomo
Léopardi* (1913), *L'Italie vivante* (1913), *Lamartine*
(1925), *La vie de Stendhal* (1927), *Sonnets de
Michel-Ange* (1929), *Don Quichotte* (1930), and *Histoire de la littérature française illustrée* (1949).
His *La crise de la conscience européenne* (1935) has
been translated into English under the title *The
European Mind 1680-1745*, Cleveland: Meridian Books,
1963.

HEBEL, Johann Peter (1760-1826): German poet, teacher,
and pastor.

HEINE, Heinrich (1797-1856): German poet and journalist. The article "Romantische Schule," included
in the collection *Über Deutschland* (1861), was
written in 1833.

HELVETIUS, Claude Adrien (1715-1771): French philosopher.

HERBELOT DE MOLAINVILLE, Barthélemy d' (1625-1695):
French Orientalist, author of the encyclopedic
dictionary *Bibliothèque orientale* (1697), which
contains a diversity of information on the Middle
and Near East.

HERBERT, Edward, of Cherbury (1583-1648): English
philosopher, historian, poet, and diplomat. He
considered religious thought an innate capacity of
man, independent of experience.

HERD, David (1732-1810): Scottish writer and collector
of ballads. In his letters on chivalry and medieval novels, he tried to prove that medieval poetry
surpasses ancient Greek poetry, and he opposed the
prevailing enthusiasm for French classicism.

HERDER, Johann Gottfried von (1744-1803): German
critic, author, theologian, and philosopher who
was extremely influential in shaping German roman-

tic thought during the *Sturm und Drang*. In his
three-part *Fragmente über die neuere deutsche
Literatur* (1766-67), he differentiated between
poetic and scientific speech and attacked Germany's
worship of other languages and literatures. Opposing Enlightenment and neo-classical theorists, he
argued in *Abhandlung über den Ursprung der Sprache*
(1772) that poetry is originally identical to language, is found in all social classes as an inherent "necessity" of man's innermost nature, and is
a spontaneous expression particularly reflected in
folksongs. The central theme throughout his works
is the necessity of viewing each nation and each
national literature in light of historical development rather than in light of absolute standards.

HERODOTUS (ca. 484-ca. 425 B.C.): Greek historian.

HEYNE, Christian Gottlob (1729-1812): German philologist and archeologist.

HIRN, Yrjö (1870-1952): Finnish folklorist.

HUET, Pierre Daniel (1630-1721): French scholar and
theologian, bishop, member of the French Academy.
His most significant works are *De Interpretatione
libri duo* (1661), *Lettre sur l'origine des romans*
(1670), *Censura philosophiae Cartesianae* (1689),
and *Histoire du commerce et de la navigation des
anciens* (1716).

HUGO, Victor (1802-1885): French poet, dramatist,
novelist, and critic who led the romantic revolt
in France against classicism. His collection of
poems entitled *Les Orientales* (1829) championed
the cause of romantic poetry and the aesthetic concept of "art for art's sake." *Cromwell* (1827) and
Hernani (1830) were radical and controversial de-
partures from the classical drama. And such later
novels as *Les misérables* (1865), *Les travailleurs
de la mer* (1866), and *L'homme qui rit* (1869)
reflect his interest in the mystical and the
romantic, especially as they exist in the lower
social classes.

HUMBOLDT, Wilhelm von (1767-1835): German linguist
and politician. His earliest critical works are
collected in *Aesthetische Versuche* (1799), which

includes his assessments of Schiller's *Spaziergang* and Goethe's *Reineke Fuchs*. He is perhaps best known for his studies in comparative linguistics; in his chief work on oriental languages, *Über die Kawi-sprache auf der Insel Java* (1836-40) he suggested the importance of studying the structure of language rather than its history, thus giving impetus to structural linguistics.

HUME, David (1711-1776): English philosopher, historian, and economist who attempted to frame general laws of human behavior. As is revealed in his major work, *A Treatise of Human Nature* (1739-40), he thought that human behavior was a result of environmental forces operating on irreducible and common aspects of human nature. In studying history, economics, and religion, he attempted to account for man's beliefs about empirical facts and events--beliefs that, in his view, result from a psychological (rather than a necessary) connection or association of facts or events. His works include *Essays Moral and Political* (1741-42), *An Inquiry Concerning the Principles of Morals* (1751), *Writings on Economics* (1752-58), and *The History of England*, 3 vols. (1754-62).

IMBRIANI, Vittorio (1840-1886): Italian poet, writer, and literary historian. His works on songs and fables include *Canti popolari delle provincie meridionali* (1871-72), done in collaboration with Antonio Casetti, *La novellaja fiorentina* (1871-77), and *XII conti pomiglianesi, con varianti avellinese, montellesi, bagnolesi, milanesi, toscane, leccesi* (1876).

INSTITORIS: See SPRENGER.

JAHN, Friedrich Ludwig (1778-1852): German educator and patriot who founded the turnverein movement to consolidate national resistance to Napoleonic rule.

JAMES, Richard (ca. 1592-1638): English priest, in 1618 member of the Embassy in Moscow. His notebook, in which someone recorded six historical and verse-epic Russian songs, was found in 1845.

JOHANNEAU, Éloi (1770-1851): French philologist and folklorist; one of the founders of the Celtic Academy.

JONES, William (1746-1794): English scholar who studied the languages, literature, and culture of ancient India. He was among the first to suggest a relationship among Indo-European languages.

JUNGMANN, Josef Jakub (1773-1847): Czech philologist and nationalist. His works include a Czech-German dictionary, *Slovnjk česko-německy* (1835-39), and a history of Czech literature, *Historie literatury české* (1825).

KARADŽIĆ, Vuk Stefanović (1787-1864): Serbian poet and folklorist who helped to fashion the modern Serbian literary language. His collections of Serbian folksongs include *Mala prostonarodnja slaveno-serbska pjesnarica* (1814) and *Srpske narodne pjesme* (1823). He also edited proverbs and folktales.

KARAMZÍN, Nikolaĭ Mikhaĭlovich (1766-1826): Russian writer and historian, one of the creators of the Russian literary language.

KELTUĬALA, Vasiliĭ Afanasevich (1867- ?): Scholar of old Russian literature and folklore. His history of Russian literature, *Kurs istoriĭ russkoĭ literatury*, was published in 1906. He edited the *Song of Igor* (1928) and *Biliny* (1928).

KER, William Paton (1855-1923): English literary historian, scholar of medieval literature, author of *Epic and Romance* (1897) and "On the History of Ballads, 1100-1500" (1909-10).

KIRCHER, Athanasius (1602-1680): German natural philosopher, mathematician, linguist, and theologian.

KIREEVSKIĬ brothers: Ivan Vasil'evich (1806-1856), and Petr Vasil'evich (1808-1856): Russian publicists and philosophers, theoretical leaders of the slavophiles, and F. Schelling's followers in philosophy. Petr also collected folksongs, publishing the religious ones in *Russkie narodnie pesni* (1848).

KLOPSTOCK, Friedrich Gottlieb (1724-1803): German romantic and nationalist poet who opposed Gottshed's classicism. In his many odes (published in book form in 1771) and his epic entitled *Der Messias* (completed in 1773), he employed a natural German poetic idiom. In his German songs (*Geistliche Lieder*, 1758) and his historical and philological study of German poetry (*Die Gelehrtenrepublik, Fragmente über Sprache und Dichtkunst*, 1779), he championed the cause of a poetry free from external influence and artificial convention.

KÖHLER, Reinhold (1830-1892): German literary historian and folklorist who collected and annotated folktales and produced several scholarly comparative studies of epic motifs.

KOLBERG, Oskar (1814-1890): Polish folklorist, ethnographer, and composer. His works include a collection of Polish folk materials, *Lud, jego zwyczaje, sposób zycia, mowa, podania, przystowia, obrzędy, gusta, zabawy, pieśni, muzyka i tańce* (The People, Their Customs, Way of Life, Language, Legends, Proverbs, Games, Songs, Music and Dances), 28 vols. (1865-90), and a collection of Polish folksongs, *Pieśni ludu polskiego* (1842, 1857).

KOLLÁR, Jan (1793-1852): Czech poet and author of works on Slavic linguistics, history, and mythology. In 1823 he and Pavel Josef Šafárik edited a collection of Slovakian folksongs.

KOPITAR, Bartholomäus (1780-1844): Slavic philologist of Slovenian origin.

KREUTZWALD, Friedrich Reinhold (1803-1882): Estonian writer and folklorist; compiler of the *Kalewipoeg, eine estnische sage* (1861), a collection of Estonian legends.

KROHN, Ilmari (1867-1960): Finnish composer, folklorist; Julius Krohn's son.

KROHN, Julius (1835-1888): Finnish writer and philologist; professor at Helsingfors. His scholarly study of origins of the runes in the *Kalevala*, fully discussed by Cocchiara in Chapter 17, section 7, is entitled *Kalevala* (1891-95). This study gave rise to the historical-geographical method of tale analysis.

KROHN, Kaarle (1863-1933): Professor of folklore and comparative folklore at the University of Helsinki.

He was the founder of the Finnish school, which
examines the diffusion of folktale motifs and
attempts to reconstruct the original form of a
tale on the basis of a comparison of all existing
oral versions of a given type, with due regard to
their geographical distribution. This historical-
geographical method is described in his *Die folkloristische Arbeitsmethode* (1926).

KUHN, Adalbert (1812-1881): German linguist who
attempts to reconstruct the culture of primitive
peoples on the basis of comparative Indo-European
studies.

LA BRUYÈRE, Jean de (1645-1696): French writer and
moralist. As the instructor of the grandson of
Count Condé, he was familiar with the courtly life
that he often satirized. He published his notes,
epigrams, and portraits under the title *Caractères*
(1688).

LACHMANN, Karl (1793-1851): German philologist, early
proponent of textual criticism, a disciple of Wolf.
In his philological study of the *Niebelungenlied*
he differentiated twenty independent songs.

LAFITAU, Joseph François (1681-1746): French missionary
who studied the life and customs of North American
Indian tribes. He was the first to describe the
primitive communal system of the Iroquois and the
Hurons. He discovered that some of their characteristics were shared by many other peoples.

LA FONTAINE, Jean de (1621-1695): French poet. He drew
upon classical themes (as in Aesop and Phaedrus) and
folk traditions for his fables.

LAHONTAN, Louis Armand de Lom d'arce, baron de (1666-
1715): French traveler. In 1683, yearing for
adventure, he traveled to the French settlements in
Canada as an enlisted man. He later organized two
expeditions to the upper Mississippi.

LALLEMANT, Charles (1587-1674): Catholic missionary to
Canada (17th century).

LANDAU, Marcus (1837-1918): Austrian philologist who
was primarily interested in the Italian literature
of the Renaissance.

LANG, Andrew (1844-1912): English writer, historian, and folklorist. He explained myths as a reflection of a prehistoric way of life and attempted to isolate the general psychological conditions for the creation of myths. His chief works are *Custom and Myth* (1884), *Myth, Ritual and Religion* (1887), *Modern Mythology* (1897), and *The Making of Religion* (1898).

LAZARUS, Moritz (1824-1903): German philosopher and psychologist.

LE BRUN, Pierre (1661-1729): French theologian. His work on the history of superstitions, *Histoire critique des pratiques superstitieuses*, was published in 1701-02.

LEIBNIZ, Gottfried Wilhelm (1646-1716): German philosopher, mathematician, and psychologist. In his most comprehensive work, *Théodicée sur la bonté de Dieu, la liberté de l'homme, et l'origine du mal* (1710), he attempted to demonstrate the conformity of faith and reason. His emphasis on "miracles of reason" (the expression to which Cocchiara alludes in Chapter 4, section 4) is also reflected in his *Principes de la nature et de la grace fondés en raison* (1714).

LE JEUNE, Paul (1592-1664): Jesuit missionary who lived in Canada for seventeen years. His works, *Brième relation de voyage de la Nouvelle France* . . . (1632) and *Relation de ce qui c'est passé en la Nouvelle France* . . . (1640), contain interesting information on the customs and morality of Indians.

LENARTOWICZ, Teofil (1822-1893): Polish poet and sculptor.

LEOPARDI, Giacomo (1798-1837): Italian romantic poet who was interested in linguistics and folklore.

LÉRY, Jean de (1534-1601): French preacher, the first Protestant missionary. In 1556 he was sent to Brazil to preach to Huguenot settlers and Indians. After his return he wrote the *Histoire d'un voyage fait en la terre du Brésil* (1578).

LESCARBOT, Marc (ca. 1580-ca. 1630): French lawyer, writer, and traveler who left his practice as a lawyer in 1604 to participate in an expedition to

New France (Canada). After his return, he published his *Histoire de la Nouvelle France, con-
tenant les navigations decouvertes et habitations
faites par les Français et Indes occidentales*
. . . (1609).
LESSING, Gotthold Ephraim (1729-1781): German writer
and critic who attacked classicism and the reflection of political absolutism in German literature
and art, especially in his *Emilia Galotti* (1772),
which contains a sharp denunciation of the social
and political difficulties arising from an absolute
system of government. He defended national and
democratic traditions and criticized Klopstock's
religious poetry.
LÉVY-BRUHL, Lucien (1857-1939): French philosopher
and sociologist. In various works, including *Les
fonctions mentales dans les sociétés inférieures*
(1910), he explained his theory of "prelogical
thinking," which he believed could be found in
primitive and underdeveloped nations.
LIEBRECHT, Felix (1812-1890): German scholar, literary
historian, folklorist, and ethnographer.
LIPIŃSKI, Karol Józef (1790-1861): Polish violinist
and composer who published a collection of Russian
and Polish folksongs, *Piésni polskie i ruskie ludu
galicyjskiego* (1833).
LOCKE, John (1632-1704): English philosopher, political theorist, psychologist. His political thought
is best revealed in his *Two Treatises of Government*
(1690), in which he argued that man has a natural
right--on the basis of natural law established by
God and vested in every individual--to life, liberty, and property, and that as man progressed from
the state of nature to civil society he consented
to a social contract with the communal power of
government, whose sole function is the protection
of man's natural rights. The two essays to which
Cocchiara refers--*Essay Concerning Human Understanding* (1690) and *The Reasonableness of Christianity* (1695)--treat contingent concerns. In the
former essay, Locke explored the limits of human
knowledge, concluding that man derives his ideas

from sensation, reflection on sensation, and intuition; in the latter essay, he argued that in-
tuitional understanding includes that offered by
Christian revelation, which provides the fulfillment and explanation of the moral law of nature
that man's reason can confirm but not otherwise
fully discover.

LOLLIS, Cesare de (1863-1928): Italian philologist
and critic; professor of romance linguistics at
the University of Geneva, later at the University
of Rome.

LÖNNROT, Elias (1802-1884): Finnish folklorist and
linguist who collected the runes of the *Kalevala*,
mainly in the Eastern part of Finland and in
Karelia, between 1828 and 1844. He edited a collection of folksongs, *Kanteletar* (1829-31), and a
collection of proverbs and idioms.

LOWTH, Robert (1710-1787): English bishop, professor
of poetry at Oxford University.

LUBBOCK, John (also known as Baron Avebury) (1834-
1913): English banker, statesman, and naturalist.
He was chiefly concerned with the study and description of wildlife.

LUCRETIUS CARUS, Titus (ca. 99-55 B.C.): Ancient
materialist philosopher, poet, and author of the
philosophical poem *De rerum natura*.

LUTHER, Martin (1483-1546), CALVIN, John (1509-1564),
and ZWINGLI, Ulrich (1484-1532): Leaders of the
Protestant Reformation. Rejecting clerical authority and the supremacy of the pope, Luther organized
a new church in Germany based on the concept of
justification by faith and good works. His polemical tracts *An den christlichen Adel deutscher
Nation* (1520), *De captivitate Babylonica ecclesiae
praeludium* (1520), and *Von der Freiheit eines
Christenmenschen* (1522) became the fundamental
documents of the Protestant Reformation. His
translation of the Bible into German, in accordance
with rules which he later set forth in *Sendbrief
vom Dolmetschen* (1530), standardized the German
language, contributing to the linguistic and cultural unification of Germany. Zwingli extended the

Reformation into Switzerland, establishing a church based on a simplification of Church ritual, a symbolic interpretation of the Eucharist, and an appeal to Biblical authority and the will of God. Calvin, a French theologian, solidified Zwingli's reform movement by establishing a Protestant Church in Geneva along the lines of principles that he set forth in his *Institution de la religion chrestienne* (1536). Based on Lutheran doctrine, Calvinism emphasizes scriptural authority, unconditional election, limited atonement, and God's irresistible grace.

L'VOV, Nikolaĭ Aleksandrovich (1751-1803): Russian scholar, poet, painter, member of the Academy of Arts and Sciences. He studied folk music and in 1790 published a collection of Russian folksongs, *Sbornik russkikh narodnykh pesen*, with his own introduction. The group of writers formed around him (including Derzhavin and Dmitriev) was also interested in folklore.

McLENNAN, John Ferguson (1827-1881): Scottish historian of religion. He introduced the term *exogamy*, but he erroneously attributed this characteristic to the tribe instead of to the clan. Independently of Bochofen, he reached similar conclusions about the importance of matriarchies and matrilineal descent. He also studied totemism.

MACPHERSON, James (1736-1796): English poet. He published his own poetry under the name of the legendary Ossian, translated allegedly from Celtic. Macpherson doubtlessly drew upon the folk poetry of Scotland and Ireland.

MAISTRE, Joseph Marie, Comte de (1754-1821): French statesman, writer, and philosopher; a leader of the Neo-Catholic anti-revolutionary movement. Responding to the anarchistic tendencies in Revolutionary religion and politics, he argued for a restoration of royal power and the re-establishment of the pope as the infallible religious sovereign. His writings include *Lettres d'un royaliste savoisien* (1794), *Considérations sur la France*

(1797), *Essai sur le principe générateur des constitutions politiques* (1814), *Du Pape* (1819), and
De l'église gallicane (1821).
MALLET, Paul Henri (1730-1807): Swiss historian. He
was a professor of French literature at the University of Copenhagen. In his works he explored the
history, folklore, and ethnography of Denmark, Germany, and the Celts. His most important work is
*Introduction à l'histoire de Dannemarc où l'on
traite de la religion, des loix, des moeurs et des
usages des anciens Danois* (1755), which was revised
and issued in two volumes in 1763.
MANGOURIT, Michel Ange Bernard de (1752-1829): French
diplomat and scholar, one of the founders of the
Celtic Academy.
MANNHARDT, Wilhelm (1831-1880): German folklorist.
At the beginning of his career he was a follower
of the mythological school. He was chiefly interested in pure folk superstitions (the so-called
"lower" mythology). Later he agreed with the followers of the diffusion theory, and in his *Wald-
und Feldkulte* (1875-77) he came closer to the
principles of the anthropological school. His
other works include *Germanische Mythen* (1858) and
Mythologische Forschungen aus dem Nachlasse (1884).
MANZONI, Alessandro (1785-1873): Italian poet and
writer, a leader of Italian Romanticism. He argued
for the unification and independence of Italy. In
1868, in a memorandum to the Minister of Education,
he defended the idea of a unified Italian language.
MARANA, Giovanni Paolo (1642-1693): Italian historian
and writer. He influenced Montesquieu, the author
of *Lettres Persanes*.
MARETT, Robert Ranulph (1866-1943): English historian
of religion who proposed the preanimistic theory.
He believed that religion takes its origin in
cultic activities (mainly dances). His principal
work is *The Threshold of Religion* (1900; 3rd ed.,
1909).
MARILLIER, Léon (1842-1901): French scholar, philosopher, and historian of religion.
MARTIRE, Pietro (1459-1526): Historian and geographer

of Italian origin at the court of Isabella, Queen
of Spain. In his *Decados de orbe novo* he described
the history of the discovery of America.

MEDICI, Lorenzo de' (1449-1492): Italian patron of
art and literature, poet, Governor of Florence.
His *I canti carnaschialeschi*, which did not appear
as a published collection until 1925, consisted of
"carnival songs" sharing some similarities with
folk poetry.

MEIER, John (1864-1953): German folklorist and ethnographer. In 1914 in Freiburg he founded the German
Archive of Folksongs. From 1911 to 1949 he was
the leader of the Verband deutscher Vereine für
Volkskunde, a union of German folklore societies.

MEINECKE, Friedrich (1862-1954): German historian
whose main work, *Das Zeitalter der deutschen
Erhebung, 1795-1815* (1906), concentrates on Germany's struggle for independence from French
domination.

MELI, Giovanni (1740-1815): Italian poet who wrote in
the Sicilian dialect. He authored satirical fables
and lyric poems.

MENÉNDEZ PIDAL, Ramón (1869-1968): Spanish ballad
scholar, professor of romance philology at the University of Madrid; president of the Spanish Academy
of Arts and Sciences and founding editor of *Revista
de Filología Española*. In his works he emphasized
the native roots of Spanish culture (including
Basque, Gothic, and Arabic ingredients) and the importance of conserving Spanish traditions. His
major works of folkloristic interest include *Cantar
de Mío Cid* (1908-11, 1944-46), *La España del Cid*,
2 vols. (1929), and *Romancero hispánico*, 2 vols.
(1953).

MERCIER, Louis-Sébastien (1740-1814): French writer,
author of philosophical novels and sketches of the
life and morals of Paris. He was influenced by
Rousseau.

MÉRIMÉE, Prosper (1803-1870): French critic and writer
who is best known for such novellas as *Colomba*
(1840) and *Carmen* (1845). The *Guzla* pieces, to
which Cocchiara refers in Chapter 13, section 5,

were alleged to be translations of twenty-eight
"Illyrian" ballads supposedly gathered in Dalmatia,
Bosnia, Croatia, and Herzegovina. Set against the
historical backdrop of the Serbian war of independence and permeated with romantic motifs of violence
and vampirism, these ballads, according to Mérimée,
were authentic ballads told to him by an old story-
teller, Maglanovic. The forgery was so successful
that a number of scholars and writers (including
Goethe and Mickiewicz) were completely taken in,
and Pushkin went so far as to translate some of the
ballads into Russian.

MEYER, Paul (1840-1917): French scholar who edited
many collections of old French and Provençal songs
and literary texts.

MICHEL, Francisque Xavier (1809-1887): French literary
historian, expert on medieval French literature.

MICHELET, Jules (1798-1874): Major French historian
and publicist.

MILÁ Y FONTANALS, Manuel (1818-1884): Spanish literary
historian and folklorist, professor at Barcelona.
He dealt chiefly with Catalan folklore and published a collection of folksongs, *Romancerillo
Catalan* (1853).

MILLER, Orest Fedorovich (1833-1889): Russian literary
historian and folklorist, professor at Petrograd.
He was a member of the mythological school. His
doctoral dissertation on Illya Maromets and the
State of Kiev, *Il'ia Muromets i bogatyrstvo
kievskoe*, was published in 1869.

MILLER, Vsevolod Fedorovich (1848-1913): Russian
linguist, folklorist, and ethnographer. At the
beginning of his career he believed in the diffusion theory. Later, he created his own "historical school," which, beginning in 1890, dominated
Russian scholarship for a quarter of a century.
He attempted to relate folk poetry to Russian
history. Among his works are his study of Russian
folk poetry, *Ocherki russkoi narodnoi slovesnosti*,
3 vols. (1897-1924) and his Ossetic studies,
Osetinskie etiudy (1881-82).

MILTON, John (1608-1674): English poet and publicist.

As a political figure, he supported the Puritan
overthrow of Charles I, served as Latin Secretary
to Cromwell's Council of State during the Protec-
torate (1649-1660), and authored several controversial tracts, including his arguments for divorce
(*The Doctrine and Discipline of Divorce*, 1644), for
freedom of the press (*Areopagitica*, 1644), and for
the right of the English people to depose the king
(*Eikonoklastes*, 1649). As a poet he employed a
complex lyrical style and a variety of traditional
forms (sonnet, lyric, epic) to explore many Biblical and classical themes. His major poetic works
include *Comus* (1634), *Lycidas* (1637), *Paradise Lost*
(1667), *Paradise Regained* (1671), and *Samson
Agonistes* (1671).

MINNESÄNGER: German poets of the 12th-13th centuries,
originators of courtly poetry. Their poetry was
initially related to folk poetry, but later they
turned to the motifs of exalted courtly love.
Their works were first published by Bodmer and
Breitinger in *Sammlung von Minnesängern aus dem
schwäbischen Zeitpunkt* (1758-59).

MÖRIKE, Eduard Friedrich (1804-1875): German poet and
writer who belonged to the Swabian school.

MÖSER, Justus (1720-1794): German publicist and historian, legal counselor of the Princedom of Westphalia. He opposed the ideas of the Enlightenment,
idealized the feudal order and medieval guilds, and
defended the isolation of the little German states.
Among his works are *Osnabrückische Geschichte*
(1780-1824), which deals with the early Middle
Ages, *Patriotische Phantasien* (1775-86), which
attacks Gottshed, and *Über die deutsche Sprache und
Literatur* (1781), which is a study of German language and literature.

MONACI, Ernesto (1844-1918): Italian philologist and
critic.

MONBODDO, Lord James (1714-1799): English scholar and
anthropologist. In his *Of the Origin and Progress
of Language* (1773), he stated, among other things,
that man is a descendant of apes.

MONTAIGNE, Michel de (1533-1592): Renaissance writer

and thinker whose principal work is *Essais* (1580).
He argued against religious dogma, denied the
principle of the immortality of the soul, and opposed the atrocities of the Inquisition. His
Epicurean ideal was the quiet enjoyment of spiritual and physical pleasures. He was interested in
the life of "natural man," the primitive man.

MORGAN, Lewis Henry (1818-1881): American ethnographer,
archeologist, and scholar of classical history who
lived for years among the Iroquois. He was concerned with kinship, and he provided the first
scientific chronology of the development of primitive society.

MÜLLENHOFF, Karl (1818-1884): German philologist and
ethnographer who participated in the editing of
medieval folklore collections. His principal work
is *Deutsche Altertumskunde*, 5 vols. (1870-1900).

MÜLLER, Friedrich Max (1823-1900): English philologist
and historian, of German origin. He began his
scholarly activities by editing Old Indic texts
(*Hitopadesa, Rig-Veda*). He was a member of the
mythological school, but, unlike the brothers
Grimm, he devoted his attention to the origin of
myths. Müller developed comparative mythology and
the theory of solar mythology, according to which
most myths are derived originally from ideas about
the movements of the sun. His views had a substantial influence on many scholars, including the
Russians A. N. Andreev and O. F. Miller.

MÜLLER, Johannes von (1752-1809): German historian.
He served the prince-elector of Mainz, the Austrian
and the Prussian governments. After the defeat of
Jena, he gave his allegiance to Jérome Bonaparte,
King of Westphalia. In addition to his *Die
Geschichten der Schweizer*, 5 vols. (1786-1808),
he published his lectures on world history, *Vier-
undzwanzig Bücher allgemeiner Geschichten* (1810).

MÜLLER, Karl Otfried (1797-1840): German scholar,
expert on ancient history, art, mythology, and
culture. In his *Prolegomena zu einer wissenschaft-
lichen Mythologie* (1825), he connected the origin
of Greek myths with several areas of Greece.

MURALT, Béat-Louis de (1665-1749): Swiss writer and
traveler who visited almost every country in Europe.
MURALT, Johannes von (1645-1733): Swiss physician and
writer, author of works on medicine and other topics.
MURATORI, Lodovico Antonio (1672-1750): Italian historian; collector and publisher of medieval Italian
source materials. He wrote introductions and notes
to his publications. *Antiquitates Italicae Medii
Aevi*, 6 vols. (1738-42) and *Annali d'Italia*, 12
vols. (1744-49)--the two works that Cocchiara cites
in Chapter 6, section 8--contain a large number of
political and historical documents.
MUSORGSKIĬ, Modest Petrovich (1839-1881): Russian composer who often drew from folk music for his compositions.

NAUMANN, Hans (1886-1951): Germanist; professor at
Jena, Frankfurt, and Bonn. One of the originators
of the theory concerning the aristocratic origin
of folklore materials, he coined the phrase
Gesunkenes Kulturgut.
NERI, Ferdinando (1880-1954): Italian literary critic.
NIBELUNGENLIED: German epic, also known as the *Song
of the Nibelung*. It came into being most probably
on Austrian territory near the beginning of the
thirteenth century, but it is based on a much
earlier epic tradition. It was published by Bodmer as *Chriemhildens Rache, und die Klage* (1757).
NICOLINI, Fausto (1879-1965): Italian scholar, historian, and philologist. He was a friend of Croce
and devoted several works to Vico, including
Giambattista Vico et Ferdinando Galiani (1918),
La filosofia di Giambattista Vico (1935), and *La
religiosità di Giambattista Vico* (1949).
NIEMCEWICZ, Julian (1757-1814): Polish writer, publicist, and politician.
NIETZSCHE, Friedrich Wilhelm (1844-1900): German
philosopher and poet. His *Die Geburt der Tragödie*
(1871), which Cocchiara mentions in Chapter 22,
section 5, refutes the traditional view that Greek
civilization was an age of noble simplicity and
genteel grandeur; focusing on the more turbulent

Greece of Aeschylus and Pindar, he argued that
Greek tragedy combined Apollonian and Dionysian
elements into a powerful musical and visual drama
that one could also find in the *Musikdrama* of
Wagner—a thesis that many philologists attacked
as being merely a tract of Wagnerian propaganda.
In his later philosophical works, beginning with
Menschliches, Allzumenschliches (1878), he repudiated his earlier romantic aesthetic and his
high regard of Wagner, emphasizing instead the
power of the human will and the necessity of
achieving self-transcendence as a means of survival. Among his later works are *Also sprach
Zaranthustra* (1883-91), *Der Fall Wagner* (1888),
and *Der Wille zur Macht* (1894).

NIGRA, Constantino (1828-1907):   Italian politician
and diplomat, ambassador to France, Russia, England, and Austria. His works include *Relique
celtiche* (1872) and *Canti popolari del Piemonte*
(1888).

NOBILI, Roberto de (1577-1656):   Italian missionary.
He worked on the west coast of India (Malabar)
and was an expert in Sanskrit and many other
Indic languages.

NOVALIS (also known as Baron Friedrich Leopold von
Hardenberg) (1772-1801):   German romantic poet,
writer, and mystic who collaborated with the
Schlegel brothers in establishing the theoretical
foundations of German romanticism. His poetry
collections include *Hymnen an die Nacht* (1799) and
Geistliche Lieder (1799). His interest in romantic
medievalism is reflected in the essay *Die Christenheit oder Europa* (1799) and in the novel fragment
Heinrich von Ofterdingen (1799-1800), which is set
in the Middle Ages.

NOVATI, Francesco (1859-1915):   Italian philologist and
author of works on the Middle Ages.

NYERUP, Rasmus (1759-1829):   Danish scholar, historian,
and philologist.

ODOACER (killed in 493):   Germanic commander of merce-
naries in the service of the Roman Empire, and the

first barbarian king of Italy. In 476 he forced
Romulus Augustulus, the last Roman emperor, from
his throne.

OLRIK, Axel (1864-1917): Danish folklorist and ballad
scholar who, following Grundtvig, served as editor
of *Danmarks gamle Folkeviser* from 1888-1917. He
also employed a historical-cultural approach to
analyze Scandinavian heroic poetry, legends, and
mythology in such works as *Kilderne til Sakses
oldhistorie*, 2 vols. (1892-94), *Danmarks helte-
digtning*, 2 vols. (1903-10), *Ragnarök* (1902-14),
and *Nordisk Aandsliv i Vikingetid og tidlig
Middelalder* (1907). His interest in the Scandinavian folktale or *sagn* is reflected in his early
monograph *Märchen in Saxo Grammaticus* (1892) and
in his study of epic laws and folktale principles,
Nogle grundsaetninger for sagnforskning (1921),
which summarizes his basic approach to the historical-geographical study of folklore materials.

OSSIAN: A legendary hero of Celtic folk epic who
lived, allegedly, in the third century in Southern
Ireland.

OVID (Publius Ovidius Naso) (43-17 B.C.): Roman poet.
The six books of his *Fasti* that have come down to
us are important sources for the study of Roman
religion and customs.

PALACKÝ, František (1798-1876): Czech nationalist
historian and politician. His main work is his
history of the Czech people, *Dějiny národu českého
v Čechách a v Moravě* (1848-76), which promoted the
stabilization of the Czech national consciousness.

PANCHATANTRA: A collection of Indic tales and parables
that dates back to the sixth century or earlier.

PARIS, Gaston (1839-1903): French philologist, follower of the historical-comparative school. Many
medieval pieces were edited under his direction.
He accepted Lachmann's view that the *Song of Roland*
was a collection of short cantilenas. His chief
works are *Histoire poétique de Charlemagne* (1865)
and *La littérature française au moyen âge* (1888).

PARIS, Paulin (1800-1881): Gaston Paris's father,

professor at the Collège de France. He edited the
texts of a number of epics.

PARSIFAL: Hero of an epic dating to the 12th-14th
centuries. The legends concerning him were treated
by French, German, and English courtly poets, among
them Chrestien de Troyes and Wolfram von Eschenbach.

PASCAL, Blaise (1623-1662): French mystical writer and
philosopher, physicist, and mathematician. In 1656
he published his *Lettres écrites à un provincial*,
in which he criticized the casuistic ethic of the
Jesuits. This tract had a great impact on the
development of French theater and literature.

PAULUS DIACONUS (ca. 720-ca. 797): Historian of noble
Lombard origin. His *Historia Langobardorum*,
written between 787-797 and published in 1878, is
the most important source for the history of the
political and social system of the Lombards.

PAUSANIAS (2nd century A.D.): Greek writer. His
Description of Greece contains ample material on
art history and on local customs and beliefs.

PERCY, Thomas (1729-1811): Poet, antiquarian, and
bishop. In 1763 he issued some translations of
Icelandic runic poetry, *Five Pieces of Runic
Poetry*, and in 1765 he published his *Reliques of
Ancient English Poetry* (see Cocchiara, Chapter 8,
sections 5-8). *Bishop Percy's Folio M.S.*, edited
by J. W. Hales and F. J. Furnivall, appeared in
1867-68, and in 1770 Percy published his *Northern
Antiquities*, which included a translation of the
Edda, along with other ancient Icelandic pieces.

PERRAULT, Charles (1628-1703): French writer and literary theoretician, member of the French Academy.
His own tales and his adaptations of folktales made
him world famous. His name was connected with the
late seventeenth-century "Querelle des Anciens et
des Modernes" between the devotees and opponents
of classicism, a debate to which he gave impetus
with the reading of his poem "Le Siècle de Louis
XIV" before the French Academy in 1687. Other
defenses of the modernist position include his
Parallèle des anciens et des modernes (1690),
L'apologie des femmes (1694) and *Les hommes*

illustres (1696-1700). His collection of Mother
Goose tales, *Contes de ma Mère l'Oye* (1696-97),
consists of eleven tales, the best known of which
are "The Sleeping Beauty," "Red Riding Hood,"
"Bluebeard," "Cinderella," and "Tom Thumb."

PICTET, Adolfe (1799-1875): Swiss scholar, founder of
"linguistic paleontology." In his *Les origins
indo-européennes, ou les Aryas primitifs* (1859-63),
he attempted to determine the character of the culture and way of life of the ancient Indo-European
people. His scientifically undocumented works were
criticized by many scholars.

PIGAFETTA, Antonio (ca. 1491-1534): One of Magellan's
fellow travelers who provided a description of his
journey.

PITRÈ, Giuseppe (1841-1916): Italian folklorist, ethnographer, and archeologist. He was an advocate
of the diffusion theory. He was strongly influenced by A. N. Veselovskiĭ, and he opposed narrow
aesthetic interpretations of folklore. Together
with S. Marino, he founded the periodical *Archivio
per lo studio delle tradizioni popolari* in 1882.
His principal works are *Biblioteca delle tradizioni popolari Siciliane*, 25 vols. (1871-1913) and
Bibliografia delle tradizioni popolari d'Italia
(1894).

PLINIUS, Gaius Secundus (ca. A.D. 23-79): Roman
scholar, popularly known as Pliny the Elder, who
attempted to collect all cosmogonical, minerologi-
cal, botanical, zoological, medical, rhetorical,
and philological knowledge. For his *Historia
Naturalis* (1469) he used more than two thousand
rolls of papyrus. For many centuries this work was
considered the main textbook of natural science.

POLIER, Antoine (1741-1795): French Orientalist and
engineer. He spent more than thirty years in India
in the service of the East Indian Society. When he
returned in 1789, he brought with him an ample collection of manuscripts--among others, the complete
list of the *Vedas*.

POLÍVKA, Jiří (1858-1933): Czech philologist and editor of Czech and Russian folktales. His area of

research was the comparative linguistics of Slavic
languages, history, literature, and folklore. He
was an advocate of the diffusion theory. The list
he attached to the tales of the brothers Grimm
contains parallel themes in the tales of other
peoples. (See J. Bolte.)

POLIZIANO, Angelo (1454-1494): Italian humanist poet
who belonged to Lorenzo de' Medici's circle. He
worked ancient heroes into his folk poetry.

POLO, Marco (1254-1323): Venetian traveler who went
to China with his father and uncle through Asia
Minor, Iran, Afghanistan, the Pamir, and Sinkiang.

POPE, Alexander (1688-1744): English neo-classical
poet who, following neo-classical criteria, translated the *Iliad* and the *Odyssey* and published an
edition of Shakespeare's plays.

POPOV, Mikhail Vasil'evich (1742-ca. 1790): Russian
writer, translator, and composer, author of *Aniuta*,
the first opera with a popular theme. His works
include a collection of short stories, *Slavianskie
drevnosti* (1770-71), a description of some ancient
Slavic legends, *Opisanie drevnego slavianskogo
basnosloviia* (1768), and a collection of Russian
songs, *Rossiiskaia Erata* (1792).

POST, Albert Hermann (1839-1895): German jurist, exponent of legal ethnology (or ethnological jurisprudence). He explained the differences in the
jurisdictions of different nations by using racial
and psychological characteristics.

PUFENDORF, Samuel (1632-1694): German jurist, advocate of natural law, although he attempted to
justify serfdom and absolutism. In addition to
his work on natural law and the right of nations,
De jure naturae et gentium (1672), the following
are important: *Elementarum jurisprudentiae uni-
versalis*, 2 vols. (1660), and *De officio hominis
et civis juxta legem naturalem*, 2 vols. (1673).

PULCI, Luigi (1432-1484): Italian Renaissance poet
who belonged to Lorenzo de' Medici's circle. His
poetry is filled with popular humor.

PYPIN, Aleksandr Nikolaevich (1833-1904): Russian
philologist, literary critic, and folklorist.

Pypin's world view was formed under the influence
of Belinskiĭ and Chernishevskiĭ, but he remained
liberal. He was a member of the Russian historical-
cultural school.

QUINET, Edgar (1803-1875): French politician, philosopher, poet, and historian of literature and religion. In his youth he was a republican and a follower of Herder.

RADLOV, Vasiliĩ Vasil'evich (1837-1918): Russian linguist, ethnographer, and archeologist; expert on
Turkic languages and literature. He published many
folklore texts, including his study of the patterns
of folk literature found in Turkic tribes, *Obraztsy
narodnoi literatury Tiurkskikh Plemen* (1860-1907).
RAHBEK, Knud (1760-1830): Danish poet and critic.
RAJNA, Pio (1847-1930): Italian Romanist. He was
primarily concerned with medieval French and Italian literature and Renaissance courtly novels as
is reflected in such works as his *Le fonti dell'-
Orlando furioso* (1876) and *Le origini dell'epopea
francese* (1884).
RAMSAY, Allan (1685-1758): Scottish poet, originally
a wigmaker. He collected ballads, many of which
were included in his *Evergreen* (1724). He was a
publisher, librarian, and founder of the Theater
of Edinburgh.
RAMUSIO, Giovanni Battista (1485-1557): Italian
scholar and statesman. In his three-volume *Delle
navigationi et viaggi* (1556-1606), he used the
descriptions of famous sailors and travelers.
RATZEL, Friedrich (1844-1904): German geographer and
ethnographer, professor at Leipzig. Founder of
the anthropological-geographical school, he thought
that geographical surroundings were the crucial
factors in social development. Attempting to apply
biological laws to social relations, Ratzel explained every phenomenon by the "innate" capacities
of the race. He considered even the state to be a
biological organism which had a tendency toward
further development (this was a justification for

imperialistic expansion). The similarity among
cultural features of different nations he explained
as the result of borrowings. Ratzel's views influenced the representatives of the historical-
cultural school.

REINACH, Salomon (1858-1932): French archeologist and
historian of art and religion. In the course of
his archeological expeditions (e.g., in Tunis), he
excavated settlements from the Stone Age. He
worked on the classification of cultural-historical
relics. In collaboration with I. I. Tolstoĭ and
N. P. Kondakov, he wrote *Antiquités de la Russie
méridionale* (1891-92). His principal work is
Cultes, mythes et religions, 5 vols. (1905-23).

RENAN, Ernest (1823-1892): French historian of religion and philosopher. A subjective idealist and
politically a monarchist, he dealt chiefly with
the history of Christianity and the languages and
cultures of the Near East. His major works include
Histoire des langues sémitique (1848), *Études
d'histoire religieuse* (1857), *Essais de morale et
de critique* (1859), and *Histoire des origines du
christianisme*, 7 vols. (1863-81).

RICCI, Matteo (1552-1610): Italian Jesuit missionary.
He lived in India (Goa) and later in China (Macao,
Canton). He was the Portuguese ambassador in
Peking when he died.

RIEHL, Wilhelm (1823-1897): German publicist, writer,
and conservative politician who, in 1858, became
the first to suggest *Volkskunde* as a scientific
discipline. Several of his sociological works were
included in *Die Naturgeschichte des Volkes als
Grundlage einer deutschen Sozialpolitik*, 4 vols.
(1855-92).

RITSON, Joseph (1752-1803): English critic and folklorist. He dealt with folk poetry in such works
as *Robin Hood* (1795), a collection of ancient
poems, songs, and ballads about Robin Hood, and
A Select Collection of English Songs (1783).

ROBERTSON, William (1721-1793): English historian,
priest, friend of Hume and Gibbon. His works include *The History of Scotland, during the Reigns*

of Queen Mary and of King James VI (1759) and *The History of the Reign of the Emperor Charles V* (1769).

ROGERS, Woodes (d. 1732): Eighteenth-century English sailor. In the course of his journey of 1708-1711, he found Alexander Selkirk on the Juan Fernández Islands.

ROHDE, Erwin (1855-1898): German philologist who dealt with ancient and contemporary literature. He was friendly with Nietzsche.

RUSSO, Luigi (1892-1961): Italian historian and scholar of literature.

RYCAUT, Paul (1628-1700): In the 1660's he was Secretary of the British Embassy in Constantinople and later Consul in Smyrna. In addition to his work mentioned in the text, he wrote *Histoire des trois derniers empereurs des Turcs, depuis 1623 jusqu'à 1677* (1684).

SAINT-ÉVREMOND, Charles (1613-1703): French writer and critic; witty free thinker who promoted Epicureanism and criticized absolutism and the Catholic Church. He was imprisoned and later banished for his opposition to the government and his pamphlet against Mazarin.

SAINT-PIERRE, Jacques Henri Bernardin de (1737-1814): French writer, exponent of French sentimentalism. He exaggerated the primitivism and nature-worship deriving from Rousseau. In his famous novel *Paul et Virginie* (1788), virgin nature provides the background for a romance between two young people who die as a result of their encounter with modern civilization.

SAKHAROV, Ivan Petrovich (1807-1863): Folklorist, paleographer. In his attempts to popularize the theory of official ethnic identity, he was not above engaging in a bit of forgery. His main works are his collections of Russian legends, *Skazaniiã russkago naroda o semeĭnoĭ zhizni svoikh predkov* (1836-37), Russian folksongs, *Pĩesni russkago naroda* (1838-39), and Russian folktales, *Russkĩiã narodnyĩã skazki* (1841).

SALLUSTIUS CRISPUS, C. (84-ca. 34 B.C.): Roman historian and politician, popularly known as Sallust.
SANCTIS, Francesco de (1818-1883): Italian critic,
philosopher, participant in the national liberation movement and the Revolution of 1848; opponent
of Romanticism and the clergy.
SAND, George (Aurore Dudevant, 1804-1876): French
woman novelist. In the thirties and forties she
was influenced by the utopian theories of the
Saint-Simonists. Her works include *Indiana* (1832),
Valentine (1832), *Lélia* (1833), *La mare au diable*
(1846), *François le Champi* (1848), *La petite
Fadette* (1849), and *Contes d'une grand'mère* (1873).
SARPI, Paolo (1552-1623): Italian scholar and politician. He opposed the secular power of Jesuits and
the popes and was persecuted by the Inquisition.
His main work, a history of the Council of Trent,
was placed on the *Index Librorum Prohibitorum*.
SAVIGNY, Friedrich Karl (1779-1861): German jurist,
one of the founders of the historical school. He
opposed the codification of civil law, in effect
defending the fragmentation of the country. He
also denied that new legislation can cause change
and rejected the possibility of legislative reform.
SCHERER, Wilhelm (1841-1886): German philologist and
literary historian, professor at Vienna and Berlin.
SCHIEFNER, Anton (1817-1879): Russian philologist who
studied Finnish, Turkish, Caucasian, and Tibetan
language and literature. He wrote several works
on Tibet and published literary relics of that
country.
SCHLEGEL, August Wilhelm von (1767-1845): German
literary historian, critic, and translator. Like
his brother, he was a theoretician of Romanticism.
He gave addresses on literary history at the universities of Jena and Berlin (1791-1804) and later
at the University of Bonn (beginning in 1818). He
is especially known for his translations of Shakespeare, Calderon, Petrarch, Boccaccio, and Cervantes.
SCHLEGEL, Friedrich von (1772-1829): German critic,
philologist, writer, and ideologist of German

Romanticism. In his youth he was influenced by the
Enlightenment, and he sympathized with the French
Revolution; as reactionism strengthened in Germany,
however, Schlegel changed his views. In 1808 he
moved to Vienna where, together with Metternich, he
became the champion of Catholic traditionalism.

SCHLEIERMACHER, Friedrich (1768-1834): German idealist
and philosopher, theologian, and politician; a
friend of Friedrich Schlegel. Schleiermacher examined the Old and New Testament critically, without
giving up faith in God. He called Christianity the
most perfect religion.

SCHMIDT, Wilhelm (1868-1954): Austrian ethnographer
and linguist. He attempted to prove that monotheism came into being as a result of divine revelation. He also considered the institutions of the
monogamous family and private property to be ancient in origin. On his initiative, several expeditions were organized to the Pygmies, to Tierra
del Fuego, and to the Indians of Brazil to prove
the ancient character of monotheism. Schmidt's
principal work is *Der Ursprung der Gottesidee*,
6 vols. (1926-35). Beginning in 1906, he edited
the periodical *Anthropos*.

SCHWARTZ, Friedrich Leberecht Wilhelm (1821-1899):
German ethnographer and folklorist. He collected
legends, customs, and superstitions in Brandenburg
and Northern Germany.

SCOTT, Walter (1771-1832): English writer. He began
his literary activities by publishing collections
of Scottish folksongs. He began writing his
romantic historical novels in 1814.

SÉBILLOT, Paul (1846-1918): French painter, writer,
and folklorist who collected folksongs in Brittany.
His works include *Littérature orale de la Haute-
Bretagne* (1881), *Contes populaires de Haute-
Bretagne* (1881), *Traditions et superstitions de la
Haute-Bretagne* (1882), *La Bretagne enchanteé* (1899),
Le folk-lore des pêcheurs (1901), *Le folk-lore de
France*, 4 vols. (1904-07), *Le paganisme contempo-
rain chez les peuples celtolatins* (1908), and *Le
folk-lore; littérature orale et ethnographie*

traditionnelle (1913).

SÉNANCOUR, Étienne Pivert de (1770-1846): French writer.

SEPÚLVEDA, Lorenzo: Spanish poet (first half of the 16th cent.). He wrote romances that were published as *Romances Nueuamente sacados de historias antiguas de la crónica de España* (1551) and included in the *Romancero general*. He took his themes from old chronicles.

SHAFTESBURY, Lord Anthony Ashley Cooper (1671-1713): English moralist philosopher, the third Earl of Shaftesbury, not to be confused with Anthony Ashley Cooper (1621-1683) who was the first Earl of Shaftesbury.

SHELLEY, Percy Bysshe (1792-1822): Great English romantic poet, representative of revolutionary Romanticism. Like Byron, he represented the politically radical strain of English Romanticism.

SILVESTRE DE SACY, Antoine Isaac, baron (1758-1838): French Orientalist who studied the countries of the Middle and Near East.

SMITH, John (1580-1631): One of the founders of the English colony in Virginia (1607) and explorer of the coasts of New England. Pocahontas, the Indian girl whom Smith described in his *General History of Virginia*, belonged to the Powhatan tribe, which lived at that time in Virginia.

SMITH, William Robertson (1846-1894): English Orientalist who dealt with Jewish and Arabic history, linguistics, and ethnology. The Church brought action against him for his articles on the Old Testament.

SNEGIREV, Ivan Mikhaĭlovich (1793-1868): Russian ethnographer and folklorist, professor at Moscow University. His published collections provided detailed commentaries on proverbs, folk customs, rituals, and historical monuments.

SOKOLOV, IUriĭ Matveevich (1889-1941) and Boris Matveevich (1889-1930): Soviet folklorists, authors of a study on the tales and songs of the Belo-Ozero Region, *Skazki i pesni Belozerskogo Kraia* (1915). On the trail of Rybnikov and Gil'ferding they

traversed Onega Province to observe the development of the Russian popular epic. As students of
V. F. Miller, they initially followed the historical school's theory that heroic epics and fairy
tales have an aristocratic origin, a view that they
revised later. Iùrii Sokolov published about two
hundred works on Russian and Soviet folklore. He
wrote the textbook *Russian Folklore*, trans.
Catherine Ruth Smith, New York: Macmillan, 1950
(rpt. Hatboro, Pa.: Folklore Associates, 1966).
Cocchiara's references are to the English translation rather than to the original Russian text,
Ruskiĭ fol'klor (1938).

SOLŌMOS, Dionysios (1798-1857): Famous Greek poet.
Starting in 1821 he wrote in the popular language.
Many of his poems became folksongs.

SOREL, Albert (1842-1906): French conservative historian who concentrated on the period of the French
Revolution, especially the aspects of the Revolution related to foreign policy. His works include
Histoire diplomatique de la guerre franco-allemande,
2 vols. (1875), *Essais d'histoire et de critique*
(1883), *Montesquieu* (1887), *Études de littérature
et d'histoire* (1901), and *L'Europe et la révolution
française*, 8 vols. (1885-1904).

SPAMER, Adolf (1883-1953): German folklorist and ethnographer. His later works include *Die deutsche
Volkskunde* (1934-35), *Deutsche Fastnachtsbräuche*
(1936), *Weihnachten in alter und neuer Zeit* (1937),
Hessische Volkskunst (1939), and *Deutsche Volkskunst, Sachsen* (1943).

SPEE, Friedrich von (1591-1635): German Jesuit and
religious poet. As a protest against witchhunts,
he anonymously published his *Cautio criminalis* in
1631.

SPENCER, Herbert (1820-1903): English philosopher,
psychologist, and sociologist. In philosophy he
was a positivist and an agnostic. A founder of
what came to be known as social Darwinism, he considered social phenomena and the laws of historical
development in biological terms, concluding that
those biologically superior would naturally dominate

their inferiors. As early as 1858, he conceived
the idea of developing a "synthetic philosophy"
by applying the principles of evolution to the
fields of biology, psychology, sociology, and
ethics; many of his subsequent works--beginning
with *First Principles of a New System of Philosophy* (1862) and including *The Principles of Biology*,
2 vols. (1864-67), the second edition of *The Principles of Psychology*, 2 vols. (1870-72), and *The
Principles of Sociology*, 3 vols. (1876-96)--demon-
strate his attempts to realize this philosophy.
For the most part, he viewed political and social
institutions and the concepts of "progress" and
social "change" as mechanistic evolutionary results
of the interplay between cultural and environmental
factors--a view that has had some impact on twentieth-century functional and cultural anthropology.
SPENCER, John (1630-1693): English theologian.
SPRAT, Thomas (1635-1713): English writer and theologian whose main works are *The Plague of Athens*
(1659) and *The History of the Royal Society* (1667).
SPRENGER, Jakob (d. 1494), and INSTITORIS, Henricus
(ca. 1430-ca. 1500): German Dominican theologians,
inquisitors, and authors of the *Malleus maleficarum*
in which they studied the nature of Satan, cases
when men were tempted by the Devil, and the transformation of people into animals. They also published charms that had been used to break the power
of the Devil.
STAËL-HOLSTEIN, Anne Louise Germaine, baronne de (1766-
1817): French romantic writer.
STAL'SKII, Suleĭman (1869-1937): Folk poet of Dagestan
U.S.S.R.
STASOV, Vladimir Vasil'evich (1824-1906): Russian musi
and art critic. Although he was not a folklorist or
ethnographer, he wrote several works on the archeology of Old Russia, the northern coast of the Blac
Sea and the Caucasus; on decorative art; and on the
origin of Russian byliny (*Proiskhozhdenie russkikh
bylin*, 1868). He was an advocate of the diffusion
theory, and he thought that Russian byliny were of
Oriental (Turkic-Mongolian) origin.

STEIN, Charlotte (1742-1827): Goethe's friend. The
poet's letters to her were published in 1848-51.
STEIN, Heinrich Friedrich Karl (1757-1831): Prussian
statesman, from 1807 to 1808 head of the government.
In order to re-establish the Prussian state and
prevent peasant revolts, he introduced several
progressive but moderate reforms: he abolished the
peasant's personal dependence on a *Feudalherr* (but
not socage), and he reformed the city government
and the army. At Napoleon's insistence and with
the pressure of the nobility, he was discharged
with a pension.
STEINTHAL, Heymann (1823-1899): German linguist, one
of the originators of the so-called psychological
school.
STRABO (ca. 63-25 B.C.): Ancient Greek geographer.
His *Geography* (in seventeen volumes) contains
valuable ethnological and historical information.
STRAPAROLA, Giovanni Francesco (last quarter of the
16th cent.): Italian writer. His *Le piacevole
notte* (*The Nights of Straparola*, 2 vols., trans.
W. G. Waters, London: Lawrence and Bullen, 1894)
is the first systematic collection of European
folktales and fairy tales.
SYDOW, Carl Wilhelm von (1878-1952): Swedish philologist and folklorist; professor of Scandinavian and
comparative folklore at Lund University; founder
of the journal *Folkminnen och folktanker* (1914).
He studied the origin of beliefs and customs found
in Scandinavian folk narratives. Later in his
career, he became interested in methodological
problems of defining and dating folktales and accounting for their diffusion. Opposing what he
saw as the artificial categories and invalid
premises of the Finnish school, he argued for the
dominant importance of the individual "bearer of
tradition" in the diffusion process and for the
necessity of studying folklore materials within
more sharply delimited cultural and national con-
fines--points made most clearly in his essays
"Finsk metod och modern sagoforskning" (*Rig*, 1943)
and "Om traditionsspridning" (*Scandia*, 1932). He

developed his own system of terminology for defin-
ing and grouping various kinds of folk narratives.
His most important articles have been collected
and translated into English in *Selected Papers on
Folklore Published on the Occasion of his 70th
Birthday*, ed. Laurits Bødker (1948).

TANUCCI, Bernardo (1698-1783): First Minister of the
Neapolitan Kingdom (1759-1776). He believed in the
politics of "enlightened despotism."

TASSONI, Alessandro (1565-1635): Italian poet and
publicist who criticized the morality and taste
of courtly nobility. His works include *La secchia
rapita* (1615-22), *Pensieri diversi* (1608), and
Considerazioni sopra le rime di Petrarca (1609).

TAVERNIER, Jean Baptiste (1605-1689): French jeweler.
His journeys to the Orient--to the Ottoman Empire,
Iran, India, and Indonesia--are described in his *Les
six voyages de Jean Baptiste Tavernier* (1681-82).

TELL, William: Legendary Swiss freedom fighter. The
legend concerning him originated at the beginning
of the fourteenth century, when the peasants of
the Swiss cantons fought against the reign of the
Hapsburgs. It is possible that William Tell was
modeled after Stauffacher, the leader of the people's uprising.

TERESHCHENKO, Aleksandr Vlas'evich (1806-1865):
Russian ethnographer, exponent of the theory of
official ethnic identity. His work on the Russian
people's social life and customs, *Byt russkago
naroda* (1848), is still valuable. Tereshchenko
idealized the past, and, like the slavophiles, he
considered the people to be "mild and forbearing."

TERTULLIANUS, Quintus Septimius Florens (ca. A.D. 155-
ca. 220): Carthaginian theologian, popularly known
as Tertullian. He devoted his life to defending
and preaching Christianity. In opposition to
ancient thinkers and scholars, he professed that
there was no need for research into the mysteries
of the Christian religion.

THIBAUT, Anton Friedrich Justus (1772-1840): German
jurist.

THIERRY: See GUIZOT, François.

THIERS, Jean Baptiste (1636-1703): French theologian
and professor. In addition to his study on superstitions, he wrote *Histoire des perruques* (1690).

THOMASIUS, Christian (1655-1728): German jurist and
philosopher who believed in natural law. He rejected the divine origin of state and law and
attempted to distinguish morality from the norms
of law.

THOMS, William (1803-1885): English antiquarian and
folklorist. He coined the term "folklore" in an
1846 article that has been reprinted in *The Study
of Folklore*, ed. Alan Dundes, Englewood Cliffs,
N.J.: Prentice-Hall, 1965.

THOMSON, James (1700-1748): English poet and playwright. In his poem *The Seasons* he gives an
idyllic depiction of nature and the patriarchal,
diligent country life as opposed to the vapidity
of urban life. He was one of the earliest of the
English eighteenth-century sentimentalists.

TIECK, Johann Ludwig (1773-1853): German romantic
poet and writer. Initially he endorsed the principles of the Enlightenment, a position that he
later abandoned. Like Novalis, he praised the
Middle Ages and considered Catholicism to be the
best of all religions.

TOLAND, John (1670-1722): English philosopher of
Irish origin. His *Christianity not Mysterious*
(1696) was burned by order of the Irish Parliament.
He fled to England to escape being imprisoned. His
Letters to Serena (1704) dealt with the origin of
prejudice, the belief in the immortality of the
soul, and religion in general.

TOMMASEO, Niccolò (1802-1874): Italian writer, philologist, and politician, born in Dalmatia. He participated in the civil war of 1848 and was a member
of the Venetian revolutionary government. In addition to his four-volume *Canti popolari toscani,
corsi, illirici e greci* (1841-42) he published an
Italian dictionary and a dictionary of synonyms.
He also published Serbian poems in the original and
in his own translations.

TOURNEMINE, René Joseph (1661-1739): French writer,
Jesuit.

TOURS, Gregory of (ca. 538-594): Bishop, author of
Historia Francorum, a history of the Franks.

TRAJANUS, Marcus Ulpius (A.D. 52-117): Roman emperor,
popularly known as Trajan, who ruled from A.D. 98
to 117.

TREITSCHKE, Heinrich (1834-1896): German historian
and publicist.

TREVELYAN, George Macaulay (1876-1962): Liberal English historian. His works include *History of
England* (1926) and *England Under Queen Anne* (1930).

TROUBADOURS: Lyric poets and musicians attached to the
courts of Provence and northern Italy in the twelfth
and thirteenth centuries. Their principal theme
was courtly love. Although the source of their art
was folk poetry, they developed their own traditions and canons. Troubadour poetry had a great
influence on the development of poetry and music
in many western European countries.

TYLOR, Edward Burnett (1832-1917): English ethnographer, devotee of the evolution theory, one of the
founders of the anthropological school. His *Primitive Culture*, which is fully discussed by Cocchiara
in Chapter 21, was first published in 1871 and reissued in two volumes (Vol. 1: *The Origin of Culture*; Vol. 2: *Religion in Primitive Culture*) in
1958. Tylor's first major work, *Researches into
the Early History of Mankind* (1965), applied the
comparative method to cultural phenomena in an attempt to find the origins of language, magic, and
myth through a detailed reconstruction of specific
historical sequences--an approach that he subsequently used in *Primitive Culture* in an effort to
demonstrate that human culture and religion have
evolved in a natural, regular, and continuous progress. The major contributions of *Primitive Culture*
are generally agreed to be Tylor's methodological
concept of survivals and his theoretical concept of
animism. His only other major work, *Anthropology:
An Introduction to the Study of Man and Civilization* (1881), is a demonstration of evolutionary
principles in various areas of human culture.

UHLAND, Ludwig (1787-1862): German poet and folklorist. He belonged to the Swabian school (late Romanticism).

USENER, Hermann (1834-1905): German philologist, professor at Berlin and Bonn. He was concerned with classical philosophy, linguistics, and the history of religion. Among his works are *Das Weihnachtsfest* (1889), *Götternamen* (1896), and *Die Sintfluthsagen* (1899).

VALLE, Pietro della (1586-1652): Italian traveler and Orientalist. From 1614 to 1626 he traveled in the countries of the Near and Middle East, returning with manuscripts and copies of Oriental inscriptions. In his *Viagi di Pietro della Valle*, 3 vols. (1650-63), he describes, among other things, Oriental folk customs.

VEDEL, Anders (1542-1616): Under the title *Et hundrede udvalde danske viser*, Vedel published the first collection of Danish folksongs. He also translated Saxo Grammaticus's famous fourteen-volume history of Denmark, *Gesta Danorum*, from Latin into Danish under the title *Den Danske Krønike af Saxo Grammaticus* (1575).

VERDI, Giuseppe (1813-1901): Italian composer remembered especially for his operas; he drew a great deal upon folk music.

VERGA, Giovanni (1840-1922): Italian verist writer who described the misery and defenselessness of peasants.

VERRI, Alessandro (1741-1816): Italian writer and poet. He belonged to the same group as Beccaria and was friendly with the French Encyclopedists.

VESELOVSKIĬ, Aleksandr Nikolaevich (1838-1906): Russian scholar. He was primarily concerned with medieval and Renaissance literature and with folklore. His early folklore scholarship was dominated by the diffusion theory. Later, influenced by the anthropological school, he attempted to make the two theories compatible. He explained the origin of folktale motifs in terms of "spontaneous creation" and themes containing several motifs in terms of borrowing. He also commented briefly on

the problem of the reciprocal influence of folk
poetry and literature.
VESPASIANUS, Titus Flavius (A.D. 9-79): Roman emperor,
popularly known as Vespasian, who reigned from A.D.
79 to 81.
VICO, Giovanni Battista (1688-1744): Italian philosopher, historian, jurist, critic, poet, and founder
of the study of aesthetics. His first major work,
De antiquissima Italorum sapientia (1710), emphasized the importance of inductive learning, imagination, and feeling in the acquisition of knowledge.
His famous cyclic theory of history was propounded
in his three-volume metaphysical treatise on universal law, *De uno universi iuris principio et fine uno*
(1920-22). His most significant work, however, is
the *Scienza Nuova*, first published in 1725 and then
revised in 1730 and again in 1744 with the addition
of new sections on Homer and on poetic knowledge.
The *Scienza Nuova*, the first survey of the social
evolution of man, suggested that poetry was the first
language and that the poet, one who imaginatively
transformed his ideas into portraits and ideal truths,
was the first and truest historian. An excellent
English translation of the *Scienza Nuova* has been
provided by T. G. Gergin and M. H. Fisch (1944).
VILLEGAGNON, Nicolas Durand (1510-1571): French admi-
ral who founded a Huguenot colony in 1555 on the
shores of the Guanabara Bay (present-day Rio de
Janeiro).
VOIART, Élise (1786-1866): French woman writer.
VOSSLER, Karl (1872-1949): German philologist who
studied the literature of countries with Romance
languages. In the area of folklore and linguistics, he believed in the "genius theory."

WACKENRODER, Wilhelm Heinrich (1773-1798): German
romantic writer.
WAGNER, Richard (1813-1883): German composer, known
especially for his operas. Many of his works are
based on folk legends.
WAITZ, Theodor (1821-1864): German anthropologist,
philosopher, and educator. His *Anthropologie der*

Naturvölker, 6 vols. (1859-72), classified an abundance of ethnographical material. According to Waitz, four factors influenced the development of human beings: the physical features of the race, the peculiarities of the people's spiritual life, the natural surroundings, and the sum of social circumstances and relations.

WARTON, Thomas (1728-1790): English poet and literary historian, a forerunner of the English romantics. He introduced medieval elements into literature, and his enthusiasm for the past is quite evident in his *The History of English Poetry* (1774-81).

WEBER, Albrecht Friedrich (1825-1901): German Orientalist and Sanskritologist. From 1849 to 1864 he published the periodical *Indische Studien*.

WEBER, Karl Maria (1786-1826): German romantic composer, music critic, and director. He fought for the creation of the German national opera and in his work relied on folk music, folk epics, legends, and tales.

WESTERMARCK, Edvard Alexander (1862-1939): Finnish sociologist and ethnographer; professor at Helsinki, London (1907-30), and Turku. His *The History of Human Marriage* (1889) was translated into many languages. He attempted to apply the laws of Darwinism to family history and to explain such phenomena as monogamy and exogamy on an entirely biological basis. Among his works are *The Origin and Development of the Moral Ideas*, 2 vols. (1906-08), *The Goodness of Gods* (1926), *Marriage* (1929), *Early Beliefs and Their Social Influence* (1932), *Ethical Relativity* (1932), *The Future of Marriage in Western Civilisation* (1936), and *Christianity and Morals* (1939).

WIELAND, Cristoph Martin (1733-1813): German writer, devotee of "enlightened despotism," a friend of Goethe and Herder. He lived in Weimar as the instructor of the future Prince Karl August.

WILAMOWITZ-MOELLENDORFF, Ulrich von (1848-1931): German classical philologist, of Prussian Junker origin. In politics he was conservative, in philology an idealist.

WINCKELMANN, Johann Joachim (1717-1768): German art
   historian and philologist. He considered classical art the supreme achievement of man.
WOLF, Friedrich August (1759-1824): German classical
   philologist. In his *Prolegomena ad Homerum* (1795)
   he attempted a scientific justification for the
   idea that the epics of Homer are collections of
   short folksongs.
WORDSWORTH, William (1770-1850), and COLERIDGE, Samuel
   Taylor (1772-1834): English romantic poets of the
   "Lake School." In their youth, both were strongly
   influenced by the French Revolution (Wordsworth
   went to France twice during the Revolution), but
   later, as a result of their increasing disillusion-
   ment and conservatism, they opposed it. The
   critical manifesto of the "Lake School" is Wordsworth's preface to the second edition of *Lyrical
   Ballads* (1800), which argued that poetry, the
   "spontaneous overflow" of feelings "recollected in
   tranquility," should use a natural, unadorned language to describe nature, the common man, and
   "humble and rustic life"--premises that greatly
   influenced the course of English Romanticism.
WUNDT, Wilhelm Max (1832-1920): German physiologist,
   psychologist, and folklorist; professor at Heidelberg and Leipzig. Although he was the founder of
   experimental psychology, he was convinced that many
   areas of psychology could not be approached through
   laboratory experimentation; his *Völkerpsychologie*,
   10 vols. (1900-09), which Cocchiara cites in Chapter 25, section 7, was his attempt to discuss such
   areas as language, myth, religion, art, customs,
   and law in order to give an account of the "natural
   history of man." Wundt insisted that only by examining all aspects of human culture can we achieve
   an understanding of how humans think. In addition
   to his extensive work in psychology, he is also
   known for his *Logik*, 3 vols. (1880-83), *Ethik*
   (1886), and *System der Philosophie*, 2 vols. (1889).

YOUNG, Edward (1683-1765): English poet, country
   clergyman, and satirist. His long poem *The Com-*

plaint, or Night Thoughts on Life, Death and
Immortality (1742-45) was the beginning of "grave-
yard poetry." He is also known as a writer of
satires.

ZHUKOVSKIĬ, Vasiliĭ Andreevich (1783-1852): Russian
romantic poet.
ZOLA, Émile (1840-1902): French naturalist writer and
democratic publicist.
ZWINGLI: See LUTHER.

INDEX

INDEX